Educational Administration

A Problem-Based Approach

William G. Cunningham
Old Dominion University

Paula A. Cordeiro
University of San Diego

Allyn and Bacon

Boston ■ London ■ Toronto ■ Sydney ■ Tokyo ■ Singapore

Series Editor: *Arnis E. Burvikovs*
Marketing Manager: *Brad Parkins*
Sr. Editorial Production Administrator: *Susan McIntyre*
Editorial Production Service: *Nesbitt Graphics, Inc.*
Composition Buyer: *Linda Cox*
Manufacturing Buyer: *Suzanne Lareau*
Cover Administrator: *Jenny Hart*
Electronic Composition: *Omegatype Typography, Inc.*

Copyright © 2000 by Allyn & Bacon
A Pearson Education Company
160 Gould Street
Needham Heights, MA 02494
Internet: www.abacon.com

Between the time Website information is gathered and published, some sites may have closed. Also, the transcription of URLs can result in typographical errors. The publisher would appreciate notification where these occur so that they may be corrected in subsequent editions.

Library of Congress Cataloging-in-Publication Data

Cunningham, William G.
    Educational administration : a problem-based approach / William G.
Cunningham, Paula A. Cordeiro.
        p.   cm.
    Includes bibliographical references and index.
    ISBN 0-205-18459-6
    1. School management and organization—Study and teaching
(Higher)—United States.   2. Problem-based learning—United States.
3. School administrators—Training of—United States.   I. Cordeiro,
Paula A.   II. Title.
LB1738.5.C86   2000
371.2'071'1—dc21   99-14377
                                                                              CIP

Printed in the United States of America

10 9 8 7 6 5 4 3 2   04 03 02 01 00

CONTENTS

11   Schools and the Law   316

PREFACE

Educational Administration: A Problem-Based Approach provides a comprehensive discussion of the field of educational administration. The book describes how successful and effective schools and administrators operate in an increasingly challenging and demanding environment. Readers are offered an integrated view of the knowledge base, research, and practice of administration within a context of multiple perspectives and a wide range of thinking. The activities, collected artifacts, and reflective writings emphasized in each chapter will help readers build a personal, professional portfolio as they proceed through the course.

The content is for anyone who wants to understand and effectively practice leadership in an educational setting and to improve his or her understanding of education, the role of educational administration, the forces that are moving education into a new era, the transitions that are occurring, and the use of the latest, best practices to improve the education of all children. This book makes the job of the educational administrator come alive.

The book's format allows the reader to choose among areas of concentration and those of review. Some chapters are important to a reader because of his or her present professional status, whereas others may be simply informative. Although the topics flow logically from one chapter to the next, selected chapters and even portions of chapters can be studied separately, or in a different sequence depending on the needs of the reader or instructor.

Earlier chapters can be skipped without losing touch with the essence of later chapters, although we recommend that you scan them to obtain a sense of their content. Each topic is introduced and placed in a practical perspective as part of an integral system of leadership that is developed throughout a person's professional life. This text provides a comprehensive reference of key information useful in improving educational practice.

Each chapter follows the same basic format and begins with a vignette that reflects the life of a school administrator. Questions and comments are located throughout each chapter to make overall theory-practice connections, to encourage readers to enrich their understanding of problems in practice, and to suggest how leadership might be applied in a variety of settings. Illustrations, expert opinions, quotes, Internet addresses, and examples are often used to highlight key points, trends, and issues.

Each chapter concludes with suggested activities through which readers can begin to build their educational leadership platforms. Artifacts can be collected to demonstrate a reader's ability to connect knowledge to his or her responsibilities. The portfolio artifacts and reflective writings can be collected for each chapter to create a cumulative portfolio documenting the reader's growth and understanding of administrative practice.

A number of nationally noted scholars and practitioners from a variety of fields have provided original, expert reflections on critical topics within each chapter. These contributions provide insights into many key areas of educational administration from those who have been involved in the most promising activities within the field. The objective of providing these important insights is to model and encourage readers in the development of well-thought-out and supported analysis of key issues. They also allow the reader to relate his or her reflective thinking to that of noted experts in the field. Each contribution encourages the reader to think through, discuss and debate key issues surrounding educational administration.

The first chapter explores and develops theories, values, issues, and practices in educational administration. The next three chapters examine context, sociocultural issues, major reform initiatives, cultural diversity, and community relations. Chapters 5 to 7 focus on school district organization, successful leadership, and the moral and ethical dimensions of leadership. Readers are asked to assess their own leadership styles using the instruments provided. Attention then shifts to operational responsibilities and legal regulatory issues in Chapters 8 through 12. The book explores major leadership responsibilities related to curriculum, instruction, and program development; pupil personnel; human resource management; legal and compliance issues; and finance and stewardship. A brief overview of problem-based learning (PBL), two expert inquiries, and four PBL projects comprise the final chapter.

The four PBL projects can be used in a variety of ways. One approach is to schedule a project before reading the text. The text can serve as a resource when readers select only chapters that are necessary to address issues adequately and appropriately. Another way to incorporate the projects is for readers to complete a project approximately midway through the book. This approach permits students to become comfortable with the content, begin the development of an administrative platform, and possibly begin developing a portfolio. Alternatively, a PBL project could be used as a culminating activity after students have read a good part of the text. No solutions are provided. The PBL projects are designed to stimulate inquiry, to create deep reflection, and to challenge perspectives regarding key issues, values, and needs.

The original idea for this book evolved through a series of conversations with Ray Short, Educational Editor at Allyn & Bacon (now happily retired). Ms. Karin Huang has nurtured our efforts throughout the writing process. Much of the content of this book is drawn from the life work of researchers, scholars, and practitioners who have dedicated their professional lives to an improved understanding of education and administration. We appreciate their dedication and critically important insights. We are also indebted to the reviewers who provided invaluable feedback, insights, and resources: Bruce Barnett, University of Northern Colorado; Martin Burlingame, Oklahoma State University; Maria-Luisa Gonzalez, New Mexico State University; Larry W. Hughes, University of Houston; Richard A. King, University of Northern Colorado; Ulrich C. Reitzug, University of North Carolina–Greensboro; and L. Nan Restine, Oklahoma State University. Special thanks go to each of the experts, who contributed original pieces reflecting on the contents of the chapters and who have made such significant contributions to our field. We also wish to acknowledge Paula Short, Gene Carter, Donn Gresso, Joe Murphy, Bruce Barnett, Fred Bateman, Karry Lambert, Donald Walker, Bill Katzenmeyer, Frank Sellew, Bob MacDonald, Mark Shibles, Patrick Mullarney, Denny Wolfe, and Bob Sinclair, who provided key input into the completion of this work. Particular thanks go to Georgia Belaire, Sheila Jones, and Dawn Hall, whose proofreading and typing helped to make this book a reality.

Many friends and colleagues who teach and practice educational administration provided counsel, inspiration, and direction as they have given of their time and interest. Last, but certainly not least, are the thousands of educational leadership students who first breathe such exciting life into this subject and then into our schools. We wish them Godspeed on their noble journeys. To them all, we offer appreciation and great thanks.

We would also like to thank our parents, Jerry and Margaret Cunningham and Manuel Cordeiro, sister, Gail Penn, spouse, Sandra L. Cunningham, children Kerri, Michael and his wife Dottie, and grandchildren, Cierra, Merrick, Keenan, and Shealyn for their continuing encouragement and support and the happiness and love we enjoy. Many, many thanks to David J. O'Brien for his careful editing of the first drafts. His insights and support are deeply appreciated.

We hope you find this book worthy of the greatness of the people who have had such profound influences on our lives. Part of each is in this work.

William G. Cunningham
Paula A. Cordeiro

1 Administrative Theory and Leadership Responsibility

Vignette: Leadership Differences in Flem Snopes School District

Superintendent Vivian Armstid of the Flem Snopes school district wanted to develop a leadership structure within the school division that would support the upcoming school renewal effort. She had argued and obtained support for the internal development and implementation of needed new curriculum and instructional reforms. Some believed that externally developed approaches would be safer because local knowledge and conflicts could be avoided. Superintendent Armstid believed that a large part of the reform effort would be to improve teaching and learning and that this improvement would best occur if the staff struggled with thinking about and developing the reforms themselves. A majority of the school board agreed, and the internal school renewal effort was born.

Dr. Armstid knew that school leadership would play an essential role in this endeavor and invited a good sampling of Flem Snopes principals to serve on a committee to discuss leadership platforms and the role of the principal in the renewal effort. The first two meetings of the leadership committee were used to further define the renewal effort, lay out a time line, define the purpose of the committee, and establish working relationships. For the next meeting, each member was asked to be prepared to discuss his or her theory and philosophy of leadership and how it would influence school renewal.

At the third meeting, the participants described their thoughts about administration and leadership and the role of the principal. Superintendent Armstid said, "Introducing new changes to our established practices and overcoming past thinking will be one of the toughest leadership challenges that you will face. Let us see, then, if we can identify our beliefs about leadership and the role of the principal in our renewal effort. Mr. Wayne, why don't you begin, being as brief as possible, and we will work around the table." After a short discussion of several key points about leadership, the participants provided their views:

■ Mr. Wayne stated, "The leader must be the role model for his teachers. He is strong and courageous, willing to take risks and try new things, with a desire to excel. Charisma is very important. You view the principalship as a character you play that models the expectations you have for your staff. You must be a person of action, engaged in great deeds, eliminating negative forces at every turn, and inspiring your employees. You show them you're willing to work as hard as you want them to work. Leaders must be people of action modeling excellence at every possible opportunity."

■ Mrs. Taylor thought she viewed leadership slightly differently, explaining, "You must carefully lay out standards, divide the work that must be done, and identify those who have the expertise to be productive and efficient. Success depends on getting the small day-to-day operations functioning well. If you can't get the bills paid and have people arrive on time, return phone calls, and have schedules that work, you won't go very far. Effective management and effective leadership are somewhat the same. Both require that people know what is expected of them and have the organization and resources needed to get the job done."

■ Mr. Newton offered a different perspective: "Leadership is first and foremost about making effective decisions. If the leader makes good decisions, everything else will fall into place. The leader must ensure that the organization objectively evaluates what is known and makes his or her decision on the basis of research, facts, and rationality. Relationships between decisions and the aims to be achieved must be carefully established and evaluated. Standards are used to define the expectations related to the level of performance deemed acceptable. When people know the leader will ensure that decisions are logical and objective and based on the latest knowledge and research, they will support him or her because they are the best possible decisions given the circumstances. Leaders must know about key subjects like development, curriculum, and finance and study them in depth. Leadership is using the right information for making decisions. Such leaders have a strong knowledge base, are aware of the latest research, and have a clear focus on the goals. Leaders are persuasive and convince others that the goals are worth achieving. Once that has occurred, the work will be achieved in an effective and efficient manner."

■ Mrs. Maynard was surprised that her colleagues held such different views and suggested, "It is the formal structure, communication networks, the relationships of people, and organizational climate that are important in leadership efforts. The employee's strongest motivation is for survival, status, power, and recognition; and leaders help those within the organization to obtain such motivators. Leaders create productive relationships within the organization and sometimes outside. It is the patterns and operating procedures of the organization that shape the people who work within it. Leaders must understand and be able to work through the inner structures to accomplish results. It's who you call, when to be nice, when to bite the bullet and decide. Good relationships and collaboration certainly help. Who you are and the power you have are important, but people's behaviors are shaped by policies, procedures, job descriptions, organizational hierarchy, and other such structural components. They must believe the mission will benefit all members of the group and is compatible with formal organizational beliefs. Leadership depends on running a tight organizational ship."

■ Mr. Browne smiled and said, "Leaders do not deal with matters that are scientific or even orderly but those that are philosophical and ethical. Leadership is being fair and honest and having a sense of what is right and what is wrong. That means issues like human rights, justice, loyalty, trust, integrity, respect, duty, and other such virtues are important. A person's moral responsibility and duty are very important. The job of the leader is consciousness-raising and ensuring good moral behavior on the part of all employees and a sense of collective responsibility. Leadership requires critical reflection and analysis of the human condition and all human action to determine what is important, right, and helpful. Employees should be responsible, inquisitive, probing, reflective, and critical in their thinking. Leaders are fair, honest, moral, and consistent, and thus earn and grant respect. Leaders increase sensitivity to moral issues that arise and develop moral, ethical, and legal responses."

■ Mrs. Gilligan countered suggesting that, "Leadership is caring for and being sensitive to the needs of others and understanding responsibilities and relationships. It should emphasize feelings, compassion, generosity, assisting, nurturing, and caring for others. We all bear a responsibility for the ethical perfection of others. You have to be willing to listen to people and set aside your agenda; just because it's good for you does not mean it's good for others. Decisions are good when they help others in their personal and professional lives. Leaders must be ethical, sincere, and encouraging. Leadership's primary purpose is developing the best in staff so they will benefit children."

■ Mr. Newman was not surprised at the diverse views, stating, "Organizations are fluid, with no final destination possible and therefore no certainty—no possibility of a true or accurate account. As a result, leadership becomes the management of discourse that is influenced by multiple interpretations, multiple realities, changing views, and different perspectives, even about leadership for school reform. Uncertainty, instability, differences, disagreements, or volatility often throws organizations into chaos; under proper conditions, however, this chaos is a catalyst for renewal and enhancement. Leadership can come from just about anyone, and conflict and dissention are not necessarily a bad thing. Individual differences can often be used as a learning tool. The leader must provide those proper conditions and comfort levels to allow such knowledge and instability to do its work. Order does not come from avoiding differences; people must be free to interact with the turbulent changing environment in order to respond and regenerate. This means a willingness to listen to people and set aside your own personal agenda. Listening is the fuel for reflecting and reframing situations. Leadership organizes complexity, provides information, remains fluid, and encourages constant improvement."

Mr. Newman suggested to the superintendent, "We need a further discussion of the widely divergent views regarding the type of leadership needed in Flem Snopes schools." Mr. Newton disagreed and expressed concern about "the totally different ways in which each of us is looking at this same concept. There is enormous pressure to develop an effective leadership and renewal process. But how can we do this under the present divergence within the committee? Maybe we should revisit the idea of developing internal reform efforts and adopt an existing model. It's impossible to identify any convergent themes that might provide guidance for needed leadership in school renewal." The superintendent realized there was a great uncertainty and lack of consensus about leadership and the relevant knowledge base. The principals reflected little agreement on their respective roles and held very different beliefs about needed leadership behavior. In fact, there was now concern that leadership within the district might actually be in disarray.

Superintendent Armstid was no longer sure how to move the committee or the renewal effort forward. She had wanted to build capacity and direction and provide some shared beliefs and skills and instead had a sharp contrast on how different principals within the district thought in regard to leadership. Yet they had taken an important first step toward defining types of leadership and knowledge that might be needed. The principals' positions could serve as the platforms for further reflective thinking and practice. They were possible frames for thinking about leadership and renewal. She decided that the principals would need to further develop platforms to clarify their thoughts about leadership and education, to share them with other people, and to foster systematic inquiry. She could not expect other employees in the division to do so if her administrative team had not. She realized this process was long overdue.

Why did Superintendent Armstid first focus on leadership rather than on needed reforms? How much will these different perceptions among principals hinder reforming the schools?

Administrative Process and Knowledge

Henri Fayole (1949) described administration as a process concerned with planning, organizing, activating, coordinating, and controlling resources within an integrated system designed to accomplish predetermined objectives. These famous five elements of administration are repeated, adapted, and extended and are widely accepted within most business, education, government, hospital, and military institutions.

Administration is often divided into two major areas of responsibility—leadership and management. Leadership has to do with guiding improvement and infusing an organization with meaning and purpose, whereas management is involved with stewardship and accountability for all types of resources. Management also focuses on implementing routines in an organization and ensuring its smooth operation. Joel Barker (1992) states, "you manage within a paradigm, you lead between paradigms" (p. 164). The line between these two concepts remains fuzzy for some, and the terms are occasionally used synonymously.

The study of administration is grounded in science and philosophy, in theories and ethics. According to Barnett (1991), many with an interest in educational administration believe it is very important for administrators to understand and develop belief systems and philosophies for their practice. Administrators have a knowledge base, a way of thinking about things, that needs to be understood. Administrators cognitively organize and classify beliefs, thoughts, and knowledge so they can better process and ultimately understand the overwhelming amount of information and number of possibilities that continuously confront them.

These classification devices serve as prisms through which people interpret and respond to presenting circumstances and therefore need to be conscientiously understood. Thus a person's epistemology—the way a person thinks and determines reality and the way that person approaches work—is critically important. Bolman and Deal (1993) conclude,

> Wise and effective leadership is more important than ever, but it requires a complex array of lenses to distinguish traps and deadends from promising opportunities. Multiframe thinking reduces administrators' stress and enhances their effectiveness. In the long term, the measure of success will be how well [leaders] can reframe the problems they face so as to discover and invent new solutions that significantly enhance the performance of their schools. (p. 31)

The premise is that good theory provides useful knowledge to guide effective practice. The administrator's skills and abilities are improved by both theory and practice. As John Dewey suggested long ago, there is nothing as practical as a good theory. Theories provide the conceptual tools to focus the work of the administrator: guides to action. They provide a reasonable base for tactics and strategies that might improve the educational administrator's success. William Greenfield (1995) states, "more complete knowledge of these two realms (the nature and centrality of leadership in schools and the demand environment [context] to which it responds) will provide a basis for more powerful theories about school administration, more informed preparation curricula, and more concrete guidance regarding the specific intentions, strategies, behaviors, and process associated with effective leadership in schools" (p. 80). Evers and Lakomski (1996) concur, believing that much benefit will be gained by providing "a systematic framework for approaching problems and issues in administrative practice; matters such as leadership, administrator training, decision-making, organization and structure, organizational change, planning and policy, ethics, power, culture, and organizational learning" (p. 279).

Without theory there is virtually no basis for knowledge. At the same time, educational administration theory formulations are not a totally clear or accurate source of knowledge for understanding organizations and administration. There are too many conflicting views on the subject. Each view, though, offers insights that allow for greater understanding, given a set of conditions that might exist. Theory formulations help administrators draw inferences that will result in a much better prospect of success. The emphasis on reflection and discourse regarding the educational administration knowledge base is described by some (English, 1994) as "meta-narrative" analysis.

How might Flem Snopes principals begin to clarify their different thinking regarding the role of the principal?

Meta-Narratives

Meta-narratives provide a general overview of the development of prominent conceptualizations and transformations of ideas about administration. The focus is on the introduction of ideas, because once ideas are introduced they are continuously developed, transformed, and applied over time. Meta-narratives provide knowledge from a rough historic discourse within the field of administration. There are a number of different typologies of knowledge in educational administration. Fenwick English (1993, 1994) provides a comprehensive typology that exemplifies the contours of the discipline. Table 1.1 on pages 6–7 provides English's set of meta-narratives for educational administration. Effective administrators "must be aware of some of the key epistemological ideas that underlie what we know and how we know it" (Owens, 1995, p. 5).

Examination of Table 1.1 suggests that the earlier, more scientific approaches assume that administrative concerns can be identified, studied, and measured through methods derived from the natural sciences and empiricism. The behavioristic narratives develop a science of human behavior focusing on extrinsic motivation. The structuralists are interested in learning about how institutions work and how they might work more efficiently and smoothly. However, Thomas Greenfield challenges this scientific-logical-positivist tradition. (Evers and Lakomski, 1991). Greenfield (1978, 1979, 1980) studies influences that are subjective in nature such as domination, alienation, exploitation, and repression.

Subjectivism and critical theory argue that administration is a social science and is thus irreducibly subjective and requires some degree of interpretation. According to these theories there is no such thing as scientific, objective choice; we augment decisions with taste, value, subjective preference, and will. Feminist poststructuralist theory

TABLE 1.1 Tentative Landscape of Narratives in Educational Administration

Meta-Narrative	Typology	Archetypical Works/Authors
I. Prescientific	Myths provide spiritual and traditional wisdom about human survival	Mythology; Legend; J. Campbell, *Hero with a Thousand Faces*; C. Estes, *Women Who Run with the Wolves*
II. Protoscientific	Historic, biographical, and literary portraits providing testimony on leadership	Homer's *Iliad* and *Odyssey*; Thucydides, *History of Peloponnesian War*; Plato, *The Republic*; Plutarch, *Lives*; Machiavelli, *The Prince*; Shakespeare, *Othello, King Lear, Hamlet*
III. Pseudoscientific	Economy and efficiency analysis of work methods based on ideological, systematic, and engineering approaches	Trait theory; Taylor's scientific management; Deming's total quality management; Henry Gantt, Frank and Lillian Gilbreth
IV. Emergent Scientific	Insights from multiple disciplines regarding foundational understanding of organizations and administration functions	Mary Parker Follet; Elton Mayo; Chester Barnard; Henri Fayol
V. Behavioristic	Analysis of influences on and consequences of behavior centered on logical positivism	Simon's *Administrative Theory*; Halpin's *Theory in Educational Administration*; McGregor's *Human Side of Enterprise*; Fielder's *Theory of Leadership*; Chris Argyris
VI. Transitional Views (hybrid between behavioralism and structuralism)	Study of organizations or structures as they influence behaviors	Katz and Kahn, *Social Psychology of Organizations*; Likert, *New Patterns of Management*; Cohen and March, *Leadership and Ambiguity*
VII. Broad Fields	Study centered on broad disciplines that examines individual traits as critical parts of leadership in given situations	J. M. Burns, *Leadership*; Barber, *The Presidential Character*; Keegan, *The Mask of Command*; Lightfoot, *The Good High School*
VIII. Structuralist	Structure as the center of analysis for understanding why people behave as they do within organizations	Blau and Scott, *Formal Organizations*; Gailbrath, *Designing Complex Organizations*; Mintzberg, *Structure in Fives*; Bolman and Deal, *Reframing Organizations*; James Thompson

TABLE 1.1   Continued

Meta-Narrative	Typology	Archetypical Works/Authors
IX. Critical Theory	Examination of linkages between organizations and the larger socio-political context and forms of power, thus expanding boundaries of thinking	Foster, *Paradigms and Promises*; Giroux, *Crisis of Democratic Culture*; Hodgkinson, *Educational Leadership*; Maxcy, *Educational Leadership*; Thomas Greenfield
X. Postmodernism	Abandonment of certainty and study of the intertextual interactions as an ontology using art, politics, culture, philosophy, morality, and so on to redefine leadership and followership	Foucault, *Archeology of Knowledge*; Foucault, *The Order of Things*; Derrida, *On Grammatology*; DeMan, *Blindness and Insight*; Wheatly, *Leadership and the New Science*

Source: English, F. (Spring, 1993). A post-structural view of the grand narratives in educational administration. *Organization Theory Dialogues.* Bloomington, IN: Organizational Theory SOG (AEFA) Indiana University.

stresses the importance of the context and perspective, and the competing ways of giving meaning to situations. Power, language, and assumptions are always viewed in terms of situations—experience, access, authority, history, and so forth. Postmodernism characterizes administration as uncertain, unstable, complex, and often unique. Postmodernists challenge existing assumptions, values, and beliefs, making "them explicit, questioning them, and seeking to forge consensus around new assumptions on which to rebuild our thinking about truth, knowledge, and epistemology in organizational behavior" (Owens, 1995, p. 9). Postmodernism highlights the multiplicity of voices, questions, and conflicts that call into question traditional bases of knowledge.

The dominance of science as a "grand or master narrative" has been eclipsed in the postmodern age. The claim that administration is a closed "scientific" system faces severe challenges (Callahan, 1962; Greenfield, 1988; Willower, 1979). Griffith (1979) criticizes science and the "cult of efficiency" for failing to provide ethical guidance and theorize gender issues, and for being unable to support political analysis or to adjudicate conflicts of interest. He suggests that educational administration as a field is in intellectual turmoil. Feminist criticisms of Carol Gilligan (1982) and Charol Shakeshaft (1986) demonstrate the neglect of gender issues in administrative theory and research. Concern is later expressed by James Banks (1993) that educational administrative research may also be racially biased.

Most criticism of logical empiricism and science has come about because of difficulties with empirical adequacy as a criterion of theory choice (Greenfield, 1993; Hodgkinson, 1991; Evers and Lakomski, 1996). Useful patterns to explain organization and educational administration "draw on more criteria than just empirical adequacy—such as consistency, simplicity, comprehensiveness, unity of explanation, learnability and fecundity" (Evers & Lakomski, 1996, p. 386). Wayne Hoy (1994) describes the turmoil produced by the debate over the appropriate theories and methodologies for knowing about educational organization and administration, as the "great paradigm wars." Logical empiricism, traditional science, behaviorism, critical theory, subjectivism, feminism, and postmodernism all provide alternative and often conflicting perspectives within administrative theory. Some, however, argue that these alternative perspectives supplement one another and provide a more comprehensive view of the profession.

> What does Superintendent Armstid want to achieve by trying to define the knowledge or belief systems on which her principals base their leadership practices?

Scientific Approaches

Theory is a coherent set of propositions used as explanations for a class of phenomena that can be tested using some form of scientific or empirical methodology. A theory is conjectural until evidence begins to prove that it is true and thus fact. The theory provides a conceptual view for testing and thus is the foundation of scientific inquiry. Over time, theories can become verified as explanations accounting for the properties of something, such as administration. The ultimate purpose is to reach the truth. Decisions made and actions taken will be congruent with a person's belief system or theoretical explanations.

Paradigms come from the traditional sciences; they are frameworks of thought that rest on a belief system and some scientific data and facts. Paradigms are the way we understand and explain our world. They are our way of perceiving, thinking, valuing, and achieving based on our particular explanations of complex behavior. Barker (1992) states, "A paradigm is a set of rules and regulations (written or unwritten) that does two things: (1) it establishes or defines boundaries; and (2) it tells you how to behave inside the boundaries in order to be successful" (p. 32). We see the world through our paradigms. "What may be perfectly visible, perfectly obvious to persons with one paradigm may be quite literally invisible to persons with a different paradigm" (p. 86).

In its simplest form, a paradigm is the set of rules by which something operates. When an organization's paradigm changes, the way it operates changes as well. This shift usually results in confusion, turbulence, and chaos as the changes dramatically upset the existing theoretical explanation and status quo. The changing of the rules, theory, or paradigms is the earliest sign of a significant change in our understanding of the world.

Scientists see unfounded explanations as ideologies. Under the influence of ideologies decisions are based on personal interpretation and not on rational inquiry and analysis and scientific methods. Usually politics, not science, is used to mediate discordant ideologies, disparate value systems, and conflicting points of view. Scientists do not hold ideology in high regard because it is often based on speculation or a body of unproven doctrine. Scientists do not accept ideologies as truth because they often rest on "self-evident" or "unexamined" truths (English, 1994, p. 49). English suggests that paradigms in the social sciences are highly likely to emerge from meta-narratives that are ideologies rather than scientific theories because they cannot be tested against objective realities. Scientists suggest that paradigms based on ideology are much less challengeable and thus less provable than those that are based on theory (Barker, 1992). Basing decision on thought processes other than science can result in an organization's continual floundering, as it is buffeted by constantly shifting and unproved ideologies.

> Which of the principals seem to take the more scientific approaches? On what basis did you draw this conclusion?

Transitional: Realism, Subjectivism, Naturalism, Structuralism

Thomas Greenfield (1978, 1979, 1980, 1985, 1988) forcefully attacked many assumptions embedded in the scientific-rationality movement. He believed that ends cannot be separated from means, facts from underlying values, or rational thinking and action from preferences, passions, and ideologies. Each type of thinking and acting is subjective rationality—justifiable from the thinker's perspective. Greenfield recognized as important the truly irrational outbursts that influence our everyday lives and the course of history—that drive humans to do what they do. Inquiry must proceed from a variety of perspectives, and not solely the sciences. Greenfield suggested that educational administration can benefit from philosophy, history, law, political theory, sociology, and anthropology as well (see Table 1.2 on pages 10–11).

Investigation that adequately grasps administrative and organizational complexity must identify motives, emotions, attitudes, abilities, intentions, preferences, values, beliefs, relationships, and many other factors that complicate administrative practice. Understanding organizational structures, functions, and roles requires critical examination of ideology, power, force, authority, legitimization, and conflict.

William Greenfield (1995) suggested that the school is unlike other institutions because of its highly educated, autonomous, and practically permanent teacher workforce; the moral character of the school as an institution; and a milieu characterized by continuous and unpredictable threats to its stability. Schools are what Evers and Lakomski (1996) describe as a human invention or naturalistic system.

Critical Theory: Values, Ethics, and Control

We expect much more of our leaders than mere unreflective focus on policy, procedures, tasks, and other structural matters. Administrators must have an awareness of competing value orientations if they hope to survive. The same individuals who develop statutes, policies, procedures, practices, and tasks on moral grounds are themselves subject to these laws. It may not make sense for those who do not believe in the laws to change their moral beliefs for legal reasons even if the laws must be temporarily followed. Heslep (1997) suggests,

TABLE 1.2   Beyond Greenfield's Subjectivism Theories of Social Reality

Dimensions of Comparison	A Natural System	Human Invention	Naturalistic Coherentism
Philosophical basis	*Realism:* the world exists and is knowable as it really is. Organizations are real entities with a life of their own.	*Subjectivism:* the world exists but different people construe it in very different ways. Organizations are invented social reality.	*Naturalism:* The natural world exists because that is the best, most coherent explanation of phenomena. Organizations are real patterns of human association.
The role of science	Discovering the universal laws of society and human conduct within it	Discovering how different people interpret the world in which they live	Discovering empirically adequate compression algorithms for capturing comprehensively the regularities in social life
Basic units of social reality	The collectivity; society or organization	Individuals acting singly or together	Individuals responding to other individuals or groups and the natural world
Method of understanding	Identifying conditions or relationships that exist; conceiving what these conditions and relationships are	Interpretation of the subjective meanings of actions; discovering the subjective rules for such actions	Exploring networks of expressions that fit the behavior of individuals and account for their own theories of behavior
Theory	A rational edifice built by scientists to explain human behavior	Sets of meanings that people use to make sense of their world within it	The most coherent network of claims about the world
Research	Experimental or quasiexperimental validation of theory	The search for meaningful relationships and the discovery of their consequences for action	Search for nonrandom features of the world
Methodology	Abstraction of reality, especially through mathematical models and quantitative analysis	The representation of reality for purposes of comparison. Analysis of language and meaning.	Full range of techniques that will establish the existence of patterns.
Society	Ordered. Governed by a uniform set of values and made possible only by those values.	Conflicted. Governed by the values of people with access to power.	Patterned. Governed by networks of causes describable in various ways.

TABLE 1.2   Continued

Dimensions of Comparison	A Natural System	Human Invention	Naturalistic Coherentism
Organizations	Goal-oriented. Independent of people. Instruments of order in society serving both society and the individual.	Dependent upon people and their goals. Instruments of power that some people control and can use to attain ends which seem good to them.	Dependent upon individual and resultant collective goals, with stability ensured by memory and records.
Organizational pathologies	Organizations get out of kilter with social values and individual needs.	Given diverse human ends, there is always conflict among people acting to pursue them.	Dissonance among individuals and between organization and society.
Prescription for curing organizational ills	Change the structure of the organization to meet social values and individual needs.	Find out what values are embodied in organizational action and whose they are. Change the people or change their values if you can.	Promote structures for enhancing organizational learning.

Source: Collin W. Evers and Gabrele Lakomski. *Exploring Educational Administration,* New York: Pergamon 1996, pp. 139–140. Reprinted with permission from Elsevier Science.

being committed to the principles of moral value, moral rights, and moral duty as the fundamental standards for their judgments, those engaged in educational leadership must not approve ends and means that are inconsistent with these principles.... What they necessitate is that in forming judgments those engaged in educational leadership appreciate the knowledge, freedom, purposefulness, deliberativeness, and so on of all affected moral agents, respect the rights of such agents to these matters, and be cognizant of the duties of all concerned to foster freedom and knowledge in leadership of that kind. (pp. 77–78)

Critical theorists challenge certain entrenched meanings, motives, or values. Such challenges open up possibilities for new types of responses and free us from habitual unreflective reactions. The result can be an educative and transformational process in which organizational aspects such as vision, goals, practices, rewards, structures, policies, and controls might be altered. However, those in power often must be motivated to consent to such changes. This usually requires relinquishing traditional concepts and practices that are well established, defined, and defended (Robinson, 1994).

Because revolution is impractical, change will require the supportive involvement of those who control and benefit from the present conditions. Some critical theorists believe that creating a moral theory base will alleviate such difficulties. Others question whether a morality base can work for both the oppressed and the oppressor simultaneously. Certainly mutual acknowledgment of common interests can sustain a transformation, but what occurs when such acknowledgments do not exist? Participants either sacrifice debate and conflict in the interest of collaboration, or they exercise power in a way that jeopardizes collaboration (Bridges, 1986). Regardless of such power struggles over renewed and reformed practices, critical theorists argue that administrators are not neutral, rational bureaucrats. They operate from a value base that affects their views, decisions, and actions.

Foster (1986) and Sergiovanni (1992) believe that administrators have a clear responsibility to articulate their values and take moral stands. Critical theorists argue against the exclusion of ethics from administrative science. The more radical critical theorists contend that leadership protects all sorts of inequalities in societies so as to favor particular groups. "Behind leadership's benign mask of social efficiency lies the ugly face of human oppression" (Slater, 1995, p. 469). Leadership should be "a matter of getting them to want to do what they should do, that is, what is right." The ability to effect such a change begins with a clear understanding of the administrator's values, which can be used to examine both direction and results.

Gender and Race

Feminist theorists begin with a desire to offer a reconceptualization of administration based strongly on the beliefs and values of women. The present administrative knowledge base developed under a white male perspective. This knowledge base is universal only to the extent that women and people of color respond like white males do. Carol Gilligan (1982) challenges the ethics of justice and proposes an ethic of care that conceptualizes moral maturity as caring for and sensitivity to the needs of others. She writes,

> As we have listened for centuries to the voices of men and the theories of development that their experience informs, so we have come more recently to notice not only the silence of women but the different voice of women lies in the truth of an ethic of care, the tie between relationship and responsibility, and the origins of aggression in the failure of connection. The failure to see the different reality of women's lives and to hear the differences in their voices stems in part from the assumption that there is a single mode of social experience and interpretation.
>
> …While an ethic of justice proceeds from the premise of equality—that everyone should be treated the same—an ethic of care rests on the premise of nonviolence—that no one should be hurt. (1993, pp. 173–174)

Feminist critique (Noddings, 1992) stresses the importance of all people and an ethics of relationships and care. The emphasis is "on living together, on creating, on maintaining, and enhancing positive relations" (p. 21). Feminist theories encourage administrators to challenge the conflicts between self-interest and the desire to "act on behalf of others." Noddings suggests that administrative decisions are related to how we are situated, who we are, and to whom we are related. Feminist critique stresses the importance of engaging in public, moral deliberation and making and revising decisions according to the results of such debate and not solely on technical, rational, and political expertise. The emphasis is on responsibility and relationships as much as on rights and rules.

Charol Shakeshaft (1995) focuses on differences in the way male and female administrators perceive situations. Her work is based on the belief that gender and race differences influence behavior and perspective. For example, male supervisors evaluate women more harshly than do female supervisors, and male administrators are less likely to promote women into positions of close working proximity because they feel uncomfortable in a close working relationship and are concerned with image problems among colleagues, subordinates, and family members. Women seem to value community and relationship building more than men do. Men typically receive more feedback, and more types of feedback, than women do. Furthermore, women often receive positive feedback even when their performance is less than ideal, depriving them of an equal opportunity to improve their performance. Males fear the prospect of women's tears and often hold back negative comments. The work environment of women is also one that has elements of sexual fear and threats that can be perceived as unsafe. Shakeshaft concludes,

> The point of examining these differences is not to say one approach is right and one is wrong (the way theory and practice up to now have done), but rather to help us understand that males and females may be coming from very different places, and that unless we understand these differences, we aren't likely to work well together.
>
> …The traditional literature of educational administration not only leaves women without a clear understanding of issues important to them, but also deprives men of understanding how their cultural identity as males interacts with women's cultural identity as females and the effects this interaction has on organizational dynamics. (pp. 153–154)

Starratt (1991) suggests that educational administrators need to draw on both care (understanding, sensitivity, nurturing) and justice (rationality, rights, laws) to create ethical schools.

Recent concern has been expressed (Banks, 1995, 1993) that administrative epistemologies used in research and practice may be racially biased. Banks suggests that "all knowledge reflects the values and interests of its creators" (1993, p. 4). With our meta-narrative understanding of educational administration, views from other races or cultures can be relegated to the margins in terms of legitimacy. Schewick and Young (1997) state,

> as we teach and promote epistemologies like positivism to post-modernism, we are at least implicitly teaching and promoting the social history of the dominant race at the exclusion of people of color, scholars of color and the possibility for research based on other race/culture epistemologies. We can, however, use our opposition to racism to consider the question of whether our dominant epistemologies are racially biased and, if they are, to begin to change the situation. (p. 11)

These authors provide an example of an Afrocentric feminist epistemology (Hill, 1991) that is theoretically grounded in concrete experience, dialogue, caring, and personal accountability. The bottom line is that a person's perception of truth can be blurred by his or her system of beliefs, assumptions, values, contexts, words, and ultimately decisions.

Foster (1986) suggests that a transformation occurred in which administrators became "concerned with justice and equity rather than efficiency and economy" (p. 23). Critical theory seeks to understand administration by how it reflects on human relationships—how administrators affect those they encounter. In the objective world of fact, conclusions are based on empirical evidence; in the moral world of rightness, they are based on sanctioned discourse and debates about values such as truth, justice, and equality. Foster approaches administration and leadership as praxis—a practical action aimed at clarifying and resolving social conditions:

> Praxis must be thought of as practical action, informed by theory, that attempts to change various conditions. In one respect, then, change involves a raising of consciousness about possibilities by penetrating the dominating ideas or total ideologies and analyzing the possible forms of life. This orientation, while political and cultural, is also critical, because it suggests that we attempt to cut through the 'natural' taken-for-granted status quo to explore new arrangements. (p. 167)

For Foster, leadership requires critical reflection and analysis by all in a process of empowerment and transformation.

Critical theory dictates that all decisions have values as well as factual premises. Administrators must reflect on and consider the moral consequences of their actions. Their decisions affect the interest and welfare of a large, diverse group of people. Administrative decisions must be grounded in deliberate reflection and consideration of moral issues and the consequences of actions based on those decisions. The well-being of the child serving as the fundamental value, "…persons along the axis of oppression (whether teachers, administrators, students, or staff) must endure first-hand the discriminatory polices and practices engaged in by majority group members unaware of the influence of their actions on others" (W. Greenfield, 1993, p. 269).

Administrators have a unique moral responsibility to all whom their decisions involve and influence. The difficulties administrators often face grow out of competing and often conflicting moral values. In education, issues such as inclusion, school prayer, and family life education have generated these types of debates. Decisions ultimately are made from complex alternatives and require effective moral reasoning. We will return to this subject in later chapters.

Postmodernism, Broad Fields, and Beyond

Feminist and critical theorists continue to attack empiricist, objectivist, structuralist thought and patterns of inquiry in educational administration. They argue that scientific methods provide only small insights—and not always accurate ones—into organizations. On the other hand, postmodernists suggest that no foundations exist for knowledge and therefore no successful way to represent reality exists. "Postmodernists argue that all forms of knowing have equal legitimacy, all expressions are acceptable forms of voice, and there are no hierarchies of wisdom." (Glickman, 1998, p. 40). Postmodernists seek to understand divisions stressing knowledge's importance to inquiry while at the same time deconstructing incumbent forms of knowledge production and dissemination. "Those who write from a postmodern perspective tend to question the value of rationality, to reject grand theory, to favor local knowledge over systemic understanding, to eschew large-scale studies, and to view the world as an indeterminate place beyond coherent description" (Constas, 1998, p. 27). Postmodernism rejects the idea of meta-narratives altogether denying that there is a "totalizing reality to be determined" as acceptable truths.

Willower (1996), argues however,

> what we've had in educational administration is the articulation by a few of a borrowed positivist view followed by an aggressive subjectivist and critical theory reaction, against a backdrop of epistemological neglect occasioned by preoccupation with other matters and lack of philosophical awareness or interest or both. (p. 172)

The critics seem to be demanding a broad-fields or theory view of administrative practice. For the practitioner, who confronts the day-to-day operation of the school, utility can be the only criterion under the pressure of today's environment. Cornel West (1992, p. 65) suggests, "…new cultural politics of difference…align themselves with demoralized, demobilized, depoliticized, and disorganized people in order to empower and enable social action."

Postmodernism addresses the importance of creativity, imagination, and vision. In a rapidly changing environment, organizations must articulate realistic, credible, attractive futures. Progress is the "realization of a vision" that is used to guide successful improvement. It begins as a statement of dreams that develop from inspiration and creative insights. Such thinking is more imagery than words, more perception than conception. It is the presentation of scenarios and visions that express dreams, and are tempered with an understanding of what is possible—a belief in what should and can be.

Thomas Greenfield himself uses this approach to create passionate arguments using the discursive arts. He brings other ways of seeing to the field of educational administration (Harris, 1996).

> Really massive gains over experience come from manipulating theory formulations so that they apply to matters beyond experience, enabling us to think hypothetically and act accordingly. The imagination so augmented can explore policy and decision option spaces that have not been lived through, perhaps not with precision, owing to the friability of current administrative theory and its context dependence, but with a modest prospect of beating chance. (Evers & Lakomski, 1996, p. 140)

There is joy in creating something of lasting value and the feeling that we have added something special to the world. Bolman and Deal (1995) suggest that leaders have lost touch with some of these precious gifts, with what gives our lives passion and purpose. As they suggest it is "about the search for something bigger…. Seek new sources of vigor, meaning, and hope to enrich your life and leave a better legacy for those who come after you" (pp. 11–12). These sources animate, inspire and, transform as they operate on the emotional and spiritual resources and on its values, commitment, and aspirations. They provide a deep, noble sense of purpose and inspiration.

Other recent lines of research focus on studying the culture of organizations and the leader's role in developing and modifying that culture. Most argue that the cultural focus is closely akin to the subjectivist and critical theory view in its underlying assumptions regarding the importance of the shared values, beliefs, and ideology.

A minority express concern that such cultural approaches are simply an expansion of the behaviorist and structuralist control models espoused by the scientific, rationalist community. They attempt to influence thought as well as action, to make a shift toward ideological control. Foster (1986) worries that it is the leader's conception of organizational culture that is promoted. The existing culture, however, may protect the status quo and need to be changed to stimulate the imaginative process. It may have to rescue itself from the perils in which it exists (Cunningham & Gresso, 1993). The culture must be changed if we hope to create a new and better future and to establish links between dreams and actions.

Even the critics of postmodernism recognize that it too has something to offer to our understanding of epistemology and knowledge development. Constas (1998) states,

> …we are meant to believe that postmodernism can rescue us from the dominant and oppressive conditions created by modernist/scientific discourse. There is, however, reason to believe that postmodernism (deconstruct, interrogate, genderize) itself contains a measure of veiled censorship that regulates the discourse of educational inquiry…. We need to consider the idea that the postmodern version of educational inquiry is just another variety of discourse in education and should not be granted special privileges…because I believe that an overreliance on any one disciplinary perspective is necessarily confining, it is worth exploring the way educational research may be situated, explained and enlivened. (pp. 30–31)

The debate continues between subjectivity and objectivity, values and facts, and empiricism and philosophy. The most reasoned position seems to suggest that all these perspectives offer the possibility for improved understanding of educational administration. As growth in all forms of knowledge occurs, it supports an improvement in our reasoning and decision making, and ultimately in our administrative ability. A balanced perspective (Willower, 1996) suggests that science, ethics, and practice should not be sharply separated but should be allowed to inform each other. We should not cut ourselves off from any of the knowledge sources that can inform wise choices. Science, ethics, philosophy, and creativity should not be sharply separated and placed in mutually exclusive warring camps.

Much can be learned from the typology of many "meta-narratives," and pursuit of that learning makes the development of educational leadership challenging and rewarding (Griffiths, 1988). As Willower (1996) states,

> indeed, it is ironic that subjectivists and critical theorists who tout the importance of values but reject science, cut themselves off from the very processes and insight that can inform value choices in concrete situations…. Morals have to do with the common problems of living, and separating morals from life in favor of an abstract creed creates social problems rather than resolving them…. The time for polemics in educational administration is ending and scholars should now devote more energy to a revitalization of scientific work in the field. (pp. 173–174)

Meta-narratives need not be mutually exclusive; considered in concert, they all contribute to theory development and practice, in the spirit of the broad-fields position. Sirotnik and Oakes (1986) combine structural functionalism, interpretivism, and critical theory into a practical, educational approach they term "critical inquiry." Prestine (1995) states,

> the debate over knowledge-base issues needs to be continued. Basic questions regarding what 'knowing' administration means needs to be raised along with political ques-

tions such as 'whose knowledge is legitimated?' and 'why is such knowledge being legitimated?'

...This multifaceted conception of knowledge contrasts sharply with a convergent linear and hierarchical approach to knowledge, which distorts practice. These and other issues caution us that in the debate over the establishment of a knowledge base, it would seem to be wise to err on the side of inclusion rather than exclusion, divergence rather than convergence. If educational administration is to remain a vibrant and dynamic field, one that pushes on the edge of the envelope, as it were, we must not be confined by rigid prespecification of boundaries or meticulous categorization of knowledge. (pp. 281–282)

Multi-narratives can often better guide practice than can any single theoretical perspective. Not all are equally useful in all situations, but each may have something to offer in different facets of educational administration. Informed administrators can value multiple ways of viewing situations from differing epistemologies and take actions beyond those offered by any single perspective (Capper, 1993).

> Characterize each of the following individuals' meta-narratives, and comment on their strengths and weaknesses: (a) Mr. Wayne, (b) Mrs. Taylor, (c) Mr. Newton, (d) Mrs. Maynard, (e) Mr. Browne, (f) Mrs. Gilligan, (g) Mr. Newman.

Administrative Platforms

The earlier sections describe the many frames of reference, conceptual understandings, ways of knowing, and ethical beliefs relevant to the enormously complex job of administering an organization. They include a set of contrasting beliefs, opinions, values, and attitudes that can provide a foundation for practice. It is thus important that administrators and those whom they influence have a clear understanding of the foundational principles, conceptualizations, philosophy, and narratives on which they base their judgments.

Sergiovanni and Starratt (1983) refer to this personal philosophy as an *educational platform*. An individual's platform

> comprises fundamental beliefs about human development, the nature of learning, and the relationship between schooling and adult life in society.... The elements of the platform make up the roots of the vision.... Both leaders and administrators need to act out of a set of beliefs and values, and these are what make up their platforms. (Starratt, 1995, pp. 71–72)

Barnett (1991) stresses the importance of platform development in helping administrators "to identify the moral dilemmas they will face as administrators and to articulate the standards of practice they will use in judging situations" (p. 135). Administrators often begin to construct preliminary platforms by examining the purpose of education, the nature of children and learning, and the teaching process. Next come their ideas of how supervision and administration are related to these processes (Kottkamp, 1982). Administrators should give themselves the opportunity to consciously articulate their educational and administrative philosophies and moral standards of practice.

Educators carry on their work, make decisions, and plan instruction on the basis of their educational platforms; thus, these platforms should be clearly articulated and espoused. This concept is based on the political model in which parties are expected to develop platforms to aid supporters and voters to make the clearest, best, most informed choices for themselves. Knowing the platform and being aware of any inconsistencies with practice or other platforms is immensely helpful. Argyris and Schön (1978) refer to these inconsistencies as differences between espoused theory and theory-in-use. Espoused theories detail philosophies, beliefs, values, assumptions, theories, and paradigms underlying behavior; theory-in-use represents the way people actually implement them. Argyris and Schön state:

> When someone is asked how he would behave under certain circumstances, the answer he usually gives is his espoused theory of action for the situation. This is the theory of action to which he gives allegiance and which, upon request, he communicates to others. However, the theory that actually governs his actions is his theory-in-use, which may or may not be compatible with his espoused theory; furthermore, the individual may or may not be aware of the incompatibility of the two theories. (p. 11)

Argyris and Schön (1978), Cunningham (1982), and Blake and McCanse (1991) suggest that the best first step in improving organizational functioning is for practitioners to discover and make explicit any differences between espoused theory and theory-in-use. An administrator needs to clearly state his or her espoused theory, that is, his or her administrative platform. The administrator then compares this platform to his or her behavior within the organization. When platform and behavior are incompatible, the administrator decides which to alter. It is best for all concerned when actual behavior is compatible with espoused values and theories. When it is not, trust breaks down and the organization becomes ineffective. Thus the development of an educational and administrative platform is essential for all administrative action.

By creating a platform and clarifying the underlying rationale for action, the administrator should evaluate its cogency, consistency, comprehensiveness, compatibility, and compare it with his or her convictions (the five Cs). Meta-narratives can help in determining orientation and epistemology. Individual platforms should be in general agreement with the philosophy, mission, goals, and direction of the school system. When they are not, administrators should endeavor to explain why such differences exist.

Sergiovanni and Starratt (1988) describe how to get started:

> Once we have written down the elements of our platform, we can with further reflection begin to group them in clusters and place them in some order of importance....
>
> [Some] will find the writing exercise too tedious and will seek out a colleague to discuss this whole question. The free flow of shared ideas frequently stimulates the process of clarification.... Still others may go to a formal statement of goals that the school or system has in print to begin the process.... (p. 244)

They go on to suggest that regardless of how individual platforms are developed, administrators should compare them with those of other colleagues to provide themselves an opportunity to reflect on "areas of agreement or disagreement." Sometimes this comparison leads to modification and sometimes to acceptance of greater diversity in perspectives. It usually helps to build collegiality, understanding, alignment, and, when the platform is compatible with behavior, trust, integrity, cooperation, and continuous improvement, that creates organization effectiveness (Cunningham & Gresso, 1995).

> Select one of the principals from the vignette whose views are closest to your own and develop his or her administrative platform.

School Improvement

DONALD J. WILLOWER
The Pennsylvania State University

Most educators, parents, and community members want their schools to be good ones, so school improvement is a major function of educational administration. It is necessarily an ongoing activity because past successes are no guarantee of future ones.

School administrators and teachers typically care about students and want to help them. But caring, although important and desirable, is by itself not enough. The basic problem is how to keep a school moving in directions that will actually benefit the students. Improvement has two main elements: the choice of desired directions and aims, and strategies for attaining them.

The examination of potential directions is a philosophical problem because some rather than others will be chosen. The selection of directions can be made in a number of ways, including considering philosophical values, exploring educational goals and objectives, or scanning for current problems in the setting in question. The direction finally chosen will depend on its relevance in terms of desired ends, but also should be based on its feasibility as determined by the examination and analysis of implementation strategies.

The selection of strategies for implementation is scientific, because actually achieving worthwhile aims depends on effective strategies. Here, the use of theories or explanations of how things work will be crucial. Organizational change has psychological, sociological, political, and economic sides, and concepts and explanations from such fields can be helpful in making judgments about how things are likely to play out in a person's own situation. This kind of analysis can reveal what could have been unanticipated and unintended sequences.

Further, it provides a dimension of realism to choices about the direction of school improvement. There are risks in efforts to move a school ahead, which educational administrators should accept willingly and even joyfully, but it would be irresponsible to expend energy, time, and public funds on the essentially unattainable. Hence, the value of the approach suggested.

Of course, it helps when the kinds of procedures cited are accepted as part of the organizational culture of the school. Because these procedures are fundamentally problem-solving methods, they can be applied to all sorts of school issues. When such an approach becomes a key part of the way educators address their school's future, hierarchy, personalities, fads, panaceas, and pet projects take second place to inquiry and critical thought. However, given the nature of people and organizations, incorporating such practices as part of an organization's routines can be a major challenge. What the ancient Greeks called praxis, or thoughtful practice, is often as elusive as it is desirable.

Moral Issues

An important aspect of administration is a sensitivity to the types of moral issues that may arise. The focus of this chapter thus far has been on the reasoning that underlies principles, practices, and decisions. Now we need to consider the types of ethical issues that confront administrators and often help to clarify and support reasoning and make it concrete. In its most basic form, the challenge of administration is to do what is right in regard to the ethical issues it faces. What are those ethical issues?

Our beliefs regarding major moral issues are often deeply ingrained by the time we reach adulthood, and we do not always consciously understand platforms or issues. Beliefs about issues shape our views about how we treat people and places. These are our ideals of individual and social justice. In addition many laws exist that govern the way we handle moral issues. Laws regarding segregation, civil rights, due process, and privacy rights provide directives that all must follow to avoid the imposition of legal penalties, whatever the administrator's value system. Laws will continue to emerge as new issues are addressed; the role of leadership, however, must consider more than the letter of the law or compliance with the law.

Bull and McCarthy (1995) suggest,

> Within their own jurisdictions (e.g., classroom, school and school, district) educators play an important role in interpreting and applying the law, and they retain considerable discretion to make decisions and establish policies. Knowledge of how the law works should lead to the realization that educators, not courts or legislatures, must determine what actions are reasonable and just in most school situations. (p. 620)

In fact, courts are reluctant to interfere with judgments of educators, and the judiciary will defer decisions to school personnel and policy makers unless legal rights clearly hang in the balance. It is at this point that reason, judgment, ethics, and moral responsibility become entwined with issues and decisions.

Almost all issues that an administrator faces are value based: All issues and actions have ethical and moral connotations. Although the context and ideological frames of reference seem to be infinite, certain issues seem to receive more attention than others. Many of these moral issues concern a combination of the following:

I. Individual rights
   a. Majority/minority interests
      1. race and ethnicity
      2. social class
      3. gender
      4. disability
      5. sexual orientation
      6. religious practice (separation of church and state)
   b. Individual/collective interests
      1. subject matter, pedagogy, and standards
      2. welfare
      3. discipline and punishments
      4. poverty

      5. resources

      6. assembly

II. Democratic society

    a. Representation (shared power)

    b. Family values

    c. Economic opportunity

    d. Common good

    e. National character

    f. Politics and governance

III. Healthy and safe environments

    a. Air, water, and land quality

    b. Crime and violence

    c. Human and social rights

    d. Public services

Knowledge of competing values and other complexities surrounding issues helps sensitize administrators to the moral and ethical dilemmas to be faced. The best decision on such issues is not always clear. Determining how such value collisions are resolved within an organization is one of the key responsibilities of administrators.

> Select a moral issue and discuss how each of the principals might deal with that issue based on their meta-narratives.

The Knowledge Base of Educational Administration

As the diverse meta-narratives suggest, there is considerable debate and little agreement regarding a specific knowledge base for educational administration (Hoy, 1994). Obviously, no "cookbook" tells practitioners what meta-narratives, values, methods, or models to use, what issues and operational areas to address, or how to apply specific skills in various different contexts. Administrative knowledge is a complex array of meta-narratives, theories, ideologies, skills, ethical principles, paradigms, and practices, which are applied to a diverse set of issues. Bernard (1938) made the first concerted effort to create a complete and integrated explanation from the tangled literature on administration. In the field of education, Edwin Bridges, Roald Campbell, Luvern Cunningham, Fenwick English, Daniel Griffith, Mark Hanson, Wayne Hoy, Ralph Kimbrough, Stephen Knezewich, Cecil Miskel, Joseph Murphy, Robert Owens, Thomas Sergiovanni, and Donald Willower, to name but a few, have made similar efforts. These scholars noted that each approach, although offering different insights and different perspectives, helps to provide a more complete explanation of the administrative process.

    The synthesis of knowledge in educational administration can be conceptualized as comprising six factors: functions, skills, ethics, context, operational areas, and issues. Table 1.3 on page 221 presents a comprehensive model of the complexity of

TABLE 1.3 Key Factors in Effective Administration

Administrative Functions	Skills	Ethical Standards	Structure and Organization	Operational Areas	Context	Issues
Plan	Leadership	Honesty	President	Finance	Community	Safe schools
Organize	Problem analysis	Integrity	U.S. Department of Education	Curriculum and instruction	Taxpayers	Multiculturalism
Actuate/direct	Decision making	Promise keeping	Secretary of Education	Human resource development	Special-interest groups	Inclusion
Coordinate	Implementing	Loyalty/fidelity	Governors	Research and development	Teachers/parents/kids	School prayer
Control/evaluate	Delegation	Fairness	State school boards	Business and logistics	Chamber of commerce	Technology
	Supervising and motivating	Concern for others	State superintendents	Physical plant	College professors/researchers	Standardized testing
	Interpersonal sensitivity	Respect for others	State departments of education	Pupil personnel	Media/TV	Assessment
	Oral communication	Law-abiding/civic duty	Local school boards		City council	Vouchers
	Written communication	Pursuit of excellence	Superintendents		Religious organizations	Charter schools
	Research measurement evaluation	Personal accountability	Central Administrators		Private business	School reform
	Legal, policy, and political applications		Principals		Professional associations	Productivity
	Public relations		Teachers		Textbook manufacturers	Family values
	Technology		PTA		Industry	Social capital
					Government	Constructivist curriculum
					International groups	Global education
					Technologists	Environmentalism

educational administration. Even though in practice factors cannot be separated, it is probably best to focus on and integrate one factor at a time. Each leads to some truth, but none by itself affords an adequate understanding. Together they provide a more complete understanding of educational administration (Flood, 1990).

Few issues in America today engender more controversy than does education. Educational administrators face "unpredictability, rapid change, and potential for exhilaration and disaster" (Porlin, 1997, p. 4). Certainly responsiveness to diverse demands is high on the list of responsibilities for all educational leaders. The role is shifting (Goldring, 1990) from one of directing and controlling to one of guiding, facilitating, and coordinating. Leaders are required to build direction, alignment, a culture of visionaries; to encourage risks and experimentation; to set the pace; and to maintain high standards

The Interstate School Leaders Licensure Consortium: Standards for School Leaders (ISLLC) were developed by key personnel from twenty-four states and nine associations representing the educational administration profession to improve policy, practice, and research throughout the country. These efforts build on previous work (discussed in Chapter 6), since the 1960s, by professional organizations representing the field of school administration. The standards are focused on what the committee called "the heart and soul of effective leadership." All standards support the essential importance of the learning environment. Each of the standards places special emphasis on vision and promoting the success of all students. Box 1.1 on page 24 presents the six ISLLC standards.

Effective leaders understand all elements of educational administration and create a shared vision of school excellence that is translated into classroom practice. They raise teacher expectations for students, they support continued curricular and instructional improvement, and they reward and recognize all forms of excellence. Sergiovanni (1991) concludes,

> Schools must be run effectively and efficiently if they are to survive. Policies must be in place. Budgets must be set. Teachers must be assigned. Classes must be scheduled. Reports must be completed. Standardized tests must be given. Supplies must be purchased. The school must be kept clean. Students must be protected from violence. Classrooms must be orderly. These are essential tasks that guarantee the survival of the school as an organization. But for the school to transform itself into an institution, a learning community must emerge. Institutionalization is the moral imperative that principals face. No matter how relentlessly administrators pursue their managerial imperative, reliability in action, firmness in conviction, and just disposition are the consequences of the moral imperative. Without tending to the moral imperative there can be no organizational character, and without character a school can be neither good nor effective. (pp. 329–330).

What will be the principals' responsibility in the Flem Snopes school renewal effort?

BOX **1.1**

ISLLC Standards for School Leaders

Standard 1

A school administrator is an educational leader who promotes the success of all students by facilitating the development, articulation, implementation, and stewardship of a vision of learning that is shared and supported by the school community.

Standard 2

A school administrator is an educational leader who promotes the success of all students by advocating, nurturing, and sustaining a school culture and an instructional program conducive to student learning and staff professional growth.

Standard 3

A school administrator is an educational leader who promotes the success of all students by ensuring management of the organization, operations, and resources for a safe, efficient, and effective learning environment.

Standard 4

A school administrator is an educational leader who promotes the success of all students by collaborating with families and community members, responding to diverse community interests and needs, and mobilizing resources.

Standard 5

A school administrator is an educational leader who promotes the success of all students by acting with integrity, with fairness, and in an ethical manner.

Standard 6

A school administrator is an educational leader who promotes the success of all students by understanding, responding to, and influencing the larger political, social, economic, legal, and cultural context.

Source: Interstate School Leaders Licensure Consortium (1996). *Standards for School Leaders.* Washington, DC: Council of Chief State School Officers.

Leadership Qualities for Our Schools

GENE R. CARTER, Executive Director
Association for Supervision and Curriculum Development

As we stand on the threshold of a new millennium, we are in the middle of a great shift in world history. Our society is going through some of the most intense social, political, economic, and educational upheavals we have ever known, and this turmoil endangers virtually all institutions and their leaders. Education, broadly

defined as from kindergarten through graduate school, is seen as America's solution. Whatever the problem, educational institutions are viewed by many as the nation's first line of defense.

Today, education leaders find themselves leading organizations and groups across a rapidly shifting landscape toward new destinations—

often under provocative conditions. These groups are increasingly diverse and challenged to deal with undefined problems, grapple with theoretical and emotional issues, and make decisions so new that the organizational consequences are unknown. And education leaders must help individuals and groups make sense and increased meaning in often fragmented, overwhelming, and fast-moving situations characteristic of the new millennium. In the face of these demands, education leaders are realizing that they can no longer rely on traditional management techniques to satisfy the requirements of their roles—they must draw on a deeper source of guidance, strength, and influence.

Education in the nineteenth century was designed to produce workers and citizens who would advance the economy by following the rules. Education in the twenty-first century must be grounded in a decidedly different agenda—it must be built on a strong foundation of connectivity, coherence, shared and mutually created meaning, relationships, and the human experience itself.

To realize this vision, education leaders for the twenty-first century must reinvent themselves and their institutions. We must change our reductionist thinking about schools and learning, and we must change the way we interact with one another. Our challenge is to reframe the agenda around the issues and challenges of learning, rather than primarily around schooling and training. We must think of learning as an integral part of human life rather than something reserved exclusively for the classroom, and we must consider all situations as potential opportunities for learning.

We now know enough about learning systems to propose a significant rearrangement of current practice. According to the new vision of reality, relationships and interdependence are central. Our responsibility as education leaders is not to reengineer a new, fixed education structure, but to enable the creation of mutable structures that adapt to the dance of life.

We are in the midst of a sea of change that is challenging us to rethink our basic assumptions about the changing of schools. For too long we have tried to fix the curriculum, the schedules, the students, and the tests. Now we realize that we must first change the way we think and relate to one another. We must change the discourse occurring in and around schools by stimulating inquiry, questioning, and problem solving, and by focusing on learning for everyone in the system—not just the students.

With the many changes that are occurring in our society and our world, a new approach to leadership is necessary at every level, particularly in our educational institutions, organizations, and agencies. Leadership becomes a matter of *how to be* rather than *how to do*. And the signs of effective leadership appear primarily among the followers. Are they reaching their potential? Are they learning? Consequently, education leaders must model a range of behaviors, including:

- Creating and communicating a core set of beliefs and values, while understanding and meeting short-term goals
- Building bridges among people and their ideas, and assisting people in discovering their creative potential
- Challenging traditional ideas, assumptions, and structures
- Embracing ambiguity and applauding serendipity
- Reflecting on current activities and events
- Seeking new perspectives in their lives
- Engaging in lifelong learning

Those who are able to release this spirit of greatness within themselves, their colleagues, and their constituents strengthen their ability to be leaders in educational transformation.

We know the story of the phoenix rising from the ashes—it serves as a symbol of transformation and rebirth. This symbol is particularly potent for us as we enter the next century. We are in the midst of rapid change, of demands to destroy old ways of doing things and to create new more powerful and vibrant ones. The message of the phoenix tells us that we can find, within ourselves, the means to transform our leadership. For us, as the generation that will pass its collective soul to the next, the time to lead is now.

Conclusion

We now know enough to develop the schools we need, but, our current thinking is holding us back. We must change our frames of reference, our paradigms, our mental models, and our meta-narratives when they no longer meet the needs of our times. They are invisible elements that influence the way we think, and our ability to envision the future. We can operate "without thinking" in a habitual state because our meta-narratives, our belief systems, are so familiar to us. However, they also hold us back from seeing that present situations do not support practice as usual, that our existing philosophical beliefs and related knowledge have blinded us. New frames can accentuate previously unnoticed possibilities; new relationships, previously unseen, can become viable. For these reasons administrators should continually revisit and reflect on their platforms.

Significant improvements can start with the system that is already in place, but it always can be radically improved (Rhodes, 1997). Our practice is held captive by our theory, our knowledge base, and our experiences. We must ensure that the ideas, positions, and theories that enjoy privileged positions of unquestioned supremacy and thus are viewed as the "truth" are themselves questioned when new ways of seeing things evolve. The challenge is in how we pursue knowledge and how knowledge is expanded.

Knowledge grows within those who discipline themselves to think about what is known and what still needs to be known. In this way, we learn from one another and we develop new insights. Edward Deming (1993) found it appalling that we so underuse and misuse the knowledge and skills of employed workers at all levels. A group encompasses more knowledge, expertise, and information than any single member. We are called to learn from those who have come before us and from our contemporaries so that we can be prepared to leave our imprints on our organizations and professions. This is the real stuff of leadership.

Leadership consists in providing information and new knowledge, maintaining interactions, creating new alignments, connecting people, continuously improving and learning, assessing results, sustaining capacity, and institutionalizing improvements. Leaders should encourage collaboration within the school and school district and across district lines. Thus a cross-fertilization of ideas occurs and new research, knowledge, values, and best practices can be synthesized into a schoolwide plan. Cunningham (1994) suggests that effective schools should:

- focus on improvements that positively influence what happens to students;
- encourage collegiality, trust, and integrity, and allow sufficient time for open, free-flowing communication;
- foster a climate of mutual trust, support, growth, and innovation;
- promote staff development as an essential component of school improvement;
- provide for continuous improvement that is incremental and systematic;
- empower and encourage staff to experiment, innovate, and share success;
- work with values, interests, and expertise;
- continuously monitor and provide feedback of results
- provide central administrative support of individual school efforts;

- nurture cooperation among home, school, and community;
- develop a mutually shared vision of the ideal school;
- encourage face-to-face involvement of appropriate stakeholders. (p. 25)

The ultimate assessment of all effort to improve education remains whether student learning has improved. That is the lasting core value that guides administrative and organizational growth.

> What frames of reference and approaches to knowledge development might work best in renewing Flem Snopes Schools?

PORTFOLIO ARTIFACTS

1. Write a one-page statement of your philosophy of education.

2. Write a one-page statement of your philosophy of leadership.

3. Define the values or ethics that guide your behavior as an educational leader.

4. Serve on or examine the results of a school improvements committee.

5. Examine past agendas of school board meetings or attend a school board meeting and relate the work of the school board to your philosophy and values.

6. Read on the subject of education and administration and write annotated bibliographies.

7. Attend a conference or a superintendent's administrative meeting and report back on the content and what you learned.

8. Develop a new and improved approach to some aspect of schooling.

9. Develop a comprehensive administrative platform.

TERMS

Administrative platforms	Management	Postmodernism
Ethics	Meta-narratives	School renewal
Feminist critique	Modernism	
Leadership	Paradigms	

SUGGESTED READINGS

Beck, L. G. (1996). *The four imperatives of a successful school.* Thousand Oaks, CA: Corwin Press.
Capper, C. A. (Ed.). (1993). *Educational administration in a pluralistic society.* Albany: State University of New York Press.

Donmoyer, R., Imbar, M., & Schewich, J. (Eds.). (1995). *The knowledge base in education administration*. Albany: State University of New York Press.

English, F. (1994). *Theory in educational administration*. New York: Harper Collins.

Evers, C. W., & Lakomski, G. (1996). *Exploring educational administration*. New York: Pergamon Press.

Gordon, S., Benner, P., & Nodings, N. (1996). *Care giving: Reading in knowledge, practice, ethics, and politics*. Philadelphia: University of Pennsylvania Press.

2 Context and Perspective for Educational Administrators

Vignette: Scrivner Middle School—Understanding the Context

You are principal of Scrivner Middle School, a position you have inherited from a string of very short term principals. Previous principals, unable to turn this school around to the satisfaction of the community and parents or have it meet state and national standards, were quickly replaced. The school is located in a poor urban ethnic community with a proud past that has been severely hurt by layoffs at the telephone company and other smaller industries within the community.

In discussing this position with you, Superintendent Melville said, "Low state assessment scores, decreases in federal funding for special programs, court rulings, ideological differences particularly related to expanded student services, state mandates, changing demographics, and a decline in the students' support systems have resulted in rapid decline at Scrivner and this situation must be turned around." There is state and national pressure for meaningful reform, and your initial assignment is to get a handle on shifting politics and pressures and see that the school is better able to respond to these demands and meet state standards.

Melville continued, "Previous principals were unable to read the federal, state, and local demands and generated resistance, divisiveness, and mistrust, which ultimately ended in ideological battlegrounds and no school improvement." Melville made reference to a quote he had read that change is "technically simple and socially complex," and he stated, "This certainly seems to be the case at Scrivner. You must use the present politics and context to take charge of the needed improvements and not become a victim of them."

Your first visit with community members quickly demonstrates their mistrust of you as an educator. They let you know that, as money got tighter within the community, per-student expenditure nearly doubled, student–teacher ratios declined, and student achievement deteriorated badly according to state and local assessments. Mrs. Peltzman, a local member of the state school board who is very critical of the state's schools cites Scrivner as evidence that, "throwing money at the problem does not work." She argues, "For an ordinary business to almost double its resources, yet somehow manage to produce less, is unthinkable. But that is what happened at Scrivner over the past ten years."

The school is also regarded as part of the social breakdown within the community—assault, robbery, auto theft, substance abuse, teenage pregnancy, the number of single-parent homes have all significantly increased, while community cohesiveness has declined. In the past, the school was a focal point of activity and pride for the community but it is no longer. The community is placing strong pressure on the board to reduce property taxes, get more money from the state and federal governments, and become more entrepreneurial.

This slump is a particular sore spot because the community believes that more affluent neighborhoods are not experiencing community and school decline. The community is very concerned since it has recently lost a possible new business, because of "a serious concern about education in the community and the need to provide remedial education for school graduates." The community sees the problems as irreversible and has given up on Scrivner and is encouraging board members to examine vouchers, privatization options, or possibly reforming Scrivner as a charter school.

In expressing the concerns brought out by the community to the teaching staff, you sense strong hostility toward state and federal interference and lack of local appreciation. Scrivner's teachers attack the community's parenting skills, discussing poor student behavior and state and local expenditure on weapons detection, security systems, police patrols, health clinics, truant officers, before- and after-school programs, special educators, counselors, discipline officers, and safe school and other behavior-related programs as taking up a lot of time and money. The school has spent money on major hazard removal, litigation regarding several suspensions, and a school accident, and significantly increased state and local accountability requirements that the teachers believe were testing for the wrong things and not adjusting for their student population. The staff believes that the state assessment system is holding back local efforts to respond to changing needs.

Federal and state mandates have clogged the school with unneeded and often half-abandoned programs. The board and superintendent are constantly providing reports to state and federal agencies that require time for meetings, assessments, and special reports from teachers and principals. A particular point of contention is the belief that actual salary adjusted for the cost of living has decreased as has the money available for instructional support. The little money available is all going into technology, which is not even a major part of the curriculum. Mrs. Rivera, a science teacher, says, "Superintendent Melville wants us to reform this school, but the teachers in this district have given him very low marks on reforms that have been tried. In addition, the board will be getting rid of him fairly soon."

Recent efforts at state and federal assessment seem to be a particular bone of contention for Scrivner teachers. The standards-based system is not compatible with many of the reforms they have recently made at the school, and thus the students do not perform well on assessments. There is considerable disagreement among people at the local, state, and national levels on what students need to know and be able to do, how this material is best taught and learned, and how student performance should be assessed. The history of outside pressures seems to be one of constantly shifting attitudes and beliefs and a lack of consistent direction. The school is now defined by strife and conflict, mistrust, criticism, and low morale. Teachers believe the school's problems are caused by lack of parental responsibility, inadequate resources for demanded improvements, inability to see differences in schools that might explain differences in tests results, power politics, micromanagement, lack of concern for social issues, a never-ending system of roadblocks, leadership instability, and an inability to agree on what Scrivner should look like as an ideal school.

In reiterating that he does not want you to follow the path of previously unsuccessful principals at Scrivner, Superintendent Melville states, "You realize that if you do not understand the context in which you operate, you could find yourself at the center of a flurry of controversies. Many events, political decisions, and economic situations have had a strong influence on what is going on at Scrivner Middle School. You cannot narrowly focus attention on the school or even the immediate community if you want to succeed at educating Scrivner students. What occurs at Scrivner is part of the larger events that are occurring outside the school. You will not succeed if you ignore this larger context for Scrivner education."

What individuals and groups seem most important in obtaining a clear understanding of the existing conditions at Scrivner?

The Federal and State Role

Most experts today recognize and accept the importance of context to the practice of educational administration. They may not agree on how best to characterize context, but few question its importance. Duke (1998) states, "as people interact, they are guided by their perception of context. These perceptions, by shaping speech and action, help to generate context, even as context influences interactions" (p. 172). He later reinforces this point, "one clear message from the preceding review of recent scholarship is that leadership is situated. It cannot be understood, in other words, apart from context. The context of leadership, however, may be characterized in various ways" (p. 182). Leaders today cannot be successful without having a broad understanding of the social, political, and economic dynamics that influence and are shaped by American education. Administrators must at least be aware of the ideologies, political pressures, shifting economic and social conditions, if they are to provide effective educational leadership.

The sheer number of groups offering ideas on how to improve education has drastically increased as have the number of competing reform agendas. Efforts to improve education have been described as waves of reform with each washing over an education system that is having a hard time gaining its balance. Because of general disappointment regarding most of these reform efforts, there is now a call for shifting the responsibility for reform. Not only may schooling change but so may the roles, responsibilities, and procedures of the educational leaders.

To a great extent, the quality of American education depends on the effectiveness of school leaders to be able to respond to diverse groups and pressures as they continuously work to improve schools. The call is for leaders with political savvy, a moral compass, who understand the social, economic, and human demands, the governmental and community agendas, as well as the professional expectations and responsibilities of the work. Schools are part of a much larger global system, linked to society through both formal and informal structures of governance and influence that shape almost all educational decisions. (For more information see: **www.ed.gov/**.)

What are some major factors that might have a strong influence on the future success of Scrivner Middle School?

Broad, Complex Context

Schooling is a federal interest, a state responsibility, and a local operation. The United States has fifty systems of public education that are being strongly influenced by world, national, state, and local pressures and expectations (see Chapter 5 for greater detail). James W. Guthrie and Rodney J. Reed (1991) capture the complexity of the system:

> The United States maintains an educational system which is probably more diverse, disparate, decentralized, and dynamic than any other in the world. This system depends only slightly upon national government to make education policy or to provide financial support for educational institutions. Instead, governmental authority for American education is distributed primarily among the fifty states, which in turn, delegate administrative responsibility to thousands of local school districts. The consequence is fifty systems of public tax-supported lower and higher education in which most policy is made by fifty sets of state officials, governors, legislators, judges, state boards of education, and their counterparts in thousands of local communities. As if this were not sufficiently complex, there exists a parallel system of private or nonpublic institutions, generally outside of government, for both higher and lower education. (p. 22)

Add to this the significant number of interest groups—the *Encyclopedia of Associations* lists 1,221 national and international education associations—and you begin to understand the diversity of thinking local school leaders must be prepared to contend with, even before they face students and their parents.

Citizens across the nation are becoming increasingly interested in what is taught, read, viewed, and discussed in our public schools. A policy network newsletter of the National School Boards Association states:

> Parents, students, school board members, and administrators all have an obvious interest regarding what goes on in our schools, but so do people with no local affiliation or direct connections to the district. People representing the political spectrum of ideas and beliefs, people worried about social mores and the future of a sometimes less than admirable society look to the public schools as a mechanism to foster change or to stifle it. (Morris, 1992, p. 1)

People use pressure, legislation, mandates, and other forms of political action to make decisions conform to their interests. The educational leader is responsible for ensuring that the final decisions are representative of the whole and are in the best interests of the children.

Educational leaders are caught among conflicting desires of elected and governmental officials, diverse communities, teachers and staff, boards of education, interest groups, students and families, educational experts, and others, all of whom have their own agendas. The related pressures seem to be increasing along with the ever-growing number of social problems and issues that find their ways into the schools. As educators become enmeshed in the web of issues being debated by various constituencies, they can find themselves at the center of the controversies, particularly if they do not understand the history and objectives of the groups with which they are dealing.

This broad and complex context have caused a number of writers to suggest that there has never been a more important time for our educational institutions to have effective leadership. Razik and Swanson (1995, pp. 70–71) suggest:

> For better or for worse, this is, indeed a dynamic and exciting period in human history. Because of the fluidity of the situation, it is a period of unparalleled opportunity and potential danger. To capitalize on the opportunities and to minimize the dangers demands extraordinarily wise leadership in all sectors and in all enterprises including education....
>
> The context of educational leadership today is different from any other time in history. It is essential that contemporary issues and processes be understood if leadership is to result in relevant action.

> With which individuals or groups should the principal at Scrivner Middle School meet on a regular basis?

Educational Origins

Education was not mentioned in the U.S. Constitution. As a result of the Tenth Amendment, ratified in 1791, it became a responsibility of each state. As states adopted constitutions, they consolidated powers over education that had been exercised by local communities. The states established minimum standards and guidelines, leaving a large amount of the power for operating the school systems to local communities. The American school system was built on a concept of universal opportunity for education to all of its citizens. Thousands of acts and laws passed in each of the states placed schools in the public domain, granting compulsory taxing power, setting schools up as quasi-municipal corporations, establishing legal rights, setting up standards, providing for governance, and so forth.

Names like Horace Mann, Henry Barnard, William H. McGuffey, Johann Herbart, and later John Dewey were powerful forces in shaping American education. The American people began to look to public education to meet the challenges of a rapidly changing civilization. School enrollments increased by geometric proportions, and public education became one of the great enterprises in the nation. At the same time, social and economic concerns in a changing world were making new demands on schooling.

Because the constitution is silent about support for public education, the federal government must use implied powers for which it does have responsibility to support involvement in education. These implied powers come from the general welfare clause, parts of the First Amendment, and both the due process and equal protection clauses of the Fourteenth Amendment. To date, five major federal responsibilities have been used to justify federal involvement in education: (1) land grant, (2) public relief and welfare, (3) national defense, (4) equal opportunity, and (5) economic competitiveness and school safety as shown in Table 2.1 on pages 35–37. This table is not inclusive but provides a sampling of legislation related to education. In addition, a number of pieces of legislation, although not directed specifically at education, certainly have a significant impact—such as the Fair Labor Standards Act and the Equal Employment Opportunity Act.

> How can you as principal gain a historic perspective on what has occurred at Scrivner Middle School?

Land Grant

As early as 1785, with the orderly distribution of public land through surveying and setting land aside for specific purposes, land-grant schools came into being. The Ohio Statehood Enabling Act was the first of the enabling acts that provided land grants for public schools in newly created states. Each of these enabling acts, by which territories became states, required provisions for a system of public education. Later, in 1862, the Morrill Act provided lands for the establishment of colleges and universities. In 1867, the U.S. Office of Education was created under the Department of the Interior for the purpose of collecting "statistics and facts as shall show the condition and progress of education in the several states and territories...." Henry Barnard was instrumental in the creation of this office and served as the first U.S. Commissioner of Education.

Relief

The country was entering into the Great Depression of the 1930s and initially relief acts were more to help the youth of the country who could not find jobs than they were to improve education. This legislation began with the development of vocational programs through the Smith–Hughes Act in 1917, but the heart of this legislation was in the New Deal activity in the 1930s, intended to train youth and place them in meaningful employment. The Impact Aid laws were enacted to help school systems that have a large amount of nontaxable federal property within the school district. The results of these laws include the familiar school lunch and school milk programs.

National Defense

In 1939, the U.S. Office of Education was transferred to the Federal Security Agency. The first act passed under the national security and defense emphasis was the National Science Foundation Act in 1950. This act provided funds for study and research in scientific fields and was administered by the National Science Board composed of twenty-four members and a director. The Hoover task force, Commission on Government

TABLE 2.1   Federal Involvement in Education

Law		Purpose
Land Grant, Agriculture, and Vocation		
Land Ordinance	1785	Provided for orderly distribution of public land by surveying the land.
Northwest Ordinance	1787	Encouraged use of public monies for the maintenance of public schools in the newly created townships.
Ohio Statehood Enabling	1802	First of the enabling acts, which provided land grants for public schools in newly created states.
Smith-Lever Act	1914	Created Agricultural Extension Service to "aid in diffusing… useful and practical information on subjects pertaining to agriculture and home economics."
Smith Hughes Act	1917	Provided matching funds to help states develop high school vocational programs.
Relief		
"New Deal" Activity	1930s	Encouraged education as part of the Public Works Administration, Civilian Conservation Corps, National Youth Administration, Works Progress Administration, and others.
Lanham Act	1941	Provided funds to construct and operate schools where federal activity created burdens on local governments; expanded in 1980 *by Impact Laws 815* and 874, which provided money for school construction and district operating costs, respectively.
National School Lunch Program	1946	Provided funds for school lunch programs in public and nonpublic school; expanded in 1954 to include a school milk program.
National Defense		
Cooperative Research Program	1954	Authorized federal funds for educational research in institutions of higher education.
School Construction Act	1957	Provided $325 million/year for four years for financing school construction.
National Defense Education Act	1958	Provided graduate fellowships in education—particularly in the sciences, mathematics, and foreign languages; extended in 1964. (Supported student loans, local-state-national partnership, encouraged curriculum reform.)
Peace Corps Act	1961	Established a program to supply teachers and technicians for underdeveloped nations for two-year time periods.
Manpower Development and Training Act	1962	Established up-to-date training programs for youth whose lack of education prevented them from obtaining employment.

(continued)

TABLE 2.1 Continued

Law		Purpose
Equal Educational Opportunity		
Vocational Education Act	1963	Extended 1950 impact laws and NDEA and provided funds for construction of vocational schools and development of expanded vocational education offerings.
Economic Opportunity Act	1964	Provided the legislative weapon for the War on Poverty; intended to improve the lot of the disadvantaged through educational and community projects: Head Start, Job Corps, Neighborhood Youth Corps, VISTA, and other work-experience and community programs.
Civil Rights Act	1964	Intended to discourage racial discrimination throughout society with particular emphasis on hastening desegregation in the nation's schools.
Juvenile Delinquency and Youth Offenses Control Act Amendment	1964	Intended to research fully the effects of compulsory attendance, and juvenile offenses, and child labor laws on juvenile delinquency.
Elementary and Secondary Education Act	1965	Provided large sums of money for a broad range of educational concerns. Improved state department of education, compensatory education, and innovative programs.
International Education Act	1966	Provided grants to institutions of higher education for establishment, strengthening, and operation of research centers for study of international education.
Education Professions Development Act	1967	Amended the 1965 Higher Education Act to improve the preservice and inservice training of educational personnel.
Bilingual Education Act	1968	Provided funds for instruction of children with limited English proficiency.
Emergency School Aid Act	1972	Provided federal support for voluntary desegregation of local schools.
Rehabilitation Act	1973	Provided for accommodation of the disabled student with the service necessary to provide high-quality education.
Family Educational Rights and Privacy Act	1974	Established a student's right to privacy.
Education for All Handicapped Children Act (PL 94-142)	1976	Forbade exclusion of or discrimination against persons solely because of their handicapping condition. (Provided some funds for children in poverty.)
World Class Economic Competitiveness and Safety		
Education Consolidation Improvement Act	1981	Provided for block grants that state and local education agencies could use for certain broadly defined educational programs.

TABLE 2.1   Continued

Law		Purpose
National Assessment of Educational Progress	1983	Created a national testing program for the assessment of educational results.
Education for Economic Security Act	1985	Provided for education and development to maintain economic position regarding high-technology.
Tax Reform Act	1986	Lowered the taxes on high-income earners and raised the taxes on middle- to upper-middle wage earners.
American with Disabilities Act	1990	Protected the rights of individuals with disabilities through high standards, accommodations, and employment practices and services.
Job Training Partnership	1991	Designed program to help at-risk youth be successful in schools and jobs.
Civil Rights Act	1991	Extended punitive damages and jury trial to those who have been discriminated against.
Family and Medical Leave Act	1993	Allowed employees to take twelve weeks a year of unpaid leave for circumstances such as childbirth, adoption, illness of family member.
Goals 2000: Educate America Act	1994	Established eight national goals for public education (two new goals concerning teacher education and parental participation). Provided funds for standards-based reforms.
School-to-Work Opportunities Act	1994	Encouraged integrating challenging standards and workplace skills needed for schools-to-job transition.
The Violent Crime Control and Law Enforcement Act	1994	Attacked youth crime, including tough enforcement provisions and crime prevention programs oriented toward youth.
Improving American Schools Act	1994	(Reauthorization of the ESEA Act) Strongly encouraged state and LEA's involvement in education, especially in setting high standards. Moved ESEA toward school-based reform. Promoted innovative programs.
Safe and Drug-Free Schools and Communities Act	1994	(Reauthorization of title IV), Supported school and community efforts in the war against drugs.
Amendments to the Individuals with Disabilities Education Act	1997	Attempted to overcome barriers that have prevented children with disabilities from being educated effectively.
Education Flexibility Partnership Act	1999	Provided for greater flexibility in applying certain federal education regulations.

Organization, created in 1955, concluded that the U.S. Office of Education had "meager influence and no control." In addition, of the 3 billion federal dollars being spent on education at the time, only 1 percent went through the U.S. Office of Education. The rest went through a number of blue-ribbon boards and commissions and over twenty other federal agencies. The commission recommended a number of changes in the executive branch of government and in 1953 the Department of Health, Education, and Welfare was created, placing greater responsibility for the administration and control of educational matters within this office. The 1954 cooperative research program was enacted under the leadership of U.S. Commissioner Samuel Brownell.

The Soviet Union's launching of *Sputnik* in October 1957 opened the floodgates of seething criticism of the American educational system. It was a rude awakening to Americans who had been taught that most Soviets did not have access to electricity or running water; unfairly or not, the schools were blamed for the Soviets' technical success over America. From all sides came demands for changes in the way Americans were schooled. National security and defense were increasingly used as a justification for greater federal involvement in education. The result was the passage of the largest federal legislation to date as the National Defense Education Act (NDEA) of 1958. This act was to address changes in curriculum, methods, and requirements, including higher standards, more training in science and mathematics, better provision for bright students, and harder study for all students. The act was particularly designed to strengthen science, mathematics, and foreign languages. This legislation introduced the era of excellence with its emphasis on enrichment, ability grouping, gifted education, and accelerated and enrichment programs. It also established more local-state-national partnerships to improve American education. This was the first piece of legislation aimed specifically at improving instruction in academic or nonvocational subjects and in broadening the involvement of those influencing curriculum and instruction.

Equal Educational Opportunity

Before the 1950s, inner-city poor urban communities, particularly black communities, saw education as their only hope for improved quality of life. The education system had shown some signs of meeting their needs through the approaches that grew out of progressive child-centered education. Progressive educators argued that teachers had the responsibility of making education relevant to the needs and background of the child. John Dewey was identified as the leader of this movement. Dewey believed that society should be interpreted to children through their daily living in the classroom, in a framework that is genuine and meaningful to them as students. It was during this time that education began to become accessible to all, enabling students to progress at their own speed. The reforms that grew out of the NDEA act and related thinking reversed the progressive child-centered focus and reverted to a subject-centered focus on basics, achieving excellence, with major focus on math, science, and foreign language skills. The curriculum was expanded to include much more learning within each grade level. Those who could not keep up often failed and later dropped out of school.

At the same time, U.S. Supreme Court and legislative activity was placing greater attention on equal opportunity without discrimination. The 1954 U.S. Supreme Court decision in *Brown v. Board of Education of Topeka* made integration law and increased the number of African Americans and other minorities entering public schools. Some of the U.S. Supreme Court decisions at this time included the invalidation of school prayer, equality of voting rights and representation, a number of antidiscrimination decisions, and reaffirmation of the freedom of religion, speech, press, and association.

Amid the sense of volatility regarding fundamental civil liberties, especially within urban communities, legislators and others were providing a powerful political push to address growing concerns. Crime, especially among juveniles and young adults, had increased significantly. The signs of problems were easily seen in New York, Cleveland, and other cities in early 1964 through boycotts of city school systems. Redevelopment, education, and jobs were the major themes. A two-year period of rioting and looting began in the summer of 1964 in the Harlem and Bedford-Styvesant sections of New York. Other cities in which this tragic pattern was repeated were Rochester, Los Angeles (Watts), Springfield, Massachussetts; Chicago; Atlanta; San Francisco; Cleveland; Pittsburgh; Baltimore; St. Louis; Omaha; Milwaukee; Pompano Beach, Florida; Birmingham; and Tuscaloosa. Demonstrations and marches were also occurring throughout the nation.

The Kerner Commission on Civil Disorders was created in 1967 to investigate the riots. The report (U.S. Riot Commission, 1968) concluded that the typical rioter was an underemployed school dropout whose hopes were raised by earlier student-centered improvements, only to be later crushed by experiences with NDEA-supported school changes. These conditions created a climate that resulted in violence. The typical citizen within the community who tried to stop the riots—the counterrioter—was a high school graduate with a job. Education and income were the only factors that distinguished the counterrioters from the rioters. General practices of racism were also high on the Kerner list of causes.

This was the beginning of federal involvement in education for the purpose of encouraging equality of educational opportunity. The most significant piece of legislation under the equality movement is the Elementary and Secondary Education Act (ESEA) of 1965, a broad program of support to children from low-income families. The first six titles of this bill supported compensatory education, instructional materials, supplementary services, innovative programs, strengthening state departments, and libraries. Literature such as, Charles E. Silberman's *Crisis in the Classroom*, describing school as a "grim, joyless place" where spirit is repressed and the joy of learning and creating is lost, added support for student-centered innovations. The programs created under the ESEA legislation were now complemented by progress in Head Start programs, desegregation, student-centered education, and open classrooms.

In the 1970s, the busing of children to schools outside their neighborhoods to improve racial balances overshadowed all other education issues. The significant *Swann v. Charlotte-Mecklenburg Board of Education* decision in 1971 established that there was "no basis for holding that the local school authorities may not be required to employ bus transportation as a tool of school desegregation. Desegregation plans cannot be limited to the walk-in school." This decision launched busing as a legal approach to achieving school desegregation when housing patterns blocked them from occurring naturally. This was another very turbulent period in American education. One of many examples of the backlash to racial busing occurred in the South Boston and Hyde Park sections of Boston, where police and National Guardsmen were required for approximately five weeks to establish order in the communities and schools. This experience was very similar to what was occurring in southern cities such as Birmingham, Alabama, and Little Rock, Arkansas.

The 1970s ended with a concern that a significant number of American youth did not perform satisfactorily on standardized tests of reading, writing, and arithmetic—the three Rs. The first major international comparison of achievement in mathematics revealed that U.S. student scores fell below those of Japan and Britain. At the same time, significant cutbacks were made in funding for public schools, the equalization of state educational funding formulas were challenged, and the integration of American schools met with considerable success and optimism. A separate cabinet-level U.S. Department of Education came into existence on September 24, 1979. There were a string of teacher strikes over issues such as salary increases, cost-of-living clauses, lesson-preparation time, class size, and extra-duty pay. This new cabinet position was to fulfill a promise to the National Education Association (NEA) and to improve relations with American teachers.

Perhaps most evident amidst the turmoil occurring in education since the 1950s was the minimum influence educational leaders were able to exert. They were constantly being whipsawed by political and judicial decisions and the social and economic conditions within their communities. They found themselves constantly reacting to political and community forums in which they were not partners. Educators had always seen themselves as apolitical, as experts and professionals in pedagogical matters. They began to realize that political issues outside education were having a profound impact on what was happening within education and that they had lost control of the agenda.

Responding to political demands, educators had built an integrated system of education, where a very high percentage of youth graduated from high school, meeting or exceeding minimum standards in schools that were barrier-free and open to all American youth regardless of race, gender, physical ability, or IQ. In the 1980s, educators were to learn that what Americans now wanted were students who are globally competitive with the top students attending schools in other first-world industrialized nations. At the same time, educators were expected to become more political and to broaden the involvement of community members within the education process. In this way, educational leaders could be more responsive to their communities' and nation's needs.

World Class Economic Competitiveness—
1980 to Present

The 1980s began with teachers openly expressing dissatisfaction with their jobs—41 percent responded to an NEA teacher poll that they would not become teachers if they had it to do over again. For three decades there had been unprecedented growth in U.S. enrollment. But by 1980, enrollments began declining slightly while the costs of education continued to increase. Educators argued that the tax revolt of the 1970s had reduced state and local funds to education, and federal cuts only contributed to the difficulties within local districts. For example, in 1980, the insolvent Chicago school board failed to meet payrolls, forcing severe budget cuts and layoffs. The Los

Angeles Unified School District endured a string of financial cutbacks in the 1980s and early 1990s. These were only two of many budget crises that occurred in large school districts across the country.

A blitz of national reports criticized U.S. education, including one by the U.S. Secretary of Education's appointed National Commission on Excellence in Education (1983). The report, entitled *A Nation at Risk*, charged that American students tested poorly in comparison with those of other industrialized nations. The report, purposefully alarmist in tone, began,

> Our nation is at risk. Our once unchallenged preeminence in commerce, industry, science and technological innovation is being over taken by competitors, throughout the world. The educational foundations of our society are presently being eroded by a rising tide of mediocrity that threatens our very future as a nation and a people.... If an unfriendly foreign power had attempted to impose on America the mediocre educational performance that exists today, we might well have viewed it as an act of war.

American students compared unfavorably to foreign students and were weaker in inferential skills, science and math achievement had declined, and illiteracy was a huge national problem. The recommendations were to launch a core curriculum, raise academic standards, lengthen the school day and year, improve teacher quality, and attract capable teachers. National attention turned to the need for higher academic standards, tougher subjects, rigorous testing, and stiffer high school graduation requirements. Also important were high-level cognitive skills, critical thinking skills, active and authentic learning, technology application, logic and reasoning skills, functional and operational literacy, interpersonal skills, work ethic, multicultural respect, problem solving and reasoning, and analytical skills. Educators found that the collective American mood had swung once again—excellence was more important than equality of opportunity and equity. President Ronald Reagan was urging prayer in public schools, legislation for tuition tax credits, vouchers, choice in public and private schools, and a smaller federal role in education.

The National Commission report was followed by hundreds of national, state, and local commissions, task forces, study groups, committees, hearings, and legislative reports that were critical of education, offering all forms of suggestions for how to improve the American educational system. Many of the recommendations were stated in the form of mandates to which boards, superintendents, and local school divisions were expected to respond. From all over America, reforms, suggestions, proposals, and policy propositions were being suggested.

Educational leaders had never seen such a large volume of different suggestions from so many vocal groups regarding how American education could be improved. U.S. Office of Education staff, superintendents, and later researchers were to use the term *waves of reform* to describe the efforts of the 1980s. The waves seemed to increase in size as each new one washed over public school systems that were ill-prepared for such turbulence. Assessing his first term in office President Reagan reflected, "If I were asked to single out the proudest achievement of my administration's first three and one-half years in office, what we've done to define the issues and promote the great national debate in education would rank up near the top of the list" (1984, p. 2).

Amid all the criticism of the schools there was a bright spot: 80 percent of the nation's school-age population now graduated from high school, far more than in most other countries. In addition, the decline described in education closely paralleled a national decline in domestic industrial output, international competitiveness, productivity and overall product quality, and governmental fiscal decline. A debate ensued on whether the slump was a cause-and-effect relationship as *A Nation at Risk* suggested or in reality just another part of a general U.S. decline. For the first time in American history, a generation was to face a standard of living lower than that of their parents. Education had entered the political arena full swing, and regardless of causes, politicians felt compelled to make their mark on education. There is no sign that they will retreat from this position any time in the near future.

The National Governors' Association 1986 report, *Time for Results*, states early on that, "Better schools mean better jobs." Governor Alexander's summary of the report (1986, p. 7) reaffirmed the governors' readiness to provide "the leadership needed to get results on the hard issues that confront the better school movement…(and) to lead the second wave of reform in American education policy." The governors shared the belief "that real excellence can't be imposed from a distance. Governors don't create excellent schools; communities—local school leaders, teachers, parents, and citizens—do." The states would work on recommendations, standards, assessment, and accountability.

At the same time, the Carnegie Forum on Education and the Economy (1986, p. 26) found that many teachers were "immensely frustrated—to the point of cynicism" by reform activities that they saw as bringing about very little change and showing a lack of respect for classroom teachers. They observed bureaucratic structures becoming more rigid, opportunities for exercising professional judgment decreasing, few or no real gains for students, and lack of professional respect for teachers. In a report entitled *Results in Education: 1987*, the members of the National Governors' Association (p. 3) noted that "states will have to assume larger responsibilities for setting educational goals and defining outcome standards, while, at the same time, stimulating local inventiveness."

Effective-schools research by Ron Edmonds (1979), Lawrence Lezotte (1988), Michael Rutter (1979), Wilbur Brookover (1979), and many others has supported greater local autonomy in education. Programs mandated by those who spend their professional lives outside the classroom often generate hostility, frustration, and helplessness among teachers. Local educators, the experts who are involved with the education of American youth on a long-term basis, must believe in what they do if they are to be effective. Dr. Lawrence Lezotte (1988) developed a set of premises that seemed to capture the themes reported in the effective-schools research. They include decentralized decision making, collaboration, staff empowerment, school accountability, and school-based planning efforts.

The Tax Reform Act of 1986 places the financing of public programs more squarely on the backs of middle-class taxpayers. This act has effected a 53 percent tax decrease for the wealthy and an 18 percent increase in federal taxes for middle- to upper-middle-class taxpayers (Barlett and Steele, 1994). The middle class carry an ever-increasing burden of fiscal responsibility for governmental activity. Politicians are unwilling to raise taxes on the wealthy and are unable to gain support for higher taxes on the tight dollars of the middle class. Budgets for education and other public enterprises have become extremely tight, adding to the existing frustration of educators. Communities are calling for reform and demanding higher standards, but at the same time they are unwilling to provide the needed financial support, especially America's high-income earners.

By the beginning of the 1990s, Razik and Swanson (1995) suggested that educational leaders realized they were no longer in command and control positions but served more as guides, supporters, facilitators, coordinators, assessors, and politicians. The leadership base would be broadened to include teachers and other front-line staff who would exert greater leadership within the schools. Principals and teachers would have greater discretion, as the role of the central office would be more of a service provider. The federal role in education would decline significantly, the state would establish and assess standards, and localities would be responsible for continuously improving the education process. At the same time, parents and community groups would have a greater influence on the operation of the school and the teaching and learning experience. Strategies would be developed to eliminate barriers, to facilitate communication, and to bring people together in comprehensive and cohesive ways to improve education.

> Select the contextual elements you believe are having the most pronounced influence on Scrivner Middle Schools today.

Establishing National Goals

In 1989, school reform was developing from the most ideologically conservative political process of our times. In this setting, President George Bush and the nation's governors came together at the historic Educational Summit in Charlottesville, Virginia. All agreed that "the time has come, for the first time in the United States history, to establish clear national performance goals, goals that will make us internationally competitive." There was a clear call for a "renaissance in education." The participants articulated six national goals for public education to be realized by the year 2000.

In 1991, the national goals were expanded and relabeled by the Clinton Administration as Goals 2000, which became the driving force for all federal initiatives. They were later adopted and approved by all states except Virginia, which lost significant federal funding as a result and approved the standards the following year. The Educational Goals panel recommended national standards and related systems for student assessment. States and school districts are required to set standards for curriculum content and student performance to qualify for federal Chapter I funds. The Goals 2000 are as follows:

- All children in America will start school ready to learn.
- The high school graduation rate will increase to at least 90 percent.
- All students will leave grades 4, 8, and 12 having demonstrated competence in challenging subject matter in the core academic subjects.
- U.S. students will be first in the world in mathematics and science achievement.
- Every adult American will be literate and will possess the knowledge and skills necessary to compete in a global economy and exercise the rights and responsibilities of citizenship.

- Every school in the United States will be free of drugs, violence, and the unauthorized presence of firearms and alcohol and will offer a disciplined environment conducive to learning.
- The nation's teaching force will have access to programs for the continued improvement of their professional skills and the opportunity to acquire the knowledge and skills needed to instruct and prepare all American students for the next century.
- Every school will promote partnerships that will increase parental involvement and participation in promoting the social, emotional, and academic growth of children.

An essential element in restoring competitiveness is the improvement of the education future front-line workers receive in elementary and secondary schools and the implementation of mechanisms for smoothing the school-to-work transition. Redesigning schools would require educational leaders to work together with their counterparts in the community at large and in business. There has been considerable doubt, however, as to whether the schools are prepared for these responsibilities.

The mood, as we entered the last decade of the century, was best summed up in a February 9, 1990, article, which appeared in the *Wall Street Journal*'s first education supplement.

> Jobs are becoming more demanding, more complex. But our schools don't seem up to the task. They are producing students who lack the skills that business so desperately needs to compete in today's global economy and doing so, they are condemning students to a life devoid of meaningful employment.
>
> Better corporate retraining may serve as a stopgap. But ultimately the burden of change rests with our schools. While debate rages about how change should come, almost everyone agrees that something has to be done. And quickly. (p. R1)

The Job Training Partnership Act in 1991 and School to Work Opportunities Act in 1994 were part of several initiatives by the federal government to help schools better address the needs of the workplace.

Thoughts for Leaders of Education Institutions in Transition

LUVERN L. CUNNINGHAM
Novice G. Fawcett Professor of Educational Administration (Emeritus)
The Ohio State University

This is a personal story invoking the privilege of experience and age.

Time, its inexorable movement traced across a half century. After one year as a teaching-

principal in a small high school on the prairies of Nebraska, I was hired as a superintendent. The hiring took place on a Saturday night in the back room of a poolhall. I was 24. It was 1949. Nine years later, two superintendencies, one year as director of admissions at Midland Lutheran College, a master's degree at the University of Nebraska at Omaha, and a doctorate from the University of Oregon under my belt, I arrived at the University of Chicago. I was appointed assistant professor and assistant director of the Midwest Administration Center, probably the most prominent and respected center for research on problems and issues of school administration in the country. Later, in 1967, I became dean of the College of Education and Professor of Educational Administration at Ohio State University.

The late 1950s and 1960s were a period of intellectual ferment and excitement in school administration across the nation. The University Council for Educational Administration was created and thrived under the leadership of Jack Culberston. Its offices were at Ohio State. Students and faculty at Chicago had built up a full head of steam, generating fresh thinking about the theory and practice of school administration. It was a movement, and Chicago was in the thick of it. Research was underway. Important books, monographs, and articles were written. Regional, national, and international conferences were convened on matters germane to educational administration. Students on completion were taking important positions in school systems and universities across the United States and Canada.

An inspiring transition to some, an enervating struggle to others, was underway in the 1950s. Concentration within the field of school administration from its humble beginnings to that point had been on technical matters. "Budgets, buildings, and buses" was a phrase often cited as a descriptor of the field. Textbooks of prominence focused on the nitty-gritty of running schools. Such topics as these were emphasized: courses of study, heating and lighting of buildings, selecting sites for schools and playgrounds, hiring and firing of employees, budgets, paying for schooling, legal questions, ordering books and supplies, organizing and reorganizing school districts and attendance areas, and preparing the school calendar. For the first forty years of the twentieth century, pencils, paper, blackboards, and chalk constituted technology; hectographs, mimeographs, typewriters, and A-V came

later. Minimum credentials were required to be a principal or superintendent of schools.

In the 1950s, the center of gravity began to shift away from those items to such interests as leadership, political behavior, change process, decision making, policy development, policy analysis, administrative behavior, organizational behavior, attributes of leaders in educational administration, and administration as a social process. New theories and their advocates began to appear. The whole of the social sciences became the source of new ideas. Theories were drawn from economics, sociology, psychology, political science, even anthropology. Professional fields such as public administration, health administration, and business administration were explored for useful ways to think about administrative practice. Drawing from such disciplines and centers of practice is now commonplace, but it was not then.

The political, economic, and social context within which schooling was taking place was changing. The Russians launched and orbited *Sputnik*, the first artificial satellite, in 1957. Enrollments were growing, classrooms were needed, double sessions were widespread. There was a severe teacher shortage.

Collective bargaining entered the picture, and rumblings of dissatisfaction with school performance began to appear. A single book, *Why John Can't Read*, stirred people and aroused indignation across the country. The federal government stepped up its interest in education, prompted in some measure by *Sputnik*, leading to the national Defense Education Act and a spate of other federal programs aimed at improving academic achievement, reforming the curriculum, addressing problems of poverty, technology (language labs for example), special education, and career.

Of singular significance in the 1950s was *Brown v. Board of Education*, the celebrated Topeka desegregation case of 1954, which changed public education profoundly in the United States. The decision launched the civil rights movement within public education. It, along with subsequent desegregation litigation, contributed to the 1967 Civil Rights Act and other public policy to follow. Nearly a half century later, its impact is still registering on the nation and its educational system. In some respects the struggle over issues

(continued)

Continued

of race and social class is only beginning. The dark cloud of poverty versus privilege, haves versus have-nots is more menacing than ever, burdening this generation as well as future generations of educational administrators.

In the new millennium, school administrators face continuing and emerging challenges. Finding money, spending it wisely, having standards and living up to them, intensifying the concentration on student learning, staying accountable, involving parents, leading and following in good balance are ongoing needs. Maintaining personal and professional focus; achieving comfort with chaos; making change your ally, not your enemy; locating the constructive place of technology in the scheme of things; carving out time for reflection; holding firm to values, traditions, and practices that sustain schools as democratic institutions; standing tall, more than ever before, for children, youth, and their families; facing squarely issues of race and social class; walking and sustaining the moral and ethical high ground: These are today's and tomorrow's imperatives.

External forces have always pounded educational institutions at all levels. Ironically, one of those forces, probably the most transforming was the evolution of digital computing, centered ini-

tially at the University of Illinois and MIT. The "digitalization of civilization," a phrase borrowed from a recent issue of *Daedalus*, characterizes our current circumstances. It began in the 1940s, continuing through the decades at a blistering pace, outstripping the capacity of analysis to surmise its significance for the future. One person's reading of the tea leaves often seems as good as another's. The impact of digitalization at the change of centuries is so profound on all aspects of life and living that it seems unnecessary to belabor its presence except to say that administrators cannot relax in their struggle to tease out its meaning for their institutional stewardship.

My doctoral work at the University of Oregon in the middle 1950s was anchored heavily in the social sciences, especially political science and sociology. I moved from the intellectually familiar to the intellectually unknown. I found the stimulation exhilarating. These experiences have enhanced my thinking, research, writing, and administrative performance ever since. I urge administrators in the process of becoming to find a conceptual system that will guide them through a host of contextual and virtual realities and help them contain and understand the excitement of their experience. Otherwise, why make the trip?

The 1990s and Beyond

The 1990s constituted a period of rapid turnover for school superintendents. A front-page article in the *New York Times* on December 26, 1990, characterized the condition of the superintendency:

[S]chool superintendents around the country have been quitting in droves or have been dismissed or have retired early, often because they have failed to deliver the quick educational fixes demanded of them. More than fifteen major cities are now scrambling to find school chiefs, nearly three times the usual number in a given year, experts say. And, the searches for superintendents are getting harder. Cities are finding fewer candidates willing to apply for these jobs, despite salaries that in many cases top $100,000 a year. (p. A1)

In 1991–92, a total of thirty superintendents of urban school districts—Los Angeles, Atlanta, Boston, Cleveland, Columbus, Charlotte-Mecklenburg, Charleston, St. Louis, Kansas City, and Washington, DC, to name a few—lost their jobs. A 1991 *Executive Educator* nationwide survey found that more than 53 percent of the superintendents in the United States had been in their present position for five years or less. Only about 40 percent of the superintendents felt that they had much job security in their present positions. In the 1950s the average term in office for incumbent superintendents in large school districts was 6.5 years. By the 1980s it had dropped to just over four years (Cuban, 1989, p. 46). Reports by the National School Board Association suggested that the average term of large-district superintendents in the early 1990s was 2.5 years.

As reported in *Urban Dynamics: Lessons Learned from Urban School Boards and Superintendents* (1992), released by the National School Boards Association (NSBA):

> During 1991, approximately thirty school boards governing some of the nation's largest school systems replaced their superintendents. Some of these vacancies were due to retirements, others to new opportunities and upward mobility; but most were attributed to the pressures of an extraordinarily stressful job. As vacancies occur, urban school boards are finding fewer applicants willing to assume the considerable demands of administering these multimillion-dollar education systems with their greater number of social problems and political factions, proportionately less funds per student, and intensive public scrutiny. (p. 5)

Carter and Cunningham (1996) suggest that the cost of turnover has weighed heavily on local school districts and the staff who are trying to hold them together. The superintendent is often the casualty of the political infighting that often occurs at the school-district level. Paul Houston, executive director of the AASA, suggests:

> The current role is indeed a troubled one. The condition of children in this country has deteriorated, while the challenges facing them have escalated. And the critics are in full force. Superintendents find themselves defending the system they lead, demanding accountability so they can keep the doors open and morale up, while at the same time they must search for ways to transform the system to meet an uncertain future.... Imparting motion to a system that is nearly immobilized by vested interests, history, and the multiple expectations placed on it—a system that places many hands on the wheel, is most difficult. Retooling is not merely a matter of putting in new technology; it requires changing the minds and sometimes the hearts of those who are doing the work.... There has been a lot of scapegoating of schools by business and political leaders, and this very vocal pressure has led to loss of credibility and diminished faith in the (educational) institutions. Much of the solution to this problem rests in the ability of school leaders to build conditions of support for schools from among those most interested in seeing schools succeed. (Carter & Cunningham, 1997, ii–iv)

By 1993, the push was to achieve greater understanding through the exchange of information and ideas among both internal and external groups. The goal was to ensure that all groups necessary to the support of public education were full partners in the process. The Goals 2000: Educate America Act encourages "communities to develop their own reform plans and [provide] seed money to support these efforts." The bill requires innovation in teaching and learning, increased parental and community involvement, professional development of teachers, and reduction in education bureaucracy. President Clinton and the U.S. Office of Education worked to obtain more funding for innovative and charter schools.

The focus of the 1980s was on shifting responsibility for education to state and local bureaucracies, but the shifts in the 1990s seemed to be to the local schools and communities. As Ted Sizer (O'Neil, 1995) suggested,

> Lasting reform requires creating a climate for local educators and community members to craft their own improvement strategies.... Our research suggests that you're not going to get significant long-term reform unless you have subtle but powerful support and collaboration among teachers, students, and the families of those students in a particular community...but we strongly believe you have to look at reform school-by-school-by-school. (p. 4)

The 1990s were also a period of great concern regarding the large increase in juvenile violent crimes. More and more of our young were lost to crime and violence. Research suggested that strategies encouraging commitment to school and academic success—especially success in reading—reduced delinquency. An aggressive and proactive response was initiated at both the federal and state levels.

Federal agencies forged collaborative approaches to delinquency, such as the Empowerment Zones/Enterprise Communities Initiative, Pulling American Communities Together, The Violent Crime Control and Law Enforcement Act, Gun-Free Schools Initiatives, Safe and Drug-free Schools and Communities Act, and the Family Preservation and Support Program, to name a few. The major emphasis of these activities was to promote collaboration, mobilize agencies, create safe and effective schools, strengthen families, and create youth programs. These efforts were successful, and by the late 1990s juvenile crime was on the decline. Youth violence, however, was on the increase.

In March 1996, forty-nine corporate leaders; forty-one governors; and thirty educators, staff advisors, and policy experts (observers) attended the second national Education Summit. Louis V. Gerstner, CEO of IBM and cochair of the summit, stated, "Until we set standards and learn how to measure against them we can't assess the effectiveness of all the ideas that bounce off the walls of educational establishments." The attendees endorsed the idea of each state developing "internationally competitive academic standards" and rigorous new tests to measure whether students meet the standards.

What might be some of the internal problems occurring at Scrivner Middle School and how might the history and existing contextual elements influence these problems?

Responding to New Educational Needs

The Congressional Office of Technology Assessment reported in 1995 that although the private sector demands workers with the skills needed to compete in the "information society," most schools lack key technologies. They also lack teachers who are properly trained to use the equipment that is readily available in other institutions. Educational leaders are now being asked to make technology a key part of the learning process. There is potential for radically different methods of teaching and learning by using the range of technological possibilities—changing what is learned, how it is learned, how it is measured, and what the teacher does in the classroom.

The General Accounting Office reported that schools don't have facilities to make full use of computer, video, and other communications. More than half the schools, lack modems and phone lines and were not linked to external networks; one-third complained of problems with electrical wiring; and less than 1 percent of the classrooms had access to voice mail. Vice-President Al Gore called for a data superhighway that can change the way students learn and teachers teach. Although overoptimistic, there was a clearly stated goal of connecting every school to the National Information Infrastructure (NII) by the year 2000 and providing training for how to use this tremendous information communication library. As a result, activities nationwide—from distance learning services to Internet online network distribution and teacher training—are on the increase. This information superhighway brings the world to the classroom. FCC Universal Service Funds are also being used to provide technological services to schools and libraries. The role of educational leadership is to find ways to harness the power of these new technologies for teaching and learning.

Business executives and state leaders are taking a much more active role in improving local education. At the same time, teachers are also being seen as leaders who should be given considerable latitude to exercise judgment and to experiment with ideas that have great potential. Turbulent times demand the strongest and best leaders, but the change process requires broadening the base and decentralizing to give principals and teachers more authority and responsibility for improving schools. The call is for local schools and communities to develop and implement massive changes and for them to be held accountable for needed improvements.

Teaching for understanding and developing the ability to apply knowledge and concepts to new situations is also receiving much more attention than in the past. Curriculum should provide opportunities to test ideas, explore relevance, develop multiple perspectives, evaluate results, apply and use technology, and cross discipline lines. Technology opens up access to massive amounts of current information and communication networks with people around the world as communication and computer technologies converge. The Business Coalition for Educational Reform suggests that "introducing new approaches to an established education infrastructure [and] overcoming a general fear of educational change" are the two most important challenges facing today's educational leaders. (For more information see: www.ncrel.org/sdrs/.)

> What do you see as the primary educational needs at Scrivner, and whose support will be needed to successfully address these needs?

State Roles and Responses

Education is mentioned in every state constitution. The legislatures in every state other than Hawaii, a state school system, continue to follow the original pattern of local control of public education (see Chapter 5 for greater detail). State boards of education date back to 1784, and the first state superintendent of public instruction temporarily emerged in New York in 1812 and reemerged permanently in 1854. State superintendents have been successful in marshalling public opinion, lobbying state legislatures, providing professional leadership, establishing direction, and setting minimum standards. Although the state legislature is charged with the primary responsibility of maintaining a system of public education, the governor's desires are not lightly ignored. Governors influence education through their platform positions, educational appointments, and proposition and veto of bills. The state board of education is often appointed by the governor and determines policies and the chief state school officer. The state department of education is responsible for implementing these policies. The state department of education originally collected data. It then expanded into setting and maintaining minimum educational standards, inspecting and ensuring appropriate compliance, providing leadership through mandates and program development, and finally facilitating and supporting local efforts to improve education.

State education departments did not really come of age until after the passage of the Elementary and Secondary Education Act in 1965. Title V of this act provided money to significantly increase the number of state department officials as well as providing training, equipment, and encouragement for research and development efforts. Within three years after the passage of this act, many state departments of education doubled in size, with much of the support coming from federal funds. These federal allocations were eliminated in 1981 when the federal government began to implement federal "block grants" under the Education Consolidation and Improvement Act (ECIA) of 1981. The ECIA gave the state departments of education more responsibility for determining how and where to spend money, but it also reduced federal funding, placing more financial responsibility on the states.

The major areas of focus at the state level are academic standards, instructional programs, textbook selection, certification of personnel, facilities standards, financial support, data collection and distribution, testing, and regulation of nonpublic schools. The 1970s began an era of unprecedented extension of state influence into issues of local school performance. Susan H. Fuhrman (1994, pp. 30–31) concluded:

> During the 70s and 80s, legislatures generated volumes of statutes related to education. In the 1970s, they revised school financing statutes to address wealth-related disparities among local districts; and they provided special programs, such as compensatory education, for the neediest students. In the early 1980s, they turned their attention to the performance of all students, increasing standards for high school graduation and mandating more testing to assess student progress…twenty-eight states enacted school finance reform measures between 1971 and 1981. By 1979–80, twenty-three states provided funds to local districts to support services for disadvantaged students; the same number offered financial assistance for instruction of limited English proficient students; and all fifty states had enacted special education programs that conformed to Public Law 94-142, although they varied in financing mechanisms. In the early and mid-1980s, education reform spread so rapidly from state to state that some elements of reform were addressed by virtually every state.

One of the increasingly complex and disquieting aspects of state involvement in education is the shifting winds of policy development that cause programs to be canceled, amended, modified, shifted, redirected, or go unfunded. These shifts have caused educators at the local level to question the staying power of state initiatives. The attitude sometimes seems to be "wake me up when this one's over!" In addition, state departments of education have been hampered in the 1990s by downsizing and having limited funds to support initiatives (John Murphy, 1993).

In the 1990s, state departments of education focused on student outcomes and the curriculum. In fact, states across the country have devised new standards of learning and assessment, and almost half require the successful completion of a competency test for high school graduation. An increasing number of states have mandated statewide tests, typically at the fourth, eighth, and twelfth grades, to establish whether students are meeting national standards. A few states have included time-consuming, complex portfolio assessment programs as part of the state testing requirements. The intended purpose of the standards is to provide guidelines for curriculum and teaching and to ascertain what percentage of students are developing the knowledge base believed to be necessary for their future success. In expressing some concerns regarding the standards movement, Linda Darling-Hammond and Beverly Falk (1997, p. 198) state:

> Ultimately, raising standards for students so that they learn what they need to know requires raising standards for the system, so that it provides the kinds of teaching and school settings students need in order to learn. Grade retention as a solution to low achievement is merely a symbol of the failure of the system to teach successfully. Given the effects of retention, such a strategy for accountability foreshadows greater educational failure in the years ahead. Genuine accountability requires both higher standards and greater supports for student, teacher, and school learning. Only this more comprehensive view will allow us ultimately to succeed at educating all children in ways that have never before been attempted.

Most states have also upgraded their standards for teacher and administrator preparation and endorsement. North Carolina has set minimum student pass rates for schools in order to maintain state school endorsement. Arizona has decentralized teacher certification; it will now be determined within the local districts. Most state department initiatives are now dominated by standards and testing programs to provide records of the students' progress and in some cases to hold people accountable. (For more information see: www.mcrel.org.)

Recent concerns have been expressed about the domination of teachers' unions, central offices, school boards, and state and federal governments over the operation of public schools. Efforts are under way to find ways to allow schools to operate beyond the reach of all these controls, thus liberating them to experiment and innovate beyond the "shackles of policy and tradition." By 1995, nearly half the states had authorized charter schools, and many were looking at various forms of school choice programs, school vouchers, year-round learning, and magnet schools. By 1998, sixteen states had passed "school choice" laws; there were approximately 4,000 "magnet" schools and 900 charter schools in twenty-three states. These numbers continue to increase as states search for ways to encourage improvements in the education of their children.

Of all these reforms, charter schools have attracted the most interest because they present the greatest potential for departure from traditional schooling. State charter laws can be distinguished by the amount of autonomy granted to schools. If charters require local school board approval before state approval, little change may occur.

The state also plays a dual role: it provides resources and technical support and is responsible for assessment and rigorous accountability (Loveless and Josin, 1998). Students are now allowed to attend schools outside their geographic borders and to select schools with special teaching or curriculum. Beginning in 1994, Title I funds could be used for schoolwide change. The National Alliance for Restructuring Education, a partnership of states, school districts, and national organizations, emphasizes that systemic reform should be standards based. According to Fashola and Slavin (1998), the key reforms now needed are in curriculum and instruction, programs for at-risk students, and family support.

If the present conditions in education do not change, we can expect to see a push toward increased privatization through charters, vouchers, public funding for private and parochial schools, and various forms of school takeovers. French (1998) believes that privatization can be avoided if state education agencies "use their leverage and resources to marry rigor and diversity, equity and democracy, high expectations and multiple intelligences instead of uniformity, rigid standards, and narrow high-stakes tests. Our educational institutions need to act democratically" (p. 190).

Because property tax bases vary among districts within each state, the amount the districts raise to educate each child, even when putting in equal financial efforts, varies significantly. General fund revenues place the state in a good position to smooth out local differences in revenue-raising capacity. Even though the Supreme Court in *Rodriguez v. San Antonio Independent School District* found that this practice is not illegal, several states are still examining these issues. Correcting inequities among districts while maintaining the vitality and responsiveness of decentralized governance is one of the many challenges facing state departments of education. (For more information see: www.ed.gov/programs/bastmp/sea.htm.)

> What role will your state most likely play in Scrivner's renewal efforts?

The Federal View of Education

GERALD N. TIROZZI, Assistant Secretary
Office of Elementary and Secondary Education
Washington, DC

Education of our nation's young people is a national priority, but it is and must remain a state responsibility and a local function. The U.S. Constitution appropriately established these roles. The reality is that there are now 15,000 school districts across the nation containing some 100,000 schools. No one can advance the mission of public education or address problems and issues more readily than can local school boards and school district personnel with ongoing state support.

Few would question that there is a national interest in education today. Education is the key to economic prosperity, especially as it becomes increasingly tied to one's livelihood. As we participate in an increasingly global economy, an educated workforce is America's greatest source of competitive advantage. A solid education system is also critical for creating lifelong learners who participate in a democracy, build vibrant communities, and make discoveries and innovations. It is an essential tool for improving equity across communities. To ignore the national interest in education risks dividing our nation as disparities increase and our future growth is stifled.

Given that federal funds support only 7 percent of the total cost of elementary and secondary education, the federal role is by its very nature a strategic one; the strategies embraced are vigorously debated.

I see the federal role in education as one of promoting equity and excellence in schools across the nation through funding for programs, providing leadership in promoting high standards for all students, and disseminating information on research and evaluation. The federal role is essential in energizing the discourse for equity and excellence throughout the nation. The use of the "bully pulpit" is a critical tool in this effort.

Promoting Equity

Federal funds are used strategically to promote equity in educational opportunities. Most federal K–12 dollars go to states to support Title I programs under the Elementary and Secondary Education Act (supplementary funds that are distributed based on school poverty rate and are used to support reading and math instruction) and special education programs funded through the Individuals with Disabilities Education Act (IDEA). Federal funds supplement state and local dollars, rather than supplanting them, and are for the most part targeted to schools serving low-income populations. These funds can influence how other funds are used in ways that improve equity for all students. For example, schools that receive compensatory education funds under Title I or special

education funds must now include all students in their education reforms; they cannot hold groups of disadvantaged students to lower standards than other students. Such a policy affects the way schools structure their programs and the expectations they hold for children.

Providing Leadership

The President and the U.S. Secretary of Education advocate the importance of education, thus raising national attention to the educational needs of our nation and increasing investments in education. From their influential vantage point they create a vision for high-quality education that can shape educational policies and debates in states and communities. They have also promoted research and development and stimulated school changes through the dissemination of innovative program and practices and the establishment of national goals.

I encourage all educators and administrators to seize the challenges offered by the national education goals with a sense of urgency and a relentless pursuit of excellence and equity in your schools. An initial step in achieving the national educational goals is for every community to focus on the essentials of schooling. Some beginning steps are outlined below. They are by no means comprehensive, but they provide a focus for the intense effort that is necessary to raise student achievement for all students.

First, articulate clear, challenging standards for student performance in the core academic subjects. Focus all district and school efforts on improving teaching and learning in ways that help all students master the standards. Aligned assessments and a clear accountability system should accompany the standards so that everyone can monitor progress and make improvements.

Second, ensure that all students are reading independently by the end of the third grade. Research emphasizes the importance of gaining early literacy and reading skills. Currently only 60 percent of our fourth-graders are meeting such a standard. Addressing the needs of the many children who are not reading independently will require substantial investments in developing well-trained teachers, focused reading programs, and family involvement in learning. We know that we must also

(continued)

Continued

address the need for high-quality, developmentally appropriate preschool programs to support early literacy. The exciting research on the development of the brain underscores the importance of early childhood programs for all children.

Third, strengthen mathematics programs. We know that students who take algebra in eighth grade are more likely to go to college, and we know that today's society demands a higher degree of mathematical understanding. The U.S. standing internationally for twelfth-graders is abysmal in the Third International Study of Math and Science (TIMSS). Schools must race to strengthen their core academic programs to ensure that all students are being exposed to a rigorous, focused curriculum.

Fourth, invest in the quality of teachers and principals. If students are to reach challenging standards, teachers must be equipped with the knowledge and skills for helping them get there. They must be exposed to the best research and practice available for improving their instructional programs. And principals must view their role as instructional leaders.

Fifth, use technology as a learning tool as well as a tool for management. Technology can greatly expand the boundaries of the classroom and offers incredible learning opportunities to support the core curriculum.

Sixth, ensure that schools create environments that are conducive to learning. All schools should be safe and free of drugs and alcohol. No matter how high standards are, if students are preoccupied with fears about their safety, they will not learn. Creating safe places that support learning is fundamental for school success.

And finally, engage families and communities in the learning process. Learning does not end with the schoolday or on weekends, nor does it take a summer respite. Our schools often ignore the incredible resources available outside their doors. We need to expand the schoolday and offer rich summer programs and invite families and communities to partner with schools to improve learning throughout the day and year.

We have the knowledge and skills to improve our schools; it is now time to summon the will in our communities to overcome the incredible challenges before us. The federal, state, and local roles in education are all important in the never-ending quest for equity and excellence in our schools. The potential to realize the promise of public education will be greatly enhanced by a meaningful, collaborative partnership among all educational stakeholders to raise student achievement.

Challenges in the Twenty-First Century

According to a number of reports, many parents and communities are not attending to their children. Marian Wright Edelman, founder and president of the Children's Defense Fund, calls them "back seat" children. Two-parent income earners, single-parent homes, mobility, divorce, and very busy lifestyles have changed the experience children have within the family. They are often confronted by social issues such as crime, neglect, poverty, abuse, disease, addiction, violence, and unemployment. In *Beyond Rhetoric*, the National Commission on Children (1991) says of American children,

> [A]mong all races and income groups, and in communities nationwide, many children are in jeopardy. They grow up in families whose lives are in turmoil. Their parents are too stressed and too drained to provide nurturing, structure and security that protect children and prepare them for adulthood. Some others are unsafe at home and in their neighborhoods. Many are poor, and some are homeless and hungry. (p. 5)

In the 1990s, the nation was becoming more self-centered and absorbed in exclusive attention to personal economic improvement and gratification. Today parents who feel guilty for not spending enough time with their children tend to be permissive and overspend on them. This practice has not resulted in happier children. Students have expensive cars, stereos, and $100 sneakers; they rent limousines, hotel rooms, and "entertainment" at proms. Dr. Edelman, expressed her deep concern for the nation's "back seat" children in a report on the state of American children (Children's Defense Fund, 1991).

> Our children are growing up today…where instant sex without responsibility, instant gratification without effort, instant solutions without sacrifice, getting rather than giving and hoarding rather than sharing are the too-frequent signals of our mass media, popular culture, business, and political life…. Nowhere is the paralysis of public and private conscience more evident that in the neglect and abandonment of millions of our shrinking pool of children, whose future will determine our nation's ability to compete and lead in a new era. (p. 7)

In 1996, Dr. Edelman participated in a march in Washington, DC, that attracted almost one million participants to rally for improving the conditions of children in America.

America is moving from a labor-intensive to a knowledge-based industrial economy. Industry is moving to rural areas, creating significant problems for industrialized cities that developed on the backs of large labor-intensive enterprises. At the same time, organizations are being delayered and downsized to create greater efficiency in operation. The real buying power of American families is decreasing except among approximately 30 percent of the wealthiest Americans. Manufacturing and white-collar employees in America receive some of the lowest compensation among the industrialized world while chief executive officers receive the very highest. Income and economic power are being concentrated in fewer and fewer hands. When you look at average incomes you see two lines, one going up for a decreasing number of very wealthy Americans, and the other going down for the large majority.

Some of the quality-of-life factors that are worsening include child abuse, the number of children in poverty, drug abuse, health insurance coverage, out-of-pocket health costs, anger, selfishness, urban poverty, and crime. A study published by the Harwood Group, a research firm in Bethesda, Maryland, found two major areas of concern emerging in American society—economic security and threats to the family. Other significant trends that affect education are national and global interdependence, increasing institutional change in both pace and complexity, the obsolescence of knowledge, and a worsening ecology. The world in which we live is shrinking, and we need a better understanding of other countries and cultures. Futurists suggest that the next two decades will produce more change than has occurred in the last century. The half-life of knowledge is approximately eight years—that is, half of what you learn will be obsolete in eight years. The world store of knowledge is growing at a geometrically increasing rate.

Minority, particularly Hispanic, populations will continue to increase faster than the overall population. As more Americans marry across racial lines, however, such categories will perhaps be less meaningful. Dr. Harold L. Hodgkinson (1995, p. 179) suggests, "Had we spent the forty years since the *Brown* decision systematically seeking to lower the poverty level for all American children, we would be in a different, and probably better, condition today. As racial and ethnic characteristics blur over the coming decades, poverty will become an even more obvious problem than it has been."

The number of older Americans—the graying population—is increasing within our society. Today only one household in four has a school-age child. As fewer adults have contact with children in their daily lives, there will probably be less political support for children in the future. A huge increase in the numbers of the elderly population requires those in the workforce to support those who have retired. It is imperative, therefore, to ensure that every young person becomes a productive member of society. Labor-intensive work is being outsourced to other nations, forcing American labor to compete with low-income workers in third world countries.

Harold Hodgkinson (1993) provides a good profile of where we are:

> Today we've got a lot of change at the margins, with more Asians, Hispanics, Blacks, and Indians. We have high- and low-pay jobs and only a few in the middle. We have single parents and nonfamilies, rich and poor, more elderly, fewer kids, and a mosaic as opposed to a melting pot. We have self-contained suburbs that are able to totally ignore the city that made them possible. Put that together and you have a pretty tough agenda, it seems to me, for the schools. That's the challenge for the next decade. (pp. 205–206)

(For more information see: www.lcweb.loc.gov.)

> What are some of the changing conditions that you need to consider in planning future school reforms?

Conclusion

Federal and state involvement in American education centers around the reccurring themes of educational excellence and educational opportunity. Educational excellence seeks to set higher standards; strengthen the curriculum, particularly in math and the sciences; set higher requirements for course work and graduation; increase time for learning and homework; develop more rigorous grading, testing, homework, and discipline; and provide more choices regarding education. Educational opportunity prompts efforts to improve school attendance, provide needed services, ensure that all Americans achieve minimum standards, and provide for multiculturalism, inclusiveness, and diversity. Money can be spent for enrichment programs directed toward gifted students or for special education and inclusion programs for disabled students, or for both. Seeing the current state of education as a dichotomy oversimplifies the diverse interests and initiatives that have been prominent in developing federal and state education policy. The demand is growing to offer more choices for kids with different learning styles and abilities. The bottom line is to create schools that are constantly improving themselves and meeting the ever-changing demands of our youth.

There seems to be a movement toward greater centralization of control of educational policy resulting in decreased power at the local level. Policy formation develops out of political battles among interest groups, politicians, and educators. Joel Spring (1998) found that the types of struggles that occur depend on the perceptions of the parties involved.

> Conservative interest groups such as the Christian coalition and Eagle Forum advocate reduction in federal regulations and control. On the other hand, some interest groups such as those representing the disadvantaged and the disabled feel protected by strong federal control. The new professionals at the state and local levels are concerned with any changes in regulations that threaten their interests.... Although state politicians welcome control over federal programs, they worry about reduced federal spending. (p. 107)

Education also is used to enhance economic opportunities and increase political power. The schools are needed to produce workers for the global economy or to win votes for the politicians. Educators must teach children within this very competitive context of control.

Local school leaders are often challenged by conflicting desires, expressed at the federal, state, and local levels as part of the "great national debate on education." These conflicts have become more intense under the criticism education has received in the 1980s and 1990s. Educators have never had to deal with the diversity of suggestions and mandates about how to improve the American education system. Diverse values are being articulated by an increasing number of special-interest groups that have an interest in education. A flood of reforms, proposals, and practices from all over America are suggesting how education can be improved.

As research indicated links among education, economic competitiveness, technological advancements, and excellence, national performance goals were established to make students internationally competitive. Responsibility for achieving these goals was placed in the hands of the local districts and schools. Teachers began demanding opportunities for exercising professional judgment and wanted greater respect. With this decentralization has come greater accountability for results. The Goals 2000: Educate American Act encourages communities to develop their own reform plans while establishing national education standards. States have followed the national lead and established state goals, standards, and assessments.

Few issues on the American scene engender more experts, more controversy, and more conflicts than does education. Carl Glickman (1998) concludes,

> In a democracy, one person's ideas should never make the greatest difference. Instead, what I hope for is that Americans will become tired—tired of yelling at and retreating from one another; tired of the political left and the right accusing each other of immorality; tired of cultural, racial, and gender groups accusing each other of genocide; and tired of religious and secular groups slinging conspiratory theories about each other back and forth.... I want educators, parents, and local citizens of all persuasions, politics, groups, and beliefs to participate as equals in helping schools reach and create a generation of citizens that will make us all proud. (p. 181)

Despite the crush of competing agendas and distractions, educational leaders must help to bring everyone's attention and efforts to bear on important educational goals for the future. All who have a stake in successful schools must be involved in the efforts to improve them. Being able to make connections with others, to share plans and visions, and to elicit help in developing an effective teaching and learning process are basic to educational leadership and the future of our schools.

How will you build the needed political support for Scrivner Middle School?

PORTFOLIO ARTIFACTS

- Join and actively participate in a civic organization or the Chamber of Commerce.

- Work with a state or city legislature to write a bill and get it passed.

- Shadow the mayor, a domestic relations judge, a police officer, or an emergency room physician.

- Join and actively participate in a political party.

- Select a good cause within the community and provide leadership in improving existing conditions.

- Become an officer in the Parent Teacher Association at a school.

- Volunteer to serve the citizens of your community.

- Attend a Senate, House of Representatives, or city council meeting.

TERMS

"Back seat" children
Block grants
Brown decision
Business partners
Context
Decentralizing
Desegregation
Downsizing

Elementary and Secondary
    Education Act
Equal educational opportunity
Graying of America
National Education Standards
National goals
National mosaic (not a
    melting pot)
Safe School Plan

School effectiveness research
*Swann v. Charlotte-Mecklenburg
    Board of Education*
U.S. Department of Education
Vested interests
Vision

SUGGESTED READING

Backarach, S. (1990). *Educational reform: Making sense of it all.* Needham Heights, MA: Allyn & Bacon.
Campbell, R. E., Cunningham, L. L., Nystrand, R. O., & Uslan, M. D. (1980). *The organization and control of American schools.* Columbus, OH: Charles E. Merrill Publishing.
Goodlad, J. I., & McMannon, T. J. (Eds.). (1997). *The public purpose of education and schooling.* San Francisco: Jossey-Bass.

Murphy, J. (1991). *Restructuring schools: Capturing and assessing the phenomena.* New York: Teachers College Press.

Murphy, J., & Forsyth, P. B. (1999). *Educational administration: A decade of reform.* Thousand Oaks, CA: Corwin Press.

Sergiovanni, T. J., Burlingame, M., Coombs, F. S., and Thurston, P. W. (1999). *Educational governance and administration.* Boston, MA: Allyn & Bacon.

Spring, J. H. (1998). *American education: An introduction to social and political aspects.* New York: Longman.

School Reform

Vignette: Reform at Prufrock School

Prufrock School has been involved in various forms of capacity-building activities for the past five years, but none have seemed to have any impact on the classroom or student learning. Reforms include such capacity-building activities as the institution of local school planning councils, customer focus, higher standards, improved assessment programs, educational choice, increased technology, greater parental participation, inclusion, and others. Most would agree that these changes were conducive to needed reforms, but there was little evidence of any reforms occurring in the classroom or in the teaching/learning process.

The 728 students now attending the school represent a fairly stable population. The racial composition is 50 percent white, 35 percent black, 10 percent Hispanic and 5 percent Asian. The school is fairly middle class and does not qualify for any externally funded enrichment programs. It has a relatively low dropout rate, however; almost 12 percent of the students fail at least one grade level because of poor academic performance. Prufrock students are professionally oriented and about half plan to attend college.

Prufrock, like many of the schools in the district and across the state, has a very traditional curriculum. Except for a few minor changes in the delivery system and a content update, the curriculum and instructional strategies have remained relatively stable. The school takes pride in its literacy across the curriculum and classroom management programs, which have been widely recognized as strengths. The faculty are considered to be quite strong, but still the school climate has been rated low by both teachers and students. Part of the school climate problem is caused by a growing split within the community and among teachers about the future directions the school should take.

A growing majority are in support of a major transformation of the academic programs to include a new emphasis on thinking, understanding, and building and applying knowledge; collaborative, combined, team efforts; active, authentic learning; technology, distance learning, and access to the Internet; an achievement, demonstration, and performance focus; and, interdisciplinary approaches. This shift in attitude is caused by a recognition that school system graduates are not well prepared for the teeming, technological, information-rich worlds of work and higher education.

The other group, which is dwindling, believes that the schools need to emphasize basics and academic content. This group believes the focus should be on rote learning; acquiring essential knowledge and skills; lecturing, reading, and intense study; printed media; grade focus with lots of assessment using paper-and-pencil tests; independent, individual work; and a strong back-to-basics discipline focus. This group wants increased systemwide standards so all teachers and students would be doing the same thing throughout the district. They believe that the schools can be improved by doing what they have always done, only better.

All agree that student achievement and academic relevance must be the focus of all decisions at Prufrock. If the staff could not draw a connection between a new effort and the improved performance of students related to twenty-first century needs, the effort would not be supported. At the same time, all existing programs and efforts would be evaluated by the same standards used to evaluate new programs and approaches. The challenge would be to create legitimate programs that maintain integrity and incorporate what educational researchers and others know about learning and the future for which we are preparing students. Comparative studies suggest that innovative alternative schools are superior to traditional schools (Raywid, 1994) like Prufrock.

This new reform emphasis has resulted in a recognition that few if any within the school or district know what a twenty-first century school might look like. The school feels it is well organized and structured to meet the challenges of rethinking and re-creating itself, but it really has no vision of a transformed school. The staff and community are unprepared to take on the creative challenge of rethinking and transforming the curriculum and instruction.

Certainly part of the reason so few within the district have thought about designing and developing new approaches to teaching and learning is the belief that the district maintains a single standardized program and staff are not expected to or even allowed to look into the research and alternative practices, much less design and experiment with new curricula. Designing and experimenting with curriculum and instruction, however, is exactly what is being encouraged. The educational challenge for a twenty-first century principal is to lead the redesign of curriculum and instruction. All are surprised by the school board chairperson and superintendent's joint statement that "sometimes it's easier to change everything in our academic program than just one thing." You have been called on to lead this massive reform for Prufrock.

Do you think Prufrock is ready to begin a major reform effort?
What knowledge base will be most helpful in successfully reforming Prufrock?

Reform Models and the Twenty-First Century

Researchers, who often disagree on almost all aspects of education, agree on a need for fundamental school reform. The Southern Regional Education Board believes that schools are outstanding at doing what they have always done, but that is not what is needed for the future. The U.S. Chamber of Commerce, the Business Roundtable, the Alliance of Businesses, and the Committee for Economic Development contend there is a need to fundamentally reform American schools. The North Central Regional Education Laboratory suggests that schools focus on traditional models that do not meet the needs of twenty-first-century students. The National Education Goals panel believes a general stagnation exists in the nation's schools. The challenge to today's educators is to build school systems that are consistently rethinking and recreating schools as institutions that are responsive to the changing needs of society.

According to a report on school reform published by the U.S. Office of Education Research and Improvement (OERI), recent reform efforts "have targeted all stages of education, from preschool to school-to-work transition and have addressed nearly every aspect of the public elementary and secondary education system: curriculum and assessment, teachers' preparation and their professional lives, school organization and management, technology, and parental and community involvement" (Goerty, Floden, & O'Day, 1996, p. iii). The Improving America's School Act requires states to develop school improvement plans that establish high content and performance standards in at least mathematics and language arts, and assessment aligned with these content standards. By 1997, more than forty-five states were involved in various stages and forms of school reform. In early 1998, the call was "to meet the challenge of massive fundamental reform." These demands have continued into the new century (For more information see: www.edweek.com/context/orgs/.)

Leading Innovative Schools

STEPHANIE PACE MARSHALL, PH.D.
Aurora, Illinois
Mathematics and Science Academy

What does it take to lead an innovative school (and by that I mean a transformative and generative learning community) for the twenty-first century? What are the conditions that leaders-in-learning must create, to prepare students to be pioneers in an unknown land? Perhaps a bit of history is important. For three centuries, the dominant scientific worldview was the image of a static, repetitive, predictable, linear, and clockwork universe. This "Newtonian" worldview has influenced and defined almost every dimension of our own cultural and organization life, including our schools.

Consequently, as leaders we focused on predictive cause-and-effect models of human learning; we became preoccupied with things and efficiently managed our schools by reducing them to discrete observable and measurable parts. Deriving our insight from "Newtonian" science, we behaved as if we actually believed that by understanding the parts we would discern the behavior of the whole and that analysis would inevitably lead to synthesis.

By design, we constructed and operated our "Newtonian" schools as we understood our world, and this produced learning-disabled institutions that have suppressed reflective thought, creativity, and the innate and inexhaustible capacity for lifelong learning.

The unexamined application of "Newtonian" laws to learning environments diminished our capacity for continuous growth and change because it diminished our capacity to grow the individual and collective intelligence, spirit, and hope of the whole system.

We designed a linear system built on predictive models of change and a belief that learning was incremental, when in fact human systems are not predictable; change is nonlinear and learning is dynamic and patterned. Human beings do not follow the logic of cause and effect. We crave connectedness and meaning, we seek lasting and deep relationships, we grow by sharing and not by keeping secrets, and we need to trust and be trusted to feel safe enough to dare.

As a result, leaders of innovative learning communities need to create learning and teaching environments that enable learners to direct their own learning toward greater rigor, coherence, and complexity; to increase their intellectual, social, and emotional engagement with others; and to foster collaborative and dynamic approaches to learning that enable learners to develop thoughtful and integrative ways of knowing.

We must create a learning culture that provides a forum for risk, novelty, experimentation, and challenge and that redirects and personalizes learning. We must create learning communities for learners of all ages that can give power, time, and voice to their inquiry and their creativity. Such a community is governed by the principles of learning, not school, and is:

- *Personalized, flexible and coherent.* Questions that are significant to the human condition drive the curriculum, and knowledge is not separated in distinct and unconnected disciplines.
- *Internally and externally connected.* It is not bounded by physical, geographic, or temporal space (because learning happens everywhere, student learning must transcend classroom and school boundaries).
- *Rich in information and flexible and diverse learning experiences.* It has pathways for all learners (students are actively engaged in meaningful research and inquiry; they study "big and important concepts in the context of interdisciplinary problems that matter and that are relevant to the real word; students are engaged in meaningful research and serious inquiry).
- *Intergenerational in the configuration of learning experiences.* Margaret Mead has said that the healthiest learning environment occurs when three generations are learning together.
- *Grounded in collaborative inquiry.* Students engage with adults and peers and draw on the experiences of the entire group; learners are honored as capable of creating and generating knowledge, not just acquiring information.
- *Focused on complex cognition, problem finding and problem resolution.* Students are engaged in authentic and meaningful dialogue with members of the internal and external community; they are taught skills that enable

them to deal with complexity and with ambiguity and paradox.

Creating these conditions for generative learning is the work of innovative leaders and it is fundamental to the creation of an environment that enables exceptional learning for all students.

Parker Palmer (1998), in his simple, yet profound book *The Courage to Teach*, offers the following essential insight about leaders and leading within a learning setting:

> If we are to have communities of discourse about teaching and learning—communities that are intentional about the topics to be pursued and the ground rules to be practiced—we need leaders who can call people toward that vision.
>
> Good talk about good teaching is unlikely to happen if presidents and principals, deans and department chairs…do not expect it and invite it into being…. This kind of leadership…involves offering people excuses and permission to do things that they want to do but cannot initiate themselves…. (page 156) Becoming a leader of that sort—one who opens, rather than occupies, space—requires [an] "inner journey"…beyond fear into authentic self-hood, a journey toward respecting otherness and understanding how committed and resourceful we all are.
>
> As those inner qualities deepen the leader becomes better able to open spaces in which people feel invited to create communities of mutual support…leaders call us back to the heart of teaching and learning, to the work we share and to the shared passion behind that work. (p. 161)

Lee Bolman and Terry Deal (1995) in their book *Leading with Soul*, confirm Palmer's assertion, "Leadership is a relation rooted in community…." (page 56) [whose essence is] "not giving things or even providing visions, it is offering one's self and one's spirit" (p. 102).

As leaders we have been trying to fix the parts. We now realize we must first change the way we think and relate with one another. We must create a new way of seeing and being in the world and this will cause us to change what we do.

(continued)

Continued

The seventeenth-century Newtonian world-view created a mechanistic and machine-based metaphor for leadership. Now we know much better. We must take our metaphor for leading, not from a machine but from the biologic of living systems in the natural world.

As leaders we must seek to gain insight from the paradoxes that continuously confront our systems. We must:

- Create comfort with ambiguity.
- Create opportunities to allow energy, information, and the human spirit to flow within and throughout the system by facilitating authentic dialogue about teaching and learning.
- Promote diversity of all kinds.
- Establish communal relationships of meaning by inviting the hearts and souls of people into the learning environment.
- Look for patterns and relationships and explicitly identify and name them in order to promote the organization's sense of self and integrity.
- Celebrate the power of community and the human spirit.
- Create common language to build common meaning.
- Create trusting response-able and love-able learning communities.

For leaders in innovative schools our role is not to control but to facilitate authentic learning by creating conversations that matter. Conversations of community that invite the entire organization into shaping its future and into answering questions:

1. What is possible now?
2. What do we want to be in the world?
3. How can the world be different because of us?

Until recently threats to organizational survival were largely external in nature and driven by precipitous events leaders could strategically defend against. Now our threats are mostly internal, and their dynamic and systematic complexity requires leaders who can think and act in integrated, systematic, and spiritful ways.

The vision of educational leadership for innovative schools has changed from knowing what to do in order to control and manage to knowing how to live in order to unleash the synergy of the system. This is both our greatest challenge and our greatest opportunity.

We need courageous leaders who can think and act in integrative, systematic, and soulful ways and who are not afraid to create transformational learning communities that learn their way into the future by inviting and engaging in development of the fullness of human capacity.

An Assessment of School Reform

In examining the reform movement, Joseph Murphy (1991) found that "In the early 1980s, a concerted effort to reform American public education began. The impetus for these attempts was primarily economic. Analysts from all walks of society concluded that the United States was on the verge of being displaced as a major player in the world economy. The belief that we were falling behind other industrial powers in development, productivity, and quality was a theme that laced the pages of the various reform reports (see, for example, Carnegie Forum, 1986; Education Commission of the States, 1983; National Commission on Excellence in Education, 1983; National Governor's Association, 1986; National Science Board, 1983; for a review see Murphy, 1990). It did not take reformers long to draw the connection between this economic impotence and the education system. Nor was the potential for schooling to restore the economic preeminence of the United States ignored" (p. vii).

The concerns of the analysts are that the times have changed and yet education has not. Schools have greatly improved student access but remain basically the same when almost all other aspects of our lives have been revolutionized. American students compared unfavorably to foreign students and were weak in inferential skills. Science achievement had declined, and a national problem of illiteracy existed. The response to these concerns was rapid and dramatic. A flurry of legislative action established goals, standards, accountability, teacher qualification, and new structures. Many scholars across the United States joined in a search for a cure-all for American education and provided general recommendations regarding opportunity, vision, empowerment, standards, expectations, resources, goals, decentralization, technology, outcomes, and accountability. Universities completely restructured their teacher and principal preparation programs, and superintendents and school boards experimented with new approaches and structures within their school districts to be more responsive to needed changes.

Although we have learned much from these efforts, few scholars have observed significant improvements. Terrel H. Bell, the secretary of education who established the National Commission on Excellence in Education (1983), which authored *A Nation At Risk*, concluded,

> The ten years since the publication of *A Nation at Risk* have been splendid misery for American education. We have learned much. We have suffered many disappointments. But we have not given up the quest to shape education into the super-efficient enterprise that it must become if America is to keep its proud place of leadership in the marvelous Information Age of this decade and beyond. Perhaps we should have made much more progress than we have. But at least we have stayed with the task. (p. 597)

David T. Kearns, former chairman and CEO of Xerox Corporation, after fifteen years of active interest in American education states, "The U.S. once was ranked no. 1 in the world in education. Now we're 13th or 14th...only about 50 percent of our kids who get a high-school diploma do so at more than an eighth-grade level" (Third International Mathematics and Science Study, 1995, p. 12).

It is becoming clearer that the existing model that served us well in the 1800s and the first half of the 1900s will no longer be effective in the 2000s. Educators are being asked to embark on an important voyage into an entirely new educational system. We have created structures, we better understand the process, and we have established significant new standards and measures of assessment; the most important journey, however, still lies ahead of us. Now that we have built the needed capacity to change we must begin to rethink all aspects of schooling, given new needs and expectations and new technologies. The call is to transform the classroom, curricula, instruction, staffing, and relationships to parents and community (Martin, 1993; Noddings, 1992; Carter & Cunningham, 1997).

In an analysis of reform efforts since the 1950s, Fullan (1993) concludes,

> We have learned that neither centralization (federal, state, or district) nor decentralization (school) by itself works. We also see that reform strategies struggle between overcontrol and chaos. The realization that initiating multiple innovations is the problem has shifted our attention to more comprehensive perspectives but has failed to provide a solution. Evidently, change is more complex than we realized. (p. 122)

Rand Institute research found little evidence that schools have changed. Theodore Sizer's experiences suggest that change in schools is exceedingly difficult and incentives are weak. The Business Coalition for Educational Reform found that introducing new approaches in education is very difficult. The National Science Foundation maintains that schools have minimum technology, which typically services existing practices. In general, research suggests reforms have had minimal impact on the long-range functioning of classrooms and schools (Carter & Cunningham, 1997).

On the other hand, the demand for school reform has intensified in the 1990s, and there is no letup in sight. Educational leaders will be expected to facilitate the rethinking of education and the creation of altogether improved places of learning where the needs of the next century will be better met. This will be a process of continuous improvement through massive change. Schlechty (1997) is concerned that "unfortunately, too many educators seem to lack the sense of urgency it will take to bring about the kinds of reforms that are needed if public education is to be a vital force in American life into the twenty-first century" (p. 17).

> What is your motivation for making the type of pedagogical reforms being called for at Prufrock School?

Finding New Directions

Past changes in American education have been slow, haphazard, incremental, and often have been effected only at the edges of existing curriculum and instruction. These marginal changes are being made at a time when there is a strong need to rethink the purpose, nature, structure, process, and practices of teaching, learning, and schooling (Goodlad, 1991). The improvements that are now called for address "what and how" subjects are taught, as well as how progress is measured and evaluated. They get at the technical core of the teaching and learning process. Students' performance, experiences, preparation, and outcomes become the driving force for the new reforms. The question becomes: "What are the needs of students as they assume the responsibilities of full citizenship in the twenty-first century?"

Teaching, curriculum, and technology have substantial knowledge and experience bases that cannot be ignored in developing schools for a new century, but this knowledge and experience should serve as a foundation for innovation and experimentation (Joyce et al., 1992). We cannot borrow models that have worked well in some school districts and implement them lock, stock, and barrel. Nor can we ignore the ideas that show great promise for improving American schools. Improvement occurs when teachers are made aware of the great possibilities to improve education and are encouraged to experiment with these ideas in their own classrooms and schools. It is essential that teacher efforts to improve schools be directly inspired by and in the context of school leadership, as well as by the vision for schooling by the best minds in education.

Certainly no educational improvements will occur if an organization has not built in the capacity to change. To succeed the people in it must use a great deal of care to create a culture and approach that motivates and supports participants, encourages wide participation, addresses complexities, and maintains a systemic view. But improvements will not occur unless educators are encouraged to think about the significant opportunities that exist for their schools. Without a strong vision of what great twenty-first century schools look like, it is highly unlikely that capacity-building efforts will have much impact on classrooms, schools, or students. Capacity and vision must proceed hand in hand if we are to achieve any level of success.

Much of the research on planning and innovation has focused on decision making and the implementation process (Allison, 1971; Hughes & Achilles, 1971; Cohen & March, 1974; Etizoni, 1986; Janis & Mann, 1977; Lindblom, 1980; March & Simon, 1968; Mintzberg, 1989). In relating this literature to education, Michael Fullan (1991) found a problem with thinking in terms of a single innovation as a means to improvement. He found such an outlook excessively limiting. Fullan states,

> Instead of tracing specific policies and innovations, we turn the problem on its head, and ask what does the array of innovative possibilities look like.… Changes that increase schools' and districts' capacity and performance for continuous improvement—is the generic solution needed.
>
> Taking on one innovation at a time is fire fighting and faddism. Institutional development of schools and districts increases coherence and capacity for sorting out and integrating the myriad of choices, acting on them, assessing progress, and redirecting energies. (p. 349)

Other authors see innovation as a series of choices that organizations and thus individuals are constantly confronting in order to decide what is better than the idea it supersedes (Rogers, 1995; Hall & Hord, 1987). The newness and the uncertainty involved distinguishes innovation from other types of decision making. Reinvention is the degree to which innovations are modified to meet the specific needs of the clients and those in the organization through the process of adaptation. Probably the most important factor related to the speed of adoption and its ultimate success is the relative advantage as perceived by those who influence the decision and its ultimate success. However, a key issue in all of this is where innovations come from.

Innovations typically begin with the recognition of a need or problem. This recognition can occur through the political process, the rise of social problems, or a sense of present difficulties and future needs. Certainly all of these were a part of the *A Nation at Risk* report, which was meant to stimulate research programs to seek solutions for education. Everett Rogers (1995) states,

> Many but not all, technical innovations come out of research" (p. 160). The purpose of research is to advance knowledge, practice and/or to solve practical problems. Rogers defines development as "the process of putting a new idea into a form that is expected to meet the needs of an audience of potential adopters.… This represents an arena in which researchers come together with change agents. How are innovations evaluated? One way is through clinical trials, scientific experiments that are designed to determine prospectively the effects of an innovation in terms of efficacy, safety and the like. (p. 160)

Eventually, when innovations are successful and are an improvement on what currently exists, they are implemented by leaders who serve as the innovative catalysts in their disciplines.

The focus of capacity building has been on staff development, governance, empowerment, site-based decision making, community participation, school culture, accountability, collaboration, networking, resources, standards, assessment, and the restructuring of existing systems. Certainly these efforts are essential to any future school improvement in order to support innovative practices. They create an environment of change or at least help it along. They are, however, only tools; it takes the genius of creative ideas, vision of the future, a knowledge of where we need to be to spark individuals to improve schools. The capacity is essential, but so are the ideas. An essential role of leadership is the innovation of improvements to the existing system through the creation of capacity, vision, innovation, development, and adoption (For more information see: eryx.syr.edu.)

> How would you begin to reform the curriculum and instruction as the principal at Prufrock School?

Championing the Cause

Ideas and knowledge from the work of others serve as a catalyst for thinking through classroom and school improvements. Ideas that have strong promise for a particular school will need to be discussed, experimented with, and assessed. In this way, educators are working together by testing and sharing ideas to better meet the needs of a changing population of students, increased economic and social pressures, advancing technology, and the demands of an uncertain future. Those participating in the improvement of schools will need to orient their common efforts toward a shared vision of improvement as they develop creative insights, invent new schools, and prepare all students for life in a knowledge society (Carter & Cunningham, 1997).

The creation of effective new schools ultimately depends on the ability of educators to visualize how improved schools look. Vision converts ideas, knowledge, experience, and futurist thinking into a reality that is clearly understood and achievable by practitioners. Vision provides the bridge between innovative ideas and purposeful, coordinated action. Therefore, it is critically important that educators be aware of the latest thinking, of what holds the greatest promise for improving education. The vision of an ideal school helps them to rework and reshape existing curriculum content, instructional methods, and delivery systems.

Educators must stop tinkering with the existing paradigm of education and rethink all aspects of schooling, given new needs and expectations and new technologies and to make the shift to a new paradigm (Sparks, 1997). Educational leadership will be required at all levels to help schools to transform themselves (For more information see: www.alsr.brown.edu/html/builproj.html.)

What will be needed to support educators and community members as they envision a more modern Prufrock School?

Common Themes in a Changing World

Professionals need some school-reform guidelines in order to know what to keep, what to throw away, and what to build anew. We must begin with the nature of teaching and learning, the structure of the pedagogical process, and the design of curriculum and instruction, given modern technological innovations. Recent studies suggest that it will be imperative for schools to emphasize lifelong learning, thinking, and problem solving. They must also stress actively applying learning, moral reasoning, writing and speaking effectively, researching information, using new technologies, and listening to and understanding others. The traditional emphasis on acquiring knowledge and skills is giving way to a greater emphasis on learning how to think intelligently and the application of knowledge as needed within a specific context. The most recent guidelines are based on Bloom's (1956) higher order of learning: analysis, synthesis, and evaluation.

New schools are expected to provide many more learning options for students who have different learning styles and brain functioning. They must incorporate what we have learned from recent brain research, including that on infant and toddler development and learning (Gardner, 1993). Teachers need to help students develop understanding, inferential skills, and strategic knowledge and advance their thinking skills. The most powerful models in instruction are interactive and generative—engaging and encouraging the learner to construct and produce knowledge in meaningful ways. Students teach others interactively and interact generatively with their teachers and peers. Reformers hope that by rethinking education, given a common set of outcomes, schools will be better prepared to meet the needs of all learners and the communities in which they live (Education Commission of the States, 1991).

More than ever before, technology is at the forefront of a rapidly changing world. Information technology is driving change at an accelerated rate. Like their forebears, children must become pioneers as they move into a future of change and great adventure, where technology allows them to access information from anywhere in the world in a matter of seconds, and where the roles and responsibilities of the populace present new challenges and opportunities. Some futurists predict that large systems (such as education) that do not respond to this paradigm shift are in particular danger of becoming irrelevant to the needs of the present generation and future ones.

The American Association of School Administrators (1993) completed a study ranking critical elements in "preparing students for the twenty-first century." In part, the top-ranked items included:

1. *Academic content.* Use of math, logic, reasoning, and writing skills, functional/operational literacy; critical interpersonal skills; use of technology to assess or process information.

2. *Behaviors.* Exercise of honesty, integrity, the golden rule, respect for effort, the work ethic, discipline; respect for multiculturalism and diversity; appreciation for individual contributions, ability to work with team members.
3. *Essential skills.* Teaching of oral/written communication; critical thinking, problem solving, reasoning, analytical skills; responsibility for one's actions, discipline and ethics; ability to assess one's goals.
4. *Changes in schools.* Incorporation of "marketplace" technology in learning and as part of exit criteria; accommodation of new technology; promotion of active versus passive learning; provision of more time for professional development, particularly in technology; clarification of students' goals and standards; incorporation of more real-world projects; and increase in parental and community involvement in schools.

A child's education should be authentically grounded; subjects should be integrated (NCTAF, 1997). It is clear that we need citizens who can think strategically to create visions, learn in a constantly changing environment, build knowledge from a wide range of sources, understand systems in diverse contexts, and collaborate both locally and globally using technology.

The President's Committee of Advisors on Science and Technology's Report to the President (1997) stated that although the private sector demands workers with the skills needed to compete in the "information society," most schools lack key technologies. They also lack teachers who are properly trained to use the equipment that is readily available in other institutions. Educational leaders are being asked to make technology a key part of the learning process. There is a potential for radically different methods of teaching and learning using the range of technological possibilities—changing what is learned, how it is learned, how it is measured, and what the teacher does in the classroom. There is a clearly stated goal of connecting every school to the National Information Infrastructure (NII) and providing training on how to use this tremendous information communication library.

Technology will be a major supporting tool for all learning, and students will work on projects through distance learning with other students and professionals at diverse locations. They will use technology to access needed resources both beyond and within the school. The technology will be based on powerful learning paradigms that allow students and teachers to work on authentic and challenging problems, interact with data in ways that allow student control, build knowledge within a learning community, and involve practicing professionals and community mentors. Virtual reality will be used to bring life to knowledge and classroom activities. The classroom will be a knowledge-building learning community.

The types of reforms required are major in scope, discontinuous with the past, and transformational. Box 3.1 summarizes some of these major new demands on education. Students need to be able to build their own knowledge and advance their thinking skills. They need to learn to work cooperatively in teams using interpersonal skills and key values such as integrity. Students will research information using the Internet, distance learning, and all forms of information media and will make multimedia presentations. They will develop multiple perspectives and a sense of responsibility for their own de-

---

B O X **3.1**

New Demands to Change Pedagogical Models

From	To
Teacher–Curriculum-centered	Learner-centered
Acquisition of knowledge and skills	Intelligent thinking and knowledge application
Individual tasks	Collaborative work
Passive learning (listener)	Active learning (collaborator)
Printed media	Technological tools
Grade focus	Achievement focus
National perspective	Global perspective
Independent efforts	Combined efforts
Abstract learning (facts)	Authentic learning (relationships, inquiry, invention, understanding)
Rote learning (drill and practice)	Problem solving (communication, access, expression)
Paper-and-pencil tests (norm-referenced)	Demonstrations and performances (criterion-referenced)
Discipline-based	Integrative/interdisciplinary/transdisciplinary approaches

---

velopment. They will be actively involved in relevant, real-world projects and will be assessed on results, work ethic, use of information, and knowledge application.

The Needed Reforms

Schools deal with a wide range of students, including the highly motivated, well prepared, and bright as well as those who lack commitment to learning, have no preparation, and do not demonstrate a high degree of ability. After examining restructuring experiments in elementary schools, Peterson, McCarthery and, Elmore (1996) concluded,

> If researchers, reformers, and teachers understood and agreed on what kind of teaching practices they wanted, and if they understood what would need to be learned to create these practices, then they might create structures that would support this learning and these practices. While some might continue to map forward from structural changes in schools to changes in teachers practice we prefer to map backward. Why not begin by attempting to understand teaching practice? (p. 151)

Teachers must eliminate what is getting in the way of advancing the teaching/learning process and meeting the needs of twenty-first-century citizens and replace it with completely new, successful practices. The needed reforms are not structural changes that come from the top down, but innovations that change what occurs in the classroom in educating our young.

Current research on restructuring suggests that the learning/teaching process that occurs in the classroom and school receives the least attention (Peterson, McCarthy

& Elmore, 1996; Murphy & Hallinger, 1993; Murphy, 1991; Goety, Floden, & Oday, 1996). In general, little effort has been made to link capacity-building reforms to changes in classrooms; relationships between teachers and students; instructional content, style, or approach; application of technology; and the interconnectedness of curriculum, instruction, and student outcomes. The new reforms must prove themselves in the classroom, and when successful they must be woven into the basic fabric of the school and school district (Cunningham & Gresso, 1993).

How do we best address the classroom needs of educationally disadvantaged students? gifted students? average students? learning disabled? How do we help more students to function on the highest level of thinking? How do we improve students' work ethic and moral reasoning? How do we best prepare students for a technological, knowledge-based, fast-paced society? These and many other such questions must be addressed in the next cycle of reform (For more information see: www.temple.edu/iss/csr-info.htm.)

> What mission and goals would you suggest to have an impact on the classroom and student learning?

Innovative Programs

A number of promising ideas are emerging to improve classroom instruction. Many are tied to the work of highly visible educational leaders who are involved in efforts to fundamentally reshape what occurs in classrooms and schools. What follows is a brief description of a few of the luminary efforts underway in the early 2000s with a vision toward the future (For more information see: www.aasa.org/reform/approach.htm.)

Accelerated Schools (Hank Levin).   Classrooms are organized around constructivist lessons, which give students much more responsibility for and input into their learning. Students are actively involved through hands-on activities and open-ended problem solving. They build connections between their school activities and what they do in their own lives. Teachers help guide students through exploration and discovery. Students work in teams, receive feedback from other class members, and often develop criteria on which they will be graded. Lessons are designed to enrich learning experiences and are based on high expectations for all students. The accelerated approach has three underlying structural principles:

1. *Unity of purpose.* The whole school community has a unified focus.
2. *Empowerment and responsibility.* The entire school community makes important educational decisions and takes responsibility for them.
3. *Capacity building.* Effort is directed at building on the strengths of the entire community. (Hopfenberg & Levin, 1993; Keller, 1995)

Schools use a variety of instruction, such as cooperative learning, socratic discussion, interdisciplinary curriculum, higher-order thinking, nongraded schedules, team teaching, and technology integration. Levin (Brandt, 1992) states, what we do is plant the seed and offer the philosophy that people in the school decide to try, and as they succeed with the philosophy, it turns things around.... We don't start by changing attitudes; we start by changing behavior; asking the staff to try things. And they've got to work them out. We don't tell them precisely what to do, we just outline general principles. But then—as the school begins to succeed—it takes on a life of its own. (p. 23)

Essential Schools (Ted Sizer).   Schools should teach many fewer subjects, topics, and skills, but they should teach them more thoroughly. The curriculum should focus on things that children can demonstrate and that set high intellectual standards. The stress in essential schools is on important information and the ability to use knowledge gained to make relevant decisions in a real-world setting. Sizer's nine common principles include focus on helping adolescents to master a limited number of essential skills and knowledge areas (less is more); using means that vary and are personalized; helping students to learn how to learn and thus to teach themselves; providing ways for students to demonstrate mastery of central skills and knowledge; building a culture of trust, respect, and high expectations with parents as essential collaborators; encouraging principals and teachers to be generalists first and specialists second; taking time for collective planning; having competitive salaries; and carrying student teaching loads of fewer than eighty-one; and, maintaining competitive per-pupil costs. These principles were originally designed for secondary schools but have also been cast in terms for elementary school practice.

Students are assessed on the basis of work portfolios. Because student performance cannot be as easily compared, we must place greater trust in educators. This process is best implemented when teams of teachers work with each student. Programs also constructively integrate separate subjects such as chemistry, physics, biology, mathematics, and technology. Teachers then work as coaches to help students, who have greater power and responsibility for their own learning. The delivery system is much more flexible in terms of the number of periods each day and the age-grade assignments.

In essential schools students are to display mastery in core skills such as "distinguishing between evidence and opinion" and "applying measurements in a variety of practical, scientific, and mathematical ways." Teaching emphasizes problem solving over rote learning, engaging students in individual and collective work, and connecting academic work with important matters in the community, nation, and world. Students are engaged in their work through a series of questions, and the results are presented in public exhibitions. Students are heterogeneously grouped but placed on a personal track that encourages them to aim high in what is called "teamstreaming." The schools have explicit standards, usually organized by domain, that students must attain. The five habits of mind, which are the touchstones of essential schools, are evidence, viewpoint, connection, suppositions, and relevance.

In contemplating "what matters" Sizer (1996) suggests,

...students are more likely to accrue success from the culture of their school—its clear convictions and the way in which those convictions are honored in practice—than from its formal technical structure. Good structures (such as enough time to do important work in class) are needed, for obvious reasons, but what the students do within those structures is what counts. That doing rests on the attitudes and confidence of the school's staff—indefinable, fleeting qualities, ones as impossible to mandate as they are important. That fact makes large-scale school reform profoundly difficult." He goes on to say, "The attitudes and commitments and relationships among a school's faculty, its students, and its parents are crucial. Without these, the best-laid plans for exhibitions, flexible schedules, advisory periods and the rest of the familiar paraphernalia of Coalition practice and that of similar reform efforts come to very little. (p. 106)

School Development Program (James Comer).   The major goal of James Comer's school development program is to advance students' social, emotional, and academic development so that they become successful citizens. Students are expected to meet high academic standards. A major theme is the creation of an inviting, engaging school climate that begins with teachers earning the trust and respect of their students' families and welcoming and supporting students in the classroom. Social events in the schools are very important, and each school must create a social calendar of events that includes various combinations of students, parents, and community members. These include breakfasts, luncheons, workshops, shows, formal dress-up parties, cotillions, reading fairs, and others. Reading is a major theme within the Comer model. In fact, the model often suggests hiring a home–school community coordinator and any needed reading recovery teachers.

A very important part of the teaching/learning process is to hold each teacher and student accountable for every student's progress. Figure 3.1 presents the overall guide for the school development program. A crucial aspect of this model is the provision of training.

Schools are improved by increasing parental presence in schools and through the use of child-centered concepts and belief for all students. Other factors include applying

Parent's Program	School Planning Management Team	Mental Health Team
Involves parents at every level of school activity	Plans, coordinates school activities	• Addresses schoolwide prevention issues • Manages individual student cases
GUIDING PRINCIPLES		
"No Fault"	Consensus Decision	Collaboration
Comprehensive School Plan	**Staff Development**	**Assessment and Modification**
Systematically addresses: • Academic achievement goals • Social climate goals • Public relation goals	Addresses needs identified in goals of Comprehensive School Plan	Creates new information and identifies new problems

FIGURE 3.1   Comer School Development Program

Source: Yale Child Study Center, 1991.

action-research; increasing instructional time and student engagement; providing cooperative learning; matching curriculum, instruction, and tests; and using a developmental approach. In the epilogue of a book on the SDP model, Comer and coauthors conclude,

> We should insist that a respect for kindness and justice be reflected in all our schools' activities. It is mandated; it is not negotiable. To this end, we must be action oriented. And as we act, we must act as servant leaders. To ask the best of children means that we always have to ask the best of ourselves. (Comer, Joyner, & Haynes, 1996, p. 168)

In 1992, Comer combined his SDP model with Edward F. Zigler's *Schools for the Twenty-First Century*. This new CoZi model offers a set of comprehensive family support services linked to the school through a child-centered collaborative decision-making structure. The guiding principle of SDP and ZIG is to bring all the adults in the community into the process of forging a common mission that keeps the child's development at the heart of all planning and decision making. The model includes programs for children as young as three, every day from 7:00 A.M. to 6:00 P.M. It includes school-based services that focus on all aspects of child development, including physical, social, emotional, verbal, and intellectual development. The combined model integrates child care and family support into the school.

Success for All (Robert Slavin).   One of the most important aspects of the "success for all" programs is, as the name suggests, a constant focus on the success of every child. Students begin with "Reading Roots," a program that emphasizes repeated oral readings to partners as well as to the teacher. Reading teachers read children's literature and engage students in a discussion of the stories. They move on to "Reading Wings," in which cooperative learning activities are built around core skills (Slavin et al., 1994). Students engage in partner reading and work in teams toward mastery of the vocabulary and content of stories. Roots and Wings engage students in activities that enable them to apply everything so they can see the usefulness and interconnectedness of knowledge. Every eight weeks student progress is assessed to determine who needs to receive tutoring or other types of intervention. The program stresses preventive services in a strategy called "neverstreaming."

Slavin's approach also includes "Math Wings" for mathematics and "WordLab," a program that integrates social studies, science, writing, and other subject areas. Students become active participants in scientific discovery and historical events. They use fine arts, music, computers, videos, and other technology to prepare all forms of multimedia reports. They participate in simulations that help to make what they learn immediately relevant. In "Math Wings" students work in cooperative groups to discover, experiment with, and apply mathematical ideas in such a way that the concepts come to life. In "WordLab," students take on roles as people in history, in various occupations, and in different countries. Students carry out experiments, investigations, and projects. An after-school program is offered to all children to further supplement regular classroom work. Family support and integrated services are provided to improve student attendance and class adjustment, coordinate health and social services, and provide tutors, mentors, and activity leaders. The concepts are now being used to begin developing a middle-school curriculum (Slavin et al., 1996).

Project Zero and the Teaching for Understanding Project (Howard Gardner).
Understanding is being able to carry out a variety of "performances" that shows both
understanding of a topic and ability to advance it. The mainstay of the Teaching for Understanding Project is engagement in performance built around carefully selected generative topics and goals. Generalizing, finding new examples, carrying out applications,
working through "understanding performances," and other activities press learners to
think well beyond what they already know. Learning is often structured around consequences, impact, dramatizations, connectability, relationships, insights, responsibilities,
and alternations, which help to induce understanding.

The basis of all efforts is to develop pedagogy that allows students "to do a variety of thought-demanding tasks" related to a topic of study. Students are expected to
find evidence and examples, generalize, analogize, apply, and represent topics in creative new ways. Needed focus for each topic and the ensuing instruction is created by
establishing specific understanding goals along with performances that support the
goals. Rubrics provide criteria for ongoing assessment throughout the learning process to support reflective activities. Students as well as teachers are involved in defining the criteria. Portfolios are an example of ongoing assessment. They illustrate the
evolution of a student's work through cycles of revision. The emphasis is on students'
active engagement with teachers in the assessment of their own and classmates' work
and record of understanding. Taking time to reflect on and improve one's work is an
essential part of the understanding process.

Teaching for understanding ensures that students understand the usefulness of
what they have learned. Thus, use of generative topics, an understanding of goals and
performances, and ongoing assessment are the core elements of all teaching for understanding. This curriculum is driven by pressing learners to think well beyond a
specific knowledge base. The greatest challenge in this approach is that it takes more
time to engage students in performance of understanding (Perkins & Blythe, 1994;
Gardner & Boix-Mansilla, 1994; Simmons, 1994).

EFG Curriculum (Joel Barker and Barbara Barnes).   Joel Barker, of Infinity Limited, Inc., and Barbara Barnes, CEO of the Ecology, Futures, and Global (EFG) Curriculum Collaborative, are developing a new transdisciplinary curriculum for "preparing
our children for the twenty-first century." A major theme of this approach is the development of pathways to competence and the commitment to stick with students until they
learn what they need to know (K-competence). The curriculum takes a constructivist,
thematic approach, allowing students to go along at their own pace. Information is
taught when needed for each student's specific instructional project. The three major
themes are:

1. *Ecological (relation with nature).* The focus is on who we are, with overall stress on
the concepts of life. All of the sciences are included in projects within this theme.

2. *Future (relation with time).* The focus is on where we are, why we are here, and
where we want to go. Subjects incorporated into this theme include physical education, philosophy, history, music, economics, nutrition, psychology, studio arts, innovation, and science fiction. Community service is often included as an important part of
these projects.

3. *Global (citizens of the twenty-first century).* The focus is on who we are and how we fit into the world. Students develop knowledge of culture, fluency of language, and an understanding of how they fit into civilization. Subjects incorporated into this theme are language, history, religion, anthropology, geography, political science, world literature, and sociology. Interaction with people in diverse locations, as well as foreign travel, is encouraged as part of this theme.

Everything taught is always connected to and made relevant by meaning, context, and use. Core values in this program include mathematics, reading, information acquisition and management, teamwork, values clarification, analytical systems, project planning, and thought presentation.

Assessment is completed through demonstrations; paper-and-pencil tests are seldom used. Student are assessed through the use of portfolios, which typically contain products, peer assessment, reports, exhibitions, demonstrations, and juried presentations. All projects include a description of relevant competency along with a rubric clearly describing not only expectations but also how outcomes will be evaluated. Computer resources are integrated with other resources to individualize and pace activity, build skills, and allow for both group and individual activity. Narrative report cards are provided to monitor student progress. (For more information see: www.efgedu.org.)

Other Innovative Models and Their Benefits

This brief review provides limited information on a few of the major reform efforts existing in America today. Other efforts underway include John Goodlad's School Renewal Project, Phillip Schlechty's Leadership for School Reform, Carl Glickman's League of Professional Schools, Dorothy Rich's Mega Skills, William Glasser's Quality School, Laurence Lezotte's Total Quality Effective Schools, Alfred Alschuler and Stephen Meyer's Global Youth Academy, Mortimer Adler's Paideia Group, Gordon Cawelti's Project on Redefining General Education, William Spady's Transformational Approach to Outcome-Based Education, Ernest Boyer's The Basic School, John Brever's Schools for Thought, E. D. Hirsch's Core Knowledge, Chris Whittle's Edison Project, as well as ATLAS Communities, Reading Recovery, Co-NECT, Expedition Learning, Outward Bound, Modern Red Schoolhouse, Direct Instruction, Consistency Management, America's Choice School Design, High Schools that Work, School Achievement Structure, and Individually Guided Education. In addition, many companies, such as Jostens Learning, IBM, Apple Education, Computer Curriculum Corporation, and many others, have introduced a number of new courseware systems for improving education. The New American Schools Development Corporation tested ideas on school reform and settled on seven designs that it is broadly marketing. In 1998, more than 900 charter schools were experimenting with innovative new approaches. The American Institutes for Research, based in Washington, DC, developed *Consumer Reports*–style effectiveness ratings for many of the various reform models. We will learn much from this work over the next five to ten years.

The extinct National Diffusion Network listed more than 500 replicable programs with some evidence of effectiveness. In evaluating some of these schoolwide reform models, Fashola and Slavin (1998) conclude, it is apparent from the discussion of the currently available schoolwide reform models that much more research is needed to make available a substantial 'shelf' of proven models. Yet what we do know now is that schools need not start from scratch in designing effective schoolwide plans. A wide array of promising programs are available, backed up by national networks of trainers, fellow users, materials, assessment and other resources.... Once a school has chosen to affiliate with a national program, it can then work out how to implement the national model with integrity, intelligence, and sensitivity to local needs and circumstances. (p. 378)

The use of preexisting models and related networks serves as an organizing tool and gives teachers the confidence to try out new ideas in their own classrooms. The network provides needed staff development, program support, and professional affiliation. Teachers can often visit other sites that have implemented the same model to learn from one another. New successes at any one location can be quickly shared among all classrooms and schools using the same model.

Networks reduce costs by sharing successes and thus avoid reinventing ideas in existence elsewhere and create efficiencies of scale that support needed development efforts. Models can be assessed at multiple sites and in different contexts. Perhaps the most important aspect of a network is being part of a broader team of experimenters, which provides teachers with greater confidence and perspective in trying different approaches. Those who are a part of the network establish a sense of identity with each other. Innovation cannot be supported in isolation from the majority of teachers (Sizer, 1996). Innovation needs a support network or group of educators who have jointly agreed on and are experimenting with new designs. Principals and teachers need to work with networks of professionals on creative innovations.

The cooperative energy of groups of people learning, planning, experimenting, and sharing acts as a catalyst for successful innovation. Margaret Mead said, "Never doubt that a small group of thoughtful committed people can change the world. Indeed, it's the only thing that ever has." Progress occurs when leaders increase the numbers of people who believe in, advocate, and practice new, successful approaches. Transformation needs people to champion the cause and when successful to display, demonstrate, report, promote, and develop other experts.

Modern pedagogy is a complex process requiring a delicate and insightful type of teaching. The new curriculum establishes a common knowledge but allows students to pursue interests and build their own curricula in a constructivist and technological approach. Students produce knowledge, teach others interactively, and interact generatively with their teachers and peers. The role of the teacher is to provide the rich environment and learning experiences needed for interactive, generative, collaborative study to occur. (For more information see: web66.coled.umn.edu.)

How would you link and support new classroom curriculum and instructional strategy with experimentation in the development of an innovative pedagogical program for Prufrock?

A Framework for School Improvement

CARL GLICKMAN, LEW ALLEN, AND JAMES WEISS
The University of Georgia

School leaders need to ensure that the focus, structure, and process of their work with faculty and staff is always focused on teaching and learning. In more than a decade of successful collaborations with more than one hundred K–12 public schools ("The League of Professional Schools"), we have found that a commitment to the beliefs and practices of democracy in learning and in governance is essential. This is accomplished through a three-part framework.

The framework consists of a covenant of teaching and learning, a shared governance process, and an action research process. The goal of implementing this three-part framework is to create a school that is a self-renewing, learning community that is focused on students. All three parts of the framework are of equal importance; neglect of any one will greatly compromise a school's efforts.

Covenant of Teaching and Learning

A covenant captures the beliefs that people in a school and its immediate community hold about exemplary teaching and learning. A school's goals, objectives, activities, curriculum, and instructional practices are filtered through the question: Are they within the letter and spirit of our covenant?

A covenant of teaching and learning allows a school to embrace certain instructional practices that are consistent with the beliefs of the school community, as well as to discern practices that are not. Without a covenant to help define and clarify a school's beliefs and practices, the collective energy of the individuals in the school is often fragmented or focused on the immediate issues of the day rather than on what all would agree, in their more reflective moments, should be done to achieve the long-term goals of the school community.

It is important that a covenant of teaching and learning reflect the voices of everyone in the school. The collegial discussions and deep reflections about teaching and learning that go into creating a covenant are crucial. A covenant written in isolation deprives those not involved of the experience of participating in a collegial dialogue about their deeply held, and often unexamined, beliefs about teaching and learning. A covenant that doesn't reflect all voices in the school will not likely serve as a guide to people's work.

Shared Governance

Shared governance is the process through which people democratically decide how to bring the covenant to life in the school. The shared governance process includes agreements as to how decisions are made and which roles will be assumed by administrators, teachers, staff, students, parents, and community members. Defining the structure and composition of decision-making bodies and the process by which decisions are made are crucial components. Time and energy must be taken to ensure that everyone understands the rules so that all can benefit from them. Rules of governance must be democratically established before decisions are made, not as decisions are being made.

A clearly written shared governance model that lays out how decisions are to be made ensures that all in the school know the rules, and the processes and procedures will not change on the whims of a few or for expediency. Schools trying to implement a new decision-making process sometimes find themselves with two decision-making processes functioning at once: the old process and the new process. Creating a specific shared governance model can help a school pick its way through this difficult transition.

Action Research

Action research can first help a school identify, clarify, plan, and evaluate actions that will bring the beliefs articulated in its covenant to life. A school's ability to bring about schoolwide renewal that benefits students is closely tied to its capacity to study and reflect on how its practices are affecting students.

(continued)

Continued

Staying focused on student goals is remarkably difficult. It is easier to document whether programs, new initiatives, or new structures have been put in place than it is to study what is happening to students. For example, it is much easier to study whether teachers are using more cooperative learning techniques in their classrooms than it is to gather data on the effects that cooperative learning is having on students. An action research process that is focused on students can help keep a school on track while informing the decision-making process as to what is working and what needs further attention.

Summary

A school renewal framework will provide a school with a structure that allows it to define for itself where it wants to go (covenant), how it wants to get there (shared governance), and how it will know if it is making progress (action research). Everyone in the school is systematically and collegially learning about and getting better at creating experiences for students that support this concept. Teachers are part of a community of learners working together to bring about a common vision of what their school is all about.

Harnessing Technology

Computers will customize educational instruction to fit each user's learning style, interests, and needs. Technology will make information and learning available to students, keeping them abreast of the latest developments in the field. Nancy Hechinger, one of the principal designers of the Edison Project, notes that technology plays multiple roles in supporting teaching and learning. It integrates access, connectivity, exploration, and research into a knowledge-building classroom environment (Hechinger, 1993). Voice, data, and images will be available from throughout the nation and world and integrated into a total educational system. Students will talk to people around the world, exchange ideas and documents, work collaboratively, and see one another simultaneously.

Students, teachers, and others can have instant access to student work and create notes or comments or talk directly to the originator via the computer. People can create networks to participate in discussions or conferences on shared topics and interests. Volunteers in various organizations can answer students' questions, comment on their work, and pose questions for students to address. Students are also able to experience history, geography, museums, and the like through virtual learning.

Louis V. Gerstner, Jr., chairman and CEO of IBM Corporation, states, "We don't want to focus on technology, we want to focus on the objective of education. IBM wants to help develop solutions that will create fundamental change." As a result, IBM launched "Reinventing Education" designed to support high academic achievement using new technology solutions. By 1998, IBM had invested $35 million to help schools reorganize themselves to achieve higher standards. IBM's Reinventing Education program is designed to develop cutting edge technology solutions for education. For example, "Wired for Learning" is used to create curriculum and lesson plans, to compare students' work against standards, and to complete parent-teacher conferences, and so forth on a computer network. Other systems are being designed to allow students to progress at their own pace and accumulate credit on the basis of demonstrations of what they know. "Watch Me Read" offers children individualized reading instruction utilizing advanced voice recognition for monitoring and evaluating student progress. IBM has also created on-line professional development materials, data mining, and warehousing solutions to improve school decision making. (For more information see: **www.ibm.com**.)

Some see an ever-expanding role for technology as education advances in the twenty-first century. One possible scenario suggests that students will have writing boards within the classrooms—large visual screens that can be connected to sites throughout the world. Their writing on the boards or on hand-held pads or their recorded verbal input could be translated and reported to diverse locations. They may also be able to speak directly to those individuals appearing on the large screens in their classroom, and the audio can be translated for foreign locations. This technology will allow students to construct their own learning systems.

Communications with parents can occur through the computer. Parents will have access to student assignments and work and be able to leave notes and schedule appointments (through distance conferencing). Parents can work with their children at home and have computer access to classroom materials twenty-four hours a day. The computer will accept voice dictation from administrators, teachers, and students and create needed formats (e.g., letters, memorandums, reports, research papers, tests). Teachers can instantly voice access students' performance records to determine what students are having trouble learning. They can access a resource repository for advice on how to best reach students who are having trouble and apply specific content, curriculum, and instructional strategy.

Students can check out computer disks that allow for direct learning from faraway libraries. Students will be able to abstract information from different sources and include it in their multimedia reports and presentations. The computer becomes a window to the whole world. Students partner with children in other cities, states, and nations to complete research and reports, working together via the computer. Students in classrooms at diverse locations talk directly with other students presenting joint multimedia reports and other presentations. Constructivist types of learning accelerate as we move the limits beyond those of classrooms.

Apple Computer, Inc. has been experimenting for more than ten years with a computer project entitled Apple Classrooms of Tomorrow (ACOT). Probably the greatest and most obvious realization from this project was that computers allowed "more children more ways to become successful learners" and "technology itself is a catalyst for change." Research has found that technology encouraged more collaboration, engaged students in generating ideas and products, developed positive student attitudes toward themselves and learning and improved performance on standardized tests. Teachers interacted differently with students, more as guides or mentors and were more open to new possibilities for redefining how students best learn.

> Learning activities in ACOT classrooms increasingly incorporated interdisciplinary studies, team teaching, and accommodations for students with different learning styles.... As teachers become comfortable with a shift in classroom roles, they may extend their pedagogical repertoires. With appropriate support, they may also adjust their approach to teaching and learning from curriculum-centered to learner-centered, from individual tasks to collaborative work, and from passive learning to active learning. (Fisher, Dwyer, & Uyocam, 1996, pp. 8–9)

Technology presents unprecedented opportunities for educators to create new paradigms of education that greatly expand the limited possibilities that exist in traditional schools. Technology provides access to much more and recent information, involving a greater number of people and assisting in instruction for both students and staff. The new technology will require new curricula, new instruction, and new staff development strategies. The need is to integrate new technology—palm-sized, wireless, voice-controlled computers, multimedia-capable laptops, digital technology, virtual reality, headsets—with other types of reforms. Educators must create a technology culture that parallels those students find outside schools. The key is to think technology and educational improvement, not only computers. (For more information see: www.cnet.com or www.zdnet.com.)

The use of technology as an integral part of the classroom opens up possibilities of redefining how schools now provide opportunities for student learning. They work with current data from many organizations, agencies, and institutes, sometimes downloading from satellites. Students typically use video cameras, VCRs, animation tools, scanners, sound digitizers, robotics, telecommunications, databases, and all forms of graphics. In a well-designed system the computer and other technologies are a major part of the core curriculum and instructional strategy. Complex assignments then become feasible.

Collectively these concepts hold many of the keys to developing improved schools. They will require educators to take a more holistic approach to educational improvement as they translate new successful practices into an integrated system of improved education. Michael Tucker (1990) states, "Very few of these things are in and of themselves new…but they have not been put together in a strategy for changing the entire system." (For more information see: www.ncrelorg/sdrs/areas/teocont.htm.)

Envision the type of technology that will be an integral part of the new innovative pedagogical program at Prufrock.

Wilson Elementary School District: Five Steps to a Successful Technology Program

JANE M. JULIANO, PH.D., Principal
Wilson Primary School, Phoenix, Arizona

You have just been hired as a principal of an elementary school and are charged with implementing a technology program. Although this is a daunting task, you can accomplished it if you involve a technically competent staff and key stakeholders in the school to develop and implement a long-range technology plan. The Wilson Elementary School District in Phoenix, Arizona, is an example of a school district that has successfully implemented the first five years of an eight-year technology plan. Currently, all students have their own computers and teachers are able to meet each student's curriculum goals by integrating subject-matter software activities into the classroom curriculum.

Step One: The Vision

The most important part of the technology plan is the statement of the reason for the technology program and how its success will be measured. For the Wilson District, which has a high minority, low socioeconomic population, the overriding goal for the technology program is to increase student achievement scores. It is also to give students, who otherwise would not have access to computers, the skills necessary to compete in a technological world. Of course, goals must be in line with the budget, and together these factors will set the vision for your plan and guide each aspect of the implementation.

Technology plans and budgets are never static. When you involve key stakeholders in your plan, you will obtain the support needed to implement the plan and keep it moving forward. At Wilson, following the superintendent's vision of a computer for every student, all administrators along with school board members, parents, teachers, students, and technology staff were included in the development of the plan. The technology coordinator for the district continued to hold monthly meetings with the superintendent, administrators, technology staff, and teachers to keep the plan on track.

Step Two: Design the Implementation

Next, your plan needs to specify what the implementation will look like. Will reaching your technology goals translate into installing a computer lab in your school, distributing a certain number of computers in every classroom, or both? What software will you purchase to meet your goals? The software you choose will determine the hardware to purchase and whether the computers will need to be networked or stand-alone. A total software curriculum package was purchased at Wilson so teachers are able to customize activities for each student based on his or her instructional needs. This type of implementation meant that all 1500 computers would be networked and distributed into every classroom. Teachers are able to print reports that evaluate student performance on the prescribed activities as well as track the information the district needs to measure the effect of the program on student achievement.

Step Three: "Wheeling and Dealing"

During the next stage of your implementation, you will be making all of the major purchases to get started. The technology team at Wilson learned much during this stage. They quickly realized that hardware and software continually change and that a portion of the budget needs to be reserved for updates and replacements. It also became apparent how dynamic the turnover rate of personnel is in the technology industry. Everything negotiated with a salesperson needs to be specified in your contract so agreements will stand through any changes in company salespeople, CEOs, or ownership.

Budget planning and purchasing is ongoing; be creative when you look for funding. At Wilson, two major bond elections three years apart have supported the costs of the technology program. Grants have helped finance teacher training activities. Every purchase, big or small, needs to be evaluated in terms of the big picture. For instance, although the network infrastructure at Wilson required a lot of capital up front, it was less expensive to complete the entire project than to install it piece by piece over four years' time. Student safety and hardware security also required a large portion of the budget. Customized student desks were built to house each computer. The monitor sits below a glass panel and the CPU and all wires are locked behind side and back doors. Custom shelving units were installed in the classrooms with tubing to house the wires that connect the computer to the network. These design strategies reduce the possibility of damage, theft, or vandalism. They also increase student safety and facilitate integration of computer activities into a teacher's daily curriculum.

Step Four: Staff Development

Now, with your vendor contracts in hand, and installation imminent, a long-term teacher training plan must be set in motion. At Wilson, with a teaching staff of 100, a full-time teacher trainer became part of the technology team from the beginning of the implementation. Not only do teachers need to learn new ways of teaching, they also need to learn the new software updates, programs, and operating systems, as well as how to implement the new phases of the technology plan

(continued)

Continued

such as the addition of the Internet. The teacher trainer at Wilson individualizes training as much as possible so that all teachers feel successful and supported. Throughout the school year, teachers are released from their classrooms for two-hour blocks of training. In addition, the teacher trainer often works collaboratively in the classroom to model and facilitate the overall management of the classroom technology.

Mentor teachers are trained to assist their colleagues. Any annual pay incentives are given to teachers who increase their computer literacy skills by taking community college technology courses.

Step Five: Show Your Success
Finally, plan for community access to the computers at your school, and promote what you have accomplished. Evenings at Wilson are busy with adult computer classes. Parents are invited to improve typing skills and learn word processing. Elementary and high school students work on homework projects. International and national visitors tour the two Wilson District campuses on a regular basis. Members of the technology team present the district technology plan at national conferences and submit articles to national publications. Teaching with technology has become part of the district's culture, and so can it become yours, if you plan with the future in mind before you take the first step.

The Leadership Challenge

Educators are being called on to translate what is now known about teaching and learning into a new system of education (Murphy, 1991). We already know enough about what future schools need to look like. Now we must clearly describe and create those schools. Gene Carter (1993) challenges educators in his belief that

> public schools must become very different than they are today if students are to possess the skills and attitudes necessary to function in an ever changing national and global society.... A coherent, congruent, shared vision or design for the future of public schools requires thinking about long-range possibilities rather than narrow specialties. The imagination needed to design an education for envisioning wider human fulfillment must come from educational leaders who are futurists themselves. (p. 187)

The challenge is to create an educational model that addresses current knowledge and needs and that the average teacher is capable of implementing. Teachers and students also must be provided the time to conduct intensive learning experiences. Time is also needed to develop curriculum and school experiences that relate to and build on the experiences of children. Teachers need to have opportunities to network with similar types of teachers—to plan, refine, teach each other, and learn. (For more information see: www.techedlab.com/k12.html.)

Define the role of administrators, teachers, and the community in the Prufrock renewal and reform effort.

Conclusion

Quantum physics suggests that order is inherent in all living systems, such as education. Stimulus or opportunities disturb and threaten that order or equilibrium. Under proper conditions, the system responds and evolves to a new, improved order, one that is much better suited for the new environment (Wheatley, 1992). Proper conditions suggest that (1) those within the system take advantage of the opportunities or possibilities for renewal and re-creation and (2) the entire system must be allowed to adapt and improve itself. When the system recognizes that the existing idea of organizational performance does not seem to be working, the system can resist, retreat, tune out, tighten control, create rigid structure, and return to traditions, or the system can regenerate, reform, renew, reconfigure and re-create itself to better suit its new environment. Linda Darling-Hammond (1997) believes

> It is critical to remember that reform is never completed because everyone continually changes and everyone continually learns, experiencing fresh insights from practices, from research, and from the synergy of teachers, administrators, students, parents, and others inquiring together. Although policy supports are essential reform can never be enforced from the top down, because people must create change in locally appropriate ways at the school and classroom levels. The importance of both context and commitment mean that local invention must be supported by policies that provide a mix of top-down support and bottom-up initiatives. (pp. 336–337)

Casey Stengle once advised, "If the horse you're riding dies, it's best if you get off." Traditional education seems to be dying a slow death and perhaps it is time to get off. Al Shanker (1990) stated it this way, "If you don't restructure, public education is going to be finished in five to ten years." The concern is that students will be locked into the 2000s with 1950s skills and behaviors. The call is for educators to rethink education and to create new, more effective paradigms that improve the entire system. Box 3.2 on page 86 presents the implications of this call for our future leaders.

Educational leaders need to build direction, alignment, and a culture of visionaries to encourage risk taking and experimentation, to set the pace, and to lead by example. Leaders must focus on planning, effective innovation, the classroom, student learning, and the twenty-first century. They must discuss and translate knowledge and research for excellent schools. Schlechty (1997) concludes,

> The capacity to establish and maintain a focus on students and the quality of the experiences they are provided, the capacity to maintain direction, and the capacity to act strategically are the most crucial components to be attended to if we are serious about developing an action plan to improve the quality of America's schools. (p. 222)

Progress occurs when we increase the number of people who believe in, advocate, and practice new, successful approaches to education. We must develop the capacity within school systems to make needed changes. But most of all, we must ignite the spark of individual and group genius required to really make a difference in education. (For more information see: **www.maec.org/mag-schl.html**.)

BOX **3.2**

Implications for Leaders

We need to:

Have a positive impact on student learning and the classroom.

Connect district, school, and staff development plans.

Encourage bold and creative undertakings (discourage tinkering, which wastes resources and short-circuits reform).

Provide vision and encouragement (take the long view).

Ensure adequate resources.

Rethink and re-create schools.

Keep everyone informed about research and practice.

Attract powerful constituents for support.

Make information technology a driving force (an integral part of school reform).

Measure performance.

Implement improved approaches.

PORTFOLIO ARTIFACTS

- Evaluate an innovative program described in this chapter or one being implemented in a local school district.

- Select an innovative program that you believe in and join the network, collaborate and become an expert on that program, and begin to experiment with it in your existing setting. Obtain appropriate permission before beginning an innovative program in any school or district.

- Join or start an innovative book club, in which everyone reads a book on innovative curriculum or instructional approaches each month and participates in a monthly discussion of the book.

- Videotape innovative classrooms in your surrounding areas, and lead a group discussion to evaluate the effectiveness of the approaches appearing on the videotape.

- Participate on a curriculum development and review committee.

- Write a proposal for curricular and instructional reform for a specific grade level.

- Distribute notes from workshops, conferences, and inquiry group meetings that stress school reform.

- Search the Web for innovative programs such as:
  Accelerated Schools
  Essential Schools
  CoZi Schools

Success for All

Project Zerro

EXCEL

EFG Curriculum

League of Professional Schools

(What are the strengths of their programs? What services do they provide? etc.)

(For more information see: pzweb.harvard.edu/hpzpages/whatsnew.html; www. waterw.com/~lucia/awlinks.html.)

TERMS

Accelerated learning
Active learning
Authentically grounded
Constructivist learning
Distance learning
Generative instruction
Interdisciplinary

Internet
Multimedia presentations
National Information
    Infrastructure (NII)
Paradigm shift
Portfolio
Reading recovery

Reform
Roots and Wings
Rubric
Site-based
Virtual reality

SUGGESTED READINGS

Bennis, W., & Mische, M. (1997). *The twenty-first century organization: Reinventing through reengineering.* San Francisco: Jossey-Bass.

Goodlard, J. I. (1994). *Educational renewal: Better teachers, better schools.* San Francisco: Jossey-Bass.

Hall, G, & Hord, S. (1987). *Change in schools: Facilitating the process.* Albany: State University of New York Press.

Lloyd, K. & Ramsey, P. (1997). *Reclaiming our nation at risk.* New York: Lloyd Ramsey Bell.

Marsh, D. D. (1999). *Preparing our schools for the twenty-first century.* Alexandria, VA: The Association for Supervision and Curriculum Development.

Pounder, D. G. (1998). *Restruturing schools for collaboration: Promises and pitfalls.* Albany: State University of New York Press

Rogers, E. M. (1995). *Diffusion of innovation.* New York: The Free Press.

Schlechty, P. C. (1990). *Schools for the twenty-first century.* San Francisco: Jossey-Bass.

Sizer, T. R. (1996). *Horaces' hope: What works for the american high school.* Boston: Houghton Mifflin.

Withrow, F. (1999). *Preparing schools and school systems for the twenty-first century.* Arlington, VA: The American Association of School Administrators.

CHAPTER

4 Cultural Diversity and Community Relations

Vignette: Cultures Clash in Fairhaven

The trouble didn't start in October. The brief but fierce brawls only announced it. Minutes after school let out at Fairhaven's Oakes High on October 29, hundreds of students poured into the street. The melee was on. Between twenty and thirty teenagers went at each other with shoes, sticks, belts, rocks, and canes.

Combatants were from virtually every ethnic group in attendance at the high school. "But," Assistant Principal Henry Barros suggested, "the two predominant groups were African American and Somali." It lasted about ten minutes, by the estimate of Brent O'Brien, Oakes's principal. Police and staff intervened, and a Fairhaven police helicopter ordered the crowd to disperse.

A second street fight broke out the following afternoon at the edge of Memorial Park, a few blocks away. Police cars and the vehicles of private citizens were pelted, and one motorcycle officer was struck with a rock. Tensions have receded in the last two weeks, but everyone involved has seen these lulls before. No one's offering a guarantee that this one is permanent.

For Somalis, the brawls were simply the latest eruption of an ongoing series of smaller conflicts that could be titled "Somalis versus Everybody Else." In the past, many Somalian children in the Fairhaven neighborhood of Mesa Grande have found themselves at odds with students of various ethnic backgrounds, particularly Indochinese and Latino.

The causes for conflict are many, subtle, and complex. The Somalis' experience provides a window into exactly what difficulties can arise as a cultural group is introduced into American society. It began among the children with name-calling, taunts, and bullying. In discussing these issues with Somali community members and students, Principal O'Brien learned that it started in 1991 when Somalis began arriving in Fairhaven. Thousands of miles away, their African homeland was being consumed in violent clan warfare, anarchy, and mass starvation after the collapse of the government. Somalian refugees arrived in Fairhaven in significant numbers with little or no advance notice. Such is often the case with refugee groups who are literally airlifted out of countries in turmoil and deposited in the United States perhaps a mere twenty-four hours later.

Somalian students say that practically from the beginning, other students have made fun of their cultural dress, with remarks such as "It's not Halloween." They are picked on, they say, and attacked when they pass through Memorial Park on their way to and from school.

For the most part the Somalian refugees who have come to Fairhaven have settled in Mesa Grande, an area that is often called a "Little U.N." in which more than thirty-five different languages are spoken.

Last spring, according to school district officials, Oakes High School, which draws much of its population from Mesa Grande, was 29.7 percent Indochinese, 27.3 percent Hispanic, 26.3 percent African American, 13.3 percent Anglo, 1.5 percent other Asian groups, and 1.9 percent other. Included in the African American population are 270 Somalian students.

According to Omar Jama, president of the East African youth Center, Somalian children tend to keep to themselves at school. Somalis are relatively new to the United States and find the culture very different. In school, Somalian children form a distinct group. Most are Muslim. Women and girls wear veils and scarves that cover their hair. But, Mr. Jama argues, these are superficial differences, and the divide goes much deeper than appearance.

In Somalia few women work outside their homes or drive cars. Men generally do not take direction from women. Islamic law forbids alcohol, drugs, and premarital sex; violations incur severe penalties. Somalis do not touch members of the opposite sex who are not related to them. They follow certain dietary restrictions; for example, they eat no pork. As Muslims they pray several times a day.

These cultural differences have led other students to consider Somali students standoffish, and many take offense. Somalian parents complain to school administrators that students deliberately poke and touch Somalian girls to provoke reaction. Boys of other ethnic groups try to speak to them. "That's just not possible," comments Mr. Jama.

For school officials, police, and outside groups, issues are magnified because of communication difficulties presented by language and customs. Mr. Jama comments that Somalian parents of all clans are anguished and alarmed at the tensions their children are experiencing: "Somalis come from a country ruined by civil war. We are looking for peace."

Assistant Principal Barros believes that the public is not accustomed to distinguishing between immigrants and refugees. He maintains that how the Somalis arrive in the United States plays a role in how they are received.

Last year Somalian parents took their complaints to Rawlins Middle School, a feeder to Oakes. The Somalis expected the school to decree an end to the taunting and name-calling. The school did not do as they expected. Meetings were convened, and attended by members of the Somalian community, school staff, Fairhaven police, parents of other ethnic groups, and various interested parties. "Steps were taken," says Mr. Jama, "But they were not deep enough. The Somali parents came away very disappointed in school officials."

The Somali parents also believe the police have failed them. "The perception is that the police are only doing things against the Somali kids," says sergeant David Melholf of the Fairhaven juvenile services team. "The kids are telling just one side of the story to their parents."

Various groups such as the Urban League of African Students at Fairhaven College have offered their services to Oakes and to the Somalian community since last month's disturbances. Hardly anyone believes the troubles are over for good. "They are only over," says Mr. Jama, "until the next incident, which could be next week or next year."

If you were Principal O'Brien, how would you go about decreasing the likelihood that these incidents will recur?

In what ways might parents, family members, and community groups be involved in dealing with these issues at Oakes?

Is there basic content knowledge in areas of cultural diversity that all involved should have? If so, what is it?

Diversity in Schools

Diversity is the norm in all schools. Staff and student populations are diverse, whether a school is located in North Dakota or along the border between the United States and Mexico, whether it consists predominantly of one racial or ethnic group or of a variety of cultural groups. Diversity includes differences in age, gender, sexual orientation, political beliefs, socioeconomic status, religion, physical and mental ability, language, and ethnicity. Although some schools have greater diversity than others, all schools must acknowledge and act on the diversity found in their populations, the community itself, the state, the nation and on our planet. Staff and students need to (a) be aware of diversity, (b) have knowledge and understanding about diversity, and (c) on the basis of that knowledge, take action or *praxis*.

Many educators, when talking about culturally diverse schools, assume that urban schools are the most heterogeneous. The words *diversity, urban,* and *minority student,* however, are not synonymous. For example, an inner-city school with a student population of all Mexican American students, who are from a low socioeconomic background, may have less diversity than a typical suburban school.

Socioeconomic Status and Social Class

Socioeconomic status (SES) refers to stratification that can be measured by factors such as economic status, family background, and job prestige. A broader term is *social class,* which involves large categories of people of similar SES who have in common such attributes as cultural identification, lifestyle, and attitudes.

SES is strongly correlated with academic success. When we talk about correlation, we are not addressing causation. Instead, researchers have found that children coming from socioeconomically low backgrounds are *more likely* to do poorly in school than children coming from high socioeconomic backgrounds. This does not mean that all children who are poor will do less well in school because they are poor. Families that are financially stable or affluent have greater access to resources, while families struggling to survive are more concerned with paying rent than buying a computer. This correlation has been found to be true in nearly every nation in the world and certainly is not a surprise to anyone. Generally, the greater the socioeconomic resources available to children, the better will be the children's educational attainment (Luster & McAdoo, 1994).

Inequities in social class intersect with other areas of difference in U.S. society. According to Parker and Shapiro (1993), "Social class plays a strong role in the struggle by people of color to achieve equal educational opportunity and vertical equity in school resources" (p. 42).

U.S. Population Demographics

Let us take a look at the U.S. population by race and ethnicity. As Table 4.2 depicts, it is estimated that by the middle of the twenty-first century, just over half of the U.S. population will fall into the category of white (this category includes persons not of Hispanic origin). An increase among nonwhite populations is projected for the next fifty years, with dramatic increases in the number of Hispanics.

TABLE 4.1   **A Child's Chances of Being Poor in the United States of America**

If white	16.9%
If African American	43.8%
If Latino	41.5%
If Native American	38.8%*
If Asian American	18.2%†
If in a female-headed family	52.9%
If younger than six	25.1%
If the head of the family is younger than 25	55.0%

*1989 data from the 1990 Census

†1993 data

Source: U.S. Department of Commerce, Bureau of the Census, www.census.gov/

Let us spend a moment discussing the categories of race and ethnicity. Table 4.3 on page 92 indicates the change in U.S. census categories between 1960 and 1990. In 1960 Americans were asked to put themselves into two categories: white and non-white. By 1990 there were six major categories including "Other." We often hear reference to four ethnic or racial groups in the United States: whites, Native Americans, African Americans, and Hispanics. The terminology used to describe people is constantly changing (For more information see: www.ericsp.org/intdiv.html.)

A Word about the Language We Use

The Spanish-speaking population in the United States comprises people from several countries and regions of the world. The words *Hispanic* and *Latino(a)*, which are used interchangeably, are the current preferred labels. These terms refer to people whose homeland was originally the Iberian Peninsula, Latin America, or the Caribbean.

TABLE 4.2   **Percent Distribution of U.S. Population by Race and Hispanic Origin**

	1990	2005	2010	2015	2030
White	75.7	81.3	80.5	79.7	77.6
Black	11.8	13.2	13.5	13.7	14.4
American Indian	0.7	0.9	0.9	0.9	1.0
Asian	2.8	4.6	5.1	5.6	7.0
Hispanic	9.0	12.6	13.8	15.1	18.9
White, not Hispanic	—	69.6	68.0	66.1	60.5
Black, not Hispanic	—	12.4	12.6	12.7	13.1
American Indian, not Hispanic	—	0.8	0.8	0.8	0.8
Asian, not Hispanic	—	4.4	4.8	5.3	6.6

Source: Bureau of the Census, www.census.gov/population

TABLE 4.3   U.S. Census Categories 1960–1990

1960	1970	1980	1990
White	White	White	White
Nonwhite	Black	Black	Black
	Other	American Indian	American Indian
		Eskimo, Aleut	Eskimo, Aleut
		Asian, Pacific Islander	Asian, Pacific Islander
		Other	Chinese
		Hispanic	Filipino
			Japanese
			Asian Indian
			Korean
			Vietnamese
			Malaysian
			Indonesian
			Samoan
			Cambodian
			Other
			Other:
			Hispanic
			Mexican
			Puerto Rican
			Cuban
			Other

Source: Bureau of the Census, www.census.gov/

In recent years the terms *Native Indian* and *Indian* have been used more frequently than *Native American. Native American* can be a confusing term because it could include indigenous people from either of the Americas. Perhaps the confusion also lies within the word *American.* What does it mean when people identify themselves as American? North America includes other countries besides the United States. Some South American people call themselves American. Unfortunately we do not have a word in English to describe people born in the United States that is based on the words *United States.*

Asian American is the term commonly used to refer to people who trace their origin to the many countries of the huge continent of Asia, including the Pacific Islands (and excluding Australia and New Zealand, of course). Labeling by ethnic heritage is somewhat more accurate than using a term such as *Asian American.* For this reason the 1990 census included categories such as Vietnamese and Korean under the term *Asian/Pacific Islander.*

Another example of how language is constantly changing can be found among the people who used to identify themselves as black or Afro-American. *African American* is currently the term preferred by the majority of people whose ancestry is African.

Educators (indeed all of us) must bear in mind that there is great danger in so categorizing people. As we explore some of the theories that explain differential academic success using race or ethnicity as the main factor, lumping people as disparate as African Americans who have lived for many generations in the United States with people who have recently immigrated from the West Indies can be highly misleading. Native language is but one of the many factors differentiating these groups.

When you deal with labels related to special education populations we recommend using *people-first* language. For example, instead of saying "the deaf child" or "the dyslexic student," you might say "the child who is deaf" or "the student with dyslexia." Using people-first language focuses on the humanity of an individual rather than the disability. Finally, and perhaps most important, a student's name, pronounced correctly, is always the best "label."

Racial Categories: What's in a Name?

Carolus Linnaeus in 1758 classified people by geography into four groups: *Americanus, Europeaus, Asiaticus,* and *Afer* or African. In 1795 Linnaeus's student, German anatomist and naturalist Johann Friedrich Blumenbach, invented the name "Caucasian" to designate the "light-skinned people in Europe, western Asia, and North Africa" (Gould, 1995, p. 65). He added one category, Malay. Blumenbach's five categories included: Caucasian, Mongolian, Ethiopian, American, and Malay.

So what is race? Is the word important? We all can agree that all humans are members of the genus and species *Homo sapiens*. In reality no traits are inherently associated with any one group of people. Thus there is only one race—the human race.

"Race" is a blank we fill out on forms for the U.S. government. The medical world uses racial classification in organizing data. But as Shreeve (1994) wonders: Are these studies pointing at genetic differences between races, or are researchers using race as a convenient scapegoat for health deficiencies whose causes should be sought in a person's economic status and environment? The same question could be asked about research conducted in education. We often hear about "black" students' low test scores or "Asian" students who do surprisingly well despite the odds against them (e.g., refugee status, language barriers).

Dividing people by racial categories can be an insidious activity and has little value for educators. Instead of discussing the variable of race let us turn to the concept of cultural identity.

Cultural Identity

In Chapter 6 we discuss organizational culture, which differs in many respects from national or ethnic group culture. Countless authors have defined the word *culture* in a variety of ways. Anthropologists Levinson and Holland (1996) maintain that emphasis should be "placed on culture as a continual process of creating meaning in social and material contexts, replacing a conceptualization of culture as a static, unchanging body of knowledge 'transmitted' between generations" (p. 13).

Anthropologist Renato Rosaldo (1989) argues that culture is open-ended, dynamic, and permeable. About a cultural group he was investigating he writes, "Immigrants and socially mobile individuals appeared culturally invisible because they were no longer what they once were and not yet what they could become" (p. 209).

Rosaldo discusses the concept of *borderlands*, liminal zones where cross-cultural encounters take place, often for the first time. Public schools are certainly one of these borderlands. Children representing nearly every ethnic group on this planet can be found in U.S. public school classrooms.

Bullivant (1989) believes that in the borderlands, groups' cultural programs evolve historically as their members adapt to changes in the social environment. A growing number of classrooms typify borderlands where children and adults from diverse backgrounds influence each other. In these borderlands, students forsake some aspects of their native cultures if the cultures conflict with the values and behaviors that produce social acceptance and success in school. It is important for educators to remember that often schools are the first places in which children internalize their ethnicity as a category for describing themselves.

If we accept the definition of culture as "a continuous process of creating meaning in social and material contexts," then each of the areas included in the elements of what compose cultural identity (see Box 4.1) has the potential to change considerably over time.

> How might issues of cultural identity be addressed at Oakes High School?

What, then, does the borderlands concept mean for schools and school administrators? One implication is that since new "cultures" are constantly being created, educators must discard the notion that they need to *understand* children's ethnic cultures (or countries). Because (1) the culture or country a child came from two years ago is not necessarily the same today; and (2) the child himself or herself is not necessarily the same person he or she was two years ago because of entering a new culture, the notion of *understanding* or *knowing* other cultures is as complex as the notion of understanding one's own culture. Thus, although Box 4.1 discusses various aspects of cultural identity, the notion that together these factors make up cultural identity is far too simplistic. Cultural identity, too, is constantly in a state of flux, especially in the borderlands.

Gender roles differ substantially from culture to culture. We can see within the United States how the roles of males and females, as well as people's views about sexuality, are in a constant state of change. Acceptable gender roles in one culture may not be acceptable in another. Why a girl from a particular ethnic group does not speak in class may have little to do with language proficiency. The explanation for her hesitation or reluctance to raise her hand in class might be because the female role in her culture may be to always allow boys to speak first.

In recent years, a subtle change with major implications is occurring in the area of religion in the United States where the majority of citizens are Christian. Several religious populations are increasing significantly. For example, the number of people in the United States who call themselves Muslims is more than 6 million (*1990 World Alma-*

BOX **4.1**

Elements of Cultural Identity

Language
Dominant language (English) versus native
   language
Nonverbal communication: kinesics
   and proxemics
Linguistic style

Gender Roles
Male and female relationships and roles
Views of sexuality

Religious/Spiritual Beliefs and Practices
Religious beliefs
Religious holiday observances

Family and Kinship Patterns
How are people related?
Close versus distant relations; extended families
Familial expectations and duties

Behavioral Norms/Moral/Social Practices
Rules and norms of the culture
Appropriate versus inappropriate activities
   and behaviors
Dress

Diet; food and eating-related issues
Personal hygiene

Adult-Child Relationships
Acceptable/unacceptable behavior between
   adults and children

**Learning Styles/Educational Beliefs/Views
of Intelligence**
Preferred learning modality (auditory,
   visual, kinesthetic)
Cooperative versus competitive approaches
   to learning
Value of education/schooling
Country of origin education system
Ways of knowing

Cultural Traditions
Mores and customs
Holidays

View of the Individual and Life Views
"Rugged individualism" versus collectivism
Historical awareness of the culture

nac). Most educators know little about the Muslim faith and its beliefs. What are the implications for schools with Muslim students who are called to pray five times each day?

Another key element of cultural identity involves behavioral, moral, and social practices. Cultures differentiate themselves by dress, diet, mores, and norms. What are the implications for school policies when students, such as Sikhs, wear turbans, when the school policy states that no hats can be worn? What does it mean to a teacher or fellow students when deodorant is not typically used in a particular culture, and the group believes a student "smells"?

Family and kinship patterns differ within many cultures as well. In some cultures the extended family plays a major role in the raising of a child. This family may include a grandparent, cousin, aunt, uncle, older sibling, or a non-blood relative. These kinship patterns can have considerable implications for family involvement in schools.

Learning styles and beliefs about how people learn, as well as beliefs about what constitutes intelligence, differ widely from culture to culture within the United States. Research supports that cultural groups differ in their preferred learning style (Ramirez

& Casteñeda, 1974; Stodolsky & Lesser, 1971). Additionally, children come to U.S. schools from many different educational systems. Helping families understand how the U.S. educational system is structured is crucial to obtaining their participation in their children's learning process.

Some educators take for granted that most U.S. schools have grades from PK through 12, with most students having different teachers each year. This is not the case in many countries, where teachers, especially in elementary grades might move for a few years with their classes. In some countries secondary school curricula are not segmented into different courses each year. Algebra, geometry, algebra II, and trigonometry might not each be offered in a different year of high school. Instead some educational systems integrate each of these areas of mathematics into one school year, with lessons each subsequent year reaching a higher level of complexity. Thus, cultural identity is a concept that has major implications for children and schooling.

Although all children deal with issues of identity, immigrant children often feel torn between worlds. One Mexican American high school student said she felt "like a jalapeño in a candy jar" (Cordeiro, Reagan, & Martinez, 1994, p. 105). One of the challenges for educators is to know how to respond, within the school environment, to the marginalization of ethnic groups in the mainstream culture.

Cultural Transitions

People experience stages as they encounter new cultures. One helpful frame for exploring these stages is Adler's (1975) five-stage model of culture shock (see Table 4.4). The stages include (1) initial contact with the culture, (2) disintegration of the familiar, (3) reintegration of new cues about the culture, (4) new identify formation with this new culture, and (5) biculturalism. People's perceptions, emotional ranges, and behaviors change depending on which stage they are in. These stages are not unidirectional; an event may trigger a person's returning to an earlier stage.

Adler's framework can be applied by educators to students in U.S. schools who come from other cultures. A student's ability to reach the stages of autonomy and independence in the United States is related to many factors. The culture of the school (see Chapter 5) and the school's relationship with the student's family are key factors in minimizing the negative behaviors that may result from culture shock.

> If most people experience stages of cultural transition as they move from culture to culture or place to place, what implications do these stages have for students, staff, and families at Oakes High School?

Prejudice and Discrimination

Prejudice is a negative or narrow attitude or belief toward an entire group of people. It is related to the use of stereotypes—generalizations about people.

TABLE 4.4 The Five Stages of Culture Shock

Stage	Perception	Emotional Range	Behavior	Interpretation
Contact	Differences are intriguing Perceptions are screened and selected	Excitement Stimulation Euphoria Playfulness Discovery	Curiosity Interest Self-Assurance Impressionistic Depression Withdrawal	The individual is insulated by his or her own culture. Differences as well as similarities provide rationalization for continuing of status, role, and identity.
Disintegration	Differences have impact, are contrasted Cultural reality cannot be screened out	Confusion Disorientation Loss Apathy Isolation Loneliness Inadequacy	Depression Withdrawal	Cultural differences begin to intrude. Growing awareness of being different leads to loss of self-esteem. Individual experiences loss of cultural support ties and misreads new cultural cues.
Reintegration	Differences are rejected	Anger Rage Nervousness Anxiety Frustration	Rebellion Suspicion Rejection Hostility Exclusiveness Opinionatedness	Rejection of second culture causes preoccupation with likes and dislikes; differences are projected. Negative behavior, however, is a form of self-assertion and growing self-esteem.
Autonomy	Differences and similarities are legitimized	Relaxation Warmth Empathy	Self-Assurance Self-Control Independent Comfortableness Confidence	The individual is socially and linguistically capable of negotiating most new and different situations; he or she is assured of ability to survive new experiences.
Independence	Differences and similarities are valued and significant	Trust Humor Love Full range of previous emotions	Expression Creativity Actualization	Social, psychological, and cultural differences are accepted and enjoyed. The individual is capable of exercising choice and responsibility and is able to create meaning for situations.

Source: Adapted from D. R. Atkinson, G. Morten, & D. W. Sue (1993) *Counseling American Minorities,* 4th ed. New York: McGraw Hill.

Henry Triandis (1971) differentiates between stereotypes and sociotypes. Socio-types are accurate characterizations about social and cultural groups, and stereotypes are inaccurate and possibly dangerous beliefs about a group.

Where do stereotypes and prejudices come from? Aboud (1988) argues, "the less that is known about a group, the easier it is to assign to it negative attributes" (p. 21). Thus, one possible cause for prejudice against a certain cultural group may be lack of contact and firsthand experience with that particular group.

Gordon Allport (1979) believes that children begin categorizing and stereotyping certain kinds of differences among people at a very young age. Later, in adolescence and adulthood, they learn to modify their categories by incorporating exceptions into their stereotypes. Depending on a person's environment and experiences, however, some stereotypes may be reinforced instead of disregarded.

According to Allport, prejudices are rigid and exaggerated preferences. All people hold prejudices. Allport argues that if a prejudice is not acted on, then it does "no great harm. It merely stultifies the mind that possesses it. But prejudice expressed leads to discrimination...." (p. 127). Allport develops a continuum of social relationships among human groups that ranges from friendly to hostile. He believes that "we define the degrees of hostile relationships that are readily distinguishable, starting with predilection, the mildest and most normal form of group-exclusion, through active prejudice and discrimination, to scapegoating itself" (p. 127). This process could be viewed as a continuum of relationships, with cooperation at one end and scapegoating at the other extreme.

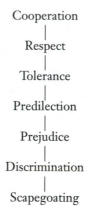

Cooperation
|
Respect
|
Tolerance
|
Predilection
|
Prejudice
|
Discrimination
|
Scapegoating

Allport refers to scapegoating as "full-fledged aggression," in which "the victim is abused verbally or physically." If, as Allport states, "No child is born prejudiced. His prejudices are always acquired" (p. 307), the focus for educators should not be on discerning *how* children acquire prejudices but, instead, on helping them to question *why* they hold these prejudices.

Discrimination occurs when people act on their beliefs. When teachers develop grading criteria that are as fair as possible and then decide that one student's paper is better than another's, they are discriminating. Discrimination is not only acceptable, it is also, in fact, necessary.

Problem discrimination arises when people's beliefs and actions are not based on evidence. For example, if a teacher has certain criteria for grading and arbitrarily changes the criteria or uses inappropriate criteria, then any resulting discrimination is harmful. When we discuss the problems of societal and educational discrimination, we should concentrate on inappropriate kinds of discrimination.

Allport identified ten sociocultural conditions that foster prejudice:

1. Heterogeneity in the population
2. Ease of vertical mobility
3. Rapid social change with attendant anomie
4. Ignorance and barriers to communication
5. The relative density of minority group populations
6. The existence of realistic rivalries and conflict
7. Exploitation sustaining important interests in the community
8. Sanctions given to aggressive scapegoating
9. Legend and tradition that sustain hostility
10. Unfavorable attitudes toward both assimilation and cultural pluralism (p. 233)

When we think about international and national problems such as race riots in Los Angeles (Watts in the 1960s), the ethnic unrest in Bosnia, or the Rodney King case in the 1990s, we can identify many of Allport's sociocultural conditions as possible explanations for them. Similarly, as we look at school bias incidents, we can identify several of these sociocultural conditions as possible explanations.

> Which of Allport's types of sociocultural conditions may have contributed to the bias incidents at Oakes High School?

Discrimination in Schools

It is rare in schools to find purposeful discrimination against students based on Allport's categories. For example, barring an African American child from a public school on the basis of skin color is prohibited by law. However, as Nieto (1992) argues, "the discrimination that children face in schools is not a thing of the past. School practices and policies still continue to discriminate against some children in very concrete ways" (p. 24). Nieto has identified nine educational structures in which prejudice and discrimination affect student learning:

1. Tracking
2. Testing
3. Curriculum
4. Pedagogy
5. The physical structure of the school

6. Disciplinary policies
7. The limited role of students
8. The limited role of teachers
9. The limited role of parents

Bullock and Stewart (1978, 1979) identified what they call "second-generation discrimination," which includes practices that deny minority students access to education and limit integration of schools. Academic grouping and disciplining students in a discriminatory manner are examples of second-generation discrimination. In an in-depth study of Hispanic students in 142 school districts, Meier and Stewart (1991) found that second-generation discrimination exists because Hispanic populations lack the political power to prevent certain conditions that would preclude discrimination. According to their research, "School districts with greater Hispanic representation on the school board and among teaching faculty experience significantly less second-generation discrimination against Hispanic students" (p. xvii).

Educational leaders need to ask critical questions about the educational structures in schools. If a secondary school, for example, has a high dropout rate, educators must ask a variety of questions. A school administrator might ask: Who is dropping out? Are there differences in ethnicity, social class, or gender of the students who drop out? What reasons do these students report for dropping out? Are there program structures (e.g., bilingual programs, special education classes) that these students were a part of? For example, Meier and Stewart found, "Hispanic high school graduation rates are negatively associated with corporal punishment and bilingual classes, and positively associated with gifted classes. Hispanic dropout rates are positively associated with suspensions and negatively associated with gifted class enrollments" (p. 177).

Additionally they noted, "The pattern that Hispanics receive more corporal punishment, more suspensions, and more expulsions when blacks receive less, and vice versa, implies that administrators compensate for disciplining one group by lessening discipline of the other group" (p. 154).

Educational leaders must be advocates for students. They must ask critical questions about the nine structures identified by Nieto to eliminate second-generation discrimination in schools.

What types of records could Oakes High School staff keep to ensure they are not guilty of various forms of second-generation discrimination?

Competing Perspectives: Theories, Models, and Approaches to Race, Class, and Gender

Educational institutions can approach issues of cultural diversity in a number of ways. Theories, models, and approaches to learning about diversity are categorized into five areas. None of these approaches is independent of the others; each category overlaps and draws on other theoretical areas. The approaches are cultural deficiency, cultural difference, single-group studies, multicultural education, and social justice education.

Cultural Deficiency Approach

Historically U.S. educators have viewed students from backgrounds other than the dominant culture in two ways: the deficit perspective and the cultural difference perspective (see Box 4.2). Some educators believe that students from other cultures come to U.S. schools with deficiencies. They might argue, for example, that students are *deprived* because they have minimal proficiency in the English language, or they might believe that because students are from low-socioeconomic backgrounds or single-parent families they are *disadvantaged*. Identification of students as deprived or disadvantaged implies that they have deficiencies that must be remediated. Similarly in recent years the term *at-risk* has become a popular label.

An example of a deficiency perspective can be found in Bernstein's (1964) research, which refers to middle-class language as "elaborated" because of its complexity of vocabulary and structure. He argues that this complexity allows speakers to communicate in hypotheses, abstracts, and relationships. He views lower-class language as "restricted" because it uses a preponderance of short, simple sentences.

BOX **4.2**

Deficit and Difference Theories in Education

Deficit Perspectives	Difference Perspectives
The child's language is considered to be a "restricted code" of the dominant language or a less developed language than the dominant language.	The child's language is considered to be different from but comparable to the dominant language.
The child's learning style is seen as an impediment to proper academic socialization and should be adapted to culturally dominant norms.	The child's learning style is an individual matter that should be seen as a tool to help the child learn.
The child's family is often seen as "broken" or dysfunctional and as a barrier to the child's success in school.	Family patterns are understood to vary, but the child's family is seen as a key player in the child's education.
The child's behavior is problematic and the child is seen as a discipline problem.	There is often a conflict between the behavioral norms of the home culture and the school culture.

Source: Cordeiro, P., Reagan, T., & Martinez, L. (1994). *Multiculturalism and TQE: Addressing Cultural Diversity in Schools.* Thousand Oaks, CA: Corwin Press (Reprinted by permission of Corwin Press, Inc.).

Educational researchers such as Beth Harry (1992) and Henry Trueba (1989) have argued that language-biased educators have incorrectly placed language-minority students in classes for the learning disabled or mentally retarded. Because language-biased educators think such students have "language deficiencies" (i.e., they are not highly proficient in English), they put them in remedial classes.

Meier and Stewart (1991) found that minority students are overrepresented among those who are expelled, disciplined, or drop out. Their research argues that Hispanics and African American students are denied access to high-quality education.

Another deficiency perception that many educators hold is that children from low socioeconomic backgrounds lack appropriate role models for their development. In a 1992 article in the *New York Times National,* Gross stated, "A mother is sometimes present in these homes, but she is often a drug addict or a teen-ager who comes and goes.... Scarred by years of abuse and neglect, many of these children are angry and disruptive" (pp. 1 & 166). Many minority groups (e.g., African American males) are blamed for abandoning their families, thus causing these families to be *deprived* or *deficient*. A more enlightened way to frame these issues is to focus on access to resources and support systems instead of focusing on lack of morals or family psychological instability. The deficit perspective has been severely criticized in recent years.

Cultural Difference Approach.   According to Sleeter and Grant (1993), "The main idea behind Teaching the Culturally Different Approach...is to ensure as much cultural compatibility as possible" (p. 44). The focus is on building bridges between the two cultures because there is a *cultural mismatch*. For example, if a child has been labeled as needing special education services (i.e., the child is a member of the culture of special education) then s/he will need special assistance (e.g., a resource room) in order to bridge the gap in his/her knowledge. Another example might be a child who has minimal proficiency in English. Programmatic response might be to include partial, or full day ESL classes, or sheltered English classes. Providing a sign language interpreter in a regular classroom for a child who is deaf might be a programmatic response for his/her cultural difference.

As we look at ethnic minority groups, according to the cultural difference approach, some minority students fail because they do not adapt themselves to the dominant cultural style of the school or as Trueba states (1988) the schools have not provided appropriate "activity settings" to accommodate the minority student. While this approach is important because it offsets the racist *cultural deprivation* approach or *genetic inferiority* approach it ignores the historical and social factors responsible for the reproduction of "cultural differences" in schools.

John Ogbu (1992) was one of the first researchers to criticize the cultural difference approach. He argued that there has been a lack of critical analysis among educators and this absence of critique has allowed educators to attempt to approach school conflicts in cultural styles through remediation programs.

Human Relations Approach.   Sometimes referred to as *intergroup education*, the major goal of a *human relations* approach is to help *all* students develop more positive attitudes toward people who are members of different racial, cultural, and gender groups. This approach concerns the relationships that students have with one another. Another objective of a human relations approach is to help students become better communicators. Group processes and group facilitation, which are part of *cooperative learning*, are methods of achieving these goals.

A human relations approach is supported by theories and concepts developed by research that started in the 1940s. Researchers were originally interested in studying the nature of racial prejudice. Gunnar Myrdal (1944) and others such as Deutsch (1963) discovered that interaction across racial lines tended to increase racial tolerance. Several explanations were given for the finding that contact reduces prejudice.

Cognitive dissonance theory argued that dissonance occurs when an individual's behavior or experience clashes with the views he or she holds. In other words, individuals want to align their attitudes with their experiences, so they try to bring their behaviors and attitudes together. Another explanation is found in the theory of *interpersonal attraction*. This theory holds that people are attracted to others whose beliefs and values they share. Hewstone and Brown (1986) contend that contact with persons and the opportunity to learn about them will eventually "neutralize the negative relationship that formerly existed…" (p. 5).

Another possible explanation for increases in racial tolerance that result when racial lines are crossed is based on the notion that contact can have an educational benefit. Interaction with others can provide more knowledge and can identify false thinking. Thus it is argued that contact might reduce prejudice because it expands an individual's knowledge and experiences.

In his seminal book, *The Nature of Prejudice*, Gordon Allport (1958) formulated a hypothesis that attitudes change most often if contact occurs between individuals of equal status. Allport made a crucial point—contact does not automatically reduce prejudice. He believed that contact across racial lines of individuals with similar educational or occupational status would have more positive effects on people's attitudes than would contact among individuals of different status.

This belief supports more recent work conducted in schools by Hallinan (1979). He found that students' friendship patterns developed on the basis of a match between classes and subjects they had in common. Recent work in anthropology by Levinson (1996), who studied students in a Mexican *secundaria*, found that

> students in their first and second years from the *pueblitos* [villages close to the city]…forge ties with one another across and within *grupos escolares* [heterogeneous cohorts who pass through the four years of middle school together]. The shared position that appears to bring them together is that of "country" or "village" dweller in relation to the school's predominantly urban culture. (p. 227)

The work of other researchers, such as Purkey and Novak (1984) and Johnson and Johnson (1975), has also contributed to our understanding of human relations. Johnson and Johnson advocate *cooperative learning*, which they believe will improve intergroup relations. Purkey and Novak have written about *invitational education*. They argue that educators and schools must be intentionally inviting. If the policies, people, practices, places, and programs are inviting, schools will be more conducive to learning, according to Purkey and Novak.

Single-Group Studies Approach

Another approach to addressing cultural diversity in education is what Sleeter and Grant (1993) call *single-group studies*. The curriculum is the main focus of this approach. A single-group focus might be a course (Asian literature), program (women's studies), or an entire school with a particular focus on one group (Afrocentric schools). According to Sleeter and Grant, the goal in these programs is to "reduce social stratification and raise the status of the group" (p. 123). This approach was instituted in response to a curriculum that has traditionally emphasized the contributions of white, middle-class males.

Many advocates of single-group studies use arguments based on reproduction theory. Two classic books are part of the first wave of critical studies of schooling: *Schooling in Capitalist America: Educational Reform and the Contradictions of Economic Life* by Bowles and Gintis (1976) and Bourdieu and Passeron's (1977) *Reproduction: In Education, Society, and Culture*. Their authors argue that schools are not passive sites where culture is simply transmitted. To the contrary, schools actually perpetuate, or *reproduce*, the inequalities that exist in society. Instead of equalizing people, schools reproduce the inequities that separate them. Educators began to ask: What does schooling mean to children who are not members of the dominate societal group (white, middle class)? This kind of thinking may be one reason, in the last twenty years, that we have seen a renewed interest in single-sex and African American immersion schools.

Multicultural Education Approach

The term *multicultural education* is most often used inappropriately. Many educators who approach cultural diversity through a *cultural difference, human relations,* or *single-group* approach describe their efforts as multicultural education. Banks and Banks (1994) state that multicultural education is "at least three things: an idea or concept, an educational reform movement, and a process" (p. 3).

Davidman and Davidman (1994) have identified six interrelated goals for multicultural education:

1. Educational equity;
2. Empowerment of students and their parents;
3. Cultural pluralism in society;
4. Intercultural/interethnic/intergroup understanding and harmony in the classroom, school, and community;
5. An expanded knowledge of various cultural and ethnic groups; and
6. The development of students, parents, and practitioners whose thoughts and actions are guided by an informed and inquisitive multicultural perspective.

Equity involves not only access to learning opportunities and physical and financial conditions within the school and district, but also "educational outcomes for both individuals and groups" (p. 4).

Empowerment requires members of the school community to take active roles, whether at the local or national level. The acknowledgment of parents as a child's first teachers is a key goal of the multicultural education approach. Schools that have a multicultural approach involve parents in many ways, both in the school and in school-related areas. The empowerment of students and parents is key to a multicultural education approach.

Cultural pluralism indicates an acceptance of cultural diversity as a valuable and worthwhile facet of society. Teachers who accept cultural pluralism constantly ask themselves how to help students respect and appreciate cultural diversity in the classroom, school, and society.

Included in the goals of a multicultural education approach are some of the goals of the human relations approach. The idea that all students with appropriate guidance can develop positive attitudes toward members of various cultural groups is one way these approaches overlap. Thus, according to Sleeter and Grant, "The Multicultural Education approach seeks to reform the entire process of school for *all* children" (1993, p. 153).

Social Justice Education Approach

Borrowing heavily from each of the previous approaches, the social justice education approach "deals more directly with oppression, social structural inequality based on race, social class, gender and disability" (p. 153).

In one of the most informative books on cultural diversity in education, *Affirming Diversity: The Sociopolitical Context of Multicultural Education*, Sonia Nieto (1992) states,

> Multicultural education is a process of comprehensive school reform and basic education for all students. It challenges and rejects racism and other forms of discrimination in schools and society and accepts and affirms pluralism (ethnic, racial, linguistic, religious, economic, and gender, among others) that students, their communities, and teachers represent. Multicultural education permeates the curriculum and instructional strategies used in schools, as well as the interactions among teaches and students and parents, and the very way the schools conceptualize the nature of teaching and learning. Because it uses critical pedagogy as its underlying philosophy and focuses on knowledge, reflection, and action (praxis) as the basis for social change, multicultural education furthers the democratic principles of social justice. (p. 208)

According to Nieto, multicultural education has seven basic characteristics. It is: (1) antiracist education, (2) basic education, (3) important for all students, (4) pervasive, (5) for social justice, (6) a process, and (7) critical pedagogy.

Let us examine the concepts of social justice and critical pedagogy in more detail. Figure 4.1 on page 106 is a model developed by James Banks (1994) describing the levels of integration of ethnic content that can be used in curriculum reform.

At the contributions level educators might celebrate Cinco de Mayo or Martin Luther King Day. The focus is on the particular contribution that a group of people (Hispanics or African Americans) or a person made toward a movement, cause, or cultural group. Most U.S. schools have a variety of activities that could fall within this approach. As Banks states, at the contributions level "Students do not attain a global view of the role of ethnic and cultural groups in U.S. society" (p. 207).

The next level Banks (1994) calls the ethnic additive approach. In this approach concepts, themes, and various perspectives are added to the curriculum, but the curriculum

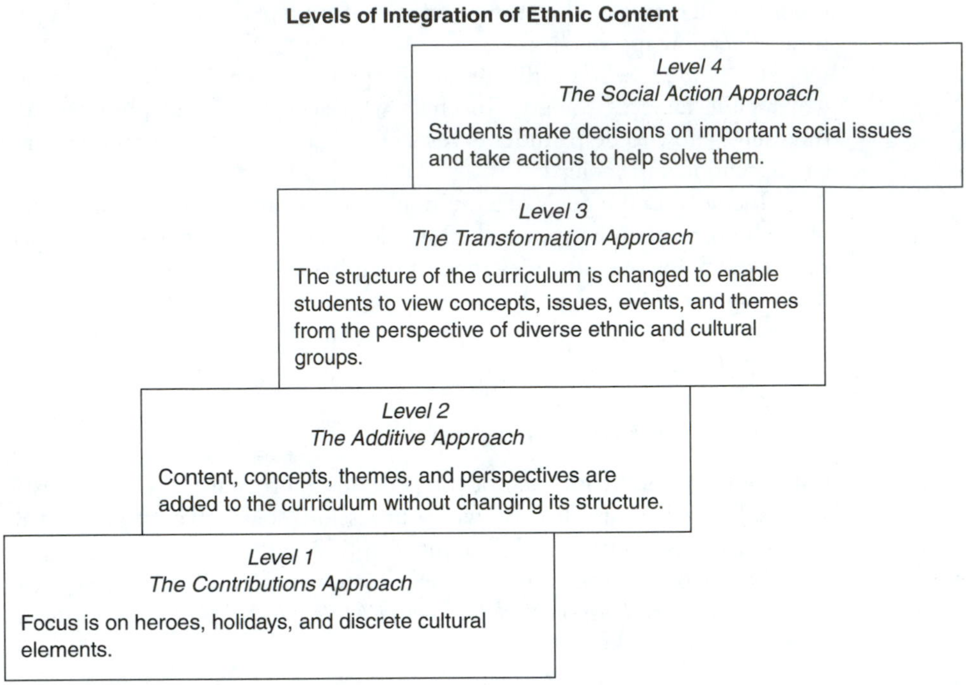

Levels of Integration of Ethnic Content

Level 4
The Social Action Approach

Students make decisions on important social issues and take actions to help solve them.

Level 3
The Transformation Approach

The structure of the curriculum is changed to enable students to view concepts, issues, events, and themes from the perspective of diverse ethnic and cultural groups.

Level 2
The Additive Approach

Content, concepts, themes, and perspectives are added to the curriculum without changing its structure.

Level 1
The Contributions Approach

Focus is on heroes, holidays, and discrete cultural elements.

FIGURE 4.1   Approaches to Multicultural Curriculum Reform

is not restructured. Adding another perspective, however, does not necessarily enhance the curriculum. For example, if the class is studying a unit entitled "Columbus's Discovery of the New World" and the teacher includes a discussion of how people indigenous to the West Indies might have responded to Columbus, an alternative perspective is not necessarily being presented. The title of the unit itself implies that it took a European to *discover* people who already had a long-standing culture. Thus, such an approach still presents only a Eurocentric perspective.

Use Fairhaven's Oakes High School to discuss alternative ways in which the lesson on Columbus might have been given a greater multicultural emphasis.

At the transformation level, a restructuring of the curriculum occurs. Students are provided with ideas, issues, themes, and challenges from a variety of perspectives. Study of the U.S. Civil War, for example, places emphasis on how our many cultures formed the overall culture of the United States at that time in its history. There is a complex weaving of diverse cultural elements (e.g., from language, music, art) that originated from the wide variety of racial, gender, ethnic, cultural, and religious groups. This level is transformational because it transcends the dominant perspective and gives voice to the many cultural elements present in our society.

Banks' fourth level, social action, incorporates each of the three earlier levels, but the concept of social justice is the main criterion of this level. Encouraging social action and developing decision-making skills in students is a key goal. Gordon (1985) would include emancipatory pedagogy. She believes that "Categories such as 'critical emancipatory or liberatory pedagogy,' may work as descriptors that not only expand the narrow frames of reference, but also move them from pejorative to self-reflection, critique, and social action…" (p. 29).

Some of the research and theory that informs this approach can be found in the works of Henry Giroux (1992), Michael Apple (1986), Paolo Freire (1985), John Ogbu (1992), and Jean Anyon (1980).

The terms *critical teaching* and *critical pedagogy* come from critical theory. According to Giroux (1992),

> Critical pedagogy refers to a deliberate attempt to construct specific conditions through which educators and students can think critically about how knowledge is produced and transformed in relation to the construction of social experiences informed by a particular relationship between the self, others, and the larger world. (pp. 98–99)

Brazilian educator Paolo Freire (1985) maintains that critical pedagogy promotes greater understanding of this approach.

> A pedagogy will be that much more critical and radical, the more investigative and less certain of "certainties" it is. The more "unquiet" a pedagogy, the more critical it will become. A pedagogy preoccupied with the uncertainties rooted in the issues we have discussed is, by its nature, a pedagogy that requires investigation. This pedagogy is thus much more a pedagogy of question than a pedagogy of answer. (Cited in Macedo 1994, p. 102)

Therefore, if a social justice approach is used, students must gather, analyze, synthesize, value, and judge data they collect as they study social issues. The result will be student empowerment and the acquisition of "a sense of political efficacy" (Banks, 1993, p. 209).

What are the implications of these approaches for Oakes High School? Would one approach or combinations of several approaches better match Oakes's context?

Segregation, Desegregation, and Integration

The U.S. educational system has responded to issues of desegregation and integration in a variety of ways. Programmatic options include magnet programs, programs for "at-risk" children, bilingual programs, and Afrocentric programs or schools, to name but a few. Since *Brown v. Board of Education* (1954), school desegregation has become one of the most hotly debated education issues nationwide. Some argue that prior to *Brown*, school segregation was legal and that it is still present in the form of single-sex schools, single race and ethnic schools (i.e., Afrocentric schools), some bilingual programs, and alternative schools or programs that separate "special-education students."

It is evident that an educational leader must not only understand the programmatic possibilities and their context, but also the social and cultural factors that influence program development decisions. Clearly, the needs of the community as Laurel Tanner discusses in Chapter 8 are one of the key issues at the heart of a school's curriculum.

Magnet Schools

Magnet schools can be found at all grade levels in both private and public schools. Magnet programs are differentiated by their curriculum, special focus area, and instructional approach (e.g., Montessori, Paideia). The formats of magnet schools vary. Some programs are schoolwide, or whole-school magnets, in which all students would be involved in the "magnet" area (e.g., in a schoolwide global education magnet, all students would in some ways be involved in the global education curriculum). Another type is often called a "school-within-a-school program" (SWAS) or "program within a school" (PWS). Only some students in a particular school are involved in the magnet program. Another format might be a grade-level magnet in which only certain grade levels are offered a particular curricular focus.

The first magnet schools appeared in the 1970s as a means of desegregating school systems. Acceptance into magnet school programs was predominantly based on race. Today nearly all large school districts have magnet schools. In the 1991–1992 school year, there were 2,433 magnet school nationwide, offering 3,171 magnet programs (some schools house more than one magnet) (American Institutes for Research, 1994). Five basic factors led to the growth of magnet schools:

1. They have represented a voluntary approach to school desegregation.
2. As people call for school choice, magnet schools are alternatives to the local school with a "regular" curriculum.
3. Like a magnet they *attract* students from outside their assigned neighborhood attendance zones.
4. In recent years greater attention has been paid to the outcomes of education.
5. Magnet schools often provide knowledge that is supposed to be helpful to a particular career choice.

Language Diversity in U.S. Schools: Program Options

Although a few earlier examples of bilingual programs in U.S. history can be identified, bilingual education is a relatively recent phenomenon. In 1968 Congress passed the Bilingual Education Act (later, Title VII of the Elementary and Secondary Education Act, ESEA). The Bilingual Education Act states that "no person shall be subjected to discrimination on the basis of race, color, or national origin." School districts are required to take affirmative steps to provide children with the language skills they need to participate in school. The Bilingual Education Act and the landmark U.S. Supreme Court decision *Lau v. Nichols*, 1974, provided a legal basis for equitable treatment of limited-english-proficient children in U.S. schools. It placed non–native-English-speaking children at the forefront of an often hotly debated topic.

Bilingual Education. *Bilingual* refers to proficiency in at least two languages, and *biculturalism* is participation in two cultures. Bilingual education usually refers to an educational approach involving the use of two languages of instruction at some point in the student's schooling.

For decades educators and policy makers have wrestled with questions related to bilingual education: What are the best ways to teach children whose native language is not English? How can the achievement of students with limited proficiency in English be enhanced? There is no debate over the issue that proficiency in English is essential to school and workplace success. Instead the debate deals with the most appropriate ways for students to learn English as a second language and what roles, if any, the first language should play.

School districts offer several types of programs to students in the United States (Box 4.3). These include ESL, structured immersion, sheltered English, transitional bilingual education, two-way bilingual education, and maintenance bilingual education.

BOX **4.3**

Program Options for Non–Native-English-Speaking Students

English as a Second Language

A systematic, comprehensive approach to teaching English to students whose native language is not English. It is usually an important component of a bilingual program, but it can also exist by itself.

Options
- full/partial day
- pullout
- sheltered English
- English for special purposes (ESP)

Sheltered English

In what are sometimes called transition or bridge classes, students cover the same content offered in classes in which native English proficiency is assumed. The language component of these classes is adapted to suit the English proficiency levels of the language-minority students.

Transitional Bilingual Education (TBE)

The Bilingual Education Act of 1968 defined transitional bilingual education as "structured English language instruction, and to the extent necessary to allow a child to achieve competence in the English language, instruction in the child's native language." Ideally access to a comprehensible curriculum is assured by providing basic instruction in the child's native language until the student attains English competency and comprehension in speaking, writing, and reading. The goal of these programs is for students to learn English as quickly as possible so they can exit the programs.

Two-Way Bilingual Education

Two-way bilingual programs offer a means of encouraging bilingualism in both language minority and language majority students.

Maintenance Bilingual Education

The goal in maintenance bilingual programs is to provide students with instruction that helps the development of the native language.

Submersion or Immersion

Sometimes referred to as the "sink or swim" approach, submersion (immersion) places students in a totally English-speaking environment with no use of their native language. It is not a form of bilingual education.

It is important for educational leaders to determine which of these approaches is most appropriate for the children in their schools or districts. Language proficiency, the number of students whose native language is not English, the ages of children, and whether or not they are able to speak and read their native language proficiently are but a few of the factors that need to be examined. Most bilingual educators favor maintenance programs; the majority of existing programs, however, are transitional.

Promoting Linguistically Diverse Learners' Academic Success

VIVIANA ALEXANDROWICZ
Assistant Professor of Education
University of San Diego

Providing comprehensible education to linguistically diverse students in the different subject areas has become a pedagogical challenge for teachers, particularly in states with a large immigrant population. In states like California, one out of four K–6 students was classified as a "Limited English Proficient" (LEP) student and of all new students who enrolled in California schools between 1987 and 1992, 69 percent were nonfluent in English. Research has shown that it can take immigrant students up to nine years to acquire the necessary language competence to successfully deal with academic tasks that are required to perform at grade level in English (Cummins, 1989). What can teachers and administrators do to help immigrant children succeed in school?

The Importance of Understanding Second-Language Acquisition

Belief is widespread at all levels in the school community—from government elected officials to school administrators, teachers, and parents— that second-language learners can acquire competence in a second language fast enough to keep up with academics within two years of arrival in the United States. This belief reflects a lack of understanding of how difficult it is to learn all the aspects of language—pragmatics, semantics, morphology, phonology, and syntax—to effectively function in academic settings. It also suggests the need for increasing educators' awareness about the factors involved in acquiring a second language.

For instance, students' prior education and literacy in their native language affects learning in a second language. Students who speak and write in a primary language that uses an alphabet and characters similar to those of English tend to acquire the English language more easily than those who do not. In addition, sociocultural factors such as family members' levels of education, parental support, living conditions, and attitudes of the host society toward the student's language and culture play a critical role in the student's motivation and academic achievement. Moreover, the student's personality and learning preferences call for a careful assessment of each child as an individual who has diverse social, affective, cognitive, and linguistic needs.

When this complex array of issues related to placement of linguistically diverse students is overlooked in U.S. schools, second-language learners often find themselves in a "sink or swim" situation. In other words, they are "integrated" in mainstream English classrooms so they can be "immersed" in authentic language environments, which supposedly allow them to "pick up" English after a period of time. As a result of these situations, we have children who, day to day, learn survival English at the expense of the rest of their education.

Usually, it is not until individuals have reached an intermediate level of language competence that they are likely to cope with and complete academic work, let alone fully participate in classroom activities in a second language. In many instances, administrators and teachers place a child who has acquired a "native like" accent within a year in a regular English classroom because "he is doing so well in English." The same teachers and administrators are "puzzled" when these children are "failing" in different subject areas, and a large number of second-language learners end up in special education classes.

Effective Programs Are Key to Academic Success

In "additive" programs, students add a second language to their native language in speaking, reading, and writing, becoming not only bilingual but, more important, biliterate. Examples of such programs are the "two-way" bilingual program or the "late-exit" maintenance program. In two-way bilingual programs, all students become biliterate in two languages, and in late-exit programs, students move gradually from instruction in their native language in all subject areas to instruction in transitional English until they become proficient enough to transfer to mainstream English classrooms. By the time students reach junior high school, they are receiving all instruction in English except in one subject area such as language arts, which allows them to maintain and enrich their primary language. All bilinguals know that once one has acquired knowledge and skills in the primary language one does not have to acquire most of them again in the second language.

The programs most often implemented, which have proven highly ineffective, are those that transfer students to all-English classrooms before they are ready—for instance after two years of primary instruction in all subject areas. Tragically, in many of these "subtractive" programs, where one loses one's primary language to gain a second one, students do not receive the strong English as a second language (ESL) component that would enable them to succeed in their new all-English "sink or swim" classrooms.

Implementation of poor-quality programs has created the perception that "bilingual education" in general does not work. The "English only" movement that reemerged in the 1990s reflects this perception. Proponents of English-only classrooms tend to promote the idea that

"if our grandparents made it without bilingual education, these children can make it too" (a critical question is how we define success in today's society compared with the skills people needed to succeed forty years ago). Furthermore, bilingual education (effective and ineffective programs) serves only about 30 percent of the second-language student population; therefore, other factors must account for the high dropout rates among certain culturally and linguistically diverse populations.

When effective bilingual programs are not viable for different reasons (for example, if there is a scarcity of teachers who speak the language of their students), an alternative is to provide students comprehensible instruction using Specially Designed Academic Instruction in English (SDAIE). A SDAIE teacher may have a contained SDAIE classroom if there are enough second-language learners at that grade level, or he or she may just have a few of these students in a "mainstream" classroom. SDAIE teachers have strong professional preparation in the areas of second-language acquisition, cultural diversity, and in classroom management in classrooms with multiple levels of academic backgrounds and languages.

Effective programs employ trained teachers who go beyond "good" teaching. They know that directions, modeling, and explanations that may be clear and sufficient for most of their fully proficient English speakers are not sufficient for their second-language learners. These teachers use a greater number of contextual clues such as pictures, graphic organizers, and manipulatives and they carefully plan for the use of language by prioritizing vocabulary, paraphrasing, and repeating, to add comprehension of content. Moreover, when they have few second-language learners who are integrated in "regular" mainstream classrooms, these teachers must assess their students' language competence and plan instruction accordingly.

These teachers hold high expectations for their students and understand that a student's ability to produce in a second language does not necessarily reflect his or her capacity to think cognitively. They also promote critical thinking early in the process of second language development,

(continued)

Continued

but hold realistic expectations for their students' ability to deal with academic tasks in English.

It is imperative that educational leaders promote a community of learners where teachers, students, parents, and staff foster compassion, fellowship, and respect for others. Most important, everyone involved must sincerely believe that anyone can and should learn a second language and become biliterate and bicultural and that anyone can succeed academically in school.

English Only, English Plus, and Programs for Nonstandard English Speakers. In recent years some states and organizations have called for English to be the *only* language used in state documents, in business transactions, and in schools. Other groups have pointed out the importance of being multilingual. The latter group takes a view that some call English Plus: People should not only speak English, but they also should have fluency in another language. Although these state and national debates may be important, they have not yet had a direct impact on schools.

One debate that garnered considerable attention in 1997 was the controversy surrounding a decision by the Oakland, California, School Board to offer African American speakers of Ebonics, or black English, special instruction. Additionally, during the debate, other school districts such as that in Los Angeles were found to already be offering "Ebonics" programs. Once the issues were dissected, several common factors could be identified regardless of the voices in the debate: (1) African American students were lagging behind other ethnic groups in academic achievement, (2) something had to be done to address this lack of achievement, and (3) everyone involved (parents, teachers, students, and community members) agreed that all students must be able to speak standard English. Clearly, many programmatic options may prove successful in helping low-achieving African Americans who speak nonstandard English, or other nonstandard-English speakers, to succeed academically. Most linguists agree that a student who develops awareness of his or her own variety of English will make a better learner of standard English.

In volatile situations such as these, the challenges for school leaders include examining the complexity of the issues, identifying needs, identifying options, and working collaboratively to choose the best option(s).

Fostering School, Family, and Community Partnerships

When asked how families are involved in a child's education, educators typically respond that parents are invited to a variety of school functions—open houses, parent conferences, school assemblies, sports activities—and to participate as classroom volunteers. Many of the rituals, activities, and roles for parents have changed little in this century. These activities have been institutionalized to involve parents in limited ways. They tend to relegate all the power to the school and usually ignore the needs of the groups, particularly those families representing different cultural groups who might not be proficient in English or who are unfamiliar with the school's expectations.

Many educators believe that schools need to increase the numbers of parents who attend school-based activities, even though many parents cannot, and do not, participate at the school site. Often educators comment:

> We hardly ever get very many parents from juniors and seniors attending open house.
>
> The parents who attend parent conferences are not necessarily the ones we need to see.
>
> These parent don't really care about their children.
>
> [Racial/ethnic group's name] don't value education.

Families are not directly involved in their children's school activities for many reasons. In order to alter the paradigm of parent involvement, we need to begin by talking about *family* involvement. Given the changing demographics of families, schools can no longer think only about mom and dad. Simply by expanding our definition of *family*, as we think about involvement, the possible participation net is enlarged. In many families, older siblings, a grandparent, or an aunt or uncle have primary responsibilities of child care.

A second part of the paradigm needing change is the relationship between schools and families. Schools need to think of family member as *partners*. Partnerships are by definition voluntary. Two or more independent agents agree to work together to accomplish a common purpose that is mutually beneficial. A partnership involves sharing and membership. A partnership means that all voices will be heard and that reciprocity of some type is involved.

For schools and educators partnership means that family and school share power. Family members are given opportunities to provide ideas and advice just as educators are. Both partners are obliged to be committed and are responsible for doing their part.

Another part of the old paradigm requiring change is the way educators have traditionally viewed involvement—attendance of parents at school functions and volunteering at school. If educators continue to think about involvement in these limited ways, little will change in the relationship between schools and families.

Epstein (1992) has created a typology of parent involvement. The six types of family involvement include:

1. parents as providers of the child's basic needs;
2. communication between the school and the home;
3. parents as volunteers at the school;
4. parents as instructors in the home;
5. parents involved in school governance; and
6. parents working in collaboration with the entire community.

Another framework that can assist educators in changing their perspective of involvement is Swap's (1993) four models of home–school relationships, which include:

1. the protective model;
2. school-to-home transition model;
3. curriculum enrichment model; and
4. the partnership model.

In the protective model, parents delegate to the school the responsibility for educating their children. Swap contends that the goal of this model is primarily to reduce the possible conflict that can result between schools and families.

The school-to-home transition model involves enlisting parents in supporting the school's goals. It then becomes the responsibility of the family to reinforce these goals in the home.

The curriculum enhancement model involves families in developing and enriching the school curriculum. Parents are encouraged to take a child to an aquarium or a museum if related topics are being covered in the curriculum.

The partnership model attempts to reshape the school environment by emphasizing two-way communication and joint problem solving. In this model families and educators work to enhance all aspects of the school, rather than certain parts of the curriculum.

Henderson and Berla (1995) report that the protective and school-to-home models are common practice and that the curriculum enrichment and partnership models are coming into wider use. The partnership model described by Swap could include the typology described by Epstein. Schools incorporating Epstein's typology and Swap's partnership model would be creating a new standard for family involvement.

Developing Programs of School, Family, and Community Partnerships: Administrators Make a Difference

JOYCE L. EPSTEIN

Director, Center on School, Family, and Community Partnerships
Johns Hopkins University

Over and again we learn that principals, district administrators, and state education policy leaders make the difference between successful and unsuccessful schools. Administrators have different leadership styles, but all effective leaders focus on important goals, encourage hard work, inspire excellence, and recognize the efforts and contributions of others. Only with outstanding support will all teachers, students, parents, community members, and others remain committed to improving schools, classrooms, and children's learning. This support is especially necessary for developing comprehensive programs of school, family, and community partnerships.

What is a comprehensive program of partnerships? First, such programs are *theory driven*. The theory of "overlapping spheres of influence" recognizes that students learn and grow at home, at school, and in their communities. Students are at the center of this model, because they are the main actors in their education. Second, comprehensive programs of partnership are *research based*. From the results of many studies in elementary, middle, and high schools, I developed a framework of six major types of involvement:

Type 1—Parenting: Assist families with parenting skills, family support, understanding child and adolescent development, and setting home conditions to support learning at each age and grade level. Assist schools in understanding families' backgrounds, cultures, and goals for children.

Type 2—Communicating: Communicate with families about school programs and student progress in varied, clear, and productive ways. Create two-way communication channels (school to home and home to school) so that families can easily communicate with teachers, administrators, counselors, and other families.

Type 3—Volunteering: Improve recruitment, training, activities, and schedules to involve families as volunteers and as audiences at the school or in other locations. Enable educators to work with regular and occasional volunteers who assist and support students and the school.

Type 4—Learning at Home: Involve families with their children in academic learning activities at home, such as homework, goal setting, and other curriculum-related activities and decisions. Encourage teachers to design homework that enables students to share and discuss interesting work and ideas with family members.

Type 5—Decision Making: Include families as participants in school decisions, governance, and advocacy activities through school councils or improvement teams, committees, PTA/PTO, and other parent organizations. Assist family and teacher representatives to obtain information from and give information to those they represent.

Type 6—Collaborating with Community: Coordinate resources and services for families, students, and the school with community businesses, agencies, cultural and civic organizations, colleges or universities, and other community groups. Enable students, staff, and families to contribute their service to the community.

There are hundreds of practices for the six types from which elementary, middle, and high schools may choose. Each type of involvement has explicit challenges that must be met in order to turn an ordinary program into an excellent one. Each type of involvement leads to different results for students, families, teachers, schools, and communities.

From many studies, we have learned that schools make progress in home-school-community connections if plans are written and if progress is charted by an action team for school, family, and community partnerships. The team of teachers, parents, administrators, and others completes an inventory of present practices, constructs a three-year vision, and writes annual one-year action plans that address school goals with good practices from the six types of involvement.

What results will good programs of partnership produce? Many studies indicate:

- Families are important for children's learning, healthy development, and school success from preschool through high school.
- State, district, and school policy statements about partnerships are not enough. Schools need assistance, support, recognition, and ongoing guidance to develop, improve, and maintain successful programs of school, family, and community partnerships.
- All communities have resources to promote students' social and intellectual development and to assist schools and families. Community resources must be organized, mobilized, and incorporated in comprehensive programs of partnership.
- Students are more positive about school and learning and do better in school if their families and communities are involved in their education in productive ways. Specific results (e.g., improved attendance, behavior, homework completion, reading, writing, math, or other achievement) are linked to goal-oriented and subject-specific activities for family and community involvement.
- When elementary, middle, and high schools develop excellent programs of partnership, families become involved, including those who would not become involved on their own or who are typically "hard to reach."

How can administrators organize and improve their leadership on school, family, and community partnerships? Leadership for school, family, and community partnerships requires understanding, action, and persistence and includes understanding the framework of the six types of involvement, the challenges that must be met to

(continued)

Continued

reach all families, and the connections of involvement to specific goals and results.

Guidelines for action are available from the National Network of Partnership Schools at the Center on School, Family, and Community Partnerships at Johns Hopkins University. This network assists schools, districts, and states to plan and conduct positive, productive, and permanent programs of partnership. Members receive handbooks, newsletters, training workshops, assistance by phone, e-mail, and Web site and opportunities for research and sharing best practices. There are no fees for these services, but members must invest in their own staff, identify budgets, implement annual plans, develop comprehensive programs, and share progress with the center.

Developing excellent home, school, and community partnerships is an ongoing process that takes time, organization, and effort. Progress is accelerated if efforts in school, family, and community partnerships are targeted in annual professional evaluations of teachers, principals, and superintendents.

No longer a separate topic off to the side of "real" reform efforts, school, family, and community partnerships now are seen as a central component of whole-school change and school improvement. Information for families and their involvement and input are needed for students to succeed with bilingual programs, challenging curricula, innovative instruction, and new tests and assessments. In sum, good programs of partnerships help improve schools, strengthen families, energize communities, and increase student success. Administrators are key to whether this happens.

Notes: This work is supported by grants from the U.S. Department of Education and the DeWitt Wallace–Reader's Digest Fund. The ideas are the author's and do not necessarily represent the policies of either funding source. For information on the National Network of Partnership Schools or lists of related publications, contact: Center on School, Family, and Community Partnerships, Johns Hopkins University/CRESPAR, 3003 North Charles Street, Suite 200, Baltimore, MD 21218. Phone: 410-516-8818; fax: 410-516-8890; e-mail: *sfc@csos.jhu.edu* or Web site: *www.csos.jhu.edu/p2000*.

Connecting Schools and Community Organizations

The unifying purpose for schools, individuals, and organizations that collaborate in the development of educational partnerships is best depicted by the much-quoted African proverb "It takes an entire village to raise a child." Partnerships exist because individuals from separate businesses and agencies seek to address the academic, social, emotional, physical, and ethical development of children.

In education, partnerships are either school-linked or school-based. These partnerships range in complexity from a school's forming a collaboration with one person, organization, or agency to multilayered alliances. Recent literature supports the observation that partnering is a service model that is not only useful, but in today's economic and social climate is also quickly becoming recognized as mandatory (Cordeiro & Loup, 1996; Gardner, 1993; Jehl & Kirst, 1993).

Figure 4.2 depicts the numerous human service agencies and community organizations that make up what some researchers call "cultural capital" or "sociocultural

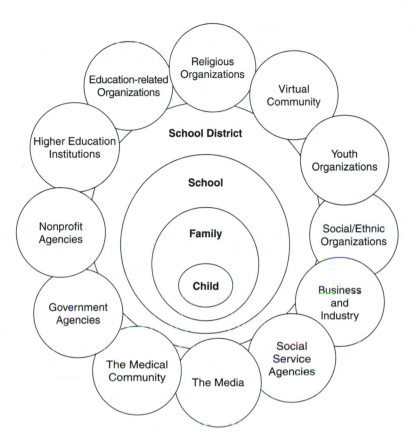

FIGURE 4.2   Educational Partnerships

capital" (Bourdieu & Passeron, 1977, p. 90; Coleman, 1993; Cordeiro, Reagan, & Martinez, 1994). At the center is the child, encompassed first by family, then by school and school district.

A variety of other entities influence the child's school and family life either directly or indirectly. These include religious organizations, higher-education institutions, nonprofits, such as museums and local arts organizations, government agencies, the medical community, the media, social service agencies, business and industry, social and ethnic organizations, youth organizations, such as the YM/YWCA, boys and girls clubs, and parks and recreation department programs, education-related organizations, and the rapidly growing outside world—the virtual community. Each of these agencies or organizations is part of a network of services available to all children. One fairly new role that schools and school districts need to play is the coordination of these many entities not only with the school, but also with the family (see Chapter 9).

Cordeiro and Monroe-Kolek (1996) identified five key factors among these organizations and schools that are preconditions for successful partnerships: leadership, trust, stability, readiness, and a common agenda. These factors interact to form a foundation on which partnerships can be constructed. Without this basic framework it is doubtful that solid school-community partnerships will improve the lives of children.

Cordeiro and Monroe-Kolek's (1996) research found four conditions that support collaboration if the above preconditions exist. Crucial to any partnerships are issues of communication. The form of communication does not appear to be the key factor, but rather the fact that regular and sustained communication occurs. The notion that both partners are benefiting in some way so that there appears to be reciprocity is another element in maintaining successful partnerships. Aligning and pooling of resources is another factor. Johnson and Galvan (1996) argue that the interests and transaction costs associated with such efforts suggest that certain partnerships may in fact increase the actual costs for both organizations involved. Thus, it is imperative that partners not duplicate services but instead fill in the gaps in service provision.

The final element these authors identify as crucial to maintaining and sustaining a partnership is the notion of knowing the community. One way to address this issue is McKnight and Kretzmann's (1993) concept of asset mapping. Especially in urban and low socioeconomic communities, there is a tendency to look at what is *not* present to support the growth and development of children. McKnight and Kretzman argue that poor neighborhoods have a multitude of assets, such as schools, ethnic and religious organizations, institutions of higher education, churches, and libraries, to name but a few.

Because children's needs know no boundaries, the urgency for services and initiatives to cross and merge boundaries, to fill in gaps, is crucial to successful partnerships. In this way, the focus moves from centering on the organization itself to focusing on the child.

What types of community partnerships should the faculty and administration of Oakes High consider developing?

Conclusion

A number of social and cultural factors affect children's learning. Ethnicity, social class, gender, disability, family, home environment, and language are but some of the many factors that must be better understood by educators. Thoughtful consideration of these factors will assist educational leaders in analyzing issues, so that prudent decisions regarding educational programming can be made. Educational leaders must create conditions for forming meaningful partnerships with families and the plethora of community agencies. These partnerships have the potential to assist educators and community members in providing services to children so that all will be better able to learn.

PORTFOLIO ARTIFACTS

1. Revisit your educational platform. What does your platform say about your beliefs regarding issues of educational equity? How does it address issues related to multicultural education?

2. Interview a person working in a community agency that partners with a school. How does this person's perspective influence your views on schools and their communities?

3. Arrange for an internship with a person leading an organization that partners with schools.

4. Examine a curriculum. Is that curriculum reflective of the issues of diversity discussed in this chapter?

5. Spend time with people who are different from you in regard to race, socioeconomic status, ethnicity, ability/disability, and reflect on the experience (for example, switch jobs for a week with someone in a school serving a population different from yours).

6. Spend a period of time riding along with a police officer in a community that is different from the one in which you live. (Many police departments have special programs for citizens.) Reflect on the experience.

7. Travel to a community or country different from your own.

8. Search the Web for: National Association of Multicultural Education. **www.inform. umd.edu/NAME**. In what ways might a educational administrator find this website helpful?

TERMS

Afrocentric schools
Assimilation
Bilingual education
Critical teaching (pedagogy)
Cultural deficit theory
Cultural difference theory
Cultural diversity
Cultural pluralism
Cultural relativism
Culture
Culture identity/
    Ethnic identity
Culture shock
Desegregation
Discrimination

Ebonics
English as a second
    language (ESL)
English for special (or specific)
    purposes (ESP)
English language
    learners (ELL)
Integration
Intergroup education
Language minority student
Language proficiency
Lau v. Nichols
Learning style
Limited english
    profciency (LEP)

Magnet schools
Prejudice
Race
Racism
Second-generation
    discrimination
Segregation
Sheltered English
Socioeconomic Groups
Specially designed academic
    instruction in English
    (SAIDE)
Stereotypes

SUGGESTED READINGS

Bennett, C. I. (1998). *Comprehensive multicultural education: Theory and practice.* Boston: Allyn & Bacon.
Capper, C. (Ed.) (1993). *Educational administration in a pluralistic society.* Albany: State University of New York Press.

Cordeiro, P. (Ed.). (1996). *Boundary crossings: Educational partnerships and school leadership.* San Francisco: Jossey-Bass.

Cordeiro, P., Reagan, T., & Martinez, L. (1994). *Multiculturalism and TQE: Addressing cultural diversity in schools.* Thousand Oaks, CA: Corwin Press.

Nieto, S. (1996). *Affirming diversity: The sociopolitical context of multicultural education.* New York: Longman.

Nieto, S. (1999). *The light in their eyes.* New York: Teachers College Press.

Reyes, P. E., & Scribner, J. (1999). *Lessons from high-performing Hispanic schools.* New York: Teachers College Press.

Sleeter, C., & Grant, C. (1993) . *Making choices for multicultural education: Five approaches to race, class and gender.* New York: Merrill.

Smrekar, C., & Goldring, E. B. (1999). *School choice in urban America: Magnet schools and the pursuit of equity.* New York: Teachers College Press.

West, C., & Sealey, S. (1997). *Restoring hope: Conversations on the future of black America.* Boston: Beacon Press.

5 School District Organizational Structure and Leadership

Vignette: Challenging Old Behaviors at Ophilia High School

You are the new principal of Ophilia High School, which has had a long-standing tradition of excellence. Students have consistently scored in the 65th to 75th percentile on national normed tests. More than 88 percent of the students pass state assessment tests. The school has a high number of merit scholars, and nearly 65 percent of the graduates go on to college even though the school serves a relatively middle-class neighborhood. The school is especially proud that they have the highest graduation rate within the state and very nearly the lowest dropout rate. The school has been previously selected as a Presidential School of Excellence. The staff at the school have been there for quite a while and have shared in the struggle to create an outstanding high school. The previous principal's motto was, "You have to win over students' hearts before you can win over their heads." The staff have focused both their hearts and minds on "excellence at Ophilia."

Recently, superintendent Robert Ford, chairman of the school board, stated, "We have been doing what we have always done better than ever; however, we are doing the wrong things." The new school superintendent has challenged each of the principals in the district to redirect the focus of schools toward more application of knowledge and enhancement of analytical skills, critical thinking, and creative capacity. He asked, "Is what we are doing today right for tomorrow?" His answer was "No!" He told central office staff to support those working in the schools to create major paradigm shifts in the way students are being educated. He explained that schools have "drawn lines and boxes to simplify instruction and to create discrete, measurable content. The problem is that the world does not work in boxes, and students are unprepared for the application of what they have learned to the challenges that lie beyond schooling. Principals and teachers must rethink education, and central office staff must facilitate this effort."

The board's and superintendent's notion has wide support among chamber of commerce members and the general business community. The faculty at Ophilia are finding that many of their givens—things like academic subject areas, grade levels, self-contained classrooms, nine-month school years, textbooks, testing, technology applications, and A through F grading—are all being challenged. Local teachers were shocked when the president of the local chamber of commerce accused the schools of having "massive institutional inertia during a time demanding massive reform." She went on to say, "Schools have not changed one iota from when I went to high school almost forty years ago."

Superintendent Ford addressed the board's new focus and the chamber's concerns at the most recent principals' meeting. He challenged the staff within the schools to develop a more "vigorous, complex content" and to focus on "applications in challenging contexts of all kinds." He has been reorganizing the central administrative staff to facilitate and support these school efforts. Major themes discussed included interdisciplinary approaches; authentic contexts; skills made relevant by applications; use of information from the Internet and distance-learning technology; evaluation by demonstration, products, exhibits, and so on; constructivist thematic approaches; integrated on-line and off-line technology; self-paced, individualized activity; use of experts; application-based indicators of progress; oral and written literacy; and portfolio assessment. Superintendent Ford has asked you to provide "transformational leadership" and to "develop an effective site-based model of school reform." He acknowledges, "This will be difficult, because teachers believe what they are doing is good. Your challenge will be to get your teachers to develop the capacity for meeting new demands and to work with others to build new paradigms. We want to create a smooth-functioning dedicated team from the boardroom to the classroom."

In reflecting on the new vision, you believe it to be the right direction but are overwhelmed by the massiveness of the improvement effort required. In the school's effort to improve test scores and school report cards, little thought had been given to the types of students needed in the new century and millennium. Computers have been used as glorified typewriters; the school has had no telecommunication or Internet capabilities; business partners have had no input into instruction; learning has been fragmented into assessment and subject areas; there has been no authentic evaluation of competence or skills; no one on the staff has much technological expertise; and staff are neither prepared nor configured to begin the journey to a totally new approach to schooling. In fact, neither parents nor central office and school staff really understand the need to reform. The focus has been on school-based performance indicators.

The school board, superintendent, central office staff, and school personnel are being asked to rethink education at Ophilia High School. No one is quite clear on what role each might play in the reform effort. You wonder what each person's role should be in the school reform effort and what types of assistance you will need.

> Have you as principal been given the needed authority from the appropriate sources to begin the reform effort? Whose assistance and support might you seek?

The Local Role

Lawrence and Lorsch (1969) described organizations as "the coordination of different activities of individual contributors to carry out planned transactions with the environment" (p. 3). The organization is a structure within which individuals work to pursue identified goals and objectives. "In addition to defining work roles and authority relations, formal organizations also explicitly define and codify such details as the organization's channels of communication, policies and procedures, and norms and sanctions" (Loveless and Jasin, 1998).

We can identify the structure of an organization and the positions within it. What makes organizations unique are the people who hold these positions, people with unique personalities and unique approaches to the formal roles and structures provided. As a result, an organization always has visible and invisible aspects. The invisible aspects are often unique to the organization and time, and the visible, formal structure is fairly consistent across all organizations and thus is easier to describe and understand. The formal organization defines the structure in which people work, and the informal organization addresses the less tangible human factors and groupings within an organization.

Even though the formally defined structures do not depict total reality, being aware of them goes a long way toward helping people understand the operation of an organization. Two important aspects of formal organizational structure are norms and roles. Scott (1992) defines these two elements: "*Norms* are the generalized rules governing behavior that specify, in particular, appropriate means for pursuing goals; and *roles* are expectations for or evaluative standards employed in assessing the behavior of occupants of specific social positions" (p. 16). Scott goes on to say these are "organized so as to constitute a relatively coherent and consistent set of beliefs and prescriptions governing the behavior of participants" (p. 16). There is a constraining nature to organizational structure but also an enabling one that allows humans to accomplish more than they could through randomness and lack of structure. Each member of an organization can produce a larger outcome than he or she would be able to accomplish separately. Organization promotes the synergy effect.

Peter Blaw (1970) suggests, "Formal structures exhibit regularities that can be studied in their own right without investigating the motives of the individuals in organization" (p. 203). The focus of this chapter is the typical local school district with its bureaucratic structures and the roles of two of its key incumbents—the superintendent and principal.

The Local School Division

The decentralization of public education in the United States has resulted in substantial diversity in regard to specific school division structure. The primary units of structure for U.S. education are the local school divisions, which number some 15,000. Even across such a diverse system, however, some general structural patterns and issues remain fairly constant. These include authority structures, political patterns, norms, roles, and assignments. Typically, in school divisions, the major layers of responsibility within the organization are school board, superintendent, central office administration, school administration, and instructional staff.

Education is usually the largest single budgetary component of local government and in total employs more people than state and federal governments. The local district operates all the public schools within it and serves as the unit by which the community influences local education. The local school district is a quasi-municipal corporation that serves as an extension of state government and derives its authority from the state. It has a perpetual status, acts as an individual, survives the death of any member, and, as long as officers and employees act in good faith and fraud and collusion are absent, it has limited liabilities.

The school district is set apart from other government bodies in that it has its own board and school governance. Education is a state function, and the local board of education represents the state as well as the residents within the district. The board represents the community interests within statutory and constitutional law. A school district is either fiscally independent or it must gain approval on fiscal matters from some other governing body. Dependent boards can be appointed by the mayor (with the consent of council) or the board of county supervisors. In some cases, board members can be elected by the voting residents within the district. Independent boards must be elected. Most urban districts have dependent school boards. These boards must get prior approval from elected or appointed municipal officials to determine finally and legally the size of the local levy, the tax rate, and the size of the school division budget.

The interface between the superintendent of schools and the school board is critical to the success of the educational program within the district. Yet, only about half the states' school codes contain language defining this relationship between the board of education and the school superintendent. This lack of legislative guidance has resulted in some confusion about the status, authority, and responsibility of the superintendent of schools.

In general, the board is given the freedom to determine the level of trust placed in the superintendent's judgment to guide the direction of schools. The American Association of School Administrators (AASA) has continually expressed concern over the ambiguous role of the superintendent. The association states in its 1994 resolutions:

> AASA believes there is a vital relationship between effective school district leadership and successful schools and learners. This relationship is enhanced when roles and responsibilities between superintendents and boards of education are clearly defined and implemented. (p. 19)

Most educational administrators know how important administrator–school board relations are to the success of the schools. Many have experienced the impossibility of the job when relations begin to deteriorate (Carter & Cunningham, 1997).

Board members typically have limited influence on the operation of the schools, inasmuch as they often hold demanding full-time jobs and have limited time and staff to devote to school board responsibilities. This condition is compounded by large enrollments, state and federal statutes, community politics, educational professionalism, and tight budgets. As a result, school boards leave much of the decision making to the superintendent and school district staff as long as there is no evidence of community concern. Not that board members are powerless—since they can apply sanctions of far-reaching consequences including the hiring and firing of the superintendent.

Administrators at the central office and school level are expected to provide leadership and stewardship so as to ensure that policies, laws, and regulations are adhered to, that effective education occurs, and that desired goals and outcomes are achieved. The power exerted at various levels within the administrative structure is dynamic and often in a state of flux. For example, in the 1990s, power shifted somewhat from the central office administrative staff to the schools, but not across all school districts. Principals, like superintendents, are generalists (line personnel) and are expected to set the tone and develop the culture for the district's schools. Central office staff are typically organized around specific operational areas—finance, pupil personnel, staff personnel, curriculum and instruction, business and logistics—and are considered specialists (all discussed in later chapters).

The concept of line and staff responsibilities grows out of the hierarchical structure that often exists within organizations. Authority (power) and responsibility (obligation) are delegated from the very top of the organization to the bottom. Those serving in line positions are delegated the authority and responsibility required to discharge operational functions. Communications, gradation of power, and relationships are defined by the line between superior and subordinate. Staff authority comes from the need to have experts in specific areas to provide support for line officers. The staff relationship is usually a staff-to-line managerial one that can occur at any level within the school division. The staff concept gives a horizontal dimension to the organization. The line officer typically asks for the assistance of a staff person in helping with a very specific area of responsibility.

> At what level(s), within the local school division, does the driving force for school reform exist? Does it seem to be a problem?

The School Board

In theory, the board of education is the policy-making body, and the superintendent and school staff execute policies. In practice, however, boards sometimes micromanage schools and educational administrators sometimes develop policy statements. The "fuzziness" of the demarcation of responsibilities often causes discontent, which can erode the effectiveness of the school division. School boards in fact are empowered to provide strategic planning and policy for the school system, and most board members take this civic responsibility quite seriously.

The powers of local boards are: (1) those expressly granted by statute; (2) those fairly and necessarily implied in the powers expressly granted, and (3) those essential to the accomplishment of the objectives of the school district. The board has no choice but to comply with the statutes of the state. It can, however, work through established legislative channels to amend, abolish, or modify statutes that it finds are not in the best interest of the school district. The laws provide a great deal of opportunity for board members to exercise individual discretion and judgment. School boards answer to the citizens in their local communities and provide an effective mechanism through which communities can address their concerns. Public schools can, however, become the political arena in which ideological, social, economic, and religions differences are reconciled, sometimes actually at the expense of student needs. Serving on the board can be a stepping stone to a higher-level political position.

All boards have legal authority to determine salary and working conditions within the school division. They almost always hire and fire the superintendent of schools and approve the hiring of all other staff. They must approve the final budgets for schools and assist in obtaining needed resources. They also make decisions related to the financing of capital purchases. They resolve issues that are closely related to interpretation of community values, like family life and sex education, religious issues, acceptable moral behavior, character education, and other issues of community concern. They keep the community informed about the general condition of schools and help to build local support for school systems. They approve all policies by which the schools are governed.

School boards are involved in determining school sites, selecting architectural designs and contractors, determining attendance boundaries, entering into contracts, and bargaining with employee groups. Much of a board's time is spent interpreting rules made at other levels of government. The board provides minutes from all meetings, which serve as the official record and are open to examination by taxpayers. All board meetings must be open to the public except for special "executive sessions" in which school personnel matters are discussed. Even though meetings are open, past research suggests that fewer than 6 percent of Americans have ever attended a school board meeting (Boardman and Cassel, 1983, p. 740).

The AASA critical issues report, *Building Better Board-Administrator Relations* (McCurdy, 1992), points to increasing pressures on and between boards and superintendents. It suggests that boards have become more actively involved in school leadership. The report concludes, "A broad array of survey findings, expert analysis, and opinions of superintendents, board members, and others all indicate that while the relationships remain solid by and large, board-superintendent tensions have risen in recent years" (p. 30). Some of the leadership factors that were found to add to tension and friction include misunderstandings about each others' roles and favoritism among individual board members. There is also a problem when the superintendent spends insufficient time communicating to board members or loses contact with them between meetings. If the board does not feel involved in the thought process, or the superintendent overwhelms the board with information or is domineering, there is further alienation. Problems the board causes include interference in management functions (micromanagement); the presence of single-issue, single-region, or single-interest members; the leaking of discussions from executive sessions; involvement in personnel matters; attempts to get favorable treatment for friends and relatives; lack of skill, knowledge, and experience; and the pursuit by board members of political power, careers, and activism.

Many researchers have suggested that board turnover is a major reason that relationships deteriorate. New members on a board may not support the initiatives underway or the personal qualities that previous board members felt were important. The turnover of board members is often cited as a main reason that school initiatives are abandoned and mistrust develops. This situation is especially difficult when a new member has a mandate from constituents that he or she pursues with significant energy.

Board members are increasingly paying attention to their political constituents and getting reelected. Very active political board members' decisions are viewed, in the opinion of many superintendents, as "more with an eye to what will gain the support of voters rather than what is best for the children." Tough decisions that alienate voters can result in loss of support from the board, even if the decisions are best for the school system over the long haul. Educational leaders have learned that they must have board support if they or their initiatives are to weather the heat that accompanies almost every decision.

An example of this phenomenon occurred in a very hotly debated vote to approve condom distribution in Philadelphia and New York. Philadelphia superintendent Constance Clayton was able to get the school board to propose and support the idea. New York Chancellor Joseph Fernandez was eventually unseated by his political battles with the board and community over issues such as condom distribution. He was called "King Condom" by a number of board and community members. Superintendents necessarily face controversial issues, and they will be in trouble if their boards do not stick with them and provide support.

Superintendents suggest that the balance has shifted to a point where political astuteness matters more than job performance. "Absolutely, politics plays a big role," said Dr. Frank Petruzielo, superintendent of the Houston Independent School District. "Competency in many instances is not the issue, and that's what makes these jobs more difficult to perform than any other in public or private sectors" (Carter & Cunningham, 1997, p. 104).

In New York City, where problems have been blamed (although not completely) on the five chancellors over the past ten years, a number of community members have called for a total restructuring of the school board. In fact, across America, school boards are being criticized by state governments, education experts, and the public in general. Reports from the Institute for Educational Leadership (IEL), the Committee for Economic Development, and the Twentieth-Century Fund have all recommended changing school boards into education policy boards or children and youth coordinating boards, improving relationships with local government, improving involvement in school boards and board elections, and setting state-established performance criteria to hold boards accountable. Kentucky, West Virginia, and Massachusetts have enacted laws that have modified the responsibilities of local school boards. The January 1994 issue of *Phi Delta Kappan* dedicated a section to school board reform and school governance. That single section contained more than twenty-five recommendations for changing school boards.

Perhaps the volatility of the school board reform movement was best demonstrated during a heated debate between reform advocate Michael Kirst, professor at Stanford University, and Thomas Shannon, past executive director of the National School Boards Association, at the 1993 AASA Annual Conference in Orlando, Florida. Kirst suggested that school boards relinquish a number of responsibilities so that they can become better policy-makers and visionaries for schools. Boards should hire superintendents, establish district plans, determine funding priorities, set staff development policies, approve major construction projects, and develop curricular framework, he argued. They should not preside over grievances, approve competitive bidding contracts and payments, make personnel decisions, and generally micromanage schools. In his *Phi Delta Kappan* article, Kirst (1994) stated, "While it is impossible to separate policy and administration in general terms, the change to education policy boards, as proposed by the IEL study, would precisely define the limits and appropriate focus for the future role of the local school board" (p. 381).

Thomas Shannon accused Kirst and other reformers of trying to make school boards scapegoats for educational failures. He said that boards encourage improvements, but neither the funds nor the public are there to support needed changes. He argued that Kirst's reform proposals would undercut representative governance of public education by eroding the powers of school boards. Shannon asked, "Does the public want a substantial part of a district's decisions made by the superintendent in the privacy of his or her executive offices or with the superintendent and the board in the bright light of a public room?"

Danzberger (1998) states,

> The Institute for Educational Leadership has worked hard to raise general reform higher on states' reform agendas and among national leaders of education reform....
>
> State policy makers avoid tacking comprehensive local governance reform, even though it is critical to achieving states' own education reform objectives. The political risks appear too great.... There certainly is not broad grassroots pressure to reform local school boards, but there are those who would organize quickly, or use existing organized networks, to fight any change perceived to weaken the power of a representative body close to the people and strengthen the power of professional educators. (p. 208)

Regardless, boards and superintendents owe it to their communities and children to forge real partnerships and to develop the best possible education system for their communities.

Policy formation and overseeing schools is a very difficult job, and most school board members deserve a great deal of credit for being willing to serve the schools. They serve as the decision makers among conflicting ideologies, political pressures, and shifting economic and social conditions. They work with business, government, and community organizations to continuously improve the schools and promote student welfare. There are many opportunities for missteps in a highly public forum. In fact, many board meetings today are televised to the local community and receive full media attention. Board members are peppered with questions by critics and supporters alike and feel the same pressures that superintendents do.

The school board is an essential part of our democratic form of government. Howard Good (1998), a board member, states,

> What some see as a major weakness of school boards—that they are directed by well-meaning amateurs—may actually be a strength. The American school board is a unique institution. Nowhere else in the world is the control of education so close to the people.... I don't think it is an exaggeration to say that today, when bureaucratic rules are proliferating and far-off highly centralized corporations control many areas of our lives, the local school board is one of the few remaining examples of grassroots democracy. (p. 151)

What responsibilities does the school board have in supporting the reform agenda at Ophilia High School? How can the school obtain the board's support?

The School Division Superintendent

The superintendent is the chief educational leader and spokesperson for the school district. The key role of the school board is to support effective leadership, but the superintendent has the expertise, responsibility, and position to manage the schools' future. The AASA (1993) Commission on Standards for the Superintendency has stated:

> To a great extent, the quality of America's schools depends on the effectiveness of school superintendents. These executives of our nation's schools have complex leadership responsibilities, and those who hold the position must be among the brightest and best our society has to offer. Their vision and performance must focus on creating schools that will inspire our children to become successful, caring Americans, capable of becoming contributing citizens of the world.
>
> The superintendency requires bold, creative, energetic, and visionary school leaders who can respond quickly to a myriad of issues ranging from dealing with social changes, diverse student populations, and demands for equity, to improving school quality for every child and making effective use of new technologies. (p. 3)

The call in American education is for leadership, political savvy, reform, community responsiveness, and improved twenty-first century education. The superintendent has become the chief executive officer for the board serving as the professional adviser to the board, leader of reforms, manager of resources, and communicator to the public. Thus, the superintendent has become the most visible, most vulnerable, and potentially most influential member of the organization. Educational decisions are usually made in an environment of strong pressure from various segments of the community, state, and nation. A major responsibility of the superintendency is to deal with conflicting expectations, multiple political agendas, and varying ideas without unduly creating enemies or distrust. The superintendent's success as chief executive officer is determined largely by his or her ability to deal with these pressures while running an effective and efficient school system.

Larry Cuban (1988) defined the core roles of the superintendent to be instructional, managerial, and political. The instructional role is one of shaping the mission, establishing climate, designing rituals and structures, creating and emphasizing curriculum and instructional strategy, setting standards, and directing future reforms. Superintendents are also involved in management through planning, carrying out policy, providing information, budgeting, supervising resources, and managing conflict (Cunningham & Hentges, 1982). Perhaps the fastest-growing responsibility is the political role. Superintendents are expected to meet with a burgeoning constituency who want to influence school policy and to be able to influence people and groups. Cuban states, "All three roles form the core of superintending. Much diversity exists, however, among school executives in how these roles are enacted" (p. 142).

Major functions of the superintendency, in descending order of time commitments devoted to the activities, are instructional leadership, finance and business management, general planning, personnel administration, school plant management, communication and public relations, and pupil services. Many superintendents have difficulty scheduling their day and often find themselves reacting to issues and crises that seem to occur on a daily basis. The majority of superintendents' interactions are with members of the school organization and board members, but there is an increasing demand from a wide variety of community groups—parents, vendors, mass media, chambers of commerce, city officials, special interest groups, civic leaders, business community, ministers and church members, police, and others.

Superintendents and local school boards are feeling pressure and counterpressure from all these very powerful agents, who often hold differing views. At the same time they are balancing these conflicting expectations and responding to mandates, superintendents are asked to empower teachers so they can both design and carry out the curriculum. Greater decentralization has resulted, as well as involvement of school administrators, teachers, and parents in determining what will work best in the schools. They are also being asked to respond to the statewide standards-based reforms. This state focus on what young people are learning and how well they are learning it has become a driving force in many school divisions across the United States. Some states have connected performance on academic standards to graduation from high school and whether schools maintain their accreditation. The report Quality Counts '99 (*Education Week*, January 11, 1999) states, "The pressure is on. After years of exhorting and cajoling schools to improve, policy makers have decided to get tough. States are taking steps to reward results and punish failure in an effort to ensure that children are getting a good education and tax dollars aren't being wasted" (p. 5). From 53 to 77 percent of employers and parents "agree" with these standards/assessments/accountability approaches; 64 to 76 percent of teachers, however, "disagree."

The modern-day challenge of the superintendency is to manage all the various national, state, and local pressures for improving school performance while working with the local school board, central office administrators, and school staff to develop the most effective schools possible. As Norton, Webb, Dlugosh, and Sybouts (1996) suggest, "It is in the public school arena where administrators and board members alike must listen to constituents and advocate the welfare of children by designing and implementing sound educational policy through a system of defensive processes" (p. 104).

Each entity has a legitimate role in the process of education; however, the superintendent and board are responsible for deciding how those roles play out within their school districts. This process has proved to be very difficult. Each decision further shapes the school agenda in a direction that favors one group, often to the disadvantage of another. Yet, superintendents must be capable of walking into the fire to reach decisions on controversial matters and to articulate and defend the basis of those decisions so they are well understood and supported. Decisions should be based on a clear understanding of the positions taken by all interested parties and an accurate assessment of the conditions and desired outcomes. The superintendent's decisions should be based on well-grounded core values and policies and should not be pressured reactions to pressure-filled situations.

The AASA and the National School Board Association (NSBA) first met in 1980 and again in 1992 and 1994 to develop jointly approved guidelines regarding roles and responsibility of the superintendent. These guidelines (AASA–NSBA, 1994, pp. 11–12) are presented in Appendix 5.A at the end of this chapter.

To further define the superintendency as a profession, the AASA Commission on Standards for the Superintendency developed a set of professional standards (AASA, 1993). The commission stated, "All superintendents should be held accountable for the eight professional standards." The Professional Standards for the Superintendency can be summarized as follows:

- *Standard 1: Leadership and District Culture*
  This standard stresses executive leadership, vision, shaping school culture and climate, empowering others, and multicultural and ethnic understanding.

- *Standard 2: Policy and Governance*
  This standard centers on developing procedures for working with the board; formulating district policy, standards, and regulations; and describing public school governance in our democratic society.

- *Standard 3: Communications and Community Relations*
  This standard emphasizes skill in articulating district vision and purpose to the community and media. Also, it stresses responding to community feedback and building consensus to strengthen community support.

- *Standard 4: Organizational Management*
  This standard calls for skills in gathering, analyzing, and using data for decision making; framing and solving problems; and formulating solutions to problems. It also stresses quality management to meet internal and external customer expectations and to allocate resources.

- *Standard 5: Curriculum Planning and Development*
  This standard tests the superintendent's skill in designing curriculum and a strategic plan to enhance teaching and learning, using theories of cognitive development, employing valid and reliable performance indicators, and testing procedures and describing the use of computers and other learning technologies.

- *Standard 6: Instructional Management*
  This standard measures knowledge and use of research findings on learning and instructional strategies and resources to maximize student achievement. It also centers on applying research and best practice to integrate curriculum for multicultural sensitivity and assessment.

- *Standard 7: Human Resources Management*
  This standard assesses skill in developing a staff evaluation and assessment and supervisory system to improve performance. It also requires skills in describing and applying legal requirements for personnel selection, development, retention, and dismissal.

- *Standard 8: Values and Ethics of Leadership*
  This standard stresses the understanding and modeling of appropriate value systems, ethics, and moral leadership. It also requires superintendents to exhibit multicultural and ethnic understanding and to coordinate social agencies and human services to help each student grow and develop as a caring, informed citizen.

The role of the superintendent is shifting from one of directing and controlling to one of guiding, facilitating, and coordinating. Superintendents are asked to build direction, alignment, and a culture of visionaries as they encourage experimentation. Superintendents bring attention and efforts to bear on important educational goals. They are expected to cultivate a culture that promotes effective teaching and learning. They must show what students in their division have learned. Superintendents must instill learning as a core value of American society.

How can the superintendent best support the needed reforms at Ophilia High School? How can the school obtain the superintendent's support?

Central Office Operations

The titles of those in central office administration include deputy superintendents, assistant superintendents, directors, coordinators, and supervisors. The central office staff usually operates under the bureaucratic model with major emphasis on planning, compliance, development, and accountability. Most staff in the central office provide expertise to those serving at the school level. Although central office staff personnel do not have direct control over the school, they have considerable power through their positions, knowledge, time, and resources.

The central office staff is usually broken up into various divisions or departments based on their operational responsibility and school division size. Departmentalization is used to subdivide tasks among the central administrative staff. Organizational charts, available in almost all school districts, portray a rough description of this departmentalization. The chart shows the formal relation of various positions to all other positions using organizational channels through which authority and responsibility flow to members within the departments. When a person is assigned to a position, he or she should report to only one boss (unity of command) and have the needed authority to complete whatever responsibility he or she has been assigned. A person's authority should always equal his or her responsibility.

Departments typically include various combinations of human resources management, curriculum and instruction, administrative and logistical services, finance, technology, pupil personnel services, information and community relations, transportation, and planning, assessment, and developmental services. Most are staff positions providing support to such people in line positions as superintendent, deputy superintendents, principals and teachers. Individuals in staff positions usually help in the handling of details, locating data requirements and offering expertise in specific areas.

A person in a staff position provides special services or fulfills certain responsibilities that a person in a line position would perform if he or she had the time and expertise. The line officer is typically a generalist, while the staff person is a specialist. The authority over operations is given to line officers, with staff officers providing advisory and consultant services. Those working in central offices complement the work of those working in the schools. The main duties of central office staff are to:

1. Provide technical expertise in new areas under development.
2. Recommend courses of action.
3. Discuss plans with others in the organization to promote the exchange of information and collegial decision making.
4. Prepare written documentation to support work efforts.
5. Explain and interpret decisions made by supervisors.
6. Conduct evaluations and research, and assemble, summarize, and interpret results.
7. Provide assistance to line position personnel in their efforts to initiate new plans.
8. Inform and advise others what is occurring in the field.

In theory, central office staff should depend on expert knowledge, persuasion, and prestige to influence the decisions of those responsible for operations.

Because of the superintendent's busy schedule, he or she often has to depend on central office administrators to keep the school district running smoothly. Superintendents often have little time to supervise central office administrators directly and have to depend on their staffs' ability to follow up on the vision established by the superintendent and board. In very large school districts regional or deputy superintendents and their staffs have direct responsibility for a specific set of schools within the school district. It is important that the board, superintendent, and assistant superintendents focus on the strategic objectives of the school, allowing the central office staff to support operational areas and the deputy superintendent(s) and school personnel to be responsible for day-to-day operations (Glass, 1992).

Central office operations are being overhauled in a number of school districts to provide greater support to school-based initiatives. These districts are shifting the purpose, structure, and nature of the work of central offices. When school districts decentralize their operations or undergo systemic reform, the responsibilities of people in the central office change (Murphy, 1994; Fullan, 1993). Central office personnel often feel caught in the middle, between state authority and local autonomy (Crowson, 1988; Murphy & Hallinger, 1993; Elmore & Fuhrman, 1994). Decentralization has brought "significant changes in the role of central office administrators, and supervisory staff. The central office must come to see itself not as a regulator or initiator but as a service provider. The function of the central office must be to ensure that individual schools have what they need to be successful" (Carlson, 1989). Some have expressed concern about school-based management's "potential to slip into political debates over power and control and lose sight of the original purpose: to improve educational opportunities for students" (Carlson, 1996).

With decentralization, central office staff members must take on new roles as supporters and facilitators of work taking place in the schools. They focus on helping schools achieve their improvement goals. As Fred Wood, former dean of education at the University of Oklahoma, put it, "the central office's role becomes one of facilitating and supporting and making sure there is implementation of change." Success at the central office is now dependent on educational leaders' ability to create new knowledge together with colleagues at the school sites.

Central office personnel must embody the best in current practice and research. More than any other body of workers within a school system, they should be informed about the latest research in educational trend literature. In turn, they should make efforts to articulate this body of information to schools in such a way that school staffs can understand and use this data.... Supervisors and central office specialists must become knowledge workers if they are to survive and prosper. (cited in Brown, 1995)

Central office educational leaders create learning communities to illuminate the knowledge that will be needed in the new millennium. Other ways in which the central office administrators can coordinate and provide support and assistance to schools is by (Glickman, 1993):

- defining the district's core beliefs about teaching and learning;
- defining the goals and objectives of an educated student;
- providing the money, technical services, and human consultation to allow schools to figure out how to get the job done;
- providing information and identifying common needs, and;
- coordinating and linking resources.

In 1993, the Cross City Campaign for Urban School Reform released a report entitled *Reinventing Central Office: A Primer for Successful Schools*, which calls for a radical shift of authority and funds from the central office to local schools. Cross City's report outlines a strategy for improving schools by decentralizing funds, authority, and accountability. In the report's vision, "central office departments are entrepreneurial, competing with other vendors to provide services. By existing only to serve school needs, departments that perform useful services quickly and cost-effectively continue to grow." Most of the responsibilities of a reinvented central office include ensuring equity, intervening in failing schools, and taking responsibility for significant or fluctuating costs so risk is spread among all schools.

The Cross City campaign envisions that the central office will remain the site for:

- Goals and standards
- Equity assurance
- Assistance
- Budget
- Management information systems
- Emergency funds
- Legal assistance
- Personnel functions
- Competitive services (for example, transportation, food, payroll)

The major theme is decentralization and support for local schools in their efforts to improve themselves. The central office is becoming a service center for the school. This means moving away from uniformity across schools and supporting the diversity that actually exists. (For more information see: www.mcrel.org.)

Central administrative staff are being called on in a number of districts to work directly with principals and teachers to improve students' test scores. The responsibility for improving test scores is being placed solidly on the principal and teachers, calling on central administration for needed financial and technical support. In these cases, job security, salary, and incentive pay are sometimes tied to the school's ability to improve scores. A key will be working together to attain high-quality professional development that is focused on improving student achievement. Expectations for low-performing schools include developing plans for improvement, imposing sanctions for failure to implement improvement plans, developing partnerships for improving schools, and supporting the state's accountability systems (*Quality Counts '99*, January 11, 1999).

Define the role of the central office staff in supporting the needed reform efforts at Ophilia High School.

Local School Structures and Arrangements

MARILYN TALLERICO, Professor
Syracuse University

Future educational leaders face a number of challenges related to how schools are structured and the arrangement among local schools and their school districts. These arrangements affect where and how key decisions are made that touch the core functions of schools: teaching and learning.

One issue that school leaders must grapple with is how to balance needs for autonomy at the local school level against coordination or standardization among schools at the district level. Scholars often refer to this as a tension between centralization and decentralization of authority over decision-making processes.

School arrangements that structure these decisions can be better understood if we look at them from a variety of perspectives. One perspective views schools as bureaucracies, characterized by formal organization based on a hierarchy of authority, multiple divisions of labor, specializations of functions, an overall impersonal orientation, and rules and regulations. While some see these features as important means of maximizing rational decision making and efficiency, others emphasize the potential dysfunction of such a

system (for example, when chains of authority become unbreakable or when regulatory controls are excessive).

From another perspective, local school structures are viewed as loosely coupled, open to a variety of internal and external influences, and more like organized anarchies than tightly connected hierarchies. In this view, schools are characterized by unclear and diffuse goals, uncertain technologies of teaching and learning, nonrational decision making behaviors, loosely connected structural elements, and fluid participation of teachers, administrators, students, parents, and community members. Thus, in the bigger picture, school districts are more like federations of largely autonomous schools, which in turn represent federations of autonomous individual classrooms. An assumption underlying this perspective is that administrators and teachers, as professionals, have broad discretionary decision-making power within existing school structures.

From a more eclectic perspective, school structures may be understood as having aspects of: (a) hierarchical order and bureaucracy;

(continued)

Continued

(b) collegiality, personal autonomy, and professionalism; (c) political features, such as conflicts among different interests; and (d) cultural and symbolic dimensions. An assumption underlying the latter is that shared beliefs, values, symbols, rituals, and traditions drive human behavior and may be the "glue" that holds together loosely or variably coupled school structures.

What does this all mean for you as a school leader? First, it's important not to limit your sights to just one perspective on whatever school structure in which you find yourself. Second, it is highly likely that dual decision-making systems will coexist in your school and district, some centralized and some decentralized, with relative dominance of each dependent on the particular context. Third, as a school leader, you can and will both affirm and shape your school's culture. It's important to use this influence wisely and intentionally. Fourth, it is equally important to be aware that distinct constituent (e.g., teachers', students', administrators') and department *sub*cultures will likely constrain the development of a school-wide culture. It will be important for you to understand—and exercise leadership through—both the information organization and formal school structures.

Whether schools and school districts are tightly coupled bureaucracies or loosely knit confederations, the reality remains that principals stand at a pivotal point of interchange between central office–school board decision-makers, teachers, parents, and students. Because of this critical positioning, an important role of principals is to buffer teachers and students from the dysfunctional aspects of large, impersonal school organizations and to use the system's structures effectively to acquire resources for the school's learning priorities.

Recent literature emphasizes the moral and ethical responsibilities of school leaders, including teachers, principals, and other educational administrators. Whatever the particular cultures and organizational systems you may inherit, it is important to continually question those cultures and structures. More specifically, I suggest raising and attending to at least two questions: (a) Who benefits from the way this school is structured and (b) who occupies the positions of leadership within those structures?

The assumptions underlying the first question are that not all students or adults in schools benefit equally from extant organizational arrangements. A significant leadership challenge is to uncover and remedy such inequities. Which students are put at a disadvantage, for example, by how schools are organized by grade levels or special programs? Which gain an advantage from certain labels or course-taking tracks?

You will also have to consider the limited integration of many educational leadership roles when analyzed by gender, ethnicity, race, and other variable. Why is this so? What evidence of improvement has there been in recent years? What needs to happen to ensure diversity and the optimization of all talent pools for leading our schools? Although these certainly are not the only questions that might be raised in the course of providing moral and ethical leadership of schools, they are ones that are directly related to the topic of local school structures. And they challenge us all to think about taken-for-granted organizational arrangements.

The School Administrator

A school's *attendance zone* is that portion within the school district served by a particular school building as designated by the local school board. Although attendance zones seem as though they should be straightforward, they often elicit much public response and have been used to resolve a number of issues—such as integration. As a result, attendance zones are not always uniform or simply defined.

Each school building is staffed by a principal and, as size warrants, any number of assistant principals, teachers, and a number of others in staff and clerical positions. The principal carries out all the duties necessary to run an effective school. Generally these duties include administering all policies and programs; making recommendations regarding improvements to the school; planning, implementing, and evaluating the curricular and instructional programs; hiring, coordinating, and developing staff; organizing programs of study and scheduling classes; maintaining a safe school environment; providing stewardship for all school resources; and providing for cocurricular and athletic activities. Principals usually serve in elementary (K–5), middle (6–8), or high (9–12) schools. It is generally agreed that the high school principalship is the most demanding job, followed by the middle school and then the elementary principalship, and this is reflected in the difference in principal pay scales.

Research has shown that the principal is the single most important individual to the success of any given school (Miller, 1995). School effectiveness research in the 1980s pointed to the importance of the principal and teachers as the main determiners of school success. Allan Glatthorn (1994) states that principals

> play a very active part in developing special curricula for their school within district constraints. Regardless of the committee structure used for curriculum work at the school, there will be a need for strong leadership, which is typically provided by the principal. (In some schools, however, the assistant principal or another individual assumes major responsibility for curriculum leadership.) (p. 66)

These researchers suggest that effective schools exist in districts that have decentralized decision making, leaving it to the schools to support curriculum work, to perform evaluation, and to provide learning materials and professional development. The key to all improvements is the vision and energy of the principal. Some of the qualities of effective schools are:

- Teaching for learning and student outcomes
- High expectations and accountability for measurable results
- Collaboration, staff empowerment and development, and direct teacher influence on decisions
- Utilization of research and best practice
- Use and application of technology to accelerate learning, feedback, monitoring, and administration
- Establishment of high standards and expectations
- Availability of adequate resources
- Continuous improvement of the curriculum and instruction.

The principal is at the very heart of school improvement. In the report *America 2000: Where School Leaders Stand* (1991), the AASA states: "Effective schools have at least one thing in common; sound leadership. School administrators have never had a more crucial role in American society; they must be the ones who stimulate the debate and help develop a vision of what our schools should become in communities across the nation." (p. 6)

Considerable effort has been expended in recent years to spell out the specific functions of the school principal. One of the key themes that evolves in this analysis is that management functions and clerical chores must not be allowed to dominate the work of the principal. In fact, the most important responsibilities focus on vision and developing and motivating staff to achieve optimum student learning outcomes. Both the National Association of Elementary School Principals (NAESP) and the National Association of Secondary School Principals (NASSP) have established proficiencies that they believe to be critically important to principals' leadership. The idea is to provide targets toward which principals can focus their efforts. It is generally agreed that these proficiencies are constantly evolving to fit the context in which schools operate. The NAESP revised proficiencies for principals (1991) are:

- *Leadership Proficiencies*—Exercise vision, recognize individual needs, encourage and develop leadership, analyze information, delegate responsibility, make decisions, coordinate resources, enhance teaching and learning, bond school community, and participate in professional groups.
- *Communication Skills*—Articulate and defend decisions; write clearly and concisely; utilize research, facts, and data; apply current technologies; use mass media; actively listen; promote higher-level thinking skills; model effective behavior; and provide time to constituents.
- *Group Process*—Involve staff, parents, students, and community; resolve conflict; identify decision-making procedures and techniques; develop consensus; and achieve outcomes.
- *Curriculum*—Apply community values, encourage faculty input, seek resources and demonstrate knowledge, honor diversity, and enhance student learning.
- *Instruction*—Apply principles of growth, development, and learning; assess methods and strategies and articulate effective classroom planning, management, and instruction.
- *Supervisory Proficiencies*—Set high expectations and goals, honor diverse styles, implement behavior management, design staff development programs, encourage staff participation, and employ appropriate support services.
- *Evaluation*—Assess performance, progress, and effectiveness; encourage input; foster continuous improvement; apply observation and conferencing skills; inspire teachers; utilize formative and summative evaluation; develop professional growth plans; and follow due process.
- *Organizational Management*—Identify and accomplish school mission; develop and implement procedures; select, assign, and organize staff; capitalize on research; facilitate professionals; attract volunteers; provide safe climate; coordinate community services; develop equitable schedules, manage time, delegate tasks; respond to issues and concerns; develop policies and practices; use technology; know school laws; and maintain the physical plant.
- *Fiscal Management*—Understand school district budget, establish budget priorities, prepare school budget, employ and monitor accounting procedures, use cost control procedures, and find new resources.
- *Political Management*—Attract community and financial support, involve influential community members, address political issues, develop effective political strategies, and participate in legislative activities.

The National Association of Secondary School Principals (NASSP) was one of the first organizations to look into the needed proficiencies for principals. The NASSP completed a study of secondary school principals and listed the twelve most important skills of a principal (see Assessment Centers in Chapter 10). They developed an assessment center to evaluate the abilities of potential candidates and a series of training activities to help future and practicing administrators to improve these skills. They placed considerable stress on the ability to lead schools that will be serving a demographically different nation in the twenty-first century. They saw schools of the future being more technologically advanced, managed on-site, globally focused, accountable, linked with the community, and culturally diverse. The NASSP (Walberg & Lane, 1989) believe that to lead these schools, new school leaders will need to:

- *Develop teams and delegate responsibilities* and include team members from the community;
- *Initiate and manage change* and deal with ambiguities resulting from a dynamic system;
- *Design effective learning environments* for a wide range of students;
- *Comment orally and in writing* with acute sensitivity to a diversity of publics;
- *Take risks and innovate*, providing for a changed environment in schools;
- *Motivate* students and staff to reach high expectations;
- *Use technology* to assist in instructing students and to manage the school;
- *Evaluate* programs and be accountable for student learning;
- *Value and integrate culturally diverse* students and staff into the life of the school, creating a positive school culture;
- *Work within the political forces* which shape schooling.

Principals must also be prepared to handle critical incidents that typically occur with little or no advance warning. Difficult issues such as racial disharmony, violence, sexual misconduct, religious freedom, educational equity, drugs, and violence have found their way into schools across the United States. Principals can misjudge the nature, direction, and scale of the conflict resulting in the underestimation or exaggeration of existing conditions. How effectively the principal deals with critical incidents ultimately determines his or her effectiveness and that of the school.

One of the hundreds of thousands of examples of such a critical incident occurred in a Minnesota high school. The school principal did not recognize the volatile nature of a sexual harassment issue in the community and did not respond quickly enough to a female student's complaint about defamatory graffiti about her that had been written on the bathroom wall. All the principal had to do was have maintenance remove the graffiti, but he did not respond to the student's complaint. The student sued the school district and created a costly stir throughout the state of Minnesota. Principals need an instinct to recognize potential "time bombs." Many principals who lose their jobs have experienced some form of "critical incident" that turned the tide against them. The successful handling of such incidents is embedded in the core values of the community, knowledge of the political power base, and common sense.

Principal: Instructional Leader or School Manager?

An age-old debate revolves around whether the role of the principal is primarily as instructional leader or school manager. Instructional leadership is focused on curriculum and instructional development; staff development; instructional supervision; program, teacher, and student evaluation; and the continuous improvement of teaching and learning. The business manager focuses more on facilities, equipment, supplies, schedules, procedures, stewardship, critical incidents, and general compliance with efficient behavior and practice and district policies, procedures, and programs. Research tends to suggest that principals must first and primarily be the instructional leader, but not at the expense of effectively managing the school. Drake and Roe (1999) state,

> very often principals feel as if they face a dilemma as management duties interfere with educational leadership. This concern is real because role expectations of the school and community may often shape the principal's activities, with emphasis on managing people and things. However, a carefully selected principal candidate, properly prepared and motivated, can run a well-managed school and still consider and effect educational leadership as his or her major function. (p. 38)

Some practitioners argue that principals cannot do both jobs and tend to get drawn into general management at the expense of instructional leadership. This problem is compounded as a result of downsizing central office administration. However, Smith and Andrews (1989) found that effective principals were more likely to communicate about instructional matters, to pay attention to test results, to discuss curriculum and instruction, to focus on how well learning objectives were mastered in communication to students, teachers, and parents, and to be a visible presence in and around the school.

A key to successful schools is the development of schoolwide instructional leadership working for the benefit of all students. Again, the focus of instructional leadership is on curriculum, staff development, program and staff evaluation, staff and pupil assistance, research and experimentation, accountability and remediation, and provision of resources. Krug's (1992) synthesis of major tasks includes defining mission, managing curriculum and instruction, supervising teaching, monitoring student progress, and promoting instructional climate. Achilles and Smith (1999) conclude,

> The stimulation of pupil academic performance is a continuing challenge for the principal. Improvement will not occur without the principal's time and attention, for 'as is the principal, so is the school.' The principal is the coordinator of the learning environment and must demonstrate a commitment to pupil performance. The principal, the teachers, and the pupils are a learning team. (p. 242)

In 1999, approximately twenty states rated the performance of all schools and held expectations that principals and teachers would work together to continuously improve that performance. The demand is for instructional leadership within all schools.

Another related area of debate and discussion is whether curriculum and instructional reform should be centralized or decentralized. The difference lies in where the primary power, information, and decision-making capacity exists. As has been suggested, school districts are moving more toward a decentralized or site-based approach. Much research suggests that decentralization is most effective, although all are not convinced of the benefit of these shifts in power (Murphy, 1995). It is important that the board and superintendent be clear about what authority has been delegated if site-based and decentralized instructional leadership approaches are to work. The approach selected has a profound effect on the organizational structure, the type of demands placed on the principalship, and the school's effectiveness. Drake and Roe continue,

> one serious way we can improve schools is by revamping their structure. Structure must be developed that keeps citizens in close communication with schools and allows individual schools to be more responsive to students and parents. Greater decentralization can bring schools closer to the people so that the schools may make decisions that will immediately affect the local area and provide the opportunity for their 'customers' to have a reasonable impact on the decision-making process. (p. 111)

We end this chapter with a vignette of a typical day for many principals, which illustrates the impact that administration at all levels has on the school. It also raises awareness and sensitivity to the challenges and vital importance of principals.

> How can you develop staff confidence in your ability to lead this major reform effort at Ophilia High School?

Putting "C's" into the Village

PAUL C. HOUSTON, ED.D., Executive Director
American Association of School Administrators

It is important to remember that the role of system leadership is changing, and that success will come from doing the job very differently from the way it once was done. Many leaders are currently caught in the trap of trying to emulate the success achieved by earlier generations of "command and control" administrators. Today, you cannot command the staff or community—you can't even get them to take a number.

Rather than try to lead by command, administrators must develop and nurture relationships. I am fond of reminding my colleagues that if you stand in the middle of the road, you get hit by traffic going in both directions. However, that is also the best place from which to direct traffic. You can either get the plate number of the truck that just ran you down, or stand up and wave your arms to move the flow in a positive direction.

Educators are particularly fond of saying "It takes a village to raise a child," but the real question for school leaders is "What does it take to raise a village?" The villages of yesterday are gone and must be rebuilt in the new era we face. Schools are the connect points for communities. They can, and must, play the role of creating the needed network of support for children. School leaders must be the connectors, the bridge builders who bring diverse elements of the community together to support children.

School leaders must move from the "B's" from past days of school administration (bonds, building, buses, budgets—the "stuff" of education) to the "C's" (connections, collaborations, communication, children—the building of relationships). School system leaders must create a balance between being courageous champions

(continued)

Continued

for children and communities and collaborative catalysts who use their pivotal roles to bring people together to make things happen. I have called this shifting role as moving from being a superintendent of schools to being a superintendent of education. It implies reaching out beyond the traditional walls of schools and school districts to embrace a broader set of responsibilities and relationships.

School leaders will of necessity behave very differently from the way they do today. Proactive leadership is required that initiates contact and issues and demands both human and political sensitivities. Changed attitudes and new skills will be required as well as change in the organizations supporting schools such as district offices. District offices must reduce their oversight and monitoring role and replace it with the building of capacity for schools. Schools need guidance and support; they do not need control. Savvy school district leaders will make it their business to transform district offices into places of support.

School management in the next century will be the management of relationships: the relationship of child to learning, child to child, child to adult, and school to community. There can be no barriers. It is all interconnected. Education is organic in nature and the pieces cannot be mechanically separated. The role of school leadership will be to foster and nurture the old relationships and to create new ones necessitated by the changing social conditions facing children and schools.

I have always thought that leadership comes from the ability to comfort the afflicted and afflict the comforted—helping the public understand that schools are more effective than they think and helping staff understand that they are not as effective as they think. Successful leaders find the balance between the demands and expectations of those working on the problems, and those who depend on the problems to be solved. Like a performer at a sea park who rides a pair of dolphins, you must have one foot on the back of the community and the other on the back of the staff. If you lean too far in either direction, you fall off.

There is one final relationship that must be fostered—the relationship with the board of education. In essence, the real role of school boards is to translate the values of the community into policy for the system. It is a crucial role that, too often, is not being played appropriately. School boards are often not asked to focus on the very thing that they are there to provide—insight into what the community hopes and dreams for its children. Boards need to be helped to move away from a preoccupation with the "stuff" of education, to its higher purposes. School superintendents must use their positions to help school boards play this role if any success is expected.

Successful school district leaders are moving from acting like sharks to behaving like dolphins. The role is no longer one of the lone predator, swimming menacingly through the water in search of the next meal. It is one where sophisticated communication and sonar are used, where collaboration and cooperation are stressed and where a bit of playfulness doesn't hurt. For all those people who would hold onto the shark behavior out of fear of being swallowed up in the dangerous waters of the next century, it is good to remember that dolphins kill sharks. You do not have to be a predator to be successful. Swimming fast and not taking yourself too seriously also do not hurt.

A Typical Day

Perhaps the best way to understand the challenges facing educational administrators is to get a feeling for a typical school day—if such a day exists. The typical work day begins at 6:30 A.M. Most principals usually treasure this time because the morning tends to be quiet, allowing a little time to finish paperwork held over from the previous night, make some calls, and leave some voice and e-mail messages. At 7:00, the principal begins to return some calls to parents that he or she was unable to contact the day before. There is also a need to find substitutes for absent teachers and sometimes rearrange schedules.

Around 7:30, the principal stands out in the office to greet teachers and parents. Sometimes both come into the office to discuss pressing matters. This morning the band teacher comes in and explains that the science club left the stage a mess last night and the band had to straighten it up before they could begin band practice. She is getting pretty fed up with club sponsors leaving this space messy. The principal writes a reminder to look into this and check with the janitor to see if this space is being cleaned at night. The secretaries are arriving and the telephones are already ringing. The principal checks the status of a report that must be sent to the deputy superintendent today. Finally, the first bell rings and the schoolday officially begins.

A morning walk through the halls allows the principal and assistant principal to spot current problems and discuss the day's activities. This morning the janitor explains that the plumbing failed in the boys' restroom on the west wing and he had no choice but to turn off the water. It will be fixed by the following morning, but the restroom cannot be used today. The assistant principal comes up with an alternative restroom for the boys on that hall to use and mentions it as part of the brief morning announcement over the P.A. system. The administrator drops by a few classrooms in response to notes left by teachers.

One teacher wants a student who is constantly disrupting her class removed and assigned somewhere else. The student's father had come into the school intoxicated and belligerent for a meeting with the teacher the previous day. There is no parental support for this child, who has an above-average IQ and a total lack of motivation for schoolwork. The teacher was asked to talk to the guidance counselor to see if anything could be done for this student. The principal agrees to talk to the student and let her know the consequences of continued misbehavior. The school is seeing an increasing number of misbehaving, mean spirited students, and a committee is being formed to discuss this problem.

Checking with a teacher who has returned from a week of illness, the principal realizes that the substitute hired to fill in for him was unsatisfactory. The principal then rushes to a meeting to discuss an individualized educational plan (IEP) with a parent, assistant principal, and school psychologist.

Some days it's off to a central office meeting, but today the principal is going to observe in three teachers' classes and complete formative evaluations. Follow-ups will be scheduled to discuss the evaluation and formalize plans for teacher development. Next, the principal meets with relevant staff to discuss new issues and the status of existing assignments, and to share information and examine short- and long-term goals. One issue of concern is the number of enrollments. It was much larger then expected this year, and class sizes are very large.

Following this meeting, the principal checks with the secretaries regarding the report due to central administration and to discuss afternoon meetings, pending reports, and correspondence. The bus monitor interrupts to discuss discipline problems on bus 13 and a recent call from an irate parent who is concerned about the bickering and unpleasantness that his daughter is experiencing on that bus. This problem takes priority and must be dealt with as soon as possible. Before this problem can be addressed, however, a teacher explains, with some irritation in her voice, that the clock in her room has still not been fixed. The principal writes a quick note on both matters and places it in the assistant principal's mailbox.

The principal ends the morning with a call to personnel to see if enrollment increases justify the hiring of one teacher this year and two for next year. The response is an explanation of how tight the budget is and that it is very unlikely that many new staff will be hired next year. In confidence, the personnel director states that each principal may be asked to cut about one percent from the school budget by the end of the school year. The personnel director explains she will look into the request and that a possible solution is a long-term sub, who would be less expensive and could be canceled more easily, if the superintendent cannot come up with additional funding. The principal, who believes it is important to be visible to students and teachers, goes to help monitor the cafeteria at lunchtime.

Chatting with students and teachers comes to an abrupt halt when the assistant principal's schedule will not allow for handing the two students now in the office who got in a fight on the school grounds. One is being seen by the nurse because of injuries from the fight. Both students are still very agitated, cursing, and generally being insubordinate. Arriving in the office are parents who are early for their conference regarding their daughter's behavior problems. They look concerned about the behavior of the two students involved in the fight. The parents wait while the principal talks briefly to these students. The secretary calls the boys' parents to pick them up because they have been suspended.

The conference with the girl's parents goes quite well, and the parents promise to support the teacher in trying to improve their daughter's attitude toward her studies. The teacher agrees to get back to the parents and principal regarding how things are going.

The principal's next meeting is with the PTA board. The board members have ideas for increasing fundraising and business sponsors—important issues in light of an already tight school budget that might be decreased even further. One of the school's business sponsors is attending this meeting to determine how his company might help. The sponsor expresses concern about the computer technology in the school and wants to help improve on the capabilities and the use of the equipment.

The principal checks back with the secretary, who has a question about a purchase order for some classroom equipment. The balance in the budget is enough to cover it, and the needed entries are made in the disbursements journal and the principal signs off on the purchase order. The central office director of planning calls regarding the staff development activity after school. The school staff have been involved in the development of a mission statement for the school. They now plan to develop a concrete vision of what they want the school to look like in the future. The director for planning is going to address the site-based planning team this afternoon and she verifies the purpose, time, and place of the meeting. She plans to talk about how test data can be used to help diagnose and treat trouble areas. All handouts have been prepared, and the room is ready for the afternoon meeting.

Three more parent meetings await the principal. The head of the teachers task force sticks her head in to discuss the short presentation of results of their work that she will be making at the planning team meeting this afternoon. The next parent conference is with a habitual offender; this student is very close to expulsion. The school psychologist and counselor attend this meeting to make it clear that something must be done to change this child's behavior or he will be expelled or placed in an alternate setting. The principal then returns some telephone calls before going out into the hallways to be visible during dismissal.

One of the telephone calls is to a board member whose grandchildren attend this school. She tells the principal that she voted against the approved plan for the school to pick up 127 kids from a low-income apartment, and she has gotten the board to relook at this rezoning plan. She wants a school representative to present a case on why it is not advisable to include these children in an already crowded school. The superintendent backs the plan to include these students and has asked the principal to come to the meeting prepared to support the plan. The board member ends the conversation by confidentially explaining there are serious concerns about the superintendent and that she will probably not last as long as our last superintendent—that was three years. In hanging up the telephone, the principal realizes that in this case everyone on the school staff agrees with what the school board member is suggesting. The principal also understands, however, that it is important to follow the leadership of the superintendent and, as suggested, provide a "united front." Some teachers catch the principal in the hall, and they go back to one of the teacher's rooms to talk with the principal, briefly bouncing ideas around on some new directions for the vision of the school. The principal hurries back to the office to meet the director of planning, who is already there with a cup of coffee in hand. The Planning Council meeting is a lively one with lots of teacher debate on how best to use the testing and assessment information in developing school programs for the twenty-first century.

The principal returns to the office to attack a large amount of paperwork and to respond to some final phone calls. On the way home, the principal reflects on how to approach a number of issues that were confronted today. The principal is particularly concerned about the political climate and the general belief that this is the most political school in the district. Another is that although the media have supported the faculty in the past, there is concern about their coverage of the school's academic standards, assessment, and teaching quality. The superintendent is particularly concerned.

The community also does not seem to be quite as supportive recently. Teacher support is there, which is very important, but community support is also vital. The principal believes that the local school board member is annoyed that the school leadership has not taken a stronger stand against the attendance rezoning and is turning parents against the principal and the staff. The principal also is concerned that more students seem to be misbehaving and that teachers do not seem to be prepared for the discipline problems.

As this typical day suggests, much of the day-to-day work of the principal remains somewhat reactive. The principal must deal briefly but effectively with the rapid events that occur and communicate in brief encounters and often unscheduled meetings. The principal places high priority on current "emergencies" and problems that occur on a daily basis. The principal also spends a good deal of time on management of school matters, instructional and curricular leadership, pupil control, teacher development, and community relations. The principal understands the need to be sensitive to parents and strives to gain strong community support. The principal also is concerned with staff issues and recognizes how necessary it is to have staff support to succeed. The biggest principal concern is how often urgent matters (crises, pressing problems, deadline-driven activities) have gotten in the way of what is important (planning, preparation, empowerment, development). Principals recognize how difficult it is to be a proactive instructional leader rather than a reactive manager.

Effective principals are active participants in the daily operations of their schools and they are visible and enthusiastic. Pride in the schools is evident in their work. They try to keep problems from reaching the superintendent but at the same time are careful to keep him or her informed. What underlies a principal's successful leadership is the creation of a school culture that promotes and sustains the continuous improvement of the school. Fullan (1997) concludes:

> counting on oneself for a good cause in a highly interactive organization is the key to fundamental organizational change. People change organizations. The starting point is not system change or change in those around us, but taking action ourselves. The challenge is to improve education in the only way it can be—through the day-to-day actions of empowered individuals. This is what's worth fighting for in the school principalship. (p. 47)

Conclusion

The basic operating unit of American education is the local school. It is at this level that teaching and learning occur and that services are provided. The role of the school board and school division staff is to support and facilitate the development of outstanding schools. At the same time, parents, employers, and community leaders are seen as partners in this process.

Existing school division structures tend to be bureaucratic with rigidly coded roles, rules, and procedures. Studies (Johnson, 1996) suggest that leaders who use these structures to encourage initiatives, the free flow of ideas, and information have been more successful in promoting improvements than those who restrict access and encourage centralized control. As a result, many school divisions are shifting the roles of all those within the district, freeing the superintendent to work more closely with the board and community power structures, sharing greater authority and responsibility with local schools, and expecting the central office staff to provide the needed support for both. The superintendent is in the most important position for establishing the tone for the local school district. The principal holds the similar position for the individual school.

As the demands on education have increased, the roles of those responsible for education have shifted. The desire to develop schools that are responsive to student and family needs has resulted in a move toward greater decentralization and responsiveness. The principal and teachers within the school are expected to be more entrepreneurial, having the power and authority to come up with needed school improvements and seeing them through to success. The central office administrators are to facilitate, support, and assess these efforts. The superintendent and board are to articulate core values and outcomes, obtain political support, develop alignment, create learning organizations, provide resources, and maintain accountability for results. This entire process works best when it is open, allowing for input from parents and community members as well as public, nonprofit, and private organizations.

Organizational authority structures, norms, routines, roles, and assignments may need to be changed as we work to continuously improve education (Singh, Tucker & House, 1986). Robert Owens (1995) states,

> Organizations of all kinds often once revered, are now suspect, viewed with hostility, and often described as oppressive.... This is, of course a marked departure from traditional thinking and is based on the conviction that overemphasis on bureaucratic structures, top-downward exercise of power, and centralized control have demonstrably failed to produce the organizational results the advocates of traditional organizational theory claimed it would" (p. 327). He goes on to conclude, "Bureaucracy is far from dead in educational organizations, and many people are confident that centralized direction is the most effective way to reform them. On the other hand, nonbureaucratic approaches to organizing and administering have been rapidly gaining support in recent years. These two approaches will continue to compete in the marketplace of ideas.... (pp. 327–328)

Many argue, however, that the school board remains the best example of grassroots democracy in action, and bureaucracy is not and never has been a problem in education.

If schools are to meet the needs of twenty-first century students, they will be required to make "second-order changes," those that alter the fundamental nature of the structure of the school system and its approach to student learning. Any reform effort that focuses only on the people and not on the organizational structure is a recipe for failure. Ineffective organizational structure can doom the best of efforts. Senge (1990) suggests that the "new work" of leadership is designing, teaching, envisioning, creating, improving, advocating, defusing, assessing, and stewarding. All who have a stake in American education must be encouraged to rethink and clarify what organizational structures will be needed to support this "new work," to prepare students for the twenty-first century, and to encourage continuous improvement in our schools.

PORTFOLIO ARTIFACTS

- Attend a school board meeting and select and research an issue being discussed.
- Interview a school board member.
- Shadow a superintendent, associate or assistant superintendent, school lawyer, or principal.
- Participate in a school audit.
- Develop a transportation plan for a school.
- Work with research and testing staff to plan and conduct a testing/assessment activity.
- Become a member of a school planning or curriculum review team.
- Review and update your school system's organizational chart and job descriptions.
- Participate in a job classification audit.

■ Search the Web for organizations such as:

AASA—*www.aasa.org*

NAESP—*www.naesp.org*

NASSP—*www.nassp.org*

NMSA—*www.nmsa.org*

NSBA—*www.nsba.org*

ASCD—*www.ascd.org*

Who are their target audiences? What do they offer to members?

■ Write a "typical day" vignette for a principle in your school district.

TERMS

Accountability

Authority and responsibility

Decentralization and delegation

Dependent and independent
school board

Instructional leadership

Leadership and management

Line and staff

NSBA, AASA, NASSP,
NAESP, NMSA, ASCD

Operational areas

Policy and procedures

Principal skills
and proficiencies

Service centers

Stewardship

SUGGESTED READING

Carter, G. R., & Cunninghan, W. G. (1997). *The American school superintendent: Leading in an age of pressure*. San Francisco: Jossey-Bass.

Drake, T. L., & Roe, W. H. (1999). *The principalship*. Upper Saddle River, NY: Merrill.

Hughes, L. W. (Ed). (1999). *The principal as leader*. Englewood Cliffs, NJ: Prentice-Hall.

Kimbrough, R. B., & Burkett, C. W. (1990). *Principalship: Concepts and practices*. Englewood Cliffs, NJ: Prentice-Hall.

Norton, M. S., Webb, L. D., Dlugosh, L. L., & Sybouts, W. (1996). *The school superintendency: New responsibilities, new leadership*. Boston: Allyn & Bacon.

Owens, R. G. (1995). *Organizational behavior in education*. Boston: Allyn & Bacon.

Sergiovanni, T. G. (1995). *The principalship: a reflective practice perspective*. Boston: Allyn & Bacon.

Short, P. M., & Green, J. T. (1997). *Leadership in empowered schools: Themes from innovative efforts*. Upper Saddle River, NY: Merrill.

Smoley, E. R. (1999) *Effective School Boards*. San Francisco: Jossey-Bass.

Speck, M. (1999). *The principalship: Building a learning community*. Upper Saddle River, NY: Merrill.

A P P E N D I X   5 . A

The Joint AASA–NSBA Superintendent Guidelines

- To serve as the school board's chief executive officer and preeminent educational adviser in all efforts of the board to fulfill its school system governance role.
- To serve as the primary educational leader for the school system and chief administrative officer of the entire school district's professional and support staff, including staff members assigned to provide support service to the board.
- To serve as a catalyst for the school system's administrative leadership team in proposing and implementing policy changes.
- To propose and institute a process for long-range and strategic planning that will engage the board and the community in positioning the school district for success in ensuing years.
- To keep all the board members informed about school operations and programs.
- To interpret the needs of the school system to the board.
- To present policy options along with specific recommendations to the board when circumstances require the board to adopt new policies or review existing ones.
- To develop and inform the board of administrative procedures needed to implement board policy.
- To develop a sound program of school/community relations in concert with the board.
- To oversee management of the district's day-to-day operations.
- To develop a description for the board of what constitutes effective leadership and management of public schools, taking into account that effective leadership and management are the result of effective governance and effective administration combined.
- To develop and carry out a plan for keeping the total professional and support staff informed about the mission, goals, and strategies of the school system and about the important roles all staff members play in realizing them.
- To ensure that professional development opportunities are available to all school system employees.
- To collaborate with other administrators through national and state professional associations, to inform state legislators, members of Congress, and all other appropriate state and federal officials of local concerns and issues.
- To ensure that the school system provides equal opportunity for all students.
- To evaluate personnel performance in harmony with district policy and to keep the board informed about such evaluations.

- To provide all board members with complete background information and a recommendation for school board action on each agenda item well in advance of each board meeting.
- To develop and implement a continuing plan for working with the news media.

CHAPTER

6 Successful School Leadership

Vignette: Failing Health at Atlas Shrug High School

You are in the second year of your first principalship at Atlas Shrug High School. Atlas Shrug has an enrollment of 1600 students and 65 full-time teachers. This old school has had a number of problems; you were brought in to take command. The new superintendent of the district has expressed concern about the school. The new superintendent has given you considerable freedom in determining how to turn Atlas Shrug around but has indicated that the school must be more responsive to student needs and the district's new reform agenda.

Recent standardized test scores indicate that the students, most from middle-class homes, are scoring slightly below the national and state averages. Only 52 percent are performing at or above grade level in mathematics and science, two areas of particular concern. The superintendent has noticed that a much higher percentage, over 65 percent of the students, receive A's and B's in their course work, and ninety percent earn C's or above. The teachers explain away these inconsistencies. One highly influential teacher states, "The tests do not measure the skills that we have traditionally believed to be important at Atlas Shrug. We have prepared students for a long while and know a lot more about these students and their parents than can be learned from any tests." In general there are few complaints from either the teachers or the community about Atlas Shrug High School.

Few improvements have been made in the school, and teachers often express concern at how difficult and traumatic it is to try anything new at Atlas Shrug. A number of innovative teachers have requested transfers. The new superintendent has charged the Office of Research to help the district gain a better understanding of the overall health of the schools within the district and their readiness for renewal efforts. The Research Office is beginning with the Organizational Health Instrument (OHI), developed by Dr. Marvin Fairman and associates (Fairman, et al., 1979; Hardage, 1978; Lucas, 1978; 1982; Johnston, 1988), to look into the critical dimensions of school health. The following ten dimensions focus on the preparedness and probable success of any improvement effort within the schools:

1. *Goal focus* measures the degree to which members of the organization clearly perceive and share system goals and objectives.
2. *Communication adequacy* refers to the extent to which information flows freely and without distortion, vertically and horizontally, within the organization.
3. *Optimal power equalization* relates to the distribution of influence between subordinates and superiors within the work group.
4. *Resource utilization* measures the extent to which resources within the organization, particularly personnel, are obtained and used effectively.

5. *Cohesiveness* measures the extent to which members of the organization feel attracted to and wish to remain with the organization.
6. *Morale* measures the degree to which members of the work group experience feelings of well-being, satisfaction, and pleasure in being part of the organization.
7. *Innovativeness* relates to the extent to which members of the work group believe the organization to be open, responsive, innovative, diverse, and supportive of creative thinking and risk taking.
8. *Autonomy* refers to the ability of the organization to deal with external pressure while maintaining its ideals and goals.
9. *Adaptation* relates to the degree to which the organization can tolerate stress and maintain stability while coping with the demands of and responses to the external environment.
10. *Problem-solving adequacy* measures the members' perceptions of the organization's ability to solve problems completely and efficiently.

The results were reported by dimension percentile score, a measure from 0 to 100 percent of the degree to which each characteristic exists in a school as compared with a normal set of schools (70 percent and above is an acceptable score). The results for Atlas Shrug High School are as follows:

Dimension	Percentile Score
Resource utilization	88
Goal focus	83
Problem-solving adequacy	80
Communication	74
Innovativeness	35
Cohesiveness	32
Autonomy	30
Morale	27
Adaptation	25
Optimal power equalization	17

"These can't be right!" responds Guy Francon, your assistant principal, who has been at the school more than seven years. The director of research assures Francon that the data were collected very carefully and have been double-checked and that these in fact are the perceptions of the teachers. Francon continues, "I don't mean that your figures are wrong but that the teachers are wrong. We are able to cope with external demands, the teachers do have influence, there are clear school expectations, and the morale is much higher than this shows. They say they want to be involved but they seem very passive and unwilling to put in the time. They seem satisfied with existing programs. Sometimes their recommendations are unacceptable, and we have to be accountable that good decisions have been made. After all, the administration is responsible for this school." The director of the research department explains, "The teachers' responses are not right or wrong. This is an expression of their perceptions of the school. If you don't think these perceptions are correct, it is important to find out why the teachers hold these perceptions. It is important that the profile is interpreted, along with other information regarding your school."

Other data suggest that very little change has taken place at Atlas Shrug High School over the past ten years. Test scores are still low, grade inflation is still high, teacher evaluations and development is uninspiring, curriculum and instruction have not changed, community involvement is limited, and although there have been few complaints, morale is not good. There is no spirit or responsiveness in this school. Although no one makes waves and there are not obvious problems, the school seems to lack energy or excitement, and, worst, it seems to produce mediocre results, with little being done to improve them. You begin to ask yourself, "What is wrong in this school?"

What might explain the wide range in the percentile scores on the ten dimensions of organization health?
Are teachers' perceptions of their organizations' health, ethos, and culture important? Why or why not?

Assessing Leadership Characteristics

Success in administration depends on one's overall leadership ability. Northhouse (1997) defines leadership as "a process whereby an individual influences a group of individuals to achieve a common goal" (p. 3). The National Policy Board for Educational Administration describes educational leadership as

> giving purpose and direction for individual and group processes; shaping a school culture and values; facilitating the development of a strategic plan and vision for the school; formulating goals and planning change efforts with staff; and setting priorities for the school in the context of community and district priorities and student and staff needs. (Matthews, 1994, p. 11)

An administrator's leadership to a large extent determines how successful his or her organization will be in delivering appropriate services and winning community support.

To better understand the literature and the field, let us begin by drawing distinctions between administration, management, and leadership. Although the meaning of these terms is often debated, there is some agreement that *administration* is the broadest term related to organizational responsibility, *management* focuses on efficient use of resources, and *leadership* focuses on organizational direction and purpose. Leadership is doing the right things, management is doing things right, and administration is responsible for both. Administrators are expected to be effective leaders and efficient managers.

Leadership concentrates on vision, the direction an organization should take. It draws others into the active pursuit of the strategic goals. Management focuses on the nuts and bolts of making the organization work, such as hiring, distributing resources, and enforcing policy and procedures (Hanson, 1991). Northhouse (1997) states, "management is about seeking order and stability; leadership is about seeking adaptive and constructive change" (p. 8). Researchers (Sergiovanni, 1991; Lewis & Miles, 1990; Cunningham, 1982) suggest that leadership relates to vision, mission, purpose, direction, and inspiration and management to implementing plans, arranging resources, coordinating effort, and generally seeing that things get done. You can have strong leaders who are weak managers and vice versa. Strong administrators are good at both, leadership and management.

Leadership, by far the most studied aspect of administrative behavior, is especially important because we have entered a time of transition. Reform in education is a continuous process of improvement to meet the needs of a dynamic society. Leadership in this new "era of change" requires the ability to envision an improved school and the spark to energize and lead staff to bring it about. Improvement requires perseverance, nurturance, and problem solving. Leaders must be entrepreneurial in the sense that they empower employees to meet new challenges.

What is effective leadership? What is the utility of the many different conceptualizations about leadership? How does a person want to operate in a leadership role, and how might he or she naturally behave in this role? Research has begun to provide a more complete knowledge base regarding effective leadership. Frederick W. Taylor (1947), often called the father of scientific management, is given credit for developing a scientific approach to the study of leadership. Since Taylor's day, many paradigms have been developed to make leadership more rational and therefore more understandable. In the last fifty years, thousands of studies have been completed on leadership. What follows is a brief review of some of the seminal works.

Are you, as principal of Shrug High School, serving more as a manager or a leader? On what basis did you draw this conclusion?

Paradigms of Leadership: A Growing Knowledge Base

A person brings a personal style to any administrative position that permeates all that he or she does within the organization and serves as the screen through which he or she views organizational activity. Style influences and is influenced by the way leaders view people, tasks, and organizations. These three factors have been extensively studied, discussed, written about, and taught to help leaders improve their style.

The qualities of leadership are similar whether your discipline is education, business, health, government, criminal justice, higher education, engineering, or any other field. Frederick Taylor's theories are classic examples of the scientific, postpositivist views of administration (see Chapter 1). This scientific management approach views people as interchangeable parts of a machine (the bureaucracy) and studies physiological aspects and organizational structure, such as time and motion, human engineering, policy, procedure, tasks, delegation, control, and specialization (Taylor, 1947; Weber, 1947; Fayol, 1949; Urwich, 1937). These ideas are all important, but today it is widely recognized that they are by no means an adequate explanation of organizational leadership and productivity.

Mary Parker Follett (1942) was among the first to critique the mechanistic interpretation of organizations and the disregard of the human factor in the structuralist approach to leadership (see Table 6.1). She was particularly concerned with the scientific belief that there is no place for debate, conflict, ambiguity, and perhaps chaos within organizations. Follett (1924) stated that these were "not necessarily a wasteful

TABLE 6.1   Benefits and Problems with Empirical Positivist Theory

Classical Theories	Benefits	Problems
Division of labor	Expertise	Boredom
Unity of command	One immediate supervisor	None
Hierarchy of authority	Disciplined coordination of power	Communication blocks
Operating procedures and regulations	Continuity and uniformity	Rigidity and lack of responsiveness
Standardization of tasks	Rationality	Lack of morale
Impersonal, objective orientation	Competition, incentive to produce	Conflict, lack of teamwork

Source: Hoy, W. & Miskel, C. (1991). *Educational Administration: Theory and Practice*. New York: McGraw-Hill. (Reproduced with permission of McGraw-Hill).

outbreak of incompatibilities, but a normal process by which socially valuable differences register themselves for the enrichment of all concerned" (p. 300). Her work was later to influence the critical feminist and postmodernist theories of leadership.

Follett and others' concern spawned the human relations and organizational behavior movement. The development of this movement is usually traced back to Elton Mayo and the studies completed in the Hawthorne plant of the Western Electric Company in Chicago (Roethlisberger & Dicksin, 1939). Perhaps the most important achievement of these findings was the tempering of the focus on organizational structure and the realization that the classical scientific theorists did not have all the answers.

Mayo's work directly challenged the concept that human beings could be viewed as passive cogs in a machine. One set of experiments held all other conditions constant and changed the frequency and duration of rest periods. The classic theories suggested that if people took more rests, the level of their output would go down because they would have less time to spend on the task. These experiments indicated, however, the actual productivity (output) of the employees went up when their rest pauses were increased. These puzzling findings later led to a number of other such discoveries that one by one established the importance of the study of organizational behavior. Behavioralism is concerned with psychological satisfaction, social interaction, motivation, job satisfaction, climate, ethos, group dynamics, interpersonal relations, empowerment, and organizational culture.

Which narrative principles—those of scientific management and scientific and structuralist theory; those of organizational behavior, human relations, and behavioralistic theory; those of values, ethics, and control; or those of broad fields and postmodernism—best describe the perceived qualities at Altas Shrug High School? On what basis did you draw this conclusion?

Leadership Instrument Analysis

Following are some of the most popular theories of leadership among educational administration practitioners along with some associated self-diagnostic instruments. Complete the instruments first, and analyze your results. Be advised, however, that conclusions based on the following type of leadership instrument analysis can be deceptive; people tend to record their intentions rather than their actual behavior (Blake & McCanse, 1991; Argyris & Schon, 1978). The purpose of instrument analysis is to lay the groundwork for people to initiate discussions about values and attitudes and to stimulate reflective thinking about behavior.

You might want to give colleagues the instruments and ask them to evaluate your leadership. Then discuss differences between their perceptions and yours. Discussions should include examples that support the responses you and colleagues provide, examples that frame behaviors first and then describe the effects of the behavior. This technique will help you see yourself as others see you while revealing how others view leadership.

McGregor's Theories X and Y

Douglas McGregor (1960) perceived an administrator's style as closely associated with his or her fundamental beliefs about human beings. He devised two contradictory views of human behavior, which he described as theory X and theory Y (Box 6.1). [Please respond to the X–Y scale presented in Box 6.1 to determine your X–Y beliefs about people (the scoring key appears in Appendix 6.A at the end of this chapter)]. Box 6.2 on page 158 presents the properties of X–Y belief patterns, which have been related to autocratic and democratic styles of leadership. The *autocratic style* is based on theory X assumptions in which leaders announce decisions, sell decisions, and invite questions about what is expected of others. In some cases they might even test their ideas to learn how subordinates will respond, in order to plan a strategy for forcing compliance. This approach relies heavily on the institutional authority of bureaucracy by carefully controlling the workforce, structuring the work, following standard operating procedures, emphasizing the importance of respect for positions of authority, threatening economic and professional harm to those who do not follow directives, and praising those who do. The leader is granted the power to force followership.

The *democratic style* is based on theory Y assumptions, in which leaders delegate authority and responsibility and permit subordinates to function within defined limits. This form of leadership is collaborative; it encourages team effort to narrow possibilities and make final decisions. Leadership based on theory Y beliefs structure organizations and use leadership to facilitate and support efforts of subordinates to develop and express themselves and to act in the best interests of the organization. Theory Y leaders emphasize self-control and development, motivate through encouragement and recognition of achievement, and expect quick response to and correction of any failures that occur (Tannenbaum & Schmidt, 1958). Organization members develop themselves and prepare for and accept ownership of their jobs. The

B O X **6.1**

The X–Y Scale

DIRECTIONS: As an administrator (manager, leader) you may engage in various types of behavior in relation to subordinates. Read each of the following items carefully, and then put a check mark in the appropriate column to indicate what you would do: 1 = make a great effort to do this, 2 = tend to do this, 3 = tend to avoid doing this, 4 = make a great effort to avoid this.

	1	2	3	4
1. Closely supervise my subordinates to get better work from them.				
2. Set the goals and objectives for my subordinates and sell them on the merits of my plans.				
3. Set up controls to ensure that my subordinates are getting the job done.				
4. Encourage my subordinates to set their own goals and objectives.				
5. Make sure that my subordinates' work is planned out for them.				
6. Check with my subordinates daily to see if they need any help.				
7. Step in as soon as reports indicate that the job is slipping.				
8. Push my people to meet schedules if necessary.				
9. Have frequent meetings to keep in touch with what is going on.				
10. Allow subordinates to make important decisions.				

The scoring instructions for the X–Y scale appear in Appendix 6.A at the end of this chapter.

leader shares power, provides evaluative data, develops staff, and expects continuous improvement.

Leadership style may, in fact, influence the behavior of subordinates in such a way that the subordinates' behavior actually supports the use of the leader's preferred style, becoming a self-fulfilling prophecy. Thus, the leader's assumptions about a person and the way he or she treats that person may actually create the behavior—the Pygmalion effect—rather than vice versa. Autocratic approaches actually cause individuals to move toward immature behaviors, and democratic approaches cause people to move toward

---

BOX **6.2**

McGregor's Two Major Belief Patterns

Theory X	Theory Y
1. People dislike and will avoid work if they can.	1. People find work as natural as play and prefer it to doing nothing.
2. People will shirk responsibility, are inherently lazy, lack creativity, and are unreliable, and therefore a leader must coerce, direct, and threaten them to make them work.	2. People are capable of self-direction and self-control; are naturally creative and, strive for excellence and therefore will make personal commitments to shared organizational goals.
3. People desire security, external direction, and rigid structuring; resist change and avoid responsibility; and have little ambition.	3. People seek and accept greater self-direction and new challenges and can be trusted with both authority and responsibility

(*Source:* McGregor, D. (1960). *The Human Side of Enterprise.* New York: McGraw-Hill.
(Reprinted with permission of McGraw-Hill.)

---

mature behaviors, whatever their initial starting points (Meyer, Kay, & French, 1965). Box 6.3 presents a continuum of immature and mature behaviors. Autocratic styles might actually trigger the lazy, indifferent, and intransigent reactions that are described as type X behaviors. Democratic leadership styles might motivate the more active, responsive, and self-directed approaches described as theory Y behaviors.

BOX **6.3**

Continuum of Immature and Mature Behaviors

(Type X) *Immaturity*		*Maturity* (Type Y)
Passive	_____	Active
Dependent	_____	Independent
Limited skills	_____	Diverse skills
Erratic, shallow interest	_____	Well supported, strong interests
Short-term perspective	_____	Long-term perspective
Unempowered, subordinate mentality	_____	Empowered, equal position
Lack of awareness of potential	_____	Awareness and control of self

Are the perceived behaviors at Atlas Shrug High School more related to Theory X or Theory Y beliefs?

The Ohio State Studies

Among the earliest of the vast research completed on leadership were the Ohio State Studies (Stogdill, 1974, 1981; Fleischman, 1953; Fleischman et al., 1956; Hemphil & Coons, 1950). These studies helped shift thinking away from a single-axis paradigm of leadership, often with democratic and autocratic at either ends of the continuum, to a two-dimensional paradigm of leadership that includes two continuums: consideration and initiating structure. *Consideration* includes behavior indicating mutual trust, respect, and a certain warmth and rapport between the administrator and the work group. This dimension appears to emphasize a deep concern for group members and their development. It stresses such behavior as participation in decision-making, encouraging communication, developing staff, supporting independent thinking, and keeping staff informed about the quality of their output.

Initiating structure includes behavior in which the supervisor organizes and defines group activities. The leader defines the role he or she expects each member to assume, assigns tasks, plans ahead, establishes work methods, pushes for improved productivity, emphasizes deadlines, encourages use of procedures, keeps staff informed of what is expected of them, and follows up to ensure that staff is working up to capacity. These two dimensions were found to be independent of one another; thus a person could operate in one of four different quadrants—high on both dimensions, low on both or high on one and low on the other. Previous research had suggested that these two approaches were opposed to one another on a single continuum, but Halpin and others showed how they were complementary in effective leadership approaches.

Well over one hundred studies of leadership have examined this model. The general findings suggest that consideration and initiating structure are positively related to various measures of group effectiveness, cohesiveness, and harmony. A leader who scores high on both of these dimensions would be considered more effective based on traditional values held by organizations. For example, Andrew Halpin (1956, 1966) completed a study of superintendents and found that the most effective were described as being high on both of these dimensions; Box 6.4 on page 160 presents a leadership behavior instrument based on this research. [Complete the instrument before you examine the scoring instructions, which appear in Appendix 6.B at the end of this chapter.] The most desirable approach to leadership, according to these researchers, is to stress both the importance of the individual and the importance of the task.

In which of the four quadrants defined by the Ohio State Studies do you believe the administration at Atlas Shrug High School would fall? Why? What benefits and what problems might this style cause?

BOX 6.4

Leadership Behavior Survey

Instructions: Place a check mark in the column that most closely describes your behavior in group activities. Scale: 5 = always, 4 = often, 3 = occasionally, 2 = seldom, 1 = never

Behavior	5	4	3	2	1
1. I make my attitude clear to the group					
2. I do personal favors for subordinates					
3. I try out my new ideas with the group					
4. I do little things to make it pleasant to be a member of the group					
5. I rule with an iron hand					
6. I am easy to understand					
7. I speak in a manner not to be questioned					
8. I find time to listen to subordinates					
9. I criticize poor work					
10. I mix with subordinates rather than keeping to myself					
11. I assign subordinates particular tasks					
12. I look out for the personal welfare of individuals in my group					
13. I schedule the work to be done					
14. I explain my action to subordinates					
15. I maintain definite standards of performance					
Column Total					

Behavior	5	4	3	2	1
16. I consult subordinates before taking action					
17. I emphasize the meeting of deadlines					
18. I back up subordinates in their actions					
19. I encourage the use of uniform procedures					
20. I treat all subordinates as equals					
21. I make sure that my part of the organization is understood					
22. I am willing to make changes					
23. I ask that subordinates follow standard rules and regulations					
24. I am friendly and approachable					
25. I let subordinates know what is expected of them					
26. I make subordinates feel at ease when talking with them					
27. I see to it that subordinates are working up to capacity					
28. I put suggestions made by my group into action					
29. I see to it that the work of subordinates is coordinated					
30. I get group approval in important matters before acting					
Column Total					

(*Source:* Halpin, A. *Theory and Research in Administration.* © 1966. Adapted by permission of Prentice Hall, Upper Saddle River, New Jersey.)

The New Managerial Grid

The managerial grid (Blake & Mouton, 1964, 1978; Blake & McCanse, 1991) is a two-dimensional model that closely resembles the one in the Ohio State Studies. The Grid, which was the popularized version, includes various phases of training to help leaders become proficient in both dimensions of leadership. For these researchers, initiating structure was a "concern for production" and consideration was a "concern for people." Blake and McCanse (1991) identified seven different leadership styles, which they believe encompassed all the most important differences among leaders. These styles are:

1. *Control and Dominate (Dictatorial).* A 9,1-oriented person demonstrates a high concern for results and a low concern for people. The resulting style is autocratic; the person comes across like a steamroller, pushing for results without considering how his or her behavior influences others. "People" concerns, such as benefits, training, flexible work hours, and career paths, are given a low priority. Human qualities of relationships are seen as issues that slow down or impede the main focus of achieving sound results. The 9,1 does not mean to attack people, but he or she truly believes this is the only way to get the job done—and "all that other stuff is frills, anyway" that distract people from working hard.

2. *Yield and Support (Accommodating).* The 1,9 person demonstrates a low concern for results with a high concern for others. The resulting style comes across as warm and friendly, but lacking in strength and purpose. This leader is the "nurturer" who is genuinely concerned about what people think and feel, and sees his or her role as generating enthusiasm and building morale rather than generating results. The 1,9 and 9,1 styles are diametrically opposed. While they both understand the difference in the two perspectives, they are unable to appreciate that these styles are equally harmful. Each of these orientations leads in a narrow and single-focused manner. The Achilles' heel in the 1,9 thinking is that "as long as I'm keeping people happy, results will follow." The evidence shows the opposite: Because there are never any serious consequences for poor performance, people respond by not really caring about personal or team effectiveness.

3. *Balance and Compromise (Status Quo).* The 5,5 style is located in the middle of the Grid figure with a medium level of concern for both results and people. Like the 9,1 and the 1,9, the 5,5 person believes there is an inherent contradiction between the two concerns. This contradiction is resolved by balancing the needs of people with results, through compromises and trade-offs rather than trying to achieve the soundest possible results. The objective is not to strive for excellence but to play it safe and work toward acceptable solutions. The 5,5 is often very informed, but his or her efforts are weakened by the objective of fitting in with popular trends. Information gathered is not used for challenging standards and searching for creative solutions but is used to reduce or suppress controversy.

4. *Evade and Elude (Indifferent).* The 1,1 indifferent evade and elude style, located in the lower left corner of the Grid, represents the lowest level of concern for both results and people. This is the least visible person in a team; he or she is a "follower" who maintains a distance from active involvement whenever possible. The key word for this style is *neutral*. Such a person goes through the motions of work rituals, doing enough to get by and rarely making a deliberate effort to do more. 1,1 survival is possible in structured workplaces where the boundaries of effort are clearly defined and communication is minimal. This sort of workplace allows the 1,1 to blend in without attracting attention. In fact, he or she often seeks work that can be done independently in order to carry on at a steady pace without being disturbed.

5. *Prescribe and Guide (Paternalistic).* The [1,9; 9,1] or paternalism style results from the coming together of two individual Grid styles in a way that produces a unique, joined style. Relationships with the paternalists are like parent to child where reward comes from the 1,9 influence and punishment comes from the 9,1 influence to dictate behaviors. The resulting style is a controlling and dominating person who also seeks approval and admiration. The paternalist holds himself or herself up to high standards of performance, and expects the same from others. A person who complies receives rewards in the form of praise, advantage, and benefits that is more characteristic of the 1,9 style. This person is still expected to maintain the high standards of performance, but receives more support, guidance, encouragement, forgiveness, and overall "help" from the paternalist along the way. A person who does not comply receives more of a 9,1 treatment as seen in increased scrutiny, "prove to me you are worthy of my support," and "this is for your own good" attitude regarding expectations for performance.

6. *Exploit and Manipulate (Opportunistic).* The opportunist is a person who uses whatever Grid style is needed to advance his or her personal goals. This person has little concern for what is best for others or the company and instead is driven by the ever-present question "What's in it for me?" The opportunist uses whatever Grid style is needed to help him or her along. The 1,9 is appealed to with 1,9 values, and the 9,1 is appealed to with 9,1 values. The opportunist succeeds by using and deceiving people in order to gain trust and support and move on. Since people learn fast, the opportunist cannot make a lasting impact without being exposed as self-serving. Opportunists operate best in short-term relationships where exposure is less likely, or in situations of unilateral authority where it doesn't matter what others think.

7. *Contribute and Commit (Sound).* The 9,9 demonstrates a high concern for both results and people. 9,9 leadership is based on examining "what's right" not "who's right?" The 9,9 leader rises above politics and fears to constantly evaluate actual effectiveness against standards of excellence. These leaders utilize feedback and criticism to develop shared understanding of objectives, learn from experience, and find ways to strengthen team performance. Every member is encouraged to contribute to and challenge ideas without fear of retaliation. This attitude of openness generates strong commitment to results because members feel a personal stake in outcomes. The candor present in 9,9 teams also builds a high degree of mutual trust and respect where people are not afraid to take risks and test the limits of creativity.

Blake and Mouton's and Blake and McCanse's findings are very similar to those of the Ohio State studies with the "contribute and committed" management style being positively associated with productivity, profitability, and success. Table 6.2 on page 164 discusses the various approaches used in these seven leadership styles. [Box 6.5 on pages 165–170 provides an instrument that can be used to suggest which of these seven management styles you would most naturally apply in practice. Complete this instrument and then check your responses using the scoring key in Appendix 6.C at the end of the chapter.] Research suggests that it is important to become a team-participation (contribute and committed) manager.

> Which of the Blake and Mouton and Blake and McCanse leadership styles should be used at Atlas Shrug High School in planning, organizing, activating, directing, and controlling? Why?

Situational and Contingency Leadership

Fiedler (1967) found that a leader's effectiveness in a given situation depends on the fit between his or her style and the task, authority level, and nature of the group. The interactions between these various combinations yield different results in different situations. A key condition is the maturity level of the followers. Immature followers need more structure; as maturity increases, they need less structure and more human-relations-oriented behavior. In the most favorable situation, relations between leader and followers are good, when tasks are well-defined and the leader is in a position of power.

Fred Fiedler and Martin Chemers (1974) suggested that leadership style is a fixed personality-based trait that no amount of training will modify. Their model assigns the "right" people to situations that best fit their style. These "leader match" models became known as contingency theories of leadership. Leadership is, to a large extent, determined by characteristics, such as power, that are vested more in the position than in the person and in the leader's personal ability to establish effective relations with appropriate people within the organization. Contingency theory suggests that both high- and low-power and control positions call for task-oriented leaders. Moderate power and control positions call for human-relationship-oriented styles (Fiedler & Garcia, 1987). These researchers expanded the study of leadership to include the qualities of the leader, the group, the task, and the situation.

Fiedler and Chemers maintain that one cannot change his or her style, but Hersey and Blanchard (1977, 1982) suggest that leaders are expected to readily modify their styles to cope with changes in the work environment. The situational style of leadership is influenced by the maturity and development level of the work group and the individual subordinates, and it varies from subordinate to subordinate. Situational theorists answer the question "What is excellent leadership?" with the reply "It depends."

Contingency and situational leadership theorists reject the conclusion that there is one best approach to leadership. They suggest that time available, task specificity, competence and maturity of the staff, need for involvement, and dynamics of the situation determine what style should be used. Other contextual factors include group size,

TABLE 6.2 Grid Styles Description Table

Grid Style	Integrated Level of Concern	Leadership Approach	Creates a Team Culture Where…
1. Control and dominate (Dictatorial)	Concern for results: High (9) Concern for people: Low (1)	I expect results and take control by clearly stating a course of action. I enforce results that support production and do not permit deviation.	Members are suppressed, hidden, and sullen. People become resentful and antagonistic and feel little motivation to do more than they are told. Tensions and low commitment are obvious.
2. Yield and support (Accommodating)	Concern for results: Low (1) Concern for people: High (9)	I support results that strengthen happy, warm relations. I generate enthusiasm by focusing on positive and pleasing aspects.	Members are complacent but also insecure and solicitous. People are friendly and accommodating as long as problems don't arise.
3. Balance and compromise (Status quo)	Concern for results: Medium (5) Concern for people: Medium (5)	I endorse results that are popular but caution against unnecessary risk taking. I test my opinions with others involved to ensure ongoing acceptability.	Members are accessible and outgoing but cautious and guarded when controversy arises. Creativity is inhibited by an overdependence on protocol, procedures, and bureaucracy.
4. Evade and elude (Indifferent)	Concern for results: Low (1) Concern for people: Low (1)	I distance myself from taking active responsibility for results to avoid getting entangled in problems. If forced, I take a passive or supportive position.	Members are apathetic and prefer working in isolation whenever possible. Members feel little or no personal commitment to results.
5. Prescribe and guide (Paternalistic)	Concern for results: 9 and 1 Concern for people: 1 and 9	I take control of results by defining initiatives for myself and others to take. I offer praise and appreciation for support and discourage challenges to my thinking.	Members are polarized by the favoritism in place. Favored members are not held up to the same high standards as others, which causes resentment, antagonism, and lower mutual trust and respect.
6. Exploit and manipulate (Opportunistic)	Concern for results: Inconsistent Concern for people: Inconsistent	I persuade others to support results that benefit me personally. If they also benefit others, that's even better in gaining support. I rely on whatever approach is needed to ensure collaboration.	Members operate independently with little to no mutual trust and respect. People resist sharing resources for fear of losing personal gain. Destructive competition is high.
7. Contribute and commit (Sound)	Concern for results: High Concern for people: High	I demonstrate my commitment to sound results by initiating team action. I explore all facts and alternative views to reach a shared understanding of the best solution.	Members demonstrate high levels of mutual trust and respect with each other, and creativity flourishes. Members feel high levels of commitment to results.

Source: Grid Style Description table, Copyright 1998 by Scientific Methods, Inc. Reproduced by permission.

BOX 6.5

Measuring Preferred Management Styles

Leader Behavior

Name _____   Date _____

The Managerial Grid

Please complete the attitude survey below before turning to Appendix 6.C for scoring instructions.

Instructions: For each of the statements below select the alternative (A or B) that is more characteristic of your attitude or actions. You are to distribute a total of 3 points across the two alternatives in each question according to your preference. If you would always choose A you would assign A 3 points and B 0 points. If you would most often select A but sometimes select B you would assign A 2 points and B 1 point. This same logic applies to selecting B. Indicate your answers in the spaces provided. Remember the responses to each question should total to 3.

1. When a subordinate disagrees, the executive should

    _____ A. shift to another position to maintain cooperation.

    _____ B. see to it the subordinate follows orders.

2. When an executive is planning an operation and gets some of the ideas from subordinates, the executive should include

    _____ A. the suggestions that are thought to be acceptable, remembering to thank all contributors for their interest.

    _____ B. all suggestions in some modified form, whether initially good or not.

3. When a subordinate presents a new idea that goes against the boss's convictions, the boss should

    _____ A. listen but reinforce the soundness of his or her own convictions.

    _____ B. let the subordinate know that the boss will solicit ideas when needed.

4. When direct reports are in conflict, an executive should

    _____ A. stand aside as far as possible unless he or she anticipates gaining personal benefit from a successful outcome when intervention is critical.

    _____ B. let them work it out alone; everyone should be responsible for himself or herself.

5. When a subordinate runs into trouble carrying out a job, the boss should

    _____ A. give support and encouragement; the subordinate should learn that the boss can be relied on.

    _____ B. work with the subordinate for a common understanding of the problem so that the difficulty can be corrected and eliminated in the future.

(continued)

Continued

6. The executive who gets best results is one who tells subordinates what is expected

    _____ A. and holds the line.

    _____ B. but realizes that since people are people, they won't be able to meet full expectations.

7. To keep within budget, the boss should

    _____ A. try to maintain a balance between cost considerations and meeting subordinates' desires.

    _____ B. continually remind subordinates of cost considerations and thank them for compliance.

8. When planning a new project not previously undertaken, an executive should

    _____ A. seek input from others before decision making while maintaining a vigilant attitude toward new information that might modify previous plans.

    _____ B. avoid making decisions until the positions of others are evident, then adopt plans that are likely to be supported and that also reflect favorably on his or her executive expertise.

9. When an executive and a subordinate disagree, the executive should

    _____ A. not force the issue unless it becomes a crisis.

    _____ B. bring the disagreement into the open and seek to resolve the subordinate's reservations to achieve understanding and agreement.

10. An executive who really understands people will plan a job by

    _____ A. giving subordinates the overall picture—encouraging them to handle the task in the way they would be most comfortable.

    _____ B. checking with each subordinate individually to get ideas and then pull these together to make a plan.

11. In planning the boss should

    _____ A. establish the plan but make a positive effort to see that subordinates embrace it in a positive manner.

    _____ B. solicit cooperation of subordinates to establish a plan that keeps work flowing at a level congruent with good feelings.

12. When promoting new ideas or procedures it is important to

    _____ A. gain in advance the support of those likely to embrace the ideas and circumvent those who might offer opposition.

    _____ B. help people accept that these ideas have been carefully thought through by those responsible to act in the best interests of the corporation.

13. An executive should recognize that if people try to do as little as possible

    _____ A. they should be pushed hard, even if it generates dissatisfaction.

    _____ B. there is not much that can be done about it except to live with it.

14. To get highest respect when reporting to a boss, a subordinate should relate

_____ A. matters that the boss needs to know in depth, whether things are going well or not.

_____ B. only things that are out of line and require direct action from the boss.

15. Executives should exercise control in such a way that

_____ A. subordinates are more or less on their own unless chronic problems becomes crises.

_____ B. detailed reporting is expected with expressions of approval for those who cooperate.

16. When making decisions that may be resisted by others, the executive should

_____ A. meet with those affected to gain their points of view; implementation can then be adjusted to accommodate dissenting opinions.

_____ B. let people know that in this give-and-take world their support on this issue will be repaid at a later time.

17. Production should be

_____ A. high even though it places demands on subordinates.

_____ B. whatever it takes to keep oneself out of trouble.

18. When a subordinate disagrees with the boss, the boss should listen to understand the

_____ A. points of agreement as well as disagreement; then reach a sound agreement with the subordinate to establish the best course toward the goal.

_____ B. points of disagreement, then after explanation persuade the subordinate that the boss's approach to the goal is sound.

19. When exercising authority, the boss should

_____ A. be direct but gracious, persuading doubters that those in higher positions have thought it through and know what is best for the organization.

_____ B. reach decisions by gaining the involvement of those who can contribute to quality of implementation.

20. When reviewing an operation that has a number of recurring problems, an executive should

_____ A. leave no stone unturned in getting to the bottom of a mistake and pinpointing the responsible party; then make clear that there is no room for any more mistakes.

_____ B. be cautious so as not to offend those whose future support might be critical; it is better to downplay problems than to create enemies who can undermine future operations.

21. A boss can avoid trouble by

_____ A. accepting, without comment, the work tempo subordinates set for themselves.

_____ B. asking subordinates to set their own work tempo in order to create positive feelings toward their job.

22. When dealing with a difficult colleague in a situation that might provoke conflict, it is

_____ A. more productive to avoid direct confrontation and to work around him or her.

_____ B. better to back off rather than to run the risk of creating hostile feelings.

(continued)

Continued

23. To promote best effort, important decisions should be developed

    _____ A. in a team made up of both the executive and subordinates to ensure coordination of effort.

    _____ B. on a one-to-one basis between executive and subordinates to ensure efficiency and accountability.

24. When asked for an opinion on a difficult matter, the executive should

    _____ A. review past practice or precedent in an effort to offer a tried-and-true position that accommodates different points of view.

    _____ B. avoid spontaneous reactions to gain more time to assess where others stand and what response is likely to engender their support for his or her position.

25. When a special assignment is given to a subordinate, the executive should

    _____ A. outline the job for completion within a predetermined time schedule and tolerate no deviations or excuses for failure to deliver.

    _____ B. assign the project a part at a time so that progress can be praised and the executive can introduce corrections as needed.

26. Where there is conflict, an executive should

    _____ A. offer to help to ease the disruptive tension.

    _____ B. not get involved if possible.

27. When a new project is to be undertaken, an executive should

    _____ A. gather the relevant information and seek ideas from those who will carry out the project.

    _____ B. analyze the facts and request recommendations from subordinates, then present a solution to subordinates, gaining their commitment to it by showing how the boss has taken their ideas into account.

28. When dealing with bosses on a high-stakes issue

    _____ A. it is important to find out what they want and to tailor one's actions and responses accordingly.

    _____ B. one should remain on the sidelines and let those in positions of authority make the final decisions.

29. When evaluating performance it is necessary for the executive to

    _____ A. keep a constant watch on subordinates in their own best interest to help them avoid repeating mistakes and errors.

    _____ B. offer praise for positive performance while withholding demoralizing criticism.

30. After a difficult job has been completed, an executive should

    _____ A. show appreciation by easing off to relieve whatever tensions may have been generated.

    _____ B. have plans made for the next job and move people on to it as fast as they finish the previous task.

31. The way to handle suggestions is to

_____ A. defer reacting to them, either positively or negatively, until your boss has evaluated them, then pass his or her reactions along to your subordinates.

_____ B. listen to them with a positive attitude and pass those on to your boss that imply no serious criticism; sit on the rest.

32. When approving training and development activities for subordinates, an executive should

_____ A. permit subordinates to choose the path they prefer since it is more likely to motivate them.

_____ B. encourage subordinates to move in directions that are likely to forward the executive's objectives.

33. When communicating with subordinates an executive should

_____ A. see that official information passes through organizational channels and use informal channels to communicate unofficial information.

_____ B. pass through organization channels what it is in the best interest of others to know and use informal channels to deal with the rest.

34. An effective way for a boss to handle mistakes and errors on the part of a subordinate is to

_____ A. get the mistake fixed by influencing third parties to put pressure on the erring subordinate.

_____ B. seek out the underlying causes for the problems and work with the appropriate parties to gain understanding and commitment to correction.

35. When planning, an executive should call in the people affected

_____ A. but let them arrive at their own plan, since they are more likely to follow it.

_____ B. and work with them until the best plan is devised.

36. Quality standards are

_____ A. a reflection of the boss's values, which team members are expected to embrace wholeheartedly.

_____ B. given tongue-in-cheek recognition; actions may not be consistent with words.

37. When an executive and a subordinate disagree on a decision, the executive should

_____ A. explain reasons for the decision and affirm apologetically that the decision must stand.

_____ B. tell the subordinate that the decision will stand.

38. When unable to resolve a disagreement with a subordinate's decision, the executive should

_____ A. disengage by tabling the discussion.

_____ B. make the decision and let the subordinate know that his or her acceptance of it is appreciated.

39. Effective coordination among subordinates can be achieved through

_____ A. actively engaging them in solving problems of work.

_____ B. letting them know that people come first.

(continued)

Continued

40. One way to spur performance of subordinates is to

_____ A. encourage competition among them to increase the effort of each.

_____ B. pressure individuals to put forth maximum effort.

41. In reviewing a subordinate's performance, an executive should realize

_____ A. that it is important for the subordinate to understand how he or she is performing.

_____ B. that since most formal appraisals are touchy and can lead to hard feelings, experience on the job is the best teacher for correcting poor performance.

42. When conducting a meeting an executive should

_____ A. listen to subordinates to gain their support, while reserving the right to make final decisions.

_____ B. see to it that decisions are based on shared understanding and agreement.

Source: An Evaluation of Organization Culture, Copyright 1991 Scientific Methods, Inc. Reproduced by permission.

rewards, leader status, method of appointment, and technical background. For each level of development among the workforce the leader should adopt a specific style of leadership; thus leaders demonstrate a strong degree of flexibility regarding approach.

Vroom and Yetton (1973) developed yet another relatively complex model for determining different situations and their relationship to subordinate participation in leadership. Decision making is on a continuum that runs from unilateral at one end to a shared model in which all group members participate in the decision at the other. Factors such as quality requirements, potential conflict, acceptance, information availability, and structure are used to determine which approach should be applied in a given situation.

Vroom and Jago (1988) presented a decision tree to help leaders determine the "best" approach under different combinations of circumstances. Ubben and Hughes (1997) expanded the factors involved and stressed the importance of time available as a consideration to leadership approach.

Yukl (1989) differentiated the situational approach on the basis of whether the requirement was for a "leader" or a "manager." In the capacity of leader a person needs an advanced repertoire of skills, and different skills are used in different situations. Participation of the workforce is important to the development of knowledge, skills, and a shared vision. Also important are gaining subordinate understanding and commitment and encouraging experimentation. In the capacity of a manager, that person is more directive, sending messages, establishing channels of command, and closely monitoring work. Followers comply with the perceived legitimacy of the leader to manage the organization. Yukl strongly argues that no single approach will suffice for all situations.

The formulas devised for matching these variables are not simple, and recent research has done little to support their credibility. Many argue that the nature of leadership does not vary with each situation. Critics of the situational model suggest that its unpredictable aspects provoke suspicion, distrust, deceit, and confusion. What contingency and situational approaches ignore is the Pygmalion effect—the power that expectations and treatment have on the behavior of others. People often become what their leader expects them to become. Berlew and Hall (1988) found that what higher-level managers expected of lower-level managers determined the lower-level managers' subsequent performance and success. These findings are corroborated by the work of Dr. Edward Deming, (discussed later in this chapter). In fact, task-oriented, production pusher styles seem to *create* immaturity, causing subordinates to be passive, dependent, subordinate, and unaware of self. A more balanced approach that focuses on tasks and people develops greater maturity, causing subordinates to be active, independent, more committed, persistent, aware, and focused. Another matter of concern is that leaders can create situations that demand their preferred styles. For example, a leader can place short time constraints on decisions to justify more autocratic approaches.

University of Michigan Studies

Another series of studies originated with Rensis Likert (1967) at the University of Michigan Social Research Center. He was able to identify the four types of leadership styles described below.

System 1 (Exploitative authoritative). Management does not trust subordinates, who are not free to discuss matters with supervisors and whose opinions are not sought in solving problems. Motivation comes from fears, threats, occasional rewards. Communication comes down from higher management. Goals are ordered from on high, where all decisions are made.

System 2 (Benevolent authoritative). Management and employees exist in a master–servant relationship. There is some involvement of employees; more rewards than in system 1; slightly better communications up. This is a paternalistic organization, not giving much latitude to employees to "do their thing."

System 3 (Consultative). Management controls things, but employees are consulted before solutions to problems and decisions are made by management. Communication upward is better, but is still cautious. Unpleasant or unfavorable information is not offered freely. Employees feel they will perform some roles in preliminary stages of decision making and policy setting but that their contributions may not always be taken seriously.

System 4 (Participative group). Management trusts employees, regards them as working willingly toward the achievement of organizational objectives. People are motivated by rewards and are involved at all levels in discussing and deciding issues that are important to them. Communication is quite accurate and goes up, down, and across. Goals are established with the participation of the people who will have to work to achieve them.

The ideal style was identified by Likert as system 4, the participative style, which was consistently associated with more effective performance. [Table 6.3 provides an instrument that can be used to determine which of the four styles is most characteristic

TABLE 6.3 Leadership Style That Is Most Characteristic within an Organization

Organizational Variable	1	2	3	4
How much confidence and trust does management place in subordinates?	Virtually none	Some	Substantial amount	A great deal
How free do subordinates feel to talk to superiors about the job?	Not very free	Somewhat free	Quite free	Very free
How often are subordinates' ideas sought and used constructively?	Seldom	Sometimes	Often	Very frequently
Is predominant use made of (1) fear, (2) threats, (3) punishments, (4) rewards, (5) involvement?	1, 2, 3, occasionally 4	4, some 3	4, some 3 and 5	5, 4, based on group
Where is responsibility felt for achieving organization's goals?	Mostly at top	Top and middle	At most levels	At all levels
How much cooperative teamwork exists?	Very little	Relatively little	Moderate amount	Great deal
What is the usual direction of information flow?	Downward	Mostly downward	Down and up	Down, up, and sideways
How is downward communication accepted?	With a great deal of suspicion	With some suspicion	With caution	With a receptive mind
How accurate is upward communication?	Usually inaccurate	Often inaccurate	Sometimes inaccurate	Almost never inaccurate
How well do superiors know problems faced by subordinates?	Not very well	Rather well	Quite well	Very well
Are subordinates involved in decisions related to their work?	Almost never	Occasionally consulted	Generally consulted	Fully involved
What does decision-making process contribute to motivation?	Not very much	Relatively little	Some contribution	Substantial contribution
How are organizational goals established?	Orders are issued	Orders are issued, some comments are invited	After discussion, by orders	By group action (except in crisis)
How much covert resistance to goals is present?	Strong resistance	Moderate resistance	Some resistance at times	Little or none
Is there an informal organization resisting the formal one?	Yes	Usually	Sometimes	No—same goals as formal
What are the cost, productivity, and other control data used for?	Policing, punishment	Reward and punishment	Reward, some self-guidance	Self-guidance, problem solving

Source: Likert, R. (1967). *The Human Organization: Its Management and Values.* New York: McGraw-Hill. Reproduced with permission of McGraw-Hill.

of an organization.] The University of Michigan studies complement the Ohio State Studies and those completed by Blake and Mouton and Blake and McCanse.

Which of the four systems from the University of Michigan studies of leadership styles best describes what is occurring at Atlas Shrug High School?

Leadership and the Change Process

MICHAEL FULLAN
University of Toronto

What makes the principal's role so critical in the change process stems from the conclusion that neither top-down nor bottom-up strategies are effective by themselves. It is only when bottom-up and top-down forces interact and are mediated in purposeful directions that improvement occurs. The principal is the one person ideally placed to play this mediating role.

It has always been said that the principal is key to change, but only recently has research given a detailed understanding of what that role means in practice. We set forth a rationale and framework for the role of the principal in our *What's Worth Fighting For* trilogy (Fullan, 1997; Fullan & Hargreaves, 1992; and Hargreaves & Fullan, 1998). I also illustrate the role in practice from the evaluation of the Chicago schools reform (Bender, Sebring, & Bryk, 1998).

We wrote *What's Worth Fight For* to provide principals and teachers guidelines for action to enable them to take greater control over the change process in a system that is fragmented and overloaded—one that places them in dependent positions. In the first book, *What's Worth Fighting For in the Principalship* (Fullan, 1997), we argued that the starting point for reform is not to hope for or wait for "systemic change" but to look for actions that we ourselves could take. We formed a number of guidelines for action for school principals such as:

■ Avoid "if only" statements, externalizing the blame and other forms of wishful thinking.

■ Practice fearlessness and other forms of risk taking.
■ Build a vision in relation to goals as well as change processes.

In the second book, *What's Worth Fighting for in Your School* (Fullan & Hargreaves, 1992), we widened the problem to focus on the culture of the school. We suggested there are at least four cultures in schools—individualized, balkanized, contrived collegiality, and collaborative. Only the last one really makes a difference in school improvement. Since the publication of that book our analysis has been confirmed precisely in Neuman and Wehlage's (1993) careful study of school restructuring in over 800 schools. All schools were engaged in reform, but some were especially successful in increasing student performance.

The three intraschool factors that distinguished the successful schools were (1) the existence of a professional learning community (none other than the collaborative culture), (2) continual review and refinement of instructional practice, and (3) evaluation of student progress. These professional communities constantly examined student work and achievement and revised their teaching accordingly. Neuman and Wehlage concluded, as we had, that the role of the principal was to foster and shape collaborative cultures that focus on student achievement using strategies that will accomplish that goal—focused professional development, organization of teaching, use

(continued)

Continued

of data, school improvement plans as a tool of developing new school cultures and the like. We said in short that "reculturing" (creating professional learning communities) was the main goal of principals and teachers.

In the third book, *What's Worth Fighting for Out There* (Hargreaves & Fullan, 1998), we extended the analysis even further to say that the context for schools has radically changed and that the "out there" in the form of community, technology, media, government policy, and so on, is now "in here." Therefore, the roles of principals (and teachers) are extended even further. They must in this new environment not only help contend with external forces, but also *form alliances* with many of them. We acknowledged that this was dangerous terrain, but that there were inevitable, indeed sound, reasons for "moving toward the danger." The reasons were inevitable because the outside forces were relentlessly in the school anyway and sound because the job could not be done in the absence of new partnerships with the outside. Our guidelines for principals included:

- Steer clear of false certainty (don't look for the silver bullet, but create your own change models drawing on external ideas).
- Respect those you wish to silence (learn new things from resistance).
- Move toward the danger in forming new alliances.

- Fight for lost causes (be hopeful when it counts).

Our analysis has been corroborated recently by the Chicago schools' reform evaluation. Bender, Sebring, and Bryk (1998) found that "the quality of the principal's leadership is a critical factor in determining whether a school moves forward to improve learning opportunities for students" (p. 1). More particularly they found that principals who are most effective (1) focus on student learning, (2) use support and pressure to enable others to act, and (3) attack incoherence through planning that provides continuity. Moreover, effective principals moved forward on two big issues: promoting stronger social ties between school staff and community and creating a viable professional community among the school staff (p. 5).

School leadership has never been more critical. It is essential in these complex times because of the need to mediate and integrate bottom-up with top-down forces. There will be tremendous turnover in teachers and principals over the next five to ten years. This will be a difficult time for new leaders, but also an enormously exciting period with a real opportunity to make a difference in the life of students, teachers, and parents.

Recent Theories of Leadership

The elusive concept of leadership can perhaps never be fully grasped, but knowledge of its properties carries one a long way toward being an effective leader. It is beyond the grasp of a single volume to be exhaustive, much less definitive. There is too much theoretical and empirical literature to cover in a survey of this subject; however, a number of studies provide the overall recent direction in the popular literature. Much of it builds on the studies already presented in this chapter.

To judge by the best-seller lists, there is a growing interest in the topic of leadership. The success of the twenty-six books of Peter Drucker (1954, 1974, 1980, 1992, 1998), a leading management and leadership philosopher, attests to the prominence of this subject. One of Drucker's (1992) works contains essays from leadership experts around the world. The book focuses on the importance of core values—integrity, respect, tenacity, curiosity, learning, standards, friendliness, resilience, convictions, and courage. Leaders need to respect diversity, see the potential in all employees, and communicate persuasively. Leaders must be high-energy, proactive change agents with a broad, inclusive viewpoint. They must model a commitment to continuous education and self-growth. They also must have advanced computer skills. Their organizations must place a strong emphasis on performance, accountability, and results, with a focus on the consumer.

Search for Excellence

Tom Peters and Robert H. Waterman's *In Search of Excellence* (1982) was the leadership and administrative book of the century based on marketplace success, with more than 5 million copies sold in fifteen languages. The sequels, *A Passion for Excellence* (1985), *Thriving on Chaos* (1987), *The Pursuit of Wow!* (1994), and *Circle of Innovation* (1997), have also done extremely well, although none has had the impact of the first book. The basic theme of this body of work is familiar—to succeed leaders must attend to both the hard and soft components of the organization (the tasks and the people). The eight attributes of successful leadership as described in these books are presented in Box 6.6.

Peters promotes the importance of organizations being responsive to customer needs and supporting experimentation, initiative, and risk taking to accomplish goals

---

BOX 6.6

Lessons from *In Search of Excellence*

1. *Bias for Action.* A preference for doing something—anything—rather than sending an idea through endless cycles of analyses and committee reports.
2. *Staying Close to the Customer.* Learning customer preferences and catering to them.
3. *Autonomy and Entrepreneurship.* Breaking the corporation into small companies and encouraging them to think independently and competitively.
4. *Productivity through People.* Creating in all employees the awareness that their best efforts are essential and that they will share in the rewards of the company's success.

5. *Hands-On, Value-Driven.* Insisting that executives keep in touch with the firm's essential business and promote a strong corporate culture.
6. *Stick to the Knitting.* Remaining with the businesses the company knows best.
7. *Simple Form, Lean Staff.* Few administrative layers, few people at the upper levels.
8. *Simultaneous Loose-Tight Properties.* Fostering a climate in which there is dedication to the central values of the company combined with tolerance for innovation from all employees who accept those values.

Source: Attributes of leadership as specified from *In Search of Excellence* by T. J. Peters and R. H. Waterman, Jr. Copyright © 1982 by J. J. Peters and R.H. Waterman, Jr. Reprinted by permission of HarperCollins.

and satisfy highly visible customers. Slogans like "ready, fire, aim" support the try-it-now, fail, learn, shift, interact, and modify approach to leadership. "Paralysis in analysis" suggests that emphasis on long-term planning be reduced so the organization can be more spontaneous in response to quickly evolving conditions. The research stresses the importance of rich, informal communication, open forums, management by walking around (MBWA), positive reinforcement, better listening, constancy of innovation, and responsiveness to customer and employees. Mistakes are always viewed as progress, although they must be identified and corrected quickly. The bedrock of Peters's message is listening, trust, respect, innovation, and whatever else results in "turned-on" and "in-touch" people. Leaders must love change (instead of fighting it) and instill and share an inspiring vision.

> Use the eight lessons from *In Search of Excellence* to describe an effective work culture for Atlas Shrug High School.

The Seven Habits of Highly Effective People

Stephen R. Covey's book *The Seven Habits of Highly Effective People*, (1989) is similar to the works of Peters in its homey approach and has been phenomenally well received. It was a best-seller for fourteen months. Covey described the seven habits of highly effective people as:

Habit 1: Be Proactive®. Take the initiative, responding and making things happen. Realize you have freedom to choose, be aware of self, develop knowledge and integrity in choices.

Habit 2: Begin with the End in Mind®. Start with an image or paradigm of the end in mind. Have a clear understanding of where you are going, where you are, and what it is going to take to get to the destination. Leadership comes first.

Habit 3: Put First Things First®. Practice effective self-management day in and day out. Discipline comes from within and is measured by personal integrity. All truly successful people make present decisions which help achieve desired outcomes Organize your time and tie weekly goals to your principles, priorities, and vision.

Habit 4: Think Win/Win®. Have a frame of mind that always seeks to have all parties feel as though they have won—the benefits to be mutually shared. All parties feel good about decisions made and are committed to the plan of action. Cooperation is the key.

Habit 5: Seek First to Understand, Then Be Understood®. Practice empathetic listening skills so that you understand other people from their frame of reference. Listen with not only ears, but with eyes and hearts. Then, present your ideas logically, clearly, specifically, and in the context of understanding the other person.

Habit 6: Synergize®. Create new alternatives. Leave your comfort zones to confront new and unknown challenges. Value differences, respect them, and use them to build on strengths. Discard old scripts, and write new ones. You are limited only by your own imagination. Develop unity and creativity with others. Unleash new powers, create new, exciting alternatives.

Habit 7: Sharpen the Saw®. Take time to preserve the most important asset—yourself. Take the time to minister to your own physical, mental, social/emotional, and spiritual needs. Leading people requires a tremendous amount of energy. Make a constant effort to manage health needs. Model good self-help techniques. Convince others that they are valued and should value others. Enjoy and celebrate accomplishment.

(*The Seven Habits of Highly Effective People* and the Seven Habits respectively are all registered trademarks of Franklin Covey Co. Used with permission.)

Excellence in organizations, according to Covey, grows out of a commitment to achieve a shared vision of an ideal state in a logical, systematic way. "Vision is the fundamental force that drives everything else in our lives. It empassions us with a sense of the unique contribution that's ours to make. It empowers us to put first things first, compasses ahead of clocks, people ahead of schedules and things" (Covey, Merrill and Merrill, 1994, p. 116).

Many researchers have identified core values, enduring purpose, and vision as the most distinguishing characteristics of the most successful organizations. Such organizations understand the difference between what should and what should never change. In discussing vision, Collins and Porras (1994) state,

> If you do this right, you will spend only a small percentage of your time articulating the vision. The vast majority of your time will be spent bringing the organization into alignment. Yes, it's very important to stop and think about vision. But even more important, you have to align the organization to preserve the core ideology and stimulate progress toward the envisioned future, not merely write a statement. Keep in mind that there is a big difference between being an organization with a vision statement and becoming a truly visionary organization. (pp. 238–239)

Successful organizations move toward visions and practices that reinforce their core ideologies and values.

Organizations build trust and collegiality, develop people and align them toward a shared vision, and then release their creative energies to work in cooperation and harmony to achieve desired results. Communication is at the heart of successful leadership and begins by understanding what others are saying through effective listening skills. Take time to understand others; it is far less than the time needed to back up and correct misunderstandings. Do not offer suggestions until you are completely clear on what the person you are talking to means. Present ideas clearly, specifically, visually, and most important contextually so that others can understand you and your beliefs and interest in the matter, knowing you have considered all facts and positions. Covey suggests, "Involve people in the problem, immerse them in it, so that they soak it in and feel it is their problem, and they tend to become an important part of the solution" (p. 280). Synergy naturally develops as people learn from each other, as they focus on creative alternatives, opportunities, and goals.

How might you use Covey's habits of highly effective people to improve the organizational health at Atlas Shrug High School?

The Learning Organization

The "learning organization" concept developed by Peter Senge (1990) is a generative process that enhances and extends an organization's ability to create. The concept of responsiveness is an important organizational behavior, but the real payoffs come from being generative. Clarify what is important by continually learning how to see the current reality more clearly and developing abilities to move beyond it. This new learned knowledge permeates the organization and gives coherence to diverse activities. A shared vision provides the focus and energy for learning and creates commitment (not compliance). Commitment to the vision fosters risk taking and experimentation. It is central to the daily work of those within the organization.

Vision grows out of opportunities to communicate, learn, experiment, be held accountable for results, and most of all to shape the future. Although this process can be chaotic, it most often "converges on a conclusion or course of action" (p. 247). Senge stresses the importance of having teams develop fluency in the language of systems thinking. The system provides the unifying principles that serve to integrate the diverse activity occurring within the organization. Successes in one classroom influence the entire system. Like Peters, Senge stresses the importance of being able to "forgive" and "forget" mistakes and knows how hard it is to provide the needed time to allow this process—understanding complexity, clarifying vision, and learning—to occur.

Max DePree (1989) believes that although it is clear that leaders draw their inspiration and spiritual reserve from their sense of stewardship, much of the leverage leaders actually have lies in helping people achieve more accurate, more insightful, and more empowering views of reality. According to DePree, success requires that employees feel needed, involved, cared for, and rewarded with fair wages and benefits. The DePree model respects the diversity of people's gifts, talents, and skills. People, relationships, information, and communication—not structures—build organizational effectiveness. "Information is power but it is pointless power if hoarded" (p. 104). Effective leaders help their employees to understand the systematic forces that shape change and to see current reality. Effective leaders instill the confidence in their employees that together "We can learn whatever we need to learn in order to achieve the results we truly desire" (Senge, 1990, p. 399).

What motivations will be needed to convert Atlas Shrug High School into a learning organization?

The New Science of Leadership

Margaret G. Wheatly (1992; Steinberger, 1995) suggests a fundamental shift in thinking in which leaders look for order rather than control in organization. Order is inherent in living systems. It does not evolve from avoiding different or disturbing information, smoothing turbulence, defining situations, standardizing approaches, writing procedures, and telling people what to do. Order is inherent—people naturally seek to make their conditions coherent. A small change can disturb and threaten order or equilibrium and result in chaos throughout a system. But even that chaos will act within specific parameters with order and predictability. Chaos has boundaries beyond which it will not go.

Disequilibrium creates growth, and under proper conditions the system will respond and evolve to a new, improved order. Successful organizations adapt and change and are free to interact with a turbulent, changing environment in such a way that it is open, free, and capable of responding and regenerating—a viable, living, adaptive, well-ordered organization. Successful organizations take advantage of the opportunities or possibilities for renewal and enhancement. Such opportunities involve longer, more thoughtful conversations, greater participation, more risk taking, more tolerance of mistakes, more openly shared information, more acceptance of chaos, more volatility of politics, and more effort toward figuring out what works and what doesn't. The foundation of leadership is a welcoming of diverse and rich viewpoints, inclusion of many different people in the process of thinking together in self-renewal, and continuous improvement.

Living systems pass through stages of chaos as they continuously improve themselves. Leaders often become wary of these periods of turbulence and clamp on controls, retreat, tune out information, and create rigid structure to calm the waters. Some administrators focus on holding all the pieces together and smoothing the political and ideological debate. Unfortunately this "circle the wagons" mentality short-circuits the learning and improvement process that is needed for success and excellence by cutting off the uncertainty, debate, disagreement, confusion, conflict, and other elements of chaos. Administrators who react this way stop the organization from learning, responding, and regenerating itself and force it back into equilibrium—the status quo. A principal, for example, seeing that test scores are falling, might abandon a new program and go back to simpler, more basic past standard practices to avoid the debate, concern, and confusion that result. "We'll go back to the basics in order to make sense out of all of this."

This effort to gain control cuts off learning and shuts down the natural, life-enhancing processes of responding and improving. The problem cited above might in fact be with the instructional strategy that worked for the old program but doesn't work for the new one. Organizations cannot become more fit in their present environments unless leaders are willing to risk the perils of the path through chaos which leads to knowledge, growth, order, and regeneration. Leaders help the system to reform, renew, reconfigure, and recreate itself to better suit the new demands and environment. Over time, people naturally organize the complexity they face and make it coherent and easy to understand. They use it as a foundation for future improvements. Dr. Rexford Brown, from the Education Commission of the States, is fond of saying,

Educational improvements will require new kinds of leadership. We need leaders to create conversations, to change the levels and kinds of discourse going on in and around schools, and to stimulate inquiry, questioning, problem solving, and a focus on learning for everyone in the system, not just students.... The primary conditions for this type of thoughtfulness are mystery, uncertainty, disagreement, importance, questions, ambiguity, and curiosity.

> Characterize what is happening at Atlas Shrug High School using Margaret Wheatley's theories regarding disequilibrium, chaos, order, and improvement. What needs to be happening?

Total Quality Management (TQM)

Advocates of total quality management (TQM) established a foothold in Japan in the 1950s and the effects of their philosophy have been growing and spreading ever since. The fundamental messages of TQM are to improve quality, serve the customer, satisfy customer requirements, encourage employee innovation, provide for the free flow of information, attack the system (not the employees), instill pride and teamwork, and create an atmosphere of innovation and continuous improvement. Henry Mintzberg (1987) argues that organizational success is less a rational plan than an "emergent phenomenon." Successful organizations "craft strategy" according to Mintzberg, as they continually learn about shifting conditions and inclusively determine "what is desired" and "what is possible." The job of leader is to create and improve the system so that more is possible. The potential for continuous improvement lies with the staff. It evolves from their work.

Edward Deming (1986, 1991, 1993), the father of TQM, stated, "workers are responsible for only 15 percent of the problems, the system for the other 85 percent." He then added that the system is the responsibility of management. The heart of Deming's approach to improving the organization is teamwork and collaboration among managers and workers. The leader provides core values, consistency of purpose, information, support, training, integration, common language, continuing feedback, improved systems, alignment, integrity, time, trust, and resources. Employees are responsible for improving themselves and the work process in such a way that the outcomes of the organization continuously improve.

Individual performance appraisals and merit raises are eliminated (they ruin morale and force workers to kiss up to bosses), and work team performance is evaluated and rewarded instead. Other TQM tenets include eliminating numerical goals, tearing down walls between work groups, and sharing information; reducing or eliminating micromanaging; and letting work teams tackle the inefficiencies and outcome problems. Matrix teams draw workers from several departments to study something in addition to their regular work; project teams pull workers for temporary work on a project; process teams look into the way work is being completed; and vertical teams take a diagonal slice through the organization so as to include people at different levels to create organizational vision and expand abilities. Regardless of the type of team, the members work together to develop one another and thus the organization.

TQM applied to education includes commitment to aims and purpose, a shared common vision; accountability and testing designed to improve and reduce costs; continuous improvement of schools; developmental plans and training for all employees; and, the development of leadership and pride in what employees do. Fear is eliminated so that people feel free to ask questions, take a stand, make suggestions, experiment, and take risks. Leaders must build the culture within the organization to support the needed transformation.

In describing what TQM leadership in schools is all about, Sagor and Barnett (1994) suggest,

> strategic planning is never complete. Plans should constantly be updated as new data from school profiles reflect both new accomplishments and new targets. Each new advance produced as a result of staff development becomes an opportunity to open up new vistas or professional growth opportunities, and each outcome target achieved must be viewed as a plateau offering firm ground from which to mount the next initiative.... The first is developing and/or strengthening a set of cultural norms—specifically focusing on the customer, holding high expectations, using data to make decisions, and valuing collaborative work. Once these cultural changes have been accomplished, the leader will not feel that the work is done. Rather, once the tradition and expectation of continuous improvement have been institutionalized in a school, then the leader will find his or her role transformed. (p. 146)

The focus of everyone's work in the TQM model is excellent, quick, high-quality, and flawless service. The Malcolm Baldridge National Quality Award criteria are one approach that has claimed to incorporate many of these ideas. This system stresses improved outcomes, cooperation, teamwork, efficiency, productivity, and involved, informed, motivated staff. Quality improvement is the goal of every single individual within the organization. Deming provides a number of statistical models and theories to organize and present information in order to improve and streamline communication:

Tools for Quality Improvement

Action plan	Force field analysis
Block diagram	Graphs: bar, line, pie
Brainstorming	Histogram
Cause and effect analysis	Interviewing
Checklist	Pareto diagram
Consensus	Problem selection matrix
Control charts	Problem statement matrix
Cost estimation	Quality indicators
Cultivating	QIC review form
Customer needs analysis	Requirements solution selection matrix
Customer/Supplier model data gathering	Stratification
Fishbone diagram	Target and goals
Flowchart	Team project planning worksheet

Graph the percentile scores on the ten dimensions of organizational health for Atlas Shrug, using a bar graph. How might this graphical representation of the data help?

School-Based Management (SBM)

School-based or site-based leadership follows many of the same principles as total quality leadership. It empowers staff to create conditions in schools that facilitate improvement, innovation, and continuous professional growth (David, 1989). It gives the school principal and professional staff members the widest possible latitude in sustaining efforts to continuously improve the effectiveness of the teaching and learning process. Teachers would be encouraged to introduce improvements that directly affect teaching and learning and that require genuine authority over budget, personnel, curriculum, instruction, and program evaluations. The factors that affect the success consideration of this decentralized approach are the provision of opportunities for professional development and training, adequate information to make informed decisions, the institution of a reward system to recognize improved performance, and the allotment of enough time to each person to participate in shared planning and development (Odden & Wohlstetter, 1994; Gauber, 1992).

Site councils and subcommittees within schools are used to disperse power to a broader range of stakeholders. Participants have access to new knowledge and skills on a routine and ongoing basis. Information is disseminated broadly to both the schools and the community and time is provided to meet and discuss the information. This approach intensifies the need for effective leadership from the principal and others serving in leadership roles. Principals must be strong supporters of their staffs as the people who introduce innovation and move the reform agenda forward. They are constantly involved in outreach efforts, development, facilitation, support, and infrastructure. Whether SBM or TQM actually works in schools is a still unanswered question. Preliminary study by Murphy (1995) suggests that the answer may be no. Others suggest that when these two approaches are implemented correctly they are successful.

The probability of success is increased when school staff are provided guidelines and have time to acquire new knowledge and skills, to discuss and share ideas, and to formulate, implement, and evaluate ideas to improve student learning (Cunningham & Gresso, 1993). Participants are rewarded for the progress they make toward the shared goals and vision. Rewards include extra compensation for defined responsibilities, money for professional development, money for materials, reimbursements for extra time expended, stipends for council membership, and nonmonetary benefits such as notes of appreciation, recognition meals and banquets, plaques, public recognition, reduced teaching loads, and prestige of leadership. Often the process requires some kind of waiver from district authority, state rules, and collective bargaining agreements to be effective. Schools that have been provided these kinds of waivers from state and local policies are often called "charter" schools. The school charter sets out its unique character and defines its mission, policy, priorities, and standards and ultimately describes the school's program and practices.

> Would a school-based management approach work at Atlas Shrug High School? Why or why not?

Cultural Leadership

Schein (1985) suggests that the most important thing that leaders do is help shape an effective culture in which people will complete their work. He talks about shared beliefs that define basic views of an organization and its environment. He contends that culture, "influences the ways in which group members perceive, think, and feel about the world thereby serving to stabilize that world, give meaning to it, and thereby reduce the anxiety that would result if we did not know how to categorize and respond to the environment" (p. 312). In fact, culture is often defined as "the way we do things around here." Deal and Kennedy (1982) suggest that culture gives meaning to work, providing an understanding of how the organization moves from values and outcomes to work performance and finally to actual results. It is the internal system of organizational integration. Lee G. Bolman and Terrence E. Deal (1991) believe that:

> Culture is both product and process. As product, it embodies the accumulated wisdom of those who were members before we came. As process, it is continually renewed and re-created and new members are taught the old ways and eventually become teachers themselves.
>
> …Our view is that every organization develops distinctive beliefs and patterns over time. Many of these patterns and assumptions are unconscious or taken for granted. They are reflected in myths, fairy tales, stories, rituals, ceremonies, and other symbolic forms. Managers who understand the power of symbols have a better chance of influencing organizations than do those who focus only on other frames. (p. 231)

They go on to say, "Beliefs, values, practices, and artifacts define for…members who they are and how they do things" (p. 250).

Our culture is important because it shapes the different ways we recognize and react to events, gives meaning and purpose to our work, and unites people (Deal & Peterson, 1998). According to Deal and Kennedy, the goal of leadership is to make something as ill-defined as culture work for leaders and for the improvement of educational performance. New ideas and genuine improvement may be elusive unless we address the culture that underlies the operation of the school.

A number of studies (Sashkin & Walberg, 1993) of the best schools provide strategies and tactics that are useful in developing the sorts of cultures that will help to produce positive student outcomes. Cunningham and Gresso (1993) found that successful schools seem to have strong functional cultures aligned with a vision of excellence in schooling. This culture steers people in a common direction, provides a set of norms that defines what people accomplish and how, and provides a source of meaning and significance for teachers, students, administrators, and others as they work. These strong cultures are nurtured and built by the school leadership and membership. Cunningham and Gresso (1993, pp. 267–268) found that the most effective school district culture was not based on "command and control" but on school "facilitation and support" sustained by the following key elements:

- a focus on changes that positively influence what happens to students
- collegiality, trust, integrity, and sufficient time for open, free-flowing communication
- an explicit, mutually shared, concrete vision of the ideal school
- a climate of mutual support, growth, and innovation
- a three- to seven-year prospective for improvement
- face-to-face involvement of appropriate stakeholders
- decisions based on values, interest, and expertise
- continuous improvement that is incremental and systematic
- staff development, character, and skill as the essential components to school improvement
- cooperation among home, school, and community
- empowerment and encouragement of staff to experiment, innovate, and share successes
- constant monitoring and feedback of results
- central administrative support of individual school efforts

These cultural elements help leaders to achieve the continuing educational excellence being called for in almost every segment of U.S. society (Schein, 1991; Sarason, 1996; Sashkin & Walberg, 1993). Schools that develop these characteristics have received national and state awards for excellence (e.g., Magna Award, Governor's Choice Outstanding School Award). Of all the elements of school culture, Starratt (1995) stresses the importance of vision. "What is needed even more is a leadership of substance—a leadership of ideas, of vision, of commitment to deeply held human values that can be translated into farsighted educational programs and human institutional structures" (pp. 10–11). The vision provides the foundation by which the institution can be transformed. This transformation requires commitment, planning, courage, support, and reflection.

Bennis (1983) found that culture can give an organization transformative power to continuously improve itself. Bennis states,

> In sum, the transformative power of leadership stems less from ingeniously crafted organizational structures, carefully constructed management designs and controls, elegantly rationalized planning formats, or skillfully articulated leadership tactics. Rather, it is the ability of the leader to reach the souls of others in a fashion which raises human consciousness, builds meanings, and inspires human intent that is the source of power. Within transformative leadership, therefore, it is vision, purposes, beliefs, and other aspects of organizational culture that are of prime importance. (p. 70)

Bolman and Deal (1995) stressed this theme when they identified courage, spirit, and hope as the enduring elements of leadership. This is the heart of leadership. Leaders put the organization in touch with what gives it passion, purpose, and meaning. They discovered that

> Heart, hope, and faith, rooted in soul and spirit, are necessary for today's managers to become tomorrow's leaders, for today's sterile bureaucracies to become tomorrow's communities of meaning and for our society to rediscover its ethical and spiritual center. Leading with soul requires giving gifts from the heart that breathe spirit and passion into your life and organization. Seek new sources of vigor, meaning, and hope to enrich your life and leave a better legacy for those who come after you. (p. 12)

How would you characterize the organizational culture at Atlas Shrug High School? What characteristics of the organization are having a positive impact? What characteristics are having a negative impact?

Transformational Leadership

Burns (1978) proposed "transactional" and "transformational" leadership. "Transactional" leadership is based on defining needs, assigning clear tasks, rewarding congruent behavior, and having a command-and-control mentality. Followers are willing to trust the leader because they need to have problems solved and they believe the leader can solve them. "Transformational" leaders develop followers, help map new directions, mobilize resources, facilitate and support employees, and respond to organizational challenges. They see change as necessary and strive to cause it. In describing transformational leaders, Burns concluded, "Leaders engage with followers but from higher levels of morality; in the enmeshing of goals and values, both leaders and followers are raised to more principled levels of judgment.... Much of this kind of elevating leadership asks from followers rather than merely promising them goods" (p. 455).

Transformational leaders create the incentives for people to continuously improve their practices and, thus, those of the organization. Although the idea of transformational leadership was proposed by Burns (1978), Kenneth Leithwood (1992; 1999; Leithwood, Steinbach, & Raun, 1993) and his colleagues have added greatly to our understanding of it and have examined the benefits of this approach to school reform. According to these researchers, transformational school leaders are in continuous pursuit of three fundamental goals:

1. Helping staff members develop and maintain a collaborative, professional school culture,
2. Fostering teacher development, and
3. Helping teachers solve problems together more effectively.

Transformational leaders provide the mechanisms by which solutions are transferred into subsequent practice by building the capacity of the individuals and the group.

Transformational leadership is a process to shape and elevate goals and abilities so as to achieve significant improvements through common interests and collective actions (Bennis & Nanus, 1985). Successful leaders expend extraordinary efforts to achieve goals through:

Vision—knowing your desired outcomes and methods of achievement through lots of idea development and the creation of vision.

Communication—expressing your ideas through various forms of presentation, including symbolic actions and shared meaning.

Trust—being predictable, accountable, persistent, and reliable and having integrity.

Deployment—knowing and nurturing of strengths, compensating for weaknesses, evaluating in relation to job requirements, and focusing on positive goals not problems.

Transformational leaders ensure the existence of collaborative goal setting, shared power and responsibility, continued professional growth, resolved discrepancies, teamwork, engagement in new activities, a broad range of perspectives, validated assumptions, periodic reflection, monitored progress, and intervention when process stalls. School personnel are inspired to rise above self-interest goals, make commitments to continuously improve student learning, and take responsibility for instructional innovation. Bill Gates, chairman and CEO of Microsoft Corporations states, "People like to have a sense of purpose, to feel that they're doing something unique and to actually see the impact their work is having." Effective leaders encourage experimentation and risk taking to meet the challenges posed by changing social conditions. The research on transformational leadership is limited but uniformly supportive of this approach as being effective in school leadership (Leithwood, 1992). Studies by Blase (1990) and Thurston, Clift, and Schacht (1993) support transformational leadership as an effective approach for the school principalship.

The Reflective Practitioner

Schon (1983) and Sergiovanni (1992a; 1992b; Brandt, 1992) stress the importance of basing practice on findings and principles that emerge from theory and research. Effective leaders use knowledge from many sources to inform and guide their actions and those of their subordinates. This information does not prescribe practice, but it does provide the impetus for important discussion, action, and ultimately school success. Leaders pay close attention to theory, research, and successful practice in order to enhance judgment and improve the quality of decision making. Reflective practice means staying abreast of the latest research in practice, researching your own practice, experimenting with new approaches, reflecting on your own approach, and sharing your insights. Nonreflective leaders, by contrast, are so busy focusing on tasks and solving problems that they seldom give thought to their personal development or that of the organization. Effective schools have to do with what teachers and other school employees know and what they believe, their commitment to excellence, their sense of professionalism and pride, their ownership of the work, and the intrinsic satisfaction they derive from the work.

Effective leaders help to develop and support a commitment of exemplary practice among the staff. The ideas that exist within the organization are key, and therefore the leader must work to help shape those ideas by what has been successful in the past and what might be successful in the future. Principals must work with the staff to develop a set of conceptions that become an ideal structure for their schools. In this way, the principal develops instructional leadership capacity among teachers. Teachers accept responsibility for their own professional and personal growth and the continuous improvement of the school. They care about what happens in their classroom and in the entire school and school district as well. Such teachers are reading research, working together, debating about goals and purposes, coordinating lessons, observing and critiquing each other's work, sharing successes, and offering solace. The whole of reflective practitioners' collective efforts is far greater than the sum of each person's accomplishments (Johnson, 1990, p. 148).

Principals as Instructional Leaders: Modeling and Supporting Teaching and Learning

PAUL V. BREDESON
University of Wisconsin–Madison

Principals' workdays are characterized by role overload, role uncertainty, and fragmentation, which manifest themselves in literally hundreds of brief, at times highly charged, social interactions. Given the nature of schools and professional work in them, highly successful principals have learned to be selective in their professional work, balancing what others expect them to do (role taking) with their own work priorities and goals as educational leaders (role making). Thus effective leadership requires balancing many conflicting activities and responsibilities. Through their work, principals create, nurture, and sustain successful and healthy teaching and learning environments for teachers as well as students. The principal's primary role is in modeling and supporting the learning of others, the essence of instructional leadership.

Play the Ball

From the sidelines, a softball coach yells advice to the players on the field. "Play the ball. Don't let the ball play you." In other words, the players need to make the plays, not let the ball determine how they should move or play the game. This advice is as useful on the ball field as it is for principals in schools. Like players facing a number of possibilities to field balls, principals daily face countless events, some predictable, others not. What's important is that principals use their expert knowledge and skills in ways that support the primary teaching and learning goals. On a daily basis principals must deal with sick children, conflicts among staff, student discipline problems, unexpected visits by parents, telephone calls, piles of paperwork, emergencies, central office meetings, bus and cafeteria duties, and student records. In addition, let's not forget about instruction, curriculum, staff development, and school improvement initiatives. The sheer number of activities can overwhelm even the most experienced principal.

To cope, successful principals keep in mind the big picture, nurturing and supporting a healthy and successful teaching and learning environment, while simultaneously attending to

(continued)

Continued

the details of all of their administrative responsibilities. Principals influence student learning outcomes directly and indirectly by what they do, what they believe, and how they use symbols. By viewing their work through the lens of instructional leadership, principals "play the ball," knowing that what they do has the potential to ripple across the school, amplifying its effect on teaching and learning processes and on student and organizational outcomes.

Instructional Leadership in Action

For principals, keeping the focus on teaching and learning is more than the application of technical knowledge and expertise. How principals choose to spend their time, what they do substantively and symbolically, and what they believe are steeped in values, intentions, and understandings about teaching, learning, and educational outcomes for children. The fact that principals pay attention to some things in schools while ignoring or deemphasizing others infuses the continuous stream of actions, substantive and symbolic, with clarity, consensus, and commitment to what's important, in teaching and learning. Ordinary routines become expressions of values and purpose.

To illustrate how principals' behavior, values, and purposes come together, let's examine one common instructional leadership behavior: principals' visits to classrooms. For instructional leaders, classroom visits are more than opportunities to monitor teacher work. They become occasions for principals to clarify the primary mission of the school (teaching and learning), validate this mission for others (students, teachers, and parents), engender excitement and high expectations for teaching and learning, and infuse the daily routines of students, teachers, and support staff with meaning and significance.

Principals as Teachers and Learners

In addition to exercising their influence as instructional leaders on teaching and learning, principals are themselves teachers and learners. "Principals as teachers need not be omniscient paragons of pedagogy. Rather, they are coaches and facilitators who help students, teachers, and other staff understand the mental models and

basic assumptions about teaching and learning in particular schools and communities" (Hart & Bredeson, 1996, p. 137). Principals are also learners.

As Edgar Schein (1985) reminds us in his discussion of leadership and organizational culture, if you want to know what's important and valued in a school, watch what the principal pays attention to and does, rather than what he or she *says* is important. For example, principals who greet staff at the beginning of a planned in-service and then give their apologies for not staying because they have other work to do send a clear, albeit negative, message regarding the use of time and learning. If learning is important in a school, the principal will model the behaviors of an active learner. Principals who read broadly and remain knowledgeable in their fields, who participate actively in professional development opportunities, and who see their own learning as an important part of their professional work are modeling the beliefs and behaviors they espouse for others in schools.

Challenges for Instructional Leaders

Many challenges await principals as instructional leaders in the twenty-first century. Here I describe three in particular. The first centers on clarifying and articulating the values and principles that will guide you as an instructional leader. Values shape and inform your thinking, while at the same time serving as guides to action. Understanding and being committed to the values will guide you and your school colleagues as you work together to meet such challenges as inclusive education for children with disabilities, charter school competition, new state and national curriculum standards, public school choice, and bilingual education, to name a few.

A second challenge for principals in the future will be to determine work priorities. As described earlier in this piece, there is no shortage of activity and responsibility for principals. There will always be unexpected and routine tasks that need to be carried out. The question is whether you as leader let the flow of events and activities define you as an instructional leader or whether your values and beliefs about teaching and learning set the tone and substance of your work. Finally, principals as instructional leaders are confronted with the perennial paradox of continuity and change. The certainty of change may be the most predictable factor in your future work, yet the certainty of change brings anxiety and ambiguity. As an instructional leader you will be challenged to promote change and at the same time preserve and celebrate the successes of the present.

Leadership Traits or Skills

The study of leadership traits and skills that emerged in the second half of the 1980s represents an important departure from the theoretical perspectives. The driving forces behind it were many and diverse (Murphy, 1993), including practitioners, professors, commissions, professional associations, and legislatures. Perhaps one of its defining moments was a highly influential address entitled "Leaders for American Schools" given by Daniel E. Griffiths at the 1987 annual conference of the American Educational Research Association (AERA). Dr. Griffiths provided a comprehensive analysis of the qualities required in school leaders. Around the same time, the National Association of Secondary School Principals (NASSP) under Dr. Paul Hersey had identified twelve skills that were used in their Principal Assessment Center for principal selection and development. The American Association of School Administrators published guidelines for administrators in 1983, which became standards in 1993. A number of other professional associations also looked into the skills of effective school leadership (NAESP, AACTE, NCEEA, UCEA, ASCD, and NCATE).

Patrick Forsyth, executive director of the University Council of Educational Administrators (UCEA), worked to develop the National Policy Board of Educational Administration (NPBEA). The NPBEA, created in 1988 under the leadership of David L. Clark, forged a union among ten groups interested in school administration. In 1993, the NPBEA, with its new executive director, Dr. Scott Thompson, published *Principals for Our Changing Schools: Knowledge and Skill Base*, which was written by a number of teams under the direction of Wayne K. Hoy.

Yukl (1989) identified a number of skills associated with successful leadership—intelligence, creativity, diplomacy, fluency, knowledge, organization, persuasiveness, and sociability. The early 1990s produced more than fifteen different widely accepted lists of leadership skills, including one from each of the different professional associations. In 1994, Dr. Joseph Matthews, working in conjunction with the NPBEA, completed an analysis of seven frameworks of educational leadership, combining all the domains into a revised list of twenty-one (revisions of the National Policy Board domains), which are presented in Appendix 6.D. As discussed in Chapter 1, the Interstate School Leadership License Consortium (ISLLC) crafted standards (see Box 1.1 on page 24) in 1996, which have been the model most states have used in developing administrative endorsement and licensure requirements.

Other major efforts to provide direction for educational leaders include *The Handbook of Research on Educational Administration* (Boyan, 1988; Murphy & Lewis, 1999), *Educational Leadership and Changing Contexts of Families, Communities and Schools* (Mitchell & Cunningham, 1990), and *Cognitive Perspectives on Educational Leadership*

(Hallinger, Leithwood, & Murphy, 1994). The knowledge base in educational administration has reached a point at which it is sufficiently developed that it complements studies from other disciplines as it provides greater understanding of the intricacies of school administration.

Conclusion

The complex process of leadership enables people to realize their full potential and that of the organization. The creation of the ideal twenty-first-century school will ultimately depend on the staff's ability to visualize it and to work toward it. It is the leader, however, who is responsible for inspiring, developing, coordinating, and assessing staff efforts. Leaders must have integrity, honesty, trust, "can-do" spirit, personal accountability, respect for all people, and openness to change. McFarland, Senn, and Childress (1993) suggest,

> The difference between those who gain mastery and those who simply dream of a vision is their commitment to action…making a difference through finding ways to improve our family life, our organizations, our education system, our economy, our urban life, our environment—the entire array of possibilities for building a healthy twenty-first-century society. (p. 344)

The call to duty is a challenging one: providing better futures for students, overhauling outdated systems, knocking down barriers, altering culture, broadening leadership, and developing highly effective schools. The decades ahead will offer many new challenges and opportunities and require what Michael Fullan (1991) calls "a new ethos of innovation." He states,

> It is time to produce results. Individual and institutional renewal, separately and together, should become our *raison d'être*. We need to replace negativism and Pollyanna-ish rhetoric with informed action. Armed with knowledge of the change process, and a commitment to action, we should accept nothing less than positive results on a massive scale—at both the individual and organizational levels. (p. 354)

We owe it to our teachers, students, and communities to develop and use the latest knowledge and skills to be excellent leaders of excellent schools.

Effective leadership has a long tradition of research and successfully integrated ideas. Many luminaries (Griffiths, 1959, 1989; Halprin, 1958; Knezevich, 1975; Campbell, Cunningham, Nystrand, & Usdan, 1980; Culbertson, 1981; Iannacconne, Clark, & Hanson, 1979; Campbell, 1987; Hanson, 1991; Hoy & Miskel, 1991; Kimbrough & Nunnery, 1983; Lunenburg & Ornstein, 1991; Razik & Swanson, 1995, and Owens, 1995) have made significant contributions to the practioner's understanding of leadership in educational administration. In addition, a number of outstanding books are now available on the principalship and superintendency.

The approach one takes to leadership sets the stage for all activity and interactions that follow. For that reason leadership style is important in the study of educational administration. Effective leaders must be clear in the set of beliefs they plan to practice and the impact their style has on the culture, ethos, and environment in which subordinates work. Leadership style guides the action and interaction of the work group, serving as a catalyst for achievement while bringing together diverse people within an organization to work for the common good.

Research and literature on leadership will always be a growing body of understanding. The body of literature is not so much a sampling of existing work and widely accepted beliefs as it is a lifelong struggle for understanding. This point is critical because postmodern perspective, as discussed in Chapter 1, warns us to carefully examine "widely accepted" or "well-known" beliefs in relation to political conditions, power, privileges, rewards, indulgences, sanctions, exclusions, dominance, ideologies, and so on.

Existing perspectives are being viewed with suspicion, especially as increasing numbers of women and men of color are in positions of leadership. Capper (1998) argues that,

> Women and other marginalized persons are just beginning to be recognized as subjects or individuals in the first place—as individuals with power and as individuals capable of working toward change in systems. Moreover, in the past, women and other marginalized persons have been excluded from the conversation and discourse.... A leadership vision is reflective of only certain voices, is a product of multiple discourse, and should be continually reevaluated and problematized. (pp. 370–372)

The "search for knowledge and truth" present in this book depends on the perspective of those conducting and presenting the research. Bill Foster (1998) states,

> I think postmodernism allows us to acknowledge the concern that knowledge is contested and that often in the contestation, some win and some lose. In educational administration, for example, there have been, since its history, competing ways of knowing, but many of these ways have been subjugated. It is to our credit, of course, that many of these ways of knowing have been recognized, but we need also ask, 'What other ways are there?'(p. 296)

Leadership is shifting from a role of directing and controlling to one of guiding, facilitating, supporting, and coordinating efforts on behalf of schools. A wider population is now envisioned as having leadership potential, and we are flattening organizations, empowering more people, and decentralizing decision-making (Hill & Ragland, 1995). Hoy and Miskel (1991) conclude,

> leadership is cultural and symbolic as well as instrumental and behavioral. Successful leaders infuse value into organizations, thereby creating institutional meaning and purpose that go beyond the technical requirements of the job. The instructional leader is responsible for articulating the mission of the organization, shaping its culture, and protecting and maintaining its integrity. (p. 299)

Leaders need to be prepared to deal with the inevitable social, cultural, economic, technological, bureaucratic, and political obstacles that can block improvement efforts.

We are at a watershed in our history. How we function as a school system, how we exchange ideas, and how we learn will affect how we continuously improve our schools. Tomorrow's leaders will:

- Encourage and enlist broad participation and support
- Empower people, maintain direction, learn by doing, and create a results-oriented approach

- Act strategically, encourage innovation, and bring everyone's attention and effort to bear on pressing issues
- Provide continuity, training, incentives, and social and political support for continuous improvement
- Create permanent mechanisms for ongoing dialogue among all those who have a stake in the education process
- Access the consequences of actions on future generations for whom the present is held in trust

Leaders will be expected to have a leadership framework expressing their primary philosophy, beliefs, and attitudes regarding leadership, learning, and teaching. Frameworks will need to accomodate working together with people, focusing on issues in common, being inclusive, setting ground rules, setting attainable goals, implementing and evaluating programs, celebrating victories, and using modern technology.

Most of all, the new leadership will require open communication and the realization that we must work together. Research (Little, 1986) suggests that successes are more likely to occur when people talk together regularly and frequently, work together, and teach one another about new ideas and possibilities.

H. G. Wells stated, "Civilization is a race between education and catastrophe." Many historians would certainly agree. Wheatly (1992) suggests that the types of reforms needed in education are major in scope, discontinuous with the past, and transformational. In explaining his great hockey play, Wayne Gretsky stated, "You always skate to where the puck is going, not to where it's been." The call is for educators to move toward where education needs to be to improve the entire system, not regress to where it's been.

Educators will need to discuss and translate knowledge and research for excellent schools. Such planning, research, discussion, capacity-building are very important, but ultimately it takes the spark of an individual or group of individuals to make a difference. Transformation needs people to champion the cause. Words that describe such efforts are *commitment*, *zest*, *energy*, *care*, *enthusiasm*, and *extraordinary effort*. Leaders encourage and facilitate this extraordinary effort.

> As principal of Atlas Shrug High School, describe your philosophy of leadership and state how that philosophy will inspire needed school reforms.

PORTFOLIO ARTIFACTS

- Chair a meeting providing the agenda, minutes, and so forth.
- Participate in the development of an annual plan.
- Take on a leadership role within your school division, the surrounding community, or a professional organization.
- Make a formal presentation to a group within the school district or community or at a conference. Answer resulting questions.

- Shadow a leader within the school division, another organization, or the community.
- Actively participate in educational administrative or professional leadership associations.
- Develop or revise a mission statement for a school or school division.
- Organize, implement, and provide leadership for a one-time project or program that involves other people in its completion.
- Volunteer to help administer a summer school program.
- Chair a committee or serve as faculty adviser for an athletic, arts, or extracurricular program.
- Attend the school division's administrative meetings.

TERMS

Bureaucracy
Chaos theory
Cultural leadership
Delegation
Leadership and management
Learning organization
MBWA
Participatory team management

Politics
Pygmalion effect
Reflective practice
School-based management (SBM)
Situational leadership
Synergy

Total quality management (TQM)
Transformational leadership
Vision
X–Y theory

SUGGESTED READINGS

Bennis, W., & Nanus, B. (1997). *Leaders: Strategies for taking charge*. New York: Harper Business Publication.

Cunningham, W. G., & Gresso, D. W. (1993). *Cultural leadership: The culture of excellence in education*. Boston: Allyn and Bacon.

Hanson, E. M. (1996). *Educational administration and organization behavior*. Boston: Allyn and Bacon.

Hoy, W. K., & Miskel, C. G. (1995). *Educational administration: Theory, research, and practice*. New York: McGraw-Hill.

Kouzes, J., & Posner, B. (1995). *The leadership challenge*. San Francisco: Jossey-Bass.

Leithwood, K. A. (1999). *Changing leadership for changing times*. Bristol, PA: Taylor Frances Incorporated.

Murphy, J. & Lewis, K. Eds. (1999). *Handbook of research on educational administration*. San Francisco: Jossey-Bass Publishers.

Owens, R. G. (1995). *Organizational behavior in education*. Boston: Allyn and Bacon.

Razik, T. A., & Swanson, A. D. (1995). *Fundamental concepts of educational leadership and management*. Englewood Cliffs, NJ: Prentice Hall.

Directions for Scoring Box 6.1
The X–Y Scale

Depending on which column you placed a check mark on the X–Y scale determines whether you operated with X or Y beliefs on that particular question. Record an X or Y in the blank column at the end of the question based on the column that you checked. When you have scored all ten questions, count the total number of Y's you have recorded.

	1	2	3	4	X/Y
1. Closely supervise my subordinates to get better work from them.	X	X	Y	Y	
2. Set the goals and objectives for my subordinates and sell them on the merits of my plans	X	X	Y	Y	
3. Set up controls to ensure that my subordinates are getting the job done.	X	X	Y	Y	
4. Encourage my subordinates to set their own goals and objectives	Y	Y	X	X	
5. Make sure that my subordinates' work is planned out for them.	X	X	Y	Y	
6. Check with my subordinates daily to see if they need any help.	X	X	Y	Y	
7. Step in as soon as reports indicate that the job is slipping.	X	X	Y	Y	
8. Push my people to meet schedules if necessary.	X	X	Y	Y	
9. Have frequent meetings to keep in touch with what is going on.	Y	Y	X	X	
10. Allow subordinates to make important decisions.	Y	Y	X	X	
					Total Ys

$10 \geq Y \geq 9$ Strong Y beliefs
$8 \geq Y \geq 7$ Y beliefs
$6 \geq Y \geq 5$ Mild X beliefs
$4 \geq Y \geq 3$ X beliefs
$2 \geq Y \geq 0$ Strong X beliefs

See Box 6.2 for interpretation of results.

APPENDIX 6.B

Directions for Scoring Box 6.4 Leadership Behavior Survey

Total the number of checks you marked in each column of Box 6.4, the Leadership Behavior Survey and enter the totals in the square below for the appropriate column. The columns on the left side of the survey represent the initiating structure values. The right side columns represents consideration values. Record the column totals in the initiating structure and Consideration boxes below. Multiply each of these totals by the weighting factors indicated. Add weighted factor totals for a grand total, representing the initiating structure grand total and consideration grand total. Chart both of these grand total values on the Charting Leadership Style Matrix to determine the quadrant of your selected leadership style.

Initiating Structure (left-hand column)

	Column Totals		Weighted Factor Totals
Always (5)		× 4 =	
Often (4)		× 3 =	
Occasionally (3)		× 2 =	
Seldom (2)		× 1 =	
Never (1)		× 0 =	
I.S. Grand Total			

Consideration (right-hand column)

	Column Total		Weighted Factor Totals
Always (5)		× 4 =	
Often (4)		× 3 =	
Occasionally (3)		× 2 =	
Seldom (2)		× 1 =	
Never (1)		× 0 =	
C. Grand Total			

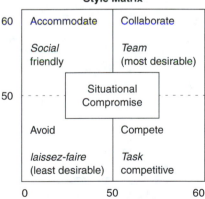

Charting Leadership Style Matrix

Consideration Value (C-TOTAL) 60

Accommodate — *Social* friendly

Collaborate — *Team* (most desirable)

50 — Situational Compromise

Avoid — *laissez-faire* (least desirable)

Compete — *Task* competitive

0   50   60

Initiating structure value (IS TOTAL)
Determine in which quadrant your scores place you.

Source: Halprin, A. *Theory and Research in Administration.* © 1966. Upper Saddle River, NJ: Prentice Hall. Adapted by permission of the publisher.

Directions for Scoring Box 6.5

Measuring Preferred Management Styles

Fill in the "answer number" from Box 6.5, Measuring Preferred Management Style, in the blanks below: Transfer the three points that you distribute across the two alternatives. For example, on number 1, if you placed a 3 by alternative A, and a 0 by alternative B, then you would fill in a 0 under B, column 9,1, and a 3 under A, column 1,9 in the answer key. Then go to Question 2. Please pay particular attention to the way the alphabetical letters are listed under each column. Sum up each column to come up with a final point total, which helps to define the leadership style you selected. When all 42 answers are transferred and each of the 7 columns is totaled, the column with the highest total (number response) represents the grid style you most value. The next highest number is the backup style. In some cases there may be ties among columns, which may suggest belief in more than one style.

A Comparison Study of Leadership Values

	9,9 (7)	9+9 (5)	9,1 (1)	5,5 (3)	OPP (6)	1,9 (2)	1,1 (4)
1			B____			A____	
2				A____		B____	
3		A____	B____				
4					A____		B____
5	B____					A____	
6			A____	B____			
7		B____		A____			
8	A____				B____		
9	B____						A____
10				B____		A____	
11		A____				B____	
12		B____			A____		
13			A____				B____
14	A____		B____				
15		B____					A____

	9,9 (7)	9+9 (5)	9,1 (1)	5,5 (3)	OPP (6)	1,9 (2)	1,1 (4)
16				A____	B____		
17			B____				A____
18	A____			B____			
19	B____	A____					
20			A____		B____		
21						B____	A____
22					A____	B____	
23	A____		B____				
24				A____	B____		
25		B____	A____				
26						A____	B____
27	A____			B____			
28					A____		B____
29		A____				B____	
30			B____			A____	
31				B____			A____
32					B____	A____	
33		B____		A____			
34	B____				A____		
35	B____						A____
36		A____			B____		
37			B____	A____			
38		B____					A____
39	A____					B____	
40			B____		A____		
41				A____			B____
42	B____	A____					

								= 126

Total Each Column

Twenty-One Combined Domains of Effective School Leadership

Domains	Definition
Leadership	Giving purpose and direction for individual and group processes; shaping a school culture and values; facilitating the development of a shared strategic plan and vision for the school; formulating goals and planning change efforts and setting priorities for the school; understanding leadership theory and organizational theory.
Problem Analysis	Identifying the important elements of a problem situation by gathering and analyzing data, facts, and impressions, identifying possible causes; seeking additional needed information; devising possible solutions, being creative in solving problems; applying conflict management techniques when needed.
Decision Making	Reaching logical conclusions founded on ethical and moral standards (judgment); making high-quality, timely decisions; analyzing alternative approaches; giving priority to significant issues.
Planning	Planning and scheduling one's own and other's work so that resources are used appropriately and short- and long-term priorities and goals are provided; managing change; establishing timelines and scheduling projects.
Implementation	Putting programs and change efforts into action; facilitating coordination and collaboration of tasks; supporting and monitoring those responsible for carrying out projects and plans.
Delegation	Assigning projects, tasks, and responsibilities together with clear authority; following up on delegated activities.
Supervising and Motivating Others	Planning and encouraging participation; facilitating teamwork and collegiality; supervising and treating staff as professionals; providing feedback and coaching on performance; providing intellectual stimulation; supporting innovation; serving as a role model.

Domains	Definition
Interpersonal Sensitivity	Perceiving the needs and concerns of others; embracing diversity; recognizing multicultural differences; dealing tactfully with others; obtaining feedback.
Oral Communication	Making oral presentations that are clear and easy to understand; utilizing appropriate communicative aids; adapting to audiences; using effective counseling skills with staff, students, and parents.
Written Communication	Expressing ideas clearly in writing; writing appropriately for different audiences such as students, teachers, and parents; preparing brief memoranda, letters, reports, and other job-specific documents.
Instruction	Creating instructional programs for the improvement of teaching and learning; recognizing developmental needs; ensuring appropriate instructional methods; accommodating differences in learning styles and achievement.
Curriculum	Understanding major curriculum design models; initiating needs analyses; aligning curriculum with anticipated outcomes; monitoring social and technological development as they affect curriculum; adjusting content as needs and conditions change.
Student Guidance and Development	Understanding and accommodating student development; providing for guidance, counseling, and auxiliary services; utilizing and coordinating community organizations; responding to family needs; planning student activities.
Staff Development	Working to identify professional needs; planning, organizing, and facilitating programs that improve faculty and staff effectiveness; arranging for remedial assistance and development activities; initiating self-development.
Research, Measurement, and Evaluation	Determining what diagnostic information is needed about students, staff, and the school environment; conducting needs assessments; drawing inferences; interpreting measurements or evaluations for others; designing, conducting, and evaluating research and evaluation studies; designing accountability mechanisms.
Resource Allocation and Management	Procuring, apportioning, monitoring, accounting for, and evaluating fiscal, human, material, and time resources; planning and developing the budget process with appropriate staff; managing all fiscal responsibilities.
Philosophical and Cultural Values	Understanding the role of education in a democratic society and accepted ethical standards; recognizing philosophical influences and values in education; understanding the values of the school and community, including current social and economic issues related to education.

(continued)

Domains	Definition
Legal Policy and Political Applications	Acting in accordance with federal and state constitutional provisions, working within local rules, procedures, and directives; recognizing standards for civil and criminal liability and intentional torts; administering contracts and financial accounts; examining and effecting policies individually and through professional groups; addressing ethical issues.
Public Relations	Responding to the electronic and printed news media; initiating and reporting news through appropriate channels; managing school reputations; enlisting public participation and support; forming collaborative relationships to promote school programs.
Technology	Advocating and using computers and other information systems as curriculum and instructional tools; applying technology in the management of school office business; promoting technology use among faculty and staff.
Personal Development	Practicing self-reflection; improving leadership and management skills; attending workshops, conferences, and so forth; reading current literature; belonging to appropriate professional organizations.

Source: Matthews, J. (January 19, 1994). *Analysis of seven frameworks of educational leadership.* Paper presented to the National Policy Board for Educational Administration.

Moral and Ethical Dimensions of Leadership

Vignette: Cuyamaca High Deals with Value Collision

With input from teachers, the administration of Cuyamaca High School radically changed the school schedule to be implemented the following year. Gone was the eight-period day, and in its place was an alternate-day block schedule. Under this system a course met every other day for extended periods of time. Further, the proposed schedule divided the year into trimesters.

Students and parents began protesting these changes the first week of the implementation year. They expressed their concern to the principal at having been left out of the decision-making process. In a meeting with parents and students, Principal Emily Schell explained that the schedule modifications had been developed with great care. School personnel had visited other campuses where similar schedules were in place and had interviewed teachers and administrators. Research data, she explained, showed strong support for the new schedule because it resulted in lower dropout rates, a better school climate, and improved teacher and student attitudes. Ms. Schell stated that she strongly believed reconfiguring the school schedule would improve student learning.

Dissatisfied with the principal's response, a group of parents spoke out at the school board meeting against "unilateral decisions without parent and student input." Several families complained that there was no evidence that block scheduling resulted in higher academic achievement. In fact, one parent created a Web site decrying block scheduling and "other fads imposed on children in America's schools." Meanwhile, Ms. Schell and her staff believed that the benefits of the scheduling changes far outweighed any negative aspects.

What is (are) the problem(s) in this vignette?

Discuss this vignette from the viewpoints of the ethics of justice, caring, and critique.

The Purposes of Leadership

In a Kellogg Leadership Project report entitled *Leadership in the Twenty-First Century* (1997), a team of researchers defined the purposes of leadership as follows:

- to create a supportive environment where people can thrive, grow, and live in peace with one another
- to promote harmony with nature and thereby provide sustainability for future generations
- to create communities of reciprocal care and shared responsibility—where every person matters and each person's welfare and dignity is respected and supported.

Comprehension of these purposes of leadership requires an in-depth understanding and analysis of one's values. For educational administrators, who will be expected to state their principles and bring them to bear on important decisions, ethical reasoning is vital. All leaders must carefully examine their values and beliefs so they can act responsibly and ethically. Ethics is the study of moral practices that are based on beliefs.

On Being Truly Human

According to Robert J. Starratt (1986), "the school promotes a moral way of being" (p. 156). A moral way of being involves three human qualities: autonomy, connectedness and transcendence.

Starratt defines autonomy as self-ownership. Being autonomous means taking responsibility for our actions within the context of our cultural filters. Although we make moral choices independent of our culture, because our culture is within us, our choices are shaped by our culture.

Starratt's second human quality is connectedness. Connectedness involves relationships, and as in the case of autonomy, it is culture that shapes our values and ultimately our network of relationships. "There appear to be certain universal demands in relationships…that define us as human beings. Every culture, for example, has categories that define 'inhuman' treatment of other people" (p. 157). Starratt's notion of connectedness is similar to some of Robert Craig's (1998) characteristics for living an ethical life that includes the ability and willingness to be concerned for others.

Another part of connectedness involves relations with nature. Noddings (1992) argues that our lives and environment are interdependent, and it is crucial that schools teach children about caring for animals, plants, and the earth. Connectedness involves not only relationships with people and culture but also with the natural environment. The motto of the IMSA High School in Illinois, "Take care of yourself, take care of others, take care of this place," is the only set of rules this high school needs to live by.

Starratt's third human quality is transcendence—that which leads us toward something greater than ourselves. Transcendence can take many forms. It might involve, for example, our participation in a collective cause such as one that focuses on issues of social justice. Another form of transcendence might be striving for excellence in a profession, in the arts, in our communities, or in any of the eight areas that Gardner (see

Chapters 3 and 8) has described as forms of intelligence. Starratt maintains that teachers should develop these three foundational qualities of being truly human in students.

Calls for character education, civics education, and service learning demand that schools focus greater attention on ethical issues. One of the purposes of education is to help young people develop and internalize a set of values required for the continuation and enrichment of our democratic culture. Schools are key institutions in the creation of a caring, compassionate, and dynamic civilization.

In an effort to broaden the focus of American education, more than forty leading educational and social service groups announced a ten-year program entitled Partnering Initiative in Education and Civil Society. A major focus of this initiative is to encourage students to explore the twin issues of character development and responsible participation in civil society. It involves integrating service learning, character education, and citizen education opportunities in the classroom.

For our democracy to work, we must ensure that our people have and practice the virtue of good character. People's character is shaped by family, faith, friends, schools, and the experiences they have throughout their lives. Through character education schools formally address the students' morality and ethics, which advance human life. "Since character education is about integrated development—encompassing head, heart, and hand—the curriculum must not only help students to know the good, it must also inspire them to want to do what is good and what is right" (Ryan & Bohlin, 1999, p. 114).

Character education is teaching children about such basic human values as honesty, kindness, generosity, courage, and respect. Students learn that their decisions affect other people and things. Service learning requires students to serve their communities. Some schools now require that students earn a certain number of credits through community service work in order to graduate.

The Role of Culture

An example of the qualities of autonomy, connectedness, and transcendence reveals how leadership and organizations are culture bound. Each of us is a part of numerous microcultures and usually one macroculture (national or societal culture), and our views and beliefs about the world are filtered through those cultures. Fukuyama (1995) defines *culture* as inherited ethical habit. According to Fukuyama, an ethical habit consists of ideas or values (e.g., bilingual education is a good), or social relationships (e.g., you should discuss ideas with the principal before going to the superintendent). Fukuyama believes that moral virtue and habit are closely related.

In *The Nichmachean Ethics*, Aristotle maintains that in order for people to be virtuous, they must habituate themselves to virtuous behavior; it then becomes second nature in which a person takes pride. Some values which transcend time are self-interest, and world boundaries. Virtues are characteristics such as honesty, cooperativeness, reliability, and a sense of duty to others. These virtues are closely aligned to Starratt's three qualities that make people human.

Figure 7.1 on page 204 depicts the many layers of culture that influence identity. Our views are shaped by societal culture, the macroculture, and the various layers that

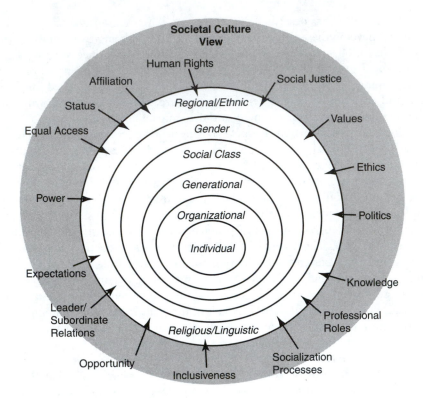

FIGURE 7.1   Levels of Culture

Source: Cordeiro, P. (1997) Up Against the Glass Ceiling: Culture and Gender in the Workplace. *School Business Affairs* v. 63 no. 4.

are part of our identity. Each person's unique identity is shaped by these cultures as he or she matures. The cultures act as filters. Individuals make independent choices but always under the strong influence of culture.

What values and cultural attributes at Cuyamaca High may be in collision with community values?

Clarifying and Resolving Value Conflicts

In *Educational Leadership: The Moral Art*, Christopher Hodgkinson (1991) maintains that "Values, morals and ethics are the very stuff of leadership and administrative life"

(p. 11). He offers an analytical model of value, which classifies values and establishes a base for the resolution of value conflicts (Figure 7.2).

Hodgkinson divides values into two parts: right and good. "Good" is a preference (e.g., I prefer teaching third grade to teaching first grade), while "right" is moral, duty bound, what *ought* to be. A sense of "right" refers to our collective responsibility or conscience. Hodgkinson sees four (actually only three) foundations of values: principles, consequences, consensus, and preferences. Consequences and consensus he regards as subtypes of a single Type II value ground. Hodgkinson calls Type III values (those founded on preference) self-justifying, "since they are grounded in individual affect and constitute the individual's preference structure" (p. 98). Thus, something is good simply because I like it.

Type II values can be "right" because they account for the will of the majority; they represent the consensus of all involved. They can also be "right" because they will bring about some desirable resultant future state of affairs. According to Hodgkinson, "Type II values enlist the reason, the cognitive faculty" (p. 98), whether it be to reach consensus by counting heads, as the "technician" does, or by assessing contingencies, as the "politician" does. The former, Type IIa, is called a consequential approach. (For further analysis of this approach, see Willower and Licata, 1997; Strike, Haller, & Soltis, 1988.) Hodgkinson states further that "Type IIa values beg

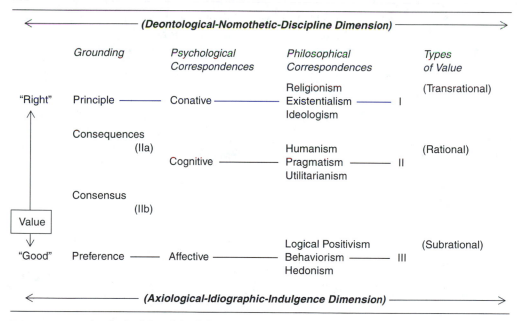

FIGURE 7.2   Analytical Model of the Value Concept

the question of grounds insofar as they project into the future the state of desirability …[which] must be adjudged on either Type I or Type IIb grounds or even…upon the collective preferential grounds of Type III" (pp. 98–99).

Type I values are metaphysical, grounded in principles that take the form of ethical codes or commandments. Type I values are based on will, rather than reasoning. To adopt Type I values, an "act of faith or commitment is necessary" (p. 99).

Each of the foundations of values has psychological correspondences. Type I values are conative, they involve our will. Type II values engage our reasoning; they are rational, cognitive; social, and collective. Type III values, rooted in our emotions, are affective and idiosyncratic, and are characterized by ego, self-interest, and self-concern.

Each also has philosophical correspondences. Type III values "lend themselves to the reductions of logical positivism and behaviorism" (p. 100). Type II values correspond to humanism, utilitarianism, and pragmatism. Hodgkinson argues, "They are buttressed by the social status quo, and the ethos, mores, laws, customs, and traditions of a given culture" (p. 100). Type I values are often found in religious or ideological systems. The moral base extends into the transrational domain of faith-activated will and sometimes illusions of perfection. Hodgkinson's model implies that Type I values are superior to and better justified than Type II or III values. He believes there is a natural tendency for administrators to solve value conflicts at the lowest level (Type III) to avoid moral issues.

According to the framework depicted in Box 7.1, which was originally developed by Beck (1984) and modified by Leithwood, Begley, and Cousins (1994), there are four categories of values: basic human values, general moral values; professional values, and social and political values. "Principles," the highest of Hodgkinson's levels are

---

BOX **7.1**

Categories of Values

Basic human values
> Freedom
> Happiness
> Respect for others
> Survival

General moral values
> Carefulness
> Fairness (for justice)
> Courage

Professional values
> General responsibility as educator
> Specific role responsibility
> Consequences
> Consequences (other)

Social and political values
> Participation
> Sharing
> Loyalty, solidarity, and commitment
> Helping others

Source: Leithwood, Begley & Cousins (1994). *Developing expert leadership for future schools.* Bristol, PA: Falmer Press. p. 103. Adapted with permission.

labeled "basic human values." They include: self-determination, happiness, knowledge, respect for others and self-preservation. These are ends in themselves. "General moral values" and "professional values" are values of consequence. "Social and political values" incorporate Hodgkinson's values of consensus because they "recognize the essentially social nature of human action and the need for individuals to define themselves in relation to others to make their lives meaningful" (Leithwood, Begley, & Cousins, 1994, p. 103).

> What value system did Emily Schell use to evaluate scheduling modifications, and what system did the parents and the community use?

The Authentic Self

"Authenticity" has become a popular concept. Educators talk about authentic curriculum and assessment; in so doing, do they mean to suggest some types are not authentic? The *American Heritage Dictionary* defines *authentic* as "worthy of trust, reliance, belief." Authenticity is the "condition or quality of being authentic, trustworthy, or genuine" (p. 88).

Trust, a key word in the definition of authenticity, is the foundation of leadership. Trust involves having faith, a confident belief in someone or something.

How does one become trusted by others? How are trusting relationships created? One must have virtue to inspire trust in the context of authenticity. *Virtue* is moral excellence and responsibility made manifest in practices or actions.

Modeling (manifestation of virtue) is a key tenet of authentic leadership. If authenticity requires trust, and trust embodies virtue, then our actions and practices become of prime importance. Our actions must be ethical if our relationships with others are to be authentic. Trustworthiness is usually associated with honesty, kindness, openness, integrity, and fairness.

Cunningham (1991) developed a model that characterizes human development as a three-stage process: self-indulgence, self-validation, and self-reliance. In *self-indulgence* the individual becomes focused on the fulfillment of needs. The individual and his or her reference group are the primary focus in the self-indulgent individual's moral reasoning. Decisions are often based on internal motives, impulses, and instinctual beliefs. Self-indulgent individuals have a strong sense of self but a limited sense of others and the world in which they live. "Good" and "bad" are totally separate, and there is no possibility that they could be aspects or perceptions of one particular situation.

In *self-validation* the individual is consumed by a desire to please others, to conform to expectations, and ultimately, to belong. Whereas the self-indulgent person's value base is self-centered, that of the self-validator is self-imprisoned as he or she depends on the outside world to provide a sense of moral authenticity. The individual seeks approval by conforming to a shared value system. The result is a value scheme based on duty, authority, obligation, legality, and the rights of society. Such individuals internalize the judgments of others as their own.

In *self-reliance* the individual develops a sense of moral and ethical conscience and universal values. The individual experiences liberation, continuity, and freedom by synthesizing and consolidating internal and external values into a more natural, productive, transcendent form of reasoning. As one sees through illusions and artificial constructs, one develops greater authenticity. Sartre equated humanness with the ability to consciously choose and act for oneself.

Victor Frankl (1984) defined three central values in life: the experiential, the creative, and the attitudinal. The *experiential* is what happens to us; we learn from our experiences, which shape our views of the world. The *creative* is what we bring into existence through planning and imagining.

The highest of the three values, Frankl maintains, is *attitudinal*. It is not what we experience or create that is most important, but how we *respond* to what we experience in life. The attitudinal value has the potential to lead us to new paradigms.

Duignan (1997) argues that authenticity includes meaningful relationships, sincerity, and genuineness. Authenticity, however, must also include awareness, trust, and priority. People become authentic to others not only when they practice what they preach, but also by the ways in which they respond to life's experiences.

Emily Schell has lost some parents and community trust. What can she do to regain that trust?

Grounding Moral Educational Leadership in the Intrinsically Moral Enterprise of Learning

ROBERT J. STARRATT
Boston College

The moral demands of educational leadership go well beyond considerations of specific acts of moral choice (when to tell or withhold the truth about what one knows about a student; whether to compromise with pressure groups who want to impose a point of view in certain areas of the curriculum or lose one's job over the issue; whether to retain a mediocre teacher with political connections, and so on). The much more essential work of moral educational leadership is to create a schoolwide learning environment that promotes the moral integrity of learning as the pursuit of the truth about oneself and one's world, however complex and difficult that task may be.

Schooling implicates learners in the enterprise of appropriating the way by which their society interprets and understands itself and the world. These knowledges help or hinder learners to identify who they are (as citizens, as workers, as gendered and racial beings, or simply as human beings), what they are worth, what they are responsible for, how they exist in nature and society, and how they might conduct themselves in their personal and public lives. Since these knowledges are received or presented as heuristic as well as an expressive cultural production of that society (McCarthy, 1997), schools ought to assist the learner in exploring how these knowledges were generated and on what assumptions that generation rests.

Learning involves an encounter with an aspect of reality, albeit an interpreted and culturally grounded reality. The learner cannot intentionally deny its existence or arbitrarily make it into its opposite without disfiguring the integrity of that reality and violating the intrinsic moral obligation to acknowledge on its own terms the reality one encounters. Learning requires a coming to terms with what a person is learning, whether it is a scientific fact such as "ice floats on water," a historical assertion that "Lincoln freed the slaves," or a depiction of a moneylender like Shylock in *The Merchant of Venice*. That learning conveys a multitude of meanings, some of which should be honored (slavery is immoral), some of which should be questioned (since most of the mass of an iceberg is below water, how can it be said to float on water? Where does money come from and how is it accumulated?), and some of which should be repudiated or denounced (Hitler's assertion of the superiority of the Aryan race).

The obligation to come to terms with what one knows, to explore its use and its misuse, to avoid its distortion or manipulation is both a moral and an intellectual obligation (if for scholars, why not for younger learners as well?). Learning is a moral search as well as an intellectual search for truth—truth about ourselves, about our community, about our history, about our cultural and physical world. The truth, of course, will never be final or complete; rather, it will be tentative, incomplete, fallible, partial, and generative. But the truth will ultimately involve human beings with choices about themselves and about the kinds of communities they want to create.

This is what schools are supposed to be about. Hence, those who would lead schools toward this approach to teaching and learning are inescapably involved in a moral enterprise. This understanding of moral educational leadership implies a different conversation between educational leaders and other teachers and parents about curriculum, about assessment of student performances, and about teacher assessment. It also implies a different kind of academic preparation of administrators, one in which the moral dimensions of their own learning are continuously explored and the ongoing creation and reconstruction of their own self-identity is pursued.

Creating Community

Bredeson (1995) defines communities as purposely chosen groups that embody values, beliefs, ideologies, goals, and shared understandings. Robert Greenleaf (1970) maintains that the first thing to do in building a community is to "build a group of people who, under the influence of the institution, grow taller and become healthier, stronger, more autonomous" (p. 30). Educators, as part of school communities, are responsible for the decisions made within their schools. As educational leaders foster the growth of the members of the school community, they must make decisions based on ethical principles of justice, caring, and critique. Starratt (1995) states, "Rather than mindless obedience to the authority—whoever they may be—the response to the call for school reform requires the moral leadership of school administrators" (p. 106).

Building an Ethical School

Figure 7.3 depicts Starratt's model (1994) of the three ethics that comprise an ethical school: caring, justice, and critique. Each of these overlapping ethics raises different questions that school leaders need to consider.

The Ethic of Caring.　The notion of an ethic of caring (discussed in Chapter 1) has been promoted by Carol Gilligan (1982) and Nel Noddings. According to Noddings (1992), "Caring is a way of being in relation, not a set of specific behaviors" (p. 17). Caring includes modeling, dialogue, practice, and confirmation. Modeling for educators means demonstrating to students that we care, rather than simply saying it. Dialogue must be in the sense that Paolo Freire (1973) espouses, open-ended and sincere. This dialogue allows teachers to show they care by listening to their students fully. Practice involves experience. Opportunities for students to practice caring must be afforded by people who can demonstrate caring. In internship settings, for example, the person with whom the student interns must be someone who demonstrates caring. Noddings's fourth component of caring, confirmation, involves affirming and encouraging the best in others. Noddings believes that "when we confirm someone, we spot a better self and encourage its development" (p. 25).

The ethic of caring involves relationships with others and the responsibilities that accompany those relationships, including our relationship with the environment. The ethic of caring empowers students to be involved in decision making. Adults use student-centered decision-making practices in which human dignity and human potential are crucial dimensions. When making a decision educators in these schools ask in what way it will benefit children. One of the tasks of school leaders is to develop the attitudes and skills required to sustain caring relationships.

FIGURE 7.3　The Multidimensional Ethic

Reprinted with permission from Falmer Press from *Building an Ethical School* by R. J. Starratt.

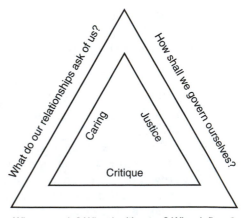
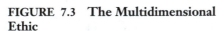

The Ethic of Justice.   Justice involves equity and fairness in relation to individual and community choice. How a school is governed is a crucial part of the ethic of justice. The ethic of justice demands that administrators serve as advocates for students, including advocating for optimal learning conditions. Chapter 8 discusses opportunity-to-learn (OTL) standards that many educators are supporting in addition to content and performance standards. OTL standards address issues of educational equity, opportunity of resources, emotional and physical security, and health and social environment.

Justice involves individuals acting impartially and a community that governs its actions fairly. With the ethic of justice, a school has fair policies that are implemented in a just fashion. As Starratt maintains, "To promote a just social order in the school, the school community must carry out an ongoing critique of those structural features of the school that work against human beings" (p. 194).

In *Democracy in America*, Alexis de Tocqueville used the term "habits of the heart" to refer to notions, opinions, and ideas that shape the mental habits of people (Bellah, Madsen, Sullivan, Swidler, & Tipton, 1995). Tocqueville believed that a democratic society requires virtue among the people in order for there to be justice; without civic virtue there can be no democracy. One habit of the heart that schools must embrace is the habit of questioning and self-criticism. If the questions raised come from the ethics of caring and justice, they are closely related to the ethic of critique.

The Ethic of Critique.   The ethic of critique is based on critical theory. According to Foster (1986) critical theory "questions the framework of the way we organize our lives or the way our lives are organized for us" (p. 72). Foster argues that the school administrator must be a critical theoretician. Through dialogue, he or she must ask and help others to ask questions that challenge the status quo. If student-centered decision making is the focus, then the ethic of critique promotes questions such as: Who benefits from this? Who holds power? Whose voice has not been heard? Who is privileged?

The ethic of critique facilitates conversation and dialogue between people in organizations. Thus, it not only permits but also encourages conflict. It is crucial to the ethic of critique that conflict be addressed with civility.

In promoting the ethics of caring, justice, and critique, educators must examine their values and the influence of those values on decision making and conflict resolution.

Ethics-Based Leadership

There are a prolific number of conceptions of leadership (Shelton, 1997):

- people leadership (Bonsignore, 1997)
- superleadership (Manz, 1997)
- brave leadership (Peters, 1997)

- limitless leadership (Tice, 1997)
- visionary leadership (Nanus, 1992)
- strategic leadership (Hesselbein, 1997)
- credible leadership (Kouzes & Posner, 1993)
- quality leadership (Deming, 1997)
- creative leadership (Eisner, 1997)
- situation leadership (Hersey & Blanchard, 1988)
- emotional leadership (Bardwick, 1988)
- passionate leadership (Bell, 1997)
- inspirational leadership (Suters, 1997)
- authentic leadership (Shelton, 1997).

Leaders have also been described as artists, architects, and commissars (Hughes, 1998); changemasters (Moss Kanter, 1983); learners (Quigley, 1997); models and mentors (Kaplan, 1997); carers (Perot, 1997); doers (Drucker, 1997). Each conception and metaphor provides insight into various aspects of what leadership involves, but none embodies ethics as its base. Recently four conceptions of leadership have emerged that emphasize values such as trust, authenticity, empowerment, and service.

Transformational Leadership

In his seminal text examining moral leadership, James MacGregor Burns (1978) differentiates between transformational and transactional leadership. Burns maintains that "the relations of most leaders and followers are transactional—leaders approach followers with an eye to exchanging one thing for another" (p. 4). Transformational leadership, he argues, is highly complex. "Transforming leadership is a relationship of mutual stimulation and elevation that converts followers into leaders and may convert leaders into moral agents" (p. 4). According to Burns, leadership is a process of morality because leaders and followers have shared motives and goals.

Transformational leadership involves specific ends to be pursued, but Burns says little about the means to those ends. He maintains that,

> …the ultimate test of moral leadership is its capacity to transcend the claims of multiplicity of everyday wants and needs and expectations, to respond to the highest levels of moral development, and to relate leadership behavior—its roles, choices, style, commitments—to a set of reasoned, relatively explicit, conscious values. (p. 46)

Servant Leadership

Robert K. Greenleaf proposed one of the most powerful conceptions of leadership in his classic *The Servant as Leader* (1970). The leader begins by being a servant. Greenleaf maintains, "Then conscious choice brings one to aspire to lead" (p. 7). For Greenleaf the important questions one must ask about leadership are: Do those served grow as people? Do they, while being served, become healthier, wiser, freer, more autonomous, more likely themselves to become servants? What is the effect on the least privileged in society; will they benefit, or, at least, will they not be further deprived?

Greenleaf states that authentic leaders are chosen by the people with whom they work. A servant leader's ability to lead with integrity depends on his or her skills for withdrawal and action, listening and persuasion, practical goal setting and intuitive prescience. The focus is on goals, success, learning, and assisting.

Principle-Centered Leadership

Steven Covey (1989), in his widely read book *The Seven Habits of Highly Effective People*, presents a conception of leadership that is centered on principle. For Covey (1997) "principle-centered leadership is based on the reality that we cannot violate natural laws with impunity" (p. 83). He maintains that we must center "our lives on timeless, unchanging principles" (p. 123) and proposes that four factors—the center of our paradigm—be security, guidance, wisdom, and power. All are interdependent and "create the great force of a noble personality, a balanced character, a beautifully integrated individual." (p. 110). People follow such individduals because they believe in them and what they are trying to accomplish. There is mutual trust, respect, and loyalty that is grounded in shared ethics and values.

Security is our identity, self-esteem, and sense of worth. Guidance means our direction in life, the standards or principles that govern our acts and decisions. Wisdom refers to how we perceive life and involves judgment, understanding, and perception. According to Covey (1997), "Power is the capacity to act, the strength and courage to accomplish something" (p. 86). He advocates centering our lives on correct principles and we will then have a "sense of stewardship in our lives" (p. 86).

Stewardship

Stewardship involves holding something in trust. According to Peter Block (1993), stewardship is "the willingness to be accountable for the well-being of the larger organization by operating in service, rather than in control, of those around us" (p. xx). Stewardship closely resembles several aspects of servant leadership, and in fact, its "underlying value is about deepening our commitment to service" (p. xx). Block maintains that service is authentic when there is a balance of power and the leader has a commitment to a larger community. Additionally, distribution of rewards must be balanced and equitable, and the defining of purpose must be done jointly. Block discusses at length the importance of accountability without control or compliance but based on his higher values such as good causes or purpose. His concept of stewardship involves ownership and responsibility based on spiritual values that must be lived.

These conceptions of leadership emphasize trust, authenticity, empowerment, and service. The core of each lies in a person's underlying beliefs and ethics.

Reflect on the sense of community that now exists at Cuyamaca High, using the models discussed in this chapter.

The Ethical Challenge of Educational Administrators: Grappling with the Complexity of Moral Leadership

LYNN BECK

University of Alabama

Recent reports of terrifying acts of violence in schools have inspired an outpouring of calls for educational settings where such events will not recur. Many blame the spate of shootings on the disappearance of "traditional" values from our homes and schools. They suggest that reinserting morality into these institutions will do much to curb violence and other social problems.

Educational leaders in this situation face enormous challenges. One, of course, is to discover ways to make schools safer. Another is to encourage students to embrace accepted social and cultural mores. These, however, in my view are not the only challenges. Indeed, they are not the most important ones.

Educational administrators, bombarded by threats of violence, drug use and abuse, adolescent pregnancy, and the like must not allow attention to these problems—all of which have moral dimensions—to lull them into thinking that frontal attacks on antisocial behaviors and attitudes are enough to create ethical schools. Certainly they must promote the kinds of values that will reduce the incidence of problems, but they must realize that the pursuit of morality is a grand and complex undertaking that requires unfailing attention to the moral dimensions of our structures, policies, and practices. School leaders must courageously confront and change cherished assumptions and traditions that have unjust and inhumane consequences. Even as they do so, administrators seeking an ethical school must also look inward as well as outward. They must attend to what some have called the state of their own "souls."

As noted earlier, recent years have been witness to a host of programs—character education, community service, multicultural education efforts, and drug awareness activities—all aimed at fostering culturally accepted values, civic responsibility, altruism, tolerance, and respect for self and others. The impulses underlying such efforts are good ones, as are most of the values they advocate. Such activities are limited, though, in their ability to encourage deep and lasting changes in the moral fabric of our schools. And they are fraught with some dangers.

Formal programs endorsing certain values, attitudes, and behaviors may tempt us to think that morality is about a few key precepts and engagement in or avoidance of certain activities. Further, the presence of such programs in schools has a tendency to lull educators, students, parents, policy makers, and the public into thinking that they are doing a sufficient job of pursuing ethics. Congratulating ourselves for our good work, we may actually avoid thinking about the many structural and cultural features of our schools that are morally troubling. As we address immediate and pressing problems, we must also continually examine our practices, norms, and policies to see if they, in fact, honor values such as justice, respect, and the full dignity of each person. Further, we must be willing to confront and change those that are unjust, uncaring, and demeaning.

As we seek to develop students' moral competence and to create ethical schools, those of us who lead face yet another challenge: to attend to our own moral development. On one level this challenge may seem to be an easy one, for it involves working on things that we believe we control—our beliefs and behaviors. Meeting it, however, is difficult, for it requires us to be active and reflective simultaneously. It demands that we have the courage to be honest and the humility to change. Meeting the challenge also requires strength to confront ourselves and others and the ability to do so gently and with love. It demands determination and persistence and the recognition that the quest for personal, professional, and institutional morality can never fully accomplish its goals.

Those who dare to embark on this quest will undoubtedly find themselves slipping and struggling. They will also experience the joy that comes with engaging in two worthwhile tasks. The first is the task of fully experiencing ourselves as moral agents, and the second involves supporting such experiences for others.

Foundations of Ethical Behavior: Standards for Good Practice

Greenfield (1990) argues that the moral obligation of educators is to serve as advocates for students and that schools must be responsive to students' needs. Greenfield (1990), Noddings (1992), Starratt (1996), Beck (1994), and others writing on the topic of ethics have identified standards of good practice that can serve school administrators as a foundation for ethical behavior. Standards of good practice include being conscious (aware and informed), encouraging dialogue, modeling, and being reflective.

An ethical administrator must be aware of current research on effective teaching and learning. Knowledge of the research allows administrators to ask questions related to the ethics of critique and justice. For example, an administrator who is conscious of good practice may ask: Why is this program being implemented when there is little evidence to support its effectiveness?

Encouraging dialogue is another standard of good practice; it supports the ethic of critique. Open-ended dialogue encourages and allows critical questions to be raised. Dialogue is the sine qua non of the ethic of critique.

Modeling, as discussed earlier, is related to the ethic of caring and to authenticity. Our moral orientation calls us to respond to students in a caring way. Modeling is one of the primary ways in which we can demonstrate that we care.

Finally, being reflective is another standard of good practice. To foster the ethics of caring, justice, and critique as a purposeful, intentional endeavor, an administrator must develop the habit of reflecting on his or her behavior. Reflection allows educators to consider the effects of their decisions before they act on them.

Each of these standards of good practice—awareness, dialogue, modeling, and reflection—can be learned. They can become "habits of the heart" that enable administrators to provide ethical leadership.

Being an Ethical Leader: Approaches to Skill Development

How does one acquire the skills to become an ethical leader? In recent years researchers have described various approaches educational administrators can use to help develop skills to function as ethical school leaders (Mertz, 1997; Shapiro & Stefkovich, 1997; Duke & Grogan, 1997; Craig, 1999). These skills and approaches include:

- examining situations from a variety of perspectives, including feminism, postmodernism, liberation theology, and critical theory

■ writing personal essays, or educational platforms, describing ethical principles or values that students subscribe to

■ examining dilemmas from consequentialist and nonconsequentialist points of view

■ utilizing data from values instruments such as the Personal Values Inventory and the Hall-Tonna Inventory that supply information on several areas of human growth

■ comparing and contrasting ethical codes of conduct from a variety of organizations

■ learning and using group dynamics training

■ reading ethical dilemmas rooted in particular contextual variables since "leadership does not exist apart from context" (Duke & Grogan, 1997, p. 145)

As Craig (1994) so aptly reports, "The ethical school administrator has a vision that includes the interrelatedness of all those involved in the school and community...viewing others as beings with respect and dignity" (p. 134). He believes that "virtue can be developed through arduous practice" and that "treating others justly and respectfully over a long period of time may result in a virtuous person" (p. 134).

Codes of Ethics

According to Shapiro and Stefkovich (1997), a legal perspective focuses on the interpretation of state and federal codes of ethics. These codes are rule bound. Box 7.2 depicts the Statement of Ethics of the American Association of School Administrators (AASA). Similar standards exist for many professional associations.

These ten standards can be viewed as a beginning step for a school administrator when developing a personal educational platform that includes the principles he or she advocates. As Covey notes (1989), "Principles are not practices. A practice is a specific activity or action. A practice that works in one circumstance will not necessarily work in another...Principles are guidelines of human conduct that are proven to have enduring permanent value" (p. 35). This AASA code of ethics contains some principles that educational administrators may want to include when developing a personal platform.

If you were the principal of Cuyamaca, what would you do immediately and in the long run to place this school on a solid moral and ethical foundation?

Building an Educational Platform

Crucial to ethical leadership is the ability to clarify one's beliefs and philosophies about education. Sergiovanni and Starratt (1988) refer to this process as developing an educational platform (discussed in Chapter 1). This platform is a work in progress and should be periodically revisited and updated. Colleagues, students and professors should chal-

BOX **7.2**

Statement of Ethics, American Association of School Administrators

An educational administrator's professional behavior must conform to an ethical code. The code must be idealistic and at the same time practical so that it can apply reasonably to all educational administrators.

The administrator acknowledges that the schools belong to the public they serve for the purpose of providing educational opportunities to all. However, the administrator assumes responsibility for providing professional leadership in the school and community. The responsibility requires the administrator to maintain standards of exemplary professional conduct. It must be recognized that the administrator's actions will be viewed and appraised by the community, professional associates and students.

To these ends, the administrator subscribes to the following statements of standards. The educational administrator:

1. Makes the well-being of students the fundamental value of all decision-making and action.
2. Fulfills professional responsibilities with honesty and integrity.
3. Supports the principle of due process and protects the civil and human rights of all individuals.
4. Obeys local, state and national laws and does not knowingly join or support organizations that advocate, directly or indirectly, the overthrow of the government.
5. Implements the governing board of education's policies and administrative rules and regulations.
6. Pursues appropriate measures to correct those laws, policies and regulations that are not consistent with sound educational goals.
7. Avoids using positions for personal gain through political, social, religious, economic or other influences.
8. Accepts academic degrees or professional certification only from duly accredited institutions.
9. Maintains the standards and seeks to improve the effectiveness of the profession through research and continuing professional development.
10. Honors all contracts until fulfillment, release or dissolution mutually agreed upon by all parties.

Source: School Administrator. (1996). Reprinted with permission.

---

lenge the leader to prove that his or her platform is more than espoused theory. The leader's theory in use must be observable in his or her actions (Argyris & Schön, 1975).

Sergiovanni and Starratt (1998) have identified ten factors that should constitute an educational platform:

1. The aims of education
2. The major achievements of students
3. The social significance of learning
4. The image of the learner

5. The value of the curriculum
6. The image of the teacher
7. The preferred kind of pedagogy
8. The primary language of discourse in learning situations (the level and quality of learning)
9. The preferred kind of teacher–student relationships
10. The preferred kind of school climate

Revisit and critique your educational platform on a regular basis; it can then become part of your ethical practice.

Conclusion

Educational leadership involves values, morals, and ethics. The purposes of education in the twenty-first century are to reflect the changing context of educational organizations. Educational administrators will have to create communities of reciprocal caring and responsibility. Creation of such communities can be accomplished only if educational leaders are authentic and truly human.

Examination of schools through the framework of the ethics of caring, justice, and critique allows educational leaders to challenge basic assumptions and enhance understanding of the issues involved. It helps ensure that all children are provided with the opportunities necessary for learning.

Conceptions of leadership such as transformational, principle-centered stewardship and servant leadership provide lenses through which educational administrators can examine their personal underlying values and beliefs. School administrators can develop standards of good practice and improve their skills as ethical leaders through numerous activities, such as writing personal platforms and comparing and contrasting codes of ethics from various organizations.

PORTFOLIO ARTIFACTS

1. Revisit your educational platform following the ten areas suggested by Sergiovanni and Starratt. What does your platform say about your beliefs concerning the ethics of caring, justice, and critique?

2. Reread the conceptions of ethical leadership in this chapter as well as other conceptions of leadership presented in this book. Write a personal essay that describes how your values influence your leadership style.

3. Become involved in a debate about a moral issue in medicine, criminal justice, religion, business, ecology, or education.

4. Critique the value system that is currently operating in a school or another organization. Compare it with the system that operates within a religious institution.

5. Get involved with character, service, or value education programs. What are the basic beliefs of the programs?

TERMS

Authenticity	Ethics	Virtue
Community	Morals	
Educational platform	Values	

SUGGESTED READINGS

Block, P. (1993). *Stewardship: Choosing service over self-interest.* San Francisco: Berrett-Koehler.

DeRoche, E., & Williams, M. (1998). *Educating hearts and minds.* Thousand Oaks, CA: Corwin Press.

Greenleaf, R. (1970). *The servant as leader.* Indianapolis, IN: The Robert K. Greenleaf Center.

Katz, M., Nodding, N., & Strike, K. (1999). *Justice and caring.* Nerw York: Teachers College Press.

Nash, R. (1996). *Real world ethics.* New York Teachers College Press.

Starratt, R. J. (1991). Building an ethical school: A theory for practice in educational leadership. *Educational Administration Quarterly, 27*(2), 185–202.

Strike, K., Haller, E., & Sottis, J. (1998). *The ethics of school administration.* New York: Teacher College Press.

8 Program Development, Delivery, and Assessment

Vignette: Program Improvement at Linton Elementary

A parent approached Principal Georgia Belaire of Linton Elementary School regarding the second grade health curriculum. This parent believed the curriculum taught by the school psychologist was inappropriate for second graders; he indicated that several other parents shared his views. The principal listened to the parent's complaints and wrote down the specific concerns.

Although in her third year as principal of Linton, Belaire was not familiar with the details of this second grade health curriculum. Following the meeting with the parent, Principal Belaire asked the opinions of the three second grade teachers. All three agreed that the curriculum was of value and well received by the students. In speaking with the school psychologist, Principal Belaire discovered that the curriculum had been introduced by the psychologist's predecessor. The incumbent was in her first year at Linton, her first position in an education setting. The psychologist stated that like the parent, she had similar reservations concerning the curriculum. Because of her lack of experience, however, she had not surfaced the concerns.

Principal Belaire immediately asked the assistant superintendent for curriculum and instruction when the school board had approved this particular curriculum. The assistant superintendent could not recall approval during her four-year tenure; eventually it was discovered that the curriculum had never been presented to or approved by the school board.

Board policy stated that the decision to retain or reject curriculum materials would be based on specific criteria, including whether the material represented life in true proportions, whether circumstances were dealt with realistically, and whether the materials had literary or social value. Policy required that factual material be included in all instructional material collections.

> How do you assess the "value and worth" of a curriculum?
> This school district's board policy had guidelines for choosing curriculum. Does your school district have board policy in this area? What does it say? How does it compare with the policy in Principal Belaire's district?

Conceptions of Academic Achievement

According to Cole (1990) there are currently two major conceptions of academic achievement. The first, called basic skills and facts, grew out of the 1950s and 1960s when behavioral psychology dominated the way educators viewed learning. The second conception of achievement involves the notion of higher-order thinking skills, problem solving, and advanced knowledge. These achievement skills could be regarded as a progression described in Bloom's (1984) taxonomy (knowledge, comprehension, application, analysis, synthesis, and evaluation).

As Cole maintains, "Conceptions of educational achievement change with the times, are influenced by many factors, and take different forms for different people" (p. 2). Cole finds the two conceptions of academic achievement inadequate in helping us to think about learning, concluding that educators need to formulate an alternative conception that integrates divergent views of achievement, carries clear instructional implications, and focuses on long-term educational goals. Choices are related to what is valued, what is teachable, how it is organized, how much time should be devoted, who should be involved, what best communicates intentions, and what goals are served, to name but a few of the elements of these alternatives (Costa, 1997).

Theories of Intelligence

In recent years, two theories of intelligence have proved particularly useful to educators: Robert Sternberg's triarchic theory, and Howard Gardner's multiple intelligence (MI) theory.

Robert Sternberg (1996) maintains that intelligence, defined by its underlying components, can be altered through instruction. Sternberg's triarchic theory of intelligence comprises three parts—synthetic, analytic, and practical—each of which is related to creativity.

The *synthetic* part of intelligence generates ideas and redefines problems. "Synthetic" relates to a person's internal thinking and consists of three processes. The first process is used in planning, monitoring, and evaluating performance of a task. The second governs behavior in the performance of the task itself; Sternberg maintains that a person can become more, or less, intelligent, by learning what to attend to and what to ignore. The final internal component of intelligence controls the previous knowledge a person brings to a new situation. According to Sternberg it is this previously acquired knowledge a person brings to the new situation that is more important than the mental speed or memory skills a person uses.

The *analytic* part of intelligence recognizes ideas, structures, themes, allocates resources, and evaluates the quality of ideas. It addresses the basics of problem solving. The *practical* part of intelligence makes ideas work. It promotes and refines ideas based on how the learner critiques the information he or she gets from others.

A key aspect of Sternberg's theory is that intelligence depends heavily on how people learn to cope with the world around them. He believes that "Academic intelligence of the kind measured by IQ tests matters, but really it doesn't matter that much" (p. 22). Sternberg (1996) argues that his concept of successful intelligence is of paramount importance because it is the type of intelligence that is used to achieve important goals and is needed in the twenty-first century.

In his 1983 seminal book on intelligence, *Frames of Mind*, Howard Gardner groups people's broad range of abilities into seven categories of intelligence: linguistic, logical-mathematical, spatial, bodily-kinesthetic, musical, interpersonal, and intrapersonal. In recent years Gardner added an eighth intelligence: a naturalist intelligence, which allows people to recognize and discriminate among living things (Checkley, 1997).

Gardner's theory is referred to as Multiple Intelligence (MI) theory. He maintains that each person possess all eight intelligences to varying degrees. Within each category are multiple ways to be intelligent. Each of these intelligences interacts with other intelligences, and the context of learning is crucial. Gardner disavows the notion that knowledge and ability in one area (e.g., musical intelligence) is less important than knowledge in another area (e.g., logical-mathematical). Table 8.1 summarizes the core components of seven of Gardner's intelligences (Armstrong, 1994).

Acceptance of the idea that (1) intelligence comprises multiple forms and (2) it can be altered through instruction challenges the traditional school curriculum, which emphasizes linguistic and logical-mathematical forms of intelligence. One need only examine the allocation of time in schools to see which disciplines are most valued. Little learning time is devoted to spatial, bodily-kinesthetic, musical, interpersonal, and intrapersonal intelligences, compared with the amount devoted to the areas of linguistic and logical-mathematical intelligences. It is a rare U.S. elementary school that does not begin the school day with reading or language arts. If, as Armstrong suggests, teaching activities, materials, and instructional strategies were to incorporate all of the intelligences, then students with "less intelligence" in one area than another would not be left out of the learning loop or made to believe they are "dumb." Confusion sometimes exists between mismatches in styles of teaching and learning being mistakenly described as poor teaching and/or lack of student ability (teachability grouping).

The traditional school curriculum also includes the notion that intelligence can be measured by an instrument. This reification of intelligence through IQ tests has had a detrimental effect on thousands of schoolchildren throughout the twentieth century. If there are numerous forms of intelligence, our goal should be to determine how people best learn certain types of knowledge.

Both Sternberg's and Gardner's theories of intelligence have important implications for teaching and learning. If people possess varying degrees of intelligence in different areas and if intelligence can be altered through instruction, then a school's curriculum can influence the degree of student learning significantly.

Types of Knowledge

What does it mean for a person to learn something? Are some ways to learn superior to others? Is a person's learning style defined by what he or she is learning? Researchers (Leithwood, Begley, & Cousins, 1994; Sternberg & Caruso, 1986; Sternberg & Frensch, 1993) suggest that there are various types of knowledge: declarative knowledge, practical and procedural or strategic knowledge, and contextual knowledge. Declarative knowledge is factual; it is knowledge about something. Sternberg and Caruso

TABLE 8.1   MI Theory Summary Chart

Intelligence	Core Components	Symbol Systems	High End-States
Linguistic	Sensitivity to the sounds, structure, meanings, and functions of words and language	Phonetic languages (e.g., English)	Writer, orator (e.g., Virginia Woolf, Martin Luther King, Jr.)
Logical-Mathematical	Sensitivity to, and capacity to discern, logical or numerical patterns; ability to handle long chains of reasoning	Computer languages (e.g., Pascal)	Scientist, mathematician (e.g., Marie Curie, Blaise Pascal)
Spatial	Capacity to perceive the visual-spatial world accurately and to perform transformations on one's initial perceptions	Ideographic languages (e.g., Chinese)	Artist, Architect (e.g., Frida Kahlo, I. M. Pei)
Bodily-Kinesthetic	Ability to control one's body movements and to handle objects skillfully	Sign languages, Braille	Athlete, dancer, sculptor (e.g., Jesse Owens, Martha Graham, Auguste Rodin)
Musical	Ability to produce and appreciate rhythm, pitch, and timbre; appreciation of the forms of musical expressiveness	Musical notational systems, Morse code	Composer, performer (e.g. Stevie Wonder, Midori)
Interpersonal	Capacity to discern and respond appropriately to the moods, temperaments, motivations, and desires of other people	Social cues (e.g., gestures and facial expressions)	Counselor, political leader (e.g., Carl Rogers, Nelson Mandela)
Intrapersonal	Access to one's own feeling life and the ability to discriminate among one's emotions; knowledge of one's own strengths and weaknesses	Symbols of the self (e.g., in dreams and artwork)	Psychotherapist, religious leader (e.g., Sigmund Freud, Buddha)

Source: Armstrong, T. (1994) *Multiple intelligences in the classroom.* Alexandria, VA: Association for Supervision and Curriculum Development. Reprinted with permission.

(1985) define practical knowledge as "procedural knowledge that is useful in one's every-day life" (p. 134). Leithwood and colleagues (1994) add the descriptor "strategic." They maintain that practical knowledge is "concerned with *how* to solve problems rather than knowledge *about* problem solving" (p. 192), which they term declarative knowledge. Contextual knowledge is knowledge that depends on context. All readers of this text, for example, speak English but, depending on the context in which they operate, may vary in vocabulary size, content comprehension, and even in rate of speech.

Psychologists argue that the separation of these types of knowledge is artificial because they overlap. Thinking about knowledge within such a framework, however, allows educators to reflect on learning opportunities and teaching strategies that may be more appropriate for different types of knowledge acquisition.

Consider, for example, the learning of a second language. If the second language is not used in a person's everyday life (procedural or possibly contextual knowledge) an educator can focus instead on declarative knowledge. In a classroom setting through a variety of teaching techniques, students can learn declarative knowledge—that is, such knowledge about the second language as its verb conjugation and vocabulary.

Visiting a local ethnic restaurant where students are required to order food in the second language or using simulations in the classroom, exemplifies procedural knowledge. Visiting a country and being required to use the knowledge in a variety of settings provides opportunities for students to obtain contextual knowledge. If, in the classroom, students are afforded a variety of teaching and learning opportunities in the second language, such as role-play and simulations that involve procedural knowl-edge, increased learning could result. Although the theory is simple, learning transfer is a far more complex process.

Learning Transfer

Transfer has been defined as "the degree to which a behavior will be repeated in a new situation" (Detterman, 1993, p. 4). Educators are often perplexed when they have a stu-dent who learned something in the recent past but is unable to transfer that learning to a similar situation. For example, in Spanish class, a student may have spent considerable time learning the past tense form of a verb and may demonstrate that knowledge on a written and oral test. Yet, the student is often unable to remember the correct verb form when required to use it in a conversation. Are there mechanisms that will increase the likelihood that learning in one situation will be transferred to another situation?

According to Sternberg and Frensch (1993) the degree of transfer from one sit-uation to another depends on four mechanisms. First, there must be *encoding specificity*. The degree of transfer depends on the original encoding of the knowledge. Retrieval of knowledge depends on how the learner has encoded it. If students are not taught (in the classroom) how to apply information, then the likelihood of their being able to transfer information to a situation is reduced. For example, most educators are well versed in adolescent development but may be unable to transfer such knowledge to raising their own children.

A second mechanism that influences transfer is *organization*—how information is originally organized in a person's memory. Sternberg and Frensch believe "that organi-zation of information from old situations can either facilitate or impede transfer to new situations" (p. 26). When we learn something in a particular way (e.g., memorizing verbs by conjugation) we must reorganize the information to apply it. For example, as one of the authors studied Spanish she was taught to conjugate verbs—*hablo, hablas, habla* (I speak, you speak, he, she or it speaks). To say "He speaks" in the early stages of Spanish language acquisition, she had to begin the conjugation process (*hablo, hablas, habla*) and then stop at the "right" form (*habla*). Next, she had to apply it to the sentence she was attempting—the learner had to reorganize what she originally learned.

A third mechanism involves *discrimination*, in which information is retrieved depending on whether it was tagged or stored as relevant to a new situation in which it might be applied. Discrimination occurs frequently, of which tagging is the key process. What makes a learner tag one piece of information and not another? Reinforcement and review of information may make it more likely that certain knowledge will be tagged by the learner.

Sternberg and Frensch (1993) label the fourth mechanism for transfer *mental set*. Whether or not a person "sees a useful way of doing something depends in part upon the mental set with which he or she approaches the task" (p. 26). In most schools, academic subjects are taught in isolation. Subjects such as algebra are infrequently made relevant to real-world use. Yet educators expect students to transfer the knowledge of the algebraic formula to practical applications. Many students study algebra for two years in high school and perceive little relevance other than that it is usually required for college entrance.

One day while sailing, a person tried to explain to one of the authors how to plot a course and stated, "This is just basic algebra." This statement enabled the author to transfer what had been learned in algebra class to an actual situation. If the learner has an appropriate mental set, transfer is more likely to occur.

Each of these mechanisms has implications for teaching and learning. Current research on teaching and learning calls for approaches that recognize students transfer of learning and that make sense of what they learn.

> What criteria should be used to evaluate Linton's second grade health curriculum and how it is being taught?

Constructivism: A New Conception of Learning

By the mid-1980s the educational community was beginning to talk about a "constructivist" way of learning. Constructivist literature calls for a marked departure from behaviorist theory, which continues to drive much educational practice today. Behaviorist theory of learning includes measurable behavioral objectives (e.g., by the end of this unit the student will have...) and sequenced curricula.

In language texts before the mid-1980s, for instance, students were taught language structure sequentially; the present tense followed by the past tense. Many language teachers believed a natural progression existed that was the best way for people to learn. Conditionals such as "can" and "may," for example, were not often presented until midway thorough a course or toward the latter part of a text, if at all. Requesting something—May I go to the restroom? May I borrow a pen?—are language statements required by beginners. A behavioral approach to language learning, however, with its tight control on presentation of grammar and vocabulary, precludes a beginner's ability to make such requests.

Behaviorist approaches segment knowledge and skills into small pieces, with an overall idea that if each of these small pieces can be mastered, they will, taken together, result in acquisition of complex language skills. It pays little attention to conceptions and misconceptions that students may hold about the knowledge or skills being introduced. We now understand that, like thinking, learning a language is more than the sum of its parts. It is possible to know all grammar tenses and possess a large vocabulary and still be unable to speak a language.

Constructivism, by contrast, is based on the belief that students learn best when they acquire knowledge through exploration and active learning. Individuals construct knowledge rather than receive it. According to Airasian and Walsh (1997), constructivism is a theory about how people learn. "Constructivism is based on the fundamental assumption that people create knowledge from the interaction between their existing knowledge or beliefs and the new ideas or situations they encounter." (p. 445)

Constructivist theory posits that students learn by actively constructing knowledge, comparing new information to previously learned information, thinking about and working through discrepancies, and ultimately reaching new understandings. Constructivist views have strongly influenced the movement toward national standards. Constructivism reminds us that ordering of information takes place in the minds of individuals, so when we as teachers impose our order on students, we rob them of the opportunity to create knowledge and understand themselves.

Building a Culture of Learning

Throughout the 1970s numerous studies explored variables that showed high correlations with increased academic achievement (Lezotte, Edmonds, & Ratner, 1974; Rutter, Maughan, Mortimore, Ouston, & Smith, 1979; Spartz, Valdes, McCormick, Meyers, & Geppert, 1977; Brookover & Lezotte, 1979; Bossert, Dwyer, Rowan, & Lee, 1982). These factors include:

- a safe and orderly environment
- an academic focus on basic skills
- close monitoring of instruction by testing and supervision
- strong instructional leadership from the principal
- high expectations and clear goals for students

Unfortunately these correlates quickly became propaganda disseminated by school districts. Teachers were "in-serviced" in these five correlates and preservice students were expected to regurgitate them on tests. The 1970s research findings, however, oversimplified the notion of effectiveness and little attention was paid to the contexts in which these studies were conducted. What may be a successful practice in one context does not necessarily transfer to another. Programs often do not travel well to other locations regardless of how meticulously they were originally crafted.

In more recent studies that longitudinally examine academic achievement, other factors related to achievement present a more comprehensive picture (Lipsitz, 1984; Stedman, 1987; Wimpelberg, Teddlie, & Stringfield, 1989; Duke, 1987; Cunningham & Gresso, 1993). These researchers discuss the broad-based conditions necessary for successful schools. Themes include leadership and management, changing school culture, and implementing challenging curricula and instruction. According to a study by Binkowski (1995) higher-performing schools include the following themes: participative leadership and management, communication and collaboration between central office and school staff regarding district and school goals, parental involvement, and staff development tied to curriculum and instruction.

In a provocative study of a school using site-based management, Beck and Murphy (1996) identified four imperatives for successful schools. These include:

- a consistent and powerful focus on learning
- strong, facilitative leadership
- a commitment to nurturing a sense of internal and external community
- resources aimed at building the capacity of people within the community to lead, learn, and teach (p. *ix*).

Beck and Murphy observed that staff members are highly motivated to increase learning in schools that have site-based management. "We found a school where promoting learning was a clear priority and, for some teachers and the principal, "a consuming passion" (p. 43). They noted that more attention was paid to student learning than to adult education. Additionally, they discovered that certain instructional strategies worked well in a particular school. These strategies matched students' interests and needs.

Beck and Murphy noted that the principal and a number of teachers exercise leadership. Additionally, parents contribute to children's success "by actively and enthusiastically supporting the work of educators" (p. 79). Finally, they found that site-based management provides more opportunities for parents to take leadership roles.

Beck and Murphy's third imperative for successful schools refers to the role of the community. Site-based management of schools creates opportunities for collaboration with organizations and agencies in the community. This comprehensive focus on children was a crucial factor in academic success.

Beck and Murphy's fourth imperative deals with capacity building. They found that site autonomy "encouraged a sense of agency on the part of teachers and parents" (p. 114). Site-based management allows teachers greater freedom to control their professional lives. Autonomy and a degree of budgetary control allows teachers to more quickly make decisions regarding curriculum, program innovations, and professional development.

A strong focus on learning, sufficient resources, strong facilitative leadership, and human capital from the school, district, and community are essential conditions for learning. Once these optimal learning conditions exist in a school, then attention must be given to the most appropriate teaching and learning approaches for the various types of knowledge that are part of the curriculum.

> What conditions must exist at Linton Elementary School to ensure that an effective health curriculum is being taught?

Teaching and Learning Approaches

A multitude of teaching and learning approaches can be used to optimize learning, and it is important to keep in mind Wiggins' (1989) idea of the futility of trying to teach everything of importance. He maintains, "Students cannot possibly learn everything of value by the time they leave school, but we can instill in them the desire to ask questions throughout their lives" (p. 44).

A number of different constructs can be used to analyze and determine what and how students should learn. Glatthorn (1994) believes that "some knowledge and skills seem to have high importance for all students, and they are the essential learning that all students need to master" (p. 27). They include major concepts, principles, ideas, and skills of a subject. Glatthorn also maintains that the structure of learning should be analyzed: "Understanding the principles of genetics is learning of high structure; it must be explicitly planned, taught, and tested. But developing scientific curiosity seems to be learning of low structure." He argues that teachers should nurture students' developing curiosity when possible, rather than simply spout facts that are taught "and then forgotten" (p. 27). Content raises questions and provides answers as it moves the learner from a basic grasp to a sophisticated and systematic view.

In this section we briefly describe learning and teaching models embedded in a constructivist approach to learning and in multiple intelligence and triarchic intelligence theories.

Apprenticeship Learning

Much has been written about apprenticeship, one of the oldest models for learning. Researchers have recently revisited the potential of this model. As Gardner (1991) states, " apprenticeships may well be the means of instruction that builds most effectively on the ways in which most young people learn" (p. 124). He posits that "the best chance for an education leading to understanding lies in the melding of certain features of apprenticeships with certain aspects of schools and other institutions" (p. 125).

Why are a growing number of educators and researchers (Moffett, 1994; Gardner, 1991; Lave and Wenger, 1993) advocating apprenticeship learning? One major reason may be that in addition to situating learning in context, apprenticeships provide interaction, which is a key part of psychologist Lev Vygotsky's (1978) *zone of proximal development*. This "zone" is the space between what a student can do when working alone, compared with what he or she can do when working with an experienced adult or peer. Learning and mastery occur through active joint participation.

This zone represents the gap between the individual learner's problem-solving ability and the total capacity demonstrated by those with whom the learner interacts.

According to Moffett (1994) natural learning methods such as witnessing, attuning, imitating, helping, collaborating, interacting, experimenting, transmitting, and investigating are all combined into the educational practice of apprenticing. Apprenticeships, however, are not the only learning formats that involve interaction in the zone of proximal development.

Cooperative Learning

Over the last twenty years professionals in education have become increasingly familiar with the practice of cooperative learning. Students are arranged in groups of heterogeneous ability levels in which they work together to accomplish shared goals. Cooperative learning can be used in any level class and subject area.

A substantial body of research documents the effectiveness of cooperative-learning strategies (Slavin, 1990; Stevens & Slavin, 1995). Children learn by piggybacking on the ideas of others through collaboration; they serve as instructional agents for one another. Work is carefully structured; students work in cooperative groups and thereby obtain a sense of positive interdependence.

Cooperative learning fosters problem solving and works best if there are five or fewer in a team. It promotes cooperative interpersonal behavior, mutual encouragement, and individual responsibility and accountability. Cooperative learning has been found to improve student achievement, intergroup relations, and self-esteem (Slavin, 1996). Cooperative learning is a sturdy platform for problem-based learning.

Problem-Based Learning

Problem-based learning (PBL) is widely used in medical education, and in recent years it has found a place in a variety of disciplines, including engineering, law, architecture, social work, and educational administration (Boud & Feletti, 1998; Bridges & Hallinger, 1995; Clarke et al., 1998). In the early 1990s PBL was introduced in elementary and secondary schools.

PBL begins with a practical problem that the student is likely to encounter in the real world. Problems are selected to illuminate core concepts in the school's curriculum. Subject matter is organized around the problem rather than around a discipline, and students have considerable responsibility and autonomy for directing their learning. Most learning is done in dyads or small teams (cooperative learning groups). Students must demonstrate their learning through a product or performance. Clearly the role of the teacher in PBL differs considerably from that of the teacher as expert. In PBL the teacher challenges, facilitates, and questions. In small groups, students work on PBL projects that are situated in a learning context and have multiple opportunities to work within the zone of proximal development.

Students are required to struggle with complicated real-world issues within the classroom setting. Problems should provide just enough information to guide investigation and student-directed inquiry. Students grapple with open-ended problems and are expected to propose solutions. They gain experience in self-direction, reasoning, problem solving, and collaboration. Teachers become facilitators, helping students understand their own thinking and guiding them as they search for new information. Students interact with others and acquire information before deciding how they will deal with the problem.

Apprenticeship learning, cooperative learning, and problem-based learning are three approaches embedded in constructivist philosophy. It is important that the school administrators understand the various approaches to learning and how to implement them in the curriculum. Other approaches related to constructivism are thematic, authentic, and differentiated instruction.

Thematic Instruction.   In a thematic instruction approach, various related disciplines are brought to bear on a theme, issue, problem, topic, or experience. It is best when the themes or problems emerge from the student's world. Teachers and students are engaged in a learning partnership to examine a specific area in-depth and from multiple perspectives. Teachers in separate disciplines are united to team-teach around a selected set of issues. Information is viewed in a holistic manner. This orientation offers a way to show how different subject areas relate, thus affirming their relevance.

Authentic Instruction.   Students learn best from actual experiences rather than from simulations. Authentic instruction requires the teacher to work with students in choosing a topic on which to focus and in obtaining needed information. Information-gathering might include contacting expert practitioners, students from another culture, and authors as well as collecting data from researchers, foundations, governments, and others. Technology is often used in obtaining, organizing, manipulating, and displaying information. The teacher serves as a coach, providing structure and actively supporting students. Some educators refer to certain types of problem-based learning as a form of authentic instruction.

Differentiated Instruction.   The approach called differentiated instruction is based on a diagnosis of student readiness, interest, and learning profile. All students are engaged in a continual progression of challenging work. Use of time, space, and groupings is flexible.

Research indicates the importance of meeting varying learning needs, even though in practice the process has proved difficult. This type of study allows students to pursue topics of interest in a direction or depth that might not be suitable for or likely to be pursued by the class as a whole. Students ready for independence from teacher direction will be released from persistent supervision, and those requiring assistance are provided greater structure. Differentiated instruction involves such strategies as curriculum compacting, independent study, interest centers or interest groups, tiered assignments, flexible grouping, mentorships and apprenticeships, learning contracts and anchoring activities. Other types of curricular and instructional approaches include brain-based, discovery, interdisciplinary, and whole language.

What instructional model(s) might work best for health education at Linton Elementary? Explain why.

Curriculum Design and Educational Programming

According to Glatthorn (1997), "principals can best discharge their leadership role if they develop a deep and broad knowledge base with respect to curriculum" (p. 3). What is it that school administrators need to know about curriculum?

Functions of Curriculum

Textbooks on curriculum development traditionally discuss four curriculum levels: state, district, school, and classroom. Box 8.1 lists the functions for each level, which is embedded in the preceding level. For example, one role of the teacher is to develop units of study. Those units of study emanate from one of the school functions—developing a program of studies. This program in turn is embedded in a district function—identifying a common program of studies. At the state level, administrators develop frameworks

---

BOX 8.1

Summary of Curriculum Functions

State functions

Develop state frameworks, including broad goals, general standards, and graduation requirements.

Develop state tests and other performance measures in required academic subjects.

Provide needed resources to local districts.

Evaluate state frameworks.

District functions

Develop and implement curriculum-related policies.

Develop a vision of a quality curriculum.

Develop educational goals based on state goals.

Identify a common program of studies, the curriculum requirements, and subject time allocation, for each level of schooling.

For each subject, develop the documents for the core or mastery curriculum guides.

Select instructional materials.

Develop district curriculum-based tests and other performance measures to supplement state tests.

Provide fiscal and other resources needed at the school level, including technical assistance.

Evaluate the curriculum.

School functions

Develop the school's vision of a quality curriculum, building on the district's vision.

Supplement the district's educational goals.

Develop its own program of studies.

Develop a learning-centered schedule.

Determine nature and extent of curriculum integration.

Align the curriculum.

Monitor and assist in the implementation of the curriculum.

Classroom functions

Develop yearly planning calendars.

Develop units of study.

Enrich the curriculum and remediate learning.

Evaluate the curriculum.

Source: Glatthorn, A. (1997). *The principal as curriculum leader.* Thousand Oaks, CA: Corwin Press. Reprinted by permission.

embodying broad goals and general standards. Thus, there is a connection, an alignment, among the functions at the various levels.

A fifth curriculum level should be added to Glatthorn's four: the emerging roles played by national professional organizations, national and international research groups, and the U.S. Department of Education in Washington, D.C. These groups can be described not only as influencing local curriculum, but also as being major players in the creation of frameworks and in the development of national tests and standards.

Principal as Curriculum Leader

ALLAN A. GLATTHORN
Professor of Education
University of East Carolina

When I told a friend that the title of one of my books was *Principal as Curriculum Leader*, she responded, "That's an oxymoron if I ever heard one." Her reaction is understandable: most principals do not believe that they have any role in setting curriculum. However, I believe that they do have a key part to play in this essential component of schooling.

Curriculum development and implementation are nested processes: the state, the school system, the school, and the classroom all have legitimate roles to play in learning enhancement. The state should identify curriculum standards for each subject; the school district should use those standards in developing coordinated curricula for grades K–12, with appropriate benchmarks. The school should develop its own program of studies, within district guidelines. The classroom teacher should operationalize the district curriculum guides in several ways: develop long-term plans, write units of study, enrich the district curriculum, and adapt it so that it responds to individual student needs.

School-level leadership functions with respect to curriculum, as follows:

1. Influencing district curriculum guides
2. Developing the school's program of studies
3. Developing a learning-centered schedule
4. Determining the nature and extent of curriculum integration
5. Aligning the curriculum
6. Monitoring the curriculum
7. Helping teachers make long-term plans
8. Helping teachers develop curriculum units
9. Helping teachers provide enrichment and remediation
10. Evaluating the curriculum

This list does not mean that the principal must do all the work. Instead, I encourage principals to play an active role but to use a team-leadership approach that recognizes the strengths and needs of classroom teachers.

While educators need to strengthen curricula at all levels, I believe that the most important challenge is to develop curriculum competence at the school and classroom levels. In responding to this challenge, principals are the key agents in curriculum reform.

The Standards Movement

Two federally funded groups, the National Education Goals Panel (no longer in existence) and the National Council on Education Standards and Testing, were established directly following the first Education Summit in 1989. The mission of these two groups was to enhance the implementation of standards-based education. In recent years a variety of national and state agencies and professional organizations have been involved in the development of curriculum standards or frameworks (see Box 8.2 on page 234). Almost all states have standards of learning in English, language arts, history/social studies, mathematics, science, and writing. Many of these frameworks have influenced the development of local school curricula. Certainly an administrator should carefully consider the standards developed by these organizations when setting curriculum at the local level.

Standards are norms for quality control. They tell us what students should know and be able to do. According to Diane Ravitch (1995) there are three types of standards: content standards, performance standards, and opportunity-to-learn (OTL) standards. Content standards are the descriptions of the knowledge and skills desired for students to learn. Performance standards refer to the level of proficiency, or degree of mastery, at which the knowledge or skill is to be displayed. OTL standards have to do with the availability of resources. The premise of OTL standards is that schools, districts, and states must provide the necessary programs, staff, and other resources to meet the basic needs of students.

What is the role of the principal and teachers at Linton Elementary School regarding the health curriculum, and how might standards help in this effort?

Curricular and Instructional Change

Whether curriculum is based on national, state, or locally developed standards, the process of change is key to understanding curriculum implementation and program innovation. Fullan (1993) argues, "It is probably closer to the truth to say that the main problem in public education is not resistance to change, but the presence of too many innovations mandated or adopted uncritically and superficially on an *ad hoc* fragmented basis" (p. 23). The successful development and implementation of programs thrives on abundant opportunity for dialogue that encourages educators to critique the curriculum. This dialogue will more than likely involve conflict. If we think of conflict in terms of "conflict with civility," then it is not only healthy, but a necessary ingredient in curriculum and program development.

Several researchers have discussed the stages of change in schools (Kilmann, 1989; Fullan, 1991; Gorton & Snowden, 1997; Cordeiro, 1998). A model for program development including four approaches to change, and the stages inherent in each, is particularly appropriate to this discussion.

As Figure 8.1 on page 235 shows, there are four overarching types of approach to change: a mandated approach ("This district will use computer technology in all courses"); a model adoption approach ("We are considering adopting the Accelerated Schools model"); a change agent approach ("Several teachers have piloted the Success for All curriculum and are recommending that it be used by the school"); and a catalytic

BOX **8.2**

Curriculum Standards Documents

Science	National Research Council. *National Science Education Standards.* Washington, D.C.: National Academy Press, 1996.
Foreign language	National Standards in Foreign Language Education Project. *Standards for Foreign Language Learning: Preparing for the 21st Century.* Lawrence, KS: Allen Press, 1996
English/language arts	National Council of Teachers of English and the International Reading Association. *Standards for the English Language Arts.* Urbana, IL: NCTE, 1996.
History	National Center for History in the Schools. *National Standards for History for Grades K–4: Expanding Children's World in Time and Space.* Los Angeles, CA.: NCHS, 1994. ————. *National Standards for United States History: Exploring the American Experience.* Los Angeles, CA: NCHS, 1994. ————. *National Standards for World History: Exploring Paths to the Present.* Los Angeles, CA: NCHS, 1994. ————. *National Standards for History: Basic Education.* Los Angeles, CA: NCHS, 1996.
Arts	Consortium of National Arts Education Associations. *National Standards for Arts Education: What Every Young American Should Know and Be Able To Do in the Arts.* Reston, VA: Music Educators National Conference, 1994.
Health	Joint Committee on National Health Education Standards. *National Health Education Standards: Achieving Health Literacy.* Reston, VA: Association for the Advancement of Health Education, 1995.
Civics	Center for Civic Education. *National Standards for Civics and Government.* Calabasas, CA: CCS, 1994.
Economics	National Council on Economic Education. *Content Statements for State Standards in Economics, K–12* (Draft). New York: NCEE, August 1996.
Geography	Geography Education Standards Project. *Geography for Life: National Geography Standards.* Washington, D.C.: National Geographic Research and Exploration, 1994.
Physical education	National Association for Sport and Physical Education. *Moving into the Future, National Standards for Physical Education: A Guide to Content and Assessment.* St. Louis: Mosby, 1995.
Mathematics	National Council of Teachers of Mathematics. *Curriculum and Evaluation Standards for School Mathematics.* Reston, VA: NCTM, 1989.
Social studies	National Council for the Social Studies. *Expectations of Excellence: Curriculum Standards for Social Studies.* Washington, D.C.: NCSS, 1994.

Marzano, R. & Kendall, J. Curriculum Frameworks *NASSP Bulletin* 1997 81:590. Reprinted with permission.

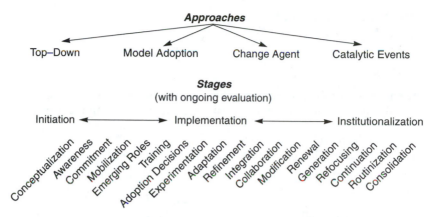

FIGURE 8.1   A Model of Program Development

events approach ("After this terrible racial incident we must consider a multicultural approach to our curriculum").

Whatever the approach, all innovations pass through a series of stages. Change proceeds along a continuum. Initiation might involve conceptualization, awareness, and commitment. Implementation might include development, experimentation, adaptation, and refinement. Finally, institutionalization might involve refocusing, continuation, routinization, or possibly consolidation.

Gorton and Snowden (1997) proposed the seven-stage change process presented in Box 8.3 on page 236. It must be remembered that this is an ideal model for change, and few innovations proceed exactly in these stages. These sequential steps, however, can serve as guidelines for administrators in helping them to think about how an innovation might be implemented.

Modification of a curriculum and educational program begins in a specific proposal to modify what already exists. Curriculum change focuses on what will be taught, and instructional change focuses on the way the curriculum will be taught. The proposal grows from the staff's knowledge of the goals, standards, and research as well as of the students and community. Participants can become knowledgeable by reading, visiting other schools, experimenting, discussing, and consulting. The formal proposal includes a rationale for change and an analysis of the change's potential impact on resources.

The proposal should be presented to all concerned, including faculty and parents, for final review before it is submitted through the school system's review process. Those involved may choose to join one of the networks to help develop the curriculum and provide needed support (see Chapter 3). The final step after approval is determining how the curriculum will be organized and delivered.

What steps should Linton Elementary School staff take to develop and refine the existing health curriculum?

BOX **8.3**

Important Stages and Steps in the Change Process

Stage I

Conduct a Needs Assessment

A. Identify the need for change. Examine the present system to ascertain which aspects need to be improved.
B. Develop or evaluate and select a new approach or system that will replace the former method.

Stage II

Orient the Target Group to the Proposed Change

A. Create an awareness of and interest in the proposed innovation on the part of the target group—teachers, for example.
B. Institute with the target group an examination of the strengths and weaknesses of the proposed change. Pilot-test and refine the new system prior to its introduction.
C. Identify, with the help of the target group, the commitments that will need to be made in terms of additional resources, in-service training programs, and/or building modifications.

Stage III

Decide Whether to Introduce the Proposed Change

A. Identify those who should participate in the decision.
B. Decide on the process by which the decision will be made.
C. Decide whether to proceed with the implementation of the proposed change.

Stage IV

Plan a Program of Implementation

A. Plan and carry out a program of in-service education for those involved in the proposed change.

B. Provide the resources and facilities necessary for successfully introducing the change.
C. Anticipate and attempt to resolve in advance the operational problems that may be encountered in implementing the proposed innovation.

Stage V

Implement the Proposed Innovation

Stage VI

Conduct In-Process Evaluation

A. Design and institute a system that will provide feedback on the extent to which the proposed change is accomplishing its objectives.
B. Diagnose those aspects of the program or its implementation that need improvement.

Stage VII

Refine and Institutionalize the Innovation

A. Modify the innovation and, if necessary, provide additional orientation, training, resources, facilities, and so forth.
B. Gain the acceptance of the innovation (if it is successful) as a regular and permanent part of the total educational program in the school or school district.

Source: Gorton, R., & Snowdon, P. (1997). *School leadership and administration* (5th Ed.) Madison, WI: WCB Brown and Benchmark.

Developing Curriculum and Programs

According to Elliot Eisner (1994) all schools teach three curricula: explicit, implicit, and null. The explicit curriculum is the actual curriculum the school uses to teach pupils. The explicit curriculum usually takes the form of curriculum guides, but all too often it consists of textbooks. The implicit curriculum is not a formal part of the curriculum, yet it is taught in school. For example, the importance of punctuality and respect for others is part of many schools' implicit curriculum. Eisner maintains that "the implicit curriculum of a school is what it teaches because of the kind of school it is" (p. 97). Eisner's thesis is that "what schools do not teach is just as important as what they do teach" (p. 97).

Eisner defines the null curriculum in two dimensions. First, educators need to look at the subjects or content areas that may or may not be present in the curriculum. Teachers might ask such questions as Why do we teach pre-algebra? Why do we have five tracks for English classes? Why are no advanced placement courses offered? Why do so few female students enroll in advanced math classes? What should students be expected to know as part of U.S. literature?

The second dimension involves the intellectual processes that the school emphasizes or neglects. Eisner maintains that "not all thinking is mediated by word or number, nor is all thinking rule-abiding" (p. 98). Critical questions educators might ask include: What forms of knowing (i.e., visual, metaphoric) are absent or marginal? In what ways do we cultivate students' imaginations?

Asking questions such as these is not only helpful in curriculum development and implementation, but also in evaluating curriculum and programs. Clearly many factors affect curriculum development.

Designing and Managing the Curriculum

According to Doll (1986) there are five curriculum designs:

- Subject designs, which stress content matter
- Interest designs, based on the needs and interests of students
- Process designs, which emphasize learning how to learn and thinking skills
- Social activity designs, which highlight social and community issues
- Competency designs, represented by behavioral descriptions and objectives

A variety of policies and factors are associated with effective programs. Whether a curriculum is based on a national, state, or local framework, the goal of curriculum development is to create a coherent educational program. Regardless of the design of the curriculum, important issues to consider are curriculum *congruity, integration, sequence,* and *access.* Administrators must foster a school environment that continuously raises questions related to these four areas. Following are some of these questions.

Curriculum Congruity

- How consistent is the curriculum across grade levels and schools?
- What criteria are used to determine whether a students has achieved mastery of a concept?
- What enables the student to understand the interpretation of knowledge and how it is used to examine authentic problems?

Curriculum Integration

- Is the curriculum socially relevant?
- Which is more important—breadth or depth of subject matter?
- Should additional time be given to a specific subject?
- Is the program balanced between essential knowledge and special interests?
- What requirements and standards should be established?

Curriculum Sequence

- Should certain topics precede other topics?
- Should a topic be taught chronologically?
- Should a topic be taught from a developmental viewpoint?
- Should a topic be taught inductively or deductively?

Student Access

- What program options are available to students?
- How are students assigned to classes and teachers?
- How do policies regarding promotion, required courses, and the like affect students?
- How is the program of studies responsive to the special needs of the students served?
- What information is provided to students and families about course and program options?
- How are students grouped or tracked into courses?
- What are the enrollments by gender and race or ethnicity in courses?

These are but a few of the questions that address issues of curriculum congruity, integration, sequencing, and access. These questions and a variety of critical factors must be investigated in the design and development of curriculum and programs. Critical factors include nature and scale of the program, community expectations, resources needed, stakeholders involved, the utilization of time, community and school demographics, incentives for teachers, timeline implementation, and program monitoring. Once a curriculum is developed or a program or model adapted to a school, the work of program improvement has begun. And it is an ongoing process.

What are some of the questions that need to be asked regarding Linton Elementary's health curriculum?

Seeing the Curriculum Whole: The Function of a Real Educational Leader

LAUREL N. TANNER
Professor, Temple University

The school administrator's task, of course, involves the entire curriculum. Nowhere is the task more beautifully set forth than in Lawrence Cremin's *The Genius of American Education*. "Someone must look at the curriculum whole and raise insistent questions of priority and relationship" (1965, p. 58). No individual, he writes, can or ought to have the sole responsibility for this concern, but it certainly must be the main business of anybody who sees himself or herself a principal, superintendent, or president of a school board.

Specialists do not look at how the parts must relate to the whole. Principals must have a larger vision and see the entire curriculum. Because we lack such a vision, schools are wrestling with some intractable problems that might have been avoided. In the famous curriculum reform movement of the 1960s, priority was given to science, mathematics, and modern foreign languages because these subjects were deemed essential for our national defense. The developers of the new curricula were advanced scholar–specialists from universities who had no understanding of the curriculum in its totality. At the same time, school administrators acted as though these three subjects were all that mattered, letting the federal funds that paid for summer institutes for their teachers (and often for themselves) drive policy.

It was this situation that prompted Lawrence Cremin to point out that when individual curriculum reform projects are under way, it should not be assumed that curriculum development is under way. Daniel Tanner and I found, as a result of the reforms that were instituted, that the schools were left with problems stemming from misguided curriculum priorities, curriculum imbalance, and failure to articulate the curriculum with the nature of the learner (Tanner and Tanner, 1995).

Two of our most difficult problems—discipline and dropping out—are due in no small way to the failure to look at the curriculum whole. For example, some school districts that reduced their offerings in the studio and industrial arts experienced an increased dropout rate (Tanner, 1997). The loss to individual students was tremendous. Unable to develop in the one area in which they excelled, they decided to leave school. The literature is filled with references to the "strong" educational leader.

The principal's strength derives from professional knowledge and experience in working out problems by using theoretical principles. It is in no sense an arbitrary thing. Three constructs provide strength for a principal to see the curriculum as an entirety.

The School's Philosophy

First, the curriculum and how it is taught must be governed by a statement of philosophy and goals—a theory of what the school hopes to achieve. Tyler (1949), whose model for curriculum development is a kind of bible—and for good reason in my view—suggests that a school have seven to fifteen broad educational goals. Without a goals statement a school is susceptible to whatever schemes are fashionable at a given time and the whims of individual faculty members.

Hoy and Tarter (1995) provide an interesting example of a high school principal who denied a member of the English faculty's request to offer an elective in Latin American literature. The department chair had already turned down the request because it was inconsistent with the thrust of the program. The school had a statement of philosophy and goals and tried to make decisions that were consistent with it.

As Cremin warned, "to refuse to look at curricula in their entirety is to relegate to intraschool policies a series of decisions that ought to call into play the most fundamental philosophical principles" (1965, p. 58). The strong educational leader derives his or her strength from a statement

(continued)

Continued

of philosophy and goals developed collaboratively with the faculty. No philosophy, however, should be a barricade against change. "Any person who is open-minded and sensitive to new perceptions, and who has concentration and responsibility in connecting them has, in so far, a philosophic disposition," observed Dewey (1916, p. 380).

What a Whole Curriculum Looks Like
The second source of strength is knowledge of what the entire curriculum looks like. Such a comprehensive vision is a difficult thing for any one person, because there are so many knowledge categories. It is little wonder that administrators regard the curriculum as specialized and compartmentalized knowledge over and beyond their domain of expertise. But there is a manageable way of looking at the macrocurriculum, in terms of five inclusive functions (Tanner & Tanner, 1995):

1. General education or the common understandings and competencies necessary for responsible citizenship in a free society
2. Specialized education that enables the learner to become a productive earner as well as a lifelong learner
3. Enrichment education—avocational instruction that enriches the life of every individual
4. Exploratory education that stimulates the individual to extend his or her reach into untried realms
5. Special-interest education that provides for intensive learning experiences beyond one's vocational and avocational pursuits

Like the fingers of a hand, these five functions are interdependent. Equipped with a comprehensive view of the curriculum, the administrator can help faculty develop a shared vision and put it into practice as an ongoing operation.

A good leader asks what Cremin called "insistent questions of priority and relationship" (1965, p. 58). The point is that a good school is always involved in curriculum development and better teaching methods. Interestingly, even top-scoring countries, with which the United States is told to compare itself, are dissatisfied with their practices in teaching science and mathematics and "are investing large sums to change" (Atkin & Black, 1997, p. 28). There is a big difference between the reform movement of the 1960s and the present one: Teachers are involved in working out the curriculum at the classroom level.

Putting the Vision into Practice
Third, how does the administrator orchestrate the vision of a whole curriculum? How does he or she bring the specializations into relationship? The best answer is an approach pioneered by Ralph Tyler (1949). It concerns what happens—or should happen—immediately after a school has firmed up its goals statement. The faculty has already answered Tyler's question "What educational purposes should the school seek to attain?" (p. v). Tyler shows the way a high school English department might use these broad goals to open up the question, How do we in the English department not just teach literature but also help achieve our school's seven or nine or twelve educational goals? Every teacher has a responsibility to deal with the school's goals—academic, social, personal, and vocational. Attention to the goals is key. The strong leader uses the goals, not just to test and screen curriculum proposals but to bring the specializations together.

As is becoming increasingly clear, curriculum is made in the schoolhouse, not the statehouse or the White House. Administrators, to a very great extent, hold the future of school reform in their hands.

Program Improvement and Evaluation

The notion of evaluation is integral to the change process. Too often it is an afterthought and is tacked on to a completed or near-completed program. Genuine program improvement requires that evaluation be built into the curriculum or program from the beginning. Program improvement may be conducted by those involved in the program itself or by an outside organization such as an accrediting agency. Regardless of the approach used, evaluation is an ongoing part of the improvement process of the school.

CRESST, the UCLA Center for Research on Evaluation, Standards, and Student Testing, proposes six steps for guiding evaluation (see Table 8.2). Two of the six steps include the involvement of key constituencies. Guba and Lincoln (1989), in their book *Fourth Generation Evaluation*, maintain that "the claims, concerns and issues of stakeholders [should] serve as organizational foci (the basis for determining what information is needed" (p. 50). Therefore, an initial step in any approach to evaluation involves identification of stakeholders.

Fenwick English (Frase, English, & Poston, 1995) developed a curriculum auditing process that is widely used by school districts and is part of an auditing approach sponsored by the American Association of School Administrators. A key concept in

TABLE 8.2   Principles of Sensible Evaluation

Step	Sensible Actions
Focus the evaluation	Involve significant constituencies
	Include improvement and accountability concerns
	Look at long- and short-term targets of change
	Look at relationships between processes and outcomes based on your theories of action
	Look for unanticipated side effects
Identify tracking strategies	Use strategies well aligned with school goals
	Use multiple indicators
	Build in checks for validity of inferences
Manage instrument development and data collection	Build measures upon existing information
	Consider accountability mandates
	Match instruments with specific evaluation questions
Score and summarize data	When appropriate, use scoring sessions for staff development
	Assure valid inferences by choosing appropriate scores
Analyze and interpret information	Involve key constituencies
	Examine progress over time
	Consider and refine your theories of action
	Be alert to unanticipated side effects
	Corroborate findings by using multiple indicators
Act on findings and continue program monitoring	Use the principles guiding focusing activities to monitor actions based on your findings

Source: Sensible evaluation. (1997) Los Angeles: Center for Research on Evaluation Standards and Student Testing. Reprinted with permission.

curriculum auditing is the alignment of goals and objectives, curriculum content, and testing. The audit determines the degree to which the written, taught, and tested curricula are aligned. The audit provides information for curriculum and instructional planning by validating what currently exists within a school district. The results of an audit are used to improve the quality of the curriculum and instruction and ultimately to improve the quality of learning.

> How might the health curriculum at Linton Elementary School be evaluated?

Utilizing Time

Perhaps the two most important jobs of a school administrator are recruiting and hiring faculty and deciding how time in a school year will be allocated. The length of the school year, day, and class session, as well as their organization, have significant impact on teacher–student and student–student relationships. In recent years there has been renewed interest in various types of scheduling. Additionally, the notion of looping—teachers moving with students over a two- or three-year period—is growing in popularity.

Year-Round Education

Year-round education (YRE) is not a new idea in the United States or in other nations. The literature on year-round education in the United States first appeared with some degree of regularity in the 1970s. Most of the discussion, unfortunately, focused on the importance of utilizing the school building, rather than on efficiency and effectiveness as has been done more recently. YRE is being revived and it is estimated that "nearly 1.5 million students in more than 25 states now attend elementary and secondary schools that function on a year-round schedule" (Levine & Ornstein, 1993).

Year-round education involves a reorganization of the school calendar into instructional blocks, with vacations (or special inter-sessions) distributed throughout the calendar year, rather than concentrated in the summer. Learning opportunities need to be continuous throughout the year. School districts can operate on single-track or multitrack schedules. The most common year-round schedule is the single-track, 45–15 day plan. Students attend school for 45 days, followed by 15 days with no school. This pattern is repeated four times. According to the research literature the several advantages to year-round education include:

- Increased attendance of teachers and students
- Lower student dropout rates, greater flexibility in instruction, greater retention of learning
- Greater flexibility in teacher planning, student assessment, and curriculum development

- Additional opportunities for remedial and accelerated classes during the inter-sessions (Doyle & Finn, 1985; Quinlan, George, & Emmett, 1987; Ballinger, 1988; White, 1988; Peltier, 1991; Gee, 1997)

Block Scheduling

In a recent book, Canady and Rettig (1995) estimated that more than 50 percent of U.S. high schools use some form of block scheduling. There are numerous formats for block scheduling. Two widely used models include the 4/4 semester plan and the alternative day or A/B schedule. In a 4/4 semester block schedule, each semester students attend four classes a day, completing the course during this time. In the alternative day, or A/B schedule, a course meets every other day for the entire school year. Figure 8.2 on page 244 depicts a typical A/B block schedule.

A powerful variation of block scheduling is the Copernican Plan (Carroll, 1994). In this scheduling model, class periods are longer so that teachers have fewer students each semester. Students have two 85- to 90-minute classes each day, lunch, and either one or two electives. Classes meet for ninety days and then another class is scheduled. In the Copernican Plan credit is awarded for mastering course objectives, and students graduate at the end of the semester in which they complete the required number of credits.

There are many reasons secondary schools are experimenting with allocating time differently from seven- or eight-period schedules. Criticisms of these schedules are numerous: time is lost passing in hallways, hallway time increases discipline problems, students are overwhelmed by having seven or eight teachers each day, teachers are overwhelmed with having 120–150 students per day, an impersonal assembly-line atmosphere is created, far too many subjects may be assigned homework for the same evening, and so on.

In a study of 820 high schools Glickman (1995) found that activity-learning methods, which are more likely to be found in schools with longer class periods, led to higher achievement. Additionally, fewer class changes resulted in fewer discipline problems and a less stressful school setting. The research data describe several advantages to block scheduling:

- Reduction in disciplinary referrals and suspensions (Carroll, 1994; Meadows, 1995; Reid, 1995; Glickman, 1995; Einedar & Bishop, 1997)
- Positive effects on school climate (Carroll, 1994; Reid, 1995; Glickman, 1998)
- Lower dropout rates (Hottenstein & Malatesta, 1993; Carroll, 1994; Reid, 1995)
- Improved student attendance (King et al., 1995; Cameron, 1995; Schoenstein, 1995)
- Improved student attitudes (Hottenstein & Malatesta, 1993; Carroll, 1994; Meadows, 1995; Einedar & Bishop, 1997)
- Improved teacher attitudes (Adam & Seick, 1994; Carroll, 1994)

Varying the structure of the school day and the school year can provide numerous academic benefits. In a study that focused on block scheduling and its effect on math instruction, Kramer (1997) noted that transitioning to block schedules can lead to achievement gain, given sufficient staff development, planning time, and curriculum modification. It is evident that when transitioning to a block schedule, the major role of the school administrator is to provide faculty with adequate support.

FIGURE 8.2 Example of a Block Schedule

Monday	Tuesday (even)	Wednesday (odd)	Thursday (even)	Friday (odd)
Period 1 7:27–8:14	**Block 1** 7:27–9:06 Period 1	**Block 2** 7:27–9:06 Period 2	**Block 1** 7:25–9:04 Period 1	**Block 2** 7:25–9:04 Period 2
Period 2 8:20–9:07				
Period 3 9:13–10:07	**Block 3** 9:13–10:53 Period 3	**Block 4** 9:13–10:53 Period 4	**Block 3** 9:11–10:51 Period 3	**Block 4** 9:11–10:51 Period 4
Period 4 10:06–10:53				
Lunch Period—A 11:00–11:30 **5** **Class Period—B** 11:00–11:49	Block 3 11:00–11:30 **5** Class Period—B 11:00–11:49	**Block 3** 11:00–11:30 **5** Class Period—B 11:00–11:49	**Block 3** 11:00–11:30 **5** Class Period—B 11:00–11:49	**Block 3** 11:00–11:30 **5** Class Period—B 11:00–11:49
		12-Minute Overlap		
Class Period—A 11:37–12:26 **5** **Lunch Period—B** 11:56–12:26	Class Period—A 11:37–12:26 **5** Lunch Period—B 11:56–12:26	Class Period—A 11:37–12:26 **5** Lunch Period—B 11:56–12:26	Class Period—A 11:37–12:26 **5** Lunch Period—B 11:56–12:26	Class Period—A 11:37–12:26 **5** Lunch Period—B 11:56–12:26
Period 6 12:33–1:20	**Block 4** 12:33–2:12 Period 6	**Block 4** 12:33–2:12 Period 7	**Block 4** 12:33–2:12 Period 6	**Block 4** 12:33–2:12 Period 7
Period 7 1:26–2:12				
After School	**After School**	**After School**	**After School**	**After School**

244

Looping

Perhaps one of the most important strategies for affording students more contact time with the same teacher, and additional opportunities for group learning, can be met through the concept of looping. Looping, or multiyear interactions between cohorts of students and a single teacher is common practice in many countries. In Spain, for example, students in kindergarten and grades 1 and 2 have the same teacher for all three years. Beginning in grade 3 the student cohort has a different teacher for the next three years (grades 3–5). Finally, this student cohort has another new teacher for grades 6, 7, and 8. Similarly, in Mexico, the heterogeneous grouping of students into cohorts facilitates students' passage through the curriculum. These *groupos escolares* remain together for three years. A growing body of research supports the notion that long-term relationships with teachers and multiyear relationships with peers can increase student learning (Cordeiro, 1990; Liu, 1997).

Time on Task

According to Stallings (1980) efficient allocation of time spent on a task can increase student achievement. The research literature has identified three levels of time: allocated time, engaged time, and academic learning time. Allocated time is the amount of time that is actually assigned for a class. Engaged time is the amount of allocated time in which the student is actively engaged in the learning activity. Academic learning time is a refinement of engaged time and reflects the quality of the learning (e.g., high, moderate, or low degree of success; appropriateness of the instructional materials).

Research indicates that the allocation of time, including models that examine the school year, day, multiple years, and time in the classroom, is an important approach that enhances learning opportunities.

Assessing Student Progress

Considerable discussion and debate centers around the best ways to assess student progress. Some of the most common forms of student assessment include standardized achievement testing (norm-referenced tests), criterion-referenced testing, and performance or alternative assessment.

Standardized tests, which are designed to compare the performance of students to the performance of a normative group, inspire much debate (Kean, 1996; Neill, 1996). The National Forum on Assessment, which included a group of eighty education and civil rights organizations, concluded that multiple-choice testing (e.g., true or false, selecting one item among several) should be only a small part of any assessment program (Marzano & Kendall, 1997; Popham, 1997). Criterion-referenced tests are meant to ascertain a learner's status with respect to a learning task. They are used to see if a student has mastered specific material.

Performance assessment is a relatively new method that provides more appropriate indicators of student learning than do multiple-choice tests. Performance assessments are sometimes referred to as *alternative assessments* and can assume many forms. Herman, Aschbacher, and Winters (1992) define alternative assessments as measures with common characteristics. Such assessments (a) ask students to perform, create, or produce; (b) tap higher-level thinking and problem-solving skills; (c) use tasks that represent meaningful instructional activities; (d) involve scoring; and (f) require new instructional and assessment roles for teachers.

Some educators maintain that assessments must be authentic. Wiggins (1990) defines authenticity as the extent to which a test, performance, or product in an assessment bears a relationship to a real-world referent.

Portfolios

A portfolio is a collection of individual students' work that results from participation in a developmental process. Decisions related to what is collected depends on the purpose of the portfolio—assessment, culmination, display, future study, to name a few. Through reflection students can become increasingly aware of themselves as learners. Portfolios tend to focus attention on what students are learning, how well they are learning it, how well they demonstrate learning, and how well they reflect on this work.

Portfolios and other types of performance assessments are a relatively recent phenomenon in education, except in arts education. Some teachers specify what goes into a portfolio, whereas others allow the student to select what will be included. This work should exhibit to the student, teacher, and others the student's progress and achievement in a particular area. A portfolio should show the various stages through which a project has passed. For example, a portfolio could contain a series of drafts of a paper. Or, it might contain video clips from different time periods showing how a dance performance has improved as the student practiced.

Assessing Student Performance

GRANT WIGGINS
President and Director for the Center on Learning Assessment and School Structure (C.L.A.S.S.)

Assessment should be educative, not merely a quick audit of performance as is now too often the case. Students and teachers need useful and timely feedback, not arcane item analysis provided in the summer when school is out. Educative assessment thus requires an approach and schedule very different from what is typically found in classroom, district, and state testing.

Assessment should be educative in two senses: It should teach students (and teachers) what kinds of performance tasks and standards are most valued. It should reflect situations in the wider world—real problems, real situations, real audiences, and real purposes. Assessment should also provide timely, ongoing, user-friendly feedback to make possible the slow but steady mastery

of such tasks (as opposed to one-shot testing and ranking).

The use of such feedback—the student's ability to self-adjust—should become increasingly central to what and how we assess. As is true of Little League, Nintendo games, karate, or cooking, the assessment system should provide ongoing feedback using standards and measures of progress over time. It should also provide opportunities to use the feedback as part of what we assess—the assessment of self-adjustment.

Four maxims about reform follow from this idea of educative assessment:

1. **Assessment must be grounded in authentic tasks if it is to inform and im-**

prove performance. To improve and not just audit student performance, we need assessment based on what adults actually do in the world. Although tests and quizzes have a place in rounding out the performance picture, they must be made secondary to more "authentic" tasks.

An assessment is authentic if it:

a. replicates or simulates the ways in which a person's knowledge and abilities are "tested" in real-world situations;

b. requires the student to use knowledge and skills wisely and effectively to solve complex, multistep problems (where the solution involves more than just following a set routine or procedure or "plugging in" knowledge);

c. asks the student to "do" the subject— to *do* science or history, not just recite or replicate through demonstration what was taught or is already known.

d. replicates the *contexts* in which adults are "tested" in the workplace, in civic, and in personal life. By "context," we mean the situations, purposes, audiences, constraints, and the "messiness and murkiness" so common to life's challenges—but so typically absent from neat-and-clean school tests;

e. tests the student's ability to use a repertoire of knowledge and skill to solve complex, multifaceted performance challenges. By contrast, most test items are "plug-in" questions—similar to the sideline drills in athletics (as opposed to the actual game, which requires integrated use of all the drills). While there is, of course, a place for drill tests, *performance is always more than the sum of the drills*; and

f. allows for *appropriate* opportunities to rehearse, practice, consult resources, get feedback on and refine performances and products.

Only by ensuring that the assessment system *models* genuine performance challenges, requirements, and feedback will student performance and teacher instruction be improved over time. This model makes teaching more appropriately like coaching athletic, artistic, and intellectual performance.

2. **Assessment must do more than *audit* performance. It must be designed to *improve* performance.** This principle exposes the weakness of one-shot typical tests. Students, teachers, and administrators need timely, ongoing, user-friendly feedback about the key performance challenges of learning and adult performance. As in athletics and the arts, students need clear, worthy, and recurring tasks that can be slowly mastered over time.

By contrast, all current testing typically "audits" student performance once. Tests use a small number of relatively simplistic indirect "items" that can be easily and quickly scored. A more direct assessment of performance would look at whether students can use knowledge in real-world ways and judge whether they can improve over time on known tasks and standards.

Consider an analogy with athletics. Imagine if basketball season consisted of one game, played on the last day of the year, in which the players did not know which plays they would be asked to make. Imagine further that they would not know if their shots went in the basket until weeks later. Imagine further that if instead of playing the game of basketball, teams of measurement experts each year invented an arcane series of drills to test with—valid to measurement experts, but unconnected to basketball playing in the minds of players and coaches. Finally, imagine a scoring system fully understandable only to the assessors and not the players and coaches. Who would improve at the game under these conditions? Yet, state testing consistently provides feedback that can't easily be deciphered or used on tasks that do not mirror real performance, where the test is unknown until test day, and where the feedback comes at the

(continued)

Continued

end of the school year, when it cannot be used to improve the performance of the student or the cohort.

3. **Assessment must be credible and open if genuine reform is to occur.** Accountability occurs only when adults not only are *responsive* to results but also feel *responsible* for them. Genuine accountability thus requires credible assessment tasks. As in athletics and the arts, where teachers typically work overtime to enable students to meet high standards, that sense of responsibility is attributable to the fact that (1) the standards and tasks are credible and worthy and (2) the assessment system (and the results generated) are open and defensible as a system. No coach complains that the "test" of the game or recital is somehow unfair or unknown; there are many opportunities to improve performance over time. A system of assessment must meet the test of local credibility if we are to get beyond local excuses for poor performance.

Assessment must not rely solely on secret test items and performance standards and one-shot tests. Although simplistic test items (kept secure until test day) are relatively inexpensive to use and easy to measure, implementing them as standard policy is counterproductive to student, teacher, and school improvement. How can anyone improve his or her performance if what specifically is going to be tested is kept secret?

4. **An effective assessment plan must build *local* high-quality assessment capacity.** An assessment system should be deliberately designed to improve the quality of local tests, standards, grading, and reporting.

Consider another analogy. The district's or state's goal should not be that of a narrow-minded doctor who merely forces patients to have an annual physical exam based on a handful of simple tests. Rather, the physician's goal should be to promote daily healthfulness. As things now stand, however, the state "doctor" seems interested only in seeing whether schools "pass the physical."

The unintended but powerful effect of the current system causes the school "patient" to fixate on the simple tasks of the physical exam rather than on attaining daily standards of health and fitness. As a result, few teachers understand how to test for genuine intellectual "health" and "fitness." Fewer still see that their own testing need not mimic the *form* of state testing. Teachers do not need to "teach to the (simplistic) test" for their students to do well on it. Teachers become (wrongly) convinced that the only way to get good test results is to teach to and practice the checkup, ignoring the fact that a multiple-choice test is based on a reverse logic: If you are "healthy" and meet high standards day in and day out, your health will show on the checkup.

The goal of improving local intellectual "fitness" thus requires a system that models good assessment practice as it audits local fitness, so that local assessment improves. Tests teach teachers and students what we value, irrespective of an intent merely to measure. The district (and the state) should provide models of "health" (good performance) and "physical fitness standards" (exemplary tests) in its assessment system. And incentives should be provided to ensure higher-quality local assessment, grounded in clear policies about design and use.

Note: A thorough discussion of these points can be found in Wiggins, G. (1998). *Educative assessment: Designing assessment to inform and improve student performance.* San Francisco: Jossey-Bass.

Reporting Student Progress

Of the many formats used for reporting student progress, letter grades (A, B, C, D, F) are the most common. Numbers (percent correct), symbols (S = Satisfactory, N = Needs Improvement, U = Unsatisfactory), or descriptors (Emerging, Developing, Maturing) are sometimes used at the elementary level.

Another format is a dual marking system. The student gets two marks in a subject—one for the student's level of achievement and the other perhaps the student's achievement in relation to personal ability (student improvement).

Pass–Fail, or Pass–No Pass, is another option for reporting student progress. One advantage to this option is that students will be more likely to explore new areas of knowledge if they know they will not receive a poor grade. A disadvantage is, some educators argue, that students will do the minimum to receive a "pass," rather than being motivated to do better by receiving a letter grade.

Some schools report success with narrative reports. A letter grade may or may not be included. This narrative is a description of the student's progress in a particular subject area and may be developed from a listing of characteristics related to the student's progress. Computer programs are often used to print out selected comments.

Presenting Student Outcomes to the Community

Who are the stakeholders in the assessment process? School administrators must ask themselves this key question to determine what types of assessment data should be shared and how those data will be understood by the different recipients. Parents, students, teachers, administrators, state officials, and community members—all of whom are stakeholders—have potentially differing expectations of program and student assessment.

Administrators must also ask what kinds of information each stakeholder needs and how that information will be used. The answers to these questions will help administrators communicate more effectively and efficiently with each stakeholder.

In his book *Student-Centered Classroom Assessment* (1994), Stiggins provides a helpful way to evaluate the users and uses of assessment results (Table 8.3 on pages 250–251). Stiggins lists the various stakeholders, the key questions that need to be answered, and the information needed to answer those questions. Staff should be informed first and oriented to the results of testing programs. Then, the community should be informed through the appropriate means. Special meetings should be held to discuss and explain test results.

There has been a national trend to move toward high-stakes student assessment, attaching real consequences to low performance. Students who do not perform well on assessment tests are required to go to summer school, retained, or awarded less than standard high school diplomas. Research has not provided evidence that such consequences improve student performance. As a result, a number of districts are looking at smaller class sizes, enriched and more rigorous curriculum, focusing on areas of weakness, and enrichment programs. Some states want to hold principals and teachers accountable by tying their evaluations and salaries to assessments of student progress.

TABLE 8.3   Users and Uses of Assessment Results

Users	Key Question(s) to Be Answered	Information Needed
Classroom Level		
Student	Am I meeting the teacher's standards?	Continuous information about individualized student attainment of specific instructional requirements
	What help do I need to succeed?	
	Are the results worth my investment of energy?	
Teacher	Which students need what help?	Continuous information about individual student attainment of specific program requirements
	Who among my students should work together?	
	What grade should appear in the report card?	
	Did my teaching strategies work?	Continuous assessment of group performance
	How do I become a better teacher?	
Parent	Is my child succeeding in school?	Continuous feedback on individual students' mastery of required material
	What does my child need to succeed?	
	Is my child's teacher(s) doing the job?	
	Is this district doing the job?	
Instructional Support Level		
Principal/Vice Principal	Is instruction in particular areas producing results?	Periodic assessment of group achievement
	Is this teacher effective?	
	What kinds of professional development will help?	
	How shall we spend building resources to be effective?	
Lead Teacher (mentor, support teacher, dept. chair)	What does this teacher need to do the job?	Periodic assessment of group achievement
Counselor/Psychologist	Who needs (can have access to) special support services such as remedial programs?	Periodic assessment of individual achievement
	What student should be assigned to which teachers to optimize results?	
Curriculum Director	Is our program of instruction effective?	Periodic assessment of group achievement
Policy Level		
Superintendent	Are programs producing student learning?	Periodic assessment of group achievement of district curriculum
	Is the building principal producing results?	
	Which programs need/deserve more resources?	

Users	Key Question(s) to Be Answered	Information Needed
Policy Level		
School board	Are students in the district learning? Is the superintendent producing results?	Periodic assessment of group achievement
State department of education	Are programs across the state producing results?	Periodic assessment of group achievement of state curriculum
Citizen/legislator (state or national)	Are students in our schools achieving in ways that will allow them to be effective citizens?	Periodic assessment of group achievement of valued achievement targets

Source: Student-Centered Classroom Assessment. by Richard J. Stiggins. (Columbus, Ohio: Merrill, 1994), a teacher's handbook distributed by the Assessment Training Institute. 50 SW Second Ave. Suite 300. Portland, OR 97204.

Some argue against, high-stakes assessment, suggesting that it works best when it is a central part of teaching, influencing the way we think about curriculum, teaching, and learning. Assessment is to "educate and improve" performance, not merely to audit it. Assessment establishes clear linkage between state and district standards and local testing and grading of students' work. Wiggins (1998) tells us that assessment is central to instruction; that authentic tasks anchor assessment, which anchors teaching; and that performance improvement is locally achieved.

A partial list of Wiggins's (1998, pp. 327–29) strategies for the future includes:

- Turn tests into prompts and prompts into performance tasks
- Change typical contextual constraints or limits on resources available during a test
- Redefine passing to ensure that a grade is standard-based
- Get colleagues to "own" the problem of quality
- Go for scoring consistency
- Establish a set of R & D task forces
- Make self-assessment and self-adjustment more central to the job
- Provide opportunities, incentives, and criteria that allow each teacher to engage in more careful research into what constitutes effective practice

School districts should devise a plan for conducting assessments to provide all stakeholders understandable and accurate information about student achievement.

Conclusion

Student assessment is a critically important topic as administrators, teachers, parents, and community members continue to work to improve curriculum, instruction, and ultimately student learning.

The curriculum provides a statement of what knowledge, skills, and moral principles students will be expected to acquire during their time at school. Program development and delivery "is a decision-making process—constantly balancing the emerging and ever-changing needs of students, society, and the content to be taught. As research adds to the knowledge base, as political systems change, as trends in society change, as technology advances, as we learn more about learning, and as we gain greater insight into the functioning of the human brain, so too must the curriculum change" (Costas, 1997, p. 49).

It is important to realize that one's perspective will determine how the results of program and student assessment will be perceived. Spring (1998) states

> A newspaper headline reads "Lower Test Scores in City Schools." A religioius-right group might give a spin that "lower scores exemplify the lack of instruction in traditional moral values." Another group might spin an interpretation that "lower scores are the result of low academic standards." Or another interested party might respond, "Poor-quality instruction is causing test scores to decline." A spokesperson for a teacher union might put the following spin on the story, "Low teacher salaries make it impossible to keep good teachers, causing test scores to fall." And a union spokesperson might blame "inadequate school funding causes a decline in test scores." A spokesperson for a group representing a cultural minority might provide the following spin: "Culturally biased curriculum causes low test scores." This means that it is very important that the school division take control by characterizing the causes for the scores and actions to be taken in the future regarding curricular and instructional changes. Otherwise they become the fuel for future ideological battles and limited improvement in student performance. (p. 24)

PORTFOLIOS ARTIFACTS

1. What does your educational platform say about teaching and learning? Developing curriculum? The allocation of time in schools? Developing assessment?

2. Analyze and critique a variety of different secondary-school schedules. What are the strengths and weakness of each? What are the implications for teachers in each of these schedules?

3. In collaboration with your internship site colleagues, devise a schedule using a computer program.

4. Participate on a curriculum development or auditing team at the state or local level.

5. Write a curriculum for a specific grade or subject level.

6. Disaggregate testing data for a school. Use different variables such as grade level, gender, native language, and so forth.

7. Implement a curriculum change at your school that has an impact on children from more than one classroom.

8. Apply for a grant for an innovative new program.

9. Work on a curriculum team focused on improving test scores.

TERMS

Apprenticeship learning	Differentiated instruction	Performance assessment
Authentic instruction	Hidden curriculum	Portfolios
Constructivism	Learning transfer	Problem-based learning
Cooperative learning	Looping	Thematic instruction
Curriculum alignment	Multiple intelligence theory	Triarchic theory
Curriculum audit	OTL standards	Zone of proximal development

SUGGESTED READINGS

Beck, L., & Murphy, J. (1996). *The four imperatives of a successful school.* Thousand Oaks, CA: Corwin Press.

Early, M., & Rehage, K. (1999). (Eds.). *Issues in curriculum.* Chicago: University of Chicago Press.

Frase, L., English, F., & Poston, W. (1995). *The curriculum management audit: Improving school quality.* Arlington, VA: AASA.

Glatthorn, A. (1997). *The principal as curriculum leader: Shaping what is taught and tested.* Thousand Oaks, CA: Corwin Press.

Ornstein, A., & Behar-Hornestein, L. (1999). (Eds.). *Contemporary issues in curriculum.* Boston: Allyn & Bacon.

9

Pupil Personnel Services

Vignette: Challenges from Thurber Middle School

Johnny Bluebell is typical of too many 13-year-olds attending Thurber Middle School. He has a poor attendance record, low grades, poor hygiene, and excessive disciplinary action. He also has a fairly high IQ and should be performing much better in school that he is. His single mother works a night shift job from midnight to 8:00 a.m. and has been unable to come in for conferences. Recently Johnny has gotten into trouble with the law for shoplifting because "his family has nothing." He discussed these problems with Mrs. Ulgine Barrows, his guidance counselor.

Mrs. Barrows is very concerned about students like Johnny. Her "taking the side" of problem and moderately disabled students in the school has annoyed a number of community members, teachers, and administrators, although she does have a small pocket of support. Mrs. Barrows is knowledgeable, dedicated, and well spoken; those who are against her, however, point out that she is an unwed mother of a three-year-old who is cohabiting with a factory worker. Mrs. Barrows sent the following letter to her superintendent and copies to the assistant superintendent of human resources, the director of pupil personnel services and her principal:

Dear Dr. Martin:

There are a number of students in our middle schools whose lives have reached the point of quiet desperation. Too many of our children show signs of neglect, such as advanced tooth decay, poor hygiene, and chronic anxiety. Many are neglected and living in overcrowded, unsanitary conditions and sometimes abusive situations. The ravages of poverty, poor health, abuse, violence, criminal behavior, and developmental disorders have reduced their chances for success in school and in life. In fact, too many fall behind academically and become severe behavior problems and even criminally dangerous. If the school does not assume a greater responsibility for the welfare of these neglected and behavior-problem children, the quality of life in our schools and communities will continue to decline.

I am requesting that a new position be created and staffed for a full-time social worker, at each of our middle schools, to work with parents, communities, and service delivery agencies to better serve the needs of these middle school children. The school nurse is kept busy from the time she arrives at school until the time she leaves by children who are hungry, ill, upset, or exhausted and by questions from parents. Some of the mothers are so young and they don't seem to have a clue about parenting and some are not literate in any language. Teachers are frustrated by these students whom they see as academically slow, uninterested in learning, associating with troublemakers, and behaving improperly. These teachers are searching for nonexisting help in developing new, more successful strategies for these students. Essentially, they are working alone in an area in which they lack the needed training or skills. The turnover rate for school nurses is high and that for middle school teachers is increasing.

We need full-time social workers at the schools, smaller class sizes, adequately prepared pupil personnel staff and teachers, reformed instructional programs, and improved staff development if we are to have any hope of meeting the new, higher standards passed by the state. It's certainly more than a school problem, but the schools are the ones blamed for the results: low achievement, major behavior problems, delinquency, truancy, a high dropout rate, and a cycle of early pregnancy, violence, and crime.

Please give this request serious consideration and treat it with the urgency it deserves. Thank you for any assistance you can provide.

Sincerely yours,

Mrs. Ulgine Barrows
Guidance Counselor
Thurber Middle School

cc: Dr. Joey Hart, Assistant Superintendent for Human Resources
    Mr. Bob Munson, Director of Pupil Personnel Services
    Mr. Peter Fitweiler, Principal

Joey Hart, the assistant superintendent for human resource development, received an irate call from Mr. Fitweiler, the principal at Thurber Middle School. Mr. Fitweiler said, "Joey, I am going to fire Mrs. Barrows by the end of the week. She has talked to me a number of times about her hare-brained ideas in the past, and I have told her they will not be supported by central administration. She has gone right over my head and embarrassed us all with the superintendent. She has even convinced a few teachers and community members to support her proposal. That liberal fool who is head of the city's social service department is even in agreement and so is the assistant district attorney, whose soft approach to these young criminals is causing a lot of problems.

I will not tolerate that, and I'm going to make an example out of this and fire her. No one likes her or approves of her lifestyle anyway. I have already called Bob and told him to ignore the letter and what I'm going to do."

Dr. Hart calmed Mr. Fitweiler down and suggested that they each take some time to think about this situation. He agreed to meet with Bob Munson, the director of pupil personnel services, Mr. Fitweiler, and a few other middle school principals to decide what to do. Dr. Hart then called Superintendent Martin to let her know that they were addressing the letter and would get back to her by the following Monday.

Dr. Hart sat back in his chair. He knew that many of the classroom teachers and guidance counselors, special-education teachers, and others hired in recent years knew little or nothing about many of the students to which they were assigned. The morale in middle schools was low and there was great concern that these schools would not meet new state testing standards. A number of influential community and board members had expressed concern regarding the behavior and performance of certain student populations.

Hart mused, *maybe we should change the recruitment, hiring, and development practices in our middle schools. Maybe a new staff position should be created to help students, teachers, and parents and to make sure students are receiving needed services. Maybe the whole issue needs a new, more integrated approach to meeting the needs of these at-risk children. The superintendent will want recommendations regarding what seems to be an escalating problem.* His thoughts are disrupted by a call from Mr. Munson.

> Which of the various pupil personnel services might be involved in addressing the concerns brought out by Mrs. Barrows, the guidance counselor?
> How will the disagreement between Mr. Fitweiler, the principal, and Mrs. Barrows, the guidance counselor, be resolved? What is the most immediate problem that needs to be addressed?

Taking Care of the Students

Erik Erickson (1998) suggested that development is a continuous growth process that challenges individuals to resolve potential demands and conflicts they confront. Erickson posited eight stages of development: infancy, toddlerhood, early childhood, school age, adolescence, young adulthood, middle adulthood, and old age. Each stage throughout the life span presents different challenges. Failure to deal adequately with any of these stages of development jeopardizes the individual's future functioning as a contributing, well-adjusted individual.

Developmentalists have described various domains of development that progress in a hierarchical-interactive-interrelated manner. Such stages are described as different self-needs (investigated by Abraham Maslow), different self-identities (investigated by Jane Lovinger), and different sets of moral responses (investigated by Lawrence Kohlberg). Whatever the model, the challenge to the individual is to complete each transitional stage in order to be productive and move to the next stage of development (Table 9.1).

The responsibility of pupil personnel services is to help individuals to progress through each transitional stage of development. Pupil personnel professionals also help students with developmental problems. Abnormal, exceptional, or handicapping behavior is defined as behavior sufficiently divergent from what typically is seen in schools or from the person's own previous actions that it cannot be classified as normal.

Pupil personnel services are a very important part of a school's ability to meet developmental needs of young people. While the demands on students are increasing, the ability of the family and community to help children succeed at school seems to be eroding. Pupil personnel's role is to help students to fully develop and to enhance their ability to be successful, whatever their life situations.

These issues can become very challenging for the estimated 14 percent of children who were classified, during the 1996–97 school year, as "exceptional." There have been increases in the identification rates of students and preschoolers with exceptionalities since that school year with attention deficit/hyperactivity disorder being one of the fastest-growing categories. When exceptionality lowers a student's chances

TABLE 9.1   **Transitional Stages of Human Development**

Needs Development	Ego Development	Moral Development
■ Physiological ■ Safety/security	■ Presocial ■ Symbiotic ■ Beginning impulsive ■ Self-protective	■ Magic wish ■ Punishment/obedience ■ Naive hedonism
■ Social affiliation/ belongingness ■ Self-esteem	■ Conformist ■ Conscientious conformist ■ Conscientious	■ Approval of others ■ Law and order
■ Autonomy ■ Self-actualization ■ Self-transcendence	■ Individualistic ■ Autonomous ■ Integrated	■ Individual rights ■ Individual principles ■ Conscience ■ Universal–spiritual
Abraham Maslow	*Jane Lovinger*	*Lawrence Kohlberg*

of success and is environmentally caused, the student is described as "at risk." When the causes of exceptionality are organic in nature they are described as handicapping conditions or disabilities.

Pupil Personnel–Student Service Team

Pupil personnel services are an essential component of an effective, modern school system. It is readily acknowledged that children's emotional, social, physical, and mental condition and their out-of-school experiences are powerful influences on their in-school performances (The Center for the Future of Children, 1992). Most all now agree that schools should address the root causes of youth disability and special needs. This service typically requires collecting pupil information, assessing pupil needs, and planning and developing comprehensive management systems to ensure that all students are receiving needed service. Changed demographics, growing poverty, more people with multiple problems, learning disabilities, health impairments, social and family breakdown, and a rising demand for competence in a high-technology society bring an increased pressure on the importance of pupil personnel services. According to David Tyack (The Center for the Future of Children, 1992):

> Once again, education reform and social pathologies have become print-time, first-page news. If Americans do not help and heal the children-at-risk, the nation's social fabric will be in quite as much danger as its standing.... (p. 30)

Research suggests that an array of deleterious conditions affect the children of rich and poor alike—conditions that will impede children's development unless they are addressed at an early age (National Commission on Children, 1991; Children's Defense Fund, 1991).

The pupil personnel services team consists of professionals who specialize in fostering the healthy career, educational, social, emotional, and intellectual development of all students. Specialists serve as counselors and as guides and provide psychological services, special education, and remedial instruction. They are concerned with child accounting and school safety, school health, speech and hearing therapy, pupil appraisal, testing and diagnostics, and school-court liaison. They also function as social workers and visiting teachers. Specialists in each of these areas often function as a team in support of the child, but each brings a unique contribution to the education of students.

> However the services and opportunities are coordinated and provided, what remains important is that they indeed are delivered. If that means that something called Student Assistance Teams or Student Service Teams need to be assembled and coordinated by school administrators, so be it. How such teams collaborate and cooperate will be a function of how the local school or district views these special programs. Knowing more about each of the special programs is a necessary prerequisite to their effective utilization in the provision of service and opportunities for students. (Zepeda & Langenback, 1999, p. 215)

Figure 9.1 lists the essential services that are part of pupil personnel.

While many may disagree with the inclusion of one or more of the functions, few would argue with their importance. Teachers (although parents and students can request services) typically arrange to consult with a specialist to discuss needs for intervention and then make arrangements to discuss the referral with parents and to complete referral forms. This referral often results in a child's being screened by the child study team, followed by a decision regarding formal evaluation. Once a child has been determined to be eligible for special education services, an individualized educational plan (IEP) is written that outlines the specific pupil personnel services a student will begin receiving. Public Law 94-142, the Education for All Handicapped Children Act of 1975 and now called the Individuals with Disabilities Education Act (IDEA), ensures the rights of children with disabilities to a free, appropriate public education, an IEP, special education services, due process procedures, and the least restrictive learning environment.

The 1997 amendments to IDEA have specifically addressed the issue of discipline for students with disabilities. In the case of a child with disabilities whose behavior impedes his or her learning or that of others, the IEP team shall consider strategies and supports to address that behavior. A behavioral intervention plan (BIP) detailing the interventions and supports must be included as part of the IEP for such students. If disciplinary action is contemplated, other new provisions of the law must be taken into consideration. For example, a determination must be made as to whether a child's behavior is a manifestation of his or her disability. Even if a behavior is not related to the disability, the IEP team must still reconsider appropriate services for the student.

Beverly Johns (1998) emphasizes the importance of teamwork if schools are to make changes in behavioral intervention options. The first step in establishing special programs and services in a school is a total staff commitment to the process. Such staff commitment may require school personnel and administrators to reevaluate the re-

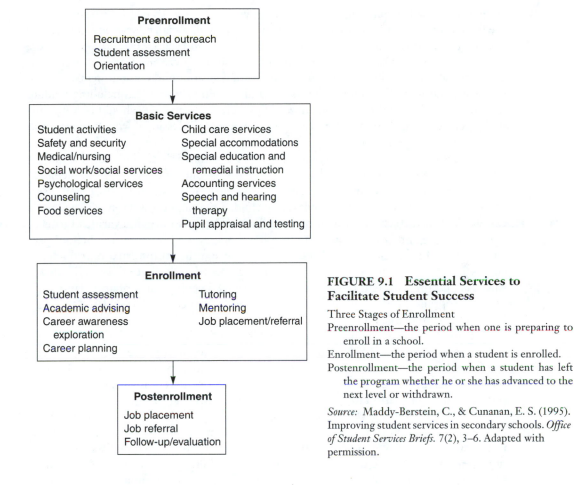

FIGURE 9.1   Essential Services to Facilitate Student Success

Three Stages of Enrollment

Preenrollment—the period when one is preparing to enroll in a school.

Enrollment—the period when a student is enrolled.

Postenrollment—the period when a student has left the program whether he or she has advanced to the next level or withdrawn.

Source: Maddy-Berstein, C., & Cunanan, E. S. (1995). Improving student services in secondary schools. *Office of Student Services Briefs.* 7(2), 3–6. Adapted with permission.

sponsibilities of various pupil personnel services to create optimum teams for meeting the needs of a wide variety of students.

What are the responsibilities of Mrs. Barrows, Dr. Hart, Mr. Munson, Mr. Fitweiler, and Dr. Martin regarding Johnny and other at-risk students at Thurber Middle School?

Counseling, Guidance, Psychological Services

The major role of counseling and psychological services is to facilitate wise choices and to promote positive adjustment, mental health, learning abilities, and development. The complexity of our society requires counseling services to play an ever-increasing role in the lives of students and their families. Students' personal, social, educational, and career needs are the focus of the work of guidance counselors and school psychologists. These professionals assist in orientation, provide information, analyze and interpret results, increase possibilities and create new ones, help with decisions and commitments, remove obstacles, and identify emotional problems and learning disabilities, including reading problems. Their role, however, in addressing severe abnormalities should be very limited. Such conditions should be referred to an external professional who is an expert in the treatment of human behavior problems.

School counselors and psychologists work with students individually and in groups and consult parents, teachers, and a diverse group of community service providers. They make recommendations regarding curriculum, instructional, and classroom management to meet the needs of the child. They suggest ways in which parents can work with the school to help their children. They also provide various forms of education programs for parents, children, teachers, and administrators. School psychologists and counselors often assist in compiling significant information, which becomes part of the student's school cumulative record. Quasi-administrative duties such as compiling student records, counting credits, keeping track of attendance, and testing programs tend to get in the way of the performance of duties related to assisting teachers, students, and parents.

Certification for counselors and psychologists is required in all states, although the requirements vary. The school counselor's professional organization is the American School Counselors Association (ASCA), which is a division of the American Counseling Association. The National Association of School Psychologists (NASP) is the professional organization for school psychologists (Neukrug, 1998).

The main function of school psychologists is to provide testing and consultation for special education students. Because the training in school psychology tends to be in testing, human development, and system change, school psychologists are usually not licensed by the state to do counseling or psychotherapy. They are experts in identifying learning disabilities, developmental disorders, physical impairments, or other special needs including the gifted. Many special-needs students are eligible to receive services under IDEA. (The culturally disadvantaged are not covered by this act and services seldom address environmental issues, social contact, or cultural barriers.)

The school psychologist works with a team to design a program of services. It blends the best methods of teaching and the most conducive learning environment for the child into a remedial plan to be implemented within the classroom. Although school psychologists spend most of their time on child study activities, they are also involved in consultation, individual and group counseling, research, and program development. They share and interpret results at parent conferences and with child-study teams and write final reports. They also follow up on the progress of students and work with others to make needed adjustments for the student.

School counseling includes developing an active public relations program for staff and the community through newsletters, local media, and school community presentations (Sears & Coy, 1991). The major role of counselors is to work with special-needs and at-risk students. They provide a diverse array of services to help these students, including advising in academic, social, emotional, and behavioral matters. They address a wide array of issues such as course selection, vocational placement, college selection, parental divorce, dating, loneliness, study habits, controlling aggressiveness, violence, depression, and many other developmental issues. While crisis and remedial counseling will always be a primary role, whole-child developmental needs and comprehensive preventive counseling began receiving more attention in the 1990s. This more comprehensive approach permits counseling programs to be seen as contributing to the growth of all students and not working only with a "special" few.

Counselors need to focus greater attention on what the William T. Grant Foundation (1988) calls "the forgotten half." Some 20 million students finish their formal education when they leave high school, with or without a diploma. Stable, good-paying jobs that do not require advanced training are rapidly disappearing. As trade barriers fall, our children will find themselves competing more directly with the citizens of other countries who work for lower wages. Educational decisions today will play a role as to whether students will be prepared to hold high-wage, high-skilled jobs or, instead, be forced to compete with workers in developing countries. The potential disparity in income and wealth could threaten the political stability our nation has long enjoyed (President's Committee of Advisors on Science and Technology, 1997).

As a result, noncollege youth need greater help in making school-to-work transitions. Career and guidance programs, geared more for the college bound, have been unable to provide these needed services. There is a need to close the growing gap between what students learn and what today's jobs require and thus enhance the quality of the employee pool. Counselors must help break down the barriers between education and the world of work and expose young people to and support programs that prepare them for job opportunities and career options.

Efforts are under way in a number of states (e.g., California, Florida) to integrate school programs with community-based interventions. Integrated programs emphasize a collaborative relationship among agencies that provide intervention and treatment programs, vocational training and placement, and school counselors and psychologists for the purpose of building a comprehensive and coordinated service delivery system. Problems that students face are beyond the scope of any single setting, because they grow out of family, community, business, poverty, health, and abuse and must be addressed at multiple levels. Intervention may be appropriate at the individual, family, community, or state level. The new role of counselors is one of facilitating a comprehensive system to recognize and help solve problems of children and families.

> Has Mrs. Barrows overstepped her authority as a counselor by writing this letter to Superintendent Martin? Who might she have involved in making this request? Why?

Special Education and Remedial Instruction

Special education benefits students who need specialized classroom assistance if they are to achieve their maximum potential. Such children are often classified as having an exceptionality. Exceptionalities include children who have giftedness, learning disabilities, emotional and behavior disorders, mental retardation, autism, health impairments, physical disabilities, speech and language impairment, hearing loss, blindness and low vision, traumatic brain injury, and severe and multiple disabilities. A number of special education personnel deal with exceptional children on an itinerant basis. Students with an exceptionality typically spend the majority of their time in regular classrooms and may be taken out of the room for short periods to receive special services. IDEA guarantees students a free, appropriate public education.

IDEA defines "special education" as specially designed services and instruction to meet the unique needs of students with disabilities and establishes six principles for governing their education. Turnbull, Turnbull, Shank, and Leal (1995, p. 53) outline five principles for educators in implementing the law.

Principle	Command to Educators
Zero rejects (nondiscriminatory evaluation)	Enroll the student. Determine if the student has a disability and, if so, whether the student needs special education and related services.
Appropriate education	Provide beneficial special education and related services.
Least restrictive environment	Include the student with children who do not have disabilities.
Due procedural process	Check to determine if schools and parents are complying with IDEA.
Parent participation	Collaborate with parents.

The continuum of services offered, from least restrictive to most restrictive, is regular classroom, resource room, separate class, separate school facility, residential facility, and homebound/hospitalized. In 1992, the National Association of State Boards of Education (NASBE) published a report entitled *Winners All: A Call for Inclusive Schools* (NASBE, 1992), which supported a massive but controversial inclusive schools movement in the United States. Inclusive classrooms places students with exceptionalities in general classrooms, and special-education resource teachers work with general classroom teachers in team-teaching modes. Children in inclusive classrooms can take advantage of cooperative learning, curriculum adaptations, classroom aides, environmental accommodations, cooperation between regular and special education teachers, proactive behavior plans, and peer tutoring. In this way the general education of all students is improved while exceptional students receive necessary supports and services in the context of general education (Turnbull et al., 1995; Goodlad & Lovitt, 1993). Requirements for educating students with disabilities in the least restrictive environment are specified in the IDEA amendments of 1997 as follows:

To the maximum extent appropriate, children with disabilities, including children in public or private institutions or other care facilities, are educated with children who are not disabled. Special classes, separate schools, or other removal of children with disabilities from the regular educational environment occurs only when the nature or severity of the disability of a child is such that education in regular classes with the use of supplementary aids and services cannot be achieved satisfactorily [(sec. 612.(a)(5)].

This presumption in favor of inclusion in and progress through the general curriculum has always been part of IDEA; the 1997 amendments, however, give the rule a new focus by linking nondiscriminatory evaluation, IEPs, and other appropriate education provisions to students' access to progress through the general curriculum and by requiring the accommodations and adjustments necessary for the students to have access to the general curriculum. Initial research suggests that such programs do not have negative effects on either general education or special education students and may actually be a positive experience for both (Salisbury et al., 1993; Baler, Wang, & Walberg, 1995; Walsh & Synder, 1994).

When evidence of an exceptionality appears, the psychologist conducts a complete diagnosis of the student to pinpoint strengths and weaknesses and to plan a comprehensive IEP. The diagnosis and classification of children is based on a comprehensive set of assessments in the areas of behavior, achievement, and functioning profiles as measured through interviews, examining records, observation, a battery of psychoeducational assessment instruments, and IQ scores. Once the school psychologist has diagnosed an exceptionality, he or she calls a coordinating conference, including all interested parties, to finalize the IEP. The student's teachers, a school psychologist, a special education teacher, the student's parent(s), and the person conducting the student's evaluation are usually present at the conference(s). The starting point for moderately to severely disabled students is to envision the ideal life for the child. The functional assessment identifies the abilities, accomplishments, conditions, potential, and full range of challenging behaviors. The results are used to develop complementary strategies that provide the greatest potential for success.

The IEP addresses evaluative information, curriculum plans, and appropriate special education placement and related services. After determining the student's educational program, placement, and need for related services, the team then determines long- and short-term objectives and specific support plans for students in general education placements. These plans match the individual student's needs while maintaining the integrity of lessons for classmates without disabilities (Giangreco et al., 1993). The students' progress is reevaluated periodically, and specialists work with the classroom teacher to obtain maximum success. The classroom teacher is key to the success of the entire process.

Giangreco, Cloninger, and Iverson (1993) provide one model for engaging in the planning process. A few of the steps include:

- Select one to three valued life outcomes
- Select a subset of curriculum areas
- Select activities needing work this year

- Rank the top eight overall priorities
- Determine the context
- Select curriculum areas and learning outcomes
- Select general support needs
- Summarize education program components
- Determine team members and assign responsibilities and identified tasks
- Develop a schedule
- Select specific lesson adaptations
- Evaluate program effectiveness and quality

They stress how important skill and care are to student success. "Such care and skill on your part will mean that you must constantly be thinking about what you are doing, individualizing to the situation you are dealing with, improving your own skills, and judging your success by the impact your team's decisions have on the lives of students and families" (p. 80).

Students may need many different, related services. Service providers may be assigned to the school or may travel to many schools, visiting exceptional children and their classroom teachers. As discussed earlier, the *school psychologist* completes the student's evaluation, helps develop plans to meet individual learning requirements, and works with teachers and parents to address special needs of the student. *The school-community worker, visiting teacher or school social worker* provides a link between the school, home, and community, rendering interpretation, support, assistance, coordination, advocacy, and investigation services. He or she also assists in the proper enforcement of all laws pertaining to juveniles. *Speech, hearing, and learning specialists* address problems such as sensory loss, speech and language delays, academic achievement delays, writing difficulties, and other communication disorders. These experts provide remediation and compensation and should be certified specialists in their respective fields.

The special-education teacher helps identify basic disabilities and develops instruction, lesson plans, materials, and tests. He or she also tests approaches to determine if they are successful and transfers the procedure and materials to the classroom teacher. The main function is to adapt curriculum materials such as assignments, tests, worksheets, reading books, and tests for individual students. Sometimes the special-ed teacher works as a coteacher, jointly planning and team-teaching lessons with the regular classroom teacher. Other times, the special-ed teacher may work with small groups or individual special-needs children within the regular classroom to provide tutorial or remedial assistance.

A special-needs student may be involved in class activities in various ways. Such activities may include the same learning outcome, multilevel curriculum and instruction, and curriculum overlapping. The special-ed teacher may pull students out of regular classrooms for intensive individualized and small-group instruction. Children with severe disabilities are frequently placed with a special-ed teacher in a self-contained classroom and also are included in the mainstream. Special-ed staff also provide consultation and training for regular classroom teachers in alternative assessment, instruction, and discipline strategies. These teachers receive specialized training and licensing to work with the special-needs population of students.

The primary objectives of all of these specialists are (1) to facilitate learning and adjustment of pupils through counseling, consultation, educational planning, program implementation, and evaluation and (2) to promote corrective and adaptive learning situations structured to the special needs of children. There are many possible disabilities, but more than 90 percent of students identified with disabilities typically are categorized as specifically learning disabled, speech or language impaired, mentally retarded, or emotionally disturbed. Some of the additional services from which special-education students can benefit are audiology, medical and health services, occupational therapy, physical therapy, recreation, transportation, and assistive technology services. Educational adaptations are often needed for the maximum development of the child. Administrators must advocate the rights of all children to receive needed services and to promote inclusive school practice.

> What role might special and remedial education play in addressing the concerns Ulgine Barrows brought out in her letter? Why do you believe these students' problems are not being addressed?

Principles of Leadership for Special Services

LEONARD BURRELLO
Indiana University

Approximately 40 percent of a school principal's job is taken up with exceptions for and about students, their parents, and teachers, who claim a need for special attention and accommodations. Forty percent of all school litigation pertains to special services complaints about due process, eligibility for services, and, of course, the appropriateness of the services being offered by the school system. Sarason (1991) has argued that the two most significant developments in school reform in the last fifty years are the right for teachers to bargain and for parents to veto professional decisions regarding the education of students with disabilities.

The purpose of special or pupil personnel services is essentially to assist and support any student who because of some disability (the inability to perform in a typical manner or on a routine task) or handicap (a set of circumstances that causes an individual to perform below his or her expected level) may not participate as fully as possible in the American experiment or dare I say the American dream. Five principles serve as keys to understanding and dealing with students who have special learning, emotional, or physical needs and their caregivers and parents.

1. *Treat and respect all students as typical students.* Always treat the student as more the same than different. A colleague of mine at Indiana University asked for my advice on how he ought to approach our local school system concerning his severely disabled child. I told him, "make sure the system and each school your son attends sees him as a child, a person who is more alike than different." He tells me it's the best advice he got in dealing with the system. Since *Brown v.*

(continued)

Continued

Board of Education and the civil rights movement of the 1960s, the inclusion of students with disabilities and students who represent cultural or racial minorities have challenged the public schools to include them in the American experiment starting with their place in the public schools. The way to operationalize the first principle is to consider the second principle.

2. *All children are in and they earn their way out.* All students belong to the local system and are the responsibility of the local school they would normally attend if they were not challenged or in need of special services. The responsibility of local school personnel is to ensure their access to the general educational curriculum and statewide assessment. If the local school can demonstrate that the student, despite special or supportive personnel services, is unable to participate in the general education curriculum, he or she may receive services in a more restrictive environment.

The determination of eligibility and the type of services needed must be decided in a case conference committee with multidisciplinary assessment and full parental consent and participation, including access to the information being used to make such a determination. Students do earn their way out of individual schools by failing to attend, exhibiting disruptive and uncontrollable or even criminal behavior. The system nonetheless has some responsibility to ensure that educational services are being provided. It is important that such a student not hurt himself or herself or anyone else.

3. *Special services are essential but they don't replace or assume the responsibility of the school to educate a diverse public.* These services are not the core and substance of what a child should experience in the public schools. The essential purpose of specialized or pupil personnel services should be to inquire about the learner and what it takes for him or her to benefit from the school's programming. Once specialized service personnel learn what it takes to support the learner to be successful, they should endeavor to support their general-education colleagues in providing those supports daily in the typical classroom environment. For example, a speech and language specialist may see students one on one for a period of time to assess speech and language proficiencies, but they should quickly try to teach others who interact with the student daily how to support the generalization of specific skill training in the classroom.

4. *These services require a collaborative relationship among professionals based on mutual respect and expectations for improving student performance and success in school.* For too long, students with special needs have too quickly, on referral, become the responsibility of the specialist. Once receiving specialized services, the student becomes labeled "different" and as someone else's responsibility as far as appropriate educational services are concerned. Our research clearly identifies principals who seek assistance from central office administrators for special education related to system-wide direction, policy, and procedures governing student and parental rights (Van Horn, Burrello, & DeClue, 1992). It also indicates that principals who accept the responsibility to educate all students create the conditions for staff to work together to make it happen.

5. *We can no longer assume that the provision of services to students with special learning needs is sufficient.* We must demonstrate that all students have valued outcomes. The shift from ensuring procedural safeguards and individual student plans for specialized educational services, guaranteed by IDEA, is no longer sufficient. As educators we must ensure student progress and success measured against a set of appropriate standards for the student with the mildest of needs to those with significant disabilities.

The best predictor of success in the provision of services to students with special needs is the attitude and disposition of the principal toward these students, their parents, and their school caretakers. School leaders must examine what they believe about these students and how these students fit into their vision of the American experiment. Public education is often the first and only place many typical students and their families get the opportunity to relate to others with significant personal and cultural differences. It is the one place where we come together to learn how to be part of a caring community.

School Health Services

The school nurse is often the first representative of pupil personnel services to have contact with the child and his or her parents. The nurse typically holds a preschool conference with the child and parents before the child enters kindergarten. At this time parents can inform the school of any unique medical problems, learning disabilities, or emotional problems that might affect the student's educational progress.

The school nurse additionally performs a large number of other services including screening for hearing and visual problems, head lice, tuberculosis, and heart defects; checking teeth and throat; teaching units on human development and personal hygiene; providing emergency first aid; consulting about health problems with teachers and students; and assisting in homebound instruction and in referring children to physicians and social workers. Physicians periodically visit schools to provide medical screening, immunization, diagnosis and referral, and health education and as medical advisers to athletic teams.

An emerging consensus indicates that present health care delivery systems do not meet the needs of children and families (National Commission on Child Welfare and Family Preservation, 1990). School administrators are expected to determine whether the health services provided within the school meet the needs of students. That means periodically assessing the current state of health delivery in the school by reviewing with the school nurse the numbers of students and teachers served, types of services being offered, and services needed. "Through our research, we believe that more schools will continue to add on health clinics to meet the increasing needs of students and, in some cases, the families of students" (Zepeda & Langenback, 1999, p. 157). As a result, some school districts have asked the school health professionals to coordinate an extensive array of health and human services through the neighborhood schools.

> What can be done to reduce the heavy load on the school nurse, and to better meet the health needs of the students and their families?

Child Accounting and School Safety

A significant amount of data is collected and stored on each student, including directory information, demographics, attendance, courses taken, grades, test scores, extracurricular activities, individualized educational plans, deportment, disciplinary action, health, recognitions, and so forth. The Family Education Rights to Privacy Act (the Buckley Amendment) restricts accessibility to student records and provides for the removal of inaccuracies. Other than directory information, principals are allowed to release student records only in clearly defined cases unless they have parent or student (18 and order) permission. Parents do not have the right to inspect counselor, psychologist, and teacher records unless these are part of the student's cumulative records. Many associated activities, such as compulsory attendance, class scheduling, follow-up services, school reports, student eligibility, and dropout prevention depend on accurate student data.

To focus on one example, attendance records can be used to ensure that the child's right to receive a free public education up to a certain age is being enforced. School attendance and other student rights are usually covered in *Students Rights, Responsibilities, and Disciplinary Rules* pamphlets each family receives, which must comply with school system policy and procedures. Good attendance habits should be established early so problems related to academics, deportment, dropout, and later employment do not develop. Irregular attendance, frequent tardiness, and low achievement are strong predictors that a child may drop out of high school and have later social and economic problems (Achilles & Smith, 1994). One of our national goals is to increase the high school graduation rate to 90 percent by the year 2000. The percentage of 18- to 24-year-olds who have high school credentials has remained at approximately 86 percent throughout the 1990s. Concern has been raised that this percentage will actually decrease if high school graduation is tied to passing state assessment tests. The attendance clerk provides monitoring and communication and triggers intervention strategy involving attendance problems.

Research suggests that negative academic experiences affect a student's self-concept and lead to counterproductive attitudes and behavior, lack of motivation, and association with other problem students. All these facts contribute to the student's absenteeism and dropping out of school (Kaplan et al., 1997). This same student also accounts for a large number of discipline problems within the school and crime problems within the community. Potential dropouts need to be identified by the eighth grade and placed in programs that help improve their academics and keep them in school. Such interventions must be aimed at encouraging and enabling students to be successful achievers and to developing positive attitudes toward academic performance and achievement. It is critical to have procedures for encouraging regular attendance that identify and remove problems related to absenteeism.

Although not often used (Schwartz, 1995), the most frequent interventions by school personnel are counseling, remedial education, peer tutoring and mentoring, adult–student mentoring, training, special placement, student advising, safe and disciplined school programs, family partnership, and comprehensive support systems. These programs have proved successful for early intervention in discipline problems and delinquency prevention. In fact, current research identifies the importance of early intervention—before grade 4—to the success of disciplinary interventions.

Student Discipline

Most schools have codes of student conduct that are to be enforced by the teachers, administrators, and pupil personnel workers. Administrators are responsible for reinforcing teacher disciplinary actions and taking responsibility for the more difficult or unusual behavior problems. Discipline and safety have been linked to pupil achievement and student attendance. Traditional methods (Kimbrough & Burket, 1990, p. 277) for correcting student behavior include (1) corporal punishment, (2) reprimands, (3) detention, (4) enforced duties, (5) suspension from school, (6) in-school suspension, and (7) expulsion from school. The disciplinarian must be consistent, tough, deliberate, fair, just, and compassionate and perceived as such. Youth, and particularly inner-city youth, want the security and predictability that accompany clear codes of conduct and consistent, clear and firm discipline. Inner-city youth seek the concern and security conveyed by strong discipline as long as they perceive the discipline as swift, certain, and fair (McLaughlin, Irby, & Longman, 1994). Many of the ideas discussed in this and other chapters suggest alternative programs that have also proved successful in the academic and behavioral development of these students. Students must be held accountable for their actions or lack of actions.

In order of teachers' perceived frequency of occurrence, school problems over the past decade include:

- Physical conflict among students
- Conflict and abuse involving teachers and other staff
- Student use of alcohol
- Student use of illegal drugs
- Vandalism of school property
- Robbery and theft
- Student possession and occasional use of weapons

Teachers also suggest that the nature of each of these school problems is more serious than in the past. All of these problems are much more serious in secondary schools than in elementary schools. Shen (1997) suggests, "when we discuss school violence, students are usually the center of concern. But given the increasing severity of verbal abuse of teachers, educators also deserve our attention" (p. 20).

Section 612 (a)(1) of the IDEA amendment of 1997 states that free, appropriate public education (FAPE) shall be available to all children with disabilities, ages 3–21, including children with disabilities who have been suspended or are expelled from school. The law has a number of provisions that basically restrict suspensions to ten school days and interim alternative education settings (IAES) to ten days except in cases involving weapons or illegal drugs. Weapons or drug violations warrant suspension for not more than forty-five days.

The expulsion and discipline provision requires a hearing to determine whether there is a manifestation (disability causes behavior). The manifestation hearing must be held in cases of (a) weapons, (b) drugs, (c) dangerous behavior, or (d) any discipline for more than ten days. If the school has not already conducted a *functional behavioral assessment* and implemented a *behavioral intervention plan* before disciplining the student, the IEP team must do so. If the school, however, has conducted a functional behavioral assessment and developed a behavioral intervention plan, the IEP team must review and modify the plan, "as necessary, to address the behavior."

The IDEA regulations, which came out in 1999, give the principal slightly more flexibility in the way the law is interpreted. The regulations allow students to be removed for ten days at a time for separate acts, no educational services required for the first ten-day suspension, and study of behavior related to disability only for suspensions that result in a change in placement and services and only to the extent necessary to advance toward IEP goals. School administrators and the special-education teacher will determine the services needed. Also, the regular classroom teacher does not have to be involved in all IEP team decisions. If a student graduates with less than a regular diploma, he or she is still entitled to educational services through age 21. Educational administration faces many challenges in regard to implementing an effective behavioral intervention system. According to Johns (1998) the answers lie in a series of action steps that school administrators should implement.

First and foremost is the establishment of total staff commitment to the process. School discipline policies and procedures must be established with input from all parties. Plans should treat students with respect, place responsibility on students, encourage appropriate choices, and teach social skills. School personnel need in-depth training, the opportunity to practice behavioral management, and technical support in these applications. Students must know what is expected of them in all school settings. Staff must recognize students who follow the rules and must establish logical consequences for those who do not. For instance, it is illogical to only suspend a student for property damage; a logical consequence is for the student to pay for or repair the property. By doing so, the student learns the cost of the property or what is involved in repairing the property. Schools must also establish crisis plans. Critical questions include: What steps will be taken if a student brings a weapon to school? and What will be done if a student becomes physically aggressive?

Promising practices that have been effective with students with challenging behaviors are conflict resolution and peer mediation, climate committee, in-school suspension or detention that teaches social skills, and teen courts in school. Bullock and Gable (1998) state,

> now, in recognition of the growing number of student behavior problems, the 1997 amendments require school-based IEP teams to address the relationship between student behavior and classroom learning. Current legislation requires that IEP teams deal with the behavior of students that interferes with their learning or that of their classmates, or require disciplinary action. (p. v)

A number of school-based discipline programs have been successful; for example, one developed by the National Institute of Justice (NIJ) is called School Management and Resource Teams (SMART). SMART is a process designed to enable local schools and school districts to resolve law and discipline violations through data collection, assessment, planning, and active monitoring. It reduces crime problems by giving school administrators specific practices, methods, techniques, and approaches to resolve law and disciplinary violations in schools.

Every school should have a safe and secure school plan to address these types of at-risk factors. Services of the school-court liaison officer permit schools and juvenile courts to unite efforts in working with youth in the community. Liaison officers investigate cases involving disruptive student behavior and poor school attendance. They sometimes provide metal detectors and security within the schools. They assist school personnel in the proper enforcement of all laws pertaining to juveniles. They also assist probationary officers in investigating and locating appropriate educational placement for juvenile offenders.

A secondary issue related to schools being safe, nuturing places for children is intraschool security. Students and staff sometimes need to be protected within their schools from the violence and ills that often surround them. Teachers report that almost all forms of problems that students confront in schools are on the increase, especially vandalism, verbal abuse, and physical conflicts (Shen, 1997). Most all agree that this trend must be reversed and schools must develop safe and secure school plans. These plans must cover not only policies and procedures to handle problems but also programs to prevent them. Such plans help schools to prevent crises and to be prepared to meet any problems expeditiously and with compassion. Schools must be prepared to deal with perpetrators as well as counsel those who are affected. Schools will not be successful unless effective discipline is maintained. (For more information see: www.ed.gov/offices/OSERS/IDEA.)

Develop a safe and secure school plan for Thurber Middle School.

Pupil Appraisal, Testing, and Diagnostics

Testing and diagnostic programs are often organized schoolwide or systemwide for administering standardized tests. These programs supplement the wide variety of teacher-made tests prepared for use in a single class or school. The information they provide is used to determine a student's performance (grade) or to help in the lesson-planning process.

Obviously, the collection of data is an essential step in any evaluation process regardless of the level at which it occurs. Tests are used to diagnose difficulties, identify aptitudes and discrepancies, appraise achievement, group students, identify needs and assess competency. They are also used to inform the public. A major part of most testing and diagnostic programs is achievement testing. A common approach is a standardized norm-referenced test. Other types of tests include criterion-referenced, objective-referenced, domain-referenced, intelligence, minimum competency, and performance assessment.

Testing helps school staff, students, and parents in assessing learning and planning educational programs and helps school students in making educational and life choices and plans. Testing is also used to compare schools and districts, plan curriculum, assess effectiveness, stimulate reform, and provide recognition. The demand for greater accountability and higher standards is increasing the importance of assessment at the same time there is growing dissatisfaction with traditional methods of assessment (Hymes et al., 1991, p. 32). These conditions provide a challenge to the testing and research staff working in most school districts to collect meaningful information and to formulate the most useful diagnosis possible.

Most states require regular or periodic testing of students. New York was one of the first states to require the successful completion of a competency test for high school graduation. Most states now have such competency tests or are moving in that direction. In 1993–94, Michigan adopted a two-tier high school diploma where students were "endorsed" if they met only minimal standards and received a "standard" diploma if they scored approximately 75 percent or above on the exam. Michigan schools cannot receive accreditation unless 66 percent of the students meet or exceed the "standard" for reading, math, and science. Schools failing to receive accreditation status may be closed or taken over by the state. At the very least, vouchers may be issued for parents to send their children elsewhere.

Many state competency tests have substantiated reports of "a bleak portrait of the current status of student achievement in the United States" issued as part of more than twenty years of assessment by the National Assessment of Educational Progress (NAEP). In fact, the Georgia State Assessment program has "embedded" NAEP items among those in its own assessment programs. NAEP findings tended to be further substantiated in the Third International Mathematics and Science Study (TIMSS). U.S. students did comparatively less well as they advanced through school, raising questions about existing exit standards and assessment.

Whether tests really measure what students need to be able to do to succeed in the twenty-first century is a growing concern. Many believe that performance assessment and demonstrations are better suited to measure the skills and abilities that students will need to be successful in a world that is undergoing significant transformation. Assessment and analysis in this case takes the form of videotapes of student performance, computer programs, written text, demonstrations, portfolios where students are measured on their ability to apply knowledge, skills, and understanding of real-world contexts. Given the debate, testing and research experts must determine the role of testing within their school districts. Perhaps the single best resource for gaining greater understanding of these and other related complex concerns is the American Educational Research Association (AERA). (For more information see: aera@gmu.edu.)

In the last analysis, each school system assumes the responsibility of planning and carrying out its own testing programs and reporting the results. It is clear that test scores and what to do to improve them will occupy significantly more time in the administrator's future. This will include choosing assessments, determining how to interpret them, providing incentives and sanctions to encourage improvement, and developing programs that will allow students to be successful on assessments. The curriculum, the standards, and the assessment must all flow together. The general purpose of all final reports is to summarize, organize, and interpret test results so that a meaningful picture of the school's or the individual's accomplishments emerge. (For more information see: www.edweek.org.)

> What types of data should Mr. Munson have to help make the best decision regarding the conditions at Thurber Middle School?

Extracurricular Activities

Athletics tends to be the most prominent of all extracurricular activities. Through athletics students set personal goals, learn to be responsible, develop self-discipline, learn to work with others, adjust to the many personalities and situations that arise, and develop lifelong physical fitness habits. Studies suggest that participation in sports contributes to better academic performance, serves to keep many students in school, and inspires greater involvement and leadership (Reith, 1989; Holland & Andre, 1991).

Sports are not the only extracurricular activities within schools. Many different honorary, service, class related, and special interest clubs relate to the particular interests of students. The primary purpose of all of these programs is to provide unique learning experiences while developing a positive school climate, school spirit, and fellowship, which add to the overall morale of the school.

Berliner and Biddle (1995) suggest,

> These activities might include, for example, various kinds of community service; hobbies; sports; music; enjoying and performing the arts; reading philosophy or history; travel; studying comparative religions; and so forth. Thus, Americans need to confront the fact that they will be spending more and more of their lives in leisure pursuits, and the schools bear a responsibility for educating students so they can fill those leisure hours with rewarding and socially useful activities. (p. 316)

Susan Gerber (1996) found that the amount of participation in extracurricular activities also was positively related to academic achievement.

These programs depend on the commitment of school staff to provide a comprehensive range of student activities that meets the needs and interests of all students. The faculty sponsor and the treasurer of each organization participate in the management of finances according to the policy of the state board of education, school board, and superintendent. Itemized day-by-day receipts and expenditures are recorded with the school bookkeeper. In many schools the student cooperative association (SCA) has a responsibility to oversee and to disseminate information about school activities. Extracurricular activities also receive support from student services, parent–teacher associations, and a number of community sponsors.

The goal is to provide a wide variety of extracurricular activities to meet the needs and interests of as many students as possible. Students involved in these kinds of cocurricular activities find opportunities to shine and are less likely to become disengaged from school. A Gallup survey showed that participation in cocurricular activity is positively correlated with high school and post–high school academic achievement as well as occupational status after graduation.

Because most of these activities are offered after school hours, transportation can be something of a problem. Usually one person is designated in each school to coordinate extracurricular activity. Sometimes students must meet specific criteria to be allowed to participate in extracurricular activity. Issues sometimes develop around adult interference, broken rules, overcompetitiveness, overemphasis, interference with academics, irrelevance, financial problems, faculty supervision, equitable treatment, transportation, and prejudice.

Some states have legislated policies that prohibit students who have failing grade point averages from participating in school-related clubs; however, this remains a hotly contested policy. Many argue that extracurricular activities provide students with avenues for expression, relevant experiences, and sometimes motivation to remain in school. Gerber states, "Indeed extracurricular activity may be one important source of identification with school, especially for academically weak students and those who are at-risk for withdrawing. Eliminating the opportunity for such participation may eliminate the last link to fostering a sense of belonging to school that some students have" (p. 50). Often both academic and extracurricular activities are recognized for excellence and high standards of achievement.

> What policies and supporting activities should exist regarding student participation in extracurricular activities at Thurber Middle School?

Integrating Services for Children and Families

Educators have long known that children don't have a fair chance to learn if they are hungry, abused, ignored, neglected, ill, afraid, or in any other form of distress. Many of the studies of the current condition of children (National Commission on Children, 1991; Children's Defense Fund, 1991) suggest that society fails to invest in children's well-being and to support and encourage families in the critical and difficult task of raising children. Americans who came of age during the Depression and World War II were far more deeply engaged in the life of their communities and children than any of the generations that have followed (Putman, 1996). Participation in most voluntary groups, including groups that help children, has declined by roughly 25 to 50 percent over the last two to three decades. A parallel drop of approximately 30 percent has occurred in social trust (trust in social institutions), along with a fading of the traditional family unit—mom, dad, relatives, and children (today only 29 percent fit the traditionally family picture).

It was unthinkable that a parent would not be home to meet a child returning from school in the 1950s; today it is a fairly common practice. In 1991, some 74 percent of women with children under 14 were working or looking for work. One in every two marriages ends in divorce. Cohabitation is one of the fastest-growing living arrangements. Participation in parent–teacher organizations dropped drastically from more than 12 million in 1964 to barely 5 million in 1982. According to Coleman and Hoffler (1987),

> the adult members are educated and individually capable, but for a variety of reasons—divorce, involvement with other adults in relations that do not cross generations, exclusive attention to self-development—the resources of the adults are not available to aid the psychological health and the social and educational development of children. (p. 225)

Safe spaces for children are shrinking as those for adults are expanding—restaurants, health clubs, tennis clubs, golf courses, sports and entertainment complexes, resorts. Many argue that technology as well as television is further privatizing lives and making needed human interactions even less available to children who desperately need them.

The Carnegie Task Force on Meeting the Needs of Young Children (1994) described this situation as the "quiet crisis." Although their report is focused on our youngest children, many of the findings are similar for all children. The task force believes that this "quiet crisis" threatens not only the healthy development of children but also our nation's well-being. The major risks are identified as inadequate parental care, isolated parents, substandard child care, poverty, and insufficient attention. The task force concluded that the "quiet crisis" requires immediate and far-reaching action. Persuaded that strong families and communities are essential to the healthy development of our youngest children, the task force calls for action in four key areas: Promote responsible parenthood, guarantee high-quality child-care choices, ensure good health protection, and mobilize communities to support children and their families. In studying these problems, policy makers and practitioners alike have become increasingly aware that schools and human service systems serve the same clients and that these clients can be better educated, socialized, and healed if different systems work together (Franklin & Allen, 1997).

Given the enormous changes occurring in families and society, it is no surprise that schools and health and other social services are being asked to take on greater responsibility in filling the evolving void in child care. The challenge is delivering the services that children and families might need in an efficient and coordinated manner. When working with the multitude of government agencies, private organizations, and special programs that are providing services, coordination is lacking, eligibility requirements are complex, categorical constraints deny services, and duplications are costly. No one is looking out for the child's needs as a whole.

A familiar Indian tale tells the story of six blindfolded men who encounter an elephant. In describing the elephant to friends, each man describes the whole based on only the one part he touches. Each man's understanding comes from his own experience—none realize the perspective or existence of the others. Staff in education, health, community, social, criminal, and recreational services are like the blindfolded men. Different professions may or may not have contact. Prescriptions they offer are based on their own disciplines, experiences, training, and reference groups. The court system wants to deal with delinquency for stealing. The school wants students to attend classes, pay attention, and improve reading skills. The mental health department is concerned with emotional problems related to sexual and physical abuse. The human services system wants to prevent child abuse through family preservation, parental training, and substance abuse counseling. The labor management system is concerned with job training and employment assistance. The welfare system is concerned that a child ran away from home. The health department is concerned with such issues as lack of nutrition, health care, and pregnancy. Professionals in each area seldom convey their own knowledge and expectations or acknowledge the expertise and contributions of the others. All of a child's problems are seldom addressed because no one is looking out for the child's needs as a whole. The irony is that none can succeed acting alone.

Each of the service systems to youth and their families provide a unique but important role. In an environment of shrinking resources, a cost-effective, efficient, comprehensive system of services is often offered as the most logical solution. Because children spend much of their time in school, the school itself is an excellent lens by which to focus on the whole needs of children. Education may serve to coordinate all services provided to children through an expanded IEP process. A comprehensive, integrated system requires creation of working partnerships among all agencies and agents who address children's needs. The justification for the needed effort is a belief that none of these professionals, including educators, can achieve their desired outcomes without addressing the needs of the entire child. Katherine Hooper-Brian and Hal Lawson (1994) conclude: "More than any one person or profession can complete, inter-professional collaboration and service integration requires us to band together in the service of children, youth, and families. A child-focused, family-centered, community development–oriented vision thus opens new avenues for success as a new century approaches" (p. 53).

A comprehensive, integrated system is one in which separate services are connected by common intake, eligibility determination, and individual family services and education planning, so that each family's range of needs is addressed. The goal is to sharply increase the number of and access to health, education, and social services for children and their families in community- and school-based programs. Dryfoos (1994) described the concept of full-service schools as those that offer a full complement of services to children and their families within the school. These schools address the social, emotional, physical, and psychological needs of the student, along with the academic needs, right in the school. This requires schools to work with outside agencies to plan for and promote student services. Integration does not typically mean merging these service systems but rather increasing the collaboration among them to form a partnership in which a number of service agencies linked to education develop and work toward a common set of goals. Typically schools are the central participant in planning and governing the collaborative effort and services. Services are coordinated (sometimes provided) by personnel at the school or a nearby neighborhood site.

These concepts received national attention in January 1991 when California Governor Pete Wilson created the cabinet-level position of secretary of child development and education with responsibility to integrate social, health, mental health, and support services in schools. Florida Governor Lawton Chiles also spoke out in favor of making schools the center for providing services to children and their families. Elementary and high schools in Miami provide full-service school-linked services. Other examples include support service coordinators in each high school in the Boston public school system and school social workers in all junior and senior high schools in St. Paul, Minnesota, public schools. The middle schools in Louisville have youth service centers. Other examples exist in St. Louis; Prince George County, Maryland; Modesto, California; and Philadelphia. The Comer/Ziegler model discussed in Chapter 3 provides for improved school-linked services.

Throughout the 1990s, Vice-President Al Gore has been a backer of this concept. He visited a number of such schools and was a strong supporter of what he called community-center school grants to design more community-oriented schools. The America's Schools Act, a revision to the ESEA, endorsed a much broader network of community-based programs within school facilities. Focus on standards, academics, and testing seems to ignore such programs, and the momentum may be disappearing.

The vision, however, calls for schools that are open to involvement by the local and the wider community and that are responsive to meeting student and family needs.

Even when services are provided off-site, strong linkages are created between school personnel and all other services. Representatives from outside agencies visit schools to provide information and make sure the school community is aware of available services and referral procedures. Centralized governance of services may be necessary if services are to be integrated within schools. Possibly most important are people who have responsibility and authority that span systems who are in a position to coordinate joint efforts.

Other key elements include staff characteristics and training, community and neighborhood support, service targeting, types of services, governance, collaboration, evaluation, information sharing, staffing alternatives, and provision of high-quality services (Center for the Future of Children, 1992). All involved must have a more holistic view of what children and families need to succeed. Franklin and Streeter (1995) point out that "benefits will be maximized as integrated service systems reduce the fragmentation in children and family services and accomplish comprehensive school programs" (p. 779).

> What might be the benefits in the development of a school-linked human services delivery system coordinated by a social worker assigned to each middle school?

Conclusion

Many programs are needed to address the social, emotional, and affective needs of students and to balance them with their educational needs. If such programs are not developed, schools will continue to experience high dropout, failure, and expulsion rates. These failures take a high toll on the future use of society's resources for remediation of social problems.

If schools emphasize these areas at the expense of academics, however, they fail to prepare the next generation academically. Underserviced students have little knowledge and few marketable skills and cannot achieve their full potential; ultimately they fail society. Their successful social and emotional adjustment will have little meaning in the context of inadequate learning. The challenge to educators, then, is to achieve the difficult and sometimes shifting balance between academics and successful human development and thus produce productive citizens.

Pupil personnel services help schools confront difficult issues that keep students from achieving academic success. All the professionals within a school are encouraged to contribute their unique knowledge and skills to the goal of achieving competent, well-educated, and well-adjusted students. Human service professionals are becoming more invested in achieving successful educational outcomes of students and helping them to become self-sufficient adults.

With the support of public policy, more and more special-needs students are receiving assistance and being accommodated in regular classes. The inclusion of a home component plan to complement classroom activity has proved absolutely essential to student success. The components, goals, and objectives of the program and curriculum plan must be clear, as well as the expected outcome within a given time frame. The total program is a long-term constant process with many important milestones along the way.

The focus of pupil personnel services is to help remediate developmental issues within a student's life and to enable the student to reach his or her full potential. When pupil personnel services are well organized and integrated into the culture of the school and community, they make a substantive contribution to student achievement by better preparing students to participate in the academic work and by improving their lives. Professionals who provide these services have a formidable responsibility to adhere to the highest professional and ethical standards. Changes within a variety of disciplines, judicial decisions, societal changes, child development research, women's and civil rights movements, educational reforms, technological and other advancements, societal and political changes, and many other forces will continue to have enormous impact on pupil personnel practices and education in general. Keeping up with the trends and issues in the decades ahead will be an exciting, challenging, sometimes frustrating, but always rewarding endeavor.

PORTFOLIO ARTIFACTS

- Chair a child-study team, and write an individualized educational plan (IEP) for a student.

- Visit a home with a school social worker and write a report on your experience.

- Participate in a group counseling session with a small group of people, and keep a reflective journal of your experiences.

- Work with a school psychologist in administering and interpreting tests.

- Volunteer to work at a group home for young adults with learning disabilities, a Ronald McDonald House, or other centers serving the special needs of youth and their families.

- Write a safe and secure school plan for your school.

- Spend a day with a social worker, juvenile court judge, pediatrician, surgeon, law enforcement officer, mental health worker, health department worker, or park and recreational worker (check insurances and protect your safety).

- Shadow the director of pupil personnel services.

- Write pupil personnel policy.

- Serve as a faculty sponsor for an extracurricular activity.

TERMS

The Education for all
  Handicapped Children Act
Extracurricular activity
"The forgotten half"
Hierarchical constructs of
  human development
Individualized educational plan
  (IEP)

Individuals with Disabilities
  Education Act (IDEA)
In-school suspension
Interprofessional cooperation
  and comprehensive service
  integration
Learning disability (LD)
Mainstreaming and inclusion

National Assessment of
  Educational Progress
Norm-referenced test
School Management and
  Resource Team (SMART)
School psychologist

SUGGESTED READINGS

Bullock, L. M. & Gable, R. A. (February 21, 1998). *Implementing the 1997 IDEA: New challenges and opportunities for serving students with emotional/behavior disorders.* Reston, VA: The Council for Exceptional Children.

Center for Effective Collaboration and Practice. (January 16, 1998). *Addressing student problem behavior.* Washington, DC: American Institutes for Research.

Dryfoos, G. (1994). *Full-Service schools.* San Francisco: Jossey-Bass.

Dryfoos, G. (1998). *Safe passage: Making it through adolescence in a risky society.* New York: Oxford University Press.

Hughes, F. P., & Noppe, L.D. (1991) *Human development: Across the life span.* New York: MacMillan Publishing Company.

Kohn, A. (1996). *Beyond discipline: From compliance to community.* Alexandria, VA: Association for Supervision and Curriculum Development.

Newkrug, E. (1999). *The world of the counselor.* Pacific Grove, CA: Brooks/Cole.

Turnbull, A. P., Turnbull, R. H., Shank, M., & Leal, D. (1995) *Exceptional lives: Special education in today's schools.* Englewood Cliffs, NJ: Prentice Hall.

Turnbull, R. & Cilley, M. (1999). *Explanation and implementations of the 1997 amendments to IDEA.* Upper Saddle River, NY: Merrill.

Zepeda, S. J., & Langenbach, M. (1999). *Special programs in regular schools.* Boston: Allyn & Bacon.

10 Human Resource Management

Vignette: Staffing Problems at Lincoln Elementary School

You are a new principal, newly appointed to Lincoln Elementary School. The assistant superintendent for human resource development (HRD) is Dr. Fred Henry, with whom you have an excellent working relationship and rapport. Dr. Henry is totally collaborative in his management style and has full confidence in you as principal. You and he agree on how to handle almost all HRD situations.

Two weeks ago, your school district announced plans to assign and bus students to Lincoln Elementary School because of its low enrollment. This is not an unprecedented action in your district. One week ago, the district held open hearings to discuss this decision. Three days ago the board reaffirmed their position. Since the busing order, you have been very aware that many parents, teachers, and children are concerned, apprehensive, and angry. Busing will begin at Lincoln in the next academic year. It is January, and staffing plans and student assignments will need to be completed over the next three months. This new plan is described as the capacity adjustment program (CAP).

Yesterday you received a call from Brad Brakeman, the school advisory chairman, and Elena Lopez, the building representative (who is the teacher elected by the faculty to represent them). They have asked that you meet with both of them to consider and address the concerns of parents, teachers, and children and to discuss your short- and long-range implementation plans regarding the busing order.

You know that you and others must address the concerns of parents, teachers, and children and gain their support for short- and long-range plans to make the change a positive experience for affected parties. You know that the school advisory chairman and building representative share many of the parents' concerns. You are very aware that it is of utmost importance that you as a new principal gain the support and confidence of these individuals.

The Receiving School: Lincoln Elementary School

Lincoln Elementary School is located in a wealthy and stable area of the city. Although the school's enrollment has been declining over the last four years, as citizens in the immediate community have become older. The building can hold 1200 students, currently only 875 children are enrolled in the school. Lincoln prides itself on its academic achievements and school spirit. It has very active parent groups and a large number of parent volunteers. It has won beautification awards and Junior Achievement awards. Many of its students go on to graduate from college.

Lincoln has a magnet program in mathematics. About 200 high-ability math students from adjacent schools are bused to Lincoln. This program has always been controversial, as parents from all schools involved are concerned about their children's safety and social acceptance at Lincoln. Others complain that the magnet program takes the best and brightest students from the sending schools. The magnet math teachers themselves have been demanding higher salaries, because those with comparable math skills in business and industry are paid so much more than they are as teachers.

The magnet math program has attracted a minority ratio slightly higher than the number that live in the school attendance zone. The student population is 1 percent Asian, 18 percent black, 21 percent Hispanic, and 60 percent white. On standardized tests, Lincoln students score in the 75th percentile in reading, the 72 percentile in oral language, and the 82 percentile in math.

The Sending School: Washington Elementary School

The students that will be identified as CAP students to attend Lincoln will come from Washington Elementary School, which is now severely overcrowded. The auditorium, library, and teachers' work area are currently being used as classrooms. It was selected as the sending school because of its overcrowding and proximity to Lincoln. The neighborhood around Washington can be characterized as "the wrong side of the tracks" compared with Lincoln's. The neighborhood is economically very poor and somewhat transient. It is not uncommon for children to come from single-parent families or homes where both parents work. There is a high rate of juvenile crime, child abuse, and child prostitution. Washington is not considered a good school. Those parents who can afford it send their children to private schools.

The school population at Washington is 55 percent Arabic, 12 percent black, 25 percent Hispanic, and 8 percent white. Most of the Arabic students don't speak English very well, since their parents recently immigrated from countries such as Lebanon, Iran, Saudia Arabia, Kuwait, and Jordan. Arabic children come from the poorest families. There is animosity among the students in these neighborhoods, especially in the junior high and high schools. Gang activities occur between the students who come from the Lincoln school area and the students who live in the Washington school area.

On standardized tests, Washington students score in the 25 percentile in reading, the 27 percentile in oral language, and the 15 percentile in math.

The table presents the school capacities, staffing patterns, and student enrollment at the two schools. To simplify this vignette, all teachers and student will return at both schools, and all students will pass to the next grade. Next year, student enrollment will grow by 210 at Washington and 65 at Lincoln, as shown in the table. The data presented in this table represent the planned pattern before the CAP decision to transfer students and implement the student busing plan. Although the total number of students will remain as shown in the table, you have been asked to reconfigure both students and staff to meet the superintendent and school board's objectives regarding the transfer of Washington students to Lincoln.

The Complaints and Concerns

Listed below are the concerns of parents, parent groups, and teachers that have been brought to your attention by Brad Brakeman and Elena Lopez:

1. Lincoln has an excellent academic environment; the bused students will lower educational standards. A third-grader in Washington is not equivalent to the third-grader in

School Capacities, Staffing Patterns, and Student Enrollments for this Year and Next Year Prior to the New Student Transfer Capacity Adjustment Plan (CAP)

Washington		Lincoln	
Capacity:	960 Students	Capacity:	1200 Students
Total enrollment:	1160 Students	Total enrollment:	875 Students
Total Classrooms:	37	Total Classrooms:	50
Student/Teacher Ratio:	29/1	Student/Teacher Ration:	24.3/1
+3-year Target:	25/1	+3-year Target:	25/1

STAFF

	Washington				Lincoln			
Grade	Teachers	Teacher Aids	Present year student enrollment	Projected Additions Next Year	Teachers	Teacher Aids	Present year student enrollment	Projected Additions Next Year
6	6	3	146	+40	8	8	200	+25
5	6	3	146	+30	7	7	179	+10
4	6	3	174	+25	7	7	174	+10
3	5	3	145	+25	5	5	118	+10
2	5	3	145	+25	4	4	91	+ 5
1	6	3	202	+35	3	3	68	+ 0
K	6	6	202	+30	2	2	45	+ 5
	40	24	1160	210	36	36	875	65

Washington	Lincoln
1 Principal	1 Principal
1 Assistant principal	1 Assistant principal
1 In-School suspension coordinator	1 Gifted-program coordinator
2 Special-education coordinators	1 Bilingual-program coordinator
1 Title-1 Coordinator	1 Special-education coordinator
2 Counselors	1 Resource specialist
2 Secretaries	1 Counselor
2 Nurses	2 Secretaries
	1 Nurse

Lincoln. They use different textbooks. The Washington school is so poor that the better students go to private schools. Lincoln will lose its famous school spirit.

2. There is too much busing. Why do so many young children's lives have to be disrupted? The values of a community school are being lost.

3. Lincoln has a magnet program in math. Teachers will not be able to effectively instruct children with such diverse abilities, and everyone concerned will suffer.

4. The communities of sending and receiving schools are complete opposites, and people in these neighborhoods have always disliked one another. Children from these communities

have totally different experiences and family environments. It will be impossible for teachers to relate their instructional objectives to children with such different life experiences.

5. Busing will require the development of a bilingual program for children who speak Arabic, and no one on the staff at Lincoln can effectively implement such a program. Arabic children have diverse dialects and often cannot understand one another. The Hispanic bilingual program is just beginning to be effective after years of effort. The district would be better off having a viable and adequately staffed bilingual Arabic program at Washington.

6. The district is trying to create social change at the expense of educational goals and children's physical safety.

Informing the Teaching Staff

It is essential that the teachers at both schools fully understand the background, purpose, and goals of the capacity adjustment plan (CAP). They should also be informed of changes that will occur in the existing staff, student configuration, and school program and be given the opportunity to ask questions. They should be told what will be done to help with the transition for teachers, students, and their families.

Additional Program Funding

A dollar amount is allocated to the receiving school for each CAP student. Additional adjustments are periodically made to account for the increased enrollment. For this reason, it is imperative that the number of CAP students be identified and reported.

CAP funds, which are in excess of regular funds, can be expended only to serve the needs of CAP students. Activities for which funds may be budgeted include, but are not limited to, the following:

- Instructional materials to address needs of incoming students
- Teaching assistants and aides for enrichment and skill building
- Coordinatorships to assist nonresident students
- Preschool counseling and programming for nonresident students
- Additional nonresident student counseling
- Clerical relief and overtime pay

Instructional materials necessary to meet the educational needs of Limited English Proficient (LEP) students transported to relieve overcrowding are also available.

The Capacity Adjustment Plan

The plan should result in enrollment numbers that place both schools close to capacity or only slightly over capacity. (Since there will be 2,211 students at these two schools next year and there is a capacity of 2,160, one or both schools will be slightly over capacity.) You have total freedom to configure the schools in such a way as to cause the least possible concern and debate among teachers, students, and families. Because of the proximity of the two schools, all students in both attendance zones can easily attend either school. Your plan should describe how students will be selected to attend which school and how decisions will be made regarding needed staff transfers. You do not have to consider the busing plan, which will be devised by others after you have decided how you will configure the two schools and which students and staff will be assigned to each school.

You must provide opportunities to encourage the parents of pupils affected by CAP to participate in school affairs. You should develop a plan that will facilitate the transition for students, parents, and staff and provide lots of support during this important first year. You should consider the training and development needs of staff and propose ideas that will help the staff to make this transition a success.

Balance

Consistent with school policies, resources and programs, classes should be organized so that (1) an ethnic balance appropriate to the school population is maintained in each classroom and (2) CAP students are assigned to all rooms to avoid isolation. These factors are in addition to all the other criteria normally considered when organizing classes and assigning staff.

> Write two needed policy statements: one for voluntary transfer and the other for administrative transfer.
>
> Explain how decisions will be made regarding which students will attend each school.
>
> Explain how decisions will be communicated.

Source: Development Dimensions International. (1985) *Assistant principal elementary school policy simulation* modified by permission. Development Dimensions International, Inc., is a world leader in providing human resource training programs and services. For more information contact DDI at 800-933-4463 (U.S.), 800-668-7971 (Canada), via e-mail info@ddiworld.com or at its Web site, www.ddiworld.com.

Taking Care of the Staff

Human resource management assumes a major responsibility for providing and maintaining a motivated, high-quality workforce. The focus is on creating an organization that serves its own goals and meets the personal needs of the school system's employees. Human resource functions run throughout the organization from top to bottom, and neglect at any level within the hierarchy ultimately reduces the chances of success. However, employees who are first entering their profession have needs that are very different from those of seasoned employees. Regardless, the focus at all levels is the achievement of school district objectives by helping individual members of the staff to reach the highest possible level of achievement and performance.

The investment in human capital or human resources is the most important one made within any organization. The human resource functions support those who work within the organization and help to link them to the organization's mission and management philosophy. Webb and Norton (1999) suggest that

> the quality of education programs in large part depends upon (1) the quality of human resources within the system; (2) the extent to which productive human relationships are realized; and (3) the development, motivation, and utilization of existing human qualities. Whereas a positive organizational climate depends upon a variety of factors, the human resource function assumes a major responsibility for providing a high quality of work life in the school system by focusing upon goals of the system in relation to its human resources. (p. 70)

Human resource management, among the oldest of the administrative functions, has undergone a resurgence in importance. Where the personnel office was once two to three levels removed from the superintendent, today most school divisions have an assistant superintendent for human resources who reports directly to the superintendent and supervises a much larger human resource staff. At the same time school division employees have recognized the importance of the proper use of human resource functions to the success of their schools. The American Association of School Personnel Administrators, founded in 1940, is the national professional association for human resource professionals in the United States and Canada. (For more information see: www.aaspa.org.)

Rebore (1998) states, "The goals of the personnel function are basically the same in all school systems—to hire, develop, and motivate personnel in order to achieve the objectives of the school district, to assist individual members of the staff to reach the highest possible levels of achievement, and to maximize the career development of personnel" (p. 11). Typically, human resource management is broken into three major functions as shown in Figure 10.1 on page 286. Today, Castetter (1996) suggests,

> Evolving models of the human resource function extend well beyond traditional tasks or recordkeeping, social work, and collective bargaining. Today's designs consider the human resources function to be a vital unit in any organizational entity. The organized and unified array of system parts interact through human performance to establish a productive public institution. (p. 30)

Which of the various HRD functions might be involved to help make the transition of staff and students as successful as possible? Explain how human resource functions may benefit this situation.

Job Analysis, Classification, and Staff Planning

The various functions of human resource management (HRM) can be viewed as sequential beginning with job analysis, job classification and staff planning, and ending with employee record keeping. This linear flow of personnel functions aids in organizing thinking about HRM functions, because; in practice, such an orderly flow seldom exists and functions are not discrete but integral aspects of a systematic process. The HRM process begins with an educational plan that has attained consensus. Implementing a new educational plan often requires a rethinking of policy and changes in the allocation of work duties and responsibilities, as well as the structure of the organization (Sredl & Rothwell, 1987).

Policies are written to provide guidance regarding acceptable practice. Policy proposals can come from any department, but those regarding employees are typically routed to the human resource department for consideration and recommendation to the superintendent's office. Ultimately the policy will be submitted to the school board

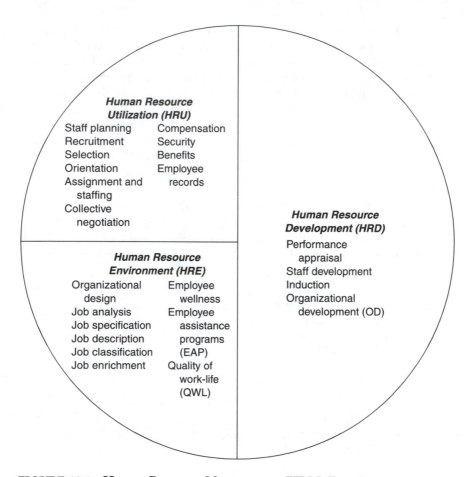

FIGURE 10.1   Human Resource Management (HRM) Functions

for adoption and, if adopted, will guide all future actions. Policies must be complete, concise, clear, changeable, and distinctive (Clemmer, 1991, p. 107). Policy must provide for consistently fair and equitable treatment. Since policy is legally binding for all district personnel, it often becomes an issue in the negotiation process with teacher associations and others. Following are two examples of typical policy statements:

■ The final judgment in all teacher transfers shall rest with the superintendent of schools.

■ In the event that it is necessary to make reductions among teachers who have attained tenure, such reductions shall be made on the basis of total seniority, which shall be determined by the total number of years under contract with the school district.

The job analysis and classification systems break down the work, group the activities into an organizational structure, define the duties and requirements for each position, and rank the position in relation to all other positions. An organizational chart is

BOX **10.1**

**Definitions of Classical
Organizational Structure**

Organizational channels—Channels of supervision and communication considered the formal lines of authority that transmit information throughout the organization.

Line authority—The major line of authority from the very top to the bottom of the organization; employees in line positions make day-to-day decisions regarding the substantive operation of the organization.

Staff authority—Those who provide advisory, specialized services to line administrators; staff duties include interpreting, recommending, discussing, explaining, evaluating, and promoting but not making line decisions.

Unity of command—The arrangement by which each individual within the organization reports and receives direction from one superior.

Delegation—The concept that authority should be given to the lowest-level individual who has the needed information, knowledge, and ability to make a decision.

Span of control—The factors that affect the number of individuals a single administrator can effectively control: time, mental capacity, complexity, number of duties, stability, capability, leadership style.

Coequality of authority and responsibility—The concept that the power (authority) and obligation (responsibility) to make and enforce decisions related to assigned duties should always be equal. Responsibilities tend to increase or decrease to the level of authority when they are not equal, thus frustrating the position holder and his or her subordinates.

Fixed responsibility—The concept that the obligation to successfully complete one's duties should be placed squarely on the subordinate to help the subordinate develop, get work accomplished, identify areas needing action, and minimize buck-passing.

---

often used to visualize the total organization, including major functions, relationships of positions, lines of authority and communication, relative authority and power, channels of supervision, and other general organizational patterns. Box 10.1 provides some classical principles for the creation of organizational structure and the assignment of duties. An important function of HRM is to stipulate the duties, authority, and responsibilities related to every position within the organization. The completion of a job analysis and job description is an essential part of the personnel activity (Webb & Norton, 1994).

Inadequate emphasis on organization, job descriptions and classification, staff planning, or recruitment and selection will decrease the ability of employees, and thus the organization, to be successful over the long run. These HRM functions are part of an integrated system, and changes in any one of these factors is bound to have an effect on all others.

Figure 10.2 on page 288 illustrates how these various elements interact. The carrying out of these important functions requires extensive knowledge of both the nature of the work organization and the workforce.

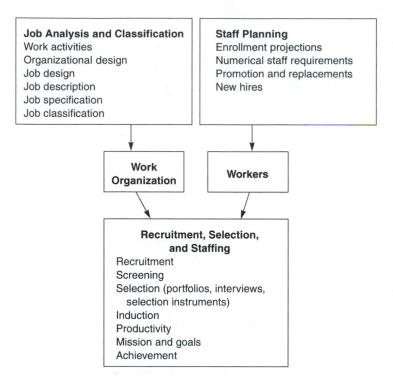

FIGURE 10.2   Creating and Defining the Needed Organization

Job Analysis

Job analysis is the process of gathering and analyzing information about the principal work activities in a position and the qualifications (knowledge, skill, abilities, and other attributes) necessary to perform those activities. It is the first step in creating and updating job descriptions for all organizational positions. People must know what they will be doing, the qualifications they must possess to be able to do it, and what they will be paid in order to feel comfortable in their hiring and employment decisions. Classifying positions into jobs and jobs into families; setting wage and salary rates; articulating standards to guide employee selection, appraisal, and training; and developing employees are all based on information collected in the job analysis. Equal employment opportunity laws also require employees to determine whether individuals with disabilities are qualified for a job.

Job analysis can be completed in several different ways. These methods include observation, work sampling, interviewing, questionnaires, or structured approaches such as role analysis technique (RAT) and functional job analysis, or commercial methods such as the Common-Metric Questionnaire (CMQ). A comprehensive review of existing documents and possible external sources such as the *Dictionary of Occupational Titles* can also be helpful. Ultimately a job description is generated for all positions for which similar tasks have to be performed. The job analysis results in a job description (i.e., title, status, relationships, nature of job, duties, tasks, and responsibilities) and a job specification (minimum qualifications).

> Obtain job descriptions for a bilingual program coordinator, a special education coordinator, and a principal. Determine how they were created and whether they fit the needs at Washington and Lincoln Elementary Schools.

Job Classification

Once jobs have been analyzed, they are grouped, according to similar work requirements, into common classes or pay grades. Henderson (1985) defines pay grades as convenient groupings of a wide variety of jobs that are similar in a number of critically important ways, even though they have little else in common. Pay grades are used to determine appropriate salary levels for each position, regardless of who holds it at present. In this way, the job classification system appraises the relative value of a position in regard to all other positions. In contrast, the performance appraisal system evaluates the merits of a position holder in relationship to others holding the same position. If an employee challenges the pay that his or her position receives in relation to other positions, it is important to have sound and rational justification for the pay scales in order to maintain effective morale and productivity. For example, if you decide to pay higher salaries to high school principals than you do to middle school principals, you will need to have sound justification to avoid harmful conflicts.

Most HRM departments use a technique that is often described as a "factor-point system" of job classification. The school system must first determine the factors that it believes are most important in determining the relative worth of all positions within the organization. Factors selected by the Virginia Beach Public School system are "education; experience; policy, methods, or procedures; program development; supervision; assets; records and reports; community contacts; student and personnel welfare; and job stress." The system establishes and defines degrees and assigns points for each of the factors. Numerical point values are assigned for each degree of each factor to reflect the relative importance of each. The following definition of degrees and point values relates to the responsibility for development and execution of "policy, methods, or procedures."

Points	*Definition of Degrees*
5	Requires execution and interpretation of existing operational policies, instruction methods, or procedures.
10	Requires development of intraschool operational policies, instructional methods, or procedures.
15	Requires development of intradivision or interschool operational policies, instructional methods, or procedures.
20	Requires development of operational policies, instructional methods, or procedures affecting the entire school district.

The total points awarded for all respective factors represent the value of the job in relation to all other jobs. Typically a diverse committee is charged with reviewing available factors and properly weighing all positions within the organization. A salary range is set for each pay grade or classification, using both internal and external comparisons to ensure that the salary schedule is internally consistent and externally competitive. It is recommended that all jobs be classified at least once every ten years.

> Consider the proposal that teachers in the magnet mathematic program should be paid higher wages than all other teachers. How would you resolve this question?

Staff Planning

Prerequisite to any efforts to recruit and select employees is an assessment of the organization's needs for employees. Staff planning is a forecast of the number and kinds of employees the organization will need in each position over a given period of time. Questions that must be answered include:

- How many and what kinds of students will be served?
- What kinds of educational programs will be needed to serve those students?
- Where will these students be located, and what existing staff will be available to serve them?
- What support services will be needed to serve the students and for the programs to be operated?
- What level of funding will be available?
- What types and how many people will need to be hired ?

Once the educational program has been determined, it is necessary to prepare enrollment projections. An error in enrollment projections will result in expensive and disruptive overstaffing or understaffing of the school system. There are many choices regarding forecasting models. Most assignments are based on the number of students expected to enroll in each school. Once these numbers are available, human resource needs can be calculated using desired personnel ratio objectives or numerical staffing-adequacy ratios. McKenna (1965) suggests that a useful gauge in arriving at the appropriate numbers of professionals is 67 professionals per 1,000 pupil units. He suggests the following breakdown:

Position	*Staff per 1,000 pupil units*
Teachers	45 (22.2/1)
Librarians	2
Guidance counselors	2
Reading/speech therapist	1
Psychologist	1
Health professionals	2
Clerical staff	9

Administrative staff	3
Instructional specialists	2
Total	67

Minimum personnel-to-student ratios are often controversial and established by state boards of education. For example, a school system with 20,000 total enrollment of which 1610 are third-graders and a teacher staffing ratio of 23 students per certified third-grade classroom teacher would require 70 (1610/23) third-grade teachers. Staff requirements are calculated for all grade levels, all schools, and the school district office. Adjustments are made for special programs and special student needs. Final hiring requirements are determined by comparing the school district's future human resource needs with the numbers of those already employed who will remain with the school district. Retirements, resignations, sabbatical leaves, dismissals, and deaths affect the number of personnel to be replaced. The totals help pinpoint needed new hires, highlight areas of overstaffing (reduction in force—RIF), identify employees for possible intra-system movement (promotions, transfers, demotions, and so on), and ultimately identify the number and kind of individuals who must be recruited to satisfy future needs.

Develop a proposal for assigning all students to Washington and Lincoln Elementary Schools. Once you know how many students will be attending each school, determine how many teachers and aides will be required for each grade level at each school. Then determine how many assistant principals, bilingual program coordinators, special-education coordinators, resource specialists, and counselors will be required at each of the two schools. How many new hires will be required at each of the grade levels and job categories? How will teacher-transfer decisions be made?

Recruitment

It is critically important to ensure that the right people, with the right skills are on hand at the right time to implement the approved educational plan. The effort to successfully match human resource demands with human resource supply is one of the most important efforts educational leaders make. The process begins with developing ways to attract qualified people to apply for open positions within the school district. Vacancy announcements, advertisements, employment agencies, university visits, professional organizations, employee referrals, job fairs, incentive programs, and other school systems are all potential sources. Perhaps the single most important factor in attracting qualified candidates is the reputation and image of the school division and community. Other factors that influence any recruitment plan are affirmative action and equal employment opportunity, professional negotiations, salary and fringe benefits, school system policy, employment continuity, employee relations, staff development, availability of opportunity, and the work itself.

Concern has periodically been expressed about the number and quality of individuals aspiring to become educators (Reagan, 1981; Kean, 1986; Task Force on Teaching, 1986). Career opportunities for minorities and women have increased in business, medicine, law, and engineering, causing a decline among this population in education. Some recruiters have anticipated the decline in applicant quality and have begun to develop programs to encourage high school students to become teachers, have expanded their geographical recruiting areas, and have worked with state departments of education to develop alternative certification programs. They are also working to determine the factors that are causing education to lose many of the best and brightest students. Higher salaries, stock option plans, and other lucrative benefits outside the public domain, although a main reason, are not the only reason—another, for example, lack of teacher respect. Obviously, the quality of the application pool is only as good as those who choose to enter the profession.

Successful recruiting requires a long-term perspective and should be a constant process for everyone employed within the organization. The process includes getting the word out and collecting application materials necessary to make initial screening decisions. Although recruitment and screening can be centralized, it is best that selection be decentralized to the unit in which the individual will work. The individual responsible for interviewing and making the final decision regarding employment is provided a rank-ordered list with information about each of the candidates eligible for appointment from which he or she selects three to five candidates for more extensive interviews. It is important to follow up quickly, particularly with strong candidates who are probably being recruited by other systems. If the desired person has not been found, it is often best, but not always possible, to maintain the vacancy rather than hire an undesirable candidate.

What qualities might be especially helpful for the new teachers that will be hired for these two schools? What will be the best source for teachers having these qualities, and how might you recruit them?

Selection

The selection process involves matching applicants' qualifications to the selection criteria, job description, specifications, and work unit. The determination to hire is related to technical skills (can he or she do the job?) and motivation (will he or she do the job?). Those involved in the interview process should be trained in its use and familiar with all legal requirements that govern employee selection. Regardless of whether a single individual or a number of staff members jointly perform the tasks of interviewing, the steps remain basically the same. The six typical steps to the structured interview process (Arons, 1998) are:

1. Introduction and welcoming
2. Obtaining information

3. Providing information
4. Responding to questions
5. Concluding the interview
6. Evaluating the candidate

The *introduction and welcoming* step begins by setting the environment and schedule for the interview. The environmental conditions should be conducive to establishing and maintaining the atmosphere of confidential relations, making the applicant comfortable and at ease, and promoting trust and free speech. Schedule enough time for the interview, and no disruptions should occur. The interviewer should form a positive relation with the interviewee while collecting all needed information and retaining control of the interview. Study information on the applicant before the interview, checking appropriate experiences and their sequence; the quality, attitude, style, and tone of the materials; and the strength of supporting documents. Make notes on items to follow up in the interview. Background investigations are very useful, but all legal requirements must be followed. The interview should begin by putting the applicant at ease and setting up ground rules related to time frame, people to be seen, use of note-taking or recording devices, and the time when interviewee's questions will be answered.

Obtaining information is the heart of the interview, with success resting on the interviewer's skills in questioning. Good interviewing is the process of getting valid and complete information related to the interviewee's ability to perform the job. A prime objective is to get the applicant to be honest and forthright during the discussion. It is best to have thought through questions in advance of the interview. Questions should be specific, probing the individual's ability to carry out the responsibilities of the position and assessing the specific characteristics sought. Questions should be open-ended, giving the applicant an opportunity to provide a fair amount of information.

The interviewer should not lead the response with any form of directive or point of view. For example, "We use cooperative education in this school. Do you think this is an effective approach?" is an ineffective question, because it is both a leading and close-ended question. A number of questions are also not in compliance with federal legislation and most state human rights laws. It is best only to ask questions that are directly related to the job. Effective listening is important to the interview process. Some common suggestions for improved listening skills are:

- Get the respondent to clarify, elaborate, and reflect (e.g., tell me more, turn a statement into a question, silence).
- Summarize or restate key points (e.g., summary bridges).
- Look at the person (good eye contact).
- Get the main points and test for understanding (e.g., paraphrase).
- Control your desire to mentally argue.
- Avoid making assumptions.
- Recognize your own prejudices.
- Do very little of the talking.
- Be accepting; there are no wrong answers.
- Watch your body language.

It is best to make brief notes during the interview to help remember what was said. Then immediately after the interview, record your observations.

In the *providing information* stage, the interviewee needs information about the nature of the position, the community, and the school system itself. Key concerns are typically about salary, benefits, working conditions, policies and procedures, colleagues, reporting relationships, opportunities, staff development, and community support. Brochures, manuals, fact sheets, and promotional materials can provide needed information to the candidate. Information allows the candidate to make better decisions regarding his or her fit within the organization. For this reason, it is very important to set a positive environment and put the best possible face on the organization, without being deceptive or overselling, which results in anger, high turnover, disruption, and loss. Always allow time for the interviewee to ask any questions and keep notes on the questions asked. Keep responses to questions brief, always maintaining control of the interview.

Concluding the interview is important to inform the candidate what happens next and give time frames in which decisions will be made and when and how the individual will be notified. Everyone who is interviewed, whether he or she receives the job or not, should receive a letter of appreciation or a telephone call indicating that the decision has been made. It is very important to successfully close the interview before showing the applicant out.

Evaluating the candidate results in the recording and rating of significant attributes of the candidate that contribute to the effectiveness of final selection. It is best to have an interviewer rating form so that information on all candidates is similarly recorded for easier comparison. Some interviewers find it helpful to construct a matrix on which to compare applicants in terms of their responses to job-related questions. Selecting employees is among the most important decision any administrator makes because an organization can be no better than the people it employs. Recording information helps in making appropriate final decisions and provides a clean audit trail against charges that decisions were based on discrimination, bias, or favoritism (Canton & Avery, 1989).

What criteria will you use to select teachers and support staff for these schools? New hires? Transfers? How will you determine whether teachers meet these criteria?

Alternative Selection Approaches

Perceiver Academy

Packaged, structured interviews ask the same series of questions of all candidates for a position, and their responses are scored. A common example are the teacher and principal perceiver systems from Gallup, Inc. Interviewers are trained to "listen for" very specific types of statements in regard to each question. If the interviewer hears the "listen for," the applicant will get a "1" for that question and, if not, the person receives a "0". Research suggests that candidates who score higher on the perceiver system are more effective in their jobs than those who have lower scores. Many school divisions that use these types of systems believe they have improved the quality of their staffs.

For example, the perceiver system might comprise five questions in each of twelve issue areas. For teachers, these twelve areas might be mission, empathy, rapport drive, individualized perception, listening, investment, input drive, activation, innovation, gestalt, objectivity, and focus. The interviewer might ask, "What is your mission? What are your beliefs about the significance of education?" The "listen for" is "the development of students, civilization's survival, or democracy depends on education." Some school systems have designed their own standard sets of questions and responses or "listen fors."

Assessment Centers

Assessment centers are geared more for promotion decisions and primarily for management positions; however, the methods they use provide a model for selection and staff development decisions. They provide an opportunity to observe candidates for administrative positions in an environment that simulates situations the individual will face as an administrator. A team of trained assessors observes and rates the candidates as they participate in various activities. The candidates are evaluated on a set of relevant skills or dimensions based on the evidence collected to identify and measure their management potential. Research tends to show that high-rated participants are two to three times more likely than low-rated participants to be promoted during following years and are significantly more likely to be described as strong administrators when promoted (Bynham, 1971; Bynham, 1978; Schmitt et al., 1983; Richardson, 1988).

The NASSP Assessment Center model typically generates behavioral data relevant to the critical skill dimensions presented in Table 10.1 on page 296 (Hersey, 1994; NASSP, 1988).

The courts have upheld selection/promotion decisions based on assessment centers (*Berry, Stokes and Lant v. City of Omaha*). The final report on each candidate describes strengths and weaknesses, skills needing improvement, recommendations for professional development, and comparison of the candidate's performance with others.

Other possible alternatives for selection are requesting videotapes, portfolios, and other forms of evaluative data.

What questions would you ask an individual interviewing for a bilingual program coordinator position? What criteria would most influence your evaluation and final decision to hire a specific person for this job?

TABLE 10.1

Principals		Superintendent	
Skills	*Dimensions*	*Dimensions*	*Skills*
Administration	Problem analysis Judgment Organizational ability Decisiveness	Encouraging innovation Strategic change Serving diverse constituencies	*Educational initiative*
Interpersonal	Leadership Sensitivity Stress tolerance	Interpreting information Judgment Complex problem analysis	*Analyzing and resolving problems*
Communication skills	Oral communication Written communication	Communicating Empowering others Balancing demands	*Team building*
Others	Range of interests Personal motivation Educational values	Knowing strengths Acquiring learnings	*Expanded learning*

Performance Appraisal and Evaluation

Performance evaluation is one of the hardest jobs in education and one of the most important. The primary goal of performance appraisal is the professional improvement of employees and thus the instructional process. It has two purposes: Formative evaluation identifies areas for improvement and designs developmental plans. The second, summative evaluation accumulates records regarding the overall quality and degree of improvement in an employee's performance in order to make and support decisions regarding the individual's continued employment, salary, and promotion potential. In this way evaluation is a continuous process throughout ones entire career in education.

Human resource management is more involved in the design, development, and maintenance of the appraisal process, which will be used by line administrators in the appraisal, development, and supervision of employees. The performance appraisal process shown in Figure 10.3 emphasizes the three phases (modified from Ellena & Redfern,1972):

Educational administrators have a responsibility to implement fair, objective, and meaningful appraisal systems.

Planning the Evaluation

Employees typically make needed adjustments if they are made aware of required performance improvements. The absence of such feedback will result in more, longer, and larger errors in their work. In this way, the purpose of the evaluation process is always related to continued improvement of employee performance. The focus is on a

Phase I. Planning the Evaluation			Phase II. Collecting Information		
Establish the purpose of evaluation	Establish basic critieria to be evaluated and standards	Establish procedures following management and legal considerations	Select evaluative techniques to be used	Train in the use of evaluation procedures	Coordinate and monitor staff evaluations
Phase III. Using Information					
Conduct an effective performance conference		Establish a developmental plan or plan of assistance ↕		Make employment and promotion decisions about personnel	
— — — — — — — Communication — — — — — — —					

FIGURE 10.3   **The Three Phases of Performance Appraisal Process**

shared belief of what the employer and employee jointly believe to be high-quality performance. The appraisal includes a feedback delivery system on employee progress along with an effective means of communication on performance and development. The system must have integrity if employees are to trust and act on the results (Joint Committee on Standards for Education Evaluation, 1988). Unless skillfully conducted, the appraisal process often results in ill feelings and misunderstandings for both parties and probably does more harm than good.

Performance appraisal planning covers the philosophy, purpose, criteria, objectives, methods, and skills needed for the appraisal process. Some of the most compelling reasons to pursue it are to:

- Help the employee assess and improve performance
- Motivate the employee to improve knowledge, skill, and methods
- Make the employee accountable for performance expectations
- Recognize and reward outstanding performance
- Identify and remediate ineffective performance
- Terminate incompetent employees
- Plan professional development and training
- Support organizational credibility

Evaluations provide an opportunity for employees to discuss their professional growth and ways they and the organization might improve curriculum, instruction, and student learning.

Communication regarding an individual's performance is by its nature important to both the organization's and the person's professional life and should not be taken lightly. Accuracy is important, along with an openness to discuss performance honestly and constructively. Evaluators need to be clear in their objectives when providing evaluative feedback (Daresh, 1992) and schedule enough time to effectively carry out this process. Job performance should be assessed by personnel familiar with the person's work. The evaluating procedure must afford due process considerations to all employees.

Collecting Information

The evaluation and evaluator's credibility is on the line. Future relationships and ability to influence one another depends on the accuracy and quality of information regarding performance. Although multiple assessment methods may be used to appraise performance, most school systems have a specific evaluative form that evaluators complete as they observe the employee's performance on the job. Both evaluator and evaluatee assume responsibility for collecting and exchanging a variety of performance data. The most common techniques are the checklist and rating scales, but recently essay approaches have gained in popularity. The essay method requires the evaluator to describe in writing how well each employee has performed. The instrument usually spells out evaluation criteria as a cue for the rater who checks, rates, or describes the level of performance.

Supervisors usually complete the instrument, but 360-degree systems, for which supervisor, colleagues, and subordinates all complete performance appraisals on an individual, have proved to improve the quality of information provided (Lepsinger & Yukl, 1995, Church & Bracken, 1997, Edwards & Ever, 1996). Additionally, traditional top-down forms of appraisal appear to be inconsistent with current developments in leadership, thought, and practice. Each source of 360-degree feedback has the potential to provide useful data on all performance traits. Employees achieve an increased self-awareness of their strengths and weaknesses. These systems sometimes include the use of technology to input appraisal data and to produce comparative reports normed on other employees.

Weller, Buttery, and Bland (1994) found that teachers, principals, and superintendents all believed that teachers could provide effective evaluations and a comprehensive and realistic view of the principal's leadership and school climate. The 360 approach in general provides a holistic approach to employee development indicators. Not everyone supports it, and some suggest it invites employees to take control of their supervisors.

Other techniques, such as portfolios, self-evaluation, cognitive coaching, parent and student evaluation, structured simulations, videotapes, test scores, transcripts, interaction analysis, and action research, are also used to provide information. The focus is on developing diagnostic habits of thinking, reflection on work process, and planning long- and short-term self-development.

New education approaches—constructivist, authentic learning, for instance—will require the gathering of more diverse data to get an accurate picture of performance (Millman & Darling-Hammond, 1990; Darling-Hammond 1997; Wiggins, 1998). Teachers being evaluated might include samples of student work over time, linked to evidence of teaching plans and activities, teacher feedback to students, and analyses of student needs and progress. The focus is on how student learning grows out of specific teaching actions and decisions and emphasizes effective performance assessment employed to measure high-level knowledge and skills (Darling-Hammond,

1998). Technology can bring in more sophisticated assessment and reporting of skills and make it easier to complete evaluations.

Using Information

In the using-information phase, evaluator and evaluatee jointly diagnose, analyze, and discuss evaluative data and they plan and agree on follow-up action. If the employee's performance meets minimum standards, a "development plan" is constructed to build on the individual's performance. If performance falls below standards, the individual is placed on a "plan of assistance" to help him or her improve performance and thus remain employed with the organization. The performance appraisal conference is the most important step in the evaluation system because this is where feedback, reflection, problem solving, and future development planning occur. Unless this step is completed, a performance appraisal has not occurred.

The first step in discussing evaluative information is identifying where increased levels of performance might occur. This step requires the creation of a supportive, open climate where everyone feels free to express interpretations, feelings, and ideas. It begins with good communication about how things are going, moves through things that are going well, and leads to areas that might benefit from further improvement. Disagreements are expected and are resolved through discussion and mutual problem solving. Both parties learn more about possible areas for future development. Performance improvement may require changes in policy, performance expectations, resource availability, or job skills, or it may require increased performance on the part of the employee. Improvement begins through a process of inquiry.

Participants actively listen to one another and discuss each idea thoroughly, agreeing on specific action to be taken by all parties and establishing a date for formal follow-up. All parties learn, because experience, knowledge, skills, and perspectives are pooled to stimulate growth, develop new ideas, and generate improvement. Feedback is focused on specific situations and exploration of alternatives to improve future performance and develop potential. The final plan should:

- Protect the individual's pride
- Show how evaluation and developmental plans are credible
- Consider the urgency relative to the area being developed
- Think about feasibility and the impact of the plan
- Consider reasonableness and manageability
- Consider sufficient duration
- Think about costs involved in the plan

All evaluations, performance improvement and developmental plans, supportive documents, and validating data are placed in the employee's personnel file along with comments, recommendations, or rebuttals of all parties. Evaluations may be used for recommending staff development, committee assignment, promotion, reassignment, dismissal, and so forth. All forms and procedures must follow due-process considerations, which require in-part that reasonable rules of conduct and disciplinary consequences be known and violations be objectively investigated. Due process also requires the existence of substantiative written documentation and credible judgments, establishment of plans of assistance, and disciplinary action that is consistent and reasonable. A hearing and appeals procedure must exist, and all law must be followed.

The most fundamental reason for a performance appraisal system is to improve both the individual's and the institution's performance so that effective service is provided to students and society. James Stronge (1997) states,

> Teacher evaluation in its myriad forms is nothing more than a process for determining how an individual, program, or school is performing in relation to a given set of circumstances. When evaluation is viewed as more than this process (i.e., evaluation as an end in itself), it gets in the way of progress and thus becomes irrelevant. When evaluation is treated as less than it deserves (i.e., superficially, with little or no resource allocation, invalid evaluation systems, and flawed implementation designs), the school, its employees, and the public at large are deprived of opportunities for improvement and the benefits that accountability can afford. All of us, whatever our relationship to the educational enterprise, deserve high-quality evaluation. A teacher assessment and evaluation system that is built squarely upon individual and institutional improvement holds the promise of filling this need and better serving our students and our communities. (p. 18)

> How might the performance appraisal system be used to increase the probability that students will have successful experiences at Washington and Lincoln Elementary Schools?

Staff Development

Shakespeare's famous line tells us, "We know what we are but not what we may be." Staff development is any activity or process intended to improve skills, attitudes, understandings, or performance in present or future roles (Fullan, 1990). Educators recognize that training is critical in helping schools to achieve the high standards that are expected of them. Training should play a transformational role within the organization. It plays a critical, integrative role as a driver of cultural change, process improvement, individual growth, job redesign, and continuous improvement. Development should address both individual learning and organizational improvement. According to Ernest Boyer (cited in Cunningham & Gresso, 1993) past president of the Carnegie Foundation for Advancement of Teaching,

> The only way we're going to get from where we are to where we want to be is through staff development....When you talk about school improvement, you're talking about people improvement....the school is the people, so when we talk about excellence or improvement or progress, we're really focusing on the people who make up the building. (p. 173)

Successful organizations promote and demand continuous professional development throughout one's career.

Successful staff development models typically interrelate district, school, and staff development plans. Each reinforces the other in a clear, coherent program. The responsibility for individual development and performance improvement must rest with the individual. The role of the human resource department is to consult and plan with employees who are involved in staff development efforts. Development activities can eliminate differences, introduce new programs, induct new staff, assist new personnel, promote continuous improvement, improve competence, reform schools, extend interests, prepare for changes in position, and provide many other benefits. Development efforts may be geared toward board members, administrators, teachers, noncertified personnel—all who are a part of the education process.

The process begins with the creation of development plans that balance both short- and long-term needs. The roles of leadership are facilitator, coach, mentor, and adviser. Most important, training must be proactive and closely tied to school values, priorities, goals, and strategies. There must be a tight fit between training and people's jobs. Training must also support the development and implementation of new, improved approaches to education. In this way, focus is on process and outcome improvement. Box 10.2 on page 302 provides a helpful checklist for those involved in planning staff development activities. By encompassing a clear vision, planning, and collegial support, staff development can be a powerful medium for continuous school improvement.

The National Commission on Teaching and America's Future (1996) found that, "Teachers consistently report that they experience much more powerful learning when they participate in new vehicles for professional development such as teacher networks, teacher academies, professional development schools, and National Board certification, as well as teaching teams, action research projects, and study groups within their schools." Electronic learning technologies to deliver information and facilitate the development of skills and knowledge will revolutionize staff development activities. Teleconferencing, for example, allows development activities to occur at multiple locations within the same time frame. The Internet can provide on-demand multimedia training at any time within a 24-hour day. Computer-based training (CBT) and CD-ROM have been and will continue to remain top choices in developmental activities. Keeping pace with the rate of change will be the biggest challenge.

Rough out three or four specific staff development activities that might improve the transition of students and teachers between schools or that will improve the staffs' ability to succeed after the capacity adjustment plan is implemented.

Employee Assistance and Wellness Programs

All school systems have employees whose health or personal problems adversely affect their performance, productivity, and job satisfaction. Now employers are providing

BOX **10.2**

A Checklist for Planning Group Staff Development Activities

A. Before in-service program planning, be sure to:

1. Identify what participants might be able to do at the end of the program (expected outcomes).
2. Consider various ways in-service programs could be delivered (i.e., workshop, independent study, college course, teleconferencing, networking).
3. Determine whether expected in-service program outcomes are appropriate for all potential participants.
4. Collect data from potential participants to be used in program planning. Determine what you think they need to know, what they think they need to know, and what they already know.

B. In planning the in-service program, be sure to:

1. Identify a planning team to include consultant and appropriate in-house representatives.
2. Identify a person with a good track record in a similar setting to lead the in-service program.
3. Summarize data collected from teachers, program evaluations, and performance appraisals, and make it available to the planning team.
4. Consult research, professional associations, networks, state and federal departments of education, business, exemplary programs, and universities as a base for planning.
5. Consider providing a variety of activities—lecture, group work, role-play, CBT, multimedia, demonstration, simulation, distance learning, networks.
6. Plan for individual differences and multiple choices.
7. Build in time for group interaction.
8. Identify ways to communicate workshop objectives and expectations to potential participants before the in-service program.
9. Select a location that would be conducive to the program and convenient for participants, and arrange for appropriate equipment and supplies.

C. In conducting (implementing) the in-service program, be sure to:

1. Allow participants to make the role change from practitioner to learner.
2. Inform participants who is here, why we are here, and what resources there are.
3. Check with participants concerning their attitudes, feelings and knowledge during the program.
4. Allow deviation from the plan for the sake of meeting emerging needs of participants.
5. Arrange for participants to work with a variety of people and resources.
6. Enable participants to relate program outcomes to their own job settings.

assistance to these employees as an alternative to poor performance appraisals, plans of assistance, and termination. This emphasis on employee assistance occurs because organizations recognize that helping otherwise good employees is much less expensive and much more motivating than replacing them. Employees who exhibit excessive absenteeism or tardiness, decreased work performance, inconsistent behavior, loss of interest, accidents, depression, physical illness, temper or substance abuse may have personal problems that cannot be resolved by disciplinary action and warrant intervention through an employee assistance program (EAP).

EAP is a free, confidential, voluntary program providing a formal structure that helps employees get counseling and clinical services for health and personal problems. It provides a method for disentangling an employee's problems from his or her performance ability. An important part of this program is selecting effective community service providers and maintaining a liaison with them. The program typically allows for self-referral, peer referral or referral by supervisor, but it is the employees who decide whether they will participate in an EAP. Directed referrals are often used as a management tool to assist the supervisor and employee in improving unacceptable job performance that may be resulting from personal problems.

The case remains open until the employee no longer receives services or the employee is placed back under disciplinary action and is terminated. Self-referrals are totally at the discretion of the employee; the employee and service provider determine when services should be discontinued. Over 12 percent of the workforce is served by some type of employee assistance. It typically spans all job classifications and includes many who are long-standing employees. According to school districts, participants reported substantial increases in functioning in work and nonwork settings, and their supervisors reported sharp increases in employee work performance. Over 90 percent of participants reported they would recommend the program.

Wellness Programs

Health care and the cost of hiring substitute teachers have escalated over the past decades and are causing many school systems to look toward wellness programs. Statistics show a significant decrease in medical care costs and employee absenteeism as a result of wellness programs (Health Insurance Association of America, 1986). The idea of a wellness program is to stimulate health-enhancing behaviors in areas such as smoking, alcohol and drug abuse, nutrition, physical fitness, safety, stress, and environmental sensitivity. Myriad wellness programs stress taking responsibility for a healthy lifestyle, practicing preventive health habits, and educating employees regarding the control of risk factors.

What assistance or wellness programs might be especially helpful to the staffs at these two schools?

Human Resource Administration in the Third Millennium

RONALD REBORE

St. Louis University

Because school districts are human service agencies, human resource management becomes a most critical responsibility, permeating all functions within every school district. Thus, the administrator who has overall responsibility for the human resource function must be committed to continual evaluation of this function and make changes in human resource practice to meet future needs. The signs are already vivid as to the future challenges facing human resource administration in public school districts. Humanizing school districts, the institutionalization of technology, decentralization of functions, and increased use of the subsidiarity principle (delegation) are all possible examples.

Humanizing school districts has become a necessity, given the following symptoms: increased stress on faculty and staff, lingering inequities, the pluralistic composition of staff; unrealistic demands from parents and taxpayers, and disruptive pupil behavior. Stress is certainly related to job ambiguity, which leads to contradictory or unrealistic expectations for employees on the part of supervisors. Ambiguity is the product of ever-changing circumstances that require teachers, administrators, and staff members to assume responsibilities that were not originally part of their job descriptions. Another factor that is equally distressing to employees is an inadequate match between a person's abilities and the responsibilities of his or her job. Stress results because the person is *under-* or *overchallenged*.

School districts that underrepresent or underutilize people because of age, disability, ethnicity, or gender will always experience poor job performance and possibly incur legal sanctions as well. Human resource administrators must focus attention on the symptoms of job-related stress identified by supervisory staff members. Remedies for this situation can be found in *employee assistance programs* for those people who are experiencing such stress. Further evaluation of administrative practices can point out systemic problems that also can be sources of stress.

The *institutionalization* of technology presents human resource administrators with many options that can enhance the human resource function. Computerization means less shuffling of paper and more effective use of staff members. Available software enable a single employee to process hundreds of applications in a timely and efficient manner. Computers can complete skills inventories for existing staff and applicants to create lists of possible candidates for new positions and promotions.

A group of school districts in a certain location or region may decide that collaboration is the most effective way to implement human resource planning and hiring. The Internet allows a potential employee the opportunity to fill out one application that can be viewed and considered by multiple school districts. Staff can scan the contents of paper applications and résumés into a network computer. Through the Internet a potential employee can apply from home via his or her computer. Employer's can review computer network files to identify possible candidates. Interviews can occur using distance communication technology. Thus, human resources planning and forecasting meld with the recruitment and selection processes to result in the more timely hiring of candidates.

In the selection process, applicants submit videocassettes of themselves—yet another instrument to provide staff members with information that can enhance a forthcoming interview. Of course, security is a major consideration not only through the unauthorized viewing of applications and related information but also in regard to the integrity of the information. Only authenticated information should be scanned into the computer.

The institutionalization of technology as set forth above will necessarily decentralize certain aspects of the human resource function. No longer will it be necessary for principals, teachers, and other staff members to travel to central office to review applications and supporting documents. Selection criteria can be transmitted by fax or printed out from a computer. The observation, comments, and rating of candidates by interviewers can be transmitted through the computer. As previously stated, the institutionalization of technology in human resource administration will accelerate the personnel function, will be more cost effective, will decentralize certain aspects of this function, and may even reduce stress for those involved in the selection process.

Finally, the result of these changes and modifications to the human resource function should enhance the implementation of the *principle of subsidiarity* (see Box 10.1 delegation). Basically, this principle holds that decisions should be made and tasks should be performed at the most immediate level within an organization. The use of computers and decentralization will allow people at various levels within the organization to complete HRD tasks that previously were centralized.

Of course, implementing the changes outlined here will require staff development, but even implementation can be enhanced through technology. The electronic or *smart* classroom setting with podium cameras that permit presenter–participant interaction at remote sites can promote greater knowledge and understanding of the changing roles and responsibilities of the human resource function.

Organizational Development

Organizational development (OD) is a planned process directed toward building and maintaining the health of the organization. It is a process of change in the organizational culture through the use of behavior science technology, research, and theory. Kurt Lewin's (1951) model is often used to challenge platform training programs and to provide support for the challenging of old attitudes, values, beliefs, or behaviors to open the mind to new possibilities. Lewin described this prelearning process as "unfreezing." The learner is much more open to "processing" new ideas and learning as a result. "Refreezing" occurs as new attitudes, beliefs, and behaviors are stabilized in such a way that the organization reaches a new, improved equilibrium state. This three-stage change process provides the general framework for all OD approaches.

Most OD requires collecting data, diagnosing the situation, providing an appropriate intervention, and monitoring and stabilizing results. The basic approach is described as action research (Lippit, Watson, & Westley, 1958). Appropriate interventions are derived from careful diagnosis and are meant to resolve specific problems and improve particular areas of organizational functioning. Possible OD interventions include team-building, process consultation, confrontation meetings, t-groups, quality circles, quality-of-work-life, and organizational health analysis. The action-research process often creates organizational or individual disruption (unfreezing) with the hope that learning (processing) will occur, resulting in improved functioning for the organization (refreezing). Many OD consultants believe that this is the only way improvements occur (Schmuck & Runkel, 1985).

How might an organizational development model be used to resolve a problem that could develop as a result of the capacity adjustment plan program?

Wage and Salary Considerations

The job classification system, as discussed earlier, groups jobs into classes or grades that represent different pay levels, ranging from minimum to maximum for a particular grade of jobs. The compensation system determines the way salary payments are allocated between and within levels. The ultimate objective is to establish proper compensation for positions as well as for individuals holding the positions. The plan should attract, retain, and motivate qualified and competent employees; remain consistent with pay plans in other industries; and meet the acceptance of the taxpayers. The compensation system takes the form of wages, salaries, and benefits.

Consistent debate has occurred over the amount of money paid to educators (Bennett, 1988; Carter & Cunningham, 1997) compared with the salaries of those in comparable positions in business, industry, and commerce. Starting salaries for educators are typically $6,000 to $10,000 less than those for comparable positions in other fields, and this gap consistently widens throughout an educator's professional career (Rollefson & Rohr, 1993). These average differences range from $200,000 to $800,000 for school superintendents when business CEO stock-option plans are included. Inequities in salaries can cause people to choose careers other than education and to feel cheated if they are in education.

In addition to salary differences across professions, salaries for educators vary across geographical regions, states, and even local school districts. The northeast and far west are consistently highest, and the south is lowest in educational salaries. Alaska, New York, and Michigan are consistently high-paying states, and Mississippi, South Dakota, Arkansas, and Maine are low-paying states. Starting salaries among different school districts in the same area can vary by as much as $5,000 for teachers and $7,000 for school principals. Better candidates tend to gravitate toward higher salaries. A major responsibility of human resource management professionals is to work with superintendents and school boards to ensure that salaries are competitive and attract competent individuals to their school districts.

The first step in creating a compensation system is to establish the economic value of each of the various job classifications or pay grades. One way to do this is to establish a base rate and to index each of the pay grades to the base figure. Salaries for all the pay grade (job) levels are slotted between the base and maximum according to their economic value. A salary range provides an opportunity to recognize variations among individuals within the pay grade for factors such as preparation, experience, and performance according to legal requirements, appropriate performance differences, and ethical obligations. The salary schedule with its accompanying rules, regulations, and procedures is an expression of the district's salary policy. The single salary schedule typically allows equivalent salaries for equivalent preparation and experience and automatic progression through the salary range within each of the pay grades. In many cases, these single salary schedules form a matrix structure of dollar salary amounts in columns and rows. The columns, commonly referred to as "scales," usually correspond to differences in academic levels or professional preparation, and the rows, commonly referred to as "steps," correspond to number of years of experience. There is no standard number of either scales or steps in a salary schedule.

There are a number of different ways to plan a salary schedule, including fixed dollar increments, variable dollar increments, simple index, and compounded index. The choice of these methods depends on how you want to allocate pay increases within the pay grade. Some methods provide a higher percentage increase for less senior employees, whereas others, such as the compounded index, ensure that everyone receives the same percent increase from step to step, regardless of level of seniority. Other compensation issues include pay for additional duties, pay intervals, and pay for performance. The resulting structure should provide reasonable relationships within and between jobs, be externally competitive to attract and retain competent personnel, recognize differences in individual employees, and arrive at reasonable solutions to a variety of compensation issues.

The problem with many compensation plans is that they do not consider performance. The most competent and the least competent teacher in the school system will be paid the same throughout their professional careers as long as they have the same preparation and number of years of experience. Some believe that this system results in lack of motivation and lower-quality performance and is inherently unfair (National Governors Association, 1986). Performance pay plans factor in merit to the automatic step increases found in most single salary schedule pay plans. Performance pay plans include merit pay, differentiated staffing, performance contracting, and incentive pay.

Merit pay is paying an educator, at least in part, according to the quality of his or her work. Merit adjusts salaries to recognize different levels of job performance. It is based on the belief that individuals should be rewarded in proportion to their contributions and; more pragmatically that sustaining productivity requires a close link between performance and rewards. The performance appraisal system is the key to a successful merit pay plan. If employees trust the appraisal plan, they often will be able to support merit pay.

In its simplest form performance increments—for rating from unsatisfactory to exceptional—are added to the single salary schedules. More complex approaches include point or unit systems and salary performance formulas. The arguments against merit pay include the creation of jealousy, envy, distrust, and conflict; breakdown of collegiality, cooperative spirit, and teamwork; places discretionary power in the hands of the evaluator; failure because of weak performance appraisal systems and insufficiently qualified evaluators; and inequitable pay for the same job.

A recent suggestion to improve the system is to emphasize group-level merit pay based on group evaluations. The focus is often on meeting customer expectations and standards. Members are jointly responsible for group performance and are more accepting of results as meaningful and relevant. Members are rewarded or penalized collectively on the basis of the group's performance. Efforts are focused on improving unit performance and enhanced commitment to the group. For example, in the last half of 1990, Kentucky rewarded team effort by providing $2,000 per certified staff member to schools who exceeded state schoolwide performance expectations. North Carolina provides $1,500 per certified staff member. School committees decide how the money is to be spent, including bonuses to teachers. Concerns are that this approach ignores individual performance and criticisms now arise from work units rather than individuals.

Differentiated staffing, or career ladders, create different roles that permit educators to assume responsibilities, initiative, authority, and pay commensurate with their interests, talents, abilities, and performance. This structure provides the opportunity to move into more complex and demanding roles as assessment of performance determines readiness. In general, differentiated staffing plans require as many promotion channels and layers as possible so as to provide for advancement in responsibility and pay. For example, there are no advancement possibilities for most teachers. Positional advancements and pay incentives do not reinforce teaching as a career; they reinforce educational administration. All promotion channels in teaching lead away from the classroom. At the same time, all teachers are treated as interchangeable parts, regardless of talent, experience, or performance because there are no structural provisions for differences among them.

Possible promotion channels within teaching might include associate teacher, staff teacher, senior teacher, and master teacher. Master teachers might work on curriculum, instruction, testing, and student support, spending only 40 percent of their time in the classroom. Master teachers would be paid comparably to the assistant principal. Programs were tried in Tennessee, Florida, Utah, and Charlotte-Mecklenburg and received mixed reviews. High tension and low morale caused Tennessee to reappraise its system, while in Utah teachers felt that the plan had improved teacher morale and student performance. In 1998, Massachusetts created a master teacher corps for high-performing teachers certified by the National Board of Professional Teaching Standards.

Incentive pay and performance contracting are salary supplements or bonuses paid for fulfilling specified conditions. This approach was particularly popular in the 1960s and 1970s; however, there seems to be a resurgence of interest in the late 1990s. The general theme of these plans is to pay people according to how much pupils actually learn. Most of these plans have not been successful, but some states—Pennsylvania, New York, and Ohio—have made efforts to tie pay to results. In 1995, David W. Hornbeck, Philadelphia's superintendent of schools linked his contract incentives to student performance (Graves, 1995). He hopes to extend similar accountability to all employees. Incentive pay was part of a failed plan for Minneapolis Public Schools.

Principals and teachers can lose their jobs and schools can be "reconstituted," requiring faculty to reapply for their jobs, in low-performing schools. Student performance is taken into account in principal and teacher evaluations and in pay-for-improvement programs. Many states have incentives for teachers to seek certification from the National Board for Professional Teaching Standards. For example, Florida offered 10 percent raises to teachers who successfully completed the process. Despite their survival, most incentive plans are considered controversial, have mixed results, and fail to receive support from teacher unions which favor guaranteed annual salary increases for all employees, regardless of their performance.

> How might wage and salary compensations be used to support and reinforce the changes that will need to occur at Washington and Lincoln schools? Do you support these ideas? Why or why not?

Benefits

Fringe benefits provide assistance and protection to all employees and are not contingent on performance. They have risen in cost to represent approximately 35 percent of total compensation paid to employees. Under the provisions of law, school districts as employers are required to provide benefits related to social security, retirement insurance, health insurance, unemployment compensation, and worker's compensation. These five along with a minimum paid vacation are often considered core benefits in a flexible-benefit, sometimes called a cafeteria or market-basket, program.

Other possible fringe benefits include leaves of absence, safety and security, duty-free lunch periods, periodic examinations, dental insurance, saving incentive plans, newsletters, legal services, four-star faculty cafeterias, wellness and health consultants, travel awards, tuition assistance, paid holidays, suggestion awards, recreation programs, and extended core coverage. Fringe benefits are an important part of all compensation programs and influence recruitment, hiring and employee motivation.

> How might teachers be rewarded for outstanding student performance?

Collective Bargaining

Collective bargaining is the process of negotiating an agreement between an employer and an employee organization, usually for a specific term, defining the conditions of employment, the rights of employees and their organization, and the procedures to be followed in settling disputes. States have legislated regulations in areas such as unfair practices, administration of labor law, determination of bargaining units, impasse procedures, and prohibiting teacher strikes in order to create a more orderly negotiation process. In addition, school boards have tightened up on the scope of negotiations with teachers. As a result, many see a decrease in the power of professional associations in the collective bargaining process. However, this condition varies by state and school district.

If there is a persistent contract disagreement between the employee organization and the employer and an agreement has not been worked out approximately 90 days before the due date for the budget, a district is automatically at impasse. In the meet-and-confer process, the bargaining unit is advisory in capacity and the school board, which has legal responsibility for the contract, writes the contract with the teachers' input. Teachers' input may have minimal impact because it can be ignored.

A significantly greater number of items reach impasse under a meet-and-confer agreement than in situations in which an appeals process exists. An appeals procedure permits the employee organization, the employer, or both to seek assistance in resolving impasses through mediation, fact-finding, arbitration, or other forms of assistance from a third party. Mediation is voluntary and advisory in order to come up with a nonbinding compromise solution. In fact-finding situations, a neutral panel gathers data, studies the impasse, publishes a report of the facts and issues involved, and makes a recommendation for settlement. Fact-finding is not binding, but it has significant power in that the results are generally published and known by all parties and may carry considerable political weight.

Arbitration is a process whereby the disputing parties at impasse submit their differences to a third party, sometimes from the American Arbitration Association, for a decision. The decision can be advisement and voluntary or compulsory and binding as agreed on by both parties. Final steps such as sanctions and strikes must follow the laws that govern the collective-bargaining process. Court-ordered injunctions can be obtained to keep individuals or groups from committing acts that the court determines to be illegal or harmful. Violators of restraining orders may be punished by contempt of court proceedings, resulting in fines or imprisonment. When strikes are legal it is important for the district to have a strike plan. The most important part of this plan is a communication component to provide information, notification, and quick response to news media, parents, staff, safety and security officials, and others in the community. The plan will also identify specific spokespersons and a decision-making center.

The collective-bargaining process generally addresses issues such as teacher workload, duties, evaluation, and development assignments; salary and fringe benefits; the school calendar; curriculum content and quality; management rights; a grievance procedure; a no-strike provision; a zipper clause (when negotiation will be reopened); reduction-in-force; class size; and check-off (collection of dues) procedures (Hoyle et al., 1990). An obvious problem that develops is determining what is negotiable and what falls under the policy responsibilities of the school board. A written agreement regarding all the issues is essential because it serves to formalize the basic rights governing the parties to the agreement and prevent controversies later. These agreements are extremely detailed and can often be more than fifty pages long. It is important that the contract is managed to ensure that no violations occur. In recent years, mutual-gain bargaining or "win-win" bargaining has emerged in an effort to eliminate harsh adversarial relations that had grown in some districts. Harris and Monk (1992) suggest:

> Faced with truths about their ability to secure additional concessions related to wages, hours, and conditions of work as they related to the funding of public education, labor leaders in the mid-1980s began to reconsider the role of collective bargaining in educa-

tion. Particularly in situations where the union and management had been at each other's throats for years, union leaders began to talk of "win-win" or mutual gains bargaining (MGB) as a way of beginning to reconcile the bitterness of former relationships.… union officials and school administrators following…MGB or similar attempts to ease unnecessary confrontation began to approach bargaining activities with the attitude that both parties represent legitimate interests. Spurred on by the realization of their own limitations in the face of declining educational resources and public demand for change, union officials and educational managers have embarked on a number of projects promoting the professionalization of teaching and school restructuring. (p. 227)

> How do collective bargaining considerations complicate or facilitate the planned changes at these two schools?

Employee Records and Reports

Effective personnel management requires collecting, maintaining, analyzing, and reporting large amounts of employee information in each of the functions of human resource management previously discussed. Recording and reporting is a routine responsibility of all staff personnel offices. It begins with job analysis, recruitment, affirmative action, and application information and covers all information through exit interviews, unemployment insurance claims, and retirement. Technology has made the collection, storage, and transmittal of information more efficient and thereby the quality of decision making has improved. For example, a skills inventory system allows position requirements to be entered into the computer, which generates a list of all present employees who meet the qualifications for a specific position. Information is more likely to be credible if it is maintained in a single automated personnel or payroll file. All updates are made to this single integrated file.

A number of laws address the importance of protecting employee privacy rights, which must be considered in record keeping and reporting. This is a relatively perfunctory task, but it is essential to the smooth operation of the school system. Accurate information is required to successfully respond to every aspect of the organization from educational planning to defending against litigation.

Employee Litigation

Among the issues that affect human resource development perhaps none is greater than the litigious nature of society. Rebore (1998) states, "Over the last decade, school districts have experienced an increase in litigation. In addition, personnel administrators are far more vulnerable today to judicial review of their actions than personnel administrations of a decade ago" (p. 333). Personnel administrators must carefully evaluate all decisions to ensure that they are ethically responsible and legally defensible (see Chapters 7 and 11). They must also maintain all needed records to support HRD decisions. Rebore continues, "Personnel policies are the key to effective human resource management. Boards of education should take deliberate approach to policy development that will ensure defensible personnel operations" (p. 334).

> What information might be collected and used to make staff transfer decisions and to protect the school system from any future litigation regarding staff transfers?

Managing Human Needs
ROBERT R. SPILLANE
Office of Overseas Schools, Washington, DC

The key to doing anything well is understanding its purpose. This statement is at least as true of management and leadership as it is of any other function. Good management and leadership must achieve some good purpose.

The primary concern in managing human needs within school systems is the purpose of schools and schooling. Two mottoes guide my thinking about the purpose of schools. The first is: "The main thing is to keep the main thing the main thing," Here the main thing is learning. Whatever an administrator does must be done to foster and improve academic learning. The second motto is: "If schools are responsible for everything, they cannot be held responsible for anything." Schools need to hold themselves responsible and be accountable for fostering and improving academic learning; everything else they do should contribute to this end.

The first motto has to do with focusing one's action on academic learning. The second has to do with taking responsibility for the results of this focus—the actual student achievement, not just the efforts to bring it about.

Anyone who has ever run a large school system recognizes that keeping this focus is not easy. Much of the time, the highest-profile issues are peripheral to the main thing, and great pressure is put on an administrator to take responsibility for every need of every student and to spend

all his or her time dealing with issues such as athletics, transportation, budget, health services, and human services. There is no question that a superintendent needs to have a handle on all these issues, but he or she also needs to send the message to everyone in the school system and in the broader community that those who work for the school system will concentrate on and be held responsible for student achievement.

This said, arguments can be made for the academic benefits of many seemingly peripheral activities. Students learn better if they are healthier and connected to the school through extracurricular activities. But schools are not—as schools—responsible for meeting physical or emotional needs of students or teachers.

This conflict between academic and other needs arises constantly in the life of a school administrator. Several years ago, when budgets were tight in my school system, the parents of students in the "swim and dive" program were among the special interests that assiduously lobbied the school board to keep their funding. These parents picketed school board meetings, spoke and wrote to every school board member, and did everything they could think of to save their program. They argued passionately that this program fostered academic achievement by citing the achievement levels of students in "swim and dive." It was pointless to argue with them about the correlational validity of such arguments; nobody wanted to hear about it—they just wanted their program. Eventually, the funding was reinstated in a budget that also substantially cut the staff development program. The whole difficult budget process that year was obviously more complex than a trade-off of staff development for "swim and dive," but the juxtaposition reflects the confusion of focus and responsibility that swirls around discussion of student "needs" in U.S. school systems.

The needs of staff members also must be sorted out with an eye toward student achievement. The most important need is for strong instructional support, including staff development, curricular materials, and on-call help from subject specialists. These kinds of support (especially staff development) are among the first things to be cut in difficult budge years as the story about staff development and "swim and dive" illustrates Too often, school board members who work for private-or public-sector employers that provide substantial staff development to their own employees see teacher staff development as an "easy cut."

Given these problems, it seems clear that an administrator needs to take two steps, neither easy,. The first is to make sure that the system of curriculum, instructional support, and staff development that the schools are using is aligned and based on solidly proved research. (Remember, the one thing schools should be held responsible for is academic learning.) The second step is to make sure that the entire school system staff, the school board, and the community understand this system and how it relates to academic learning.

Getting curricular issued right and defensible is the hard part, but doing so will be critical for future administrators, who will be under heavy demands for results. If you have curricular issues right and your staff understands them, you can defend them. The instructional support you provide to your teachers will meet their most important human need—to be successful at what they do. Accommodating this need should direct all human resource management activities.

Administrators must convey the clear message that teachers will be judged, recognized, and rewarded for their ability to foster and improve students' academic achievement. I have long been a believer in strong teacher evaluation and in financial rewards based on such evaluation. The teacher performance evaluation program (TPEP) in Fairfax County Public Schools, which I initiated and oversaw for ten years as superintendent, continues to ensure excellence in that system. The merit pay element of TPEP, which once rewarded over 2,000 teachers, was dropped, but I expect merit pay to come back throughout the United States as schools are held increasingly accountable. Everything we can do to make expectations clear and to help employees succeed helps to meet their most important need.

The main thing to remember when managing human needs is your purpose for doing so. If your purpose is clear to you and your staff, you will be prepared to make the tough choices that every school administrator will have to make in the years ahead. These will be years in which focus and accountability, at all levels, will be the watchwords of all school administration. Administrators who focus efforts on student academic achievement will be able to manage the needs of students and employees alike.

Conclusion

Robert Reich (1997) evaluates the effectiveness of the human resource function through employee attitudes: "I'd say, 'tell me about the company.' If the person said 'we' or 'us,' I knew people were strongly attached to the organization. If it was 'they' or 'them' I knew there was less of a sense of linkage." It is the "sense of linkage" that remains an important function of human resource development. Is the individual properly placed within the organization? Does he or she feel supported as part of a larger whole? If the answer is yes, the HRD function is working.

Many human resource services go beyond the functional need in that they can be symbolic, providing a tribute to the individual's relation to the organization. Structural supports reward a person's identification with the organization and the contributions he or she has made and will continue to make. Research shows that when an organization voluntarily acts to benefit members, it signals a value placed on employees and concern for their well-being, which pays off through greater productivity and loyalty. Effective HRD efforts offer a wide array of resources to attract competent workers, to develop and reward them, and to foster a relationship that retains them.

Assimilating school system employees by socializing them into the school culture continues to be a essential organizational practice. Diverse forms of support—compensation; development, and other inducements; effective hiring practice; respected, fair, and helpful evaluation procedures; and other well-established HRD functions—all contribute to a high-performance school system. Such efforts have been linked to high trust and attachment, continued organizational learning, greater responsiveness, acceptance of change, and greater organization productivity. Employees typically describe their organizations as close-knit, and employees often stay connected even after leaving the organization.

The intellectual capital of the organization is critical to its success. The HRM department is responsible for obtaining, maintaining, and developing this capital. Successful school districts consider carefully the investments they make in the organization's intellectual capital, and thus the HRM functions.

PORTFOLIO ARTIFACTS

- Collect and compare job descriptions for a principal, supervisor, coordinator, and superintendent.

- Develop a staffing plan for a school

- Pair up with someone and interview each other for the position to which you both aspire. Write up the results of your interview, and discuss the effectiveness of the interviewee and interviewer.

- Pair up with someone and complete a performance appraisal on each other. Write up the results of the appraisal, and discuss the effectiveness of the appraisee and appraisor.

- Complete a staff development plan for a school or an individual.

- Compare a salary and fringe benefit plan for a school system with that of another organization.

- Help the personnel records manager to update records and produce an affirmative action report for the school district.

- Shadow the assistant superintendent for human resource development.

- Write staff personnel policy.

- Participate in the interview, selection, hiring, and induction of new employees.

TERMS

Assessment centers
Development plan
Differentiated staffing
Due process
Employee assistance
program (EAP)
Human resource development
(HRD)

Human resource utilization
(HRU)
Job classification
Line and staff
Open-ended questions
Organizational development (OD)
Pay grade and single salary
schedule

Perceiver academies
Performance appraisal
Plan of assistance
Professional negotiation and
meet-and-confer
Staff planning

SUGGESTED READINGS

Castetter W. B. (1996). *The human resource function in educational administration*. Englewood Cliffs, NJ: Prentice Hall.

Hanushek, E. (1994). *Making schools work: Improving performance and controlling costs*. Washington, DC: Brookings Institute.

Harris, B. M., & Monk, B. J. (1992). *Personnel administration in education*. Boston: Allyn & Bacon.

Highes, F. P., & Noppe, L. D. (1991). *Human development: Across the life span*. New York: MacMillan.

Rebore, R. W. (1998). *Personnel administration in education: A management approach*. Boston: Allyn & Bacon.

Webb, L. D., & Norton, M. S. (1999). *Human resource administration*. Upper Saddle River, NY: Merrill.

CHAPTER
11

Schools and the Law

Vignette: Not Following School Board Policy

It was 7 A.M. and Principal Kathryn Cipriani was sitting at her desk contemplating her next step. Yesterday high school teacher Glenn O'Brien had chosen not to follow school board policy on field trips. The policy required that parents give written permission prior to their children's going on a field trip. O'Brien knew what the policy was, but in his own mind the circumstance was different and justified deviation from the policy. Clearly it wasn't. He had chosen not to get prior permission, and the car he was driving with the four students had been involved in an accident around 5:00 P.M. No permission slips, a clear violation.

Cipriani knew that O'Brien was not incompetent. She had worked with him for nearly fifteen years. Before she became principal Cipriani had been a teacher in this school. Cipriani and O'Brien had spent hours discussing education and how to improve schools for kids. In fact, O'Brien was one of the top teachers in the building. Two years before he had received the district's "Outstanding Teacher" award. He just hadn't thought about the possible implications of his field-trip decision.

The previous afternoon Principal Cipriani and her assistant principal had tried to find out as much as possible about the situation. One of the students was still in the hospital and was scheduled to be released today. O'Brien and the three other students had suffered minor injuries and were released from the hospital that same night. Cipriani called the superintendent to inform him of what had occurred. Since he was out of town, she left a message at his hotel.

Last night after arriving home around midnight from a work-related dinner, Cipriani had found a long message on her answering machine from Mike Canavan, the board president. Outraged by what had happened, he demanded that O'Brien be fired, tenured or not. "This is gross negligence," he clamored. There was also a message from her superintendent asking her to call him first thing in the morning. He had spoken to Mike Canavan and was very concerned about the situation.

If you were the principal, what would you do next?
Obtain a copy of your state's policy regarding the dismissal or suspension of teachers. What does it say?

Legal Responsibility

Every week federal and state courts hand down decisions that have the potential to affect every school in the nation.

It is important for educational leaders to learn about current legal issues and their potential impact on schools. School districts are involved in a number of major litigation areas, and knowledge of several key concepts in school law are essential. It is also important for administrators to understand compliance with policies and procedures and risk management.

Learning about Schools and Legal Issues

One way to begin to acquire a basic understanding of the legal system and the laws and statutes that pertain to schools is to take a basic course in school law. Although such a course provides a foundation, keeping up-to-date must become an ongoing part of professional development. School leaders should have an understanding of and appreciation for the legal rights of teachers and students.

Educators need a basic understanding of the federal Constitution and Bill of Rights as well as their state constitutions and statutes. Common law is a general, overarching statewide or nationwide precedent that derives from earlier legal controversies. It prescribes social conduct enforced by courts by the doctrine of the supremacy of law.

One of the functions of school boards is to adopt policies in accordance with state legislation. Thus, educational leaders must understand school district policies. Many professional organizations, such as the National Association of Secondary School Principals (NASSP), publish monthly updates regarding current issues in school law (see *Cases in Point; A Legal Memorandum* at the NASSP Web site, www.NASSP.org). Educational newspapers and journals have special sections pertaining to legal issues (e.g., see Kappan, PDK's monthly magazine with a special department entitled "Courtside"). Other resources include Web sites and publications that serve as guides to federal and state cases. The official newspaper of the U.S. government, the *Federal Register* (available online as well as in paper format) is the vehicle through which all federal agencies publish their regulations and legal notices.

A graduate-level university course in school law and professional reading on a regular basis will help administrators stay current about issues related to school law. For interpretations of court decisions, which can sometimes be difficult to follow, a telephone call to the school district's lawyer (most districts have legal counsel) may be appropriate.

The U.S. Legal System

Federal Role in Education

Education is not specifically discussed in the U.S. Constitution. Box 11.1 on page 318 lists those amendments that are particularly relevant to typical school legal issues. The

BOX **11.1**

Selected Amendments of the U.S. Constitution

Amendment 1 (1791)

Congress shall make no law respecting an establishment of religion, or prohibiting the free exercise thereof; or abridging the freedom of speech, or of the press; or the right of the people peaceably to assemble, and to petition the Government for a redress of grievances.

Amendment IV (1791)

The right of the people to be secure in their persons, houses, papers, and effects, against unreasonable searches and seizures, shall not be violated, and no Warrants shall issue, but upon probable cause, supported by Oath or affirmation, and particularly describing the place to be searched, and the persons or things to be seized.

Amendment IX (1791)

The enumeration in the Constitution of certain rights, shall not be construed to deny or disparage others retained by the people.

Amendment X (1791)

The powers not delegated to the United States by the Constitution, nor prohibited by it to the States, are reserved to the States respectively, or to the people.

Amendment XIV (1868)

Section 1. All persons born or naturalized in the United States, and subject to the jurisdiction thereof, are citizens of the United States and of the State wherein they reside. No State shall make or enforce any law which shall abridge the privileges or immunities of citizens of the United States; nor shall any State deprive any person of life, liberty, or property, without due process of law; nor deny to any person within its jurisdiction the equal protection of the laws.

Tenth Amendment states, "the powers not delegated to the United States by the Constitution, nor prohibited by it to the States, are reserved to the States respectively, or to the people." This does not mean that the federal government has little influence on schools—in fact, the amendments to the *Constitution*, U.S. Supreme Court decisions, and congressional acts have considerable influence on both public and private educational institutions.

Federal Courts

The three levels of federal court are shown in Box 11.2. Each state has at least one federal district court; some have several, depending on population density. Appeals from federal district courts can go to the next level, the U.S. circuit court or the U.S. court of appeals.

The procedures and functions of intermediate and the highest appellate courts differ from those of trial courts. These courts do not conduct trials, nor do they hear

BOX **11.2**
The Federal Court System*

U.S. Supreme Court
(highest court of the country)

U.S. Circuit Courts of Appeals (Appellate Courts)
(thirteen intermediate appeal courts)

U.S. Trial Courts
(eighty-nine district courts)

*For more information see: www.law.vill.edu/.)

any new evidence or conduct fact-finding. Their function is to review records of lower courts to determine whether any errors of law have occurred. Errors of law might include procedural mistakes, misinterpretations of the Constitution or statutes, and incorrect instructions to juries, to name but a few.

There are thirteen circuit courts of appeal (see Table 11.1). One, the Federal Circuit Court of Appeals, has jurisdiction to hear special claims such as those related to taxes, patents and copyrights, customs, and international trade. The remaining twelve are those to which an education-related case would be appealed.

Decisions rendered in a federal appellate court are binding only in the states that fall within that circuit's jurisdiction. For example, the first Circuit Court of Appeals includes Maine, Massachusetts, New Hampshire, Puerto Rico, and Rhode Island. A

TABLE 11.1 Jurisdictions of the Federal Circuit Courts of Appeal

Circuit	Jurisdiction
1st	Maine, Massachusetts, New Hampshire, Puerto Rico, Rhode Island
2nd	Connecticut, New York, Vermont
3rd	Delaware, New Jersey, Pennsylvania, Virgin Islands
4th	Maryland, North Carolina, South Carolina, Virginia, West Virginia
5th	Louisiana, Mississippi, Texas
6th	Kentucky, Ohio, Michigan, Tennessee
7th	Illinois, Indiana, Wisconsin
8th	Arkansas, Iowa, Minnesota, Missouri, Nebraska, North Dakota, South Dakota
9th	Alaska, Arizona, California, Guam, Hawaii, Idaho, Montana, Nevada, Northern Mariana Islands, Oregon, Washington
10th	Colorado, Kansas, New Mexico, Oklahoma, Utah, Wyoming
11th	Alabama, Florida, Georgia
DC	Washington, DC
Federal	Three specialized courts, Washington, D.C.

decision rendered in the first Federal Court of Appeals pertains to these states and territory only, however, the decisions rendered by individual courts of appeals, often *influence* the decisions of other courts dealing with similar issues.

The U.S. Supreme Court is the court of highest appeal on questions of federal law. The Supreme Court has heard numerous education cases dealing with particular provisions of the U.S. Constitution. In particular the Fourteenth Amendment's *equal protection clause* (e.g., *Plessy v. Ferguson*, 163 U.S. 537, 16 S. Ct. 1138, 41 L. Ed. 256 [1896] and *Brown v. Board of Education*, 347 U.S. 483, 74 S. Ct. 686, 98 L. Ed. 873 [1954]); the Fourteenth Amendment's *due process clause* (e.g., *Meyer v. Nebraska*, 262 U.S. 390, 43 S. Ct. 625, 67 L. Ed. 1042 [1923]); and the first Amendment's *establishment clause* (e.g., *Board of Education v. Allen*, 392 U.S. 236, 88 S. Ct. 1923, 20 L. Ed 1060 [1968]) are cited more often than other amendments in school law cases.

Understanding Court Decisions

PERRY A. ZIRKEL, Professor of Education
KATHLEEN A. SULLIVAN, Research Associate
Lehigh University

Published court opinions form an important body of law that fills in the gaps and resolves the interactions between other sources of law, such as the Constitution and legislation, in relation to specific factual situations. Not all court decisions result in published opinions. Generally, the proportion of published opinions is higher in federal than in state courts and in appellate than in trial courts.

Citations provide identifying information for published court decisions. This sample citation illustrates the key elements:

Yankton School District v. Schramm, 93 F.3d 1369 (8th Cir. 1996). The first element, the name of the case, is customarily underlined or italicized and contains the names of at least one party on each side of the case. Inasmuch as many of the published opinions, including this one, are at the appellate level, the order of the names does not necessarily convey who was the plaintiff, or suing party. Instead, at the appellate level, the first of the two names (here "Yankton") is the appellant, or the party who lost at the level below and, as a result, has brought the appeal.

The second element consists of numbers and an abbreviation that tell where to find the case. The central piece of information, here "F.3d" signifies the reporter, or set of volumes for a particular group of courts. The *Federal Reporter*, originally abbreviated as "F." and now in its third series, contains published decisions of the intermediate, appellate courts in the federal system. The number in front of the abbreviation, here "93," is the volume in that series, and the number after the abbreviation, here "1369," is the page in that volume where the court's opinion starts.

The final element, which is in parentheses, contains the year in which the decision was issued and, if not indicated by the reporter abbreviation, an abbreviation for the court that issued the decision. Since only Supreme Court decisions appear in the alternative Supreme Court Reporters, "U.S." and "S. Ct.," no additional notation beyond citation to the reporter is necessary to identify the court. As in the sample citation, the United States circuit courts of appeal, the level below the Supreme Court, are identified by circuit number. An opinion rendered by the highest state court will contain only the state's abbreviation in parentheses, and opinions from lower levels will contain further abbreviations for the name of the court.

The court opinion also has identifiable elements that help the reader understand the import of the decision. The first part, which follows the name of the judge who authored the opinion, typically contains the facts that were distilled from the evidence in the case. The facts include who did what to whom, giving rise to the specific controversy. At the appellate level, this section also includes the disposition of the case in the lower court(s).

The central element of the opinion, which may take several readings to accurately identify, is the issue of the case. Usually a single question answerable by "yes" or "no," the issue poses the relevant facts in a sufficiently generalizable form. In the *Schramm* case, for example, the issue may be stated as follows: "Whether instructional accommodations fulfill the 'special education' criterion for eligibility under the Individual with Disabilities Education Act (IDEA)."

The court's answer to this question, along with the basis, or legal source, and rationale for the decision provide the final part of the court's opinion. The court's answer is called the rule or holding in the case. In *Schramm*, the Eighth Circuit Court of Appeals answered the question affirmatively, based on the definition of "special education" in the IDEA. The rationale was that the plain meaning of the words in the definition, such as "specially designed instruction" to meet individual needs, conveyed a Congressional intent to include instructional accommodations for otherwise qualified students. Usually the court presents its rationale through a logical discussion and application of the law to the facts of the case.

Opinions also often contain statements made by the court that are not necessary for the "holding," such as a comment on how the decision might change if the facts were different. These comments, known as "dicta," should not be confused with the holding. Only those statements or observations essential to the judge's decision form the holding in the case and may be relied on for guidance.

Usually a court's decision applies both to the immediate parties and to future cases that have the same circumstances. These past cases and their effect on future cases is called precedent. Precedent is binding on courts at the same or higher level within a jurisdiction. Since our legal system contains both federal and state branches, each with different boundaries of authority, not all decisions are binding on all other courts. Decisions from outside jurisdictions, although not binding, may be persuasive to other courts.

Judicial opinions offer insight into the probable outcome of similar cases and establish boundaries to guide future conduct. Deciphering the elements of not only of the citation but, more important, of the opinion, enables school leaders to locate and use court decisions. Because they cannot afford to leave such matters entirely to lawyers, school leaders can benefit by knowing how to find and understand court decisions to answer as well as ask key questions.

In addition to federal courts, the federal government enacts legislation (federal statutes) that directly affects educational institutions. Statutes are regularly updated, supplemented, and revised by successive legislatures (see the *Federal Register*). Courts determine the validity and meaning of these legislative acts. These acts are binding for all citizens as long as they satisfy constitutional requirements. Civil rights legislation such as the Educational of the Handicapped Act (EHA) and the 1975 amendment, Education for All Handicapped Children Act, Section 504 of the Rehabilitation Act of 1973, and Title VII of the Civil Rights Act of 1964 (Title VII) are examples of federal statutes.

One example of federal legislation that has affected nearly all school districts in the country is Goals 2000. This legislation was introduced by President George Bush in 1989 and later passed by Congress and signed by President Bill Clinton in 1994. Consisting of eight goals, it appropriates federal money each year for states that adopt voluntary standards. These standards must meet federal guidelines for student achievement. It is not required that a state apply for the funding, but, if it does, it would then make subgrants to local education agencies (LEAs may include school districts, regional service centers, and others) This legislation also established two other acts: The Gun-Free Schools Act and the Safe Schools Act. (For more details about federal involvement in education, see Chapter 2.)

The Department of Education's (DOE) role is to implement the administration's policies regarding education. For example, a state that wants a GOALS 2000 grant would have to apply to the DOE. The chief executive officer of the DOE is the secretary of education. This position is one of thirteen secretaries making up the president's cabinet. The Department of Education maintains a home page on the World Wide Web. (For more information see: www.ed.gov/index.html.)

The operationalizing of the administration's policies can be seen in the federal education budget. (Chapter 12 provides an example of how federal monies are distributed to certain program areas for use in local school districts.) The federal government can penalize or sanction local education agencies that do not adhere to federal policies. Additionally, guidelines and policies from federal agencies, such as the Equal Employment Opportunities Commission (EEOC), are often cited in employment discrimination claims.

What federal laws are relevant to addressing issues related to O'Brien, the injured students, and the field trip?

The State's Legal Role in Education

Although state court systems vary, most state courts have three levels: trial courts, intermediate appellate courts, and the state supreme court (see Box 11.3).

BOX **11.3**
State Court Systems

State Supreme Court
(highest state court)

State Appellate Courts
(intermediate appellate courts)

Trial Courts
(district, circuit, or county courts)

The majority of education-related cases are heard at the state level because education is a function of the state, rather than the federal, government. A state supreme court case can be appealed to a federal court only if it involves a question of federal law. Appellate courts, whether at the federal or state level, do not review an entire case. Instead, they take appeals only on questions that the lawyers properly "preserve" for appeal. The narrowness of the appeals process explains why some school law cases are litigated several times before all the important issues are finally settled. Examining one state education case will be illustrative.

Sheff v. O'Neill was filed in 1989 on behalf of seventeen Hartford, Connecticut, schoolchildren. Milo Sheff was a fourth-grade African American student at the time (sixteen other white and Hispanic children living in the city of Hartford and the suburbs were also plaintiffs). William A. O'Neill, the defendant, was then governor of Connecticut. The plaintiffs argued that it was up to the state to alleviate the educational deprivation associated with living in a racially and socioeconomically isolated urban area such as Hartford. The case was originally filed in the lowest court in the state—the superior court. This district court ruled against the plaintiffs, Milo Sheff and the other children. The superior court ruled that because the state did not create the segregation that now held sway, it need not take measures to dismantle it.

The case was appealed by the plaintiffs to the state appellate court. The appeal was granted and in 1995 the case went to the Connecticut State Supreme Court. In 1996 this court ruled in favor of the plaintiffs. It declared that the state constitution's education and equal protection clauses require the legislature to ensure that students in the Hartford public schools are provided with integrated and equal educational opportunities. Although this case is not binding outside Connecticut, it has the potential to influence similar claims in other states.

State Legislatures, Administrative Agencies, and Local Boards of Control

States have the power to enact statutes within the limitations of state and federal constitutions. Valente (1997), in his text on school law entitled *Law in the Schools*, maintains that within the realm of education

> legislative power includes authority to (1) create, alter, and abolish school districts; (2) alter the structure and powers of school boards; (3) remove incumbent school board members and abolish offices; (4) prescribe the school calendar and curriculum; (5) determine the sources and procedures for raising school revenue and school spending; (6) fix the appointment, term, and qualifications of teachers; (7) require local schools to admit children of nontaxpayers; and (8) revoke charters of public schools for noncompliance with state regulations (p. 17).

For example, a Connecticut statute (Sec. 46b-56) regarding the rights of noncustodial parents reads:

> Sec. 46b-56. (Formerly Sec. 46-42). Superior court orders re custody and care of minor children in actions for dissolution of marriage, legal separation, and annulment. Access

to records of minor children by noncustodial parent. (a) In any controversy before the superior court as to the custody or care of minor children, and at any time after the return day of any complaint under section 46b-45, the court may at any time make or modify any proper order regarding the education and support of the children and of care, custody, and visitation if it has jurisdiction under the provisions of chapter 815o. Subject to the provisions of section 46b-56a, the court may assign the custody of any child to the parents jointly, to either parent, or to a third party, according to its best judgment upon the facts of the case and subject to such conditions and limitations as it deems equitable. The court may also make any order granting the right of visitation of any child to a third party including but not limited to grandparents.

Some statutes are designated as education statutes. For example, Sec. 10–221 of the Connecticut statutes pertains to rule prescription by boards of education:

Sec. 10-221. Boards of education to prescribe rules. (a) Boards of education shall prescribe rules for the management, studies, classification, and discipline of the public schools, and, subject to the control of the state board of education, the textbooks to be used; shall make rules for the control, within their respective jurisdictions, of school library media centers and approve the selection of books and other educational media therefore, and shall approve plans for public school buildings and superintend any high or graded schools in the manner specified in this title.

All states have a *state superintendent of instruction* or *state commissioner of education*. This person is the chief state school officer and serves as the chief executive of the state department of education (see: www.CCSSO.org/). State education departments typically comprise a variety of divisions, such as teaching and learning, educational programs, vocational-technical schools, finance and administration, and so forth. The size of the department often depends on the state's population as well as whether or not there are regional or county departments of education. For example, Texas has regional service centers with appointed directors, whereas California has county service centers that fall under the aegis of the county board of education, an elected board with an elected superintendent. The roles of these service centers vary but often include providing direct services to school districts such as special-education services, adult education programming, family service coordination, and cooperative purchasing programs, to name but a few. (See Chapter 2.)

Administrative agencies include not only the state department of education but also other state and regional agencies that may have jurisdiction over all or some schools in a given state. In some states boards of education are referred to as school committees and in others they are called school boards. States cannot implement the general supervision of schools, so it is delegated to local boards of education. (Hawaii is an exception because it is composed of a single school district.) Since local school boards have the authority to enforce federal and state policies, their actions must be within federal and state constitutions and statutes (see Chapter 5).

The statutes of each state contain provisions that concern certain aspects of teachers' and administrators' behavior. Statutes dealing with a variety of topics can be found in the state's education statutes, including information regarding teacher and administrator certification; discipline; dismissal; the denial, revocation or suspension of certification; and contract termination, for example. Table 11.2 on pages 326–327 displays the state-by-state statutory grounds for the dismissal or suspension of teachers. The school administrator must be familiar with the statutes in the state's education code and refer to them when needed.

What specifically does your state's education code say regarding the tenure, nonrenewal, or dismissal of teachers? What implications, if any, does this have for Glenn O'Brien?

School Districts and Litigation

According to a study conducted by Underwood and Noffke (1990), the number one cause for school district litigation was employee-related issues. Table 11.3 on page 328 displays the percentage of total cases initiated in three categories: employee issues, districtwide issues, and student issues.

Negligence is the primary reason for litigation. However, as Underwood and Noffke (1990) point out, "It's most likely to be settled by the parties, rather than being litigated in court" (p. 20). The authors identify the second-highest litigation area as employment-related issues. Under the category of student issues, special education ranked highest. According to the authors, litigation in this area is on the upswing.

Legal Issues and Schools

Common law, statutes, and constitutional law touch on such issues as tenure, contracts, student rights, civil rights, collective bargaining, finance, property, desegregation, intergovernmental relations, instructional programming, and teacher rights. These and other issues are governed to some extent by law. A few important issues that educational administrators may face are due process, freedom of expression, student discipline, records, and tort liability.

Due Process

According to the Fourteenth Amendment a person cannot be deprived arbitrarily of "life, liberty, or property, without due process of law." Before the state can damage these rights, due process must be afforded. According to Data Research Inc. (1991), an organization that publishes law texts, "There are many variations, and the courts do not always agree on what constitutes due process of law" (p. 92).

TABLE 11.2   Statutory Grounds for the Dismissal or Suspension of Teachers

	Incompetency	Unfitness for Service	Negligence, Neglect of Duty	Failure to Provide Designated Instruction	Failure to Attend Required Institutes	Inefficiency	Incapacity	Insubordination	Refusal to Obey School Board Regulations	Noncompliance with School Laws	Disloyalty, Subversive Activity	Contract Violation, Cancellation, Annulment, Breach	Conviction of Specified Crime	Immorality	Untruthfulness, Dishonesty, Falsification of Application or Records	Drunkenness, Intemperance	Addiction to Drugs and/or Selling Drugs	Cruelty	Conduct Unbecoming a Teacher, Misconduct in Office	Unprofessional Conduct	Violation of Code of Ethics	Revocation of Certificate	Cause (Good, Just, Sufficient)	Failure to Obey State Laws	Other
Alabama	X		X		X			X						X									X		
Alaska	X									X			X	X						X					
Arizona																									X
Arkansas											X														
California	X	X							X	X	X	X	X	X	X	X			X			X		X	X
Colorado	X		X	X				X				X	X	X									X		
Connecticut	X					X		X						X									X		
Delaware	X		X					X			X			X				X							
Florida	X		X					X					X	X		X	X						X		
Georgia	X							X															X		X
Hawaii						X		X	X					X									X		
Idaho								X					X						X						X
Illinois	X		X											X				X					X		
Indiana	X		X					X	X		X			X							X				
Iowa	X		X																				X		
Kansas																									
Kentucky	X		X		X			X						X					X						
Louisiana	X		X												X										X
Maine																							X		
Maryland	X		X					X						X					X				X		
Massachusetts						X	X	X	X		X			X					X				X		
Michigan									X						X								X		
Minnesota			X			X		X		X		X	X	X					X				X		
Mississippi	X		X									X		X		X		X					X		
Missouri	X		X			X		X	X	X			X	X											X
Montana	X	X				X			X					X											
Nebraska	X		X					X		X														X	X
Nevada		X	X			X		X		X			X	X	X					X		X			
New Hampshire														X		X									
New Jersey						X	X												X				X		X
New Mexico																							X		

State	Incompetency	Unfitness for Service	Negligence, Neglect of Duty	Failure to Provide Designated Instruction	Failure to Attend Required Institutes	Inefficiency	Incapacity	Insubordination	Refusal to Obey School Board Regulations	Noncompliance with School Laws	Disloyalty, Subversive Activity	Contract Violation, Cancellation, Annulment, Breach	Conviction of Specified Crime	Immorality	Untruthfulness, Dishonesty, Falsification of Application or Records	Drunkenness, Intemperance	Addiction to Drugs and/or Selling Drugs	Cruelty	Conduct Unbecoming a Teacher, Misconduct in Office	Unprofessional Conduct	Violation of Code of Ethics	Revocation of Certificate	Cause (Good, Just, Sufficient)	Failure to Obey State Laws	Other
New York	X	X				X		X						X					X				X		
North Carolina	X	X				X	X		X				X	X			X							X	
North Dakota						X	X		X			X	X	X					X					X	X
Ohio						X			X					X											X
Oklahoma	X	X											X	X				X							
Oregon		X				X		X	X				X	X								X			
Pennsylvania	X	X											X	X			X		X						X
Rhode Island									X														X		
South Carolina	X	X							X					X	X		X		X				X		
South Dakota	X	X							X	X			X	X	X							X			
Tennessee	X	X		X		X		X	X	X			X	X		X	X	X	X		X				
Texas		X							X		X		X	X		X									
Utah																									
Vermont	X	X							X			X				X								X	
Virginia	X	X			X		X	X						X										X	
Washington																									
West Virginia	X	X						X	X				X	X		X	X	X						X	
Wisconsin						X				X				X										X	
Wyoming	X	X	X			X								X										X	

Source: Delon, F. (1977). *Legal Controls on Teacher Conduct: Teacher Discipline.* Topeka, KS: Nolpe.

Of the two types of due process, substantive and procedural, substantive due process deals with the entire process of being fair. According to Strahan and Turner (1987) substantive due process includes the necessity for a rule not to be unduly vague, and that discipline should be based on written rules. Further, decisions should be supported with evidence, the identify of a witness should be revealed, an impartial hearing must be afforded each person, and if the accused so requests, a public or private

TABLE 11.3   Issues That Land Schools in Court

Issues	Percentage of total cases initiated	Percentage of times district prevailed
Employee issues (total)	42.6	81.4
Dismissal/nonrenewal	14.2	93.3
Contract negotiations/implementation	11.6	75.0
Discipline	10.5	88.8
Other	1.6	33.3
Hiring	1.0	100.0
Districtwide issues (total)	37.4	67.5
Negligence	22.6	63.1
District property	4.7	60.0
Desegregation	3.2	66.7
Curriculum	2.6	0.0
Finance	2.1	50.0
Other	2.1	90.0
Student issues (total)	20.0	65.4
Special education	8.9	50.0
Discipline practices	6.8	87.5
Discrimination	2.1	33.3
Grades and promotion	1.0	100.0
Constitutional issues	.5	100.0
Other	.5	33.3

Source: Underwood, J., & Noffke, J. (1990) "School law news: Your're winning." Reprinted with permission.

hearing should be offered. Procedural due process involves providing notice and fair hearing so that an impartial and just settlement of a conflict between parties can be reached; thus, procedural due process is an established system.

Notice refers to making the rules orderly and ensuring that the party involved is aware of them and how they should be followed, as well as possible penalties for their violation. Inherent in this notion is that people have a right to know the standards by which they are to be judged. It would be unreasonable and unfair to hold people accountable for meeting expectations if they are ignorant of those expectations. For example, if a school system has a teacher-evaluation system and the procedures and standards involved in that system are not explained to teachers, then it would be unfair and unreasonable to expect teachers to be evaluated using that system. Similarly, if there is a student discipline code, including the procedures and penalties for certain behaviors, and the code is not explained to a student, it is unreasonable to punish the student for not following it. Standards must be known in advance, and they should be clear so that a person knows that what he or she has done counts as meeting, or not meeting, the standards.

Fair hearing includes several aspects: a written statement of the charges and the type of evidence that should be given to the individual; explanation of procedural right; adequate time to prepare a defense; and an opportunity for a formal hearing. According to McCarthy, Cambron-McCabe, & Thomas (1997) in cases where a teacher may be terminated, the following procedural elements must be afforded:

- Notification of charges
- Opportunity for a hearing
- Adequate time to prepare a rebuttal to the charges
- Access to evidence and names of witnesses
- Hearing before an impartial tribunal
- Representation by legal counsel
- Opportunity to present evidence and witnesses
- Decision based on evidence and findings of the hearing
- Transcript or record of the hearing
- Opportunity to appeal an adverse decision (pp. 381–382)

What implications do these procedural elements have for Principal Cipriani's decisions?

Freedom of Speech and Expression

The First Amendment covers written, oral, and symbolic forms of expression, including

- academic freedom (e.g., *Keyishian v. Board of Regents of New York*, 1967)
- censorship (e.g., *Planned Parenthood v. Clark County School District*, 1991)
- community service programs (e.g., *Steirer v. Bethlehem Area School District*, 1993)
- defamatory expression, which includes slander (oral) and libel (written) (e.g., *Scott v. New-Herald*, 1986)
- symbolic expression (e.g., *Tinker v. Des Moines Independent School District*; the Supreme Court in 1985 ruled that a rule prohibiting students from wearing black arm bands in school as a protest against the Vietnam War was invalid)
- hate speech (e.g., *Doe v. University of Michigan*, 1989)
- obscene, vulgar, or inflammatory expression (e.g., *Miller v. California*, 1973; *Fenton v. Srear*, 1980)
- freedom of the press (e.g., *Hazelwood School District v. Kuhlmeier*, 1988)
- distribution of religious materials (e.g., *Stone v. Graham*, 1983)
- dress and hair codes (e.g., *Farrell v. Dallas Independent School District*, 1968)

Numerous controversies over freedom of speech erupted starting in the 1960s. Many educators argue that schools should not tolerate student speech and expression that is inconsistent with the school's basic educational mission. Given a compelling purpose, speech can be regulated; but no one can be prohibited from speaking simply because his or her ideas differ from those of the administration or staff.

Discipline and Students with Disabilities

In the expert inquiry, school law Professor Charles Russo discusses the expanded rights of students with disabilities. As previously noted in Table 11.3, for litigation areas related to students, Underwood and Noffke rank special education highest. They maintain that litigation in special education is on the upswing. Discussing the disciplining of regular and special-education students, legal expert Perry Zirkel (1996) recommends that policies and practices be "in accord with federal constitutional requirements and any procedural safeguards under state law" (p. 21). Box 11.4 contrasts federal law regarding suspensions and expulsions of students with and without disabilities.

Substantive and procedural due process must clearly be kept in the forefront as regards disciplining students. Nathan Essex (1999) states, "It has long been held that children with disabilities may not be punished for conduct that is a manifestation of their disability.... In situations where certain types of discipline are warranted, an effort must be made to ensure that the punishment does not materially and substantially interrupt the child's education" (p. 80). Exercise caution and work with the district's legal counsel to protect you schools and district from legal costs and liability awards (see Chapter 9).

The Confidentiality of Student Records

The Family Educational Rights and Privacy Act (FERPA, Public Law 93-380), enacted by the U.S. Congress in 1974, established a student's right to privacy. Also included in this act is the requirement that schools adopt and publicize the procedures for accessing and obtaining school records as well as explaining how information can be removed. FERPA stipulates that a parent's written consent is required for a third party to obtain access to a student's record. An amendment to this act, the Buckley amendment, threatens the withdrawal of federal funds if parents are prevented from seeing their children's complete records.

Administrators should formulate guidelines regarding student records that include developing procedures for allowing access to the files, keeping a log of all people who have obtained access to the records, allowing parents and students to submit outside materials to the record, and developing procedures to obtain informed consent from students and parents before data in the student's record can be released to a third party. Clearly the issue of the privacy of records is an important one, and the development of clear guidelines is not only an important legal issue but an ethical one as well.

BOX **11.4**

Summary of Federal Law on Suspensions/Expulsions

	Nondisabled students	Students with disabilities	
		Established law	*Emerging developments*
1–10 days	Give the student prior oral (or written) notice of the charges and, if the student denies them, an explanation of the evidence and an opportunity to respond. *Exception:* If the student poses a threat to persons, property, or the academic process, this notice and hearing may be delayed until as soon as practicable after the immediate exclusion. (The student has no right to know the identity of student informants)	The same procedures as for nondisabled students, unless the number, proximity, and pattern of cumulative days of suspension are the equivalent of more than 10 consecutive days—several short suspensions within a two-month period that total 35 school days, for example.	■ In-school suspensions that have the effect of depriving the student of education, as measured by his or her Individualized Education Plan (IEP), for prolonged periods may count as de facto days of suspension (*Big Beaver*, Pennsylvania Commonwealth Court, 1993). ■ Some states by legislation or regulation establish a specific numerical limit for cumulative suspensions (for example, 15 days in Pennsylvania). ■ Even if they last fewer than 10 days and are in good faith, short suspensions may violate Section 504 if they are based on misconduct relating to the student's disability (*Jonathan G.*, Federal District Court. Louisiana, 1994).
More than 10 days	Give the student and his or her parents specific written notice, sufficiently in advance, and a formal hearing before the school board or its designee. At the hearing, the student generally has these rights: ■ Right to counsel; ■ Right to testify and present witnesses; ■ Right to cross-examine adverse witnesses or substitute procedure. (No right to know identity of student accusers.) (No right to exclude hearsay evidence.) (No right to swear witnesses and adhere to formal rules of evidence.)	Have a knowledgeable group determine whether the misconduct is related to the student's disability. If it is not, use the same disciplinary procedures as for nondisabled students. Exception: Educational services may not be terminated for students covered by the IDEA but may be terminated for those students covered by Section 504 and ADA but not IDEA. If the misconduct is found to be related to the disability, provide full special education due-process procedures, including an IEP meeting and an opportunity for due-process hearing, before implementing a change of placement.	■ The district's responsibility is triggered when it has reason to suspect that the student may be covered by IDEA, Section 504, or the Americans with Disabilities Act (e.g., *M.P.*, Federal District Court, California, 1994); however, the "stay-put" is the excluded status unless a court rules otherwise (U.S. Department of Education, 1995). ■ Determining the relationship between misconduct and disability is not limited to whether the student knows right from wrong (*Pascagoula*, Mississippi Supreme Court, 1987). ■ Obtaining a *Honig* injunction requires the school district to prove (1) substantial likelihood of, and (2) reasonable steps to minimize, injury (*Light*, Federal Appeals Court for the 8th Circuit, 1994). ■ Referring a student with a disability for prosecution by the juvenile court may be a change in placement, triggering "stay-put" (*Morgan*, Federal District Court, Tennessee, 1994). ■ If the misconduct is the illegal use or possession of alcohol or drugs, students may be suspended without the extra procedural protections required under IDEA or Section 504 (OCR, 1991).

(continued)

BOX **11.4** Continued

Nondisabled students	Students with disabilities	
	Established law	*Emerging developments*
More than 10 days (No right to outside hearing officer or public hearing.) (No right to complete transcript.)	*Exception:* If the student is clearly dangerous to himself or herself or others, seek a preliminary injunction from court.	■ If the misconduct is bringing a firearm to school, an alternative placement of up to 45 days (or longer if parents request a due-process hearing) is permitted (Jeffords Amendment 1995).

Source: The Executive Educator (1996), 18:7. Reprinted with permission.

Student Rights

CHARLES J. RUSSO
Professor, University of Dayton

The legal landscape of American public education has changed greatly over the past forty-five years. The catalyst for this dramatic metamorphosis was the U.S. Supreme Court's 1954 ruling in *Brown v. Board of Education*, which struck down separate but equal educational facilities as inherently unequal. In the decades after *Brown*, the combination of judicial and legislative action has not only protected the rights of children of color, female students, and those with disabilities to equal educational opportunities, but has also defined the range of constitutional rights available to all school children.

Tinker v. Des Moines Independent Community School District (1969), decided in the middle of the civil rights era that was ushered in by *Brown* and the social unrest of the 1960s, did much more than uphold the rights of students to wear armbands as a protest against American involvement in Viet Nam. The Court's often quoted words, "[i]t can hardly be argued that students or teachers shed their constitutional rights to freedom of speech or expression at the schoolhouse gate" (p. 506), signaled the dawn of a new day in student rights.

Congressional passage of Title IX of the Educational Amendments of 1972 protected female students by prohibiting discrimination based on gender in educational programs receiving federal financial assistance. The Supreme Court has since expanded the scope of Title IX to cover students who have been victims of sexual harassment (*Franklin v. Gwinett County Public Schools*, 1992).

The Court further defined the rights of students in *Goss v. Lopez* (1975). In *Goss*, the Court ruled in favor of students who did not receive procedural due process before being suspended from school for ten days. The Court found that since a suspension of ten days (or longer) is more than a minimal deprivation of the rights of students to education, they "must be given some kind of notice and some kind of hearing" (p. 738). Although it stopped short of mandating hearings for all disciplinary infractions, the Court suggested that longer suspensions or expulsions may require more formal procedures.

Perhaps the most significant expansion of student rights occurred in special education. The passage of the Education for All Handicapped Children's Act in 1975, now the Individuals with Disabilities Education Act (IDEA, 1997), opened the door for millions of children with disabilities. Along with ensuring that all students with disabilities are entitled to free, appropriate public education in the least restrictive environments, the act includes substantive and procedural protection to assist children and their parents in safeguarding their rights.

The judicial expansion of student rights ended in 1985. In *New Jersey v. TLO*, the Court upheld the warrantless search of a student's purse because the administrator who did so satisfied its two-part test. According to the Court a search is permissible, first, as long as there is reasonable suspicion (a lower standard than probable cause, which applies to the police) to believe that a student has violated or is violating school rules or the law. Second, the Court maintained that the area being searched has to be reasonably related in scope to the circumstances that justified the interference in the first place. Following *TLO*, school officials have won all but a handful of the approximately forty cases involving searches of students, including a decision by the Supreme Court (*Vernonia School District 47 J. v. Acton*, 1995) that permits the drug testing of interscholastic athletes.

The Court cut back on the free speech rights of students in *Bethel School District v. Eraser* (1986). In *Eraser* the Court ruled that educators could discipline a high school student who delivered a nominating speech at an assembly because it contained sexual innuendoes. The Court distinguished *Eraser* from *Tinker* on the basis that the nondisruptive, passive expression of a political viewpoint in the latter case intruded on neither the work of the school nor the rights of other students.

The Court went full circle in a 1988 decision involving a dispute over a student newspaper. In *Hazelwood School District v. Kuhlmeier*, the Court concluded that educators could exercise reasonable editorial control over the style and content of student speech in school-sponsored expressive activities so long as their actions are reasonable related to legitimate pedagogical concerns" (p. 273). As such, the Court permitted educators to exclude an article on pregnancy at the high school from the newspaper, along with one about the divorce of a student's parents because they believed that these topics were inappropriate.

As American schools head into the new millennium, educational leaders must consider at least two important legal questions about the rights of students:

1. How can educators balance the need to maintain safe and orderly learning environments against the rights of students to be free from unreasonable searches of their persons and property?
2. As students familiarize themselves with technology such as the Internet and World Wide Web, not to mention software packages that facilitate desk top publishing, which will permit them to express themselves all the more, how can administrators maintain a middle ground between fostering frank and open discussion in the schools and stemming the flow of inappropriate subject matter in classes and educational activities?

How today's educational leaders answer these challenging questions will go a long way in determining the kinds of students and schools that the United States will have in the twenty-first century.

References

Bethel Sch. Dist. No. 403 v. Eraser, 478 U.S. 675 (1986).

Brown v. Board of Educ., 347 U.S. 483 (1954).

Franklin v. Gwinett County Pub. Schs., 503 U.S. 60 1992).

Goss V. Lopez, 419 U.S. 565 (1975).

Hazelwood Sch. Dist. v. Kuhlmeier, 484 U.S. 260 (1988)

Individuals with Disabilities Education Act, 20 U.S. C. A. 1400 et seq. (1997).

New Jersey v. TLO, 469 U.S. 325 (1985).

Tinker v. Des Moines Indep. Community Sch. Dist., 393 U.S. 503 (1969).

Title IX of the Educational Amendments of 1972, 20 U.S. C. A. 1681 (1997).

Vernonia Sch. Dist. 47 J. v. Acton, 515 U.S. 646 (1995).

Torts

A tort is a civil (not a criminal) wrong, not including contracts, for which a remedy in damages can be sought. According to Valente (1997) tort liability is created by federal and state law. Actions alleging failure of schools to protect students against sexual harassment and violence are being brought against schools under federal law. According to state tort law, "a person who causes injury to another through violation of some legal duty is liable to pay compensatory money damages to the injured party" (p. 443). Claims are usually covered by a district's group insurance; minimizing the potential for tort litigation, however, should be of much concern to educational leaders.

A basic concept of tort law is *fault*. Torts may be intentional, or may result from negligence or carelessness. According to Taylor (1996), three factors must be met in order for a party to be liable for negligence: (1) there must be a duty on the part of the defendant toward the victim either to act or to refrain from acting in a particular way, (2) this duty must be breached through failure to exercise a reasonable standard of care, and (3) there must be injury caused by this breach (p. 66).

All school employees are required to carry out their duties in a reasonable manner so that no damage or injury is incurred. Typical tort liability settings include laboratories, shops, playgrounds, field trips, spaces for physical education, and classrooms.

With regard to negligence:

- School employees have a duty to protect students in their care (*in loco parentis*);
- School employees must act with a reasonable standard of care;
- Once a cause of injury is established, the school leader must ask if the employee failed to act with a reasonable standard of care; and
- There must be evidence that damage to the plaintiff was the result of the injury.

What implications does the discussion about torts in this chapter have for the students involved in the accident and their parents?

Monitoring Compliance with Policies and Procedures

How can the school administrator ensure that the policies of the school district are followed and that teachers and students understand them? What systems can be put in place to monitor compliance? As schools continue developing partnerships and collaborations with individuals and community organizations, complying with state and district policies is crucial to risk management. According to Shoop and Dunklee (1992), "risk management is a coordinated, effective pre-event and post-event response to a school district's liability exposure, developed through planning, organizing, leading, and monitoring a district's activities and assets" (p. 307).

Risk management is a concept that started in the insurance industry, and the business manager of a school district should be keenly aware of its importance. It includes areas such as safety, security, transportation, and health. Given the growth of litigation against school districts and the simultaneous decentralization of management from the district to the site level, risk management is a concept with which all administrators should have familiarity. A key way of operationalizing the myriad issues involved in risk management is the development of clear and succinct policies and procedures, which are then explicated to students and teachers in school handbooks.

Another important concept is the *legal audit*. In the case of school districts, this refers to a *professional* review of the legal affairs of the district, carried out on a periodic basis and reported to the school board. Shoop and Dunklee (1992) cite two advantages of a legal audit:

1. The likelihood is increased that significant, but preventable, legal problems will come to the attention of district administrators and the board of education.
2. The flow of information to district administrators and the board of education is increased, with the assurance that the parties are receiving accurate facts on which to base preventive action.

Part of the legal audit involves examining the policies the school board has developed and the procedures for informing school district personnel and students of those policies. School-based administrators should be aware that the central office arranges for legal audits to be conducted and that these reports may have implications for the daily operations of their schools.

Box 11.5 on pages 336–337 exemplifies a school district policy regarding electronic information resources, including building-level operationalization. Lyman Memorial High School in Lebanon, Connecticut, has a "School-Community Handbook" (1999–2000) that includes items such as academic requirements, general school polices, specific conduct guidelines, and significant board of education policies.

To ensure that students have read the use policy and that their parents are aware of its existence, the school handbook also includes "Rules and Code of Ethics" (Box 11.6 on page 339) that students and parents must sign and return to the school site.

It then becomes imperative that the school site administrator develop mechanisms to monitor that all such forms are returned and filed. This is part of what is referred to as *preventive law*. Shoop and Dunklee (1992) define it as "a branch of law that endeavors to minimize the risk of litigation or to secure, with more certainty, legal rights and duties" (p. 308).

How might the school system make sure that problems like the one caused by O'Brien's negligence do not occur in the future?

BOX **11.5**

Lebanon Board of Education Internet Code of Conduct

- -

LEBANON   LOCATOR: 6141.321
Board of Education   SECTION: INSTRUCTION
POLICY   INFORMAL APPROVAL DATE: 2/27/96
                         FORMAL APPROVAL DATE: 3/26/96

- -

Electronic Information Resources (Internet)
The Lebanon Board of Education supports the use of the Internet to improve learning and teaching through interpersonal communication, student access to information, research, teacher training, collaboration and dissemination of successful educational practices methods and materials. The school system's connection to the Internet will provide access to local, national and international sources of information and collaboration vital to intellectual inquiry in a democracy.

In return for this access, every Internet user within this school system has the responsibility to respect and protect the rights of every other user in our community and on the Internet. User's are expected to act in a responsible, ethical and legal manner in accordance with the district's "Internet Code of Conduct," the missions and purposes of the other networks used on the Internet, and the laws of the states and the United States.

The Internet Code of Conduct shall apply to all users of the network. It reads:

"I will strive to act in all situations with honesty, integrity and respect for the rights of others and to help others behave in a similar fashion. I will make a conscious effort to be of service to others and to the community. I agree to follow the access usage and content rules as put forth in the district's Internet policy statement."

The Superintendent of Schools will establish and distribute to students and staff, guidelines pertaining to the use of the Internet.

In order to provide for the appropriate use of the Internet in keeping with Board of Education policy, the following "Acceptable Use Policy" has been developed. It requires student and parental agreement.

Acceptable Use Policy
Computers are used to support learning and to enhance instruction. Computer networks allow people to interact with many computers. The Internet allows people to interact with a multitude of networks and computers. All computers having Internet access must be used in a responsible, efficient, ethical and legal manner. Local community standards, as defined by the courts, will be applied by building administrators. Failure to adhere to this "Acceptable Use Policy" will result in the revocation of access privileges.

A responsible user may use the Internet to:

1. Research assigned classroom projects;
2. Send electronic mail to other users;
3. Explore other computer systems.

A responsible user MAY NOT:

1. Use the Internet for any illegal purpose;
2. Use impolite, abusive or discriminatory language, and media;
3. Change computer files that do not belong to the user;
4. Send or receive copyright material without permission;
5. Destroy, modify or abuse hardware or software

Unacceptable uses of the Internet will result in the revocation of access privileges. Unacceptable uses include:

1. Violating the statutes pertaining to student's rights to privacy.
2. Using profanity, pornography, obscenity or other language and media that may be offensive to other users.
3. Forwarding personal communications without the author's prior consent.
4. Copying commercial software in violation of copyright laws.
5. Using the networks for financial gain, for commercial activity or for any illegal activity.
6. Accessing media which violates community standards.

Source: Lebanon Public Schools, Lebanon, Connecticut (1999). Reprinted with permission.

BOX **11.6**

Rules and Code of Ethics for Lebanon Schools Computer Users

As a computer user I agree to follow the rules and code of ethics in all of my work with computers while attending Lebanon Public Schools.

I. I recognize that all computer users have the same right to use the equipment; therefore,
   - I will not play games or use the computer resources for other non-academic activities when others require the system for academic purposes;
   - I will not waste nor take supplies such as paper, printer ribbons, and diskettes that are provided by the school system; and when I am in a computer lab, I will talk softly and work in ways that will not disturb other users.

II. I recognize that software is protected by copyright laws; therefore,
   - I will not make unauthorized copies of software found on school computers, either by copying them onto my own diskettes or onto other computers through electronic mail or bulletin boards; and
   - I will not give, lend, or sell copies of software to others unless I have the written permission of the copyright owner or the original software is clearly identified as shareware or in the public domain.

III. I recognize also that the work of all users is valuable; therefore.
   - I will protect the privacy of others' areas by not trying to learn their passwords;
   - I will not copy, change, read, or use files in another user's area, without that user's prior permission;
   - I will not attempt to gain unauthorized access to system programs or computer equipment;
   - I will not use computer systems to disturb or harass other computer users by sending unwanted mail or by other means; and
   - I will not download information onto the hard drives of any school system computer for permanent storage.
   - I will download information onto diskettes if planning to store the information for more than one week.

IV. Violations of the rules and code of ethics described above will be dealt with seriously. Violators may lose computer privileges, be liable for damages done to school property and/or receive a school punishment, including out-of-school suspension.

(continued)

Continued

Please Sign and Return

_____

Student's Signature

We, the parents of _____ have read and discussed the above Rules and Code of Ethics for Lebanon Public Schools Computer Users, Guidelines for Telecommunications Use at Home, and Acceptable Use Policy with our student.

Parent's Signature: _____ *Date:* _____

Source: Lebanon Public Schools, Lebanon Connecticut (1999). Reprinted with permission.

Legal and Ethical Dimensions of Educational Leadership

MARTHA MCCARTHY, Chancellor Professor
Indiana University

An important purpose of public education in our nation is to instill core values for citizenship—values that form the foundation of a democratic society, such as love of liberty, justice, democracy, equality, and fairness and freedom of thought (Etzioni, 1993; McCarthy, Bull, Quantz, & Sorenson, 1993). A related function of public schools is to teach how our legal system and ethical codes protect these values. Many school administrators, however, currently are hesitant to engage teachers and students in reflecting on legal and ethical concerns. Legal discussions are sometimes avoided because school leaders are uneasy about their own knowledge of the law and consequently fear that such discussions will identify legal problems or make schools more vulnerable to legal challenges. Ethical deliberations may be avoided because they frequently surface value conflicts. Public schools have been faulted by some conservative citizen groups for encouraging students to clarify their values (Cohen, 1990).

Educators should not fear the law, apologize for exploring ethical concerns, or try to eliminate value-oriented material from the public school curriculum (an impossible feat). On the contrary, school leaders have an obligation to encourage their staff members and students to examine their values and the fundamental values undergirding the Constitution and laws in our nation.

All actions of school leaders have legal and ethical dimensions, yet many school administrators hold the erroneous impression that law and ethics simply set boundaries for their behavior (Bull & McCarthy, 1995). Indeed, the law is often viewed as a bothersome, external constraint—a prescriptive limitation—imposed on administrators' discretion and creativity. And some view ethical considerations as more concrete and settled—a precise list of "correct" behaviors—than they are.

Prospective school leaders should be encouraged to embrace a broader view of law and ethics. The law provides the basic framework for all interactions in an ordered society, and it specifies mechanisms for conflict resolution. The law emanates from experience, is constantly evolving, is designed to facilitate individual and collective activities, and reflects political and social changes over time. Thus, understanding the law is not simply a mechanical process of locating rules and regulations that govern our behavior. When educators do not understand the law, they often have unfounded fears of legal sanctions and they focus solely on the legal directives rather than on the process of developing, interpreting, and applying the law. Increased awareness of fundamental legal principles and the tensions between individual and collective interests leads to greater respect for the responsibilities that accompany legal rights.

Ethical deliberations also are more complex than school leaders often perceive them to be. Ethics is a social process of justifying human actions and exploring the validity of reasons for actions. By examining school situations through the lens of ethical behaviors (e.g., what is considered "just" and why), individuals can acquire a deeper understanding of their own values and biases as well as those of society. One's ethical code is more than a list of virtuous behaviors; it involves an examination of the concept of "virtue" and other concepts (e.g., "good," "moral"). To gain an understanding and appreciation of ethics, one must explore various ethical perspectives on a range of issues.

Although there are similarities between law and ethics, the commonalties should not be overstated. Some actions may be considered ethical but violate the law and vice versa. Individuals continue to be willing to suffer legal consequences for breaking laws they consider morally wrong (civil disobedience). Also, practices that some view as unethical, such as misleading a colleague regarding a professional matter, have no legal ramifications. This is why many professional organizations have developed codes of ethics in an effort to regulate behavior for which legal sanctions are not available.

If school leaders are to develop a deep understanding of law and ethics and translate such knowledge into action, these topics must be approached differently in educational leadership preparation programs. The notion is no longer widely supported that school administrators should be taught to deal with school situations as objective problems to be solved in a scientifically rational manner. Many now believe that preparation programs should guide school leaders in exploring complex, messy school situations that have no concrete answers and in understanding that personal beliefs influence what they do on the job (Beck, Murphy, & Associates, 1997).

Yet most preparation programs still do not encourage future school leaders to think critically about the legal and ethical aspects of their roles or to challenge their own values and worldviews. Preparation programs should expose future school leaders to scholarship in law and ethics and provide them ample opportunities to practice legal and ethical discourse and engage in intense personal reflection and critique (McCarthy et al., 1993; Starratt, 1994). Moreover, if school leaders become comfortable with legal and ethical deliberations during their preparation programs, their comfort level should carry over into their professional roles.

Whereas law has been a part of the educational leadership curriculum for several decades (although often too technically focused), only recently has ethics received systematic attention in some programs (Beck et al., 1997). Both law and ethics lend themselves to problem-based instruction and the exploration of legal and ethical implications of real and simulated school situations. By identifying and exploring dilemmas and considering alternative perspectives in formulating responses, school personnel can ask penetrating questions and make thoughtful decisions. Preparation programs have a responsibility to address ethical and legal concerns throughout the curriculum (not simply in a few courses), which should help school leaders to see connections between legal and ethical principles and the challenges they face every day in schools.

Conclusion

It is critically important that educational leaders keep abreast of school law issues. Administrators need a comprehensive knowledge of both education and law to make prudent judgments. Consulting professional publications and, when appropriate, contacting the district's legal counsel are important preventive measures for protecting your school from litigation. Follow these guidelines:

- Schools may regulate speech only when it is necessary to achieve a compelling purpose and when regulations are no more extensive than necessary.
- Schools cannot prohibit speech simply because the ideas expressed differ from those of the administration or staff.
- The prohibition of speech can occur only when it disrupts the school's educational purpose or if it invades the rights of others.
- Students must be given an opportunity for a hearing before exclusions from school for disciplinary purposes.
- Students with disabilities, as well as limited-English-proficient students, must be afforded an education from which they may reasonably be expected to benefit.
- State statutes establish the only acceptable bases for termination or nonrenewal of contract of a teacher after that teacher has passed a probationary period.
- It is imperative that all school personnel act reasonably with regard to the rights of others.

A related issue is the protection against unreasonable search and seizure. Nathan Essex (1999) states, "School officials should have reasonable grounds to believe a search of a particular student is necessary to provide pertinent proof that the student has violated a particular policy, rule or law. Further, the scope of the search must be limited to the incident at hand" (p. 39). The decision to complete a search is carefully balanced against the school official's need to maintain order and discipline and to protect the safety and welfare of others.

In the *International Handbook of Educational Leadership and Administration* (1966) Ann Shorten reminds readers, "Prudent administrators will establish operational mechanisms which enable the changes in the law to be brought to their notice as soon as it is possible to do so, and have in place an adequate communication system to enable that information to be disseminated to those who need to know it" (p. 83). This is sound advice, and the prospective educational administrator must be keenly aware of the importance of this type of communication system.

PORTFOLIO ARTIFACTS

1. Obtain a copy of two different school districts' policy manuals. Compare them. How are they similar and different? Scan the table of contents of each manual; what policies exist in one district that do not exist in the other?

2. Some states produce one (or several) document(s) referred to as the education code. Does your state have such a code book? If so, review a copy. Examine one topic, such as teacher evaluation and dismissal. What is the essence of the code? How many times has it been revised?

3. Interview a school principal and ask questions related to legal issues in schools. The ISSLC standards (see Chapter 1) can be used to create your questions. See Standards 3, 5, and 6 in particular.

4. Spend a day observing cases in family and domestic relations court or follow an educational case through the courts.

5. Identify an issue within a school and research the laws that relate to the issue developing a legal brief arguing for, or against, the issue.

6. Spend a day with a judge.

7. Find and read the published report on a court decision listed in this chapter or of interest to your school division.

TERMS

Circuit court
Defendant
Desegregation
Due process
Equal protection clause
Establishment clause

Family Educational Rights
  and Privacy Act
  (FERPA—1974)
in loco parentis
Libel
Negligence

Plaintiff (complainant)
Slander
Statute
Tort

SUGGESTED READINGS

Alexander, K., & Alexander, M. D. (1998). *American public school law*. Belmont, CA: Wadsworth Publishing, Co.

Essex, N. L. (1999). *School law and the public schools: A practical guide for educational leaders*. Boston: Allyn & Bacon.

Imfer, M., & Van Geel, T. (1993). *Education law*. New York: McGraw-Hill.

Lamorte, M. W. (1999) *School law*. Boston: Allyn & Bacon.

Sperry, D. J. (1999). *Working in a legal and regulatory environment: A handbook for school leaders*. Princeton, NJ: Eye on Education.

Taylor, B. B. (1996). *Education and the law: A dictionary*. Santa Barbara, CA: ABC-CLIO, Inc.

Valente, W. D. (1997). *Law in the schools*. (4th ed.) New York: Merrill.

COURT CASES

Board of Education v. Allen, 392 U.S. 236, 88 S. Ct. 1923, 20 L. Ed 1060 (1968)

Brown v. Board of Education of Topeka, 347 U.S. 483, 74 S. Ct. 686, 98 L. Ed. 873 (1954)

Brown v. Coffeeville Consolidated School District (1973)

Doe v. University of Michigan, 721 F. Supp. 852 (1989)

CHAPTER 11

Fenton v. Stear (1976), 423 F. Supp. 767 (W.D. Pa)

Farrell v. Dallas Independent School District (1968), 392 F. 2d 697

Hazelwood School District v. Kuhlmeier, 484 U.S. 260 (1988)

Keyishian v. Board of Regents of New York (1967), 385 U. S. 589

Meltzer v. Board of Public Instruction (1977)

Meyer v. Nebraska, 262 U.S. 390, 43 S. Ct. 625, 67 L. Ed. 1042 (1923)

Miller v. California (1973), 413 U.S. 15

Planned Parenthood v. Clark County School District, 941 F. 2d 871 (9th Cir. 1991)

Plessy v. Ferguson, 163 U.S. 537, 16 S. Ct. 1138, 41 L. Ed. 256 (1896)

Stone v. Graham (1983), 449 U. S. 39

Scott v. New-Herald (1986), 655 F. Supp. 1353 (S.D. Ohio)

Sheff v. O'Neill (1996), 211 Conn. 627 A. 2d. 518

Steirer v. Bethlehem Area School District, 987 F. 2d. 989 (3d Cir. 1993)

Tinker v. Des Moines Independent School District, 393 U.S. 503 (1969) 1985

12 Resource Allocation and Management

Vignette: Identifying Funding Sources for Meadows High

Oceanview School District is located adjacent to a large city in the West. It comprises seven elementary schools, two middle schools and a high school with nearly 3,000 students. Meadows High School (MHS) like many of its counterparts throughout the nation, is experiencing problems with an aging facility.

MHS, originally built in 1926, nearly doubled its size in 1980 by means of an addition. Although the facility has been well maintained, it needs retrofitting. Referring to the science and computer labs the faculty have often told Principal Carolina Martin that although safety requirements have been met, the facilities are in a "deplorable condition." The faculty say they are "completely embarrassed" about the lack of equipment, particularly when visitors pass through the rooms. A typical high school class has twenty-five students, but the computer lab has only ten computers. In science labs, students have to share microscopes and other equipment.

Martin has discussed these concerns with the central office; however, they have informed her that in the foreseeable future no additional money will be available. Martin has requested that the school-site council include discussion of these issues on the next agenda. The school-site council comprises five teachers, one student, the principal, two parents, and two community members. Because Oceanview District has decentralized authority in recent years, MHS has considerable control in budget planning and expenditures.

If you were formulating next year's budget, what approach might you use to help reallocate funds within the existing budget?

How can money be identified so that additional resources will be available to students in the science and computer laboratories?

Financing Schools

To address fiscal issues in operating a school and to speak knowledgeably with school community members, administrators should have an understanding of school finance.

The proliferation of school-based management and budgeting to an even wider audience, including teachers and community members, requires these participants to have a basic understanding of how public and private schools are financed and strategies that can be used to enhance revenue generation.

Taxes

Tax revenues are used to finance many public services, including social service agencies, police departments, fire departments, transportation systems, and schools. Public schools are primarily funded through the revenues generated from property, consumption, and state income taxes. Each of these taxes has advantages and disadvantages when evaluated on such criteria as equity, yield, tax base, economic impact, and compliance.

The *equity* of a tax refers to fairness. One of the basic assumptions since the inception of American taxation has been progressivity. The belief is that an equitable tax is one that takes a higher percentage from those whose net worth increases the most because they are gaining the most from society and that such taxes do not take away from the basic necessities of life but only from luxuries. Former Secretary of Labor Robert Reich (1997), expressing concerns about recent policies that have lowered the taxes of the wealthiest income earners stated, "I find this trend deeply disturbing. We have the most unequal distribution of income of any industrialized nation" (p. 32). This trend of lowering taxes for the wealthiest Americans occurred as part of the Tax Reform Act of 1986 and became an issue again at the turn of the century. In these cases, to maintain the present level of public services, taxes on the middle class are increased over time.

Yield refers to the revenue produced by a tax. Questions such as the following are asked with regard to yield: With this type of tax is a high yield generated at a low tax rate? Does the income from this tax increase as the economy improves and decrease as the economy downturns?

The *tax base* refers to the particular category to which a tax rate can be applied. Typical tax base classifications include income, wealth, property value, consumption, and privilege.

Economic impact is another factor used to evaluate taxation systems. Key questions to ask are: Is the tax a disincentive to the American business owner or worker? Does this tax produce any negative impacts on the economy?

The *administration of taxes* can be highly cumbersome. The question to ask is: How can maximum revenue be generated while keeping tax administration costs to a minimum?

Finally, *compliance* involves ensuring that taxes are actually paid. One example is the automatic nature of withholding of income taxes. In some countries the worker pays income taxes on a quarterly or yearly basis and the taxes are not deducted from the paycheck; thus, compliance becomes an important issue.

In recent years the federal government has moved more toward a proportional or flat tax, which reduces the taxes on the wealthy and increases the taxes on the middle class, if the expenditure remains constant. Many states have imposed limitations on certain taxes.

Proposition 13, which was passed in 1978 in California, and Proposition 2½ in Massachusetts are two examples. As states examine their school finance legislation, there is a trend toward reducing the reliance on property taxes and increasing the amount of revenue from other types of taxes (e.g., consumption taxes such as the revenues generated from state lotteries). Property taxes and some other types of taxes are often regressive—that is, they ask middle-class taxpayers to pay a higher percentage of their wages in taxes than higher-income groups. Knowledge of taxation for education and its effect on citizens is important since taxes provide much of the revenue stream for public education.

Federal Involvement in Financing Schools

Although education is a state rather than a federal responsibility, the federal government plays a role in financing specific education programs supported by the government. According to Figure 12.1 the federal government's role as a source of revenue has changed little since 1970. The percentage of a local school budget contributed by the federal government is usually less than 10 percent. This figure varies according to the type of school.

For example, large urban school districts are more likely to have federally financed initiatives such as bilingual programs, magnet schools, migrant programs, Headstart, and school-to-work programs. Thus, the percentage of their budget contributed by the federal government is larger than that in districts not offering these programs.

Table 12.1 on page 346 depicts a budget outlay for a variety of programs supported by the U.S. government. Aid is usually distributed to school districts as block grants,

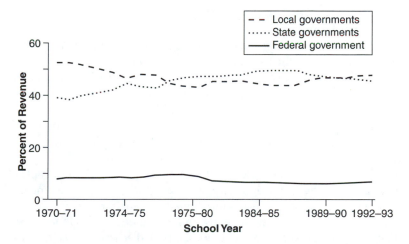

FIGURE 12.1 Sources of Revenue for Public Elementary and Secondary Schools: 1970–71 to 1992–93

TABLE 12.1   Where Do School Dollars Go?

A breakdown of average per-pupil spending by category in nine selected districts in 1967, 1991, and 1996.

Program Area*	1967	1991	1996
Regular education	80.1%	58.5%	56.8%
Special education	3.6	17.8	19.0
Food services	1.9	3.3	4.8
Compensatory education	5.0	4.2	3.5
Pupil support (attendance and counseling)	2.1	3.5	3.2
Transportation (regular education)	3.6	3.9	3.1
Vocational education	1.4	2.8	2.7
Bilingual education	0.3	1.9	2.5
Desegregation	0.0	1.9	1.5
Regular health and psychological services	1.4	1.0	1.1
After-school athletics	0.4	0.7	0.6
"At risk" youth education, alternative education	0.1	0.6	0.6
Security and violence prevention	0.1	0.5	0.6
Total	100.0%	100.0%	100.0%

*Programs listed in order of 1996 share of total per pupil spending

Source: Economic Policy Institute, 1996.

categorical aid, or as general aid. These monies are usually sent to the state office of education, which distributes funds to local education agencies.

State Involvement in Financing Schools

Most states have complex systems of funding; however, one particularly important concept is what is called the foundation program. The *foundation program* refers to the established minimum of financial support that a district receives for each enrolled student. School districts are reimbursed by the state on an average daily membership (ADM) or average daily attendance (ADA) basis. The amount, sometimes called a per-pupil allotment, may be affected by several factors, including the amount of local fiscal effort, the number of special, vocational, and bilingual education students, and the number of students from families below the poverty level.

Let's examine California's sources of revenue for schools as an example (Table 12.2).

In addition to the foundation concept, other approaches to financing public schools include a flat-grant model, power-equalizing plan, guaranteed tax base plan, and a weighted-student model. Several states use more than one method for financing schools.

With a *flat-grant model* state aid to local school districts is based on a fixed amount. This amount is then multiplied by the number of students in the district. Many people argue that this approach to funding schools is unequal because it is more expensive to educate some children than others. For example, a child requiring special-education

TABLE 12.2   **Sources of Revenue for California Schools**

	1994–95	**1995–96 (est.)**	**1996–97 (est.)**
Federal Aid	8.3%	8.15%	7.8%
State Aid	53.2%	55.6%	57.4%
Property Tax	29.1%	27.5%	26.4%
Local Miscellaneous	7.2%	6.7%	6.4%
Lottery	2.2%	2.0%	1.9%

services or bilingual education would cost a school district more to educate than a child not needing these services.

A *power-equalizing model* pays a percentage of local school expenditures in an inverse ratio to the school district's wealth. The wealthier the district, the less matching state monies it receives. The goal is an equalization between wealthier school districts and those of less wealth. Since those living in wealthy districts can pay a much lower percent of their income and yet raise considerably more money for the education of every child in average daily membership, the state tries to make adjustments for these inequities.

In a *weighted-student model* of financing public education, students are weighted in proportion to their special needs. For example, students requiring bilingual education, special-needs classes, or vocational classes, would be allotted additional money according to the costs of those services. One of the problems with this model is the complexity involved in assigning weights. For example, some children receive not only special education services but may also receive bilingual program services. Calculating weights for special programs can become highly complex.

The school financial issue that has received the greatest sustained court attention is the alleged inequities in financing public education. The issue is inequality of educational opportunity caused by educational funding that is "a function of district property wealth; whether or not a disputed financial scheme provides each child with at least a basic or adequate education; the importance of local control; and the extent, if any, of courts' involvement in providing remediation" (Lamorte, 1999, pp. 351–352).

A related issue is providing choices of educational services at public expense. Lamorte (1999) goes on to say,

> Unfortunately for discussion purposes, the notion of choice does not describe a single, well-defined plan but is an umbrella term for a host of programs.... Its proponents argue that bringing a concept—consumer choice—to education will break the alleged monopolistic stranglehold of the educational bureaucracy by introducing the necessary ingredient of a measure of needed competition, with all the positive connotations that term implies, to the public schools. (p. 374)

Charter schools are a form of choice that encourages innovative educational ideas.

Charter schools, which are public schools that have many of the characteristics of independent schools, are also financed through taxes. A certain allotment is given by the district or state directly to the charter school for each child enrolled, rather than to a district central office. If a student chooses to leave a school, he or she takes the funding away from that school.

Local Involvement in Financing Schools

Because school districts do not generate revenue from profits on sales, they have been granted by their state government the power to tax individuals and companies. The main revenue source for public schools is the local property tax. The property tax is a function of three variables: the tax base, the assessment practice, and the tax rate. The tax base includes all taxable property in the district except that owned by the federal government, public hospitals, state parks, churches, and nonprofit entities, which are not taxable.

States vary as to how they assess property. Usually a percentage rate, established by the taxing authority, is applied to the property's market value. The market value is the amount the owner would receive on selling the property. Depending on the state, the tax rate is expressed in a variety of ways: per thousand dollars of assessed valuation, dollars per hundred dollars of assessed valuation, and mills. According to William Sharp (1994), "the school district's tax rate is multiplied by the assessed value of the tax base of the community to yield the amount of money the school will receive" (p. 2).

Let's look at an example for a single home. If the market value of a home is $120,000 and the taxing authority's assessment practice is 80 percent, the assessed value of the home would be $120,000 × .80 or $96,000. This is the amount on which the homeowner would be taxed. If the rate were $2.00 per $100.00 of assessed value, the property tax on this house would be 96,000 × .02, or $1,920.00. Keep in mind, however, that the homeowner's overall tax rate includes other taxes in addition to school taxes (e.g., water district, hospital district).

This is a simplified version of the tax process. Often homeowners and businesses are eligible for certain types of exemptions. Additionally, when a community is trying to lure businesses into town, it often offers tax abatements (a lesser amount of taxes in the first few years).

Here is a typical formula for a school district's income:

General purpose (Revenue limit × ADA)
+ Special purpose (categorical aid)
+ Miscellaneous local and other (i.e., sale of assets, investment income)
+ Lottery
_____

Total District Income

Box 12.1 depicts the income and expenditures of one large city school district.

Vouchers

In the mid-1950s economist Milton Friedman proposed that every family be given a voucher of equal worth for each child attending public schools. Under his plan, a family could choose any school meeting the basic requirements set by government.

BOX 12.1

San Diego City Schools General Budget

1997–98 General Fund Budget
Income by Source

Revenue Limit

Local Property Taxes	$305,875,356	37.77%
State General Fund	186,591,509	23.04%
Total Revenue Limit	492,466,865	60.81%
Other State Revenues	212,548,919	26.25%
Federal Revenues	49,808,577	6.15%
Miscellaneous Local Revenues	8,802,213	1.09%
Carryover Balance	46,185,452	5.70%
Total General Fund	$809,812,026	100.00%

1997–98 General Fund Budget
Appropriations by Expenditure Classification

Employee Salaries & Benefits	$644,304,493	79.56%
Books and Supplies	81,012,853	10.00%
Contracted Services and Other Operating Expenses	37,399,585	4.62%
Capital Outlay	16,088,996	1.99%
Other Outgo	13,849,383	1.71%
Reserves	17,146,716	2.12%
	$809,812,026	100.00%

Appropriations by Program

Classroom Instructional Programs	$512,752,104	63.34%
Instructional Support	107,814,740	13.31%
Health, Counseling, Attendance	45,792,651	5.65%
District Administration	24,329,440	3.00%
Plant Maintenance and Operations	65,057,885	8.03%
Pupil Transportation	26,256,050	3.24%
Auxiliary Programs	5,612,541	0.69%
Interfund Transfers	5,039,899	0.62%
Reserve for Economic Uncertainties	15,853,116	1.96%
Inventory Revolving Funds	1,150,000	0.14%
Cash Revolving Funds	153,600	0.02%
Total General Fund	$809,812,026	100.00%

Source: San Diego Unified School District Statistical Report. November, 1997. Public Information Office, San Diego City Schools.

Parents could add their own resources to the voucher, and schools could set their own tuition level and admission requirements.

Throughout the last forty years, various versions of a voucher system have been debated at local, state, and national levels. Vouchers have been tied to the concept of school choice, with a voucher program being proposed as one form of schooling that should be made available to children and families.

School choice has become a major policy issue affecting schools throughout the nation. At present no state has a voucher system. Several cities, however, are utilizing voucher systems (e.g., Milwaukee, Chicago, Cleveland) with limited measures of success. In 1998, the Wisconsin Supreme Court upheld the use of vouchers and the U.S. Supreme Court declined to review the case. Florida Governor Jeb Bush proposed a voucher plan providing up to $4000 for each student attending a failing school (based on the school's test scores) that can be used to attend public, private, or religious schools. The school choice movement includes ideas such as vouchers, magnet schools, and charter schools. These movements have the potential to change the allocation of revenues and have implications for revenue generation for schools.

Nontraditional Revenue Sources

To expand services many school districts have begun to look at a variety of nontraditional sources of revenue. Meno (1984) identified three categories for nontraditional funding sources: donor, enterprise, and cooperative. Table 12.3 depicts these three categories as well as various kinds of revenues assigned to each category. According to the research of Garnos and King (1994) superintendents and principals believe that nontraditional revenues are viable ways to enhance public school budgets. As the charter school movement expands nationwide, these sources will become more commonly used. Additionally, much can be learned from independent schools (both private and religious) about alternative sources of revenue generation; in order to exist these institutions have had to utilize a variety of funding strategies. School administrators must be skilled in fostering partnerships, securing donors, and establishing enterprises.

School Foundations

A school foundation is similar to a university's development office. A foundation has a tax-free status; thus, donors can benefit from their gifts. Foundations allow community members to raise funds through gifts from individuals and corporations. Funds can be used to pay for field trips, special projects, scholarships, and awards.

Thayer and Short (1994) maintain that the principal must be a key player in forming a foundation. They recommend the following steps in creating a foundation:

- Organize a team to study the feasibility of such a move.
- Obtain 501(c)(3) status and authorization to transact business, subject to all applicable state and federal laws.

TABLE 12.3   Sources of Nontraditional Funding

Donor	Enterprise	Cooperative
1. Cash gifts from individuals 2. Real property from individuals 3. Private foundation grants 4. Corporate gifts 5. gifts from nonprofit organizations 6. Donated services 7. Donated supplies 8. Donated equipment 9. Fundraiser to support an educational program 10. Fundraiser to support a cocurricular activity	1. Services leased to other school districts or organizations 2. Facilities leased to other school districts or organizations 3. User fee payments (community education, drivers education, etc.) 4. Rental of school facilities or equipment 5. Sale of school access (vending machines, advertising, etc.) 6. Sale/lease-back arrangements	**Local Agencies** 1. Programs shared with other districts 2. Activities shared with other districts 3. Cooperative programs with universities 4. Programs or activities sponsored by service clubs or organizations **Governmental Agencies** 1. Joint facility maintenance programs with city, county (property, equipment, etc.) 2. Joint use of buses 3. Joint use of athletic facilities or swimming pool **Business and Industry** 1. Work-study programs 2. Youth job placement programs 3. Career guidance

Source: Garnos, M. L. & King, R. A. (1994). *NASSP Bulletin* **78**, 566. Reprinted with permission.

- Inform stakeholders why a foundation is needed and the history behind the process.
- Set specific, reasonable goals.

Revenue Sources for Independent Schools

Independent schools include both religious and private schools located in the United States and overseas. (Note: There are approximately 550 overseas American schools. These schools differ from schools sponsored by the Department of Defense in several ways, including funding sources [ECIS, 1998]). Independent schools are primarily funded through tuition and gifts. Alumni are among the largest sources of gifts for independent schools. One difference between independent private schools and religious schools is that for the latter, religious institutions usually support a portion of the school budget.

Much can be learned from independent schools, not only regarding their fund-raising strategies, but also in how they market their programs.

What implications do funding mechanisms have for the plans of the school-site council of Meadows High?

Obtaining Funding for Educational Programs

HARVEY B. POLANSKY, PH.D.
Assistant Superintendent of Schools
East Lyme, Connecticut

Funding has become an intricate part of district and school management. Strategies in the development, procurement, and public approval of school funds vary greatly but have one common strand: accountability. Accountability is less a process of bookkeeping and more one of intense taxpayer scrutiny of what value the public receives for its educational dollars. With the new millennium comes even greater scrutiny and criticism of school funding. Administrators will be forced to defend funding strategies and seek alternative and creative means to obtain funds. They will have to manage the funds with greater competency and preparation. Many of us started our educational journey in the spend-free 1980s. Since then a quasi-tax revolt has diminished educational dollars.

Where Do School Funds Come From?

Nationally, over 80 percent of all school funds come from local and state funding, entitlements, and tax revenue. Tax revenues have decreased, placing both tax revenues and entitlements in jeopardy. School districts seek other means to develop strategies in obtaining funds for worthwhile programs. No longer can administrators expect the municipality to cover all expenses. Creative strategies to find school funding include the following five.

Development of Educational Enterprise Zones
Schools can no longer sit back and expect tax dollars to cover the costs of innovative programs. In many cases, school must put up an "open for business" sign. Fees for extended-day programs, day-care programs, and enrichment programs often come from consumers. Principals must learn how to market and create fiscal systems of accountability to manage these programs. School will be open from 6 A.M. to 6 P.M., and the fees earned can be used for staff, materials, and building initiatives. Governance teams and building improvement teams must be coordinated to get the full "bang for the buck."

Preschool Programs
Schools will have to compete with private day-care providers. Are preschool programs educationally sound, providing the students fewer transitions? Can they be an economic cash cow? Effective preschool programs will enhance feeder programs, engage parents at early ages, and offer community outreach to a population that is politically strong. Funds can be used for school-wide initiatives. In addition, research suggests that the experience of children in the first four years has a strong influence on their future development.

Resource Sharing

School districts tend to view their existence in isolated management camps. Regional service centers attempt to develop resource sharing but are often in the market themselves. School districts should learn to share business and support side functions, such as transportation, substitute teachers, food service, custodial service, bidding services, and innovative technological and curricular programs across district lines. Sharing will diminish personnel costs and enhance district funding. Cooperative arrangement with museums, corporations, and businesses will also bring needed services to schools. Most corporate giving has ceased or is part of a competitive grant program.

Grant Writing

School administrators must turn to the Internet and find grants. Entitlements are drying up and competitive categorical grants are becoming increasingly available. Dream a little. Put your thought on paper, go online, and find out what grants are available. The National School Boards Association (www.nsba.org) and the U.S. Depart- ment of Education (www.sdoe.org) have Web sites and periodicals listing available grant programs. Local organizations may also list grant opportunities. Some administrators are hesitant to submit a grant proposal. Remember, the worst that could happen is that they reject it. You'll still be learning a great innovative approach to finding alternate funding.

Distance Learning

While most teacher unions oppose the concept of distance learning, satellite, interdistrict distance-learning programs can decrease costs (thereby allowing administrators to use funds elsewhere) and offers opportunities to charge for programs. Latin 4, French 6, and esoteric math and science courses can be taught via interactive distance-learning programs. Equipment is expensive but does tend to attract grant funding. Universities also offer programs that can reduce costs and provide much-needed studio facilities.

We can no longer rely on traditional funding sources. It is the entrepreneurial administrators who will find funds that best meet the needs of their schools and programs.

Grant Writing

Given the increase in the need for schools and school districts to obtain funding from nontraditional sources, skills in understanding grant writing are now requisite for school administrators. Ruskin and Achilles (1995) summarize the grant-writing process as follows:

1. Identify a philanthropist or foundation interested in your type of project.
2. Develop a comprehensive and individualized plan to interest this person.
3. Design a short-term strategy and a long-range plan for support.
4. Make personal contact with the funder.
5. Devise a plan to enlist support of other key people.
6. Send a letter of inquiry and interest.
7. Submit the required proposal.
8. Establish ongoing dialogue with the funder.
9. Steward the funder through various phases of your project to ensure that the funder becomes a stakeholder. (p. 30)

Not only do school administrators have to understand the process of applying for grants, but they also need to understand what information is typically found in any grant. Ruskin and Achilles (1995) provide eleven suggestions for grant writers to use when supporting their case in a grant proposal:

1. Provide a clear picture of your school site—demographics, curriculum, special programs, best features, and the problem.
2. Clearly present the needs you are attempting to meet, with supporting data about the impact of needs on the quality of education provided to students.
3. Articulate the plan you are proposing to meet these needs, including how the plan was developed. Provide a comprehensive picture of the reasons this plan is the best means to address the educational needs. Support your ideas with other successful models, and provide a timetable for implementation.
4. Outline direct and indirect educational benefits derived through successful implementation of your plan. Emphasize the impact of your project on the quality of education and its implications for the individual student.
5. List funder costs for your plan. Depending on what the funder is seeking, you may need to convince the funder that you have given careful attention to costs and that you can complete the project within your budget.
6. Provide an evaluation design for your plan as part of your implementation timeline. Tie it to measurable objectives.
7. Provide a convincing argument about the professional and personal qualifications of the proposed project director.
8. Delineate future funding needs and a strategy to secure needed resources.
9. Develop a plan to continue the project after initial funding is completed. How will you institutionalize the grant?
10. Provide appropriate support information in appendixes.
11. Develop a calendar with your agenda for grant follow-up. Specify important targeted grant deadlines and appointments on this calendar to ensure ongoing contact with the funder. Details of stewardship activities could be added here. Make it easy for the grant manager to take one glimpse at the calendar and anticipate any significant deadlines. (p. 53–54)

Budgeting, Accounting, and Facility Management

The receipt of the budget provides that moment of truth when the administration learns the type of educational program that the community can afford or is willing to support. Budgeting ensures that required resources will be available at the right time and in the right amount to accomplish the educational plan. It is a financial plan that needs to be interpreted to the school board and community so that it can be approved. In this section, we first discuss the steps in the budgeting process and then three approaches to budgeting: program-planning budgeting system, zero-based budgeting, and incremental budgeting. The final section describes budgeting in school-based management models.

The Budgeting Process

The budgeting process involves planning, formulating, presenting, administering, and evaluating. Many states follow a calendar that determines when certain stages of a school district's budget must be met. Often the process begins in September, and the budget is adopted the following June or July.

Planning. The academic program should drive the budget; therefore, in the planning stage of the budget process factors such as needs, program goals and objectives, alternatives for achieving goals, and selecting cost-effective alternatives must be considered. In Figure 12.2 Sanders and Thiemann present the specific components of the instructional and implementary costs of education.

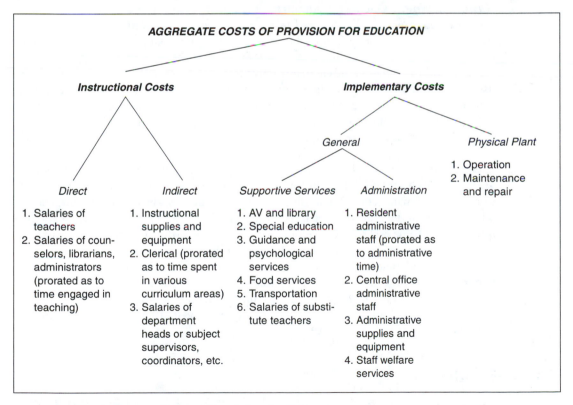

FIGURE 12.2   Aggregate Costs of Provision for Education

Source: Reprinted with permission from NASSP.

Formulating.   To formulate the budget it is crucial to have input from the many constituencies of the school. Schools can no longer jealously guard the budget, keeping secret how and why money is spent. Teachers are being asked to assume a greater role in the budget process in many school districts, especially in schools that are site managed. Creating and detailing the budget should involve input and discussion from faculty, staff, and other groups who are part of the school's community.

Box 12.2 displays a checklist for developing a school budget. It includes the process, the organizing of the budget document, and the types of data needed to compile the budget.

Presenting.   A crucial part to presenting a school budget is the development of a rationale. In most school districts, principals meet with superintendents and other central office personnel involved with the budgeting process to discuss their budget. The final school district budget is presented to the school board and, in the case of dependent school districts, to the city council or board of county supervisors. It is crucial that an administrator be able to articulate a strong rationale for budget priorities.

Administering.   One way to administer the budget is to allocate money to each program or department and allow staff to spend as they wish as long as they stay within the assigned amount. The responsibilities related to purchasing and accounting, however, are very important. Often it can take several months between the time an item is ordered and the time the bills actually arrive (encumbrances). The money that will be used is encumbered until the bill is actually paid. Thus, although the money is technically available, it should not be used. A multitude of computer programs are available to help school administrators manage the school budget and ensure that encumbered monies are not used and that the budget is not overexpended.

Evaluating.   The school budget is usually organized into categories such as programs (early childhood, bilingual, language arts), functions (instructional, transportation, facilities management), and objects (supplies, salaries, staff development, travel). These areas can be evaluated separately or in combination. Questions such as the following need to be asked: How well did the budget serve the goals it was meant to accomplish? How will we determine whether the goals and objectives were achieved? Were the goods and services purchased actually used? Should the program be expanded? Should the program be eliminated? Two key words to keep in mind are *effectiveness* and *efficiency*. As programs are evaluated, school administrators should ask if the approach used was the most effective as well as most efficient way to accomplish the goals.

Types of Budgeting

The following four types of budgets are not mutually exclusive; each can provide useful and needed information. One may become more important depending on the organizational needs and situations. If the computer system used is sophisticated

BOX **12.2**
School Budget Development Checklist

Process: Procedures for Conducting Hearings
___ Roles of board and superintendent clearly defined
___ Board finance policies updated regularly
___ Financial data accurate and timely
___ Staff adequately in budget request
___ Public hearing held with citizen participation
___ Budget document (or summary) widely distributed
___ Process complies with legal requirements
___ Community/political support generated for budget
___ Contingency strategy (budget options) exists
___ Efficient accounting/financial reporting system used

Format: Preparing the Document
___ Cover, title page, appearance attractive
___ Table of contents or index; number pages
___ Board members and officers' names included
___ Organizational chart and school administrators listed
___ Budget message or transmittal letter included
___ Graphics/artwork, charts, figures, tables
___ Clarity of style; avoidance of technical jargon
___ Manageable size and shape of document
___ Glossary of key terms
___ Concise executive summary (budget in brief)

Contents: Data Compilation
___ Feasibility of bottom-line requests
___ School system goals and objectives
___ Budget guidelines or priorities
___ Object budget summary (e.g., salaries, supplies)
___ Site budget summary (e.g., individual campuses)
___ Budget history (expenditures for previous five years)
___ Unit cost analysis (per-pupil expenditures)
___ Estimated revenue summary (all sources)
___ Explanation of tax rate impact
___ Explanation of major cost factors (contracts, inflation)
___ Budget coding system explained (account charts)
___ Performance measures included (test data)
___ Pupil enrollment projections by grade
___ Staffing history and projections
___ Long-range plans (five years) for district
___ Major decisions justified (layoffs, closings)
___ District or state comparisons
___ Capital budget summarized (improvement projects)
___ Budget detail (line-item expenditure data)

Source: Hartley, H. (1990) "Boardroom Bottom Line" with permission from the *American School Board Journal* 177(2): 31.

enough for financial records and the data are properly organized, the computer program can prepare cost and budget information in a number of different formats.

Line-Item Budgeting

An *object budget* is a listing of the objects of expense, such as salaries, supplies, equipment, services, insurance, travel, professional improvements, postage, maintenance, utilities, fringe benefits, rents, debt reduction, and so forth. A *function classification* lists estimates of expenditures in terms of the purposes for which they are made—administration, instruction, health service, pupil transportation, food service, operation, fixed charges, summer school, adult education, and so on. Today's general line-item budget has evolved from a combination of these two organizational categories.

The wide variety of classification systems used to account for school expenditures and revenues complicate the process, along with the consequent difficulties involved in securing expenditure and revenues. Additionally the difficulty involved in securing comparable data concerning the financial operation of the school systems impelled the U.S. Office of Education to issue a handbook, *Financial Accounting for Local and State School Systems*, which is periodically updated. The handbook provides recommendations regarding expenditure and revenue accounts to be used in budgeting and accounting. For the most part, state requirements and local school budgets have followed the basic recommendations made by the U.S. Office of Education.

Budget estimates are typically made from one year to the next by adding a percentage increment of the previous year's budget. The typical procedure is to record expenditures for a given budget classification for one or two years prior, enter the request for the future year, and note the additional amounts requested. Then the budget director, superintendent, and school board arrive at a final figure by taking a fixed percentage cut (or addition) in the school's requests. This is the basis of stability in the appropriations process and provides an excellent mechanism for control.

Planning, Programming, Budgeting System (PPBS)

Typically the line-item budget deals primarily with the functions and objects of expense but not with the programs. A program-budgeting system provides a method of determining the costs of programs. Sometimes called PPBS and at other times referred to as PPBES, with the *E* referring to evaluation, this approach to budgeting requires that the budget be organized around program goals and the processes to accomplish these goals. Although it originated in the 1940s, PPBS did not gain momentum until the 1960s.

According to Ubben and Hughes (1997), PPBS involves five steps:

1. Establish the general goals to be achieved.
2. Identify the specific objectives that define this goal.
3. Develop the program and processes that it is believed will achieve the objectives and goals.

4. Establish the formative and summative evaluation practices.
5. Implement a review and recycle procedure that indicates whether or not, or the degree to which, the program and processes resulted in the achievement of the objectives and the goals, and, if not, to help determine other procedures, processes, and programs. (p. 308)

Program budgets are not increased incrementally, but require leadership to decide how much to spend on achieving program goals and objectives. The administrator might select a more favorable alternative for one program and a less favorable one for another based on cost-and-benefit analysis. Candoli, Hack, Ray, and Stollar (1984) maintain that PPBES is a cyclical process that constantly requires feedback. The two-way arrows in Figure 12.3 depict the recursive nature of this budgeting approach. One disadvantage of PPBES is that it is far more time-consuming than other budgeting approaches and may not provide as efficient fiscal control; it is, however, excellent for planning purposes.

Zero-Based Budgeting

Zero-based budgeting requires administrators to justify all expenditures on an annual basis. Thus, starting with a zero amount, current and new expenditures must be fully justified so that monies can be allocated for them. Zero-based budgeting also requires yearly evaluations so that priorities based on program evaluation data can be set.

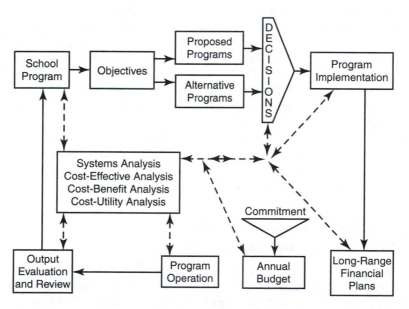

FIGURE 12.3   Illustration of way in which Planning, Programming, Budgeting, Evaluation System (PPBES) might work.

According to Bliss (1994) zero-based budgeting involves five steps:

1. Identify decision units (defined as any programs that consume resources).
2. Analyze decision packages (documents that describe a decision's objectives, activities, resources, and costs).
3. Rank decision packages.
4. Allocate funds.
5. Prepare official budgets.

One of the key benefits is that functions or programs can be ranked as to desirability and marginal activities can be identified. Administrators can reassess their operations from the ground up and justify every dollar spent in terms of current goals. However, the major focus is typically on those program increments that are just above or below the projected funding level. The heart of zero-based budgeting is, therefore, the ranking process.

This ranking procedure establishes priorities among the decision packages. The give-and-take of the political process is vital in determining priorities. Forecast revenues determine the budget amount; packages can be accepted up to this spending level. One disadvantage to zero-based budgeting is its time intensiveness. A major advantage is the elimination of expenditures that were valid in the past but are no longer relevant.

Incremental Budgeting

The most common budgeting in schools is incremental budgeting, which involves adding to or subtracting from the current year's budget. Budget development for the current year begins with the previous year's budget. An assumption is made that the upcoming year's budget will be similar to the current year's. Last year's programs are regarded as a base and allowed to grow by some fixed percent; whatever resources are left over are then assigned to new or improved programs.

Incremental budgeting does not include formal evaluation of needs and programs. Often programs that do not necessarily fulfill existing needs continue to be allocated monies, while more effective, newer programs may go underfunded. These are serious problems for a nation calling for greater accountability. Items such as special programs and facility renovations are handled separately. Additionally, money coming from federal sources is usually addressed separately.

School-Based Management (SBM) and School-Based Budgeting

School-based management (SBM), or site-based management as it is sometimes called, can be defined as a "process that involves the individuals responsible for implementing decisions in actually making those decisions" (AASA, 1998, p. 18). In general, schools that have SBM have more authority at the school site than do others. This greater autonomy at the building level may include more local control over the budget as well. In SBM schools a school council makes program and fiscal decisions.

School-based budgeting typically includes additional local control in budget planning and expenditures. It involves developing "strategies to both create a workable budget and to obtain the consensus of the staff for its approval" (Herman & Herman, 1993, p. 106).

> What budgeting approach(es) might help the school-site council at Meadows High School in reallocating funds for the science and computer labs? How might it help?

Activity Funds

Typical student activity funds include accounts for student organizations (e.g., sports clubs, student council), profit earnings (e.g., concessions and school pictures), special-purpose accounts (e.g., field trips, hospitality), and others. Monitoring accounts is essential to a well-managed school.

The Association for School Business Officials (ASBO) has recommended twelve guidelines for managing student activity accounts (Box 12.3 on page 362).

Fiscal Accounting

Fiscal stewardship is of the utmost importance and is a responsibility that no administrator should take lightly. The funds an administrator allocates each day are public funds, and there is an inherent expectation that they will be accounted for properly.

Once the budget for the school district has been approved, it is the responsibility of the administration to ensure that the money that has been appropriated is expended properly. Fiscal accountability is maintained through the district's accounting system and its reporting, auditing, and inventory procedure.

Administrators must maintain accurate records of all money spent and received during the fiscal cycle and provide an accurate accounting at the end of the budget year. Administrators must be knowledgeable and skilled in maintaining accounts for revenues and expenditures as well as for inventories of materials and equipment. The accounting system must adequately control requisitions, purchase orders, contracts, payments, claims, payrolls, and other actions influencing the assets of the organization. The expectation is that all records will be accurate and provide assurance to the board that its financial policies are being observed.

The typical accounting system is described as a double-entry system. *Double entry* means that two accounts are affected by each entry. For example, the most common entry would be to increase (purchase) an asset and to decrease capital (money) or to increase

BOX **12.3**

ASBO Guidelines for Managing Student Activity Accounts

1. All money received should be acknowledged by issuing prenumbered receipts or prenumbered tickets to the person from whom the money is received.
2. Deposits should be made daily if possible. Cash should never be left in the school over the weekend or holidays.
3. Receipts should be issued to the person making the deposit. Deposit slips should be retained by both the depositor and the school accountant or bookkeeper.
4. Purchase orders or requisitions should be initiated by the person in charge of the activity fund.
5. Payments should be made by check, prepared and mailed from the business office to the payee.
6. The principal should designate two or more persons in addition to himself or herself who will be authorized to sign checks. Two of the three authorized signatures should also be required for all withdrawals.
7. No payment should be made unless supported by a written purchase order and by a signed invoice certifying receipt of merchandise and accuracy of prices.
8. Student-activity funds should not be used for any purchase which represents a loan or accommodation to any school district employee or other nonstudent. Emergency loans may be made to students for lunches, carfare, and the like on written permission of the principal. Individuals may not make purchases through the student body in order to take advantage of better prices.
9. Student bodies may enter contracts for the purchase of supplies, equipment, and services from an approved vendor provided the term of the contract is within the tenure of the students of the school (usually three years).
10. The student body should operate on a budget reflecting past experience and future plans; like the school and school district budget, the student budget should serve as a guide for the year's financing activities.
11. Student activity books and financial procedures should be subjected to periodic internal and external audits. An annual examination by outside, independent accountants is also recommended.
12. Regular reports (monthly and annual) should be prepared and submitted to the principal, business office, or any others responsible for the supervision of student activity funds.

a liability (debt to creditors). Transactions are entered into the accounts as debits and credits. A debit typically increases an asset or decreases a capital or liability account. A credit can have at least nine different effects on the school system's financial books. The debits and credits in all the school system's accounts must be equal, and all assets, resources, and liabilities must be accounted for in the financial records. The books in which financial records are maintained are called journals or ledgers. The journal provides a historic record of all transactions, and the ledger provides all transactions made to a given account.

The following is an example of a journal entry for the purchase of laboratory equipment for $600.00 and supplies for $130.00, setting up an accounts payable category:

Sept. 18	Laboratory equipment (17)	$600.00	
	Supplies (22)	130.00	
	Account payable (86)		$730.00

When the school system receives the laboratory equipment and supplies and pays the creditor, the entry would be as follows:

| Sept. 30 | accounts payable (86) | $730.00 | |
| | cash (1) | | $730.00 |

The general ledger accounts for these transactions would look like this:

Assets		Liabilities	
Cash *(1)*		*Accounts Payable* *(86)*	
Beginning Balance	20,000	Beginning Balance	1000
Payment of A/P	(730)	Purchase of Lab Equipment	600
Ending Balance	19,270	Purchase of Supplies	130
		Payment	(730)
		Ending Balance	1000

Lab Equipment (17)	
Beginning Balance	15,000
Purchase	600
Ending Balance	15,600

Supplies (22)	
Beginning Balance	2,600
Purchase	130
Ending Balance	2,730

Each school system has its own procedures for maintaining fiscal accountability, but the administrator or his or her designee is expected to code expenditures properly and follow accounting system procedures to accurately maintain ledger accounts and a cash receipt and payment journal. One of the most important decisions an administrator makes is selecting financial officers and bookkeepers to help maintain the financial records. Nonetheless, the administrator is ultimately responsible and should understand accounting procedures.

The Audit

Checking for accuracy in accounting is referred to as auditing. Internal and external audits should be conducted regularly, and reports should be prepared. Most states require that a certified public accountant conduct an external audit on an annual or bi-annual basis. It is in the best interests of the school that audits be conducted regularly to maintain credibility and accountability. An administrator should ensure that an audit has been completed before taking responsibility for a budget.

> What accountability procedures need to be addressed at Meadows High?

Acquiring, Allocating, and Accounting for Resources

RICHARD A. KING
University of Northern Colorado

Acquisition of adequate resources to attain performance goals challenges educational leaders at all levels. Finding funds for desired programs entails several aspects of school finance: (1) gathering resources, which is often referred to as a *revenue* dimension; (2) directing appropriate resources to educational programs, which forms an *allocation* dimension; and (3) ensuring that resource use makes a difference in program outcomes, which entails both a *management* function (to be sure resources are directed where intended) and an *accountability* dimension (to relate allocations to school performance measures).

Balancing Uniformity and Local Control

The revenue dimension, once the domain of legislators, school boards, and county assessors, today involves educational leaders at all levels. As attention continues to shift from local and state governments to ever-broadening sources of money, leaders will wrestle with conflicting demands for equalization and local control. Superintendents and principals will be asked to ensure that all schools can have access to similar resources, while simultaneously striving to make each school responsive to teachers' and parents' desires for funds to support perceived needs.

Many state courts concluded that wealth-based spending inequities violate state constitutions' equal-protection provisions or articles mandating "uniform" or "thorough and efficient" educational systems. Other courts upheld finance policies, finding that revenue variations do not deny equal protection, since they are a consequence of legitimate state interests in maintaining local control over schooling. State legislatures responded to judicial and political pressures to equalize resources, and in the 1990s the average state share rose to 48 percent—exceeding the local contribution of 45 percent—with the remainder financed by federal revenue.

Partnerships with businesses, educational foundations, and sales of advertising space on facilities and buses have promised new resources. These funds, however, account for but a small portion of total revenue, and, like property taxation, they raise questions about resulting inequities when opportunities to generate new resources differ greatly from community to community.

School and district personnel continue to walk the fine line between the goal of equalized educational opportunities, as represented by somewhat equal resources for all pupils' education, and the goal of responsiveness to community demands. Leaders will be increasingly pressed to secure more revenue to expand programs, obtain essential instructional materials and technologies, finance necessary professional development, and be competitive with private schools and charter schools. Educational leaders will address such questions as: Will our school community be satisfied with the level of resources provided through traditional channels, or will we aggressively seek additional resources to meet parental demands and student needs despite resulting inequities among schools?

Deciding Priorities When Allocating Resources

Just as equality and local control goals influence revenue policies, desires to improve efficiency shape many allocation decisions. Planning and budgeting frameworks help school personnel determine goals and objectives, the most cost-effective mix of human and material resources to reach goals, the funds necessary to deliver programs, and evaluation of outcomes in relation to resources as new budget cycles begin. These budget development processes raise questions about priorities. The questions are often answered in ways that reflect program needs and productivity measures.

The difficulty of reaching consensus about priorities among stakeholders makes the allocation dimension highly political. For this reason, it is tempting to adopt an incremental approach and thus ease tensions by increasing all prior budgets by a given percentage. However, as new instructional approaches and technologies emerge, as program demands shift along with a school's demography, and as the productivity of traditional programs is challenged, discussions about resource priorities are inevitable.

In the context of school-based decision making, budget decisions will increasingly be made at building levels. Allocations among existing and proposed programs will challenge educational leaders to address many questions, including: Will we incrementally raise all current program budgets, or will we examine which instructional approaches and consequent resource allocations best enable school personnel to meet changing student needs and improve student performance?

Accounting for the Use of Financial Resources

Budget management and accounting functions within central offices and schools are concerned primarily with ensuring the lawful use of public money within designated funds. This dimension of school finance has been expanded in recent years to embrace a broader accountability function, that of relating resource decisions to improvements in program outcomes.

Relationships between human and financial inputs and resulting outcomes define a traditional view of school productivity and efficiency. Another perspective on efficiency calls for maximizing the satisfaction of consumers—parents, students, employers, and legislators—at the same or perhaps at an even lower investment of society's resources. Concerns about school performance have impelled parents to seek vouchers and the privatizing of school management and instructional delivery.

An emerging policy direction is to induce school improvement and greater efficiency through performance-based school finance. This entrepreneurial restructuring of schools aligns resources, as well as potential sanctions, with state standards and assessments. By rewarding those schools or districts whose students' performance meets desired standards or whose performance improves toward such targets, this approach is intended to stimulate school leaders and teachers to redesign curriculum and instruction in ways that achieve educational reform goals. There are concerns, however, that "high-stakes" accountability brings such unintended consequences as narrowing curricula around tested topics, displacing testing purposes from a classroom to a state accountability focus, and diminishing morale, which follows negative publicity when performance targets are missed.

(continued)

Continued

To the degree that program and financial accountability relates future school resources to performance, educational leaders will address questions such as: Will budget management be primarily concerned with proper accounting for revenue and expenditures within designated funds, or will we also lead schools in ways that help all personnel to maximize the results of programs financed by those resources—and ultimately strengthen public accountability and support for public education?

Managing School Supplies and Equipment

Managing school supplies includes purchasing, storing, distributing, and accounting. Computer programs can be particularly helpful in managing supplies and equipment. Table 12.4 describes the process of purchasing and control and enumerates those responsible for the process.

Maintaining School Buildings and Grounds

Creating a meaningful and appropriate learning environment for students is a challenge for educators. It demands not only an excellent curriculum but also designing, and maintaining the school building and grounds. Anne Bullock and Elizabeth Foster-Harrison (1997) describe twelve requisite factors of the school environment: furniture, color, aesthetics, carpet, building and grounds maintenance, decorating detail, comfort, space and design, lighting, classroom elements (e.g., ceiling fans, sinks), instructional items (e.g., areas for displaying student work), and professional items (e.g., access to a telephone).

How will you include needed improvements for the building and grounds in your proposal?

School Safety

Creating a safe and secure learning environment requires that possible threats be identified. According to Flanary (1997) security problems and climate problems are the two sources of threats. He recommends that a physical security review be conducted periodically. It should include the following locations and equipment:

Bus and transportation areas
Open areas

TABLE 12.4   The Supply Process and Its Control

Process of Purchasing and Control	Staff Member of Department Involved in Process
1. Develop standard list of supplies and equipment	1. By users in cooperation with business manager
2. Stock catalogs refined from standard list; includes all possible supplies normally handled with necessary ordering data	2. Business office
3. Annual supply and equipment request (detailed statement of requirements for year)	3. Entire staff, including teachers and custodians
4. Budget document (listing, in general, supplies and equipment authorized and money available)	4. Supply and equipment budget developed by business office, approved by superintendent and board of education
5. Requisition and approval	5. Initiated by individual approved by designated administrative officer
6. Purchase order	6. Designated purchasing office
7. Note of receipt in good order	7. Receiving clerk
8. Spot-checks made on weight, quality, and quantity; notations made	8. Business office
9. Material placed in supply or equipment accounting ledger	9. Supply clerk
10. Bill paid by accounting office	10. Sent to accounting office by purchasing officer
11. Distribution records material sent to accountable individual buildings, based on annual requests and periodic requisitions	11. Principal of school
12. Building distribution personnel records each teacher who gets basic supplies at beginning of year and periodically as requested	12. Principal administers. May be coordinated with central office computer
13. User accountability: user signs for supplies	13. Users (teacher, custodians, etc.) and equipment in room at beginning of year; list provided by supply clerk
14. User "use" chart: materials checked off as used; form provided by supply, appraisal may be computerized	14. User (teacher, custodian, etc.)
15. Spot-checks and inspections	15. Business office and principal
16. Yearly inventory of all areas of supply storage	16. Business office (supply)
17. Use charts, reports, summaries	17. Business office (supply)

School grounds
Parking lots
Athletic fields and courts
Outbuildings
Gymnasium
Main building exterior
Entrances
Hallways and stairwells
Restrooms
Cafeteria
High-value rooms (Computer storage, A-V storage, musical instrument storage)
Classroom instructional areas
Library
Science and technology laboratories
Storage rooms
Conference and common use rooms
Office areas
Interior and exterior lighting
Smoke and fire detectors
Fire alarm system
Fire extinguishers
Hazardous waste disposal equipment
Emergency chemical showers and eye baths

Develop a safe school plan for Meadows High.

Conclusion

School administrators must have a basic understanding of how schools are financed. There are various sources for school revenues, and some sources have a more important role than others in revenue generation. As the next century begins, issues in generating revenue and allocating resources for schools will continue to dominate the discussion at both the state and national levels.

As additional leadership roles expand to the building level, it becomes even more crucial for administrators, teachers, staff, and community members to better understand fiscal issues. Clearly, finding new and creative sources for obtaining funds will dominate the discussion at the local level.

In addition to the acquisition of resources, budgeting, accounting, and maintenance are vital to a well-managed school. Planning, management, and control each play their own distinctive part in the complete budgeting and accounting process. One does not operate at the expense of the other; rather they all coexist as multiple purposes of fiscal stewardship. The school administrator must work in collaboration with faculty and staff to ensure an appropriate and inviting school environment.

PORTFOLIO ARTIFACTS

1. Compare and contrast the school budgets of two schools within the same district and between two different districts.

2. Collaborate with colleagues in your school or in your internship site school in writing a small grant. When you have completed the project, describe in writing what you learned.

3. Investigate a school that has a foundation. Interview some of the people on the foundation's committee. How did the foundation first begin? How does it currently operate? Describe in writing what you learned about school foundations from your interviews.

4. Examine a safety plan for a school. What is included in the plan? Who is involved in implementing it?

5. Observe the school auditing process.

6. Work with the bookkeeper to make entries in a school's accounting records or follow a purchase order through the system.

7. Attend a school board meeting at which the budget is discussed.

TERMS

ADA	PPBS	Vouchers
Flat-grant model	PPBES	Weighted-student model
Foundation concept	SBM	Zero-based budgeting
Power-equilizing model	School foundation	

SUGGESTED READINGS

Burrupe, P., Brimley, V., & Garfield, R. (1999). *Financing education in a climate of change.* Boston: Allyn & Bacon.

Drake, T., & Roe, W. H. (1994). *School business management: Supporting instructional effectiveness.* Boston: Allyn & Bacon.

Ruskin, K. B., & Achilles, C. M. (1995). *Grantwriting, fundraising and partnerships: Strategies that work!* Thousand Oaks, CA: Corwin Press.

Schools in the middle (November/December 1997). NASSP middle level education (entire issue devoted to facilities design and management).

Swanson, A., & King, R (1997). *School finance: Economics and politics.* White Plains, NY: Longman.

Thurow, L. (1996). *The future of capitalism.* New York: Simon & Schuster.

CHAPTER

13 Problem-Based Learning Projects

This chapter contains four problem-based learning (PBL) projects. It is recommended that only one project be used in a typical 3-credit university course. The instructor and students might decide to use the same PBL project with more than one group, or different groups could complete different projects at the same time. Project selection might depend on the interests of students and the level of school (elementary, middle, or high school, or school district) in which they would like to focus their learning. Table 13.1 lists the main features of each project.

Problem-Based Learning

Problem-based learning (PBL) is an instructional approach that uses typical problems of practice as the context for an in-depth investigation of core content. According to Bridges and Hallinger (1995) PBL has five elements:

1. The starting point for learning is a problem.
2. The problem is one that students are apt to face as future professionals.
3. The knowledge that students are expected to acquire during their professional training is organized around problems rather than disciplines.
4. Students, individually and collectively, assume a major responsibility for their own instruction and learning.
5. Most of the learning occurs within the context of small groups rather than lectures. (p. 6)

A key part of PBL involves the nature of the problems used in a project. Leithwood, Begley, and Cousins (1994) categorize problems that confront educational leaders into two types: high ground and swampy. They discuss the characteristics of preparation programs for developing expert school leaders and urge programs to focus on "swampy" problems. High-ground problems are those "of a more technical nature, where a well-rehearsed procedure for solving [is] available" (p. 53). Swampy problems are complex, at least to the person who has to solve them. The authors explain that problems are swampy when "one only vaguely understands the

TABLE 13.1 Main Features of PBL Projects

Project Name	Grade Level	Related Chapters	Related Topics and Concepts
Safe Havens	K–8	1, 3, 5, 6, 9, 10, 11	Service Integration Partnerships Grant writing Site-based management Transformational leadership Facilities management and allocation Change
A Jalapeño in a Candy Jar	Middle school	3, 4, 6, 7, 8, 9, 10, 11	Cultural diversity Change Staff development Curriculum Learning theory Equity, student rights Central office and board roles
Atoms and Bits	High school	2, 3, 4, 5, 6, 8, 10, 11, 12	Technology Staff development Change Curriculum Program evaluation Instruction
Marveling at the Results	School district	1, 2, 3, 5, 6, 7, 8, 10, 11, 12	Leadership style Staff development School improvement Organizational structure Reform

present situation, has no clear way of knowing what solutions would be superior, and lacks procedures for addressing the obstacles or constraints in the situation" (p. 43). Given the vast array of constituents and needs that face school administrators, it is crucial that the preparation of future educational leaders focus on solving swampy, ill-structured problems.

At the same time, educational administration students need to have conversations with experts to probe how effective practitioners solve identical or similar problems. Working with real audiences for the culminating activity of the PBL project, as well as people used to developing solutions to problems, affords students opportunities to learn how experts engage in problem solving and reflection. The goal of such reflection is for the learner to examine swampy problems by analyzing, exploring, gathering data, and critiquing.

Leithwood (1995), for example, discusses the high level of reflection that was an integral part of the problem-solving practice of reputationally effective superintendents he studied. Similarly, Schön (1987) advocates "reflection-in-action through which practitioners sometimes make new sense of uncertain, unique, or conflicted situations of practice" (p. 39). Schön maintains that if instructors encourage reflection, students will not assume "that existing professional knowledge fits every case nor that every problem has a right answer" (p. 39). Reflective thinking is crucial to helping educational leaders improve their problem-solving expertise.

In the real world of schools, problems are not solved independently. The complexity of the problems addressed by school leaders requires collaboration. Collaboration requires learning to listen to others, collectively reviewing outcomes, and responding to and partaking of relevant discussion. Vygotsky's (1978) concept of the "zone of proximal development" may be particularly relevant to PBL. As discussed in Chapter 8, this zone is the gap between a person's individual capacity for problem solving and the capacity of the group or peer with whom the learner is working. The group processes of discussing and critically reflecting afford the individual learner opportunities to internalize the group's problem-solving capacities. Ultimately, the ability to show good judgment, take control of situations, and communicate effectively will determine the success of solutions to problems, pinpoint perceptions, rank options, and resolve the issue at hand. The leader's future effectiveness depends on how well he or she handles problems, whether they are high ground or swampy.

Because learning group-processing skills is essential to problem-based learning, peer and instructor feedback are integral components of projects. Students are usually asked to reflect on their role in the group with peers, and instructors provide feedback to students about those roles. Part of a discussion might include exploring why certain decisions have been made and how other factors might be involved. Thus, opportunities for what Argyris (1982) calls *double-loop learning* can be built into the feedback and assessment process.

Problem-Based Learning in Educational Leadership

ED BRIDGES
Stanford University

PHILIP HALLINGER
Vanderbilt University

Problem-based learning (PBL) provides a context in which participants can develop various leadership skills, acquire the knowledge needed to deal with problems of leadership, and experience what it means and feels like to be a leader. PBL develops leaders who solve problems through thoughtful deliberation with people who have a stake in the outcome and, in the end, are committed to implementing the group's decision.

When people first encounter PBL, they often initially feel "lost at sea." The sea can become rough as the group struggles with defining the problem and agreeing on what should be done about it. If a lot of wheel-spinning occurs and deep divisions develop within the group, the experience can be less than satisfying, result in a shoddy product, and thwart learning. Over the years we have learned that these undesirable consequences can be minimized or avoided by using particular methods and techniques. In this brief commentary we share some of what we have learned with you.

Group Size

Through experimenting with various group sizes, we have discovered that groups of six or seven members are ideal and are large enough to permit members to occupy and learn different roles (e.g., leader, facilitator, recorder, group member). Moreover, groups of this size afford opportunities for everyone to participate and contribute ideas. Three-person groups are especially troublesome because there is an inherent tendency in these groups for two people to form an alliance against the third. As groups increase in size beyond seven, they constrain the amount of "airtime" each member can have. The potential for problems to develop that interfere with group functioning increases unless an extremely skilled facilitator guides the discussion.

Method for Conducting Effective Meetings

The vast majority of people have worked in groups; some have undoubtedly wasted time and accomplished little, and others have worked much more efficiently and effectively. When groups go awry, people tend to attribute their difficulties to personality clashes. While these clashes may account in part for troubles in the group, more often discord is due primarily to a lack of methods for conducting effective meetings.

In our search for ways to assist groups in functioning more effectively, we have introduced them to the interaction method (Doyle & Straus, 1982). Groups that use this method initially find it too constraining; the discomfort gradually disappears, however, as group members begin to internalize the method and acquire the skills and tools. Occasionally, after trying it once or twice, groups abandon the method on the grounds that they function well together and do not need such a method. Typically, these groups run into difficulty and revert to the interaction method with a greater appreciation of the contribution it makes to effective group functioning.

Criteria for Problem Framing and Analysis

Learning in PBL, as the term implies, begins with a problematic situation. Some problems are fairly well structured, and others are ill-structured, messy, complex, and multifaceted. Identifying and stating the problem concisely poses a challenge for most people. The vast majority of PBL groups rush to solve the problem without fully understanding it. Yet, as Dewey (1910) and others have taught us, "A problem well-defined is half solved." Unless the problem is well-defined, problem solvers may follow a path that fails to remedy the existing situation while creating additional difficulties in the process because they fail to consider an adequate range of alternative courses of action.

To facilitate the problem-framing phase of the problem-solving process, we have found it beneficial to provide PBL groups with two criteria for evaluating the adequacy of a problem statement. The first criterion underscores the importance of stating the problem without embedding a solution in it. Groups commonly incorporate a solution into their statement of the problem, thus shutting off consideration of solution alternatives. A brief example may help to clarify this point.

In a Desert Survival exercise we use in our leadership program, groups either bypass the problem-framing stage or frame the problem as "Should we stay at the crash site, or should we leave and walk to safety?" Either of these formulations of the problem contains a solution to the "real" problem: "How can we survive?" The choice the group makes, to stay or leave, has profound consequences on its chances of survival. Groups that identify the "real" problem are much more likely to make the right choice of whether to stay or leave.

In addition to the solution-free criterion for judging the adequacy of a problem statement, we encourage PBL participants to look for facts in the problem scenario that support their definition of the problem. By testing their definition of the problem against the facts contained in the description of the problem, participants have a basis for evaluating their particular definition of the problem.

Use of Resources

With many PBL projects, the instructor supplies a list of resources that may have relevance to the problem; in some instances, the instructor also includes a copy of the suggested readings. Group members often decide to assign each person a

(continued)

Continued

different set of readings. At the next meeting of the group, members take turns providing brief synopses of what they have read. Having completed their reading "assignments," they turn to attacking the problem. By following this procedure, group members are apt to focus simply on the knowledge without regard to its application and may compromise their own in-depth knowledge of the content.

Because knowledge and application are of equal importance in PBL, we encourage group members to postpone reading the pertinent resources until they agree on a formulation of the problem. As individuals proceed to read the material, they ask themselves a question such as, "How does what I read apply to the problem we are facing?" When reporting back to the group, members discuss how what they have read may apply to their problem. If two members read the same material, they can share their perspectives on the same issue. We have learned that group members are much more likely to use the knowledge in solving the problem if they study the resources after, not before, they have framed it.

Facilitating Groups

The Institute for Development of Educational Activities, Inc. I/D/E/A has been involved in a number of projects that require the development of effective facilitator skills. The following discussion of group facilitation is based on the I/D/E/A projects.

The success of the group in solving problems is interrelated with the facilitator's ability to help the group work as a productive team. Group members enter the team with highly developed perspectives, knowledge, and talents, and the initial task of the facilitator is to help create a sense of collegiality that fosters personal growth and improvement efforts on a continuing basis (Cunningham & Gresso, 1993). The facilitator works with the group to establish a climate of mutual understanding, trust, and commitment to work together as a team to develop the best possible solution to the problem at hand. Facilitation requires a sensitivity to and appreciation of the diverse talents on the team and the skill to value each person's unique contribution to the group. The ability to model positive reinforcement of members but also to stick to a reasonable plan of action is essential for a successful group leader. The facilitator must be nonthreatening, supportive, and positive.

Facilitators do not provide the answers; rather, they are neutral servants of the group. Group members clarify their thinking by expressing their perspectives and attaining consensus relative to the solution to the problem. One of the key decisions a facilitator makes is when to keep quiet and when to intervene in the group.

The major role of the facilitator is to:

- Build the capacities and stature of group members
- Nurture diverse values and perspectives among group members
- Create ownership among group members
- Nurture creative thoughts of others
- Ask questions that help members rethink positions
- Ensure that team members identify resources, outside information, and ideas needed to address the problem

- Use effective, solid, time-tested group processes to maximize the efficacy of the group and its individual members
- Demonstrate effective listening, processing, and communication skills
- Encourage goal-directed behavior and foster a patient and encouraging environment

Depending on the approach used for the division of duties for team members playing various roles, the facilitator's tasks may include working with team members to develop schedules, agendas, and assignments in regard to solving the problem. There is no room for mechanistic answers in this fluid environment; success depends on everyone's using good judgment. The facilitator should begin by establishing mutual understanding of why the group exists and setting forth what will happen. Members should be encouraged to be open, take risks, share expertise, stay focused, and suspend judgment until the problem has been solved.

To be successful, group members need to be able to solve problems together and make effective decisions to which they are all committed. Cunningham and Gresso (1993) state, "The role of the group facilitator is to provide support by serving as a catalyst during the consideration, discussion, and resolution phase of team deliberation" (p. 23). The facilitator should help the group to be aware of the needs of the individual members and assisting the group to focus on its purpose. "The facilitator models appropriate forms of participation and assists the individual to be as effective as possible. The main function of the facilitator is to continuously encourage and support human development, resulting in individual, team, and organizational improvement" (p. 243).

Group and Team Processing Skills

DONN GRESSO, Professor
East Tennessee State University

According to the ISLLC Standards for School Leaders (1996; see Chapter 1) school administrators should not only possess effective problem-framing and problem-solving skills, but they should also be able to communicate effectively and use conflict-resolution skills, group-processing skills and consensus-building skills. One exciting aspect of a problem-based learning approach to educational administration is the ample opportunity for students of educational leadership to practice these skills and receive immediate feedback from instructors and fellow students.

As you work in groups during your problem-based learning projects, I suggest the following:

- Designate roles such as facilitator, manager, and recorder for each session.
- Create ground rules before beginning. Personal attacks, putdowns, and name-calling should not be allowed.
- Designate a person to set the agenda before each meeting. Include allotted times for each item.
- Adhere to the agenda unless the group decides to alter it.
- Confront behavior that diverts the group from reaching its desired outcomes.
- If there is tension, address it directly. For conflict to be productive, it should be focused on the issue, rather than on the person.

(continued)

Continued

- Agree on a process to use (e.g., the interaction method, the nominal group technique, brainstorming, force-field analysis)
- Encourage all group members to share their knowledge on the issue at hand.
- Record information in a way that is visible to all group members as ideas are discussed (e.g., use an overhead projector, chart, computer display).
- Get agreement on action steps, and responsibilities, and set dates for completion of tasks.
- Debrief all meetings. Discuss the strengths of the people who played specific roles as well as other group members. Provide at least one "stretcher" for all members including people with specific roles. A "stretcher" is a comment that will help the group member improve his or her group facilitation skills.

The role of facilitator is a key one for all groups. Each student at some point in his or her leadership preparation program should have an opportunity to serve as group facilitator. Being an effective group facilitator includes using effective listening and conflict-management skills and dealing with the many other challenges groups typically face.

Another role that the group may want to consider is that of process observer. The process observer can have a dual role, that of regular team member and observer of the group, or the process observer may be an outsider with the sole purpose of observing. The process observer examines the way the team goes about its work. This modus operandi is then reviewed during the debriefing session held at the conclusion of each group meeting. Several important objectives in this process are:

- to learn from the experiences that take place during the meeting or PBL session.
- to develop ownership in the results of the day's agenda.
- to assist members individually and as a group in developing more effective group behaviors.

- to give positive reinforcement regarding actions that contributed to the team's results.
- to think about and record the events of the PBL session as a connected whole, seeing the interrelationships between the various parts of the session—the timing and sequence; the types of activities and the level of participation—and how together they relate to the objectives of the project.

The group should charge the process observer with looking for specific characteristics of affective small group functioning. The process observer then assesses to what degree these criteria are met and provides feedback to the group that helps them in becoming more effective. Feedback includes examples of the presence or absence of each criterion. It is best to allow the process observer to report what he or she observed without discussion. All team members can reflect on the process observer's report and decide for themselves how they might alter their own behavior during the next group meeting.

An example of some of the possible criteria that the process observer can look for include:

1. The group's task is clear and deemed important by all members.
2. Group members feel free to express themselves.
3. Responsibilities involved in getting the work done are shared.
4. Actions to be taken are made clear and explicit.
5. Good communication skills are practiced.
6. The way the group goes about doing its work is reviewed periodically.
7. The problem is well defined.

Keep in mind that improving the learning from group activities is the goal. Feedback gives group members information about how effective their work or actions appear to be. Feedback should be descriptive, both positive and negative, specific, directed at performance or changeable behavior, solicited, and provided immediately after work is completed.

Texts and materials that focus on group processing, such as those by Doyle and Straus

(1982), Corey and Corey (1987), and Robbins and Finley (1995) and the many materials on working with groups published by the Study Cir-cles Resource Center (e-mail: scrc@neca.com), will assist students of educational leadership in improving their group-processing skills.

PROJECT

1

Safe Havens: Developing School-Based Health Clinics

ELLEN SMITH SLOAN
Southern Connecticut State University

The current health care crisis affecting the lives of significant numbers of children in the United States, as well as its connection to the public schools, is not a new phenom-enon. Poor health in America's underserved youth, inaccessibility to health care and health insurance, and the serious concerns about the welfare of children have resulted in "external shocks" (Jehl & Kirst, 1992, p. 27) to this country for more than two cen-turies. Furthermore, remediation for these shocks, to a greater or lesser extent, has often involved the public school system. "In 1839 Horace Mann voiced the need for [public] schools to give attention to health" (Cortese, 1993, p. 21), and as early as 1840 the populace of Concord, Massachusetts, "requested that physicians provide health care in their schools, just as they provided health care in other public institutions" (Kirby & Lovick, 1987, p. 139).

Although concern for children's health issues was voiced at this time, its expression was sporadic at best. Not until the Progressive Period (1890–1920), accompanied by mas-sive waves of immigration, did significant numbers of groups and individuals become more cognizant of the plight of America's children and begin to suggest that the public schools play a larger role. Not unlike much of the public discourse today, health care for underserved children became a topic that provoked differing viewpoints and often heated conflict (Raftery, 1992) in social and political discussions. "Activist writers like Jacob Riis...cast a bright light on the suffering of children—the wasting of a generation—and cried out for action" (Tyack, 1992, p. 20). Strong recommendations that the public school act as the vehicle for remedying these ills became an increasingly popular notion in the country (Wollons, 1992, Zigler, Kagan, & Klugman, 1983).

Today many public schools still find themselves faced with children's unresolved health issues. Social, emotional, and physical health problems all present themselves at the doorways of America's public schools. Aware of the political and fiscal realities of trying to assume total responsibility for these health concerns, schools and other community agencies have become creative in their strategies for meeting children's needs. An emerging phenomenon across the country has been the development of school-based health centers or clinics (SBHC), a type of interagency collaborative. Spurred on by recommendations from child advocacy groups urging schools and communities to collaborate in linking families with health and human service providers (Anne E. Casey Foundation, 1993; Children's Defense Fund, 1992), more than 570 SBHCs have been formed in over thirty-three states (*Education Week*, February 2, 1994), and the number continues to grow annually.

In 1967 Harvard Medical School professor Phillip Porter initiated the concept of school-based health centers in Cambridge, Massachusetts, in public elementary schools. Five separate agencies serving children were linked with these first Cambridge schools (Raftery, 1992). In 1975, impressed with the success of the Cambridge program, the Robert Wood Johnson Foundation made grants to three school systems. During this same time period, school-based health center projects were also initiated in Texas, Connecticut, Illinois, and Minnesota (Kirby & Lovick, 1987).

Great variety exists among present models of collaborative services for children; and within the generic categories of these models (school-based, school-linked, neighborhood-based, community-based) are widespread differences. Indeed, most people feel that these differences in interagency initiatives are healthy and allow those at local levels to be creative with networking, needs, and resources. Many eschew creating "cookie-cutter" designs for others to recreate. Knapp (1995) acknowledges the complexities (and the dangers) of labeling specific models and chooses to phrase the interagency process as "comprehensive, collaborative services for children and families" (p. 5).

Whatever the terminology, these efforts around the country require enormous amounts of energy and patience as well as new understandings as people from various professions and walks of life come together to plan, procure funding, designate space and services, and learn to cooperate and collaborate. Yet another dimension comes into play when these services are school based or school linked, as teachers and principals become integral players in an interagency collaborative comprising very different professions. Hooper-Briar and Lawson (1994) illuminate some of these interprofessional issues as they describe the "well-intentioned language of 'collaboration'—in reality most groups are cooperatives facing the challenge of working together" (p. 28). As Dryfoos (1994) quipped, collaboration is "an unnatural act between non-consenting adults" (p. 149).

Learning Objectives

- To broaden understanding of the concept of interagency collaboration, and specifically, the concept of a school-based health center

- To develop specific strategies for the implementation of a school-based health center
- To reflect, through group discussions, the extent to which deep beliefs and assumptions shape our "ways of doing and thinking" and hence play an important role in the decisions we make as educational leaders (see Chapter 1)
- To gain expertise in the art of discussing controversial and emotionally charged issues facing a school and its community
- To prepare short- and long-range plans for the development of a school-based health center
- To heighten the productivity of meetings through the strengthening of group interaction skills (see Chapter 6)
- To strengthen ability to conduct productive and inclusionary meetings (see Chapter 5)

Guiding Questions

1. If your school has a school-based health center (SBHC), reflect on the ways your school has involved the social worker or the school nurse in faculty meetings, social events, classroom activities, and other educational functions. Are they included? Do they feel a part of the school? Why or why not? How do you reach out to these adults from different professions (see Chapter 9)?

2. Thinking as a principal, what organizational processes, in your building, support and strengthen the work of the school nurse or social worker? What processes or structures impede their work?

3. Either before reading the following problem-based learning project or as you work on completing the project, visit a school with a SBHC. Make arrangements to talk with the principal, a professional who works in the SBHC, and a teacher. What information can you infuse into this project as a result of those conversations?

4. How would you involve parents and caregivers in the very early discussions of implementing an SBHC? Has your school involved parents and caregivers in other initiatives? Why or why not (see Chapters 5 and 6)?

5. Have you ever developed or considered developing a partnership with an outside agency? Has your school? Does the school already have a solid, albeit informal, relationship with the juvenile system or a hospital or shelter in your community? What works? What doesn't?

6. As you read this problem and gain insights from the readings and conversations with people from other professions, where do you think it best to initiate a health center for children: In the school building? On the school grounds but not inside the building? In the neighborhood or community? Explain your choice.

7. Issues always arise pertaining to what specific services should be offered to children in a health center. Reflect on your beliefs and assumptions. Learn your district's policies on what school nurses can and cannot do in regard to treating children for physical, social, or emotional needs.

The Problem

As you begin your third year as principal of A. M. McCabe School (K–8), increasing numbers of students are referred to the school nurse, the social worker, and your office. The lines of children with physical or social health concerns waiting outside these three office doors remain a persistent image in your head. Not only do you wonder how the nurse and social worker are handling it all, but you worry about the students' welfare, the academics they may be missing, and the disruptions to your teachers' classrooms. And what happens when the nurse and social worker are not in school? (Working hours for both the nurse and social worker are Monday, Wednesday, and Friday.)

The superintendent, extremely sympathetic to and supportive of your concerns at McCabe, did increase the hours of both the social worker and the nurse to the present level of three days a week. In addition, she redistributed monies to provide the K–3 grade levels with teacher aides. These improvements have mitigated teacher anxiety levels somewhat. Everyone realizes that these changes, though gratifying, barely tip the balance in favor of children. The superintendent has also broached the concerns of McCabe with the board of education, but the board cannot reach agreement on how to better meet the health needs of students.

Coupled with the discussions of scarce financial resources and the existence of twenty-five other schools in the district with similar issues is the belief many hold that schools are not in the business of resolving the serious physical and mental health needs of children; these people believe the school's focus ought to remain strictly on academic issues. Opponents also remind you that there is a community health center downtown to which all families can and should go. You've checked out that avenue as well and discovered that there are myriad reasons people do not use the city's community health center, including lack of transportation, erratic city bus schedules, its four-mile distance from the housing development where most students reside, presence in the home of infant siblings who cannot be left at home, complicated bureaucratic procedures and forms, and the absence of a concerned parent or caregiver.

Cognizant of the realities of what the district can actually do, you decide to take a grassroots approach and involve your faculty in the problem-solving process. A year ago you all met and voted to create a Faculty Council (eight of your thirty-four faculty members, the nurse, and the social worker). In addition to tackling academic issues facing the school, you encouraged the council to focus on children's unmet health needs. In the initial problem-solving sessions focusing on health issues, teachers talked about creating a business partnership with the school, with the ultimate goal that the partnership would lead to a short-term grant for additional health and human service personnel.

The pursuit of that line of thinking came up dry. Coupled with the fact that most business and industry had moved out of the city was the reality that the remaining companies were already committed to other programs and charities. Discussion also included exploring private philanthropic sources, providing children with transportation to the city's community health center, requesting pro bono work from community medical professionals, and writing to nationally based foundations. Despite roadblocks and unfamiliar territory for the council, you have felt continually buoyed up by the group's optimism, energy, and commitment to helping kids.

Two months ago you became aware of state grants to be awarded to schools and their local city boards and departments of health for the development of school-based health centers. (City boards and departments of health would actually oversee the administration of the centers.) The grant would be available for three years in the amount of $150,000 per year, per school. In addition to serving students who attended the school, the SBHC would also treat students' younger non–school-age siblings residing at home (birth to five years old).

After making the council aware of this opportunity, you requested the application materials. They arrived three weeks ago. You and the council shared the idea and application process with the entire faculty, who subsequently voted to have the school proceed with the idea.

The tenor of the faculty meeting was clearly optimistic—everyone appeared rejuvenated by this unique opportunity to change things. Without adding any doom-and-gloom comments, you also tried to balance the faculty's enthusiasm with some discussion that McCabe may not be awarded the grant. However, you could not help but feel caught up in their enthusiasm; it was like a light at the end of the tunnel. A school-based health center could be such a force in improving student health problems and afect their academic profiles as well.

You have approached the superintendent and city board of health about the grant, and they have encouraged you to pursue this path. The superintendent was impressed with your involvement of the council and faculty and believes that this ownership is a crucial step. To assist you with budgetary items and grant-writing language, she has asked the assistant superintendent to step into the process whenever you feel it appropriate. In addition, you have invited the nurse from the city's board of health, the agency that technically will be responsible for the SBHC's administrative structure, including the hiring and firing of personnel.

You've just taken a deep breath. It is time for the council's first work session toward actually completing the application. Only the nurse and social worker have some knowledge of what an SBHC is. This is new territory for your eight teachers on the council, as well as for you. The application guidelines are comprehensive, rigorous, and due in four weeks. Will the group be able to meet the deadline and do it well? Will individuals feel overwhelmed with the task or uncomfortable that the nurse and social worker know so much more than they? And in the back of your mind you are wondering whether you are leading the school down the "wrong" path. After all, you're just beginning to learn about SBHCs and haven't even had time to visit one. You also recognize a strong interest in the improvement of student performance on state assessments. If awarded the grant, how will you then deal with all the controversial health issues that are sure to arise with the board and other city taxpayers? Will you be able to gather board support? How will the sensationalizing local newspaper deal with the news? How will this affect other school iniatives?

It's 3:15 and you walk into the workroom. These questions will not stop whirling around in your head.

Grant Application: Questions and Areas to Address (Product Specifications)

1. Submit a written rationale for the creation of a school-based health center in your educational setting.

2. What children's health and human service needs will be addressed by the SBHC? Be specific about why the school has selected these needs.

3. List the people who will be involved in the development of the SBHC, including those involved in the preparation of this written application. (List people by profession and community role, not by name.)

4. Using the annual grant allocation of $150,000, outline the specific types of personnel (including hours and salaries but not names) who will be employed in the SBHC for each of the three years of the grant's duration. (*Special information for PBL participants:* Each SBHC must by law include the services of a medical doctor for at least three hours per week to oversee all medical procedures.)

5. What processes does the school plan to put into place to allow new health and human services personnel to interface with the current school nurse and social worker?

6. What processes and procedures will be initiated to encourage interprofessional understanding between the teaching faculty and health and human services professionals? How will the success of this effort be monitored over the three-year cycle?

7. Describe the process(es) by which teachers, parents and caregivers, and the media will be introduced to the concept of an SBHC.

8. Given the ethnic and cultural diversity of your school's population, how will the SBHC ensure that the health and human services needs of all children (and their families) will be best addressed?

9. What specific role(s) will the building administrator play in implementing, integrating, and sustaining the SBHC?

10. Where will the SBHC be located? Be specific about why its location is the most appropriate decision for your school. What is your rationale? (*Pertinent information for PBL participants:* The school has three options, all of which have the same square footage. The options are: (1) the room that adjoins the current school nurse's office, (2) the room that adjoins the principal's office, and (3) a modular unit on the school campus that is not accessible from the school building. Renovation costs for all three would be the same.

Profile of A. M. McCabe School

1. Grade Levels
K–8 (two classes per grade level)

2. **Total School Enrollment: 457**

   Race/Ethnicity Breakdown

Asian	10
Black	112
Hispanic	218
Native American	1
White	118

   Sex

Male	207
Female	250

3. **Average Class Size**

Kinder/Grade 1	24.5
Grades 2 and 3	25.0
Grades 4 and 5	26.5
Grades 6, 7, 8	25.0

4. **Special Program Enrollment** (by number)

Bilingual Education	180
ESL	9
Extended-Day Kindergarten	49
Special Education	
0.5 or fewer hours per week	40
0.5–15 hours per week	25
15 or more hours per week	27

5. **Other Student Needs** (by percentage)

Free or reduced-price meals	72.8%
Home language non-English	45% (approx.)

6. **Percentage of Students Returning to McCabe Each Year**

   Approximately 92%

7. **Levels of Absenteeism**

   Grades K–4—Approximately 10% of class per week
   Grades 5–8—approximately 13% of class per week

8. **Staffing**

Total Teaching Staff	34
Regular classroom	18
Art, Music, PE	5
Special education	5

Special programs
(ESL, bilingual)   6

Total administrative staff   1
Noncertified staff (aides)   8
Secretarial staff   1
School nurse (part-time)   1
Social worker (part-time)   1

9. Gender and Ethnicity of Teaching Staff
Female
    Asian   1
    African American   3
    Hispanic   5
    White   22
Male
    Hispanic   1
    White   2

10. Documented Reasons for Visits to the School Nurse
(Number per eight-month period)
    Temporary illness   202
    Chronic medical problems
    (ear, stomach, throat, eyes, bowels)   175
    Asthma related   52
    Dental pain   160
    Reproductive questions   32

Special Note: Many children with medical problems were referred to the community health center physicians or a family doctor (if the child had one). These other serious medical issues included children in need of: lead level tests, immunizations, physical examinations, respirators, ear infections leading to deafness, dental check-ups and related surgery, eye impairments, and physical injuries occurring at home or at school.

11. Documented Reasons for Visits to the School Social Worker
(Number per eight-month period)
    Reproductive questions   25
    Counseling issues with peers   180
    Family problems   125
    Substance abuse   36
    Academic issues   129

12. Family Involvement
McCabe has traditionally enjoyed family support for the school's mission of educating children, but actual involvement of parents and caregivers (e.g., conferences, volunteers, open house, PTO) has been limited. The limited involvement is due to the fact that 45 percent are from non–English-speaking homes as well as home- and job-related responsibilities. Two years ago the faculty, principal; and a small but energetic

PTO developed a plan to address these issues. A room adjacent to the entrance of the school was designated the "family room." Coffee and tea are always available, magazines and books are there for browsing, and children's work covers the walls. The principal, who also speaks Spanish, often stops in to chat with visitors. Judging from the guest book, parent/caregiver visits have become more frequent, and teachers report higher comfort levels and increased attendance in conferences.

13. Children in Single-Parent/Caregiver Homes

With mother	212
With father	8
With grandparent	18
Other caregivers	8
Total	246

14. McCabe's External Community

McCabe is a neighborhood school, and most children walk to school every morning. Homes include single-family low-income dwellings and two federally funded low-income housing developments.

The percentage of taxpayers in the city without children in school is 35 percent and the majority of this population is over 55 years old.

15. McCabe's School Governance Structure

School governance was very traditional for the twenty-five years preceding the arrival of the new principal. With the advent of the faculty council, decisions are beginning to involve the whole faculty. The principal hopes to involve parents in the near future.

RESOURCES

To obtain specific statistics and policies and procedures concerning health and related issues in your state, contact the following agencies; also refer to appropriate chapters within this book. Their data and other resources will strengthen knowledge and productivity levels of PBL project participants and instructor.

Anne E. Casey Foundation. Kids count data book: State profiles of child well-being. Washington, DC.

Children's Defense Fund. (1992). Leave no child behind: The state of America's children. Washington, DC.

Cortese, P. A. (1993). Accomplishments in comprehensive school health education. *Journal of School Health, 63*(1), 21–23.

General Accounting Office, Washington, DC.

Kirby, D., & Lorick, S. (1987). School-based health clinics. *Educational Horizons, 5*(3), 139–143.

State and City Departments/Bureaus of Health and Human Services

University of Colorado Health Sciences Center, Office of School Health. (Offers regular resource material on state and national school, health, and human service issues. Funded by U.S. Department of Health and Human Services. 4200 E. 9th Ave./Box C287, Denver, CO 80262.

Zigler, E., Kagan, S., & Klugman, E. (1983) *Children, families, and government.* Cambridge, England: Cambridge University Press.

2

A Jalapeño in a Candy Jar: Addressing Cultural Diversity

PAULA A. CORDEIRO
University of San Diego

One of the greatest challenges facing schools today is the diversity of the children at our doorsteps. The demographics of the United States are shifting in important ways. American families are rapidly becoming more diverse—the definition of what is meant by "family" is being reconceptualized. Increasing numbers of single-parent families, more families with stepchildren, more fathers raising children alone, and more mothers in the labor force are all factors. The cumulative effect of a significant influx of immigrants in the last thirty years promises to be both profound and interesting. Many of our recent immigrants represent cultural groups that have never immigrated to the United States before in significant numbers. These immigrants fall into three categories: refugees, legal immigrants, and undocumented immigrants. In absolute numbers, this migration is among the largest in U.S. history.

Most teachers and administrators have not been trained to deal with the unique needs these children bring to schoolhouse doors. The structural aspects of local governments in many cities and towns do not lend themselves easily to linking services that may be available to other community members and schoolchildren. Additionally, racism rises to the surface as jobs are lost and financial constraints on local governments increase.

School administrators are faced with these challenges in addition to continuing to promote instructional effectiveness. The success of dealing with these issues will be based in large part on educational administrators' ability to reshape schools' focus so that it ensures success for all students.

Learning Objectives

- To broaden understanding of cultural-diversity issues.
- To collaboratively develop a plan incorporating knowledge from research in multicultural education.
- To develop specific strategies for the implementation of multicultural programming.

■ To examine personal beliefs and assumptions about language and cultural issues.

Guiding Questions

1. Reflect on the ways in which your ethnic and racial background, gender, religion, ability or disability, and sexuality affect your beliefs. Share with your team some of your basic beliefs. How have they changed over time? Why?
2. Chapter 4 discusses a variety of social and cultural issues. Discuss this PBL project in relation to the deficit and difference theories discussed in Chapter 6.
3. Chapter 4 presents Sleeter and Grant's writings about five approaches to addressing cultural diversity. Reflecting on the curriculum of the school in which you are working or of schools in which you have worked, what approach to addressing cultural diversity is used?
4. What should a school administrator know about issues related to cultural diversity? Do you know these things? If so, how did you learn them? If not, how might you learn them?
5. What should a teacher know about cultural diversity? If a teacher has had little training in this area, what are the best ways for him or her to learn more?
6. What roles, if any, should parents, families, school boards, and community members play in working with schools? In the case of Seaview School District, and Silvermine Middle School in particular (see below), how might they be actively involved in multicultural educational programming?
7. How might Banks' (1994) (see Chapter 4) "Approaches to Multicultural Curriculum Model" be applied to this situation?
8. Chapters 8, 9, 10, and 11 discuss legal and ethical considerations, learning, learning transfer, pupil services, and staff development. What implications do these readings have for the development of your team's plan?

Seaview School District

Seaview School District is adjacent to a large city in the northeastern part of the United States. Seaview has approximately 2,970 students. Until the mid-1980s the demographics of the district were relatively stable. Seaview had been a predominantly white, middle-class community. However, since that time the African American and Hispanic (Puerto Rican and Mexican American) populations have steadily increased. Additionally, two local organizations have sponsored Laotian and Vietnamese immigrants. One of these groups also has plans in the near future to sponsor Hmong immigrants.

Silvermine Middle School

Silvermine Middle School has approximately 520 students and thirty certified staff members. Currently there are no bilingual programs, but as the Spanish-speaking population increases steadily the assistant superintendent has begun discussing the need to consider some type of bilingual (Spanish/English) program. The district employs two full-time ESL teachers and six aides. One ESL teacher covers the middle and high schools, and the other teacher works in three elementary schools which have the highest proportions of non–native English-speaking students. Each of the aides works in a different elementary school "tutoring" students and helping those elementary teachers who have non–native English-speaking children in their classes.

All Silvermine staff members (certified and noncertified) are white. Twenty-seven percent of the students are currently receiving free or reduced-priced meals; this percentage has doubled in the last ten years.

Silvermine offers the typical content areas found in a middle school. The staff and students are especially pleased with their technology education program. The school has a strong library information center as well as a computer lab. It does not offer any language classes except English and ESL.

The Problem

You are the new principal of Silvermine Middle School. One day last fall after your first two weeks on the job, a serious racial incident occurred on school grounds. The incident involved students from your school and from another middle school in a nearby city. Several students had black eyes and were badly bruised from having been hit with baseball bats. These students required medical attention. After a complete investigation, which included community groups, eleven students from the two schools were suspended. Two parents claimed that their children were unfairly punished. They argued that because there was a lack of evidence to prove that their children were involved and that suspension was too severe a punishment.

During the investigation you discovered that numerous racial, ethnic, and religious incidents have occurred over the last five years. Numerous "minor" incidents also have taken place throughout your first year. After exploring the curriculum and talking with your assistant principal and staff members during the school year, you have seen little evidence that issues of cultural diversity are being addressed. Additionally, you have found that more than half your staff and your assistant principal do not feel that these "incidents" were bias-related incidents. They believe them to be "typical problems encountered by adolescents."

Several African American and Spanish-speaking families have complained to you and the central office staff, both formally and informally, that their children are being treated unfairly by some teachers at Silvermine. In your observations this year, you have seen some evidence of such discrimination as well. Also, at the last school board meeting, several African American parents called these issues to the attention of the board. The school board promised to investigate and report back to the parents.

More than 60 percent of the teachers have been at Silvermine for more than seventeen years. You believe that many of these staff members are dissatisfied with the "different" kinds of children the district has now, as compared with fifteen years ago. Although most staff members have had little experience working with children from non–native English-speaking backgrounds or with children representing racial and ethnic groups other than white, several faculty members do have teaching experiences with LEP students and students from culturally diverse backgrounds. Mrs. Sasse recently told you a story of a Hispanic student who confided in her that at Silvermine she felt "like a jalapeño in a candy jar."

As a result of the information collected during the investigation of the fight as well as through exploring the curriculum, you are keenly aware that Silvermine Middle School cannot continue to be reactive in its approach to dealing with racial, cultural, and religious incidents. Meanwhile, the superintendent has sent a memo to all administrators in the district (see memorandum below).

Your Challenge

Today is June 3, and the superintendent has scheduled a meeting with you at 10:00 A.M. on June 29. You have been working with a team of staff members on the plan requested by the superintendent. She has asked you to present a draft outline of the written plan at that meeting. She and the assistant superintendent would like to familiarize themselves with what your team is proposing for your school so that they can marshal district resources.

Memorandum

June 2

To: All Principals, Assistant Principals, and Instructional Leaders
From: Valerie Blandy, Superintendent
Re: Multicultural Education

As you may be aware, the population of Seaview school district is rapidly changing. Additionally, we are seeing an increase in serious confrontations among students. There is increasing evidence of the inability of all of us in the schools to understand the nature of the new, diverse population of students in our schools.

These changes make it imperative that schools at all levels begin addressing issues in multicultural education. Multicultural education is not solely a racial issue. Rather, the focus of multicultural education is on those cultural groups that experience prejudice and discrimination in our society. The purpose is to reduce discrimination against them and to provide equal educational opportunities for all. To meet this goal, the district will:

- nurture lifelong respect and compassion in students for themselves and other human beings regardless of race, ethnic origin, gender, social class, disability, religion, and sexual orientation
- remain steadfast in guaranteeing equal opportunity for high-quality education for all students, and not unlawfully discriminate
- endeavor to secure equal opportunities for all students

(continued)

Continued

Multicultural education is a major concern, and we encourage all schools to begin to address this issue through curriculum and staff development. By beginning the process now, we can eliminate problems at a later date.

Each school is to develop a three-year plan to address these issues starting in the following school year. I will be contacting each school in the next few weeks to set up a meeting in which you will present an outline of your plan.

Seaview School District 1999–2000

School	Grade	Enrollment
Unity Elementary	K–5	380
Hope Elementary	K–5	438
Praxis Elementary	K–5	291
Seaview Middle School	6–8	468
Silvermine Middle School	6–8	522
Seaview High School	9–12	870

Silvermine Middle School 1999–2000

Total certified staff	25
Regular classroom teachers	20
Special-program teachers	2
Administration	2
Pupil personnel services	1
Noncertified staff: Instructional	**4**
Noncertified staff: Noninstructional	10
Average class size	26

School enrollment

	Numbers	Percentages	
		Now	In 3 years
Total	522	100%	(approx.)
Race-ethnicity			
Asian American	34	7	10
African American	62	11	15
Hispanic	60	12	20
Native American	5	1	1
White	361	69	51

Product Specifications

Prepare an action plan that reflects your solution to the superintendent's request for Silvermine Middle School. Your plan should be a group product and include the following sections:

a. *A definition of the problem* as you view it at Silvermine. If your team identifies more than one problem, please prioritize what you choose to address.

b. *A three-year draft plan* for addressing the important components of the problem. The plan should include sample activities, the sequence in which you intend to proceed with them, and a rationale for the selection and sequence.

c. Your *strategy* for gaining the support of faculty, staff, students, and families. It should include how you will overcome the potential obstacles you will face in implementing the plan.

(Please refer to appropriate chapters in this book as a resource.)

Four Silvermine Middle School Staff Members

Katie Bishop has been teaching social studies at Silvermine for seventeen years, and she currently serves as a team leader. Before working at Seaview, Katie taught for five years at an International American School in Spain. Katie usually spends her summer vacations in Spanish-speaking countries (Mexico, Spain, Guatemala) She has a keen interest in Latino cultures and is well respected by many of the Spanish-speaking families.

Scott Newkirk is in his eighth year of teaching English. Before coming to Silvermine he taught in New York City for ten years. Scott has spoken with the principal several times about his concerns with the LEP students. He believes that he cannot adequately meet their language needs because the ESL teacher has to cover both the middle school and high school, and many students have only one class of ESL each day.

Helen Sasse has been teaching ESL at Silvermine and Seaview High School for the last four years. Before that time she taught English three-quarter time and ESL one-quarter time at Silvermine. Helen has a master's degree in teaching English as a second language (TESOL). Last summer she attended her third special weeklong workshop, which focused on LEP students from specific language backgrounds.

Bob Infantino is a guidance counselor who has been at Silvermine for eleven years. Bob has been particularly adept in working with students involved in some of the racial and ethnic incidents in the last few years. He is married to a woman who is African American and has strong ties with the black community.

3 Atoms and Bits: A Technology Project

BARBARA S. CAMPBELL
Assistant Superintendent, Wolcott, Connecticut

"Atoms and Bits" is based on a metaphor that Nicholas Negroponte, founding director of MIT's Media Lab, uses in his book *Being Digital:*

> I [Negroponte] recently visited the headquarters of one of America's five integrated circuit manufacturers. I was asked to sign in and, in the process, was asked whether I had a laptop computer with me. Of course I did. The receptionist asked for the model and serial number and for its value. "Roughly, between one and two million dollars," I said. "Oh, that cannot be, sir," she replied. "What do you mean? Let me see it." I showed her my old PowerBook, and she estimated its value at $2000. She wrote down that amount, and I was allowed to enter the premises. The point is that while the atoms were not worth that much, the bits were almost priceless. (pp. 11–12)

The challenge of this PBL is this: Is what we are doing in our schools preparing students for productivity in a world of atoms or of bits?

Microchip technology's power to store, manage, and transmit large amounts of information rapidly has transformed all aspects of living and working in our society. Information mediated by microchips is the commodity of the future. In the past, the mission of education was to equip students with competencies that would serve as their stock in trade (e.g., in agriculture, industry) to live a productive, high-quality life. Schools currently are information-based institutions charged with the same mission, so one would expect them to be aggressive adopters and users of technology.

They have not, however, been successful in adopting and integrating technology. The reasons frequently cited are:

- insufficient hardware
- inappropriate and or insufficient software
- lack or inadequacy of technical support
- lack or inadequacy of teacher training and staff development
- lack of administrative support

- mismatch between the technology and educational need
- lack or inadequacy of initial and continuing funding

If schools are to be successful in preparing productive, informed citizens for the twenty-first century, they will have to overcome the problems they have had with integrating technology into the teaching and learning process. Administrators, who are responsible for program development, must meet this challenge.

Learning Objectives

- define the opportunities and challenges associated with technology integration
- collaboratively design a plan for adopting and implementing technology in a school that incorporates prior learning, field experiences, and best-practice models gleaned from available resources
- prepare the plan, using available computer technologies
- participate in an administrative review

Guiding Questions

1. Whom will you involve in developing the plan? In implementing it? What role will you play (see Chapter 6)?

2. Which technology is "right" for your building's initial experience? What kinds of implementation challenges are associated with the technology (see Chapters 11 and 12)?

3. What potential leverage points do you have for developing and implementing the plan?

4. What elements constitute an exemplary building technology plan?

5. Based on what you have learned about change, staff development, curriculum/instruction, and school reform, how will you address the issues that have caused previous attempts at integrating technology to fail (see Chapters 2, 3, 8, and 10)?

The Problem

As the new principal of Marietta High School, you have spent most of the year gathering information about the school's culture. Even though many of the problems are characteristic of comprehensive high schools in the area, you are beginning to feel frustrated and overwhelmed by the way in which each issue compounds another.

Marietta is the only high school in the Mountjoy district of 2,800 students. Its enrollment of 730 students is beginning to increase as larger classes make their way through the system. The district seems to be a buffer zone. It is surrounded by affluent suburban districts on one side and a large urban district on the other. From your conversations with other district principals, you sense a tension between competing with the achievement levels of the suburban schools and having to deal with more at-risk students from the inner city whose parents have moved into Mountjoy. Data show that your minority, free or reduced lunch, and special-education numbers are increasing annually.

The faculty (fifty-five certified) are a veteran staff who, for the most part, view themselves as content experts. When you began sharing thoughts and articles on learner-centered instructional strategies with the departmental leaders, most were not receptive. They informed you that their twice-a-year observations indicate that teachers have solid instructional skills that seem to meet the needs of motivated students. The head of the social studies department summed up their beliefs, "We cover our content in the limited time we have. That stuff (e.g., learner-centered methodologies, alternative assessments, technology, any of the literacies) is for the elementary and middle school teachers, anyway!"

The staff have clearly conveyed to you their attitude regarding professional development: clearly its content is the "fad-of-the-year," the timing of in-service training always accommodates the lower levels, and the presenters rarely have experience teaching high school students. They firmly believe that "this too shall pass." They note that the only ongoing "fad" has been the district's commitment to technology. However, since the initiative started at the elementary level, they believe that money and commitment will run out before the technology gets to them.

Feedback from students is conflicting. You are disturbed by the "listlessness" you feel as you walk down the halls during passing times and that you observe in class. Many students respond to your questions regarding issues affecting them with "I don't know" or a shrug. On the other hand, a few students have come to you with complaints about boring classes, the lack of computers, and the absence of student input into decision making.

You suspect that student experiences in the lower grades may be a significant contributing factor to negative student behavior and attitudes. Your conversations with other principals lead you to believe that the expectations of incoming freshmen have been dramatically changed by the success of the district's technology initiative at the elementary and middle school levels. By the time students leave the elementary schools, they are accustomed to generating their assignments using word processing, graphics, and charts in fully networked environments. Their experiences at the middle school build on this expertise. Students are used to working with a team of teachers in long blocks of time. They are accustomed to being in charge of their learning. Confronted with the technology wasteland of Marietta and lecture-style teaching delivered in 42-minute segments, students seem to respond with behaviors that rapidly degenerate into apathy or disciplinary issues.

The school's crumbling physical infrastructure compounds all these problems. It is poorly designed and poorly equipped for implementing more effective programs. Electrical wiring is inadequate; blueprints are almost nonexistent. You suspect that any facilities monies in the district have been consumed in attempting to respond to ever-increasing enrollments at the elementary and middle levels.

There is no area with computers that can accommodate a class of more than fourteen, and the average class size is twenty-three. The few computer areas in English, business, and technology education are considered exclusively for the use of those respective departments. The computers themselves are a hodge-podge of Apple IIes and GSs, DOS machines ranging from 286s–486s, and Macintoshes. Some of the DOS machines run Windows; others don't. Of the mini-networks in the building (office, technology education, and business), none connects with the others. There are no connections to the Internet.

Marietta's parents seem to be divided into two camps. One group wants to perpetuate the status quo; the other argues strongly in favor of raising levels of academic performance and expanding the program of studies. The president of Marietta's Parent Group, Karen Strong, belongs to the former. She has not found her participation in the newly formed district parent council (whose membership consists of the presidents of all of the school parent councils) worthwhile. She has told you that the group is made up of parents who think that Mountjoy schools are private technology academies. Her recommendation to drop out of the group was overturned by high school parents interested in academics and increased use of technology.

At your last meeting with Superintendent Garcia, you learned that monies will be available during the next budget year to begin the process of making Marietta High School a technology-rich environment. She has asked you to develop the first part of a three-year plan for the project and informed you that she will send you a memo outlining details.

With all of the other instructional and cultural issues, you wonder how you will ever manage this assignment.

Product Specifications

1. Develop Marietta's technology-based plan. The plan must include:
   a. a brief description of how the plan was developed (e.g., who was involved, when they met, how they organized their task, what the principal's role was)
   b. a list of the technology(ies) chosen for initial adoption and implementation with a brief rationale for the selection
   c. an outline of the adoption and implementation stages and strategies, with a brief rationale for each major stage and strategy
   d. a description of how you will monitor the progress and success of the plan

2. Prepare the plan, using computer applications.
3. Prepare for and participate in a review of the plan by the administrative council. *Note:* The review will not include a formal presentation, since the purpose of an administrative review is to refine a plan before it is finalized and implemented. The council will read your plan in advance. During the review, you must be prepared to answer questions about it.

Plan Due: _____

Memorandum

April 15

To: Deborah Carroll
From: Esmeralda Garcia, Superintendent
Re: Technology initiative

At our last meeting, I reviewed our district's technology initiative with you and asked you to begin developing a technology plan for your building. We will review your plan at the September administrative council meeting the following year. Final adoption is scheduled for the October meeting. To assist you with plan development, I am providing these conditions and guidelines:

- Consider the district's goals for technology—improved teaching, learning, and leading with technology.
- Our corporate partners and the Board of Education have been willing to provide generous funding for well-thought-out plans. Therefore:
  —the network infrastructure will be provided for your building.
  —funding to cover plan development costs (e.g., summer work by staff, consultant fees, visitations, training, materials) is readily available.
  —cost should not be a primary decision-making criterion when selecting technology(ies).
- Think long-range but develop the plan *only* for Marietta's first year of adoption and implementation. You should list "next steps" for years two and three.
- Technology coordinators and principals from other buildings stand ready to assist you at any point in your plan development.
- Please send a copy of your plan to me by September 15, so that we can duplicate and distribute it before the meeting.
- Do not hesitate to call me for assistance.

Selected Readings from the Principal's Journal

May 1
I toured my building today. Reality hit me in the face. What an ugly monster of a place! Ceiling tiles stained, floor tiles mismatched, walls painted in awful institution colors.... And those awful chairs with arms placed in rows.

According to Frank, the head custodian, Marietta has antiquated heating and intercom systems and problems with asbestos and electricity. He also informed me that he does not have enough staff to manage a building of its size.

My assistant Elaine interrupted the tour because the computer network had crashed while she was running schedules. The level of anger was incredible. I learned from Fred and Carol [assistant principals] that the network spends most of its time crashed. When I asked what we do about a crashed network, I unleashed the office staff's frustration. The contracted service responds on its time schedule, not on the basis of our needs.

May 24

I did it!!!! I got Dr. Garcia to agree to release Marietta's staff from the district in-service days. I want to spend three days with my staff to find out what their dreams, desires, needs, etc. are for Marietta's students. And I want them to have time to spend with their departments, especially since almost every department has at least one new staff member.

When I got back to the building, I ran into Kelly, our library media specialist. As we chatted, I gathered some valuable information. Although her budget is not adequate, it seems that she has been working with Fred, Nancy, and Pat to move away from textbooks to resource-based learning. Kelly implied that I might see some kind of proposal from the group. I assured her I look forward to reviewing it. She asked whether I thought funding would be available to automate Marietta's library media center in the near future. It seems the other buildings have online circulation and catalog systems, CD-ROM reference materials, and telecommunications!

May 28

Here are my initial impressions about the department leaders:

Fred Gollner (English): Articulate, seems to know the latest buzzwords. Peers tease him about being the "bleeding edge" of education; wants more computers for writing.

Nancy Heisey (Science): Greeted me the first day I was on the job. Believes her staff is doing some interesting things. Hinted at issues related to the district policy that every course must have an approved textbook. Seems to know how to help her colleagues to compromise. Listens in a group more than she speaks. Has jerry-rigged computers that others don't want; used to form a small computer-based learning lab.

Hank Keller (Social Studies): Has he read or thought about anything since the early 1960s?! Seems attached to the expression "If it ain't broke, don't fix it." Complains about all the work he has to do as department head, but has been in the position ten years.

Terry Rankin (Health and Physical Education): Terry was shocked when I insisted he attend the meeting. Apparently he has been used to excusing himself regularly from these meetings, since his area isn't an "academic" subject. Body language during the meeting ranged from apathy to hostility.

Carl Groff (Mathematics): Behaves like Hank's yes-man. Informed me that the high school has enough technology and that his math teachers are experts. How does he explain our low test scores in math? Hedges on responding whenever I bring up NCTM standards.

Jose Gomez (Foreign Language): Seems to know his stuff! Desperately needs and wants additional staff and some computer setup so that kids can interact with native language speakers. Great sense of humor.

Sally Ball (Combined Arts): What a powerhouse! Two years ago she single-handedly persuaded the BOE to fund Arts Propel and a graphics computer for kids to use and then proceeded to have kids earn all kinds of awards. She seems to value Fred's input.

George Crandall (Vocational Studies): When asked what changes he'd like to see, he replied that all students should take keyboarding. He has nothing positive to say about school-to-work transition programs. He informed me that he will not entertain revision of the home economics or automotive programs, because they meet the needs of Marietta's nonacademic kids.

Pat Green (Special Services): Seems ostracized by the group—sat alone, no one greeted her. Several times she was addressed indirectly by the phrase "your kids" or "Green's kids". She seems pleasant and knowledgeable. I wonder whether she is shunned because of the district's unpopular inclusion initiative.

May 29

Although I had met many of the staff earlier, this was the first time I had them together. I've formed some initial hypotheses: (1) new staff are regarded as outsiders; (2) most of the staff do not link what they do instructionally with student performance; (3) many staff believe that only some students can achieve at high levels; (4) staff identify strongly with their respective departments. It is amazing that some of these people don't know the names of recent hires in other departments! This is a staff of 55 teachers, not 200.

Watching the social groups during breaks and lunch, I think that I may have a fairly typical breakdown. My initial categories: the movers and shakers (a smattering of teachers across departments, Kelly, and Pat); the middle majority; and the "guys" as they call themselves, a group made up of Hank, Carl, George, and Terry. They took their lunches to the AV area to watch a baseball game.

June 3

I suppose I shouldn't be disappointed with the list the faculty brainstormed, but I am. Vision is absent but need is apparent. Imagine 4–5 intercom interruptions to class, an intercom system that doesn't work in some classrooms (liability) and having only one copier that serves administrative and instructional needs in a school this size! Another big issue is that the teachers feel that many of the meetings which they are contractually obligated to attend are meaningless.

I think I made some allies when I promised no intercom announcements during class time and rotation of events like pep rallies.

I also asked them to form a committee to make recommendations for their copying and intercom needs. Dead silence in the room. I didn't know what that meant. Finally, Greg (a social studies teacher whom I suspect is an informal leader) explained that they felt that they had too many meetings and that most committee recommendations were ignored.

Heart in throat, I countered with a promise to reduce the number of unproductive meetings and to budget for whatever recommendations the faculty approve for copiers and intercoms. Dead silence was followed by a maelstrom of complaints regarding the absence of any kind of technology in sufficient numbers and condition. Finally Kelly offered to provide me with an inventory of most of the AV equipment. Apparently no one has kept computer and software inventories.

Then Mary, the teacher association president, sarcastically noted that many of the meetings are contractual. I had been told by the superintendent that I hold teachers to their contract. However, when I reviewed the contract, the language speaks specifically about faculty and department meetings, but is vague about the content and timing of those meetings. I see some room to use time more effectively, but wasn't ready to make my ideas public. So I proposed that the teachers who volunteered to serve on the copier/intercom committee hold their first meeting during the faculty meeting, which contractually must be scheduled at the end of the school day (whose crazy idea is that?!). That went over well, and the meeting ended.

Harry (science) and Kelly, who had volunteered to co-chair the committee, came up to ask whether I would consider letting a secretary meet with the committee, since office staff also use the technologies. I agreed—much to their surprise.

June 5
I'm in trouble with Dr. Garcia. (One of the staff must be an informant.) By the time I arrived at school this morning, I had a note to call the superintendent after 9:00. When I did, I was told very firmly that I was to hold teachers to their required meetings. After I explained my rationale and plan (use the time flexibly for staff development, small study groups, etc.), she seemed to accept the idea "because you need to build a relationship with the staff" but warned me about the importance of "holding their feet to the fire." Hmmm...this is a potential area of conflict.

June 10
Harry and Kelly met with me today on the copier recommendations. I agreed to budget for their copier and telephone requests. Their report also raised some important issues regarding other technologies. The AV inventory is ancient and inadequate for our needs. There is no building inventory of computers and software because of intense department territoriality.

June 12
How depressing! Seven of the last eight observations have shown me that teachers lecture and students sit; worksheets, questions at the end of the chapter. No student engagement, no ties to their lives or current events.

I think I'll mix my observations from now on. I balance this last bunch with some of the really gifted educators I have on staff—veteran and new. I have to find a way to get the traditional teachers to see some of their techniques.

And then the departmental meetings. Hank is the group's bully. He talks a good game and dominates any discussion by his physical size and volume of voice. Having observed his teaching and some of the math staff, I do not see a connection between his words and actions so far!

The topic of discussion was the state mastery test scores—(low, low, low!). I had asked the chairs to analyze the results to see what we could do to improve our students' performance. I don't think I was prepared for their responses.

> Marietta kids are all good kids.
>
> Some Marietta kids can learn because they are motivated.
>
> We can help the motivated ones. [A group they think comprises approximately 20 percent of the student body. Like improving their scores will significantly impact our results!!]

Their teachers work hard but will try even harder. (Doing what??)

It's the middle school's fault for coddling kids rather than teaching them.

Only Fred and Nancy had even discussed the test results with their departments. Nothing I said or did could move most of the group toward linking instruction and curriculum and student achievement.

June 13

I finished my initial meetings with students and student groups. I am deeply troubled by what I heard and observed. Apathy and anger co-exist. Students feel outside the decision-making process. The present clubs and athletic programs do not seem of interest to many. On the other hand, a small group of students expressed interest in building "school spirit." This group wants to restructure everything from the extra-curricular program to the number of computers available during the day.

I reviewed my findings with both vice principals. They were defensive, citing no time to deal with the issues because of the increasing amount of time they have to spend on discipline.

I am surprised how many teachers have, in casual conversation, wanted to know whether Marietta will ever be able to have the kinds of technology-rich environments other schools in the district have. It seems they have heard from students about what other buildings have, but many have never been to the buildings themselves!!

REFERENCE

Negroponte, N. (1995). *Being digital*. New York: Alfred A. Knopf.
(Also refer to appropriate chapters within this book.)

4 Marveling at the Results: Power, Roles, Relationships, and School Reform

WILLIAM G. CUNNINGHAM
Old Dominion University

School improvements often demand new ways of thinking and behaving. If superintendents are to help school sites make the needed changes, they are going to have to develop school staff so they have the needed abilities and skills. New hires must be knowledgeable and proficient in relation to needed reform efforts and must be able to develop skills in existing staff.

Expectations of staff to learn from and work with one another have increased. Linda Darling-Hammond in a background paper for the National Commission on Teaching and America's Future (1996) states, "Time for preparation, planning, working with colleagues, meeting individually with students and parents, or working on the development of curriculum or assessment measures is rarely available and considered not part of the teacher's main job. Current efforts at school reform are likely to succeed to the extent that they are built on a strong foundation of teaching knowledge and are sustained by a commitment to structural rather than merely symbolic change." Dennis Sparks, executive director for the National Staff Development Council concurs: "Significant changes in the daily work lives of teachers must be at the core of reform efforts that are truly intended to create schools in which adults feel competent in their work and all students develop to their full potential."

Those who have opportunities for growth, development, and promotion often raise their aspirations, value their own skills, engage in improving performance, form political alliances with an improvement orientation, and actively participate in and support reforms. Those without such opportunities lower their aspirations, undervalue their skills, disengage from work improvements, form protective peer groups, and resist passively. Positive attitudes are encouraged by the ability to influence others within the organization. If the individual has very limited power, his or her knowledge and ability will not be respected. Even symbolic forms of power increase an individual's value in the eyes of his or her colleagues. Powerlessness leads to petty domination, not leadership, reform, or improved performance.

Powerlessness usually manifests itself as supervising too closely, holding back people's careers, failing to develop their talents, and being a "watchdog" not a leader. It also can mean focusing on means, not the ends, and adherence to standard operating procedures and past practices. How can leaders provide school personnel the development, opportunity, and power needed to encourage or motivate ambitious, committed staff who willingly put in the kind of work that reform efforts require? How can teachers share their knowledge so that it can be synthesized in improved practice?

Learning Objectives

- To acquire an understanding of the complexity of achieving school reform
- To examine the types of organizational structures that will promote staff development and curriculum and instructional improvement
- To determine how the daily lives of teachers must be altered for reform efforts to succeed.
- To analyze the types of leadership styles that will best promote successful school reform and the types of support these styles will need to be successful
- To examine methods by which the knowledge and ability of very different groups of people may be brought together in an ongoing, mutually beneficial way; to determine how groups can share their talents, knowledge, and resources, thus supporting each other in relationships that merge their abilities for the purpose of improving the school
- To distribute power and responsibility in such a way that it encourages mutual respect and willingness to work together to jointly improve schools

Guiding Questions

1. How can you get staff to develop their full potential and encourage their full participation in a school-improvement process? What are the characteristics of a job that provides and supports opportunities for development and advancement (see Chapters 6 and 8)?
2. Considering the concept of two kinds of employees, the "moving" and the "stuck," how might you differentiate between a person who is "stuck" as opposed to a person who is "moving"?
3. If power means the capacity to mobilize resources, influence others, and "get things done," how can different staff members be given power so they can develop the credibility needed to be respected and ultimately "get school reform done"?
4. What are the sources of order, power, and purpose within the school (see Chapters 1, 2, 5, 7, and 11)?
5. What types of efforts will facilitate complex learning, creativity, experimentation, and continuous improvement of the school?
6. How will you know that you are nurturing potential and capacity?

Hickory Ridge High School

Hickory Ridge High School is a large urban school of approximately 1800 students, 15 percent exceptional or special-needs students, 46 percent white, 40 percent African American, 12 percent Hispanic, and 2 percent Asian, of whom many are recent immigrants. The mean composite score on standardized tests such as the Iowa Test of Basic Skills have improved from the 45th to the 49th percentile, but some students score in the bottom quartile.

The graduating class comprises 420 graduates. Of these graduates, 160 received an advanced studies diploma and 147 graduated with less than a 2.0 grade point average (4.0-point system).

The faculty and school community have sought to meet the needs of the students, but those needs have significantly changed over the past four years and the system has been unable to keep pace. During the past year, the Hickory Ridge faculty, staff, parents, and business partners worked toward a variety of reform initiatives but achieved very limited success. The district's reform efforts allowed a core of Hickory teachers to participate in activities. They took technology-based industry tours and attended community forums on the implementation of pilot programs to reform the schools. Although Hickory has formulated a new mission statement and vision for the school, the teachers and administrators are in conflict about how best to proceed. The school is generally viewed as unable to meet new reform guidelines, out of date, and in serious conflict.

The makeup of the teaching staff at Hickory Ridge High School is illustrated in Table 13.2 on page 404.

A teacher profile looked at teacher beliefs related to how each of five groups respected their ability as professionals. The views of the teachers regarding the perceptions of their respect held by differing groups are shown in Figure 13.1 on page 405.

The second bar shows how each of these five groups describe their own level of respect for teachers' ability as professionals. The teachers underestimated their level of respect in all cases except for students.

Figure 13.2 on page 405 shows students' raw scores on a nationally normed test over the past twelve years.

There was considerable concern over scores that, having fallen over the past three years, had risen only slightly last year.

The major reform effort in Wingfield School District was focused on an "integrated, technologically supported curriculum." The desire was to have technology become a part of the curriculum that students use on a daily basis. All rooms at the high school were wired and each had at least fifteen computers. The district was seen as a leader in obtaining the needed equipment to make the schools technological centers. The actual use of the computers by both teachers and students, however, was disappointing and major pressure was put on the system to incorporate the computers into the curriculum and daily instruction. Even though the scores and performance of the students on standardized tests were disappointing, the school board and community believed that these changes would result in "better teaching and learning for all kids," and "give their children a head start by providing them with critical thinking and technological skills."

TABLE 13.2   Makeup of the Teaching Staff at Hickory Ridge High School

Faculty Demographics	All Teachers (percentage)
Total	100
Sex	
Male	35.0
Female	65.0
Age	
Under 26 years old	21.4
26–30 years old	16.4
31–35 years old	2.1
36–40 years old	4.5
41–45 years old	10.0
46–50 years old	11.3
51–55 years old	20.0
56–60 years old	8.0
61 or more years old	6.3
Race-ethnicity	
Asian or Pacific Islander	0.0
Hispanic, regardless of race	1.3
African American, not of Hispanic origin	20.6
White, not of Hispanic origin	75.6
Native American	2.5
Highest academic degree	
High school diploma	0.0
Business/technical school certificate	0.0
Associate degree (2 years or more)	0.0
Bachelor's degree	38.3
Master's degree	56.9
Education specialist or professional diploma	2.4
Doctorate	1.2
Professional degree	1.2

Hickory High has a very supportive parent group who are civic minded, young, technically advanced, and middle to below-middle class. The turnover in this neighborhood is high because it is considered a stepping-off point to greater affluence. The central administrative staff and you, hold the teachers at Hickory High in high regard. Most are baffled by the present state of affairs at the high school.

The Problem

You are the superintendent for Wingfield School District. You were hired four years ago to help the school district achieve its newly established vision of becoming a technologically driven, innovative school district. The focus of the reforms was to be school based, beginning at Hickory Ridge High School and spreading to other

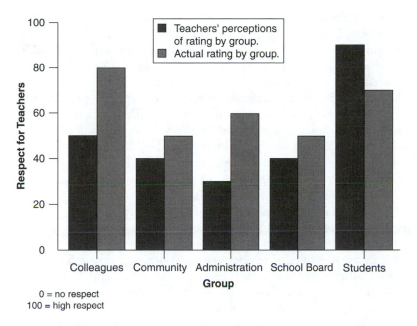

FIGURE 13.1   **Teacher Perceptions of How Others Respect Their Ability as Professionals**

schools. You have aligned the work of all schools toward a new technologically supported, constructivist curriculum.

The faculty at the high school are aging and many have been teaching for twenty years or longer. Jim O'Connor, the principal, was a teacher for sixteen years at the middle-school level before moving to the assistant-principal position. He served as an assistant principal for 10 years before being promoted last year to his present job of principal at Hickory Ridge High.

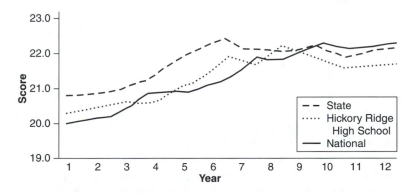

FIGURE 13.2   **Students' raw scores on a nationally normed test over the past 12 years.**

Jim O'Connor is not seen as an individual who would go any further than high school principal. His promotion was based on his loyalty to Wingfield and his extraordinary knowledge of the community power structures and policy, rules, and regulations. He is the keeper of the history and, although he relates well to children and their parents, he lacks understanding of their needs in the twenty-first century. No one, however, is more knowledgeable about the community, people, and existing programs and policies within the school district. You called on him to gain perspective on reactions of both internal and external publics to issues being considered within the school district. His staff see him as knowledgeable but not well respected and unable to understand the school district's vision for Hickory Ridge High School. He has a lot to offer, particularly to younger staff, in perspective and understanding the community. Most staff, however, and especially younger staff, see him as having limited power, importance, and promotability in the school district. They also do not see him as helping them to gain desired promotions.

Over the last four years you have placed twenty-seven new teachers at Hickory, all of whom are identified as having very high potential, although still relatively young. They have all attended top universities and been in the top 10 percent in their programs of study. They have been extremely well prepared regarding the desired school reforms and are experts in technology. These new high-potential people are highly likely to become superintendents themselves someday—they are "fast-trackers."

You placed these "fast-trackers" at Hickory in hopes that O'Connor and the aging teaching staff would learn from them regarding new, innovative programs. At the same time, you hoped that the "fast-trackers" would learn more about the community, families, and children and the school district from O'Connor and the more experienced teachers. You hoped that the younger and older staff would share their talents, resources, knowledge, and skill and support each other and the school in the achievement of needed reforms. This respect and appreciation of each others' abilities and knowledge never developed, however.

Two of the top fast-trackers, Michael Scott and Kerri Beth, have recently requested to be taken off the site-based planning team for the school. All twenty-two of the new teachers have been complaining about O'Connor's management and the attitude of a number of older teachers on the staff, first to O'Connor and then, more delicately, to Sandi Walchek, the associate superintendent O'Connor reports to, and even to you. They told Walchek that O'Connor is always looking over their work, second-guessing how they teach their classes and what they say to parents and is endlessly critical.

They are beginning to raise questions about whether Jim and a few of the older teachers can really do their jobs. They see Jim and the older teachers as being out of touch with modern times, too bureaucratic, and not respected within the system. They are concerned that the principal and staff will hold back their careers and are not in touch with the power base within or outside the school. The principal measures performance by adherence to routine procedures and community relations, not accomplishments, responsiveness, or continuous improvement. Walchek, concerned, has asked O'Connor about this situation without, of course, identifying the people involved.

O'Connor explains that he has a lot of experience and sees the new hires as not understanding the community or kids or appreciating the significant progress we have made in this school district. He complains that they seem to look down on him and everything the experienced teachers have to say. As a result, they are making a lot of mistakes and trying to do things that will not work. This negligence requires that he pay very close attention to their work and that educating children and maintaining the good relations with the community is simply too important to take chances. "Anyhow," he says, "they're not as smart as they think. It takes time, experience, and an understanding of the school's heritage to develop the skills you need to be a good educator." Although he doesn't say so, Walchek can tell that O'Connor is also very angry.

You now find yourself under some pressure from the board. You do agree with the direction that the board has established for the schools and you are empathetic with their frustration with what is occurring at Hickory Ridge High School. You have won the trust of the board, staff and community, and you do not want to lose it. You also realize that the staff and parents at Hickory seem to be beginning to divide themselves in support of either the older or the younger staff. You also know that O'Connor has many friends within the community, including some board members. You are frustrated that this perfect marriage between the younger staff, who are so technologically competent and so knowledgeable about needed reforms, and the older staff and principal, who have so much knowledge, about Wingfield children, programs, services, and families, is not working. You do not want to give up on this idea, because you see no other option that has a higher probability of succeeding.

In reflecting on the situation, you believe that perhaps you have not structurd the plan properly for success or that you can do something to get these groups to respect one another and work together on reforming the school. After all, the new teachers understand the needed reforms but do not relate well to the community, whereas O'Connor does not understand the needed reforms but does relate well to the community. You believe that the principal and teachers have the right combination of knowledge, experience, and ability to be successful if only they would work together. None of this can occur under the present conditions of defensiveness, anger, power struggles, mistrust, self-defense mechanisms, and ultimately adversarial relationships. You are now going back to the drawing board to come up with ideas to make this plan work.

Some of the problems that you see as holding back the reform efforts at Hickory High include lack of trust, confidence, and power; misunderstanding about roles; insufficient communication; lack of respect for each other and the important knowledge each has to share; principal seen as lacking power with central administration and the superintendent; neither side feels involved or important; the juniors regret the lack of opportunity for powerful mentorship; the seniors lack motivation to change what already exists. Other factors include institutional inertia; lack of respect for diversity; inability to combine knowledge, talents, and energies in the best interest of the school; and low expectations.

Your Challenge

You, as superintendent of Wingfield School District, realize that the organizational culture at Hickory Ridge High School is actually hindering the needed school reform efforts. All parties need to work together to achieve the desired curriculum and instructional improvements. The staff, from O'Connor to the newest teachers, now seem to feel a sense of helplessness and powerlessness. They are unable to act at a time when they are absolutely essential to needed reform efforts. You realize that you must identify ways to give the principal and teachers a sense of purpose, direction, responsibility, power, optimism, and mission.

You have been given a free hand by the board to see that all Hickory staff have a common direction, are working together and supporting one another, and have the time and power "to develop needed reforms and then deliver on those plans." The idea is to develop respect for each person's unique talents as an important resource so he or she can work together to create an outstanding twenty-first century school.

The plan should address "enabling factors" that will result in successful reforms at Hickory High. The plan should develop a high level of understanding, support, and assistance that runs from the top to the bottom of the school district, beginning at Hickory High.

The board chairman has challenged you: "Free up the energy, creativity, and commitment in individual schools, then step back and marvel at the results." You now realize the full meaning in the challenge of this statement. Everything you ask staff to do appears to be an add-on. They seem incapable of working together. There is a lack of respect for the principal. Energy and focus gets lost; stress and anxiety are running high. The chair has expressed concern that "anything that undermines staff confidence will result in a downward spiral at the school."

The plan should address the following elements:

1. Helping Jim O'Connor to gain the respect of the new faculty
2. Developing collegiality, honest and open communication, and support among all the faculty
3. Encouraging more design and greater experimentation and risk taking with the reform efforts now under way
4. Developing high expectations, trust, and confidence within the staff
5. Providing tangible support and empowerment for all members of the staff
6. Connecting the staff more closely so they can better appreciate, recognize, and share their unique knowledge and ability and encouraging them to reach out to the extensive research and knowledge pertinent to the desired reforms
7. Developing structures that provide administrators, parents, and teachers the opportunity for involvement in decision making and participation in the school reform effort
8. Protecting what is important and good about Hickory High while reforming it to better meet the needs of twenty-first-century students

You have been told that "it takes a few mistakes before you get it right." You want to get it right this time.

Product Specifications

You realize you must, in a way, remake Hickory High so it is better prepared to meet the demands for school reform. As one board member warned, with a smile on his face, "You can't bludgeon people into greatness." The initial focus of your plan will be building the needed relationships and exploring structural and cultural changes. You need to give O'Connor greater symbolic power so he will be seen with greater respect. You need to see that teachers work together to share knowledge and expertise. You must create a catalyst for needed reform at Hickory Ridge High School.

You are to develop a plan for "strategic alliance" that creates conditions whereby purpose, values, information, and relationships are meaningfully connected and aligned around the school system's desire to develop an integrated, technologically supported curriculum. You are to address the conditions that must be created at Hickory High School if the school is to be successfully reformed. You are to create a process at this high school that builds on the capacity of everyone in the school, so as to develop the school's collective intelligence. The plan should create continuous generative learning and staff engagement for the purpose of school reform and improvement. The plan should encourage experimentation and implementation. Your plan should build the school's capacity for participation, engagement, interconnectedness, development, and resilience. You should examine creative ways to distribute power throughout the school district so as to improve respect and each person's opportunity to make a difference.

The plan should capitalize on the strengths of employees and mobilize their energies and commitments to reform and improve the school. You must encourage and manage input from diverse stakeholders and may have to examine the roles of the staff and design new organizational structures. The existing positions may no longer seem to serve the needs of the district. The point is that you truly have been given a free hand to solve this very "swampy" problem and to begin developing an effective integrated, technologically supported curriculum.

New directions often demand new structure, new practices, new roles and expectations, new relationships, new ideas and maybe even new people. The required report addresses these changes as "strategic alignment." Alignment must take place among the school structure, the people working within the structure, and the needed educational reform so that improved technologically supported teaching and learning can be achieved. The process by which the school personnel create needed reforms is the most important element in relation to its ultimate success. You will be asked to make an oral presentation to the board on your written plan. The plan should address short-term initiatives (first year) and long-term initiatives (two to five years) and include a chronological sequence of steps to be taken.

(Please refer to appropriate chapters within this book as a resource.)

REFERENCES AND BIBLIOGRAPHY

AASA. (1993). *1994 platforms and resolutions*. Arlington, VA: American Association of School Administrators.

Aboud, F. (1988). *Children and prejudice*. New York: B. Blackwell.

Achilles, C. M. & Smith, P. (1994, 1999). Stimulating the academic performance of pupils. In Larry W. Hughes (Ed.), *The principal as leader*. New York: Merrill.

Adler, P. (1975). The transitional experience: An alternative view of culture shock. *Journal of Humanistic Psychology, 15*(4), 23–40.

Airasian, P., & Walsh, M. (1997). Constructivist cautions. *Phi Delta Kappan, 78*(6), 444–449.

Alam, D., & Seick, R. (1994). A block schedule with a twist. *Phi Delta Kappan, 9*, 732–733.

Alexander, L. (1986). Chairman's summary. In National Governor's Association, *Time for Results*. Washington, DC: National Governor's Association.

Allison, G. (1971). *Essence of decision making: Exploring the Cuban missile crisis*. Boston: Little, Brown.

Allport, G. (1979). *ABC's of scapegoating*. New York: Anti-Defamation League of B'nai B'rith.

Allport, G. (1958). *The nature of prejudice*. Cambridge, MA: Addison-Wesley.

American Institutes for Research. (1994). *Educational innovation in multiracial contexts: The growth of magnet schools in American education*. Palo Alto, CA: Prepared for the U.S. Department of Education.

American Association of School Administrators. (1993). *1994 Platform and resolutions*. Arlington, VA: American Association of School Administrators.

American Association of School Administrators (1991). *America 2000: Where school leaders stand* (Report No ISBN-0-8762-172-3). Arlington, VA: AASA (ERIC ED 344 325).

American Association of School Administrators (1988). *School-based management* (AASA Stock Number 0221-00209) Washington, DC: American Association of School Administrators, National Association of Elementary School Principals, National Association of Secondary School Administration.

American Association of School Administrators (1981). *Statement of ethics*. Arlington, VA: American Association of School Administrators.

Andrade de Herrera, V. Education in Mexico: Historical and contemporary educational systems. In J. LeBlanc Flores (Ed.), *Children of La Frontera*. Charlestown, WV: ERIC Clearinghouse.

Anyon, J. (1980, winter) Social class and the hidden curriculum of work. *Journal of Education, 162*, 67–92.

Apple, M. (1986). *Teachers and texts: A political economy of class and gender relations in education*. New York: Routledge.

Archer, J. (1994, February 2). School-based health centers. *Education Week*, 3, 7.

Argyris, C. (1982). *Reasoning, learning, and action*. San Francisco: Jossey-Bass.

Argyris, C., & Schön, D. (1978). *Organizational learning: A theory of action perspective*. Reading, MA: Addison-Wesley.

Argyris, C., & Schön, D. (1974). *Theory in practice: Increasing professional effectiveness*. San Francisco: Jossey-Bass.

Arias, B. (1986, November). The context of education for Hispanic students: An overview. *American Journal of Education*, 26–57.

Aristotle, (1962). *Nicomachean ethics*. Trans. Martin Ostwald. Indianapolis, IN: Bobbs-Merrill.

Armstrong, T. (1994). *Multiple intelligences in the classroom*. Alexandria, VA: Association for Supervision and Curriculum Development.

Arons, E. L. (1998). *Successful interviewing techniques*. Mimeographed sheet, p. 18. Rockville, MD: Montgomery County Public Schools.

Association of School Business Officials. (1986). *Guidelines for managing student activity accounts*. Reston, VA: Association of School Business Officials.

Atkins, J. M., & Black, P. (1997). Policy perils of international comparisons. *Phi Delta Kappan, 79*(1), 22–28.

Bacharach, S. B., & Mundell, B. (Eds.) (1995). *Images of Schools: Structures and roles in organization behavior*. Thousand Oaks, CA: Corwin.

Baker, E. T., Wang, M. C., & Walberg, H. J. (1995). The effects of inclusion on learning. *Educational Leadership*, (4), 33–35.

Ballew, A., & Prokop, M. (1994). *Earthquake survival*. San Diego: Pfeiffer.

Ballinger, C. (1988). Rethinking the school calendar. *Educational Leadership*.

Banks, J. A. (1995). The historic reconstruction of knowledge about race. *Educational Researcher, 24*(2), 15–25.

Banks, J. A. (1994). *An introduction to multicultural education*. Boston: Allyn & Bacon.

Banks, J., & Banks, C. (Eds.). (1994). *Multicultural education: Issues and perspectives*. Boston: Allyn & Bacon.

Banks, J. A. (1993). "The canon debate, knowledge, construction, and multi-cultural education." *Educational Researcher, 22*(5), 4–14.

Bardwick, J. M. (1997). Emotional leadership. In K. Shelton (Ed.), *A new paradigm of leadership* (pp. 191–194). Provo, UT: Executive Excellence.

Barker, J. A. (1992). *Paradigms: The business of discovering the future*. New York: Harper Collins, Publishers, Inc.

Barnett, B. G. (1991). The educational platform: Articulating moral dilemmas and choices for future educational leaders. In Barnett, B. G., McQuarrie, F. O., & Norris, C. G. (Eds.), *The moral imperatives of leadership: A focus on human decency*. Memphis, TN: National Network for Innovative Principal Preparation.

Beck, L. (1994). *Reclaiming educational administration as a caring profession*. New York: Teachers College Press.

Beck, L., & Murphy, J. (1996). *The four imperatives of a successful school*. Thousand Oaks, CA: Corwin Press.

Beck, L., Murphy, J., et al. (1997). *Ethics in educational leadership programs: Emerging models*. Columbia, MO: University Council for Educational Administration.

Bell, C. (1997). Passionate leadership. In K. Shelton (Ed.), *A new paradigm of leadership* (pp. 195–198). Provo, UT: Executive Excellence.

Bell, T. H. (1993). Reflections: One decade after a nation at risk. *Phi Delta Kappan, 74*(8), 592–598.

Bellah, R., Madsen, R., Sullivan, W., Swindler, A., & Tipton, S. (1991). *The good society*. New York: Knopf.

Bellah, R., Madsen, R., Sullivan, W., Swindler, A., & Tipton, S. (1985). *Habits of the heart*. Berkeley, CA: University of California Press.

Bender, W., Sebring, P., & Bryk, A. (1998). *School leadership and the bottom line in Chicago*. University of Chicago, Consortium on School Research.

Bennett, C. I. (1998). *Comprehensive multicultural education: Theory and practice*. Boston: Allyn & Bacon.

Bennett, K. P., & LeCompte, M. D. (1990). *How schools work: A sociological analysis of education*. New York: Longman.

Bennett, W. J. (1988). *American education: Making it work*. Washington, DC: U.S. Government Printing Office.

Bennis, W. G. (1983) *The chief*. New York: Morrow.

Bennis, W., & Nanus, B. (1985). *Leaders: The strategies for taking charge*. New York: Harper & Row.

Berliner, D., & Biddle, B. (1995). *The manufactured crisis*. Reading, MA: Addison-Wesley.

Bernard, C. I. (1938). *The functions of the executive*. Cambridge, MA: Harvard Press.

Bernstein, B. (1964). Elaborated and restricted codes: Their social origins and some consequences. *American Anthropologist, 66*, 55–69.

Berube, M. R. (1994). *American school reform: 1883–1993*. Westport, CT: Praeger.

Bilingual Education Office. (1986). *Beyond language: Social and cultural factors in schooling language minority students*. Sacramento, CA: Bilingual Education Office.

Binkowski, K. (1995). *Factors contributing to school improvement in high performing elementary schools*. Unpublished doctoral dissertation. University of Connecticut.

Birdwhistell, R. (1970). *Kinesics and context*. Philadelphia: University of Pennsylvania.

Blake, R. R., & McCanse, A. A. (1991). *Leadership dilemmas—Grid solutions*. (Formerly *The managerial grid* by Robert R. Blake and Jane S. Mouton). Houston: Gulf Publishing.

Blake, R. R., & Mouton, J. S. (1978) *The new management grid*. Houston: Gulf Publishing.

Blake, R. R., & Mouton, J. S. (1964) *The managerial grid*. Houston, TX: Gulf Publishing.

Blanchard, K. H., & Peale, N. V. (1988) *The power of ethical management*.

Blase, J. G. (1990) Some negative effects of principals' control-oriented and protective behaviors. *American Educational Research Journal 27*(4), 727–753.

Blau, P. M. (1970). A formal theory of differentiation in organization." *American Sociological Review 35*(2), 201–218.

Bliss, W. (1994). Managing budgets. *NAASP Bulletin, 78*(566), 327–344.

Block, P. (1993). *Stewardship: Choosing service over self-interest*. San Francisco: Berrett-Koehler.

Bloom, B. (1956). *Taxonomy of educational objectives: A classification of educational goals. Handbook I*: Cognitive domain. White Plains, NY: Longman.

Bloom, B., & Krathwohl, D. R. (1984). *Taxonomy of educational objectives*. Addison-Wesley.

Blumberg, A., & Greenfield, W. (1980) *The effective principal: Perspectives on school leadership*. Boston: Allyn & Bacon.

Boardman, G. R., & Cassel, M. (June, 1983). How well does the public know its school board, *Phi Delta Kappan 64*(10), 739–744.

Bolman, L. G., & Deal, T. E. (1995). *Leading with soul: An uncommon journey of spirit*. San Francisco: Jossey-Bass.

Bolman, L. G., & Deal, T. E. (1993). Everyday epistemology in school leadership: Patterns and prospects.

In P. Hallinger, K. Leithwood, & G. Murphy (Eds.), *Cognitive perspectives on educational leadership.* New York: Teachers College Press.

Bolman, L. G., & Deal, T. E. (1991) *Reframing organizations.* San Francisco: Jossey-Bass.

Bonsignore, F. N. (1997). People leadership. In K. Shelton (Ed.), *A new paradigm of leadership* (pp. 55–58). Provo, UT: Executive Excellence.

Bossert, S., Dwyer, D., Rowan, B., & Lee, G. (1982). The instructional management role of the principal. *Educational Administration Quarterly, 18*(3), 34–64.

Boud, D., & Feletti, G. (1998). *The challenge of problem-based learning.* New York: St. Martin's Press.

Bourdieu, P., & Passeron, J. (1977). *Reproduction: In education, society, and culture.* Newbury Park, CA: Sage.

Bowles, S., & Gintis, H. (1976). *Schooling in capitalist America.* New York: Basic Books.

Boyan, N. J. (Ed.). (1988). *Handbook of research on educational administration.* New York: Longman.

Bracey, G. (1995, October). The fifth Bracey report on the condition of public education. *Phi Delta Kappan* 77(2), 149–160.

Brandt, R. (1992, September). On building learning communities: A conversation with Hank Levin. *Educational Leadership, 50*(1), 19–23.

Brandt, R. (1992, February) On rethinking leadership: A conversation with Tom Sergiovanni. *Educational Leadership, 49*(5), 46–49.

Bredeson, P. (1995). A journey toward community in educational administration. *UCEA Review, 36*(1), 1, 13–17.

Bridges, E. M. (1986). *The incompetent teacher.* Philadelphia: Falmer.

Bridges E., & Hallinger, P. (1995). *Implementing problem-based learning in leadership development.* University of Oregon, ERIC Clearinghouse on Educational Management.

Brookover, W. (1979). *School social systems and students' achievement.* New York: Praeger.

Brookover, W. B., Brady, C., Flood, P., Schwirgen, J., & Wisenboter, J. (1979). *School systems and school achievement.* New York: Praeger.

Brookover, W., & Lezotte, L. (1979). *Changes in school characteristics in coincidence with changes in student achievement.* East Lansing, MI: Michigan State University.

Brown, F. (1995). Privatization of public education: Theories and concepts. *Education and Urban Society, 2*(2), 116.

Bryk, A. (1993, July). *A view from the elementary school: The state of reform in Chicago.* Chicago: Consortium on Chicago School Research.

Bull, B. L., & McCarthy, M. M. (1995, November). Reflections on the knowledge base in land and ethics for educational leaders. *Educational Administration Quarterly* 31(4), 613–631.

Bullivant, B. M. (1989). Culture: Its nature and meaning for educators. In J. Banks and C. A. McGee Banks (Eds.), *Multicultural education: Issues and perspectives* (pp. 27–45). Boston: Allyn & Bacon.

Bull, B. L., & McCarthy, M. (1995). Reflections on the knowledge base in law and ethics for educational leaders. *Educational Administration Quarterly, A,* 613–631.

Bullock, L., & Gable, R. (1998, February 21). *Implementing the 1997 IDEA new challenges and opportunities for serving students with behavior disorders.* Reston, VA: Council for Exceptional Children.

Bullock, A., & Foster-Harrison, E. (1997, November/December). Making the best decisions: Designing for excellence! *Schools in the middle: NASSP,* 7(2), 37–39, 60–61.

Bullock, C. S., & Stewart, J. (1979). Incidence and correlates of second-generation discrimination. In M. L. Palley & M. B. Preston (Eds.), *Race, sex, and policy problems* (pp. 115–129). Lexington, MA: Lexington Books.

Bullock, C. S., & Stewart, J. (1978). *Compliant processing as a strategy for combating second generation discrimination.* Paper presented at the annual meeting of the Southern Political Science Association, Atlanta.

Burillo, R. C., & Reitzug, U. C. (1993). Transforming context and developing culture in schools. *Journal of Counseling and Development, 71*(6), 669–677.

Burns, J. M. (1978). *Leadership.* New York: Harper and Row.

Bynham, W. C. (1978, November). How to improve the validity of an assessment center. *Training and Development Journal, 32*(11), 4–6.

Bynham, W. C. (December, 1971). The assessment center as an aid in management development. *Training and Development Journal, 25*(12), 10–22.

Callahan, R. E. (1962). *Education and the cult of efficiency.* Chicago: University of Chicago Press.

Cameron, T. (1995, October). Block scheduling one year later, or, what's your schedule done for you lately? *Oklahoma Association of Secondary School Principals Newsletter.*

Campbell, R. (1987). *A history of thought and practical educational administration.* New York: Teachers.

Campbell, R. F., Cunningham, L. L., Nystrand, R. O., & Usdan, M. D. (1980). *The organization and control of American schools.* Columbus: Merrill.

Campion, J., & Arvey, R. (1989). Unfair discrimination in the employment interview. In R. Eder & G. Ferris (Eds.), *The employment interview: Theory, research and practice.* Newbury Park, CA: Sage.

Canady, R. L., & Rettig, M. (1995). *Block scheduling: A catalyst for change in high schools*. Princeton, NJ: Eye on Education.

Candoli, I. C., Hack, W. G., Ray, J., & Stollar, D. H. (1984). *School business administration: A planning approach*. Boston: Allyn & Bacon.

Capper, C. A. (1998, August). Critically oriented and postmodern perspectives: Sorting out the differences and applications for practice. *Educational Administration Quarterly, 34(3), 354–379.*

Capper, C. A. (1991). Educational administration in a pluralistic society: A multiparadigm approach. In Collen A. Capper (Ed.), *Educational administration in a pluralistic society*. Albany: State University of New York Press.

Carlson, R. (1989). *Restructuring schools: International memorandum*. Washington, DC: District of Columbia Public Schools.

Carlson, R. (1996). *Reframing and reforms*. White Plains, NY: Longman.

Carnegie Forum on Education and Economy. (1986). *A nation prepared: Teachers for the twenty-first century*. New York: Report of the Task Force on Teaching as a Profession.

Carnegie Task Force on Meeting the Needs of Young Children. (1994, August). Starting points: Meeting the needs of our youngest children. New York: Carnegie Corporation of New York.

Carroll, J. M. (1994). The Copernican plan evaluated: The evolution of a revolution. *Phi Delta Kappan, 76(2), 105–113.*

Carroll, J. M. (1990). The Copernican plan: Restructuring the American high school. *Phi Delta Kappan, 51, 358–365.*

Carson, C. C., Hiwelskamp, R. M., & Woodall, T. D. (1992, April). Perspectives on education in America. Final Draft. Albuquerque, NM: Sandia National Laboratories.

Carspecken, P., & Cordeiro, P. (1995). Being, doing, and becoming: Textual interpretation of social identity and a case study. *Qualitative Inquiry, 1(1), 87–109.*

Carter, G. R. (1993). Revitalizing American's public schools through systemic change. In Stanley Elam (Ed.), *The state of the nation's public schools*. Bloomington, IN: Phi Delta Kappan.

Carter, G., & Cunningham. W. G. (1997). *The American school superintendent: Leading in an age of pressure*. San Francisco: Jossey-Bass.

Castetter, W. B. (1996). *The human resource function in educational administration*. Englewood Cliffs, NJ: Prentice-Hall.

Center for the Future of Children. (1992, Spring). *The future of children*. Los Altos, CA: The David and Lucile Packard Foundation.

The Center for the Future of Children. (1992, Spring). School linked services. *The Future of Children, 2(1), 31–43.*

Checkley, K. (1997). The first seven…and the eighth: A conversation with Howard Gardner. *Educational Leadership, 55(1), 8–13.*

Children's Defense Fund. (1991). *The state of America's children*. Washington, DC: Children's Defense Fund.

Church, A., & Bracken, D. (1997, June). Advancing the state of the art of 360-degree feedback. *Organizational Management, 22(2), 149–162.*

Cibulka, J. G. (1997). Two eras of urban schooling: The decline of the old order and the emergence of new organizational form. *Education and Urban Society, 29(3), 317–341.*

Clarke, G. H. (1998). *Real questions, real answers*. Alexandria, VA: Association for Supervision and Curriculum Development.

Clemmer, E. F. (1991). *The school policy handbook: Primer for administrators and school board members*. Boston: Allyn & Bacon.

Clinchy, E. (1995, January). Sustaining and expanding the educational conversation. *Phi Delta Kappan, 77(5), 352–354.*

Cohen, D. K., & Spillane, J. P. (1992). Policy and practice: The relations between governance and instruction. In G. Grant (Ed.), *Review of research in education*. Washington, DC: American Educational Research Association.

Cohen, D. K., & March, J. G. (1974). *Leadership and ambiguity: The American college president*. New York: McGraw-Hill.

Cohen, J. J. (Ed.). (1990). *The fundamentalist phenomenon*. Grand Rapids, MI: William B. Eerdmans.

Cohen, J. M. & March, J. G. (1977, September). Almost random careers: The Wisconsin superintendency, 1940–1972. *Administrative Science Quarterly, 22, 79–92.*

Cohen, J. M., March, J. G., & Olsen, J. P. (1972). A garbage can model of organization choice. *Administrative Science Quarterly, 17, 1–25.*

Cole, N. S. (1990). Conceptions of educational achievement. *Educational Researcher, 19(3), 2–7.*

Coleman, J. (1993, March). *Family involvement in education*. Paper prepared for The Milken Family Foundation, National Education Conference. Los Angeles.

Coleman, J. S., & Hoffler, T. (1987). *Public and private high schools: The impact of communities*. New York: Basic Books.

Collins, G. C., & Porras, G. I. (1994). *Build to last: Successful habits of visionary companies*. New York: Harper-Collins.

Comer, J. P. (1991). *A brief history and summary of the school development program*. New Haven, CT: Yale Child Study Center.

Comer, J. P., Joyner, E. T., & Haynes, N. M. (1996). Lessons learned. In J. P. Comer, et al. (Eds.), *Rallying the whole village*. New York: Teachers College Press.

Commission on the Skills of American Workforce. (1990). *America's choice: High skills or low wages?* Rochester, NY: National Center on Education and the Economy.

Commission on Standards for the Superintendency. (1993). *Professional standards for the superintendency*. Arlington, VA: American Association of School Administrators.

Committee on Labor and Human Resources, United States Senate Report to the Chairman. (1993). School-linked human services: A comprehensive strategy for aiding students at risk of school failure. (GAO/HRD-94-21). Washington, DC: General Accounting Office.

Constas, M. A. (1998, March). The changing nature of educational research and a critique of postmodernism. *Educational Researcher, 27*(2), 26–32.

Cordeiro, P. (1999). The principal's role in curricular leadership and program development. In L. Hughes (Ed.), *The principal as leader* (2nd ed.). Upper Saddle River, NJ: Prentice-Hall.

Cordeiro, P. (1998). The principal's role in curricular leadership and program development. In L. W. Hughes (Ed.), *The principal as leader*. New York: Merrill.

Cordeiro, P. (1996). *Border crossings: Educational partnerships and school leadership*. San Francisco: Jossey-Bass.

Cordeiro, P. (1990). *Growing away from the barrio: An ethnography of high achieving, at-risk, Hispanic youths at two high schools*. Dissertation Abstracts International. University of Houston, Houston, TX.

Cordeiro, P., & Loup. K. (1996). Partnering changes the roles of school leaders: Implications for educational leadership preparation programs. In P. Cordeiro (Ed.), *Border crossings: Educational partnerships and school leadership*. San Francisco: Jossey-Bass.

Cordeiro. P., & Monroe-Kolek, M. (1996). Connecting school communities through the development of educational partnerships. In P. Cordeiro (Ed.), *Border crossings: Educational partnerships and school leadership*. San Francisco: Jossey-Bass.

Cordeiro, P., Reagan, T., & Martinez, L. (1994). *Multiculturalism and TQE: Addressing cultural diversity in schools*. Newbury Park, CA: Corwin.

Corey, M., & Corey, G. (1987). *Groups: Process and practice*. Pacific Grove, CA: Brooks/Cole.

Cortese, P. A. (1993). Accomplishments in comprehensive school health education. *Journal of School Health, 63*(1), 21–23.

Costa, A. L. (1997). Curriculum: A decision-making process. In A. L. Costa & R. M. Liebmarin (Eds.), *Envisioning process as content*. Thousand Oaks, CA: Corwin Press.

Covey, S. (1997). Leading by compass. In K. Shelton (Ed.), *A new paradigm of leadership* (pp. 83–88). Provo, UT: Executive Excellence.

Covey, S. R. (1989). *The 7 habits of highly effective people*. New York: Simon & Schuster. © 1998 Steven R. Covey. Used with Permission.

Covey, S. R., Merrill, A. R., & Merrill, R. R. (1994). *First things first*. New York: Simon & Schuster.

Craig, R. (1999). Ethical frameworks to guide action. In L. Hughes, (Ed.), *The principal as leader*. Upper Saddle River, NJ: Prentice Hall.

Craig, R. (1994). Ethical frameworks to guide action. In L. Hughes (Ed.), *The principal as leader*. New York: Merrill.

Cremin, L. (1965). *The genius of American education*. New York: Vintage.

Crosby, P. B. (1996). *The absolutes of leadership*. San Diego, CA: Pfeiffer.

Crowson, R. (1988). Editor's introduction. *Peabody Journal of Education, 65*(4), 1–8.

Cuban, L. (1989). *The urban school superintendency: A century and a half of change*. Bloomington, IN: Phi Delta Kappa.

Cuban, L. (1988). *The managerial imperatives and the practice of leadership in schools*. Albany: State University of New York Press.

Cuban, L. (1976). *The urban school superintendency: A century and a half of change*. Bloomington, IN: Phi Delta Kappa Education Foundation.

Culbertson, J. A. (1981). A century's quest for a knowledge base. In N. J. Boyan (Ed.), *Handbook of research on educational administration*. New York: Longman.

Cummins, J. (1989). *Empowering minority students*. Sacramento: California Association for Bilingual Education.

Cunningham, L., & Hentges, G. T. (1982). *The American school superintendent*. Arlington, VA: American Association of School Administrators.

Cunningham, W. G. (December, 1994). The way we do things around here. *The School Administrator, 54*(11), 24–26.

Cunningham, W. G. (1991). *Empowerment: Vitalizing personal energy*. Atlanta, GA: Humanics.

Cunningham, W. G. (1982). *Systematic planning for educational change*. Palo Alto; CA: Mayfield.

Cunningham, W. G., & Gresso, D. W. (1993). *Cultural leadership: The culture of excellence in education.* Boston, MA: Allyn & Bacon.

Danzberger, J. P. (1998). School boards—Partners in policy. In R. Spillane & P. Regnier (Eds.), *The superintendent of the future.* Gaithersburg, MD: Aspen.

Daresh, J. C. (1992, May). Teacher evaluation: Are you a drive-by shooter? *Principal, 71*(5).

Darling-Hammond, L. (1998, February). Standards for assessing teaching effectiveness are key." *Phi Delta Kappan, 79*(6).

Darling-Hammond, L. (1997). *The right to learn.* San Francicso: Jossey-Bass.

Darling-Hammond, L., & Falh, B. (1997). Using standards and assessments to support student learning. *Phi Delta Kappan, 79*(3), 190–202.

Data Research. (1991). *U.S. Supreme Court education Cases.* Rosemount, MN: Data Research.

David, J. L. (May 1989). Synthesis of research on school-based management. *Educational Leadership, 46*(8), 45–53.

Davidman, L., & Davidman, P. T. (1994). *Teaching with a multicultural perspective.* New York: Longman.

Deal, T., & Peterson, K. (1998). *Shaping school culture: The heart of leadership.* San Francisco: Jossey-Bass.

Deal, T. E., & Kennedy, A. A. (1982) *Corporate cultures.* Reading, MA: Addison Wesley.

Deal, T. E., & Peterson, K. E. (1990, September). *The principals' role in shaping school culture.* Washington, DC: Office of Education Research and Improvement.

Delbecq, A. L., Van De Ven, A. H., & Gustafsan, P. H. (1975). *Group techniques for program planning.* Dallas: Scott, Foresman.

Delon, F. (1977). *Legal controls on teacher conduct: Teacher discipline.* Topeka, KS: NOLPE.

Deming, W. E. (1997). Quality leaders. In K. Shelton (Ed.), *A new paradigm of leadership* (pp. 121–126). Provo, UT: Executive Excellence.

Deming, W. E. (1991). Foundations for management of quality in the western world. In *An introduction to total quality for schools.* Arlington, VA: American Association of School Administrators.

Deming, W. E. (1986) *Out of crisis.* Cambridge, MA: MIT Center for Advanced Engineering Studies.

Deming, W. E. (1993) *The new economics for industry, government and education.* Cambridge, MA: MIT Center for Advanced Engineering Studies.

Depree, M. (1989). *Leadership is an art.* New York: Dell.

Detterman, D. (1993). The case for the prosecution: Transfer as an epiphenomenon. In D. Detterman & R. Sternberg (Eds.), *Transfer on trial: Intelligence cognition and instruction.* Norwood, NJ: Ablex.

Deutsch, M. (1963). The disadvantaged child and the learning process. In A. H. Paslow (Ed.), *Education in depressed areas* (pp. 163–180). New York: Teachers College Press.

Dewey, J. (1938). *Logic: The theory of inquiry.* New York: Holt, Rinehart & Winston.

Dewey, J. (1910). *How we think.* Boston: DC Heath.

Diangreco, M. F., Cloninger, C. J., & Iverson, V. S. (1993). *Choosing options and accommodations for children.* Baltimore: Brookes.

Diaz, C. (1992). *Multicultural education for the twenty-first century.* Washington, DC: National Education Association.

Digest of Education Statistics. (1995). Washington, DC: National Center for Education Statistics.

Dolan, L. J. (1992). Models for integrating human services into the school. (Report no. 30). Baltimore, MD: Center for Research on Effective Schooling. (ERIC Document Reproduction Service No. ED 347 244).

Doll, R. (1986). *Curriculum improvement, decision making and process.* Boston: Allyn & Bacon.

Doyle, D., & Finn, C. (1985). Now is the time for year-round schools. *Principal 65*, 29–31.

Doyle, M., & Straus, D. (1993). *How to make meetings work* (3rd ed.). New York: The Berkley Publishing Group.

Drake, T. L., & Roe, W. H. (1999). *The principalship.* Upper Saddle River, NJ: Merrill.

Drake, T., & Roe, W. H. (1994). *School business management: Supporting instructional effectiveness.* Boston: Allyn & Bacon.

Drucker, P. F. (1998). *Managing the nonprofit organization.* New York: Diane Publishing.

Drucker, P. F. (1997). Leaders as doers. in K. Shelton (Ed.), *A new paradigm of leadership.* Provo, UT: Executive Excellence.

Drucker, P. F. (1992) *Managing for the future: The 1990's and beyond.* New York: Truman Tally Books.

Drucker, P. F. (1980) *Managing in turbulent times.* New York: Harper & Row.

Drucker, P. F. (1974) *Management: Tasks, responsibilities, and practices.* New York: Harper & Row.

Drucker, P. F. (1967) *The effective executive.* New York: Harper & Row.

Drucker, P. F. (1954) *The practice of management.* New York: Harper & Row.

Dryfoos, J. (1994). *Full-service schools: A revolution in health and social services for children, youth, and families.* San Francisco: Jossey-Bass.

Duignan, P. A. (1997). *The ideal and the ethics of authenticity in leadership.* Annual Conference of the University Council for Educational Administration. Oct. 31–Nov. 2, Orlando, Florida.

Duke, D. L. (1998, April). The normative context of organizational leadership. *Educational Administration Quarterly, 34*(2), 165–195.

Duke, D. (1987). *School leadership and instructional improvement.* New York: Random House.

Duke, D., & Grogan, M. (1997). The moral and ethical dimensions of leadership. In L. Beck & J. Murphy (Eds.), *Ethics in educational leadership programs.* Columbia, MO: UCEA.

Duke, D. et. al. (1997, November). A thousand voices from the firing line: A study of educational leaders, their jobs and the problems they face. Paper presented at the 1997 Annual Conference of the University Council of Educational Administrations, Orlando, FL.

E. C. I. S. (1998). *The directory of the European council of international schools.* Petersfield, England: European Council of International Schools.

Education Week. (1999, January 11) *Quality counts: Education Week/Pew Charitable Trusts report on education in the 50 states.* Bethesda, MD: Education Week.

Einedar, D., & Bishop, H. (1997). Block scheduling the high school: The effects on achievement behavior, and student-teacher relationships. *NASSP Bulletin, 51*(589), 45–54.

Eisner, M. (1997). Creative leadership. In K. Shelton (Ed.), *A new paradigm of leadership* (pp. 105–108). Provo, UT: Executive Excellence.

Ellena, W. G., & Redfern, G. (1972). *Tentative Report: Evaluation of personnel.* Richmond, VA: State Department of Education.

Elmore, R. F., & Fuhrman, S. H. (1994). The governance of curriculum. *1994 ASCD Yearbook.* Alexandria, VA: Association for Supervision and Curriculum Development.

Elmore, R. F., Peterson, P. L., & McCarthy, S. J. (1996). *Restructuring in the classroom: Teaching, learning, and school organization.* San Francisco: Jossey-Bass.

English, F. W. (1995). Toward a reconsideration of biography and other forms of life writings as a focus for teaching educational administration. *Educational Administration Quarterly, 31*(2), 203–233.

English, F. (1993, Spring). A post-structural view of the grand narratives in educational administration. *Organization theory dialogues.* Bloomington, IN: Organizational Theory SIG (AERA) Indiana University.

English, F. W., & Steffy, B. E. (1997, February) Using films to teach leadership in educational administration. *Educational Administration Quarterly, 33*(1), 107–115.

Epstein, J. L. (1995). School/family/community partnerships: Caring for the children we share. *Phi Delta Kappan, 76,* 701–712.

Epstein, J. L., Coates, L., Salinas, K. C., Sanders, M. G., & Simon, B. S. (1997). *School, family, and community partnerships: Your handbook for action.* Thousand Oaks, CA: Corwin Press.

Erickson, E. H. (1998). *Identity and the life cycle.* New York: W. W. Norton.

Essex, N. L. (1999). *School law and the public schools.* Boston: Allyn & Bacon.

Etzioni, A. (1993). *The spirit of community.* New York: Crown.

Etzioni, A. (1989) Humble decision making. *Harvard Business Review, 67,* 122–126.

Etzioni, A. (1986). Mixed scanning revisited. *Public Administration Review, 46,* 8–14.

Etzioni, A. (1967, December) Mixed scanning: Their approach to decision-making. *Public Administration Review, 27:*385–392.

Evers, C. W., & Lakomski, G. (1996). *Exploring educational administration.* New York: Pergamon Press.

Evers, C. W., & Lakomski, G. (1996, August). Science in educational administration: A postpositivist conception. *Educational Administration Quarterly, 32*(3), 379–402.

Evers, C. W., & Lakomski, G. (1991). *Knowing educational administration: Contemporary methodological controversies in educational administration.* New York: Pergamon Press.

Fairman M., Holmes, M., Hardage, J., & Lucas, C. (1979). *Manual of the organization health instrument.* Fayetteville, AR: Organizational Health: Diagnostic and Development.

Fashola, O. S., and Slavin, R. E. (1998, January). Schoolwide reform models: What works? *Phi Delta Kappan, 79,* 370–379.

Fayol, H. (1949). Administrator Industrielle et generale. In C. Starrs (Ed.), *General and industrial management.* London: Sir Issac Pitman and Sons.

Fisher, C., Duyer, D., & Yocam, K. (Eds.). (1996). *Education and technology.* San Francisco: Jossey-Bass.

Flanery, R. A. (1997). Making your school a safe place for learning. *Schools in the Middle,* 7(20), 43–47.

Follett, M. P. (1942). *Dynamic administration.* New York: Harper.

Follett, M. P. (1924). *Creative experience.* London: Longmans Green.

Foster, W. (1986). *Paradigms and promises: New approaches to educational administration.* Buffalo, NY: Prometheus Books.

Foster, W. (1998, August). Editor's foreword. *Educational Administration Quarterly, 34*(3), 294–297.

Frank, J. (1970). *Law and the modern man.* Gloucester, MA: Peter Smith. (Original work published in 1930)

Frankl, V. (1984). *Man's search for meaning.* New York: Simon & Schuster. (Originally published in 1949.)

Frase, L., English, F., & Poston, W. (1995). *The curriculum management audit: Improving school quality*. Arlington, VA: AASA.

Freire, P. (1973). *Pedagogy of the oppressed*. New York: Seabury Press.

Freire, P. (1985). *The politics of education*. South Hadley, MA: Bergin and Garvey.

Fukuyama, F. (1995). *Trust: The social virtues and the creation of prosperity*. New York: Free Press.

Fullan, M. (1990). Staff development, innovation, and institutional development. In Joyce, B. (Ed.), *Changing school culture through staff development*. Alexandria, VA: Association for Supervision and Curriculum Development.

Fullan, M. (1991). *The new meaning of educational change*. New York: Teachers College Press.

Fullan, M. (1993). *Change forces*. Bristol, PA: Falmer Press.

Fullan, M. (1997). *What's worth fighting for in the principalship*. New York: Teachers College Press.

Fullan, M. (1993). Innovation, reform, and restructuring strategies. In G. Cawelti (Ed.), *Challenges and achievements of American education*. Alexandria, VA: Association for Supervision and Curriculum Development.

Fullan, M., with Stiegelbauer, S. (1991). *The new meaning of educational change*. New York: Teachers College Press.

Fullan, M., & Hargreaves, A. (1992). *What's worth fighting for in your school*. New York: Teachers College Press.

Fuhrman, S. H. (1994). Legislature and Education Policy. In R. F. Elmore and S. H. Fuhrman (Eds.), *The governance of curriculum*. Alexandria, VA: Association for Supervision and Curriculum Development.

French, D. (1998, November). The state's role in shaping a progressive vision of public education. *Phi Delta Kappan, 80*,(3), 184–195.

Gable, R., Baler, G., Wang, M., & Walberg, H. (1995). *Research on school effects in urban schools*. Philadelphia: National Research Center on Education in the Inner City.

Gardner, H. (1993). *Multiple intelligences: The theory in practice*. New York: Basic Books.

Gardner, H. (1983). *Frames of mind: The theory of multiple intelligences*. New York: Basic Books.

Gardner, H., & Boix-Mansilla, V. (1994, February 7). Teaching for understanding—within and across the disciplines. *Educational Leadership, 51*(5), 14–18.

Gardner, H. (1991). *The unschooled mind: How children think and how schools should teach*. New York: Basic Books.

Gardner, H. (1993). *Frames of mind: The theory of multiple intelligences*. New York: Basic Books. (Originally published in 1983.)

Gardner, S. (1993). Key issues in developing school-linked, integrated services. *Education and Urban Society, 25*(2), 141–152.

Gardner, S. L. (1992). Key issues in developing school-linked integrated services. In *The future of children* (2nd ed.) (pp. 85–94). Los Altos, CA: Center for the Future of Children.

Garnos, M. L., & King, R. A. (1994). Non-traditional sources of revenue: South Dakota's experience. *NASSP Bulletin, 78*(566), 27–38.

Garvin, J. R., & Young, A. H. (1993). Resource issues: A case study from New Orleans. *Politics of Education Association Yearbook*, pp. 93–106.

Gee, W. (1997). The Copernican plan and year-round education: Two ideas that work together. *Phi Delta Kappan, 78*(10), 793–796.

Gerber, S. B. (1996, Fall). Extracurricular activities and academic achievements. *Journal of Research and Development in Education, 30*(1), 42–50.

Giangreco, M. F., Cloninger, C. J., & Iverson, V. S. (1993). *Choosing options and accommodations for children*. Baltimore: Brookes.

Gilligan, C. (1982; 1993). *In a different voice*. Cambridge, MA: Harvard University Press.

Giroux, H. (1992). *Border crossings: Cultural workers and the politics of education*. New York: Routledge.

Glass, T. E. (1992). *The study of the American school superintendency*. Arlington, VA: The American Association of School Administrators.

Glatthorn, A. (1997). *The principal as curriculum leader: Shaping what is taught and tested*. Thousand Oaks, CA: Corwin Press.

Glatthorn, A. A. (1994). *Developing a quality curriculum*. Alexandria, VA: ASCD.

Glickman, C. D. (1998). *Renewing America's schools*. San Francisco: Jossey-Bass.

Glickman, C. D. (1998). *Revolutionizing American schools*. San Francisco: Jossey-Bass.

Goerty, M. E., Floden, R. E. & O'Day, J. (October, 1996). *Systematic reform*. Washington, DC: U.S. Office of Educational Research and Improvement.

Goldring, E. G. (1990). Elementary school principals as boundary spanners: Their engagement with parents. *Journal of Educational Administration, 28*(1), 53–62.

Good, H. (May, 1998). Then and now: The more boards change, the more they remain the same. *The American School Board Journal, 185*, 5.

Goodlad, J. I. (1994). *Educational renewal: Better teachers, better schools*. San Francisco: Jossey-Bass.

Goodlad, J. I. (1991). *Teachers for our nation's schools*. San Francisco: Jossey-Bass.

Goodlad, J. I., & Lovitt, T. C. (Eds.). (1993). *Integrating general and special education*. New York: Macmillan.

Gordon, B. M. (1985). Toward emanicpation in citizenship education: The case of African-American cultural knowledge. *Theory and Research in Social Education, 12,* 1–23.

Gorton, R., & Snowden, P. (1997). *School leadership and administration.* Madison, WI: WCB Brown & Benchmark.

Gorton, R., & Snowden, P. (1993). *School leadership and administration: Important concepts, case studies, and simulations* (4th ed.). Madison, WI: WCB Brown and Benchmark.

Gould, S. J. (1981). *The mismeasure of man.* New York: Norton.

Gould, S. J. (1995, November). The geometer of race. *Discover,* 109, 64–69.

Grant, C. A. (Ed.). (1992). *Research and multicultural education: From the margins to the mainstream.* London: Falmer Press.

Grant Foundation Commission on Work, Family, and Citizenship. (1988). *Citizenship through service.* Washington, DC: Grant Commission.

Graves, B. (1995, February). Putting pay on the line. *The School Administrator, 52*(2), 8–16.

The William T. Grant Foundation. (1998, January). *The forgotten half: Non-college youth in America.* Washington, DC: William T. Grant Foundation.

Greenfield, T. B. (1988). The decline and fall of science in educational administration. In D. E. Griffiths, R. T. Stout, and P. B. Forsyth (Eds.), *Leaders for American schools.* Berkeley, CA: McCutchan.

Greenfield, T. B. (1985). Theories of educational organization: A critical perspective. In T. Husen and T. B. Greenfield (Eds.), *International encyclopedia of education.* Oxford: Pergamon Press.

Greenfield, T. B. (1980). The man who comes back through the door in the wall: Discovering truth, discovering self, discovering organizations. *Educational Administration Quarterly, 16*(3), 26–59.

Greenfield, T. B. (1979). Ideas versus data: How can the data speak for themselves? In G. L. Immegart and W. L. Boyd (Eds.), *Problem-finding in educational administration.* New York: Lexington Books.

Greenfield, T. B. (1978, Spring). Reflections on organizational theory and the truth of irreconcilable realities. *Educational Administration Quarterly, 14*(2), 1–23.

Greenfield, T. B. (1975). Theory about organizations: A new perspective and its implications for schools. In N. Hughes (Ed.), *Administering education: International challenge.* London: Athlone.

Greenfield, T., & Ribbins, P. (Eds.). (1993). *Greenfield on educational administrations: Towards a humane science.* London: Routledge.

Greenfield, W. D. (February, 1995). Toward a theory of school administration: The centrality of leadership. *Educational Administration Quarterly, 31*(1), 61–85.

Greenfield, W. D. (1993). Articulating values and ethics in administrative preparation. In Collen A. Capper (Ed.), *Educational administration in a pluralistic society.* Albany, NY: State University of New York Press.

Greenfield, W. D. (1990). Five standards of good practice for the ethical administrator. *NASSP Bulletin, 74*(528), 32–37.

Greenfield, W. D. (1982) *A synopsis of research on school principals.* Washington, DC: National Institute for Education.

Greenleaf, R. K. (1996). *On becoming a servant leader.* San Francisco: Jossey-Bass.

Greenleaf, R. K. (1977). *Servant leadership: A journey into the nature of legitimate power and greatness.* New York: Paulist Press.

Greenleaf, R. K. (1970). *The servant as leader.* Indianapolis, IN: R. K. Greenleaf Center for Servant Leadership.

Griffiths, D. E. (1979). Intellectual turmoil in educational administration. *Educational Administration Quarterly, 13*(3), 43, 65.

Griffiths, D. E. (1969). *Developing taxonomies of organizational behavior in educational administration.* Chicago: Rand McNally.

Griffiths, D. E. (1959). *Administrative theory.* New York: Appleton-Century-Crofts.

Griffiths, D. E., Stout, R. T., & Forsyth, P. E. (Eds). (1988). *Leaders for America's schools: The report and papers on the national commission on excellence in educational administration.* Berkley: McCutchan.

Gross, J. (1992, March 29). Collapse of inner-city families creates America's new orphans. *New York Times National,* 1, 616.

Guba, E., & Lincoln, Y. (1989). *Fourth generation evaluation.* Beverly Hills, CA:

Guthrie, J. W., & Reed, R. J. (1991). *Educational administration and policy: Effective leadership for American education.* Boston: Allyn & Bacon.

Hall, G. E., & Hord, S. M. (1987). *Change in schools: Facilitating the process.* Albany, NY: State University of New York Press.

Hallinan, M. (1979). Structural effects of children's friendships and cliques. *Social Psychology Quarterly, 42,* 54–77.

Hallinger, P., Leithwood, L. E., & Murphy, J. (Eds). (1994). *Cognitive perspectives on educational administration.* New York: Teachers College Press.

Hallinger, P., & Murphy, J. (1987) Instructional leadership in the school context. In W. Greenfield (Ed.), *Instructional leadership: Concepts, issues, and controversies* (pp. 79–207). Boston: Allyn & Bacon.

Halpin, A. W. (1966) *Theory and research in administration*. New York: Macmillan.

Halpin, A. W. (1958) *Administrative theory in education*. Chicago: University of Chicago Press.

Halpin, A. W. (1956). *The leader behavior of school superintendents*. Columbus, OH: Ohio State University College of Education.

Hanson, E. M. (1979, 1991, 1996) *Educational administration and organizational behavior*. Boston: Allyn & Bacon.

Hanushek, E. (1994). *Making schools work: Improving performance and controlling costs*. Washington, DC: Brookings Institution.

Hardage, J. G. (1978). *Development of an instrument to measure the task-centered and the internal state components of organizational health*. Unpublished doctoral dissertation. Fayetteville, AR: University of Arkansas.

Hargreaves, A., & Fullan, M. (1998). *What's worth fighting for out there*. New York: Teachers College Press.

Harris, B., & Monk, B. J. (1992). *Personnel administration in education*. Boston: Allyn & Bacon.

Harris, C. E. (1996). The aesthetic of Thomas B. Greenfield: An exploration of practice that leaves no marks. *Educational Administration Quarterly, 32*(4), 487–511.

Harry, B. (1992). *Cultural diversity, families, and the special education system*. New York: Teachers College Press.

Hart, A. W. (September, 1995). Reconceiving school leadership: Emergent views. *The Elementary School Journal. 96*,(1), 9–28.

Hart, A. W., & Bredeson, P. V. (1996). *The principalship: A theory of professional learning and practice*. New York: McGraw-Hill.

Hartley, H. (1990). Boardroom bottom line. *American School Board Journal, 177*(2), 29–31.

Health Insurance Association of America. (1986). *Wellness at the worksite. A manual*. Washington, DC: HIAA.

Hechinger, N. (1993). The roles of technology. In S. Rocikman (Ed.), *The future: New visions of schooling*. Electronic School. Alexandria, VA: National School Board.

Henderson, A., & Berla, N. (Eds.). (1994). *A new generation of evidence: The family is critical to student achievement*. Columbia, MD: Center for Law and Education.

Henderson, R. (1985). *Compensation management*. Reston, VA: Reston Publishing.

Hemphill, J. K., & Coons, A. (1950). *Leadership behavior description*. Columbus, OH: Personnel Research Board, Ohio State University.

Herman, J., Aschbacher, P., & Winters, L. (1992). *A practical guide to alternative assessment*. Alexandria,

VA: Association for Supervision and Curriculum Development.

Herman, J. J., & Herman, J. L. (1993). *School-based management: Current thinking and practice*. Springfield, IL: Charles C Thomas.

Herman, J., & Winters, L. (1992). *Tracking your school's success: A guide to sensible evaluation*. Newbury Park, CA: Corwin Press.

Hersey, P. (1994, February 12). *AASA/NASSP superintendent leadership development program*. Presented at the American Association of School Administrators, Conference on Education, San Francisco, CA.

Hersey, P., & Blanchard, K. H. (1977, 1982) *Management of organizational behavior: Utilizing human resources*. Englewood Cliffs, NJ: Prentice-Hall.

Hersey, P., & Blanchard, K. H. (1988). *Management of organizational behavior: Utilizing human resources* (5th ed.). Englewood Cliffs, NJ: Prentice-Hall.

Heslep, R. D. (1997, February). The practical value of philosophical thought for the ethical dimension of educational leadership. *Educational Administration Quarterly, 33*(1), 67–85.

Hesselbein, F. (1997). Strategic leadership. In K. Shelton (Ed.), *A new paradigm of leadership* (pp. 101–104). Provo, UT: Executive Excellence.

Hewstone, M., & Brown, R. (Eds.). (1986). *Contact and conflict in intergroup encounters*. New York: Basil Blackwell.

Hill, M. S., & Raglan, J. C. (1995). *Women as educational leaders*. Thousand Oaks, CA: Corwin.

Hill, R. B. (1991). *The strengths of black families*. New York: Emerson Hall.

Hirsch, E. D. (1996). *The schools we need: And why we don't have them*. New York: Doubleday.

Hodgkinson, C. (1991). *Educational leadership: The moral art*. Albany, NY: State University of New York Press.

Hodgkinson, C. (1991). *Educational leadership: The moral art*. Albany, NY: State University of New York Press.

Hodgkinson, E. (1982). *Toward a philosophy of administration*. Oxford, MA: Blackwell.

Hodgkinson, H. L. (October, 1995). What should we call people? *Phi Delta Kappan 77*(2), 173–179.

Hodgkinson, H. L. (1993). Keynote address by Harold Hodgkinson. In S. Elarn (Ed.), *The state of the nation's public schools*. Bloomington, IN: Phi Delta Kappa.

Hofstede, G. (1991). *Cultures and organizations: Software of the mind*. London: McGraw-Hill.

Holland, A., & Andre, T. (1991). Is the extracurriculum an extra curriculum? *American Secondary Education Journal, 19*(2), 1–12.

Holland, S. (1989). (1989, September/October). Fighting the epidemic of failure: A radical strategy for educating inner-city boys. *Teacher Magazine*, 88–89.

Hooper-Brian, K., & Lawson, H. (1994). *Serving children, youth and families through interprofessional collaboration and service integration*. Oxford, OH: Institute for Educational Renewal.

Hooper-Brian, K., & Lawson, H. A. (1994, October). Serving children, youth, and families through inter-professional collaboration and service integration: A framework for action. Philadelphia: National Forum for the Danforth Foundation and the Institute for Educational Renewal at Miami University.

Hopfenberg, W. S., & Levin, H. M. (1993). *The accelerated schools resource guide*. San Francisco: Jossey-Bass.

Hottenstein, D., & Malatesta, C. (1993). Putting a schooling year with intensive scheduling. *High School Magazine, 2*, 23–29.

Hoy, W. K. (1994, May). Foundations of educational administration: Traditional and emerging perspectives. *Educational Administration Quarterly 30*(2), 178–198.

Hoy, W. K., & Miskel, C. G. (1991, 1995). *Educational administration: Theory, research and practice*. New York: McGraw-Hill.

Hoy, W. K., & Tarter, C. J. (1995). *Administrators solving the problems of practice*. Boston: Allyn & Bacon.

Hoyle, J. R., English, F. W., & Steffy, B. E. (1990). *Skills for successful school leaders* (2nd ed.). Arlington, VA: American Association of School Administrators.

Hughes, L. (1999). *The principal as instructional leader*. Englewood Cliffs, NJ: Prentice-Hall.

Hughes, L. W., & Achilles, C. M. (1971). The supervisor as change agent. *Educational Leadership, 28*(8), 840–848.

Hymes, D. L., Chafin, A. E., & Gonder, P. (1991). *The changing face of testing and assessment*. Arlington, VA: American Association of School Administrators.

Iannoccone, L. (1978). *Public participation in local school districts*. Lexington, MA: Lexington Books.

IBM. (1992, June 22) *EduQuest: The journey begins*. Armonk, NY: IBM Educational Systems.

Janis, I. L., & Mann L. (1977). *Decision making: The psychological analysis of conflict, choice, and commitment*. New York: Free Press.

Jehl, J., & Kirst, M. (1992). Getting ready to provide school-linked services: What schools must do. In *The future of children* (2nd ed.) (pp. 95–106). Los Altos, CA: Center for the Future of Children.

Joint Committee on Standards for Educational Evaluation. (1988). *The personnel evaluation standards: How to assess systems for evaluating educators*. Newbury Park, CA: Sage.

Johns, B. H. (1998). Translating the new discipline requirements of the 1997 Individuals with Disabilities Education Act into practice. In L. M. Bullock and R. A. Gable (Eds.), *Implementing the 1997 IDEA: New challenges*. Reston, VA: Council for Exceptional Children.

Johnson, B., & Galvan, P. (1996). Conceptualizing school partnerships and inter-organizational relationships: A consideration of the public choice and organizational economics frameworks. In P. Cordeiro (Ed.), *Border crossings: Educational partnerships and school leadership*. San Francisco: Jossey-Bass.

Johnson, D. W., & Johnson, R. (1975). *Learning together and alone*. Englewood Cliffs, NJ: Prentice-Hall.

Johnson, S. M. (1996). *Leading to change: The challenge of the new superintendency*. San Francisco: Jossey-Bass.

Johnson, S. M. (1990). *Teachers at work: Achieving success in our schools*. New York: Basic Books.

Johnston, E. W. G. (1988) *Organizational health instrument: Technical manual*. Fayetteville, AR: Organizational Health Diagnostic and Development Corporation.

Joyce, B., Weil, M., & Showers, B. (1992). *Models of teaching*. Boston: Allyn & Bacon.

Kagan, S. L. (1991). *United we stand: Collaboration for children*. New York: Teachers College Press.

Kanter, R. M. (1983). *The change masters*. New York: Simon & Schuster.

Kaplan, D. (1997). Leader as model and mentor. In K. Shelton (Ed.), *A new paradigm of leadership* (pp. 145–148). Provo, UT: Executive Excellence.

Kaplan, D. S., Peck, B. M., & Kaplan, H. B. (1997, August). Decomposing the academic failure–dropout relationship: A longitudinal analysis. *Journal of Educational Research, 90*(6), 331–343.

Kean, T. H. (1986, November). Who will teach? *Phi Delta Kappan, 18*, 205–208.

Kearns, D. (1995, January 9). Are we making progress? *Industry Week*, 12.

Keller, B. K. (1995). Accelerated schools: Hands-on learning in a unified community. *Educational Leadership, 52*(5), 10–13.

Kellogg Leadership Studies Project. (1997). *Leadership in the twenty-first century*. College Park, MD: University of Maryland, Center for Political Leadership and Participation.

Kilmann, R. (1989, October). A completely integrated program for creating and maintaining organizational success. *Organizational Dynamics*, 5–19.

Kimbrough, R. B., & Burket, C. W. (1990). *The principalship: Concepts and practices*. Englewood Cliffs, NJ: Prentice Hall.

Kimbrough, R. B., & Nunnery, M. Y. (1983). *Educational administration*. New York: MacMillan.

King, A., Clements, J., Enns, J., Lockerbie, J., & Warren, W. (1975). *Semestering the secondary school*.

Toronto, Ontario: Ontario Institute for Studies in Education.

Kirby, D., & Lovick, S. (1987). School-based health clinics. *Educational Horizons, 5*(3), 139–143.

Knapp, M. S. (1995). How shall we study comprehensive, collaborative services for children and families? *Educational Researcher, 24*(4), 5–16.

Knapp, M., & Shields, P. (1996). *Better schooling for the children of poverty: Alternatives to conventional wisdom.* Berkeley, CA: McCurtchan.

Knapp, M., & Associates (1995). *Teaching in high poverty classrooms.* New York: Teachers College Press.

Knezevich, S. J. (1975). *Administration of public education.* New York: Harper & Row.

Kotlowitz, A. (1991). *There are no children here: The story of two boys growing up in the other America.* New York: Anchor Books.

Kottkamp, R. B. (1982). The administrative platform in administrator preparation. *Planning and Change, 13,* 82–92.

Kouzes, J., & Posner, B. (1993). *Credibility: How leaders gain and lose it, why people demand it.* San Francisco: Jossey-Bass.

Kowalski, T., and Reitzug, U. (1993). *Contemporary school administration: An introduction.* New York: Longman.

Kozol, J. (1991). *Savage inequalities: Children in America's schools.* New York: Crown.

Kramer, S. L. (1997). What we know about block scheduling and its effects on math instruction, part II. *NASSP Bulletin, 81*(587), 69–82.

Krug, S. E. (1992, August). Instructional leadership: A constructivist perspective. *Educational Administration Quarterly, 28*(3), 430–443.

LaMorte, M. W. (1999). *School law.* Boston: Allyn & Bacon.

Lave, J. & Wenger, E. (1993). *Situated learning: Legitimate peripheral participation.* New York: Cambridge University Press.

Lawler, E. E. (1992). *The ultimate advantage.* San Francisco: Jossey-Bass.

Lawler, E. E. (1986). *High involvement management.* San Francisco: Jossey-Bass.

Lawrence P. R., & Lorsch, J. W. (1969). *Developing organization: Diagnosis and action.* Reading, MA: Addison Wesley.

Leithwood, K. (1999). *Changing leadership for changing times.* Bristol, PA: Taylor Frances.

Leithwood, K. (Ed.). (1995). *Effective school district leadership.* Albany, NY: State University of New York Press.

Leithwood, K. A. (1992, February). The move toward transformational Leadership. *Educational Leadership, 49*(5), 8–12.

Leithwood, K., Begley, P., & Cousins, B. (1994). *Developing expert leadership for future schools.* Bristol, PA: Falmer.

Leithwood, K. A., Steinback, R. S., & Raun, T. Superintendent's group problem-solving process. *Educational Administration Quarterly, 29*(3), 364–391.

Lemann, N. (1991). *The promised land.* New York: Knopf.

Lepering, R., & Moskowitz, M. (1993). *100 Best companies to work for.* New York: Doubleday Currency.

Lepsinger, R., & Yukl, G. (December, 1995). How to get the most out of 360-degree feedback. *Training, 32*(12), 45–50.

Lerner, R. (1995). *America's youth in crisis.* Thousand Oaks, CA: Sage.

Levine, D., & Ornstein, A. (1993, November/December). School effectiveness and national reform. *Journal of Teacher Education, 342.*

Levinson, B. (1996). Social difference and schooled identity at a Mexican *secundaria.* In B. Levinson, D. Foley, & D. Holland (Eds.), *The cultural production of the educated person.* New York: State University of New York Press.

Levinson, B., & Holland, D. (1996). The cultural production of the educated person: An introduction. In B. Levinson, D. Foley, & D. Holland (Eds.), *The cultural production of the educated person.* Albany, NY: State University of New York Press.

Levy, E. H. (1948). An introduction to legal reasoning. *University of Chicago Law Review, 15,* 501–574.

Lewin, K. (1951). *Field theory in social science.* New York: Harper & Row.

Lewis, A. (1992). *Urban youth in community service: Becoming part of the solution.* Washington, DC: Office of Educational Research and Improvement (EDO-UD-72-4).

Lezotte, L. (1988). Strategic assumptions of the effective school process. *Monographs on effective schools.* New York: New York State Council of Educational Administration.

Lezotte, L., Edmonds, R., & Ratner, G. (1974). *A final report: Remedy for school failure to equitably deliver basic school skills.* East Lansing, MI: Michigan State University Press.

Lieberman, A., & McLaughlin, M. (1992). Networks for educational change. *Phi Delta Kappan, 73*(9), 673–677.

Likert, R. (1967). *The human organization: Its management and value.* New York: McGraw-Hill.

Lindblom, C. E. (1995). *The intelligence of democracy.* New York: Free Press.

Lindblom, C. E. (1980). *The policy making process.* Englewood Cliffs, NJ: Prentice-Hall.

Lindblom C. E. (1959, Spring). The science of muddling through. *Public Administration Review, 19,* 79–88.

Lippitt, R., Watson, J., & Westley, B. (1958). *The dynamics of planned change*. New York: Harcourt, Brace, and World.

Lipsitz, J. (1984). *Successful schools for young adolescents*. New Brunswick, NJ: Transaction Books.

Little, J. W. (1986, September). The effective principal. *American Education*, 72, 3.

Liu, J. Q. (1997). The emotional bond between teachers & students. *Phi Delta Kappan*, 79(2), 156–157.

Louis, K. S., & Miles, M. B. (1990). *Improving the urban high school: What works and why*. New York: Teachers College Press.

Loveless, T., & Jasin, C. (1998). Starting from scratch: Political and organizational challenges facing charter schools. *Educational Administration Quarterly*, 34(1), 9–30.

Lucas, C. J. (1978). *Development of an instrument to measure form dimensions of organizational health: Innovation, autonomy, adaptation, and problem-solving adequacy*. Unpublished doctoral dissertation, Fayetville, AR: University of Arkansas.

Lunenburg, F., & Ornstein, A. (1991). *Educational administration: Concepts and practices*. Belmont, CA: Wadsworth.

Luster, R., & McAdoo, H. P. (1994). Factors related to the achievement and adjustment of young African American children. *Child Development*, 65, 1080–1094.

Macedo, D. (1994). *Literacies of power: What Americans are not allowed to know*. Boulder, CO: Westview Press.

Machiavelli (1988). *The prince*. New York: Skinner & Price. (First published in 1515.)

Manz, C. (1997). SuperLeadership. In K. Shelton (Ed.), *A new paradigm of leadership* (pp. 45–50). Provo, UT: Executive Excellence.

March, J. G., & Simon, H. A. (1959). *Organizations*. New York: Wiley.

Mark, G. (1996). Superintendency in crisis calls for system thinking: State, national leaders meet at national conference. *Leadership News*, 168, 1.

Martin, J. R. (1993). The school home: Rethinking schools for changing families. *Educational Leadership*, 52(1), 25–31.

Marzano, R., & Kendall, J. (1997). Curriculum frameworks. *NASSP Bulletin*, 81(590), 26–41.

Matthews, J. (1994, January 19). Analysis of seven frameworks of educational leadership. Charlottesville, VA: National Policy Board for Educational Administration, 1–16.

McCarthy, B. (1997a). *About learning*. Barrington, IL: Excel.

McCarthy, B. (March, 1997b). A tale of four learners: 4 MAT's learning styles. *Educational Leadership*, 54(6), 45–51.

McCarthy, M., Bull, B., Quantz, R., & Sorenson G. (1993). *Legal and ethical dimensions of schooling: Taxonomy and overview*. New York: McGraw-Hill.

McCarthy, M., & Cambron-McCabe, N., & Thomas, S. (1987). *Public school law* Boston: Allyn & Bacon. (1998).

McCurdy, J. (1992). *Building better board-administrator relations*. Arlington, VA: American Association of School Administrators.

McFarland, L. J., Senn, L. E., & Childress, J. R. (1993). *Twenty-first century leadership*. New York: Leadership Press.

McGregor, D. (1960). *The human side of enterprise*. New York: McGraw-Hill.

McKenna, B. H. (1965). *Staffing the schools*. New York: Teachers College Press.

McKnight, J. L., & Kretzman, J. P. (1993). Mapping community capacity. *Michigan State University Community and Economic Development Program Community News*, 1–4.

McLaughlin, M. W., Irby, M. A., & Longman, J. (1994). *Urban sanctuaries*. San Francisco: Jossey-Bass.

Meadows, M. E. (1995). *A preliminary program review of the four-period day as implemented in four high schools*. Doctoral dissertation. College Park, MD: University of Maryland.

Meek, J. C. (1972). *Unit cost analysis of the implementary expenditures in an urban system*. Master's thesis. University of Alberta.

Meier, K., & Stewart, J. (1991). *The politics of Hispanic education: Un paso Pa'lante y Dos Pa'tras*. New York: State University of New York Press.

Meno, L. R. (1984). Sources of alternative revenue. In *Fifth annual 1*. L. D. Webb and V. D. Mueller. (Eds.). Cambridge: Ballinger.

Mertz, N. T. (1997). Voices from the field: Principal perceptions. Presented at the 1997 Annual Conference of the University Council of Educational Administration, Orlando, FL.

Mertz, N. (1997). Knowing and doing: Exploring the ethical life of educational leaders. In L. Beck & J. Murphy (Eds.), *Ethics in educational leadership programs*. Columbia, MO: UCEA.

Metcalf, H., & Urwick L. (Eds.). (1941). *Dynamic administration and the collected papers of Mary Parker Follett*. New York: Harper.

Metz, M. (1978). *Classrooms and corridors: The crisis of authority in desegregated secondary schools*. Berkeley, CA: University of California Press.

Meyer, H. H., Kay, E. E., & French, R. P. (1965, February). Split roles in performance appraisals. *Harvard Business Review*, 48(2).

Miller, E. (1995, November/December). Shared decision making by itself doesn't make for better decisions. *Harvard Education Letter, XI*(6), 1–4.

Millman, J., & Darling-Hammond, L. (Eds.). (1990). *The new handbook of teacher evaluations: Assessing elementary and secondary school teachers.* Newbury Park, CA: Sage.

Milstein, M. (1993). *Changing the way we prepare educational leaders.* Newbury Park, CA: Corwin.

Mintzberg, H. (1989). *Mintzberg on management.* New York: Free Press.

Mintzberg, H. (1987, July-August). Crafting strategy. *Harvard Business Review, 65*(4), 66–75.

Mitchell, B., & Cunningham, L. L. (Eds.). (1990). *Educational leadership and changing contexts of families, communities, and schools.* (Eighty-ninth NSSE Yearbook, Part II) Chicago: University of Chicago Press.

Moffett, J. (1994). *The universal schoolhouse: Spiritual awakening through education.* San Francisco: Jossey-Bass.

Morris, C. (1992, December). Pressure groups and the politics of education. *Updating School Board Policies, 23*(9) 1–5.

Murphy, J. (1993). What's in? What's out? American education in the nineties. In S. Elam (Ed.), *The state of the nation's public schools* (pp. 55–56). Bloomington, IN: Phi Delta Kappan.

Murphy, J. (1995). *School-based management.* Thousand Oaks. CA: Corwin Press.

Murphy, J. (Ed.). (1993). *Preparing tomorrow's school leaders: Alternative designs.* University Park, PA: ULCA, Inc.

Murphy, J. (1991). *Restructuring schools: Capturing and assessing the phenomena.* New York: Teachers College Press.

Murphy, J. (1990). The educational reform movement in the 1980's. In J. Murphy (Ed.), *The reform of American public education in the 1980's: Perspectives and cases.* Berkeley: McCutchan.

Murphy, J., & Beck, L. (1996). *The four imperatives of a successful school.* Thousand Oaks, CA: Corwin.

Murphy, J., & Hallinger, P. (Eds.). (1993). *Restructuring schooling: Learning from ongoing efforts.* Newbury Park, CA: Corwin.

Murphy, J., & Lewis, K. (1999). *Handbook of research in educational administration.* San Francisco: Jossey-Bass.

Myrdal, G. (1944). *An American dilemma: The negro problem and modern democracy.* New York: Harper & Brothers.

Nanus, B. (1992). *Visionary leadership.* San Francisco: Jossey-Bass.

Nathan, J. (1996). *Charter schools.* San Francisco: Jossey-Bass.

National Association of Elementary School Principals. (1991). *Proficiencies for principals: Revised.* Alexandria, VA: NASPP.

National Association of Secondary School Principals. (1998). *Assessment handbook.* Reston, VA: NASSP.

National Association of State Boards of Education. (1992). *Winners all: A call for inclusive schools.* Alexandria, VA: National Association of State Boards of Education.

National Commission on Child Welfare and Family Preservation. (1990). *A commitment to change.* Washington, DC: American Public Welfare Association.

National Commission on Children. (1991/2). *Beyond rhetoric: A new American agenda for children and families.* Washington, DC: U.S. Government Printing Office.

National Commission on Excellence in Education. (1983). *A nation at risk: The imperative of school reform.* Washington, DC: U.S. Office of Education.

National Commission for Excellence in Teacher Education. (1985). *A call for change in teacher education.* Washington, DC: American Association of Colleges for Teacher Education.

National Commission on the Role of the School and the Community in Improving Adolescent Health. (1990). *Code blue: Uniting for healthier youth.* Alexandria, VA: National Association of State Boards of Education and the American Medical Association.

National Commission on Teaching and America's Future. (1996). *What matters most: Teaching and America's future.* New York: NCTAF.

National Education Goals Panel. (1991). *The national education goals report: Building a nation of learners.* Washington, DC: NAEG.

National Education Goals Panel. (1994). *The National Education goals report: Building a nation of learners.* Washington, DC: U.S. Government Printing Office.

National School Board Association. (1997). *Urban dynamics: Lessons learned from urban boards and superintendents.* Alexandria, VA: National School Boards Association.

National Governors Association. (1986). *Time for results.* Washington, DC: National Governors Association.

National Governors Association. (1987). *Results in education: 1987.* Washington, DC: National Governors Association.

National Science Board. (1983). *Educating Americans for the twenty-first century.* Washington, DC: National Science Foundation.

Negroponte, N. (1995). *Being digital.* New York: Alfred A. Knopf.

Neukrug, E. (1999). *The world of the counselor.* Pacific Grove, CA: Brooks/Cole.

Newmann, F. M., & Wehlage, G. (1993, April). Five standards of authentic instruction. *Educational Leadership, 50*(5), 8–12.

Nieto, S. (1992; 1996). *Affirming diversity: The sociopolitical context of multicultural education.* New York: Longman.

Noddings, N. (1992). *The challenge to care in schools: An alternative approach to education.* New York: Teachers College Press.

Norris, C. J. (1994). Cultivating creative cultures. In L. W. Hughes (Ed), *The principal as leader* (p. 341). New York: Macmillan.

Norris, J. H. (1994, Spring). What leaders need to know about school culture. *Journal of Staff Development, 15*(2).

North Central Regional Educational Laboratory (NCREL). (1994). *Designing learning and technology for educational reform.* Elmhurst, IL: NCREL.

Northhouse, P. G. (1997). *Leadership: Theory and practice.* Thousand Oaks, CA: Sage.

Norton, M., Webb, L., Dlugosh, L., & Sybouts, W. (1996). *The school superintendency: New responsibilities, new leadership.* Boston: Allyn & Bacon.

Odden, A. R., & Wohlestetter, P. (1994) Making school-based management work. *Educational Leadership, 51*(6), 32–36.

Ogawa, R. T. (1994). The institutional sources of educational reform: The case of school-based management. *American Educational Research Journal 31*, 519–548.

Ogbu, J. (1992). Understanding cultural diversity and learning. *Educational Researcher, 21*(8), 5–14.

Olson, L. (1997, February 12). Designing for learning. *Education Week, 16*(20), 40–45.

O'Neil, R. (1995). On lasting school reform: A conversation with Ted Sizer. *Educational Leadership, 52*(5), 4–9.

Outtz, J. H. (1993). *The demographics of American families.* Washington, DC: Institute for Educational Leadership.

Owens, R. G. (1995). *Organizational behavior in education.* Boston: Allyn & Bacon.

Pai, Y. (1990). *Cultural foundations of education.* Columbus, OH: Merrill.

Palmer, P. J. (1998). *The courage to teach: Exploring the inter-landscape of a teacher's life.* San Francisco: Jossey-Bass.

Parker, L., & Shapiro, J. (1993). The context of educational administration and social class. In C. Capper (Ed.), *Educational administration in a pluralistic society.* Albany, NY: State University of New York Press.

Payzant, T. W. (1994). Commentary on the district and school roles in curriculum reform: A superintendent's perspective. In R. F. Elmore and S. H. Fuhrman (Eds.), *The governance of curriculum* (p. 224). Alexandria, VA: ASCP.

Payzant, T. W. (1992). New beginnings in San Diego: Developing a strategy for interagency collaboration. *Phi Delta Kappan 74(2)*, 139–146.

Pedersen, P. (1994). *A handbook for developing multicultural awareness.* Alexandria, VA: American Counseling Association.

Peltier, G. (1991). Year-round education: The controversy and research evidence. *NASSP Bulletin, 75* (536), 120–129.

Perkins, D., & Blythe, T. (1994, February). Putting understanding up front. *Educational Leadership, 51*(1), 4–7.

Perman, P., & McLaughlin M. W. (1978, May). *Federal programs supporting educational change, volume VII: Implementing and sustaining innovation.* R-1589/8-HEW. Washington, DC: Department of Health, Education, and Welfare.

Perot, R. (1997). Caring leaders. In K. Shelton (Ed.), *A new paradigm of leadership* (pp. 237–240). Provo, UT: Executive Excellence.

Peskin, A. (1991). *The color of strangers, the color of friends.* Chicago: University of Chicago Press.

Peters, T. (1997). Brave leadership. In K. Shelton (Ed.), *A new paradigm of leadership* (pp. 73–76). Provo, UT: Executive Excellence.

Peters, T. (1994). *The pursuit of wow!* New York: Vintage Books.

Peters, T. (1987). *Thriving on chaos: Handbook for management revolution.* New York: Knopf.

Peters, T. J., & Austin, N. (1985). *A passion for excellenence: The leadership difference.* New York: Random House.

Peters, T. J., & Waterman, R. H. (1982). *In search of excellence: Lessons from America's best-run companies.* New York: Harper & Row.

Peterson, P. L., McCarthy, S. J., & Elmore, R. F. (1996, Spring). Learning from school restructuring. *American Educational Research Journal, 33*(1), 119–153.

Phinney, J. (1993). A three-stage model of ethnic identity development in adolescence. In M. Bernal & G. Knight (Eds.), *Ethnic identity.* New York: State University of New York Press.

Popham, W. J. (1997). The standards movement and the emperor's new clothes. *NASSP Bulletin, 81*(590), 21–25.

Porlin, B. S. (1997, November 1). Complexity and capacity: A survey of principal role change in Washington state. Paper presented at UCEA annual meeting, Orlando, Florida.

Postman, N. (1995). *The end of education: Redefining the value of school.* New York: Knopf.

Pounder, D. (1995). Theory to practice in administrator preparation. *Journal of School Leadership 5,* 151–162.

President's Committee of Advisors on Science and Technology. (1997, March). *Report to the president on the use of technology to strengthen K-2 education in the United States.* Washington, DC: Panel on Educational Technology.

Prestine, N. A. (1995). A constructivist view of the knowledge base in educational administration. In R. Donmoyer, M. Imber, & J. Scheurich (Eds.), *The knowledge base in educational administration.* Albany, NY: State University of New York Press.

Purkey W. W., & Novak, J. M. (1984). *Inviting school success* (2nd ed.). Belmont, CA: Wadsworth.

Putman, R. D. (1996, Winter). The strange disappearance of civic America. *The American Prospect, 24,* 34–48.

Quigley, M. (1997). Leader as learner. In K. Shelton (Ed.), *A new paradigm of leadership* (pp. 93–96). Provo, UT: Executive Excellence.

Quinlan, C., George, C., & Emmett, Y. (1987). *Year-round education: Year-round opportunities.* Los Angeles: California State Department of Education. (ERIC Reproduction Service No. ED 285 272.)

Raferty, J. R. (1992). *Land of fair promise.* Palo Alto, CA: Stanford University Press.

Ramirez, M., & Casteñeda, A. (1974). *Cultural democracy, bicognitive development and education.* New York: Academic Press.

Ravitch, D. (1995). *National standards in American education.* Washington, DC: Brookings Institution Press.

Raywid, M. A. (1994, September). Alternative schools: The state of the art. *Educational Leadership, 52*(1), 25–31.

Razik, T. A., & Swanson, A. D. (1995). *Fundamental concepts of educational leadership and management.* Englewood Cliffs, NJ: Prentice Hall.

Reagan, B. R. (1981, July). Teacher shortages in Texas. Presentation at the AASA Summer Instructional Leadership Conference. Washington, DC.

Rebore, R. W. (1998). *Personnel administration in education: A management approach.* Boston: Allyn & Bacon.

Regan, R. (1984). Overview of education reform issues. In C. Masshner (Ed.), *A blue print for educational reform.* Washington, DC: Free Congress Research and Education Foundation.

Reich, R. (1997). Keynote speech. Employment in the twenty-first century conference. Pittsburgh, PA: University of Pittsburgh and Carnegie Mellon University.

Reid, W. M. (1995) *Restructuring secondary school with extended time blocks and intensive courses: The experiences of school administrators in British Columbia.* Dissertation Abstracts. Spokane, WA: Gonzaga University.

Reith, K. M. (Winter, 1989). Minority athletes: Study breaks stereotypes. *National Coach 25*(2), 36.

Reitzug, U. C. (1994). A case study of empowering principal behavior. *American Educational Research Journal, 31*(2), 283–307.

Richardson, M. D. (1988, June). The administrative assessment center. Presented at the Kentucky Association of School Superintendent Annual Conference. Louisville, KY. ED 301–930.

Robbins, H., & Finley, M. (1995). *Why teams don't work: What went wrong and how to make it right.* Princeton, NJ: Pacesetter Books.

Robinson, V. M. G. (1994, February). The practical promise of critical research in educational administration. *Educational Administration Quarterly, 30*(1), 56–57.

Rhodes, L. A. (1997, January). Connecting leadership and learning. A position paper for the American Association of School Administrators. Arlington, VA: American Association of School Administrators.

Roethlisberger, F., & Dixon, W. (1939). *Management and the worker.* Cambridge, MA: Harvard University Press.

Rogers, E. M. (1995). *Diffusion of innovations.* New York: Free Press.

Rollefson, M., & Rohr, C. L. (1992). *Teacher salaries—Are they competitive?* Washington, DC: National Center for Education Statistics.

Rosaldo, R. (1989). *Culture and truth: The remaking of social analysis.* Boston: Beacon Press.

Rowan, B. (1990). Commitment and control: Alternative strategies for the organizational design of schools. *Review of Research in Education 16,* 353–389.

Rutter, M., Maughan, B., Mortimore, P., Ouston, J., & Smith, A. (1979). *Fifteen thousand hours: Secondary schools and their effects on children.* Cambridge, MA: Harvard University Press.

Ruskin, K. B., & Achilles, C. M. (1995). *Grantwriting, fundraising and partnerships: Strategies that work!* Thousand Oaks, CA: Corwin.

Ryau, K., & Bohlin, K. E. (1999). *Building character in schools.* San Francisco: Jossey-Bass.

Sagor, R., & Barnett, B. G. (1994) *The TQE principal: A transformational leader.* Thousand Oaks, CA: Corwin.

Salisbury, C. L., Palombaro, M. M., & Hollowood, P. M. (1993). On the nature and change of an inclusive elementary school. *Journal of the Association for Persons with Severe Handicaps,* (8), 2, 75–84.

Sanders, K. P., & Theimann, F. C. (1990). Student costing: An essential tool in site-based budgeting and teacher empowerment. *NASSP Bulletin, 74*(523), 95–102.

San Diego Unified School District. (1997–1998). *Statistical report*. San Diego, CA: San Diego City School Communications/Public Information Office.

Sarason, S. B. (1996). *Barometers of change: Individual educational social transformation*. San Francisco, CA: Jossey Bass.

Sarason, S. (1994). *The predictable failure of school reforms*. San Francisco: Jossey-Bass.

Sashkin, M., & Walberg, H. (1993) *Educational leadership and school culture*. Berkeley, CA: McCutchan.

Schein, E. (1991, 1985). *Organizational culture and leadership*. San Francisco: Jossey-Bass.

Schewick, J. J., & Young, M. D. (1997, May). Coloring epistemologies: Are our research epistemologies racially biased. *Educational Researcher, 26*(4), 4–16.

Schlechty, P. C. (1997). *Inventing better schools: An action plan for educational reform*. San Francisco: Jossey-Bass.

Schlechty, P. C. (1990). *Schools for the twenty-first century*. San Francisco: Jossey-Bass.

Schoenstein, R. (1995). The new school on the block. *Executive Educator, 17*(8), 18–21.

Schmitt, N., Noe, R., Meritt, R., Fitzgerald, M., & Jorgensen, C. (1983). *Criterion-related and content validity of the NASSP assessment center*. Reston, VA: National Association of Secondary School Principals.

Schmuck, R., & Runkel, P. (1985). *The handbook of organizational development in schools*. Prospect Heights, IL.: Waveland Press.

Schofield, J. W. (1989). *Black and white in school: Trust, tension, or tolerance?* New York: Teachers College Press.

Schön, D. (1983). *The reflective practitioner: How professionals think in action*. New York: Basic Books.

School Health Resource Services, Office of School Health. (1995). *School-based health centers: Recommended services*. Denver: University of Colorado Health Sciences Center Resource packet Series. [Available by writing: 4200 E. 9th Ave./Box C287, Denver, CO 80262 or calling (303) 270-5990.]

School Health Resource Services, Office of School Health. (1995). *School-based clinics that work*. Denver: University of Colorado Health Sciences Center Resource Packet Series.

School Health Resource Services, Office of School Health. (1995). *State initiative to support school-based health centers*. Denver: University of Colorado Health Sciences Center Resource Packet Series.

Schwartz, W. (1995). *School dropouts: New information about an old problem*. Washington, DC: Office of Educational Research and Development. EDO-OD-96-5.

Scott, W. R. (1992). *Organizations*. Englewood Cliffs, NJ: Prentice-Hall.

Sears, S. J., & Coy, D. R. (1991). The scope of practice of the secondary school counselor. Washington, DC: *ERIC Clearinghouse on Counseling and Personnel Services*. ED 328830.

Senge, P. M. (1990). *The fifth discipline: The art and practice of the learning organization*. New York: Doubleday Curency.

Senge, P. M. (1990, May). The leader's new world: Building learning retention. *Educational Leadership, 47*, 84–88.

Sergiovanni, T. J. (1994, May) Organizations or communities? Changing the metaphor changes the theory. *Educational Administration Quarterly, 30*(2), 214–226.

Sergiovanni, T. J. (1992, February) Why we should seek substitutes for leadership." *Educational Leadership, 49*(5), 41–45.

Sergiovanni, T. J. (1991). *The principalship: A reflective practice perspective*. Boston: Allyn & Bacon.

Sergiovanni, T., & Starratt, R. J. (1998). *Supervision: Human perspectives*. New York: McGraw-Hill.

Shakeshaft, C. (1995). A cup half full: A gender critique of the knowledge base in educational administration. In R. Donmoyer, M. Imber, & J. Scheurich. *The knowledge base in educational administration*. Albany, NY: State University of New York Press.

Shakeshaft, C. (1986). *Women in educational administration*. Newbury Park, CA: Sage.

Shanker, A. L. (1990, April). Restructuring: What is it? *Educational Leadership, 47*(7), 10.

Shapiro, J. P., & Stefkovich, J. (1997). Preparing ethical leaders for equitable schools. In L. Beck & J. Murphy (Eds.), *Ethics in educational leadership programs*. Columbia, MO: UCEA.

Sharp, W. (1994). Seven things a principal should know about school finance. *NASSP Bulletin, 78*(566), 1–5.

Shelton, K. (Ed.). (1997). *A new paradigm of leadership: Visions of excellence for the twenty-first century*. Provo, UT: Executive Excellence Publishing.

Shen, J. (1997, October). The evolution of violence in schools. *Educational Leadership, 55*(2), 18–22.

Shoop, R. J., & Dunklee, D. J. (1992). *School law for the principal*. Boston: Allyn & Bacon.

Shoop, R. J., & Sparkman, W. (1983). *Kansas school law*. Dubuque, IA: Bowers.

Short, P. M., & Greer, J. T. (1997). *Leadership in empowered schools*. Upper Saddle River, NJ: Prentice-Hall.

Short, P. M., Green, J. T. & Michael, R. (1991, April). Restructuring schools through empowerment: Facilitating the process. *Journal of School Leadership, 1*(2), 127–139.

Shorten, A. R. (1996). Law and the courts. In K. Leithwood, J. Chapman, D. Corson, P. Hallinger, & A. Hart. (Eds.), *The international handbook of educational leadership and administration*. Boston: Kluwer Academic.

Shreeve, J. (1994). Terms of estrangement. *Discover 108*, 57–63.

Simmons, R. (1994). The horse before the cart: Assessing for understanding. *Educational Leadership 51*(5), 22–23.

Simon, H. A. (1976, 1947). *Administrative behavior* (4th ed.) New York: Macmillan.

Simon, H. (1960). *The new science of management decision*. New York: Harper & Row.

Singh, J. V., Tucker, D. J., & House, R. J. (1986). Organizational legitimacy and the liability of newness. *Administrative Science Quarterly, 31*, 171–193.

Sirotnik, K., & Oakes, J. (Eds.). (1986). *Critical perspectives on the organization and improvement of schooling*. Boston: Kluver-Nighoff.

Sizer, T. R. (1996). *Horaces' hope: What works for the American high school*. Boston: Houghton Mifflin. (Excerpts from *Horace's Hope* copyright 1996 by Theodore R. Singer. Reprinted by permission of Houghton Mifflin Co. All rights reserved.

Slater, R. (1994). Symbolic educational leadership and democracy in America. *Educational Administrative Quarterly, 30*, 97–101.

Slater, R. O. (1995). The sociology of leadership and educational administration. *Educational Administration Quarterly, 31*(3), 449–472.

Slavin, R. E., Madden, N. A., Dolan L. J., & Waskik, B. A. (1996). *Every child. Every school: Success for all*. Thousand Oaks, CA: Corwin.

Slavin, R. E., Madden, N. A., Dolan L. J., & Waskik, B. A. (1994, November). Roots and wings: Inspiring academic excellence. *Educational Leadership, 52*(3), 10–15.

Slavin, R. (1990). *Cooperative learning: Theory, research, and practice*. Englewood Cliffs, NJ: Prentice-Hall.

Slavin, R. (1995). *Cooperative learning and intergroup relations*. Washington, DC: ERIC Document No. ED 382 730.

Slavin, R. (1996). Cooperative learning in middle and secondary schools. *Clearinghouse, 69*(4), 200–204.

Sleeter, C., & Grant, C. (1993). *Making choices for multicultural education: Five approaches to race, class and gender*. New York: Merrill.

Smith, W. F., & Andrews, R. L. (1989). *Instructional leadership: How principals make a difference*. Alexandria, VA: Association for Supervision and Curriculum Development.

Smrekar, C., & Goldring, E. B. (1999). *School choice in urban America: Magnet schools and the pursuit of equity*. New York: Teachers College Press.

Solomon, R. P. (1992). *Black resistance in high school*. New York: State University of New York Press.

Spartz, J., Valdes, A., McCormick, W., Meyers, J., & Geppert, W. (1977). *Delaware educational accountability system case studies: Elementary schools grade 1–4*. Dover, DE: Delaware Department of Public Instruction.

Spillane, R. R., & Regnier, P. (1998, Spring). *The superintendent of the future*. Gaitherburg, MD: Aspen.

Spring, J. (1998). *Conflict of interests: The politics of American education*. Boston: McGraw-Hill.

Sredl, H. G., & Rothwell, W. J. (1987). *Professional training roles and competencies—volume I*. New York: Random House.

Stallings, J. (1980). Allocated academic learning time revisited, or beyond time on task. *Educational Researcher, 9*, 11–16.

Starratt, R. J. (1996). *Transforming educational administration: Meaning, community and excellence*. New York: McGraw-Hill.

Starratt, R. J. (1995). *Leaders with vision*. Thousand Oaks, CA: Corwin Press.

Starratt, R. J. (1994). *Building an ethical school: A practical response to the moral crisis in schools*. London: Falmer Press.

Starratt, R. J. (1993). *The drama of leadership*. Bristol, PA: Falmer Press.

Starratt, R. J. (1991). Building an ethical school: A theory for practice in educational leadership. *Educational Administration Quarterly, 27*(2), 185–202.

Stedman, L. (1995, February). The new mythology about the status of U.S. schools. *Educational Leadership, 52*(5), 80–85.

Stedman, L. (1987). It's time we change the effective schools formula. *Phi Delta Kappan, 69*(3), 215–224.

Steinberg, L. (1996). *Beyond the classroom: Why school reform has failed and what parents need to do*. New York: Simon and Schuster.

Steinberg, E. D. (1995, January 6). Margaret Wheatley on leadership for change. *School Administration*, 16–20.

Sternberg, R. (1996). IQ counts, but what really counts is successful intelligence. *NASSP Bulletin, 80*(583), 18–23.

Sternberg, R. (1996). *Successful intelligence*. New York: Simon & Schuster.

Sternberg, R., & Caruso, O. (1985). Practical modes of knowing. In E. Eisner (Ed.), *Learning and teaching the ways of knowing (NSSE Yearbook)* (pp. 133–158). Chicago: University of Chicago Press.

Sternberg, R., & Frensch, P. (1993). Mechanism of transfer. In D. Detterman & R. Sternberg (Eds.), *Transfer on trial: Intelligence, cognition, and instruction*. Norwood, NJ: Ablex.

Stevens, R., & Slavin, R. E. (1995). Effects of a cooperative learning approach in reading and writing on academically handicapped and nonhandicapped students. *Elementary School Journal, 95*(3), 241–262.

Stiggins, R. (1994). *Student-centered classroom assessment*. Portland, OR: Assessment Training Institute.

Stodolsky, S., & Lesser, G. (1971). Learning patterns in the disadvantaged. In *Challenging the myths: The schools, the blacks, and the poor*. Reprint Series #5. Cambridge: Harvard Educational Review.

Stogdill, R. (1981). Traits of leadership: A follow-up to 1970. In B. Bass (Ed.), *Handbook of leadership*. New York: Free Press.

Stogdill. R. (1974). *Handbook of leadership*. New York: Free Press.

Strahan, R. D., & Turner, L. C. (1987). *The courts and the schools*. New York: Longman.

Strike, K., Haller, E., & Solitus, J. (1988). *The ethics of school administration*. New York: Teachers College Press.

Strong, J. H. (1997). Improving schools through teacher evaluation. In J. H. Stronge (Ed.), *Evaluating Teaching*. Thousand Oaks, CA: Corwin Press.

Suters, E. (1997). Inspirational leadership. In K. Shelton (Ed.), *A new paradigm of leadership* (pp. 199–202). Provo, UT: Executive Excellence.

Swap, P. (1993). *Developing home-school partnerships: From concepts to practice*. New York: Teachers College Press.

Takaki, R. (1993). *A different mirror: A history of multicultural America*. Boston: Little, Brown.

Talbert, J., & McLaughlin, M. W. (1994). Teacher professionalism in local school contexts. *American Journal of Education, 102*, 123–153.

Tanner, D. (1993, December). A nation truly at risk. *Phi Delta Kappan, 74*, 288–297.

Tannenbaum, R., & Schmidt, W. H. (1958) How to choose a leadership pattern. *Harvard Educational Review, 57* 92–106.

Tanner, D., & Tanner, L. N. (1995). *Curriculum development: Theory into practice*. Englewood Cliffs, NJ: Prentice-Hall.

Tanner, L. N. (1997). *Dewey's laboratory school: Lessons for today*. New York: Teachers College Press.

Task Force on Teaching as a Profession. (1986). *A nation prepared: Teachers for the twenty-first century*. New York: Carnegie Forum on Education and the Economy.

Taylor, B. B. (1996). *Education and the law: A dictionary*. Santa Barbara, CA: ABC-CLIO.

Taylor, C. (1991). *The ethics of authenticity*. Cambridge, MA: Harvard University Press.

Taylor, F. W. (1947) *Scientific management*. New York: Harper.

Thayer, Y., & Short, T. (1994). New sources of funding for the twenty-first-century school. *NASSP Bulletin 78*(566), 6–15.

Thomas, K., & Kilmann, J. (1975). Conflict and conflict management. In Marvin Dunnett (Ed.), *Handbook of industrial and organizational psychology*, vol 2. Chicago: Rand McNally.

Thurston, P., Clift, R., & Schacht, M. (1993, November) Preparing leaders for change oriented schools. *Phi Delta Kappan*, 259–265.

Tice, L. (1997). Limitless leadership. In K. Shelton (Ed.), *A new paradigm of leadership* (pp. 79–82). Provo, UT: Executive Excellence.

Triandis, H. (1971). *Attitude and attitude change*. New York: Wiley.

Trilling, L. (1974). *Sincerity and authenticity*. London: Oxford University Press.

Trueba, H. T. (1988/9). *Raising silent voices: Educating the linguistic minorities for the twenty-first century*. Rowley, MA: Newbury House.

Tucker, M. (1990, April). Restructuring: What is it? *Education Leadership, 47*(7), 9.

Turnbull, A. P., Turnbull, H. R., Shank, M., & Leal, D. (1995). *Exceptional lives*. Englewood Cliffs, NJ: Prentice-Hall.

Tyack, D. (1992, Spring). Health and social services in public schools: Historic perspective. *The Future of Children, 2*(1), 19–31.

Tyler, R. W. (1949). *Basic principles of curriculum and instruction*. Chicago: University of Chicago Press.

Ubben, G. C., & Hughes, L. W. (1997). *The principal: Creative leadership for effective schools*. Boston: Allyn & Bacon.

Underwood, J., & Noffke, J. (1990). Litigation threat has chilling effect. *The Executive Educator, 12*(3), 18–20.

Urwick, L. F. (1937). Organization as a Technical Problem. In L. Gulick and L. F. Urwick (Eds.), *Papers on the science of administration* (pp. 47–88). New York: Institute of Public Administration, Columbia University.

Valente, W. D. (1994). *Law in the schools* (4th ed.). New York: Merrill.

Van Horn, G., Burrello, L., & DeClune, L. (1992). An instructional leadership framework: The principal's leadership role in special education. *Spe-*

cial education leadership review. Albuquerque, NM: Council of Administration of Special Education.

Vroom, V. H., & Jago, A. G. (1988). *The new leadership: Managing participation in organization.* Englewood Cliffs, NJ: Prentice-Hill.

Vroom, V. H., & Yetton, P. W. (1973). *Leadership and decision-making.* Pittsburgh: University of Pittsburgh Press.

Vygotsky, L. (1978). *Mind in society.* Cambridge, MA: Harvard University Press.

Walberg, H. J., & Lane, J. E. (1989). *Organizing for learning: Toward the twenty-first century.* Reston, VA: National Association of Secondary School Principals.

Walsh, J., & Snyder, D. (1994). Cooperative teaching: An effective model for all students. *Case in Point, 2,* 7–19.

Wang, M. C., Haertel, G. D., & Walberg, H. J. (1993). Toward a knowledge base for school learning. *Review of Educational Research, 63*(3), 249–294.

Webb, L. D., & Norton, M. S. (1994, 1999). *Human resource administration.* New York: Merrill.

Weber, M. (1947). *The theory of social and economic organization* (trans. by A. M. Henderson; introduction by T. Parsons). New York: Free Press.

Weiss, C. H. (1995, Winter). The four "I's" of school reform: How interests, ideology, information, and institution affect teachers and principals. *Harvard Education Review, 65*(6), 571–592.

Weller, L. G., Buttery, T. L., & Bland, R. W. (1994). Teacher evaluation of principals: As viewed by teachers, principals, and superintendents. *Journal of Research and Development in Education, 27*(2), 112–117.

Werner E. E., & Smith, R. S. (1989). *Vulnerable but invincible: A longitudinal study of resilient children and youth.* New York: Adams, Bannister, Cox.

West, C. (1992). The new cultural politics of difference. In S. Seidman (Ed.), *The postmodern turn: New perspectives on social theory.* Cambridge, England: Cambridge University Press.

Wheatley, M. (1992). *Leadership and the new science.* San Francisco: Berrett-Koehler.

White, W. D. (1988, January). Year-round high schools: Benefits to students, parents and teachers. *NASSP Bulletin, 478,* 18–24.

Wiggins, G. (1998). *Educative assessment.* San Francisco: Jossey-Bass.

Wiggins, G. (1990). *The case of authentic assessment.* ERIC ED 328 611.

Wiles, J., & Bondi, J. (1993). *Curriculum development* (4th ed.) New York: Macmillan.

William T. Grant Foundation (1988, January). *The forgotten half: Non-college youth in America.* Washington, DC: The William T. Grant Foundation.

Willower, D. G. (1996). Explaining and improving educational administration. In C. W. Evers and G. Lakomski (Eds.), *Exploring educational administration.* New York: Pergamon.

Willower, D. G. (1979). Some issues in research on school organization. In G. I. Immegart & W. Boyd (Eds.), *Currents in administrative research: Problem finding in education.* Lexington, MA: Heath.

Willower, D., & Licata, J. (1996). *Values and valuation in the practice of educational administration.* Thousand Oaks, CA: Corwin.

Wimpelberg, R., Teddlie, C., & Stringfield, S. (1989). Sensitivity to context: The past and future of effective schools research. *Educational Administration Quarterly, 25*(1), 82–107.

Wolf, S. (1997, October). Teach our children well. *Time, 150*(17), 62–71.

Wollons, R. (1992). (Ed.). *Children at risk in America: History, concepts, and public policy.* Albany, NY: State University of New York Press.

Yetman, N. R. (1985). *Majority and minority: The dynamics of race and ethnicity in American life.* Boston: Allyn & Bacon.

Yukl, G. A. (1989). *Leadership in organizations.* Englewood Cliffs, NJ: Prentice-Hall.

Zepeda, S., & Logenbock, M. (1999). *Special programs in regular schools.* Boston: Allyn & Bacon.

Zigler, E., Kagan, S., & Klugman, E. (1983). *Children, families, and government.* Cambridge: Cambridge University Press.

Zirkel, P. (1996). Discipline and the law. *The Executive Educator, 18*(7), 21–23.

NAME INDEX

Note: The letters *b*, *f*, and *t* indicate boxes, figures, and tables, respectively.

SUBJECT INDEX

Note: The letters *b*, *f*, and *t* indicate boxes, figures, and tables, respectively.